A GIFT OF FIRE

SOCIAL, LEGAL, AND ETHICAL ISSUES FOR COMPUTING AND THE INTERNET

THIRD EDITION

SARA BAASE

San Diego State University

PEARSON

Prentice
Hall

Pearson Education International

Vice President and Editorial Director, ECS: Marcia Horton
Executive Editor: Tracy Dunkelberger
Editorial Assistant: Melinda Haggerty
Director of Team-Based Project Management: Vince O'Brien
Senior Managing Editor: Scott Disanno
Production Liaison: Jane Bonnell
Production Editor: Vikas Kanchan, TexTech
Manufacturing Manager: Alan Fischer
Manufacturing Buyer: Lisa McDowell
Marketing Manager: Margaret Waples
Marketing Assistant: Mack Patterson
Art Director, Cover: Kenny Beck
Cover Designer: Kristine Carney
Art Editor: Greg Dulles
Composition/Full-Service Project Management: TexTech International Pvt. Ltd.
Typeface: 11/13 AGaramond

© 2009 by Pearson Education, Inc.
Pearson Prentice Hall
Pearson Education, Inc.
Upper Saddle River, New Jersey 07458

10 9 8 7 6 5 4 3 2

ISBN-13: 978-0-13-501137-9
ISBN-10:   0-13-501137-X

Pearson Education Ltd., London
Pearson Education Singapore, Pte. Ltd.
Pearson Education Canada, Inc.
Pearson Education–Japan
Pearson Education Australia PTY, Limited
Pearson Education North Asia, Ltd., Hong Kong
Pearson Educación de Mexico, S.A. de C.V.
Pearson Education Malaysia, Pte. Ltd.
Pearson Education, Upper Saddle River, New Jersey

To Keith (again and again)

CONTENTS

PREFACE

This book has two intended audiences: students preparing for careers in computer science (and related fields) and students in other fields who want to learn about issues that arise from computer technology and the Internet. The book has no technical prerequisites. Instructors can use it at various levels, in both introductory and advanced courses about computing or technology. My students mostly are junior and senior computer science majors.

Scope of this book

Many universities offer courses with titles such as "Ethical Issues in Computing" or "Computers and Society." Some focus primarily on professional ethics for computer professionals. Others address a wide range of social issues. The bulky subtitle and the table of contents of this book indicate its scope. I also include historical background to put some of today's issues in context and perspective. I believe it is important for students (in computer and information technology majors and in other majors) to see and understand the implications and impacts of the technology. Students will face a wide variety of issues in this book as members of a complex technological society, in both their professional and their personal lives.

The last chapter focuses on ethical issues for computer professionals with discussion of case scenarios. The basic ethical principles in computing are not different from ethical principles in other professions or other aspects of life: honesty, responsibility, and fairness. However, within any one profession, special kinds of problems arise. Thus, we discuss professional ethical guidelines and scenarios specific to computing professions. I include two of the main codes of ethics and professional practices for computer professionals in an Appendix. I placed the professional ethics chapter last because I believe students will find it more interesting and useful after they have as background the incidents, issues, and controversies in the earlier chapters.

Each of the chapters in this book could easily be expanded to a whole book. I had to leave out many interesting topics and examples. In some cases, I mention an issue, example, or position with little or no discussion. I hope some of these will spark further reading and debate.

Controversies

This book presents controversies and alternative points of view: privacy vs. access to information, privacy vs. law enforcement, freedom of speech vs. control of content on the Net, pros and cons of offshoring jobs, market-based vs. regulatory solutions, and so on. Often the discussion in this book necessarily includes political, economic, social, and philosophical issues. I try to focus specifically on the connections between these issues and computer technology. I encourage students to explore the arguments on all sides and to be able to explain why they reject the ones they reject before they take a position. I believe this approach prepares them to tackle new controversies. They can figure out the consequences of various proposals, generate arguments for each side, and evaluate them. I encourage students to think in principles, rather than case by case, or at least to see that the same principle appears in different cases even if they choose to take different positions on them.

My point of view

Any writer on subjects such as those in this book has some personal opinions, positions, or biases. I believe strongly in the principles in the Bill of Rights. I also have a generally positive view of technology, including computer technology. Don Norman, a psychologist and technology enthusiast who writes on humanizing technology, observed that most people who have written books about technology "are opposed to it and write about how horrible it is."* I am not one of those people. I think that technology, in general, has been a major factor in bringing physical well-being, liberty, and opportunity to hundreds of millions of people. That does not mean technology is without problems. Most of this book focuses on problems. We must recognize and study them so that we can reduce the negative effects of computer technology and increase the positive ones.

For many topics, this book takes a problem-solving approach. I usually begin with a description of what is happening in a particular area, often including a little history. Next comes a discussion of why there are concerns and what the new problems are. Finally, I give some commentary or perspective and some current and potential solutions to the problems. Some people view problems and negative side effects of new technologies as indications of inherent badness in the technology. I see them as part of a natural process of change and development. We will see many examples of human ingenuity, some that create problems and some that solve them. Often solutions come from improved or new applications of technology.

An early reviewer of this book objected to one of the quotations I include at the beginnings of many sections. He thought it was untrue. So perhaps I should make it clear that I agree with many of the quotations—but not with all of them. I chose some to be provocative and to remind students of the variety of opinions on some of the issues.

I am a computer scientist, not an attorney. I summarize the main points of many laws and legal cases and discuss arguments about them, but I do not give a comprehensive legal analysis. Many ordinary terms have specific meanings in laws, and often a difference of one word can change the impact of a provision of a law or of a court decision. Laws have exceptions and special cases. Any reader who needs precise information about how a law applies in particular cases should consult an attorney or read the full text of laws, court decisions, and legal analysis.

Changes for the third edition

For this third edition, I updated the whole book, removed outdated material, added many new topics and examples, and reorganized several chapters. New material appears throughout. I mention here some major changes, completely new sections and topics, and some that I extensively revised.

Most of Section 1.2 is new. Among other topics, it addresses new phenomena such as the growth of amateur work on the Web, blogs, video sharing, collaborative works (such as Wikipedia),

---

*Quoted in Jeannette DeWyze, "When You Don't Know How to Turn On Your Radio, Don Norman Is On Your Side," *The San Diego Reader*, December 1, 1994, p. 1.

social networking, and the impact of cell phones. At the request of many users of earlier editions, I moved the section describing ethical theories and principles from the last chapter to the first chapter.

New privacy topics include access to our search queries and all sorts of data we ourselves put on the Web, location tracking, high-tech surveillance systems, increasing risks of sensitive data stolen from businesses, and some antiterrorism programs. I expanded the section on public records. They have become more important as a privacy issue because search engine companies are working to make them more easily searchable. I moved topics about communications privacy from Chapter 3 of the second edition to Chapter 2. The rest of the old Chapter 3 is removed because much of it was out of date.

Chapter 3 includes a mostly new section (Section 3.4) on political campaigns and two completely new sections, Section 3.3.4 on the ethics of companies aiding government censorship in unfree countries, and Section 3.6 on "net neutrality." Chapter 4 includes new sections on video sharing, intellectual property issues for search engine practices, patents for technology implemented in software, and new business models that ease the problem of widespread unauthorized copying of professional entertainment and software.

I greatly expanded the discussion on identity theft (Section 5.3). The new section, Section 5.6, covers the intriguing and difficult issue of determining which country's laws should apply when individuals and businesses provide material or services on the Web that are legal in their own country but illegal in others. Who is responsible for keeping the material or services out of the country where it is illegal? In Chapter 6, I expanded the section on the global workforce and offshoring of jobs.

Chapter 7 has a new section on the quality of information on the Web. I moved the section on computer models from Chapter 8 to Chapter 7 because it fits better with the section on evaluating information. Chapter 7 also has a new section considering potential threats from intelligent robots. The current Chapter 8 was Chapter 4 in the second edition. I moved it because the new Chapters 2–5 have a variety of interconnections, whereas Chapter 8 leads into the discussion of professional ethics in Chapter 9. I added discussions of electronic voting systems and legacy systems to Chapter 8.

Chapter 9 contains several new ethical scenarios for computer professionals.

This edition has more than 130 new exercises.

This is an extremely fast-changing field. Clearly, some issues and examples in this book are so current that details will change before or soon after publication. I do not consider this to be a serious problem. Specific events are illustrations of the underlying issues and arguments. I encourage students to bring in current news reports about relevant issues to discuss in class. Finding so many ties between the course and current events adds to their interest in the class.

Class activities

The course I designed in the Computer Science Department at San Diego State University requires a book report, a term paper, and an oral presentation by each student. Students do several presentations, debates, and mock trials in class. The students are very enthusiastic about these activities. I include several in the Exercises sections, marked as Class Discussion Exercises. Although I selected some exercises for this category, I find that many others in the General Exercises sections are also good for lively class discussions.

It has been an extraordinary pleasure to teach this course. At the beginning of each semester, some students expect boredom or sermons. By the end, most say they have found it eye-opening and important. They have seen and appreciated new arguments, and they understand more about the risks of computer technology and their own responsibilities. Many students send me e-mail with news reports about issues in the course long after the semester is over, sometimes after they have graduated and are working in the field.

Additional sources and Web sites for this textbook

The notes at the ends of the chapters include sources for specific information in the text and, occasionally, additional information and comment. I usually put one endnote at or near the end of a paragraph with sources for the whole paragraph. The lists of references at the ends of the chapters include some references that I used, some that I think are particularly useful or interesting for various reasons, and some that you might not find elsewhere. I have made no attempt to be complete. I include references to Web sites, some that have extensive archives of relevant material.

An italic page number in the index indicates the page on which an index entry is defined or explained. The text often refers to agencies, organizations, and laws by acronyms. If you look up the acronym in the index, you will find its expansion.

The Instructor's Manual for this book can be found at www.prenhall.com/Baase. It contains course materials (e.g., sample assignments), updates about cases and issues in this book that occurred after publication, and links to documents and other sites of interest.

Feedback

This book contains a large amount of information on a large variety of subjects. I have tried to be as accurate as possible, but, inevitably, there will be errors. I appreciate corrections. Please send them to me at GiftOfFire@sdsu.edu.

Acknowledgments

I am grateful to many people who gave me ideas, leads, and articles, answered many questions for me, and provided other assistance for this edition. They include Ivan Bajic, Susan Love Brown, Cyndi Chie, Charles Christopher, Robert Gordon, Jim Herrin, Stephen Hinkle, Richard Hollinger, Peter J. Hughes, Jamie Lawson, Jean Nelson, Carol Sanders, Jack Sanders, and Vernor Vinge. I thank Carol Sanders and Jeannie Martin for encouraging me to write the new edition.

The reviewers of the manuscript provided very helpful feedback, corrections, and suggestions. I am very grateful to them: Beth Givens (Privacy Rights Clearinghouse), Ronald Greenburg (Loyola University), Susan Keenan (Worcester Polytech Institute), Greg Lastowka (Rutgers University), Timothy Lee (Show-Me Institute), Ernst Leiss (University of Houston), Bruce Maxim (University of Michigan, Dearborn), David Post (Temple Law School), Clayton Price (University of Missouri), Sam Ramanujan (University of Central Missouri), Robert Ellis Smith (*Privacy Journal*), Daniel Tomasevich (San Francisco State University), and Jeannie M. Walsh (University of North Carolina at Chapel Hill).

I thank the following people for reviewing the second edition at the beginning of this project and providing many suggestions for the new edition: Richard J. Botting (California State University, San Bernardino), Ronald Greenberg (Loyola University), Julie L. Johnson (Vanderbilt University), Kristin Lamberty (University of Minnesota, Morris), John G. Messerly (University of

Texas at Austin), Clayton Price (University of Missouri, Rolla), Birgit Tregenza (California State University, Northridge), and Jeannie M. Walsh (University of North Carolina at Chapel Hill).

Many people at Prentice Hall and TexTech International worked on producing this book. I am grateful to those I interacted with directly—Tracy Dunkelberger, Jane Bonnell, ReeAnne Davies, Scott Disanno, Melinda Haggerty, Vikas Kanchan, and Krishna Ramkumar—and to the many others behind the scenes.

This edition includes some material from the second edition. Thus again, I acknowledge assistance from Leland Beck, John L. Carroll, Sherry Clark, Joseph F. Fulda, Don Gotterbarn, Jeannie Martin, Alan Riggins, Carol Sanders, Jack Sanders, Milton Sank, Deborah Simpson, and Vernor Vinge. Many former students suggested relevant topics and sent me articles: Cindy Clay, John Coulombe, Lionel English, Mary Dorsey Evans, Stephen Hinkle, Sang Kang, and Philip Woodworth.

Michael Schneider and Judy Gersting initiated my writing in this area when they asked me to contribute a chapter, "Social and Legal Issues," to their textbook *An Invitation to Computer Science*. Jerry Westby, West Publishing Company, gave permission to reuse portions of that chapter.

I enthusiastically thank you all!

Most of all, I thank my husband, Keith Mayers, my system administrator, editor, research assistant, and Prince Charming.

1

Unwrapping the Gift

Prometheus, according to Greek myth, brought us the gift of fire. It is an awesome gift. It gives us the power to heat our homes, cook our food, and run the machines that make our lives more comfortable, healthy, and enjoyable. It is also awesomely destructive, both by accident and by arson. The Chicago fire in 1871 left 100,000 people homeless. In 1990 the oil fields of Kuwait were intentionally set ablaze. In 2003 a lost hunter set a signal fire in San Diego County. It got out of control and burned for days, killing 14 people and destroying 2,200 homes and 280,000 acres. In spite of the risks, in spite of these disasters, few of us would choose to return the gift of fire and live without it. We have learned, gradually, how to use it productively, how to use it safely, and how to respond more effectively to disasters, be they natural, accidental, or intentional.

Computer technology, many would agree, is the most significant new technology since the beginning of the industrial revolution. It is an awesome technology, with the power to make routine tasks quick, easy, and accurate, to save lives, and to create large amounts of new wealth. It helps us explore space, communicate easily and cheaply, find information, and do thousands of other tasks. As with fire, the power of computers creates powerful problems: potential loss of privacy, multimillion-dollar thefts, and breakdowns of large, complex systems (such as air traffic control systems, communications networks, and banking systems) on which we have come to depend. In this book, we describe some of the remarkable benefits of computer and communication technologies, some of the problems associated with them, and some of the means for reducing the problems and coping with their effects.

1.1 The Ubiquity of Computers and the Rapid Pace of Change

In 1804 Meriwether Lewis and William Clark set out on a two-and-a-half-year voyage to explore what is now the western United States. Many more years passed before their journals were published; later explorers did not know that Lewis and Clark had been there before them. Stephen Ambrose points out in his book, *Undaunted Courage*, about the Lewis and Clark expedition, that information, people, and goods moved no faster than a horse—and this limitation had not changed in thousands of years.[1] In 1997 millions of people went to the World Wide Web to watch a robot cart called Sojourner roll across the surface of Mars. We chat with people thousands of miles away and instantly view Web pages from around the world. We fly at more than 500 miles per hour.

Telephones, automobiles, airplanes, radio, household electrical appliances, and many other marvels we take for granted were invented in the late 19th and early 20th centuries. They led to profound changes in how we work and play, how we get information, how we interact with our neighbors (even how we define our neighborhood), and how we organize our family lives. Although fast paced when compared to earlier rates of innovation, the changes were gradual compared to those in the computer age. Our entry into space was one of the most dramatic feats of technology in the 20th century. Sputnik, the first man-made satellite, was launched in 1957. Neil Armstrong walked on the moon in 1969. We still do not have personal spacecraft, vacation trips to the moon, or a large amount of commercial or research activity in space. Space tourism for the very rich is in an early stage. The moon landing has had little direct effect on our daily lives.

But have you used a computer today?

I used to ask my students this question on the first day of class. I had to remind them that their microwave oven or their car might contain a microprocessor. Now, so many people carry cell phones and iPods that the answer is immediate. A day without using an appliance containing a microchip is almost as rare as a day without turning on an electric light. The last few years of the 20th century and the beginning of the 21st are characterized by the ubiquity of computers, the rapid pace of change that accompanies them, and their myriad applications and impacts on daily life.

When we speak of computers in this book, we include personal computers and mainframes; embedded chips that control machines (from sewing machines to roller coasters); information, entertainment, and communications devices (like cell phones, digital video disc [DVD] players, and game machines); and the Net, or cyberspace. Cyberspace is built of computers (e.g., Web servers), communications devices (wired and wireless), and storage media, but its real meaning is the vast web of communications and information that includes the World Wide Web, the Internet, commercial services, news and discussion groups, chat rooms, e-mail, databases, and so on, that are accessible from all over the world.

The first electronic computers were built in the 1940s. The first hard-disk drive, made by IBM® in 1956, weighed more than a ton and stored only five megabytes of data, roughly the amount of space in one high-resolution photo. Now we can walk around with 150 hours of video in a pocket. Now a disk with a terabyte (one trillion bytes) of storage—enough for 250 hours of high-definition video—costs roughly $400. The 1991 space shuttle had a one-megahertz* computer onboard. Ten years later, some luxury automobiles had 100-megahertz computers. In 2006 IBM and Georgia Tech developed a 500-gigahertz chip, more than 100 times as fast as PCs.

Problems and controversies accompany the conveniences and wonders of new computer technologies and applications. With PCs and floppy disks came computer viruses and the beginnings of a huge challenge to the concept of copyright. With e-mail came spam. With increased storage, speed, and connectivity came databases with details about our personal and financial lives. With the Web, browsers, and search engines came easy access to pornography by children and more threats to privacy and challenges

---

*This is a measure of processing speed. One megahertz is one million cycles per second; one gigahertz is one billion cycles per second. "Hertz" is named for the 19th-century physicist Heinrich Rudolf Hertz.

to copyright. Online commerce brought identity theft and a variety of scams. Cell phones increase risk of car accidents. Discussions of social issues related to computers often focus on problems, and indeed we examine problems created or intensified by computer technologies throughout this book. Recognizing the benefits is important too. It is necessary for forming a reasonable, balanced view of the impact and value of the technology.

When I started my career as a computer science professor, PCs had not yet been invented. Computers were large machines kept in air-conditioned rooms; we typed computer programs onto punched cards. Library catalogs filled large rooms with racks of trays containing three-by-five-inch index cards. The point is not that I am old. It is that change is fast and dramatic. Social-networking sites were neighborhood pizza places and bars. The way you use computer systems and tools, personally and professionally, will change substantially in two years, in five, and in ten, and almost unrecognizably over the course of your career.

In the next section we look at some services and social phenomena, often unplanned and spontaneous, that computer and communications technology made possible. They have deeply changed the ways we interact with other people, find news and create entertainment, buy, sell, and give things away. In the rest of this chapter, we introduce issues and themes that show up often, and we present an introduction to some ethical theories that can help guide our thinking about some of the controversies over impacts of computer technology throughout the rest of the book.

1.2 New Developments and Dramatic Impacts

In a way not seen since Gutenberg's printing press that ended the Dark Ages and ignited the Renaissance, the microchip is an epochal technology with unimaginably far-reaching economic, social, and political consequences.

—Michael Rothschild[2]

No one would design a bridge or a large building today without using computers, but the Brooklyn Bridge, built more than 100 years ago—long before the advent of computers—is both a work of art and a marvelous feat of engineering. The builders of the Statue of Liberty, the Pyramids, the Roman aqueducts, magnificent cathedrals, and countless other complex structures did not wait for computers. People communicated by letters and telephone before e-mail. People socialized in pubs and churches before the arrival of social-networking sites. Yet we can identify several phenomena resulting from computer technology and the Internet that are far different from what preceded them—in degree, if not entirely in kind—and several areas where the impacts are dramatic. In this section, we consider a brief sampling of such phenomena. (Entire books could be written on each topic.) Some are quite recent. Some are routine parts of our lives now; the point is to remind us that a generation ago they did not exist. They illustrate the amazingly varied uses people find for new tools and technologies.

> *It is precisely this unique human capacity to transcend the present, to live one's life by purposes stretching into the future—to live not at the mercy of the world, but as a builder and designer of that world—that is the distinction between human and animal behavior, or between the human being and the machine.*
>
> —Betty Friedan[3]

1.2.1 AMATEUR CREATIVE WORKS: BLOGS AND VIDEO SHARING

Blogs and video sharing are two of the many new forms of creativity that flourish because digital and Web technology make them so easy and inexpensive. They began as outlets for amateurs who wanted to express their ideas or creativity. They are extremely popular, and they have a tremendous impact on how people get news and entertainment. They have led to new paths for jobs—with news media and magazine publishers (for bloggers) and with advertising and entertainment companies (for video makers). They have led to celebrity for some people. Some works are intended only for friends and family, and many are dull, silly, and poorly written or made. But there are many gems, and people find them.

Blogs

Blogs (a word made up from "Web log") began as online journals with frequent, sometimes daily, comments on a few topics of interest to the blogger. Many commented on news events or articles posted online, with links to the item the blogger commented on. Now you can find blogs on political issues and campaigns, celebrity gossip, news, hobbies, books, movies, dieting, economics, technology, Internet issues, climate change, and virtually any other topic.

Blogging began slowly, shortly before 2000, and took off in the early 2000s with the help of several developments: software to make blogging easy for nontechnical people, sites hosting blogs for free, sites indexing blogs, search tools, and software to alert readers whenever their favorite blogs are updated. Technorati™, a blog search and indexing site, tracks more than 50 million blogs. Blogs appeal to people for several reasons, many similar to reasons for the popularity of video sites. They present a personal view; they are often funny and creative; they provide varied, sometimes quirky perspectives on current events. The independence of bloggers attracts readers; it suggests a genuine connection with what ordinary people are thinking and doing, not filtered through major news companies or governments.

Initially, mainstream media scorned news blogs, arguing that bloggers are not trained journalists. They are unreliable (the mainstream media said). They are not objective. They are little more than gossip columnists. In fact, many blogs provide excellent writing and expert commentary. Some people argue that competition from bloggers encourages mainstream journalists to do a better job. Blogs can generate communication when war and national laws act against it. For example, people in Israel and Lebanon chatted with each other via their blogs while the two countries shot rockets at each other in 2006. There were no telephone connections between the two countries, and it was illegal for an Israeli to enter Lebanon.

The better blogs gained acceptance, and they have become a valuable accompaniment (for some, an alternative) to mainstream news media. Bloggers demonstrated their influence by digging up information before the mainstream media did and by pushing stories the mainstream media did not publish. Bloggers detect and report errors, bias, and digitally falsified news photos in mainstream media.[4] Some people criticize bloggers for creating scandals by reporting on sexual affairs of politicians that mainstream journalists chose to leave as private.

More popular blogs have 100,000 to 500,000 readers per day, and some peak at several million when they carry an important story or scoop. These figures are higher than the circulation figures of many newspapers and for political and current-events magazines. Now bloggers get invitations to fashion shows and press credentials for news events.

Businesses were quick to recognize the appeal and value of blogs. Many set up their own blogs as part of their public relations programs. These blogs often contain useful information, but they are not the independent voices people expected of early blogs. Advertisers began sponsoring some popular blogs. Some remain independent; some are influenced by sponsors. When advertising or sponsorship is obvious or announced to readers, readers can decide on an appropriate level of skepticism. Sometimes sponsorship by advertisers or advocacy groups is not disclosed.

In Chapter 7 we consider the difficulty of knowing if a blog is reliable and other criticisms of blogs.

Video sites and popular culture

People with creative talents are quick to embrace new technologies. Inexpensive, and sometimes free, image-manipulation tools powered a burst in creativity, from computer art to electronic music to computer-generated movies. With increased bandwidth, digital cameras, tools for manipulating videos, and space on social-networking sites and video sites, came an explosion of short amateur videos—often humorous, sometimes quite serious. We can see a soldier's view of the war in Iraq, someone's encounter with aggressive whales, an arrest by police. Less than two years after YouTube™'s founding in 2005, people posted more than 65,000 videos a day and watched videos more than 100 million times a day. Almost 30 million people viewed one particular video on MySpace; that is more than the number who watch most television shows. Are people wasting an extraordinary

"I'VE GOT PRESSURE"

When asked by a young man to speak more quietly on his cell phone, a Hong Kong bus rider berated the man for nearly six minutes with angry insults and obscenities. In the past, a few other riders might have described the incident to friends, then soon forgotten it. But in 2006 another rider captured the scene on his cell phone. The video soon appeared on the Internet and was downloaded nearly five million times. Others provided subtitles in different languages, set the video to music, used clips as mobilephone ringtones, and produced t-shirts with pictures and quotes. "I've got pressure" and other phrases from the rant slipped into conversations.

This incident reminds us that anything we do in a public place can be captured and preserved on video. But more, it illustrates how the Internet facilitates and encourages creativity and the quick creation and distribution of culture artifacts and entertainment, with the contribution of ideas, modifications, variations, improvements, and new works from thousands of people.

amount of time? A lot of the videos on such sites are junk, although some are truly creative and entertaining. Mundane and silly videos sometimes attract big audiences. Only a few hundred people watched a video of a U.S. Senator debating his opponent during an election campaign, but 80,000 watched a video of him sleeping at a meeting. Does this reflect superficiality and immaturity of the young people who flock to video sites or is it just another reminder of the falsity and irrelevance of most politics? Perhaps it indicates that people go to these sites mostly for fun and relaxation.

As with blogs, the popularity of video sites presents opportunities for initially unintended uses, both valuable and annoying ones. Some sites include videos of classic performances by now-dead musicians. Significant news and journalistic video could follow, eventually turning some sites into valuable video libraries. On the other hand, investigative journalists traced the origins of some amusing, politically slanted videos and found that they were posted from computers of marketing and public relations firms. Candidates for political offices hire people to follow their opponents and record embarrassing videos to post on the Web. Marketing companies post videos and profiles of fictional characters in new movies and mascots of companies to advertise to young people. Businesses and nonprofit organizations (including the United Nations) adopted *viral marketing,* that is, relying on large numbers of people to view, copy, and spread marketing messages presented in clever or amateur-seeming videos. It has become popular to post video on the Web showing people being rude, arguing, littering, and singing or dancing poorly. Is public shaming appropriate for these actions?

What are the effects of mixing fiction, advertising, politics, and authentic amateur videos in one setting? How important is it to know which is which? Television companies screen ads (to some degree) for taste, fairness, and accuracy. Is it good or bad that there is no production company, television station, or other professional decision maker making judgments about quality and choosing what to distribute on the Internet? We discuss these issues further in Chapter 7. Many videos on the Web infringe copyrights owned by entertainment companies. We explore copyright issues in Chapter 4.

1.2.2 CONNECTIONS

The Web and cell phones, keep us connected all day, virtually everywhere. Internet telephony brought down the cost of telephoning across the world. Social-networking Web sites generate millions of new connections. We briefly look at the rapid development of applications, side effects, and a few problems.

E-mail, the Web, and empowerment

E-mail and the World Wide Web are so widely and commonly used now that we may forget how new and extraordinary they are. E-mail arrives at the recipient's computer or cell phone as quickly as a phone call, but it does not interrupt important work, dinner, or a shower. The recipient reads the message when it is convenient. The sender does not have the frustration of getting busy signals, nor does he or she have to consider time-zone differences when sending messages to other countries. E-mail was first used mostly by computer scientists. In the 1980s messages were short and contained only text. As more people and businesses connected to computer networks, use of e-mail expanded to scientific researchers, then to businesses, then to millions of other people. Limits on length disappeared, and we began attaching digitized photos and documents. By 2000, Americans sent approximately 1.4 billion e-mail messages per day.

High-energy physicists established the World Wide Web in Europe in 1990 to share their work with colleagues and researchers in other countries. It had more than 10,000 sites by 1993. In the mid- and late 1990s, with the development of Web browsers and search engines, the Web became an environment for ordinary users and for electronic commerce. It grew at an astonishing rate. Today there are approximately 100 million Web sites.

The Web gives us access to information and to audiences almost unimaginable a generation ago. The Web empowers ordinary people to make better decisions about everything from selecting a television to selecting medical treatments. It empowers us to do things that we used to rely on experts to do for us. Software tools, many available online for free, help us analyze the healthiness of our diet or plan a budget. We can find references and forms for legal processes. Tax software helps us fill out our tax forms without depending on (and paying) an expert. Small businesses and individual artists sell on the Web without paying big fees to middlemen and distributors.

We can read and listen to thousands of news sources on the Web from other countries, getting different cultural and political perspectives on events. We can search archives of millions of news articles from the past 200 years. We can read the full text of government documents—bills, budgets, investigative reports, congressional testimony and debate—instead of relying on a few sentences quoted from an official news release or a sound bite from a biased spokesperson. We can read frank reviews of cameras, clothing, cars, books, and other products written by other buyers, not marketing departments. We can select our entertainment and watch it when we want to.

As astounding and empowering as the huge amount of information on the Web was, Web enthusiasts began referring to it a bit disparagingly as Web 1.0. On Web 1.0, people passively read or downloaded information. Blogs, video sharing, and wikis* introduced Web 2.0. Millions of people collaborate and post their own content on the Web. We do not have to find a publisher, sign a contract, and meet someone else's requirements.

The Web empowers innovators and entrepreneurs. A college student with a good idea and some well-implemented software can start a business that quickly grows to be worth millions or billions of dollars. Several have. The openness of the Internet enables "innovation without permission," in the words of Vinton Cerf.[5]

The Web has become a huge library, a huge shopping mall, an entertainment center, and a multimedia, global community forum.

Cell phones

At the beginning of the 21st century, relatively few people had cell phones. Business people and sales people who often worked outside their office carried them. High-tech workers and gadget enthusiasts liked them. Others bought the phones so they could make emergency calls if their car broke down. We were used to being out of touch when away from home or office. We planned ahead and arranged our activities so that we did not need a phone when one was not available.

Within a short time cell service improved and prices dropped. Millions of people started carrying cell phones—and discovering new uses for them: last-minute planning, keeping track of children, and hundreds of other uses. Cell-phone makers and service providers developed unanticipated new features and services, adding cameras, video, and Web connections. Cell phones became a common tool for conversations, messaging, taking pictures, downloading music, checking e-mail, playing games, banking, accessing the Web, tracking friends, watching videos, projecting slide shows, and sending test answers to friends in class during a test. (Of course, teachers do not approve of that one.) Companies are developing systems for using a cell phone as a "credit card." Some are designing larger, fold-up screens so you can watch movies on a phone. Some cell phone systems monitor security cameras at home or control home appliances from a distance. Businesses use enhanced cell phones to access records, manage inventory, and accomplish other business tasks while on the move. Companies are developing systems to provide doctors with mobile access to drug and treatment information and patient medical records.

---

*A wiki is a Web site, supported by special software, that allows people to add content and edit content provided by others. Wikis are tools for collaboration on projects within a business or organization or among the public.

Cell phones and cell-phone services come specialized for different budgets, usage patterns, and observers of different religions. A phone for Muslims indicates the direction of Mecca and reminds the owner when it is time for prayers. A Christian can buy ringtones with prayers or religious music. A company in Israel sells a phone without a camera and entertainment services. Hundreds of organizations offer service plans with specialized information and messages for groups such as yoga enthusiasts, cancer survivors, and nature fans.

All these examples suggest the astounding number of unanticipated applications of this one, relatively new, "connection" device. In 2006, 208 million people in the United States and more than a billion worldwide used cell phones.

To be sure, new problems showed up with cell phones as with each new technology.

When people began carrying cell phones and could call for help, more headed out into the wilderness or went rock climbing without appropriate preparation. In many areas of life, people take more risk when technology increases safety. It is not completely unreasonable if the added risk and increased safety are in balance. When rescue calls surged, some rescue services began billing for the true cost of a rescue, one way to remind people to properly weigh the risk.

Talking on a phone while driving a car increases the risk of an accident. Some studies estimate that the added risk is similar to that of other distracting things drivers do, such as eating or putting on makeup. Some indicate that the risk from cell phones is higher. Either way, it is one more distraction adding more risk. Some states responded by prohibiting use of hand-held phones while driving. Hands-free systems might reduce risk, but do not eliminate the distraction of a conversation with someone not present, not aware of the traffic situation.

Cell phones interfere with solitude, quiet, and concentration. We can turn off our own while working or relaxing in a park, but a big issue with cell phones is rudeness. Some people use them in inappropriate places, disturbing others. Theaters and courts remind people to turn off their phones. Common sense and courtesy could help reduce rudeness.

Cameras in cell phones (and small digital cameras generally) obviously have many valuable uses, but the fact that so many people carry them affects our privacy in public and nonpublic places. When cameras first appeared in cell phones, most people were unaware of them. Photos taken covertly in bathrooms or locker rooms appeared on the Web showing people undressed. Photos appeared showing religious Muslim women with uncovered faces and other people in embarrassing or awkward situations. The cameras created or contributed to some unpleasant social phenomena such as gangs of young people beating someone up while one member records the attack for the amusement of the others. More than a million people watched the execution of Saddam Hussein, captured covertly on a cell phone and posted on the Internet. Some people record and post embarrassing behavior of someone who has angered them. Will people armed with cell phone cameras distinguish news events and evidence of crimes from voyeurism, their own rudeness, and stalking?

Some critics find fault with cell phones and other technologies because some people cannot afford them or cannot use them. The criticism is misplaced; there would be no reason to complain if the product were not desirable. In fact, such situations indicate a market niche—a set of consumers who need a pared-down, inexpensive version or who need special features in the product. With many electronic devices, cost is a temporary problem; they get steadily cheaper. Older folks were slower to adopt cell phones, partly because they had difficulty reading the tiny screens and labels on the buttons, partly because they did not want the entertainment services, and partly because they had always done without them and did not see a need for them. Soon, companies produced phones with fewer frills but with large buttons, labels, and fonts, and ear cups to improve sound for those with hearing problems.

Social networking

Facebook, one of the first of the social-networking sites, started at Harvard as an online version of hardcopy student directories available at many colleges. The service was so popular that it spread to other colleges, had more than a million registered users by the end of 2004 (the year it was founded), and almost ten million in 2006. Hardcopy "facebooks" provided a photo and a little bit of information about each student. On the Web, of course, we can do much more: include pictures, video, and huge amounts of information. We can connect to other people, by linking to their profiles and via e-mail and chat. MySpace, founded in 2003, had roughly 100 million member profiles by 2006. MySpace expanded to Japan, England, France, Germany, and several other countries where people visit a site in their own language but can view profiles of and communicate with members in other countries. While many older people do not understand the appeal of social-networking sites, or worry about safety and privacy, the sites are wildly popular with young people. These sites provide new ways for people to express their personalities. People use them to keep in touch with friends, to find others with similar tastes and interests, and to find dates, jobs, and political allies.

People like to connect with other people, to chat, argue, play games. They have been doing so in online communities since the beginning of the Internet. Usenet news groups (since the early 1980s), the Well (founded in 1985), bulletin board systems, and Web discussion forums are all examples. The social-networking sites differ from the older communities in number of members (huge), amount of space available (also huge), primary focus as social sites, ability to handle sound and video, and the young age range of many members.

People found unexpected uses of social-networking sites, some good, some bad, some just quirky. Friends may post racy profiles of friends as pranks, sometimes generating laughs, sometimes generating serious embarrassment and other problems. Ex-boyfriends, ex-girlfriends, and others may post false and damaging profiles. Politicians create profiles for themselves. They find the sites a good tool for attracting donations and campaign volunteers. Advertisers request to be added to members' contact lists and then may spam their "friends." Fake celebrity profiles are common. In an example of online communities finding their own solutions to new problems, a member of MySpace took on the task of validating celebrity profiles; he provides a list of those he rates as authentic. Members and visitors who care can check his list. Stalking is a more serious problem. Concern about stalkers, spam, and the general feeling of being too exposed led some people to leave the sites. As with many new things, after the initial excitement, people see disadvantages and adjust their usage accordingly. (We consider some privacy issues for social network sites in Chapter 2.)

Social-networking software, facilitating connections among people with common acquaintances, proved valuable in business settings. Among other uses, the systems help people find the right person within their own company or another company for a particular project. They help find an acquaintance who knows a potential customer or business partner—someone who can provide a personal introduction or help to pitch an idea for a business deal. Social-networking sites are developing for a variety of other specialized populations.

How do social-networking sites affect people and relationships? It may be too early for definitive answers, but we can ask a few questions. The sites increase a member's number of friends and contacts, but are the relationships more superficial than in-person relationships? Does the time spent online reduce the time spent on physical activity and staying healthy? At least one member of MySpace has almost one million "friends." Should we view this as an indication of the superficiality of online friends? Or should we consider that the meaning of the word might be closer to "fan" than "friend" in this context? Suppose an article in a magazine about a young entrepreneur, entertainer, writer, or model impressed a reader who then wanted to follow her work. In the past, there was no simple way to do so, or to count the people who wanted to do so. Connections online help us follow someone's work and they provide feedback about its popularity in a new way.

More connections

The connections facilitated by the Web have numerous other applications besides personal communication. We cite just a few examples.

Telemedicine, or long-distance medicine, refers to remote performance of medical exams, analyses, and procedures using specialized equipment and computer networks. Telemedicine is used on long airplane flights to help treat a sick passenger and to ascertain whether an emergency landing is needed. Prisons use telemedicine to reduce the risk of escape by dangerous criminals. Some small-town hospitals use two-way video systems to consult with specialists at large medical centers—eliminating the expense, time, and possible health risk of transporting the patient to the medical center. A variety of health monitoring devices now send their readings from a patient's home to a nurse over the Internet. This technology eliminates the expense, time, and inconvenience of more frequent visits, while enabling more regular monitoring of conditions like blood sugar in diabetics, and helping to catch dangerous conditions early. Telemedicine goes well beyond transmission of information. Surgeons in New York used video, robotic devices, and high-speed communication links to remotely remove a gall bladder from a patient in France. Such systems are being developed for emergency situations. They can save lives of soldiers, wounded on battlefields, far from expert surgeons.

The Web connects students and teachers in "distance learning" programs. Many specialized high school courses and some complete college programs are offered entirely on the Web. People who live in rural areas, who work full-time, who have varying work schedules that conflict with normal class schedules, or who have small children at home benefit from the flexibility of Web courses. People who cannot travel easily because of disabilities benefit from increased learning opportunities at home.

The impact of the connections provided by the Web is more dramatic in remote or less developed areas of the world, many of which do not have telephones. Mountains and thick jungle, with no roads, separate villagers in Bario, Malaysia, from the next town. The villagers use a satellite connection to order supplies, to check the market price of rice to get a good deal when selling their crop, and to e-mail family photos to distant relatives. Farmers in Africa get weather forecasts and instruction in improved farming methods. An Inuit man operates an Internet service provider for a village in the Northwest Territories of Canada, where temperatures drop to $-40°$F. Villagers in Nepal sell handicrafts worldwide via a Web site based in Seattle. Sales have boomed, more villagers have regular work, dying local arts are reviving, and some villagers can now afford to send their children to school.

1.2.3 COLLABORATIVE EFFORTS AMONG STRANGERS

Wikipedia®, the free, online, collaborative encyclopedia, is an excellent example of collaborative projects among large numbers of strangers worldwide that produce extremely valuable products for the public. Wikipedia exemplifies another phenomenon new with the Internet: publication with no editorial board in control. Thousands of volunteers, not carefully selected scholars, write and continually edit and update Wikipedia. Anyone who chooses to participate can do so. Encyclopedias are normally written by expert scholars selected by editorial boards. We expect encyclopedias to be accurate and objective. Few would have expected Wikipedia's open model to produce a useful, reasonably reliable, well-written product. But it did. Within five years of its start in 2001, Wikipedia had more than a million entries in English and more than five million in all its dozens of languages, far more than the long respected Encyclopedia Britannica®. It is more up-to-date than a printed encyclopedia or one distributed in annual editions on DVD. Wikipedia is one of the Internet's most used reference sites. It is an excellent reference, especially for technical topics not easily found in other encyclopedias, but it also has flaws. Some articles have errors. Some are poorly written, some clearly biased. People worry that the lack of editorial control means no accountability, no standards of quality, no way for the ordinary person to judge the value of the information. We consider such criticisms and similar criticisms of the vast amount of information on the Web in Chapter 7.

The Open Directory Project™ (ODP), the directory of the Web organized by topic areas, is another valuable project created by thousands of volunteers around the world. Many popular search engines, including Google™, Lycos™, Netscape™ Search, and AOL™ Search, use the ODP to provide their directory services. The Web abounds with other examples of collaborative projects, some organized, like Wikipedia and the ODP, some spontaneous. Scientists collaborate on research with scientists in other countries much more easily and more often than they could without the Internet. Informal communities of programmers, scattered around the world, create and maintain free software. Informal, decentralized groups of people help investigate online auction fraud, murder, stolen research, and other crimes. People who have never met collaborate on creating entertainment. The number of large online collaborative projects is likely to increase significantly.

Some collaborative projects could have dangerous results. To reduce the flow of illegal immigrants, a governor of Texas proposed setting up night-vision Webcams along the Mexican border to be monitored by volunteers on the Internet. Will monitors of a border Webcam go out and attack people they see coming across the border? What training or selection process is appropriate for volunteers who monitor security Webcams? In China, a man posted the online name of another man he believed was having an affair with his wife. Thousands of people participated in tracking down the man's real name and address and encouraging public action against him.[6] Anti-abortion activists created a Web site containing the names and home addresses of doctors who perform abortions; some of the doctors were killed. Mobs and individuals emotionally involved in a political or moral cause do not always pause for the details of due process. They do not carefully determine whether they identified the correct person, whether the person is guilty of a crime, and what the appropriate punishment is. On the other hand, police departments in several countries effectively use instant messaging to alert residents who help find crime suspects or stolen cars in their neighborboods. Enlisting volunteers can be a useful new collaborative tool for crime fighting and possibly antiterrorism programs. How can the efforts of thousands of individuals be directed to useful ends while protecting against mistakes, instant vigilantism, and other abuses?

1.2.4 E-COMMERCE AND FREE STUFF

In the 1990s the idea of commercial Web sites horrified Web users. The Web, they believed, was for research, information, and online communities. A few brick-and-mortar businesses and a few young entrepreneurs recognized the potential and benefits of online commerce. Among the earliest traditional businesses on the Web, United Parcel Service and Federal Express let customers check the status of packages they sent. This was both a novelty and a valuable service. Amazon.com, founded in 1994, started selling books on the Web and became one of the most popular, reliable, and user-friendly commercial sites. Ten years after it "opened" for business, its annual sales reached almost $8.5 billion. Many Web-based businesses followed Amazon, creating new business models—such as eBay with its online auctions. Traditional businesses established Web sites. Online sales in the U.S. increased more than tenfold from 1999 to 2005. Now, people buy and sell $20 billion of merchandise on eBay each year. Forrester Research, Inc., estimated that online sales would grow to $329 billion in 2010. For Europe, Forrester projected online sales of €263 billion in 2011.[7]

Some of the benefits of e-commerce are fairly obvious: We can consider more products and sellers, some far away, in less time and without burning gasoline to get there. Some are less obvious or were not obvious before they appeared. Auction sites gave people access to customers they could not have found efficiently before. The lower overhead and the ease of comparison shopping on the Web brought down prices of a variety of products. Consumers save 10–40%, for example, by buying contact lenses online, according to a Progressive Policy Institute report. Consumers who do price-comparison research on the Web before buying a new car typically save about $400.[8]

Growth of commerce on the Web required solutions to several problems. One was trust. People were reluctant to give their credit card numbers on the Web to companies they had not dealt with or even heard of before. Enter PayPal™, a company built on the idea of having a trusted intermediary handle payments. Encryption and secure servers also made payments safer.* The Better Business Bureau® established a Web site where we can find out if consumers have complained about a company. Auction sites implemented rating and comment systems to help buyers and sellers determine whom to trust. E-mail confirmations of orders, consumer-friendly return policies, and easy packaging for returns all contributed to consumer comfort and more online sales. The University of Michigan's National Quality Research Center found that e-commerce businesses had a higher customer-satisfaction rating than any other sector of the economy.

Impacts of e-commerce on free speech and free trade: Section 3.2.4

As online sales increased, competition led traditional stores to adopt some of the practices of e-commerce, such as more consumer-friendly return policies.

Free stuff

Libraries provided free access to books, newspapers, and journals for generations, and radio and television provided free news and entertainment before the invention of computers and the Internet. But there is so much more free stuff now, a truly astounding amount on the Web, and access to it is far more convenient than it was before.

For our computers, we can get free e-mail programs and e-mail accounts, browsers, filters, firewalls, encryption software, software to manipulate photos, software for viewing documents and videos, home inventory software, antispam software, antivirus software, antispyware software, and software for many other specialized purposes. This is just a small sampling of software available for free.

We can find free game-playing programs for old games like chess and bridge and new computer games. Phone service via Skype™ is free. There are free dating services on the

---

*The ease and security of payment on the Web had a pleasant side effect: Many people contribute more to charitable organizations.

Web. Major music festivals offer their concerts for free on the Internet, a nice alternative to paying $30 to $500 for a ticket. Craigslist™, the classified ad site, one of the most popular Web sites in the world, is free to people who place ads and people who read them. Major (expensive) universities such as Stanford, Yale, and MIT provide video of lectures, lecture notes, and exams for thousands of their courses on the Web for anyone for free. We can download whole books from Google, the Open Content Alliance™, and other sources for free.* We can set up our own blog on a free blog site, and we can read other blogs, online news services, and online versions of major print newspapers from all over the world for free. MySpace, Facebook™, and YouTube are free; Google and Yahoo!® are free. Wikipedia and hundreds of other references are free.

We pay for libraries with taxes. Advertisers pay for broadcasting radio and television programs. On the Web, advertising pays for many, many free sites, but far from all. Wikipedia carries no advertising, donations pay for its hardware and bandwidth. Craigslist charges fees of some businesses that post job announcements and brokers who post apartment listings in a few cities. That keeps the site free to everyone else and free of other paid ads. Businesses provide some free information and services for good public relations and as a marketing tool. (Some free e-mail or game programs, for example, do not have all the features of the paid versions.) Nonprofit organizations provide information as a public service; donations or grants fund them. The organizations can provide more and reach more people on the Web than they could previously with brochures and radio or TV ads because the costs are so much lower. One of the distinct and delightful features of the Internet is that individuals provide a huge amount of free stuff simply because it pleases them to do so. They are professionals or hobbyists or just ordinary people who enjoy sharing their expertise and enthusiasm. Generosity and public service flourish in the Web environment.

1.2.5 ARTIFICIAL INTELLIGENCE, ROBOTICS, AND MOTION

Artificial intelligence (AI) is a branch of computer science that develops theories and techniques for making computers perform tasks that we normally (or used to) think of as requiring human intelligence. It includes playing complex strategy games like chess, language translation, diagnosing diseases, making decisions based on large amounts of data (such as whom to approve for a loan), and understanding speech (where "understanding" might be measured by the appropriateness of the response). AI also includes tasks performed automatically by the human brain and nervous system, for example, vision (capture and interpretation of images by cameras and software). Learning is a characteristic of many AI programs. That is, the output of the program improves over time as it "learns" by evaluating results of its decisions on the inputs it encounters. Many AI applications involve *pattern recognition*, that is, recognizing similarities among different

---

*Books available for free downloading are in the public domain (that is, out of copyright).

things. Applications include reading handwriting to allow automatic sorting of mail, matching fingerprints, and matching faces in photos.

Early in the development of AI, researchers thought the hard problems for computers were tasks that required high intelligence and advanced training for humans, such as winning at chess and diagnosing diseases. In 1997 IBM's chess computer, Deep Blue™, beat World Champion Garry Kasparov in a tournament. AI researchers realized that narrow, specialized, skills were easier for computers than what a five-year-old does: recognize people, carry on a conversation, respond intelligently to the environment. Work on developing machines with general intelligence continues. Here we provide some examples of specialized applications, many in medicine and other life-saving areas. This form of AI is now a part of so many computer applications that we no longer think of them as astonishing simulations of human intelligence. They were astonishing advances not long ago.

When a man had a heart attack in a swimming pool in Germany, lifeguards did not see him sink to the bottom of the pool. An underwater surveillance system, using cameras and sophisticated software, detected him and alerted the lifeguards who rescued him. A similar system alerted lifeguards in a busy swimming pool in France when a man blacked out underwater. They saved his life. The software distinguishes a swimmer in distress from normal swimming, shadows, and reflections. It is now installed in many large pools in Europe and the United States.

Search engine designers use AI techniques in their algorithms to select and rank sites for search results and to guess what the user meant if the search phrase contains typos. Automated Web sites that answer questions use AI to figure out what a question means and find answers.

Antilock braking systems (ABS) in automobiles use sensors and computers to control the pressure on the brakes to prevent skids. The ABS is more expert than human drivers at safely stopping a car. Parallel parking takes skill; luxury cars compute and plot the appropriate parking path and park themselves.

Speech recognition, once a difficult research area, is now a common tool for hundreds of applications. Computer programs that teach foreign languages give instruction in correct pronunciation if they do not recognize what the user says. Air traffic controllers train in a mock-up tower whose "windows" are computer screens. The trainee directs air traffic that is entirely simulated by computer. The computer responds when the trainee speaks to the simulated pilots. Such simulation allows more intensive training in a safe environment. If the trainee directs two airplanes to land on the same runway at the same time, no one gets hurt.

People used to think that when fingerprints were found at a crime scene, the police routinely matched them against thousands of prints on file to find a suspect. This was not true. Fingerprints of a specific suspect could be compared, but matching fingerprints was slow, painstaking work performed by human specialists. Now, AI programs process millions of prints in minutes. Human sketch artists used to make sketches of crime suspects from witness descriptions. Now, computer systems generate pictures of a suspect and search databases with criminal mug shots to find a match. Just as AI software can distinguish a swimmer in trouble from other swimmers, AI software in some video surveillance systems distinguishes suspicious behavior by a customer in a store that might indicate shoplifting or other crimes. Thus (without constant human monitoring), an AI-equipped video system can help prevent a crime, rather than simply identify the culprits afterward.

The goal of 17th- and 18th-century calculators was modest: to automate basic arithmetic operations. It shocked many people at the time. That a mindless machine could perform tasks associated with human intellectual abilities was disconcerting. Centuries later, Garry Kasparov's loss to a computer generated worried articles about the value—or loss of value—of human intelligence. People continue to debate the philosophical and social implications of AI. It seems that each new breakthrough is met with concern and fear at first. A few years later, it is taken for granted.

Implications of human-level AI: Section 7.5.3 How will we react when we can go into a hospital for surgery performed entirely by a machine? Will it be scarier than riding in the first automatic elevator? How will we react when we can have a conversation by e-mail or phone about any topic at all—and not know if we are conversing with a human or a machine? How will we react when chips implanted in our brains enhance our memory with gigabytes of data and a search engine? Will we no longer be human?

Robotics

Robots are mechanical devices that perform tasks traditionally done by humans or tasks that we think of as human-like activities. Robotic arms have been assembling products in factories for decades. They work faster and more accurately than people can. A robotic milking machine milks cows at dairy farms while the farmhands sleep. Robotic devices now are generally controlled by computer software and include aspects of AI. Just as general intelligence is a hard problem for AI, general movement and functioning is a hard problem for robots. Most robotic devices are special-purpose devices with a relatively limited set of operations.

McDonald's® and other fast-food sellers installed robotic food preparation systems to reduce costs and speed service. A robot pharmacist machine, connected to a patient database, plucks the appropriate medications from pharmacy shelves by reading bar codes, checks for drug interactions, and handles billing. One of its main goals is reduction of human error. Physicians do complex and delicate surgery from a console with a 3-D monitor and joysticks that control robotic instruments. The software filters out a physician's shaky movements. High-end gadget stores sell robot vacuum cleaners that move around the floor by themselves. Robots work in environments that are hazardous to people. They inspect undersea structures and communication cables. They search for survivors in buildings collapsed by bombs or earthquakes. They explore volcanoes and other planets. They move or process nuclear and other hazardous wastes.

Various companies and researchers are developing robots with more general abilities. For several years, Sony™ sold a robot pet dog, Aibo (robot pet dog)™. It walked (with a camera providing vision). It responded to commands and it learned. Several companies make robots with a more or less human shape. Honda's Asimo, for example, walks up and down stairs. A goal is to develop robots that can act intelligently and perform a variety of operations to assist people.

Motion sensing and control

How do robots walk, climb stairs, and dance? Tiny motion-sensing and gravity-sensing devices collect status data. Software, sometimes quite complex, using AI techniques, interprets the data and determines the necessary motions, then sends signals to motors. These devices—accelerometers, or *mems* (for microelectromechanical systems)—help robots and Segway's motorized scooter stay upright. They provide image stabilization in digital cameras. They detect when a car has crashed or when someone has dropped a laptop. The system deploys an airbag or triggers a lock on the disk drive to reduce damage. A sharp price drop for mems triggered a burst of new applications.[9]

1.2.6 TOOLS FOR DISABLED PEOPLE

One of the most heartwarming applications of computer technology is the restoration of abilities, productivity, and independence to people with physical disabilities.

Some computer-based devices assist disabled people in using ordinary computer applications that other people use, such as Web browsers and word processors. Some enable disabled people to control household and workplace appliances that most of us operate by hand. Some improve mobility. For example, some wheelchairs climb stairs and support and transport a person in an upright position.[10] Sensors and microprocessors control artificial limbs. Some technologies that are primarily conveniences for most of us provide significantly more benefit for disabled people: Consider that text-messaging devices, like the BlackBerry®, are very popular among deaf people.

For people who are blind, computers equipped with speech synthesizers read aloud what a sighted person sees on the screen. They read information embedded in Web pages that sighted visitors do not need, for example, descriptions of images. Google offers search tools that rank Web sites based on how accessible they are for blind users.* For materials not already stored in electronic form, a scanner or camera, optical character recognition software, and a speech synthesizer combine to read aloud to a blind person. The first such readers were large machines. Now portable, hand-held versions can read menus, bills, and receipts in restaurants, as well as magazines and mail at home. Where noise is a problem (or for a person both blind and deaf), speech output can be replaced by a grid of buttons raised and lowered by the computer to form Braille characters. Braille printers provide hard copy. Books have been available in Braille or on tape, but the expense of

---

*Video, graphics, and complex layouts strain the tools that help blind users. Many Web sites remain difficult to use.

production for a small market kept the selection limited. Systems similar to navigation systems in cars help blind people walk around and find their way in neighborhoods they are not familiar with.

Prosthetic devices, such as artificial arms and legs, have improved from heavy, "dumb" wood, to lighter materials with analog motors, and now to highly sensitive and flexible digitally controlled devices that enable amputees to participate in sports and fly airplanes. A person whose leg was amputated above the knee can walk, sit, and climb stairs with a new "smart" knee. Sensors attached to the natural leg measure pressure and motion more than a thousand times a second and transmit the data to a processor in the prosthetic leg. AI software recognizes and adapts to changes in speed and slope and the person's walking style. The processor controls motors to bend and straighten the knee and support the body's movement, replacing the normal, complex interplay of nerves, muscles, tendons, and ligaments. Artificial arms use electrodes to pick up tiny electrical fields generated by contractions of muscles in the upper (natural) limb. Microprocessors control tiny motors that move the artificial limb, open and close fingers, and so on.[11]

Various conditions—loss of limbs, quadriplegia (paralysis in both arms and legs, often resulting from an accident), and certain diseases—eliminate all or almost all use of the hands. Speech-recognition systems have improved enormously in quality and are an extremely valuable tool for these people and for others. (Deaf people can use speech-recognition systems to "hear" another speaker as the computer displays the spoken words on a monitor.) People who cannot use their hands can dictate documents to a word processor and give commands to a computer to control household appliances. These systems are a boon to the safety, comfort, and independence of a person with limited mobility and use of hands.

Researchers in the U.S. and Europe are developing brain–computer interfaces so that severely handicapped people can operate a computer and control appliances with their thoughts.[12] The impact of all these devices on the morale of the user is immense. Think about a person with an active mind, personality, and sense of humor—but who cannot write, type, or speak. Imagine the difference when the person gains the ability to communicate—with family and friends, and with all the people and resources available on the Internet.

One of the results of the availability of computer technology for disabled people is that people who formerly could not work now can. Many disabled people have formed and run their own businesses. People who develop computer-based tools for disabled people describe the technology as "liberating" and "empowering," and as "the Swiss Army knife for disabled people."[13]

1.2.7 WHAT NEXT?

A Microsoft researcher developed a system with which a user manipulates 3-D images with hand movements, without touching a screen or any controls. Designers of buildings, machines, clothing, and so on could use it to examine designs before implementing them.

Someone with dirty (or sterile) hands (e.g., mechanics, cooks, surgeons) could examine reference materials while working. What other applications will people think of?

Hewlett-Packard™ developed a chip smaller than a grain of rice that stores four megabits of data and can be read wirelessly. It is designed to be stuck on things. What things? Medical records could be put on a chip attached to a patient's medical bracelet. What else? What potential problems will this generate?

What will be the impact of *wearware*—wearable computers, displays in eye glasses or contact lenses, smart sensors in clothing? What will be the impact of tiny flying sensors/computers that communicate wirelessly and which the military can deploy to monitor movement of equipment and people, or which rescuers can use in a collapsed building to search for survivors, or with which police or criminals can spy on us in our homes and public places?

Biological sciences and computer sciences will combine in new ways. Already we implant or attach microprocessor-controlled devices in or on human bodies: heart pacemakers and defibrillators and the smart, artificial knees we described in Section 1.2.6. To restore control and motion to people paralyzed by spinal injuries, researchers are experimenting with chips that convert brain signals to controls for leg and arm muscles. We are likely to see more such devices to repair injuries and treat diseases. And then we will see such devices modified to enhance performance. At first it might be physical performance for athletes, for example, to help a competitive swimmer swim more smoothly. Later, implanted chips might enhance mental performance.

Thinking about the issues and arguments discussed in this book should help prepare us to face the issues these new applications raise.

1.3 An Introduction to Some Issues and Themes

1.3.1 ISSUES

Analyzing and evaluating the impact of a new technology can be difficult. Some of the changes are obvious. Some are more subtle. Even when benefits are obvious, their costs and side effects might not be, and vice versa. We use an early application, the automated teller machine (ATM), and a Web application, online banking, to introduce some issues we discuss in more detail throughout the book. Many other examples could be used as well. While reading this discussion, try to do a similar analysis for, say, cell phones or for ordering medicines from a Web site.

Why do we use ATMs and online banking? Because they are convenient. They enable us to check our account balance, withdraw cash (at ATMs), or make other banking transactions at any time of day or night, at locations that are more accessible than our bank branch. But what are the negative aspects?

❖ *Unemployment*
   Automation of the most common teller functions led to a decline in employment for bank tellers. Within a ten-year period when ATMs became widespread (1983–1993),

the number of people working as bank tellers dropped from 480,000 to 301,000.[14] Online banking services eliminated more teller jobs.

❖ *Alienation and customer service*
Automation of teller functions removes the human contact between the customer and a live teller. Instead of talking to a smiling person, we confront a screen. The ATM or bank Web site might be confusing to use. We could forget our password. We might have a question it cannot answer.

❖ *Crime*
People are robbed after withdrawing cash at ATMs. Thieves steal millions of dollars with stolen and counterfeit ATM cards. Thieves who obtain our account number and other personal information can access our account online. The anonymity of ATMs and the Web makes fraud easy. A human teller would notice if the same person made numerous withdrawals, or might know the real customer by sight, or might be able to identify a suspect after a theft is discovered.

❖ *Loss of privacy*
Because transactions at ATMs are recorded in a database at the bank, the record of a person's transactions at various ATMs can provide information about the person's whereabouts and activities. Online account information is at risk from hackers.

❖ *Errors*
An error in the computer program that operated the ATMs for a large New York bank caused accounts to be debited twice the amount of the actual withdrawal. In less than one day, more than 150,000 transactions, totaling approximately $15 million, were incorrectly recorded.[15]

Unemployment, alienation, crime, loss of privacy, errors—a lot of serious problems! Are ATMs and online banking services, on balance, bad developments? Are you going to stop using them? Probably not. Why? One reason is the benefit we get from them. Convenience might not at first seem like a very important thing, especially when compared to impressive life saving and life-enhancing applications of computer technology. Yet these examples suggest that many people do in fact value convenience very highly. For this one benefit, we are willing to accept several negative features. Another reason why most of us will not give up ATMs and online banking is that some of the problems described above are exaggerated, or would occur anyway, or have solutions. Let us reconsider them.

❖ *Unemployment*
Contrary to projections by government agencies and financial companies, the number of bank tellers rose from the late 1990s—to about 600,000 in 2006—as banks opened more branches. Many jobs involving the design, production, sale, and use of computing devices, electronic gadgets, and software (including software for online banking) did not exist when ATMs were first introduced. Automation causes changes in the kinds of jobs people do. Overall, has computing technology increased or decreased employment? In Chapter 6, we consider this question and other issues of

computers and work. For example: How have computers and the Web changed the work environment and the structure of businesses? How do they affect the privacy of workers? How does the ease of "offshoring" jobs, due to fast data transmission and inexpensive communications, affect employment?

❖ *Alienation and customer service*
Anyone who wants to talk to a human teller can go into a bank during banking hours. No one has to use an ATM machine or bank online; these are additional options. In fact, banks are open more hours now than they were before ATMs existed. In the 1960s standard bank hours were 10 AM to 3 PM, Monday through Friday. Now many banks are open later and have Saturday hours.

   On the other hand, automated telephone systems or Web sites now handle many services that people used to provide. Some have the advantage of convenience. Some are quite frustrating to use. Some banks charge a fee for teller transactions. Many banks are closing branches. Computers have a mixed impact on customer service.

❖ *Crime*
Robberies at ATMs, while serious for the victim, are not a significant crime problem. The banking industry developed many approaches to reducing ATM crime such as improved lighting, surveillance cameras, and emergency buttons connected to the 911 system. Security for online banking improves. We discuss credit card fraud, hacking, identity theft, online scams, and other forms of computer crime in Chapter 5. (In that chapter, we also look at the intriguing and difficult problem of how to deal with the fact that some activities and material on the Web are legal in some countries and criminal in others.)

❖ *Loss of privacy*
The records kept of ATM transactions are not a serious privacy problem. Transactions inside a bank are also recorded. But this mention of privacy serves to introduce issues we consider in Chapter 2. A large portion of our financial transactions, including credit card purchases, loan payments, and income, make their way into databases. Our Web surfing can be tracked. Millions of young people post personal profiles on the Web without thinking about long-term consequences. Our governments maintain huge databases with personal information on us, and they access databases maintained by businesses. Who should have access to all this information, and how should it be protected from abuse? How does the Fourth Amendment's protection against unreasonable search and seizure apply when law-enforcement agents want to access personal data or use high-tech surveillance gear? How should we balance our desire for privacy of communications with the need of law-enforcement agencies to intercept and monitor communications of suspected criminals and terrorists?

❖ *Errors*
The bank that double debited ATM accounts corrected the errors quickly. With billions of transactions each year, we must expect that there will be some errors. The

error rate for ATM transactions is quite small. The potential for damage caused by serious errors in complex computer systems is a significant problem, however. The use of computer systems leads to new kinds of errors that would not have occurred before. We need to study these and learn how to reduce them. On the other hand, computers can reduce mistakes and increase safety in some cases. In Chapter 8, we look at a variety of examples and issues related to the risks, reliability, and safety of computer systems. What about errors in news reports, medical information, and all the other information on the Web? How do we know what we can trust?

In general, when evaluating computer systems and online services, we should not compare them to some ideal of perfect service or zero side effects and risk. That is impossible to achieve in most aspects of life. Instead, we should compare them to the alternatives and weigh the problems against the benefits. Of course, as in any endeavor, we continue to seek cost-effective improvements and solutions to problems. The ideal shows us the direction to go.

The ATM/online banking example served to introduce issues we study in several chapters of this book, but not all. Here are the others.

❖ *Freedom of speech* (Chapter 3)
   How much freedom of speech do we have in cyberspace? How serious are the problems of pornography and other unpleasant or dangerous material? Should the law or company policies prohibit some kinds of material? Should we have the right to be anonymous on the Net? Should we have the right to campaign for our favorite political candidate? Does freedom of speech apply to spam? How do repressive countries control access to the Net?

❖ *Intellectual property* (Chapter 4)
   People copy billions of dollars worth of music, movies, and software illegally each year. Storage in digital form has made intellectual property easy to copy without permission of the copyright owner. What is the extent of this problem? What can or should be done about it? Do search engines infringe copyrights? What is the "free software" movement? What is open-source software? What kinds of software should get patents?

❖ *Evaluating and controlling technology* (Chapter 7)
   In addition to the quality of online information, this chapter considers how the Internet affects local community life and the quality of life overall.
   Both the technological advances brought about by computer technology and the extraordinary pace of development can have dramatic, sometimes unsettling, impacts on people's lives. To some, this is frightening and disruptive. They see computers as a dehumanizing tool that reduces the quality of life or as a threat to the status quo and their well-being. Others see challenging and exciting opportunities. To them the development of computer technology is a thrilling and inspiring example of human

progress. Does computer technology have an overall positive or negative impact? Do some applications threaten our humanity?

❖ *Professional ethics* (Chapter 9)
The first eight chapters of this book look at issues primarily from the perspective of any person who lives and works in a modern computerized society and is interested in the impact of the technology. The final chapter looks at some of the same topics from the perspective of a computer professional who designs or programs computer systems or a professional in any area who must make decisions and/or set policy about the use of computer systems. What are the ethical responsibilities of the professional? For example, do system designers have a professional responsibility to develop systems that have built-in protections against crime? The Software Engineering Code of Ethics and Professional Practice and the ACM Code of Ethics and Professional Conduct, in Appendix A, provide some guidelines.

1.3.2 THEMES

Several themes and approaches to analysis of issues run through this book. I introduce a few here.

Old problems in a new context

Cyberspace has many of the problems, annoyances, and controversies of noncyber life, among them crime, pornography, violent fiction and games, advertising, copyright infringement, gambling, and products that do not work right.

Throughout this book, I often draw analogies from other technologies and other aspects of life. Sometimes we can find a helpful perspective for analysis and even ideas for solutions to new problems by looking at older technologies and established legal and social principles. The emphasis on the fact that similar problems occur in other areas is not meant to excuse problems related to computers. It suggests, however, that the root is not always the new technology, but can be human nature, ethics, politics, or other factors. We will often try to analyze how the technology changes the context and the impact of old problems.

Adapting to new technology

Changes in technology usually require adaptive changes in laws, social institutions, business policies, and personal skills, attitudes, and behavior.

When cell phones first came with built-in cameras, privacy laws in Pennsylvania (and elsewhere) were not sufficient to convict a man who used his cell phone to take a photo up a woman's skirt. (The man was found guilty of disorderly conduct.) During Japanese election campaigns in 2005, candidates were afraid to use e-mail and blogs and to update their Web sites to communicate with voters. A 1955 law that specifies the legal means of communicating with voters does not, of course, include these methods. It allows post cards and pamphlets.

We might naturally think some actions are criminal, and some should be legal, but they were not considered when existing laws were written. Their legal status might be the opposite of what we expect or it might be uncertain. Many new activities made possible by new technology are so different from prior ways of doing things that we need a new set of "rules of the game." We have to relearn standards for deciding when to trust what we read. The major impact of computer technology on privacy means we have to think in new ways about how to protect ourselves. We have to decide when privacy is important and when we are willing to put it at risk for some other benefit.

Varied sources of solutions to problems

> Solutions for problems that result from new technology come from more or improved technology, the market, management policies, education and public awareness, volunteer efforts, and law.

The cycle of problems and solutions, more problems and more solutions, is a natural part of change and of life in general. Throughout this book, when we consider problems, we consider solutions from several categories. Technical solutions involve hardware and software. For example, ATM software can prevent the double-debit problem we described earlier. "Hardware" includes more than the computer system; improved lighting near ATMs to reduce crime is a hardware solution. Management solutions are helpful business policies. Market mechanisms, such as competition and consumer demand, generate many improvements. Computer users and Web surfers must become educated about the tools they use. That includes knowing how and when to use them safely. Legal solutions include effective law enforcement, criminal penalties, lawsuits, legislation, and regulation. For example, there must be appropriate penalties for people who commit fraud online, and there must be appropriate liability laws for cases where system failures occur.

If you review our brief discussion of problems that arose with the use of cell phones in Section 1.2.2, you will see that the solutions came from almost all the categories mentioned here.

The global reach of the Net

> The ease of communication with distant countries has profound social, economic, and political effects—some beneficial, some not.

The Net makes information and opportunities more easily available to people isolated by geography or by political system. It makes crime fighting and law enforcement more difficult, because criminals can steal and disrupt services from outside the victim's country. Laws in one country prohibiting certain content on the Web or certain kinds of services restrict what people and businesses can put on the Web in other countries because the Web is accessible worldwide.

Trade-offs and controversy

> Increasing privacy and security often means reducing convenience. Protecting privacy makes law enforcement more difficult. Unpleasant, offensive, or inaccurate information accompanies our access to the Web's vast amounts of useful information.

Some of the topics we discuss are not particularly controversial. We will sometimes address an issue more as a problem-solving exercise than as a controversy. We will look at the impact of computer technology in a particular area, observe some problems that result, and describe solutions. On the other hand, many of the issues are controversial: censorship of the Internet, legislation for privacy protection, how strict copyright law should be, the impact of computers on quality of life.

We consider various viewpoints and arguments. Even if you have a strong position on one side of a controversy, it is important to know the arguments on the other side, for several reasons. Knowing that there are reasonable arguments for a different point of view, even if you do not think they are strong enough to win overall, helps make a debate more civilized. We see that the people on the other side are not necessarily evil, stupid, or ignorant; they may just put more weight on different factors. To convince others of your own viewpoint, you must counter the strongest arguments of the other side, so, of course, you first must know and understand them. Finally, you might change your own mind after considering arguments you had not thought of before.

Differences between personal choices, business policies, and law

> The criteria for making personal choices, for making policies for businesses and organizations, and for writing laws are fundamentally different.

We can make a personal choice, for example, about whether to give out our e-mail address or other personal information, according to our individual values and situation. A business bases its policy on many factors, including the manager's perception of consumer preferences, what competitors are doing, responsibilities to stockholders, the ethics of the business owners or managers, and relevant laws.

Laws are fundamentally different from personal choices and organizational policies because they impose decisions by force on people who did not make them. Arguments for passing a law should be qualitatively different from reasons for adopting a personal or organizational policy. It might seem odd at first, but arguments on the merits of the proposal—for example, that it is a good idea, or is efficient, or is good for business, or is helpful to consumers—are not good arguments for a law. We can use these arguments to try to convince a person or organization to adopt a particular policy voluntarily. Arguments for a law must show why the decision should be enforced against someone who *does not agree* that it is a good idea. It is better to base laws on the notion of rights rather than on personal views about their benefits or how we want people to behave.

1.4 Ethics

> *Honesty is the best policy.*
> —English proverb, pre-1600

1.4.1 WHAT IS ETHICS, ANYWAY?

Sometimes, we discuss issues and problems related to computer technology from a somewhat detached perspective. We see how a new technology can create new risks and problems and how social and legal institutions continually adapt. But technology is not an immutable force, outside of human control. People make decisions about what technologies and products to develop and how to use them. People make decisions about when a product is safe to release. People make decisions about access to and use of personal information. People make laws and set rules and standards.

Should you download movies from unauthorized Web sites? Should you hire foreign programmers who work at low salaries? Should you use a friend's password to get into a computer system on which you do not have an account? Suppose you are a manager and you discover that many of your employees are spending a lot of time visiting sports, stock, and entertainment Web sites while at work. Will you install monitoring software that records what sites each employee visits and how much time he or she spends there? Will you inform employees first? Suppose you manage a Web site. What information will you collect from visitors to the site and how will you use and protect the information? In these examples, you are confronting practical and legal issues—and ethical ones. In each case you can restate a question in the form: "Is it right to . . .?" Is it right to make a significant change in your company's privacy policy without giving customers or members advance notice?

In this section, we introduce several ethical theories. We discuss some distinctions (e.g., between ethics and law) that are important to understand when tackling ethical issues.

Ethics is the study of what it means to "do the right thing." It is a complex subject that has occupied philosophers for thousands of years. This presentation is necessarily simplified.

Ethical theory assumes that people are rational and make free choices. Neither of these conditions is always and absolutely true. People act emotionally, and they make mistakes. A person is not making a free choice when someone else is pointing a gun at him. Some argue that a person is not making a free choice in a situation where she might lose a job. However, free choice and use of rational judgment are capacities and

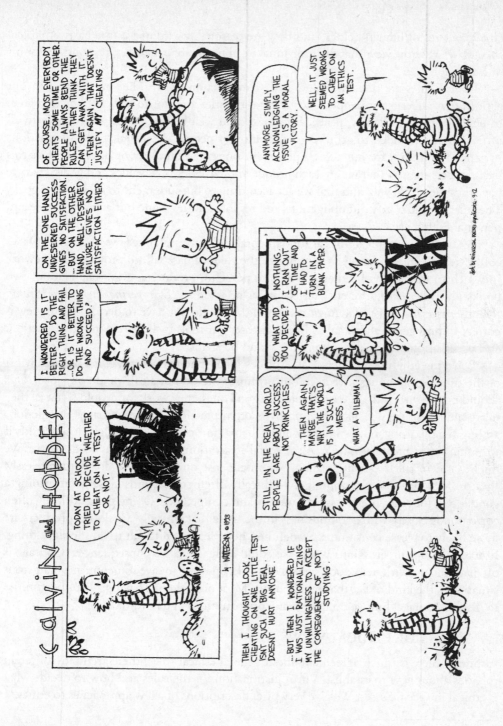

characteristics of human beings, and they are reasonably assumed as the basis of ethical theory. We take the view that the individual is, in most circumstances, responsible for his or her actions.

Ethical rules are rules to follow in our interactions with other people and in our actions that affect other people. Most ethical theories attempt to achieve the same goal: to enhance human dignity, peace, happiness, and well-being. Ethical rules apply to all of us and are intended to achieve good results for people in general, and for situations in general—not just for ourselves, not just for one situation. A set of rules that does this well respects the fact that we are each unique and have our own values and goals, that we have judgment and will, and that we act according to our judgment to achieve our goals. The rules should clarify our obligations and responsibilities—and our areas of choice and personal preference.*

We could view ethical rules as fundamental and universal, like laws of science. Or we could view them as rules we make up, like the rules of baseball, to provide a framework in which to interact with other people in a peaceful, productive way. The titles of two books illustrate these different viewpoints. One is *Ethics: Discovering Right and Wrong*; the other is *Ethics: Inventing Right and Wrong*.[16] We do not have to decide which view is correct to find good ethical rules. In either case, our tools include reason, introspection, and observation of human nature, values, and behavior.

Behaving ethically, in a personal or professional sphere, is usually not a burden. Most of the time we are honest, we keep our promises, we do not steal, we do our jobs. This should not be surprising. If ethical rules are good ones, they work for people. That is, they make our lives better. Behaving ethically is often practical. Honesty makes interactions among people work more smoothly and reliably, for example. We might lose friends if we often lie or break promises. Also, social institutions encourage us to do right: We might land in jail if caught stealing. We might lose our jobs if we do them carelessly. In a professional context, doing good ethically often corresponds closely with doing a good job in the sense of professional quality and competence. Doing good ethically often corresponds closely with good business in the sense that ethically developed products are more likely to please consumers. Sometimes, however, it is difficult to do the right thing. It takes courage in situations where we could suffer negative consequences. Courage is often associated with heroic acts, where one risks one's life to save someone in a dangerous situation—the kind of act that makes news. Most of us do not have those opportunities to display courage, but we do have many opportunities in day-to-day life.

1.4.2 A VARIETY OF ETHICAL VIEWS

Although there is much agreement about general ethical rules, there are many different theories about how to establish a firm justification for the rules and how to decide what is ethical in specific cases. We give very brief descriptions of a few approaches to ethics.[17]

---

*Not all ethical theories fit this description. Ethical relativism and some types of ethical egoism do not. In this book, however, we assume these goals and requirements for ethical theories.

Some ethicists* make a distinction between ethical theories that view certa..
good or bad because of some intrinsic aspect of the action and ethical theories u..
view acts as good or bad because of their consequences. They call these deontological
(or nonconsequentialist) and consequentialist theories, respectively. The distinction is
perhaps emphasized more than necessary. If the criteria used by deontologists to determine
the intrinsic goodness or badness of an act did not consider its consequences for people—
at least for most people, most of the time—their criteria would seem to have little ethical
merit.

Deontological theories

Deontologists tend to emphasize duty and absolute rules, to be followed whether they
lead to good or ill consequences in particular cases. One example is, "Do not lie." An act
is ethical if it complies with ethical rules and is chosen for that reason.

Immanuel Kant, the philosopher often presented as the prime example of a
deontologist, contributed many important ideas to ethical theory. We mention three
of them here. One is the principle of universality: We should follow rules of behavior that
we can universally apply to everyone. This principle is so fundamental to ethical theory
that we have already accepted it in our explanation of ethics. The Biblical instruction,
"Do unto others as you would have them do unto you," is another statement of the same
general idea.

Deontologists argue that logic or reason determines rules of ethical behavior, that
actions are intrinsically good because they follow from logic. Kant believed that rationality
is the standard of what is good. We can reason about what makes sense and act accordingly,
or we can act irrationally, which is evil. The view that something is evil because it is illogical
might seem unconvincing, but Kant's instruction to "Respect the reason in you," that
is, to use your reason, rationality, and judgment, rather than emotions, when making a
decision in an ethical context, is a wise one.

Three, Kant stated a principle about interacting with other people: One must never
treat people as merely means to ends, but rather as ends in themselves.

Kant took an extreme position on the absolutism of ethical rules. He argued, for
example, that it is always wrong to lie. For example, if a person is looking for someone
he intends to murder, and he asks you where the intended victim is, it is wrong for you
to lie to protect the victim. Most people would agree that there are cases in which even
very good, universal rules should be broken—because of the consequences.

Utilitarianism

Utilitarianism is the main example of a consequentialist theory. Its guiding principle, as
expressed by John Stuart Mill,[18] is to increase happiness, or "utility." A person's utility
is what satisfies the person's needs and values. An action might decrease utility for some

---

*Ethicists are philosophers (and others) who study ethics.

people and increase it for others. We should consider the consequences—the benefits and damages to all affected people—and "calculate" the change in aggregate utility. An act is right if it tends to increase aggregate utility and wrong if it tends to decrease it.

Utilitarianism is a very influential theory, and it has many variations. As stated above, the utilitarian principle applies to individual actions. For each action, we consider the impact on utility and judge the action by its net impact. This is sometimes called "act utilitarianism." One variant of utilitarianism, called "rule utilitarianism," applies the utility principle not to individual actions but to general ethical rules. Thus, a rule utilitarian might argue that the rule "Do not lie" will increase total utility, and for that reason is a good rule. Rule utilitarians do not do a utility calculation for each instance where lying is considered. Generally, a utilitarian would be more comfortable than a deontologist breaking a rule in circumstances where doing so would have good consequences.

There are numerous problems with act utilitarianism. It might be difficult or impossible to determine all the consequences of an act. If we can do so, do we choose acts that *we* believe will, or should, contribute to the happiness of the people affected, or let them choose themselves? How do we know what they would choose? How do we quantify happiness in order to make comparisons among many people? Should some people's utility be given more weight than others'? Should we weigh a thief's gain of utility equal to the victim's loss? Is a dollar worth the same to a person who worked for it and a person who received it as a gift? Or to a rich person and a poor person? How can we measure the utility of freedom?

A more fundamental (and ethical) objection to act utilitarianism is that it does not recognize or respect individual rights. It has no absolute prohibitions and so could allow actions that many people consider always wrong. For example, if there is a convincing case that killing one innocent person (perhaps to distribute his or her organs to several people who will die without transplants), or taking all of a person's property and redistributing it to other community members, would maximize utility in a community, utilitarianism could justify these acts. A person has no protected domain of freedom.

Rule utilitarianism suffers far less than does act utilitarianism from these problems. Recognizing that widespread killing and stealing decrease the security and happiness of all, a rule utilitarian can derive rules against these acts. We can state these particular rules in terms of rights to life and property.

Natural rights

Suppose we wish to treat people as ends rather than merely means and we wish to increase people's happiness. These goals are somewhat vague and open to many interpretations in specific circumstances. One approach we might follow is to let people make their own decisions. That is, we try to define a sphere of freedom in which people can act freely according to their own judgment, without coercive interference by others, even others (including us) who think they are doing what is best for the people involved, or for humanity in general. This approach views ethical behavior as acting in such a way that respects a set of fundamental rights of others, including the rights to life, liberty, and property.

These rights are sometimes called natural rights because, in the opinion of some philosophers, they come from nature, or can be derived from the nature of humanity. We each have an exclusive right to ourselves and our labor, and to what we produce with our labor. John Locke argued for a natural right to property that we create or obtain by mixing our labor with it. Respect for these rights implies ethical rules against killing, stealing, deception, and coercion.

Those who emphasize natural rights tend to emphasize the ethical character of the *process* by which people interact, seeing acts generally as likely to be ethical if they involve voluntary interactions and freely made exchanges, where the parties are not coerced or deceived. This contrasts with other approaches that tend to focus on the *result* or state achieved by the interaction, for example, seeing an action as likely to be unethical if it leaves some people poor.

No simple answers

We cannot solve ethical problems by applying a formula or an algorithm. Human behavior and real human situations are complex. There are often trade-offs to consider. Ethical theories do not provide clear, incontrovertibly correct positions on most issues. We can use the approaches we described to support opposite sides of many an issue. For example, consider Kant's imperative that one must never treat people as merely means to ends, but rather as ends in themselves. We could argue that an employee who receives a very low wage, say, a wage too low to support a family, is wrongly being treated as merely a means for the employer to make money. But we could also argue that expecting the employer to pay more than he or she considers reasonable is treating the employer merely as a means to providing income for the employee. Similarly, it is easy for two utilitarians to come to different conclusions ona particular issue by measuring happiness or utility differently. A small set of basic natural rights might provide no guidance for many situations in which you must make ethical decisions—but if we try to define rights to cover more situations, there will be fierce disagreement about just what those rights should be.

Although ethical theories do not completely settle difficult, controversial issues, they help to identify important principles or guidelines. They remind us of things to consider, and they can help clarify reasoning and values. There is much merit in Kant's principle of universalism and his emphasis on treating people as intrinsically valuable "ends." There is much merit in utilitarianism's consideration of consequences and its standard of increasing achievement of people's happiness. And there is much merit in the natural-rights approach of setting minimal rules in a rights framework to guarantee people a sphere in which they can act according to their own values and judgment.

DO ORGANIZATIONS HAVE ETHICS?

Some philosophers argue that it is meaningless to speak of a business or organization as having ethics. People make all decisions and take all actions. Those people must have ethical responsibility for everything they do. Others argue that an organization that acts with intention and a formal decision structure, such as a business, is a moral entity.[19] Viewing a business as a moral entity does not diminish the responsibility of the individual. We can hold both the individuals and the company or organization responsible for their acts.*

Whether one accepts or rejects the idea that a business can have ethical rights and responsibilities, it is clear that organizational structure and policies lead to a pattern of actions and decisions that have ethical content. Businesses have a "corporate culture," or a "personality," or simply a reputation for treating employees and customers in respectful and honest—or careless and deceptive—ways.

People in management positions shape the culture or ethics of a business or organization. Thus, decisions by managers have an impact beyond the particular product, contract, or action a decision involves. A manager who is dishonest with customers or who cuts corners on testing, for instance, is setting an example that encourages other employees to be dishonest and careless. A manager's ethical responsibility includes his or her contribution to the company's ethical personality.

1.4.3 SOME IMPORTANT DISTINCTIONS

A number of important distinctions affect our ethical judgments, but are often not clearly expressed or understood. In this section, we identify a few of these. Just being aware of them can help clarify issues in some ethical debates.

Right, wrong, and okay

In situations with ethical dilemmas, there are often many options that are ethically acceptable, with no specific one ethically required. Thus, it is misleading to divide all acts into two categories, ethically right and ethically wrong. Rather, it is better to think of acts as either ethically obligatory, ethically prohibited, or ethically acceptable.

Negative and positive rights, or liberties and claim rights

When people speak of rights, they are often speaking about two quite different kinds of rights. In philosophy books, these rights are usually called negative and

---

*Regardless of whether businesses and organizations are viewed as moral agents, they are treated as legal entities and can be held legally responsible for their acts.

positive rights, but the terms liberties and claim rights are more descriptive of the distinction.[20]

Negative rights, or liberties, are rights to act without interference. The only obligation they impose on others is not to prevent you from acting. They include the right to life (in the sense that no one may kill you), the right to be free from assault, the right to use your property, the right to use your labor, skills, and mind to create goods and services and to trade with other people in voluntary exchanges. The rights to "life, liberty, and the pursuit of happiness" described in the Declaration of Independence are liberties, or negative rights. Freedom of speech and religion, as guaranteed in the First Amendment of the U.S. Constitution, are negative rights: The government may not interfere with you, jail you, or kill you because of what you say or what your religious beliefs are. The right to work, as a liberty or negative right, means that no one may prohibit you from working or, for example, punish you for working without getting a government permit. The (negative) right to access the Internet is so obvious in free countries that we do not even think of it. In totalitarian countries, it is restricted or denied.

Claim rights, or positive rights, impose an obligation on some people to provide certain things for others. A positive right to a job means that someone must hire you regardless of whether they voluntarily choose to, or that it is right, or obligatory, for the government to set up job programs for people who are out of work. A positive right to life means that some people are obligated to pay for food or medical care for others who cannot pay for them. When freedom of speech is interpreted as a claim right, or positive right, it means that owners of shopping malls, radio stations, and online services may be required to provide space or time for content they do not wish to include. Access to the Internet, as a claim right, could require such things as taxes on our telephone bills to provide subsidized access for poor people.

Now here is the problem: Negative rights and positive rights often conflict. Some people think that liberties are almost worthless by themselves, and that society must devise social and legal mechanisms to ensure that everyone has their claim rights, or positive rights, satisfied, even if that means diminishing the liberties of some. Other people think that there can be no (or very few) positive rights, because it is impossible to enforce claim rights for some people without violating the liberties of others. They see the protection of liberties, or negative rights, as ethically essential.

This is one of the reasons for disagreement on issues such as some privacy protection regulations, for example. Although we will not solve the disagreement about which kind of right is more important, we can sometimes clarify the issues in a debate by clarifying which kind of right we are discussing.

Distinguishing wrong and harm

Carelessly and needlessly causing harm is wrong, but it is important to remember that harm alone is not a sufficient criterion to determine that an act is unethical. Many ethical, even admirable, acts can make other people worse off. For example, you may accept a job offer knowing someone else wanted the job and needed it more than you do. You may reduce the income of other people by producing a better product that consumers prefer. If your product is really good, you might put a competitor out of business completely and cause many people to lose their jobs. Yet there is nothing wrong with doing honest, productive work.

On the other hand, hackers used to argue that breaking into computer systems is not wrong because they do no harm. Lack of harm is not sufficient to conclude that an act is ethically acceptable. Aside from the fact that the hacker might do unintended harm, one can argue that hacking is a violation of property rights: A person has no right to enter your property without your permission, independent of any harm done.

Separating goals from constraints

Economist Milton Friedman wrote that the goal or responsibility of a business is to make a profit for its shareholders. This statement appalled some ethicists, as they believe it justifies, or is used to justify, irresponsible and unethical actions. It seems to me that arguments on this point miss the distinction between goals, on the one hand, and constraints on actions taken to achieve the goals, on the other—or the distinction between ends and means. Our personal goals might include financial success and finding an attractive mate. Working hard, investing wisely, and being an interesting and decent person can achieve these goals. Stealing and lying might achieve them too. By most ethical theories, stealing and lying are unacceptable. Ethics tells us what actions are acceptable or unacceptable in our attempts to achieve the goals. There is nothing unethical about a business having the goal of maximizing profits. The ethical character of the company depends on whether the actions taken to achieve the goal are consistent with ethical constraints.[21]

Personal preference and ethics

Most of us have strong feelings about a lot of issues. It might be difficult to draw a line between what we consider ethically right or wrong and what we personally approve or disapprove of. Imagine an organization that advocates some policy you think ethically wrong, perhaps an abortion rights group or an anti-abortion group, or a group that advocates legalizing marriages between same-sex couples, or a group that advocates banning homosexuals from teaching in public schools. Suppose the group is solely an advocacy or educational group; it does not perform abortions or block abortion clinics, for example. Now the organization asks you to set up a Web site for it. You believe in freedom of speech, but you find the job distasteful; you do not want to do anything to assist the organization.

If you decide to decline the job, are you acting on ethical grounds? In other words, can you claim that performing the job is unethical? The organization is exercising freedom of speech. Although its position is controversial and ethical issues are relevant to the social issue the organization supports, the organization is not engaged in unethical activity. Your assistance would help to further a goal you do not support. This is a matter of personal preference. There is nothing ethically wrong with declining the job, of course. The organization's freedom of speech does not impose an ethical obligation on you for assistance.

When discussing political or social issues, people frequently argue that their position is right in a moral or ethical sense or that an opponent's position is morally wrong or unethical. People tend to want to be on the "moral high ground." People feel the stigma of an accusation that their view is ethically wrong. Thus, arguments based on ethics can be, and often are, used to intimidate people with different views. It is a good idea to try to distinguish between actions we find distasteful, rude, or ill-advised and actions that we can argue convincingly are ethically wrong.

Law and ethics

What is the connection between law and ethics? Sometimes very little. Is it ethical to prohibit marijuana use by terminally ill people? Is it ethical for the government or a state university to give preference in contracts, hiring, or admissions to people in specific ethnic groups? Is it ethical for a bank loan officer to carry customer records on a laptop to work at the beach? The current law, whatever it happens to be at a particular time, does not answer these questions. In addition, history provides numerous examples of laws most of us consider profoundly wrong by ethical standards; slavery is perhaps the most obvious example. Ethics precedes law in the sense that ethical principles help determine whether or not we should pass specific laws.

Some laws enforce ethical rules (e.g., against murder and theft). By definition, we are ethically obligated to obey such laws—not because they are laws, but because the laws implement the obligations and prohibitions of ethical rules.

Other laws fall into several categories. One category of laws establishes conventions for business or other activities. Commercial law, such as the Uniform Commercial Code, defines rules for economic transactions and contracts. Such rules provide a framework in which we can interact smoothly and confidently with strangers. They include provisions for how to interpret a contract if a court must resolve a dispute. These laws are extremely important to any society. They should be consistent with ethics. Beyond basic ethical considerations, however, details could depend on historic conventions, practicality, and other nonethical criteria. In the U.S., drivers must drive on the right side of the road; in England, drivers must drive on the left side. There is obviously nothing intrinsically right or wrong about either choice. But once the convention is established, it is wrong to drive on the wrong side of the road because it needlessly endangers other people.

Unfortunately, many laws fall into a category that is not intended to implement ethical rules—or even be consistent with them. The political process is subject to pressure from special interest groups of all sorts who seek to pass laws that favor their groups or businesses. Examples include the laws that delayed the introduction of cable television (promoted by the television networks) and laws, sponsored by the dairy industry when margarine was first introduced, against coloring margarine yellow to look more like butter. After opposing resale auctions of event tickets for years, Ticketmaster accepted this popular online sales paradigm—and lobbied for laws restricting competitors.[22] Many prominent people in the financial industry reported receiving a large number of fund-raising letters from members of Congress—in the week that Congress took up new regulations for their industry. Many political, religious, or ideological organizations promote laws to require (or prohibit) certain kinds of behavior that the group considers desirable (or objectionable). Examples include prohibitions on gambling or alcohol, requirements for recycling, and requirements that stores close on Sundays. At an extreme, in some countries, this category includes restrictions on the practice of certain religions.

Copyright law has elements of all three categories we described. It defines a property right, violation of which is a form of theft. Because of the intangible nature of intellectual property, some of the rules about what constitutes copyright infringement are more like the second category: pragmatic rules devised to be workable. Powerful groups (e.g., the publishing, music, and movie industries) lobby for specific rules to benefit themselves. This is why some violations of copyright law are clearly unethical (if one accepts the concept of intellectual property at all), yet others seem to be entirely acceptable, sometimes even noble.

Are we ethically obligated to obey a law just because it is a law? Some argue that we are: As members of society, we must accept the rules that the legislative process has created so long as they are not clearly and utterly ethically wrong. Others argue that, whereas this might often be a good policy, it is not an ethical obligation. Legislators are just a group of people, subject to errors and political influences; there is no reason to feel an ethical obligation to do something just because they say so. Indeed, some believe that laws regulating personal behavior or voluntary economic transactions violate the liberty and autonomy of the people forced to obey and, hence, are ethically wrong.

Is it always ethically right to do something that is legal? No. Laws must be uniform and must be stated in a way that clearly indicates what actions are punishable. Ethical situations are complex and variable; the people involved might know the relevant factors, but it might not be possible to prove them in court. There are widely accepted ethical rules that would be difficult and probably unwise to enforce absolutely with laws—for example, "Do not lie." New law lags behind new technology for good reasons. It takes time to recognize new problems associated with the technology, consider possible solutions, think and debate about the consequences and fairness of various proposals, and so on. A good law will set minimal standards that can apply to all situations, leaving a large range of voluntary choices. Ethics fills the gap between the time when technology creates new problems and the time when reasonable laws are passed. Ethics fills the gap between general legal standards that apply to all cases and the particular choices made in a specific case.

While it is not ethically obligatory to obey all laws, that is not an excuse to ignore laws, nor is a law (or lack of a law) an excuse to ignore ethics.

EXERCISES

Review Exercises

1.1   What were two unexpected uses of social-networking sites?

1.2   What are two ways free services on the Web are paid for?

1.3   Define *artificial intelligence*.

1.4   Describe two computer-based devices that assist people with disabilities.

1.5   List four kinds of software that helped expand use of the Web.

1.6   What are two of Kant's important ideas about ethics?

1.7   Name two problems with act utilitarianism.

1.8   Give an example of a law that implements an ethical principle. Give an example of a law that enforces a particular group's idea of how people should behave.

1.9   Define negative rights and positive rights. Give an example of a negative right and a positive right that are in conflict.

General Exercises

1.10   Computer and communication technologies have deeply changed the way we interact with other people. Write a paragraph about a technological application that has affected your relationships with others. Have there been any social implications? Has this technology created any ethical dilemmas for you?

1.11   Some high schools ban use of cell phones during classes. Some require that students turn in their phones at the beginning of class and retrieve them afterwards. What are some reasons for these policies? Do you think they are good policies? Explain.

1.12   Describe a few ways computer technology has made life in a new country easier for immigrants.

1.13   What are some advantages and disadvantages of online libraries (of entire books) as compared to "brick and mortar" libraries? Give at least five distinct replies in total.

1.14   Telemedicine, or long-distance medicine, refers to remote performance of medical exams, analyses, and procedures using specialized equipment and computer networks. Describe an instance in which telemedicine has been used.

1.15   Describe a useful application, other than those mentioned in Section 1.2.7, for the system with which the user controls a display with hand movements, without touching a screen or controls.

1.16   High schools and universities across the globe are turning to distance learning and online education. Discuss some advantages and disadvantages of this type of instruction? How do you think online cheating can be prevented?

1.17   Think up some computerized device, software, or online service that does not yet exist, but that you would be very proud to help develop. Describe it.

1.18   Various advocacy groups sued various companies because blind people cannot use their Web sites. The suits argue that the Americans With Disabilities Act requires that the sites be accessible.

A judge dismissed a suit against Southwest Airlines because Web sites did not fit in any of the categories specified in the law. Another judge allowed a similar suit, *National Federation for the Blind v. Target Corporation*, to proceed.

Should all business and government Web sites be required by law to provide full access for disabled people? Discuss arguments for both sides. Identify the negative and positive rights involved. Which side do you think is stronger? Why?

1.19   List three applications of computer technology mentioned in this chapter that reduce the need for transportation. What are some advantages of doing so?

1.20   Talking on a cell phone while driving increases the risk of an accident. States, such as California, have now banned the use of a hand-held cell phone. Think of how this new law will affect commuters. Do you feel the roads will be safer because of the law? How do you think the law will be enforced? Do you think more states will soon develop similar laws?

1.21   Many elderly people have trouble remembering words, people's names, and recent events. Imagine a memory-aid product. What features would it have? What technologies would you use if you were designing it?

1.22   Which kind of ethical theory, deontologist or consequentialist, works better for arguing that it is wrong to drive one's car on the left side of a road in a country where people normally drive on the right? Explain.

1.23   Develop a code of ethics and etiquette for use of cell phones. Include provisions for cameras in phones.

1.24   Technology has allowed for advancement in digital imaging. Suppose you worked for a newspaper and were to cover a story about the ongoing war. You don't have any pictures that are right for the story, but you have a number of shots that have some of the elements you want. With the help of digital imaging, you can combine the photos to better illustrate your story. Would you do so? Do you think this would be an ethical action? What would be the implications and consequences?

1.25   With the help of the Internet, people can do things from the comfort of their own home that used to require a trip to an office or library. Give three examples of how such technology has affected your daily life. What are the advantages and disadvantages? Where do you think such technology is headed in the future? What additional technological advancements would you like to see?

1.26   Analyze the ethics of creating a fictional person on a social-networking site with no indication that the person is not a real person.

1.27   In the following (true) cases, tell whether the people are interpreting the right being claimed as a negative right (liberty) or as a positive right (claim right). Explain. In each case, which kind of right should it be, and why?
   a) A man sued his health insurance company because it would not pay for Viagra, the drug for treating male impotence. He argued that the insurer's refusal to pay denied his right to a happy sex life.
   b) Two legislators who ran for reelection lost. They sued an organization that sponsored ads criticizing their voting records. The former legislators argued that the organization interfered with their right to hold office.

1.28   Thinking ahead to Chapter 8, pick any example, application, or service mentioned in this chapter where an error in the system could pose a serious danger to people's lives. Explain how.

Assignments

These exercises require some research or activity.

1.29   Go around your home and make a list of all the appliances and devices that contain a computer chip.

1.30   Get a brochure from a car dealer for a new car. Describe the uses of computer technology in the car. For each one, tell whether its main purpose is to enhance convenience or to enhance safety.

1.31   Christie's (www.christies.com™), an international auction house, was founded in 1766. So why is eBay® a big deal? Compare the price range of objects sold in Christie's auctions and those sold on eBay. Compare the kinds of customers each business has. Mention other factors you can think of that distinguish the two in terms of their impact.

1.32   Arrange an interview with a disabled student on your campus. Ask the student to describe or demonstrate some of the computer tools he or she uses. (If your campus has a Disabled Student Center, its staff may be able to help you find an interview subject.) Write a report of the interview and/or demonstration.

1.33   Go to your campus library and get the microfilm or microfiche for the issue of a major newspaper published on the day you were born. Read a few articles. Compare the convenience of using these media (standard for research not long ago) to reading newspaper and magazine articles on the Web.

1.34   Over the next month or two (whatever is appropriate for the length of your course), collect news articles, from print or electronic sources, on (1) benefits and valuable applications of computer technology and (2) failures and/or problems caused by computer technology. The articles should be current, that is, published during this time period. Write a brief summary and commentary on two articles in each category indicating how they relate to topics covered in this book.

NOTES

1.   Stephen E. Ambrose, *Undaunted Courage: Meriwether Lewis, Thomas Jefferson and the Opening of the American West* (Simon & Schuster, 1996), p. 53.

2.   Michael Rothschild, "Beyond Repair: The Politics of the Machine Age Are Hopelessly Obsolete," *The New Democrat*, July/August 1995, pp. 8–11.

3.   Betty Friedan, *The Feminine Mystique* (W. W. Norton, 1963), p. 312.

4.   For one example, see "Adnan Hajj Photographs Controversy," Answers.com, www.answers.com/topic/adnan-hajj-photographs-controversy (accessed September 3, 2007).

5.   Statement of Vinton G. Cerf, U.S. Senate Committee on the Judiciary Hearing on Reconsidering our Communications Laws, June 14, 2006, judiciary.senate.gov/testimony.cfm?id=1937& wit_id=5416.

6.   Howard W. French, "Mob Rule on China's Internet: The Keyboard as Weapon," *International Herald Tribune*, June 1, 2006, p. 1.

7.   Carrie A. Johnson, "US eCommerce: 2005 To 2010," Forrester Research, Inc., September 14, 2005, www.forrester.com/Research/Document/Excerpt/0,7211, 37626,00.html (accessed August 21, 2006); Jaap Favier, "Europe's eCommerce Forecast: 2006 To 2011," Forrester Research, Inc., June 29, 2006, www.forrester.com/Research/Document/Excerpt/0,7211, 38297,00.html (accessed September 3, 2007). Estimates of the value of online commerce vary depending on who does the counting and whether auction sites and services like travel are included.

8.   Robert D. Atkinson, "Leveling the E-Commerce Playing Field: Ensuring Tax and Regulatory Fairness for Online and Offline Businesses," Progressive Policy Institute Policy Report, June 30, 2003, www.ppionline.org

(accessed September 3, 2007); Jennifer Saranow, "Savvy Car Buyers Drive Bargains with Pricing Data from the Web," *Wall Street Journal*, October 24, 2006, p. D5.

9. William M. Bulkeley, "Profit in Motion: Tiny Sensors Take Off," *Wall Street Journal*, May 10, 2007, p. B3.

10. John Hockenberry, "The Human Brain," *Wired*, August 2001, pp. 94-105.

11. Evan Ratliff, "Born to Run," *Wired*, July 2001, pp. 86–97; Rheo and Power Knees by Ossur, www.ossur.com (accessed August 25, 2006).

12. Various brain interface devices are described in Hockenberry, "The Human Brain."

13. Jim Fruchterman, former president of a company that makes book readers for the blind, in an e-mail message to me.

14. Joan E. Rigdon, "Technological Gains Are Cutting Costs, and Jobs, in Services," *Wall Street Journal*, February 24, 1994, p. A1.

15. Saul Hansell, "Cash Machines Getting Greedy at a Big Bank," *New York Times*, February 18, 1994, p. A1, C16.

16. By Louis P. Pojman (Wadsworth, 1990) and J. L. Mackie (Penguin Books, 1977), respectively.

17. Sources used in the preparation of this section include Joseph Ellin, *Morality and the Meaning of Life: An Introduction to Ethical Theory* (Harcourt Brace Jovanovich, 1995); Deborah G. Johnson, *Computer Ethics*, 2nd ed. (Prentice Hall, 1994); Louis Pojman, *Ethical Theory: Classical and Contemporary Readings*, 2nd ed. (Wadsworth, 1995) (which includes John Stuart Mill's "Utilitarianism," Kant's "The Foundations of the Metaphysic of Morals," and John Locke's "Natural Rights"); James Rachels, *The Elements of Moral Philosophy* (McGraw Hill, 1993).

18. John Stuart Mill, *Utilitarianism* (1863).

19. Kenneth C. Laudon, "Ethical Concepts and Information Technology," *Communications of the ACM*, 38, no. 12 (December 1995), p. 38.

20. J. L. Mackie uses the term *claim-rights in Ethics: Inventing Right and Wrong*. Another term that could be used for positive rights is entitlements.

21. Some goals appear to be ethically wrong in themselves, for example, genocide, although often it is because the only way to achieve the goal is by methods that are ethically unacceptable (killing innocent people).

22. Kent Smetters, "Ticketmaster vs. Ticket Buyers," American Enterprise Institute, October 24, 2006, www.aei.org/publications/pubID.25049,filter.all/pub_detail.asp (accessed November 1, 2006).

BOOKS AND ARTICLES

Many of these references include topics that are covered throughout this book. Some of the references in Chapter 9 also include topics covered throughout this book.

- The Alliance for Technology Access. *Computer Resources for People With Disabilities*. 4th ed. Hunter House Publishers, 2004, www.ataccess.org.

- Augarten, Stan. *Bit by Bit: An Illustrated History of Computers*. Ticknor & Fields, 1984. The early history, of course.

- Cairncross, Frances. *The Death of Distance 2.0: How the Communications Revolution Is Changing Our Lives*. Harvard Business School Press, 2001.

- Denning, Peter J., ed. *The Invisible Future: The Seamless Integration of Technology Into Everyday Life*. McGraw Hill, 2001.

- Cavazos, Edward, and Gavino Morin. *Cyberspace and the Law*. MIT Press, 1994.

- Denning, Peter, and Robert Metcalfe. *Beyond Calculation: The Next Fifty Years of Computing*. Copernicus, 1997.

- Dertouzos, Michael. *What Will Be: How the New World of Information Will Change Our Lives*. HarperEdge, 1997.

- Ellin, Joseph. *Morality and the Meaning of Life: An Introduction to Ethical Theory*. Harcourt Brace Jovanovich, 1995.

- Gershenfeld, Neil A. *When Things Start to Think*. Henry Holt & Co., 1999.

- Langford, Duncan, ed. *Internet Ethics*. St. Martin's Press, 2000.

- McConnell, Ben, and Jackie Huba. *Citizen Marketers*. Kaplan Publishing,

2006. Describes how ordinary people influence other consumers, democratizing marketing.

- Mokyr, Joel. *The Gifts of Athena: Historical Origins of the Knowledge Economy.* Princeton University Press, 2002.

- Narveson, Jan. *Moral Matters.* Broadview Press, 1993. The first chapter gives a good, very readable introduction to moral issues.

- Pojman, Louis. *Ethical Theory: Classical and Contemporary Readings.* 2nd ed. Wadsworth, 1995. Includes John Stuart Mill's "Utilitarianism," Kant's "The Foundations of the Metaphysic of Morals," John Locke's "Natural Rights," and other classical essays on various ethical theories.

- Reynolds, Glenn. *An Army of Davids: How Markets and Technology Empower Ordinary People to Beat Big Media, Big Government, and Other Goliaths.* Nelson Current, 2006.

- Rosenoer, Jonathan. *Cyberlaw: The Law of the Internet.* Springer Verlag, 1997.

- Spinello, Richard A., and Herman T. Tavani, eds. *Readings in CyberEthics.* Jones and Bartlett, 2001.

- Tapscott, Don, and Anthony D. Williams. *Wikinomics: How Mass Collaboration Changes Everything.* Portfolio, 2006.

- Vinge, Vernor. *Rainbows End.* Tor, 2006. A science fiction novel, set in the near future, that imagines how computer technology may affect communication, education, medical care, and many facets of ordinary life.

ORGANIZATIONS AND WEB SITES

- The Online Ethics Center for Engineering and Science (National Academy of Engineering): onlineethics.org

2

Privacy

2.1 Privacy and Computer Technology

2.1.1 INTRODUCTION

After the fall of the communist government in East Germany, people examined the files of Stasi, the secret police. They found that the government had used spies and informers to build detailed dossiers on the opinions and activities of roughly six million people—a third of the population. The informers were neighbors, coworkers, friends, and even family members of the people they reported on. Stasi did not store the files in computers. The paper files filled an estimated 125 miles of shelf space.[1]

Before the digital age, surveillance cameras watched shoppers in banks and stores. And well into the era of computers and the Internet, pharmacies in Indiana disposed of hundreds of prescriptions, receipts, and order forms for medicines by tossing them into an open dumpster. Private investigators still search household garbage for medical and financial information, details of purchases, evidence of romantic affairs, and journalists' notes.

Computer technology is not necessary for the invasion of privacy. However, we discuss privacy at length in this book because digital technology and the Internet have made new threats possible and old threats more potent. Computer technologies—databases, digital cameras, the Web, among others—have profoundly changed what people can know about us and how they can use the information. Understanding the risks and problems is a first step toward protecting privacy. For computer professionals, understanding the risks and problems is a step toward designing systems with built-in privacy protections and fewer risks.

There are three key aspects of privacy:

- ❖ freedom from intrusion—being left alone
- ❖ control of information about oneself
- ❖ freedom from surveillance (from being followed, tracked, watched, and eavesdropped on)

It is clear that we cannot expect complete privacy. We usually do not accuse someone who initiates a conversation of invading our privacy. Many friends and slight acquaintances know what you look like, where you work, what kind of car you drive, and whether you are a nice person. They need not get your permission to observe and talk about you. If you live in a small town, you have little privacy; everyone knows everything about you. In a big city, you can be nearly anonymous. But if people know nothing about you, they might be taking a big risk if they rent you a place to live, hire you, lend you money, sell you automobile or medical insurance, accept your credit card, and so on. We give up some privacy for the benefits of dealing with strangers. We can choose to give up more in exchange for other benefits such as convenience and personalized service.

We use the term *personal information* often in this chapter. In the context of privacy issues, it includes any information relating to, or traceable to, an individual person. It is not restricted solely to what we might think of as sensitive information, although it includes that. It also includes information associated with a particular person's "handle," user name, online nickname, identification number, or e-mail address. Nor is it restricted to text data. It extends to any information from which a living individual can be identified, including images.

For the most part, in this book, we view privacy as a good thing. Critics of privacy argue that it gives cover to deception, hypocrisy, and wrongdoing. It allows fraud. It protects the guilty. Concern for privacy may be regarded with a suspicious "What do you have to hide?" The desire to keep things private does not mean we are doing anything wrong. We might wish to keep health, relationship, and family issues private. Some health and medical information is very sensitive: information about alcoholism, sexually transmitted diseases, psychiatric treatment, and suicide attempts. We might strongly desire to keep other health problems private even if they do not have negative social connotations. We might wish to keep religious beliefs and political views private from some of the people we interact with. Privacy of some kinds of information can be important to safety and security as well. Examples include travel plans, financial data, and, for some people, simply a home address. Other risks from the compilation of huge amounts of personal data result from the fact that so much of the data are incorrect. Business and government databases contain many errors. Files are not updated. Records of different people with similar names or other similarities get commingled or confused.

Privacy threats come in several categories:

❖ intentional, institutional uses of personal information (primarily for law enforcement and tax collection in the government sector and for marketing and decision making in the private sector by both businesses and organizations)

❖ unauthorized use or release by "insiders," the people who maintain the information

❖ theft of information

❖ inadvertent leakage of information through negligence or carelessness

❖ our own actions (sometimes intentional trade-offs and sometimes when we are unaware of the risks)

Privacy issues arise in many contexts. More topics with privacy implications appear in later chapters. We discuss anonymity more fully in Chapter 3. It can protect both privacy and freedom of speech but makes crime easier. We also discuss spam, the intrusion of online junk mail, in that chapter. We address identity theft in Chapter 5. In Chapter 5, we also examine rules for law enforcement searches of computers. In Chapter 6 we discuss privacy of employees in the workplace. Chapter 8 discusses problems that result from errors in stored personal information. Privacy comes up again in Chapter 9, where we focus on the responsibilities of computer professionals.

I use many real incidents, businesses, products, and services as examples throughout this book. In most cases, I am not singling them out for special endorsement or criticism. They are just some of the many examples we can use to illustrate problems, issues, and possible solutions.

> *The man who is compelled to live every minute of his life among others and whose every need, thought, desire, fancy or gratification is subject to public scrutiny, has been deprived of his individuality and human dignity. [He] merges with the mass. . . . Such a being, although sentient, is fungible; he is not an individual.*
>
> —Edward J. Bloustein[2]

> *It's important to realize that privacy preserves not personal secrets, but a sense of safety within a circle of friends so that the individual can be more candid, more expressive, more* open *with "secrets."*
>
> —Robert Ellis Smith[3]

2.1.2 NEW TECHNOLOGY, NEW RISKS

Computers, the Internet, and a whole array of digital devices, with their astounding increases in speed, storage space, and connectivity, make the collection, searching, analysis, storage, access, and distribution of huge amounts of information and images much easier, cheaper, and faster than ever before. These are great benefits. But when the information is about us, the same capabilities threaten our privacy.

Today there are thousands of databases, both government and private, containing personal information about us. Some of this information, such as our specific purchases in supermarkets and bookstores, was simply not recorded in the past. Some, including government documents such as divorce and bankruptcy records, were in public records but took a lot of time and effort to access. It was not easy to link together our financial, work, and family records. Now, the speed and power of search and analysis tools, when applied to all the data about us in myriad databases, make it easy to produce detailed profiles of our personal characteristics, relationships, activities, opinions, and habits. In the past, conversations disappeared when people finished speaking, and only the sender and the recipient normally read personal communications. Now, when we communicate by e-mail and on Web sites, our words are recorded and can be copied, forwarded, widely distributed, and read by others years later. Miniaturization of processors and sensors put tiny cameras in cell phones that millions of people carry everywhere. The wireless appliances we carry contain global positioning system (GPS) devices and other location devices. They enable others to determine a person's location and track a person's movements. Teenagers and college students put the facts of their lives on social-networking sites. Patients refill prescriptions and check results of medical tests on the Web. They correspond with doctors by e-mail. We store our photos and videos, fill out our tax forms, and create and store documents and financial spreadsheets on Web sites instead of on our own computer. These services have benefits, of course, but they expose us to increased privacy risk.

Increased storage capacity magnifies the impact of lost or stolen data. Disks and laptops with hundreds of thousands or millions of people's Social Security and credit-card numbers disappear from banks, stores, and government agencies.

Government agencies have very sophisticated tools for eavesdropping, watching us, and collecting and analyzing data about us. They can use the tools to reduce crime and increase security—and to infringe privacy.

Example: search query data

When a person enters a phrase into a search engine, views some results, then goes on to another task, he or she expects that the phrase is gone—gone like a telephone conversation with a friend, or a few words spoken to a clerk in a store. After all, with millions of people doing many searches each day for work, school, or personal uses, how could it all be stored? And who would want all that trivial information anyway? That is what most people thought about search queries until two incidents in 2006 demonstrated that it was all stored, it could be released, and it mattered.

Search engines collect many terabytes of data daily. A terabyte is a trillion bytes. It would have been absurdly expensive to store that much data in the recent past, but no longer. Why do search engine companies store search queries? It is tempting to say "because they can." But there are many uses for the search data. Suppose you search for "Milky Way." Whether you get many astronomy pages or information about the candy bar or a local restaurant can depend on your search history and other information about you. Search engines use such information to better guess the context for your search. Search engine companies want to know how many pages of search results users actually look at, how many they click on, how they refine their search queries, what spelling errors they commonly make. The companies analyze the data to improve search services, to target advertising better, and to develop new products and services. The database of past queries also provides realistic input for testing and evaluating modifications in the algorithms search engines use to select and rank results. Search query data are valuable to many companies besides search engine companies. By analyzing search queries, companies draw conclusions about what kinds of products and features people are looking for. They modify their products to meet consumer preferences.

But who else gets to see this mass of data? And why should we care?

If your own Web searches have been on innocuous topics, and you do not care who sees your queries, consider a few topics people might search for, and consider why they might want to keep them private: health and psychological problems, bankruptcy, uncontrolled gambling, right-wing conspiracies, left-wing conspiracies, alcoholism, anti-abortion information, pro-abortion information, erotica, illegal drugs. What are some possible consequences for a person doing extensive research on the Web for a suspense novel about terrorists who plan to blow up chemical factories?

The federal government presented Google with a subpoena* for two months of user search queries and all the URLs† that Google indexes. It wanted the data to respond to court challenges to the Child Online Protection Act (COPA), a law intended to protect children from online material "harmful to minors." (We discuss COPA in Section 3.2.2.) Google protested, bringing the issue to public attention. Although the subpoena did not ask for names of users, the idea of the government gaining access to the details of people's searches horrified privacy advocates and many people who use search engines. Google and privacy advocates opposed the precedent of government access to large masses of such data. A court reduced the scope of the subpoena to 50,000 URLs and no user queries.[4]

A few months later, release of a huge database of search queries at AOL showed that privacy violations occur even when the company does not associate the queries with people's names. Against company policy, an employee put the data on a Web site for search technology researchers. It included more than 20 million search queries of more than 650,000 people from a three-month period. The data identified people by coded ID numbers, not by name. However, it was not difficult to deduce the identity of some people, especially those who searched on their own name or address. A process called *re-identification* identified others. Re-identification means identifying the individual from a set of anonymous data. Journalists and acquaintances identified people in small communities who searched on numerous specific topics, such as the cars they own, the sports teams they follow, their health problems, and their hobbies. Once identified, a person is linked to all his or her other searches. AOL quickly removed the data, but journalists, researchers, and others had already copied it. Some made the whole data set available on the Web again.[5]‡

The search query databases and these two incidents illustrate numerous points about computer technology and privacy of personal data. We list some here.

❖ Anything we do online is recorded, at least briefly, and linked to our computer, if not our name.

---

*A subpoena is a court order for someone to give testimony or provide documents or other information for an investigation or a trial.

†As is common, we use the term *URL* (short for "uniform resource locator") informally for identifiers, or addresses, of pages or documents on the Web (the string of characters one types in a Web browser).

‡Members of AOL sued the company for its release of their search queries, claiming the release violated roughly ten federal and state laws.

❖ With the huge amount of storage space available, companies, organizations, and governments save huge amounts of data that no one would have imagined saving in the recent past.

❖ People often are not aware that information about them and their activities is being collected and saved.

❖ Leaks happen. The existence of the data presents a risk.

❖ A collection of many small items of information, in this case, search queries, can give a fairly detailed picture of a person's life.

❖ Direct association with a person's name is not essential for compromising privacy. Re-identification has become much easier due to the quantity of personal information stored and the power of data search and analysis tools.

❖ The government sometimes requests or demands sensitive personal data held by businesses and organizations.

❖ Information on a public Web site will be found by people other than those for whom it was intended. It is available to everyone.

❖ Once data goes on the Internet or into a database, it seems to last forever. People (and automated software) quickly make and distribute copies. It is almost impossible to remove released information from circulation.

❖ It is extremely likely that data collected for one purpose (such as responding to a user's search query) will to be used for other purposes (such as business planning).

❖ We cannot directly protect information about ourselves. We must depend on the businesses and organizations that hold it to protect it from thieves, accidental leaks, and government prying.

2.1.3 TERMINOLOGY AND PRINCIPLES FOR DATA COLLECTION AND USE

In this section we present some terminology about collection and use of personal information. Then we present principles for responsible management of personal data.

Invisible information gathering

Invisible information gathering describes collection of personal information about someone without the person's knowledge. The important ethical issue is that, if someone is not aware that the information is being collected or how it will be used, he or she has no opportunity to consent or withhold consent for its collection and use. Invisible information gathering is common on the Web. Here is one example: A company offered a free program that changed a Web browser's cursor into a cartoon character or other image. Millions of people installed the program and then later discovered that the program sent to the company a report of the Web sites its users visited, along with a customer identification number in the software.[6]

Internet service providers (ISPs) and Web sites can invisibly collect such details of our online activities as where we went, what we did, what browser we use, and how long we stayed at a particular page. Even when we know that Web sites *can* collect such information, we often are not aware of just what information a particular site *is* collecting.

Event data recorders in cars are a non-Web example of invisible information gathering. They record driving speed, whether or not the driver is wearing a seatbelt, and other information. Other examples include satellite surveillance and sophisticated snooping technologies (discussed in Section 2.2.2).

Cookies are files a Web site stores on each visitor's computer. The site stores within the cookie, and then uses, information about the visitor's activity. For example, a retail site might store information about products we looked at and the contents of our virtual shopping cart. On subsequent visits, the site retrieves information from the cookie. Many Web sites use cookies. They help companies provide personalized customer service and target advertising to the interests of each visitor. At first, cookies were controversial because the very idea that Web sites were storing files on the user's computer without the user's knowledge startled and disturbed many people. If a Web site we visit can read cookies, what else on our computers can it read? Also, cookies can be used to track our activities on many Web sites and combine the information. Now, more people are aware of cookies, but some Web sites do not inform visitors when they use them.[7]

A program that manages a user's music files secretly sent information about the music its users played to the company that distributed the program. Similar programs offered by other companies collected similar information but informed users and let them turn off the data collection.[8] This example illustrates that the data collection itself is not always sinister or dangerous. Some people do not mind giving the information. The critical point is whether the user is told and thus can make an informed choice.

Most people who used supermarket club cards when these cards first became popular did not know that the store collected and kept a record of everything they bought when they swiped their card at the checkout stand. Now more people know, and they know that at some stores they are trading a degree of privacy for discounts. Some people know about event data recorders in cars; most do not.[9] Thus, whether or not a particular example of data collection is invisible information gathering can depend on the level of public awareness. Before 2006, collecting search query data was an example of invisible information gathering, and for many people it still is.

In many cases, customer contracts or policy statements inform customers, members, and subscribers about a business or Web site policy on collecting and using data, but many people simply do not read them. And if they read them, they forget. Thus, there can be a significant privacy impact from the many automated systems that collect information in unobvious ways, even when people have been informed. There is, however, an important distinction between situations where people are informed but not aware and situations where the information gathering is truly covert.

Secondary use, data mining, and computer matching and profiling

My most private thoughts, my personal tragedies, secrets about other people, are mere data of a transaction, like a grocery receipt.

—A woman whose psychologist's notes were read by an insurer.[10]

Use of personal information for a purpose other than the one for which it was supplied is called *secondary use*. Examples include sale of consumer information to marketers or other businesses, use of information in various databases to deny someone a job or to tailor a political pitch, use of numerous databases by the Internal Revenue Service (IRS) to find people with high incomes, and the use of a supermarket's customer database to show alcohol purchases by a man who sued the store because he fell down. We will see more examples throughout this chapter. One of the big concerns about privacy is the degree of control a person should have over secondary uses of his or her personal data. The variety of uses illustrated by the few examples we just gave suggests that different solutions are appropriate for different users and different uses.

Data mining means searching and analyzing masses of data to find patterns and develop new information or knowledge. *Computer matching* means combining and comparing information from different databases, often using an identifier such as a person's Social Security number (SSN) to match records. *Computer profiling* means analyzing data in computer files to determine characteristics of people most likely to engage in certain behavior. Businesses use these techniques to find likely new customers. Government agencies use them to detect fraud, to enforce other laws, and to find terrorist suspects or evidence of terrorist activity. They use computer profiling to identify people to watch—people who may have committed no crime but may have a "propensity" to do so. Data mining, computer matching, and computer profiling are, in most cases, examples of secondary use of personal information.

Principles for data collection and use

The first principle for ethical treatment of personal information is *informed consent*. People vary in how much they value their privacy, how desirable or annoying they find advertising, and so forth. There is an extraordinary range in the amount of privacy different people want. Some pour out details of their personal lives on television shows. Some post personal profiles and video displaying their lives and emotions to the world. Others use cash to avoid leaving a record of their purchases, encrypt all their e-mail, use services (called anonymizers) to hide their identity when surfing the Web, never give personal information on warranty cards, and are appalled and angry when information is collected about them. When people are informed about the data collection and use policies of a business or organization, they can decide whether or not to interact with that business or organization. (We have choices about participating in some government programs, but of course many are mandatory.)

After informing people about what an organization does with personal information, the next simplest and most desirable policy is to give people some control over secondary uses. The two most common forms of providing such choice are *opt out* and *opt in*. Under an opt-out policy, one must check or click a box on a contract, membership form, or agreement, or call or write to the organization to request that one's information not be used in a particular way. If the consumer does not take action, the presumption is that the organization may use his or her information. Under an opt-in policy, the collector of the information may not use it for other purposes unless the consumer explicitly checks or clicks a box or signs a form permitting the use. (Be careful not to confuse the two. Under an opt-out policy, more people are likely to be "in," that is, their information will be used or distributed, and under an opt-in policy, more people are likely to be "out," because the default presumption is the opposite of the policy name.)

Business privacy policies often describe secondary uses in general terms. Some privacy advocates argue for an opt-in policy for all secondary uses, including uses by the entity that collects the data, as well as for any transfers of data to another entity. That is, they want to require businesses to obtain explicit consent from a person for each use of his or her personal information.

Some libraries have a policy of destroying the checkout record when a borrower returns a book—an excellent protection against disclosure. Most databases cannot use this technique, but the policy is a good reminder of a goal. There is a tendency among people not to throw anything away, including information. A policy of destroying records that are old or no longer needed protects privacy.

Both the public and private sectors need strong sanctions against employees who release information without authorization. We will also see that many businesses, government agencies, and universities need to work much harder to protect sensitive data from theft and accidental loss.

Privacy experts have developed sets of principles for protection of personal data. These principles, often called Fair Information Principles or Fair Information Practices, vary in details and wording. Figure 2.1 incorporates most of the points.[11] These privacy principles are very reasonable ethical guidelines. Many business policies include versions of them. Many laws in the U.S., Canada, and European countries do also. There is wide variation in interpretation and implementation of the principles. For example, businesses and privacy advocates disagree about what information businesses "need" and for how long. Thus, application of the principles in specific cases can generate controversy. To what extent should the guidelines be voluntary and to what extent enforced in law?

You will rarely see point 8 in Figure 2.1 in Fair Information Principles, but I consider it to be an important one. Some companies and organizations turn over personal

* Inform people when personally identifiable information about them is collected, what is collected, and how it will be used.

* Collect only the data needed.

* Offer a way for people to opt out from mailing lists, advertising, transfer of their data to other parties, and other secondary uses.

* Provide stronger protection for sensitive data, for example, an opt-in policy for disclosure of medical data.

* Keep data only as long as needed.

* Maintain accuracy of data. Where appropriate and reasonable, provide a way for people to access and correct data stored about them.

* Protect security of data (from theft and from accidental leaks).

* Develop policies for responding to law enforcement requests for data.

Figure 2.1   Privacy Principles for Personal Information

data to law enforcement agents and government agencies when requested. Some do so only if presented with a subpoena or other court order. Some challenge subpoenas; some do not. Some inform their customers or members when they give personal data to the government; some do not. The entity that holds the data decides how far to go in protecting the privacy of its members or customers. The individuals, those who can be harmed or inconvenienced by release of their data, are rarely aware of the government request. Thus, the entities that hold the data have a responsibility to those people. Planning for various possible scenarios, developing a policy, and announcing it (and following it) are all part of responsible management of other people's personal data.

The privacy principles in Figure 2.1 were developed with large databases of businesses and government in mind. The principles do not fully address new privacy issues that have arisen with the increase in the use of cameras in public places (such as police camera systems and Google's Street View). They do not address the growth of user-supplied content on the Web. People supply a huge amount of information about themselves to the public (or some part of it, such as members of a social-networking site). The Facebook incident described in the box on the next page illustrates that privacy problems can arise even when a company follows reasonable privacy principles. More examples appear in Section 2.3.4.

FACEBOOK'S MINI-FEEDS

Facebook, a social-networking site, introduced "news feeds" and "mini-feeds" in 2006. Mini-feeds sent recent changes in a member's profile, friends list, and group memberships to all the member's friends. In a major misjudgment about likely user reaction, Facebook introduced the new features as cool new conveniences, helping members stay up to date on their friends' activities.[12] Facebook stated that it did not change any privacy settings. It sent the information only to people the members had already approved. Within a day or two, hundreds of thousands of Facebook members protested vehemently. Why?

As we see throughout this chapter, the ease of accessing information and the packaging of collections of facts can increase privacy (and safety) risks. On social-networking sites, many people do not bother to check the profiles of their hundreds of friends regularly. The new feeds, however, spread the information to everyone instantly. In the physical world, we might share information about a serious illness, a family problem, or the end of a relationship with a few, chosen, close friends. Gradually, as we adjust to the new situation, others might learn of the event. The mini-feed removes the emotionally protective delay. For investigation of a stalking incident, a log showing who recently read the victim's profile might narrow a suspect list. With the feeds, a much larger number of people might have seen the same information.

The mini-feed incident demonstrates how important it is, from both an ethical perspective and a business perspective, that businesses that handle personal information give careful thought to the implications of new features, even those that do not disclose information to anyone the users had not already approved.

Within three days, Facebook added detailed privacy controls for its new data feeds.

Example: considering search queries again

We return to the issue of search engine companies collecting and storing user search query data. The ideas and arguments about this issue have many other applications.

Some users and privacy advocates want to prohibit or severely restrict search engine companies from collecting and storing search query data in a way that allows identification or re-identification of users. When thinking about ethical guidelines or legal requirements for use of data about our online activity, many people make little distinction between search query data and data about other activity. However, the principle of informed consent does imply a difference. When someone joins, subscribes to, or registers with a company (such as AOL or MySpace), they are accepting the company's policy on privacy and information sharing as part of the agreement. People use search engines such as Google, AOL, and Ask.com without registering. The search engine home page, with the search box, does not have a direct link to the company's statement about data collection.[13] Most ordinary people do not expect that a search engine can or does collect and store data about their searches and their computer. Thus, one can argue that there is no agreement between the user and the company. A privacy-protecting default, from both an ethical and a legal perspective, could specify that the company may not store or use the information, beyond its immediate purpose for the search, in a way that could disclose a person's searches. On the other hand, use of the search engine is free, and many people understand that they trade information for free services. The search engine data-collection policy is available, though not obviously displayed to the user.

Performing a search for a user is a kind of transaction, or at least an interaction, between the user and the company. Clearly, companies need to use information about transactions for business purposes. It is reasonable that there are rarely opt-out options for internal business uses. As an ethical issue, because of the privacy risks, a company should not store identifiable, or re-identifiable, data longer than necessary. It is not obvious how long that is. Companies make judgments about how long an individual search history is useful for providing personalized search results. They decide how long they need data for other customer services, fraud protection, research, and so on. Perhaps legal sanctions should apply only when a company loses, discloses, or abuses the data.

The proper privacy status of search queries is not as clear as it is for data collected by companies that the consumer has joined, registered with, or otherwise has a contract or agreement with. Is collection of user search queries an example of improper invisible information gathering? Or is consent implicit when people use the free tool? Would a prominent link to the policy on the home page provide sufficient notice so that someone's use of the search engine constitutes informed consent?

Publicity about privacy risks for search query data led companies that operate search engines to compete for users based on privacy policies. Google, Microsoft, ask.com, and Yahoo announced time limits for the storage of query data in ways that identify a user. (The time periods range from 13 months to two years.)

Independent of ethical and market considerations, the U.S. government and some European countries are developing legal requirements that companies retain *Use of ISP logs to catch hackers: Section 5.2.3* such data (and that ISPs retain customer activity data) for up to two years in case a government agency wants access to the data for an investigation. Governments usually cite investigations of child pornography, terrorism, and other law enforcement purposes as reasons for retaining the records. This is one of many examples where government interests are in opposition to privacy protection.

2.2 "Big Brother Is Watching You"

When the American Republic was founded, the framers established a libertarian equilibrium among the competing values of privacy, disclosure, and surveillance. This balance was based on technological realities of eighteenth-century life. Since torture and inquisition were the only known means of penetrating the mind, all such measures by government were forbidden by law. Physical entry and eavesdropping were the only means of penetrating private homes and meeting rooms; the framers therefore made eavesdropping by private persons a crime and allowed government to enter private premises only for reasonable searches, under strict warrant controls. Since registration procedures and police dossiers were the means used to control the free movement of "controversial" persons, this European police practice was precluded by American governmental practice and the realities of mobile frontier life.

—Alan F. Westin, *Privacy and Freedom*[14]

In George Orwell's dystopian novel *1984*, Big Brother (the government) could watch everyone via "telescreens" in all homes and public places. There was little crime and little political dissent—and no love and no freedom. Today, the government does not have to watch every move we make because so many of our activities leave data trails in databases available to government agencies. The use of myriad personal-data systems to investigate or monitor people is sometimes called *dataveillance*, short for "data surveillance." When Big Brother wants to take a direct look at us and our activities, he uses sophisticated new surveillance tools. We consider the impact of these tools on privacy and look into their compatibility with constitutional and legal protections from government intrusions.

2.2.1 DATABASES

Federal and local government agencies maintain thousands of databases containing personal information. Figure 2.2 shows a small sampling. Government agencies require reporting of many types of information. In addition to what they require and maintain in their databases, they ask businesses for personal information about customers. They order businesses to provide some with subpoenas and court orders. They buy personal information from information sellers. Although homeland security and the fight against terrorism have been the most publicized reasons for the increase in data collection and surveillance in recent years, there are many other, long-standing purposes for government data mining, surveillance, demands for Web activity logs, and so on. Government databases help government agencies perform their functions, determine eligibility for

- ❖ Tax records
- ❖ Medical records (e.g., those covered by Medicare, Medicaid, and the armed services; also prescriptions for certain medications, such as pain relievers containing narcotics)
- ❖ Marriage and divorce records
- ❖ Property ownership
- ❖ Welfare records, including family details
- ❖ School records, including psychological testing of children
- ❖ Motor vehicle records
- ❖ Voter registration records
- ❖ Books checked out of public libraries
- ❖ People with permits to carry firearms
- ❖ Applications for government grant and loan programs
- ❖ Professional and trade licenses
- ❖ Bankruptcy records
- ❖ Arrest records

Figure 2.2 A Small Sampling of Government Databases with Personal Information

government jobs and benefits programs, detect fraud in government programs, collect taxes, and catch people who are breaking laws.

The scope of government activities is enormous, ranging from catching violent criminals to licensing flower arrangers. Governments are coercive by nature. They can arrest people, jail them, and seize assets from them. Thus, the use and misuse of personal data by government agencies pose special threats to liberty and privacy. It seems reasonable to expect governments to meet an especially high standard for privacy protection and adherence to their rules.

The Privacy Act of 1974 is the main law about the federal government's use of personal data. Congress passed the Privacy Act in response to government abuses, including keeping files on war protestors, wiretappings, mail openings, and harassment of individuals for political purposes. A summary of the provisions of the Privacy Act appears in Figure 2.3. Although this law was an important step toward attempting to protect our privacy from abuse by federal agencies, it has problems. The Privacy Act has, to quote one expert on privacy laws, "many loopholes, weak enforcement, and only sporadic oversight."[15]

❖ Restrict the data in federal government records to what are "relevant and necessary" to the legal purpose for which they are collected.

❖ Require federal agencies to publish a notice of their record systems in the Federal Register so that the public may learn about what databases exist.

❖ Allow people to access their records and correct inaccurate information.

❖ Require procedures to protect the security of the information in databases.

❖ Prohibit disclosure of information about a person without his or her consent (with several exceptions).

Figure 2.3 Some Provisions of the Privacy Act of 1974

Over many years, studies have found that government agencies do not always obey laws passed to protect privacy and reduce government abuse of personal information. They do not adequately protect personal information, often in violation of those laws. Our examples are from the U.S., but one can find similar examples in other free countries. In countries with oppressive governments, of course, the situation is much worse.

The Government Accountability Office (GAO) is Congress's "watchdog agency."[16] One of its tasks is to monitor the government's privacy policies. A major GAO study, released in 1990, showed lack of compliance with the Privacy Act of 1974. In 1996, Congress investigated a "secret" database that the White House maintained on 200,000 people with more than a hundred fields of data for each person, including ethnic and political information. A GAO study of 65 government Web sites in 2000 found that only 3% of the Web sites fully complied with the fair information standards for notice, choice, access, and security established by the Federal Trade Commission (FTC) for commercial Web sites. The FTC's Web site was one that did not comply. In 2005, the GAO reported that the IRS, the Federal Bureau of Investigation (FBI), the State Department, and other agencies that use data mining to detect fraud or terrorism did not comply with all rules for collecting information on citizens.[17]

The IRS is a major secondary user of personal information. For example, it matches tax data for individuals and small businesses with a variety of federal and state government records. It scans vehicle registration records for people who own expensive cars and boats. It searches professional license records for people who are likely to have large incomes. It searches a database of "suspicious" cash transactions, examining transactions of millions of taxpayers. (Banks and other businesses are required to report all large, and suspicious small, cash transactions to the government.)

Year after year, hundreds of IRS employees are investigated for unauthorized snooping in people's tax files. An IRS employee who was a Ku Klux Klan member read tax records of members of his Klan group looking for income information that would indicate that someone was an undercover agent. This and other abuses led to a law with tough penalties for government employees who snoop through people's tax information without authorization. However, a GAO report a few years later found that although the IRS had made significant improvements over prior years, the tax agency still failed to adequately protect people's financial and tax information. Unauthorized IRS employees were able to alter and delete data. Employees disposed of disks with sensitive taxpayer information without erasing files. Hundreds of tapes and diskettes were missing. An inspector general of the U.S. Treasury Department reported that the personal financial information that taxpayers provide to the IRS is "at risk" from hackers and disgruntled employees because many of the 250 state and federal agencies to which the IRS provides taxpayer information do not have adequate safeguards.[18]

As an example of the observation that the uses of databases expand over time, consider CODIS, the FBI's DNA database. The database includes information on DNA collected from crime scenes and from certain classes of criminals. Originally, CODIS contained data on the DNA of convicted sex offenders. Then rapists and murderers were added. Now laws in some states require collection of DNA from people convicted of misdemeanors. Some states also require DNA from people arrested for a crime. Forced collection of DNA from people who are arrested, but are not convicted criminals, is different from forced collection of DNA from convicted sex offenders. What privacy and other risks does it present?

Many government agencies, including the Department of Homeland Security, the IRS, the FBI, and Immigration and Customs Enforcement (formerly the Immigration and Naturalization Service), access huge amounts of personal data not in their own databases. They "outsource" collection of information it would be controversial and possibly illegal to collect themselves. At least 35 government agencies are or were clients of ChoicePoint, a huge private data-collection company. ChoicePoint culls data from credit bureaus, numerous local, state, and federal government agencies, telephone records, marriage and divorce records, liens, deeds, and many other sources. ChoicePoint bought more than a dozen other personal information companies with extensive databases. It has more than ten billion records in its system.*[19] The writers of the Privacy Act in 1974 did not anticipate the huge amount of information the government can buy from private information services. Some observers say that if the government is not allowed to collect certain data, then it should not be allowed to buy them. Government agencies argue that they are simply using a new tool to collect information and evidence they used to collect themselves before, but much less efficiently.

Several federal agencies, including the U.S. Justice Department and the Department of Homeland Security, have appointed privacy officers responsible for ensuring that the

---

*Several times, courts found that ChoicePoint (and its subsidiaries and ancestor companies) violated federal laws, regulations, and court orders concerning its data collection and selling. The company was fined $1.37 million by the state of Pennsylvania for selling driver data in breach of a contract with the state. ChoicePoint won a "Big Brother" Award at the annual Computers, Freedom, and Privacy conference. The award is given to businesses and government agencies whose practices are particularly offensive to privacy advocates.

agencies comply with privacy (and civil liberties) policies. Although the appointments are a positive step, it is not yet clear how much these officers will accomplish.

> *Quis custodiet ipsos custodes? (Who will guard the guards themselves?)*
> —Juvenal

Example: tracking college students

The Department of Education tentatively proposed establishing a database to contain the records of every student enrolled in a college or university in the United States. Colleges and universities would be required to provide and regularly update records including each student's name, gender, SSN, major, courses taken, courses passed, degrees, loans, and scholarships (public and private). The data would be kept indefinitely. Whether or not the government implements this plan, it provides a good example for analysis. The issues and questions we raise here apply in many other situations.

Supporters of the student database proposal point out its many beneficial uses: The federal government spends $80 billion on federal grants and loans to students but has no good way of measuring the success of these programs. Do students who get aid graduate? What majors do they pursue? The database will help evaluate federal student aid programs and perhaps lead to improvements in such programs. The database will provide more accurate data on graduation rates and on actual college costs. The ability to track the number of future nurses, engineers, and so on in the educational pipeline can help shape better immigration policy and business and economic planning.

The collection of so much detail about each student in one place generates a variety of privacy risks. Several of the points in the list in Section 2.1.2  *Identity theft: Section 5.3* are relevant here. It is very likely that the government will find new uses for the data that are not part of the original proposal. Such a database could be an ideal target for identity thieves. Leaks of many sorts are possible and likely. There is potential for abuse by staff who maintain the data; for example, someone might release college records of a political candidate.

There will undoubtedly be errors in the federal student database. If the data are used only for generalized statistical analysis, errors might not have a big impact, but for some potential future uses the errors could be harmful.

Some educators worry that a likely eventual link between the database and public school databases (on children in kindergarten through high school) would contribute to cradle-to-grave tracking of childhood behavior problems, health and family issues, and so on.[20]

The database is not intended for finding or investigating students who are breaking laws, but it would be a tempting resource for law enforcement agencies. A Virginia state law requires colleges to provide the names and other identifying information for all students they accept. State police then check if any are in sex-offender registries.

DOES THE PRESIDENT MATTER?

When I presented the example of the national student database in a workshop of university professors, several opposed the database immediately before identifying any benefits and risks. Perhaps, they disliked the U.S. president at the time and saw the proposal as a partisan issue. Analyzing such a proposal based on the politics of the current president is not a good idea. If a Democratic administration proposes and establishes a new federal database, it will be used by the next Republican administration. If a Republican administration proposes and establishes a new federal database, it will be used by the next Democratic administration. As we see in numerous examples, once the data are collected, they rarely go away. Many of the risks and costs are independent of politics, and a database will likely be used for purposes not in the original plan no matter who initiates it.

What else might they check for? What other government agencies might want access to the federal student database? Would the Defense Department use the database for military recruiting? What potential risks arise if employers get access? All such uses would be secondary uses, without the consent of the students.

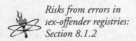
Risks from errors in sex-offender registries: Section 8.1.2

It makes sense for the government to monitor the effectiveness of the grants and loans it gives to college students. Thus, it is reasonable to require data on academic progress and graduation from students who receive federal money or loan guarantees. But what justifies demanding the data on all other students? Can some of the benefits be obtained by less intrusive means? For statistics and planning, the government can do voluntary surveys, just as businesses and organizations without the government's power of coercion must do. Are the benefits of the database central enough to the fundamental responsibilities of government to outweigh the risks and to justify a mandatory reporting program of so much personal data on every student?*

Burden of proof and "fishing expeditions"

Computer technologies have altered the nature of tax, criminal, and other government investigations. Traditionally, law enforcement officials started with a crime and used a

---

*Critics of the proposal, including many universities, point out other risks and costs besides privacy. Colleges fear that collection of the data would lead to increased federal control and interference in management of colleges. The reporting requirements would impose a high cost on the schools. The whole project would have high costs to taxpayers.

THE U.S. CENSUS

The U.S. Constitution authorizes and requires the government to count the people in the United States every ten years, primarily for determining the number of Congressional representatives each state will have. Between 1870 and 1880, the U.S. population increased by 26%. It took the government nine years to process all the data from the 1880 census. During the 1880s the population increased by another 25%. If the Census Bureau used the same methods, it would not complete processing data from the 1890 census until after the 1900 census was to begin. Herman Hollerith, a Census employee, designed and built punch-card processing machines—tabulators, sorters, and keypunch machines—to process census data.* Hollerith's machines did the complete 1890 population count in only six weeks—an amazing feat at the time. The Bureau completed the rest of the processing of the 1890 census data in seven years. It could have been done sooner, but the new machines allowed sophisticated and comprehensive analysis of the data that was not possible before. Here is an early example of computing technology enabling increased processing of data with the potential for good and bad effects: better use of information and invasion of privacy.

The Census Bureau requires everyone to provide name, gender, age, race, and relationship to people one lives with. It used to require a sample of households to fill out a "long form" with many more questions. After the 2000 census, the Bureau replaced the long form with the American Community Survey, which contains questions about marital history, ancestry, income, details about one's home, education, employment, disabilities, and other topics. Three million households receive the mandatory survey each year.

Census information is supposed to be confidential, and federal law says that "in no case shall information furnished ... be used to the detriment of any respondent or other person to whom such information relates."[21]

During World War I, the Census Bureau provided names and addresses of young men to the government to help find and prosecute draft resisters. In 1942, the Census Bureau assisted the Justice Department in using data from the 1940 census to find neighborhoods with high concentrations of U.S. citizens of Japanese ancestry. Knowing how many people to look for in each block, the army rounded up Japanese Americans and put them in internment camps. There were no computers then, but now that computers are the storehouses of census data, using the data "to the detriment of any respondent" is easier. Some cities used data from the 1980 census to find poor families who violated zoning or other regulations by doubling up in single-family housing. These people were evicted. In 2004, at the request of the Department of Homeland

---

*The company Hollerith formed to sell his machines later became IBM.

Security, the Census Bureau prepared lists showing the number of people of Arab ancestry in various zip codes throughout the United States. The lists indicated the specific country from which the people or their ancestors came. A government spokesperson said the data were needed to determine which airports should have signs in Arabic. Privacy and civil liberties organizations were skeptical.[22]

variety of techniques to look for a suspect, collecting evidence from a variety of sources. Now government agencies can search through huge volumes of information or, as we see in the surveillance examples in Section 2.2.2, through huge crowds of people, seeking people who look suspicious. One result is that, in many cases, a presumption of guilt replaces the traditional presumption of innocence. The police might detain a person whom a computer program or device considers suspicious. A person might lose benefits or be ordered to pay additional taxes. Innocent people are subject to embarrassing searches and expensive investigations and sometimes to arrest and jail.[23] On the other hand, older investigation techniques might no longer be sufficient. Fraud and other crimes are more complex. Some modern crimes are more easily hidden. Criminals can hide more easily in large, anonymous cities—or travel more easily to another city. Do databases and search technologies simply make the work of law enforcement agencies more efficient and up to date, or do they fundamentally change the relationship between citizen and government?

Data mining and computer matching to fight terrorism

Before the terrorist attacks on the U.S. on September 11, 2001, law enforcement agencies regularly lobbied for increased powers that conflicted with privacy. Sometimes they got what they wanted; sometimes they did not. In some areas, for example, e-mail privacy, Congress passed a strong privacy protection law. (We discuss it in Section 2.5.1.) Generally, people resisted privacy intrusion by government. After the attacks on the World Trade Center and the Pentagon, more people became willing to accept uses of personal data and forms of search and surveillance that would have generated much protest before. The more intrusive searches at airports are an obvious example.

The federal government initiated various data mining, profiling, and screening programs for use at airports, such as CAPPS (Computer Assisted Passenger Prescreening System), that gave the government access to passenger information in airline databases. More extreme proposals, such as CAPPS II and Total Information Awareness, would have allowed the government to collect and analyze a huge amount of data on travelers. The government abandoned them after intense opposition.

A TECHNOLOGY FOR PROTECTING PRIVACY

Federal agencies want to screen airline passenger lists for known or suspected terrorists. They want to screen other databases too (e.g., workers in the transportation industry or other sensitive infrastructure industries). They do not like to disclose their lists of suspects. Airlines and other businesses often do not want to turn over information about their passengers and customers to federal agencies. Civil libertarians and privacy advocates strongly object to collection by federal agencies of personal data about huge numbers of people who are not suspects. Here is one example of a technical tool, a software system, that can help protect privacy while enabling government and businesses to cooperate on searching for matches without disclosing data to each other. The government and the business use the same software to encode the names or identifiers in their own database (of suspects or customers, respectively). Then either side can compare coded entries to see if there is a match. The system uses a form of encryption (one-way hashing) in which knowing how to encode the names gives no information about how to decode the coded form. So the actual names or identifiers are protected. If a match is found, the government agency can take appropriate action with respect to that one person.

It does not appear that such a system is used. There might be *Errors in terrorism watch lists: Section 8.1.2* technical problems or costs that reduce its usefulness, but perhaps it is not used because the increased search powers given to law enforcement agencies by antiterror laws do not require such privacy protection.

Proposals for new data mining programs to find terrorists and terrorist plots will continue to appear. We summarize an interesting point Jeff Jonas and Jim Harper present about the suitability of data mining for this purpose.[24] Marketers make heavy use of data mining. They spend millions of dollars analyzing data to find people who are likely to be customers. How likely? In marketing, a response rate of a few percent is considered good. In other words, expensive, sophisticated data mining has a high rate of false positives. Most of the people data mining identifies as potential customers are not. Many targeted people will receive ads, catalogs, and sales pitches they do not want. Junk e-mail and pop-up ads annoy people, but they do not significantly threaten civil liberties. A high rate of false positives in data mining for finding terrorist suspects does. Jonas and Harper argue that other methods for investigating terrorists are more cost-effective and less threatening to privacy and civil liberties of large numbers of people.

When considering each new system or policy for personal data use or data mining by government, we should ask many questions: Is the information it uses or collects accurate and useful? Will less intrusive means accomplish a similar result? Will the system inconvenience ordinary people while being easy for criminals and terrorists to thwart? How significant are the risks to innocent people? To the extent that we are willing to give up some privacy, freedom, and convenience while the terror threat is high, we should also consider the question: Once high-tech devices and systems are in place and laws allow more intrusive surveillance and data access by government agencies to find terrorists, will we be able to remove these threats to privacy and freedom after the threat recedes?

2.2.2 THE FOURTH AMENDMENT, EXPECTATION OF PRIVACY, AND SURVEILLANCE TECHNOLOGIES

> *The right of the people to be secure in their persons, houses, papers, and effects, against unreasonable searches and seizures, shall not be violated, and no Warrants shall issue, but upon probable cause, supported by Oath or affirmation, and particularly describing the place to be searched, and the persons or things to be seized.*
>
> —Fourth Amendment, U.S. Constitution

The U.S. Constitution protects a right to privacy from government intrusion, most explicitly in the Fourth Amendment. The U.S. Supreme Court has interpreted other parts of the Bill of Rights to provide a constitutional right to privacy from government in other areas as well. England has a similar tradition, as expressed in William Pitt's colorful statement in 1763:

> The poorest man may in his cottage bid defiance to all the force of the Crown. It may be frail; its roof may shake; the wind may blow through it; the storms may enter; the rain may enter—but the King of England cannot enter....[25]

Here we look at how databases and surveillance technology challenge this right. Although the discussion in this section is in the context of the U.S. Fourth Amendment and U.S. Supreme Court rulings, the new technological risks to protection from intrusion by governments raise similar issues in other countries.

Weakening the Fourth Amendment

The Fourth Amendment sets limits on the government's rights to legally search our homes and businesses and seize documents. It requires that the government have "probable cause" for the search and seizure. That is, there must be good evidence to support the specific search. Two key problems arise from computer technology. First, much of our personal information is no longer safe in our homes or the individual offices of our doctors and financial advisors. Second, new technologies allow the government to search our homes without entering them and to search our persons from a distance without our knowledge. We first consider personal information.

We carry personal information on our laptop when we travel. Much personal information is in huge databases outside our control. Many laws allow law enforcement agencies to get information from nongovernment databases without a court order. Federal privacy rules allow law enforcement agencies to access medical records without court orders. The USA PATRIOT Act lets the government collect information from financial institutions on any transactions that differ from a customer's usual pattern. It eased government access to many other kinds of personal information, including library records, without a court order.

As we consider all the personal information available to government agencies now, we can reflect on the worries of Supreme Court Justice William O. Douglas about the potential abuse from government access to only the records of someone's checking account. In 1968, he wrote:

> In a sense a person is defined by the checks he writes. By examining them agents get to know his doctors, lawyers, creditors, political allies, social connections, religious affiliation, educational interests, the papers and magazines he reads, and so on ad infinitum. These are all tied in to one's social security number, and now that we have the data banks, these other items will enrich that storehouse and make it possible for a bureaucrat—by pushing one button—to get in an instant the names of the 190 million Americans who are subversives or potential and likely candidates.[26]

Today's readers should not miss the irony of the last sentence: 190 million was the entire population of the U.S. at the time.

The next several examples illustrate more ways technology erodes Fourth Amendment protection. Courts sometimes use the notion of expectation of privacy to determine when the Fourth Amendment applies. We will explain this concept and its weaknesses.

Fourth Amendment protection in crime investigation: Section 5.5.1

Automated toll collection and itemized purchase records

Many bridges, tunnels, and toll roads use automated toll collection systems. Sensors read a device in the car as it goes by without stopping, and the owner's credit card or bank account gets billed for the toll. These systems save time for drivers, reduce the costs of collection, and allow for variable charges at different times of the day to improve traffic flow. The database used for billing drivers contains a record of where and when a person traveled (and, in some cases, how fast). The privacy concern is that marketers and government agencies can use this information to track people. Some toll-road operators have an option allowing drivers to pay cash in advance, avoiding billing records. Currently, however, most of the systems do not provide anonymity.

Police use toll records in investigations. A bridge and tunnel authority in New York had a policy that it would not disclose a driver's travel information except when required by law or when presented with a court order by a law enforcement agency. A judge ruled that police could get such information without a court order. The judge said that traffic movement is in public view, a person does not have a reasonable expectation that information about his or her travel is private, and therefore the Fourth Amendment does not protect it. Let us look at this reasoning and its implications.

Yes, it is true that when we drive in public, anyone might see us. Someone could stand near a bridge and write down the license plate number of each car that passes by. If the police assigned an officer to do this, there might be a fuss. In any case, it simply was not done, not at all bridges and toll roads, 24 hours a day. We expected that our travel was mostly anonymous. Strangers saw us but did not recognize us, and no record remained after we passed by. The automated toll systems change the situation fundamentally. They keep a detailed, computerized record, 24 hours a day, of every vehicle using the system.

When we shop in a supermarket or a bookstore, we might be observed. Someone might remember what we bought. Before computerized checkout systems were introduced, no one recorded our specific purchases. If the judge's argument in the toll case were to apply, would the police have access, without a court order, to lists of all the books we buy? In fact, law enforcement agencies have asked bookstores and online sellers to turn over records of books purchased by particular people, sometimes with a search warrant, sometimes without one. These requests raise First Amendment issues as well as Fourth Amendment issues. The head of the American Booksellers Association commented that "[F]rom a First Amendment perspective, having the government be able to go in and review an individual's buying or reading patterns will have an incredible chilling effect."[27]

"Noninvasive but deeply revealing" searches

The title above is from Julian Sanchez's description of a variety of new search and detection technologies.[28] Many sound like science fiction; they are not. These technologies can search our homes and vehicles but do not require police to physically enter or open them. They can search our bodies beneath our clothes from a distance without our knowledge. What restrictions should we place on their use? When should we permit government agencies to use them without a search warrant?

We begin our discussion with a slightly older search technology, satellite imaging. Satellites use various computer technologies to take detailed photographs of Earth, detailed enough to show our homes and backyards. State governments use them to catch people who are growing ... What? Are you expecting "marijuana"? No doubt, satellites have looked for that, but they also are used to catch people growing cotton without appropriate permits. Some state government agencies use satellite images to detect building or property improvements that would raise property taxes. Some plan to use them to find people who have built backyard porches without all the required building permits.[29] Is this an intrusion into our personal space—a search of our homes—that the Fourth Amendment should prohibit without a warrant? The Supreme Court has said "maybe" in a side comment in a decision that permitted surveillance from an airplane, but so far there has been no direct legal challenge of satellite imaging. The constitutional status of searching by satellite remains open, and government agencies continue to use the images. In 2007 the federal government authorized federal and local law enforcement agencies to access real-time, high-resolution images from its network of spy satellites. Potential beneficial uses include protection of critical infrastructure and improved response to natural disasters. Such surveillance capability clearly can also threaten privacy and personal freedom.

The Transportation Security Administration (TSA) uses a new kind of X-ray machine at some airports. The machine displays on a computer screen the image of a person's body and any weapons and packets of drugs hidden under clothing and wigs. People singled out for search have a choice of using the machine or undergoing a pat-down search. A scan by the machine is faster, more thorough, and less physically intrusive than a pat-down search. On the other hand, the American Civil Liberties Union (ACLU) describes it as "a virtual strip search." In response to concerns from privacy advocates and the ACLU, TSA officials said they would adjust the machines to blur some parts of the body and that the machines do not have the ability to store images.[30] One company has plans to build machines that scan passengers as they move along on a conveyor belt—similar to the current screening method for carry-on baggage. The ease of searching people with this technology means that more people will be searched.

Other noninvasive but deeply revealing search tools (some in use and some in development) include particle sniffers that detect many specific drugs and explosives, imaging systems that detect from a distance guns under clothing, and devices that analyze the molecular composition of truck cargo without having to open the truck. These devices have obvious valuable security applications, but the technologies can be used for random searches, without search warrants or probable cause, on unsuspecting people. As Sanchez points out, we live "in a nation whose reams of regulations make almost everyone guilty of some violation at some point."[31] Before the government begins using these tools on ordinary people bringing medications home from Canada, making their own beer, or keeping a banned sweetener or saturated fat in their home (or whatever might be illegal in the future), it is critical for privacy protection that we have clear guidelines for their use—and, in particular, clarification of when such use constitutes a search requiring a search warrant.

Supreme Court decisions and expectation of privacy

> The principles laid down in this opinion… apply to all invasions on the part of government and its employees of the sanctity of a man's home and the privacies of life. It is not the breaking of his doors, and the rummaging in his drawers, that constitutes the essence of the offense; but it is the invasion of his indefeasible right of personal security, personal liberty and private property.
>
> —Justice Joseph Bradley, *Boyd v. United States*, 1886

Several Supreme Court cases addressed the impact of technology on Fourth Amendment protection in earlier contexts. In *Olmstead v. United States*,[32] in 1928, the government had used wiretaps on telephone lines without a court order. The Supreme Court allowed the wiretaps. It interpreted the Fourth Amendment to apply only to physical intrusion and only to search or seizure of material things, not conversations. Justice Louis Brandeis dissented, arguing that the authors of the Fourth Amendment did all they could to protect liberty and privacy—including privacy of conversations—from intrusions by government based on the technology available at the time. He believed that the Fourth Amendment should be interpreted as requiring a court order even when new technologies give the government access to our personal papers and conversations without entering our homes.

In *Katz v. United States*, in 1967, the Supreme Court reversed its position and ruled that the Fourth Amendment does apply to conversations and that it applies in public places in some situations. In this case, law enforcement agents had attached an electronic listening and recording device on the outside of a telephone booth to record a suspect's conversation. The court said that the Fourth Amendment "protects people, not places" and that what a person "seeks to preserve as private, even in an area accessible to the public, may be constitutionally protected." To intrude in places where a reasonable person has a reasonable expectation of privacy, government agents need a court order.

Although the Supreme Court's decision in *Katz v. United States* strengthened Fourth Amendment protection in some ways, there is significant risk in relying on reasonable expectation of privacy to define the areas where law enforcement agents need a court order. We saw that a judge used this notion to decide that law enforcement agents have access, without a court order, to the detailed tracking information automated toll systems collect. We used to have a reasonable expectation of privacy while driving around in our cars or, surely, in our own backyards, but as well-informed people come to understand the capabilities of modern surveillance tools and the mass of information in databases, we might no longer expect privacy from government, in a practical sense. Does that mean we should not have it? The Court recognized this problem in *Smith v. Maryland*, in which it noted that, if law enforcement reduces actual expectation of privacy by actions "alien to well-recognized Fourth Amendment freedoms," this should *not* reduce our Fourth Amendment protection. The Supreme Court, however, has interpreted "expectation of privacy" in a very restrictive way. For example, it ruled that if we share information with businesses such as our bank, then we have no reasonable expectation of privacy for that information (*United States v. Miller*, 1976). Law enforcement agents do not need a court order to get the information. This interpretation seems odd. We do expect privacy of the financial information we supply a bank or other financial institution. We expect confidentiality in many kinds of information we share with a few, sometimes carefully selected, others. We surf the Web in the privacy of our homes, but we share our Web activity with ISPs, Web sites, and search engine companies merely by typing and clicking. We share many kinds of personal information at specific Web sites where we expect it to be private. Is it protected from warrantless search?

In *Kyllo v. United States* (2001), the Supreme Court ruled that police could not use thermal imaging devices to search a home from the outside without a search warrant. (In this case, they were looking for heat lamps used for growing marijuana.) The Court stated that where "government uses a device that is not in general public use, to explore details of the home that would previously have been unknowable without physical intrusion, the surveillance is a 'search.'" This reasoning suggests that when a technology becomes more widely used, the government may use it for surveillance without a warrant. This standard may allow time for markets, public awareness, and technologies to develop to provide privacy protection against the new technology. Is it a reasonable standard—a reasonable adaptation of law to new technology? Or should the court have permitted the search? Or should the government have to satisfy the requirements of the Fourth Amendment for every search of a home where a warrant would have been necessary before the technology existed?

In *Illinois v. Caballes* (2005), the Supreme Court ruled that police may use a detection

Searching computers: Section 5.5.1

method without a search warrant if it is precise enough to detect only something illegal but no legal activity or intimate information. This case involved a drug-sniffing dog and a search of a car, not a house. Is this a reasonable principle for warrantless searches of homes or of people in public places?

The USA PATRIOT Act and national security letters

The USA PATRIOT Act (passed soon after the terrorist attacks in 2001) and other antiterrorism laws have many controversial provisions. Many of the controversies are beyond the scope of this book, but some involve access to personal information in databases. We discuss national security (NSLs) letters as an example.

Before the PATRIOT Act passed, the FBI could obtain various kinds of records, including telephone, e-mail, and ISP records, without a court order or any court oversight, using a document called an NSL. The FBI could use NSLs only when it had reason to believe that the customer or entity whose records it sought was a foreign power or agent of a foreign power. Only certain senior FBI officials at its headquarters could issue NSLs. The PATRIOT Act significantly expanded FBI authority to issue NSLs. It allows any field office to issue them. It eliminated the requirement that the information sought must pertain to a foreign power or an agent of a foreign power. It allows use of NSLs for information relevant to terrorism or espionage investigations. Also, the PATRIOT Act expanded the kinds of information the FBI could obtain with NSLs to include a person's full credit report. Recipients of an NSL are prohibited from telling anyone except their lawyers about the order or even that they received one.[33] The level of secrecy and the lack of court review clearly present opportunities for abuse.

A review by the Department of Justice Inspector General found that the FBI issued more than 143,000 NSLs between 2003 and 2005. It found "widespread and serious misuse of the FBI's national security letter authorities."[34] The review found that, in its required reports to Congress, the FBI seriously underestimated both the number of NSLs it issued and the number of improper uses. The review also found that the FBI misused its emergency authority to get some information in situations that were not emergencies. The report did not find that FBI agents intentionally misused NSLs. Instead, it concluded that the problems resulted from "mistakes, carelessness, confusion, sloppiness, lack of training, lack of adequate guidance, and lack of adequate oversight."[35] In some cases, because of confusion, businesses provided more personal information than the FBI requested or had authority to request. For example, some ISPs provided contents of e-mail when asked for header information about senders and recipients.

The report points out that in the period studied, the FBI was reorganizing and conducting numerous investigations in response to the increased terrorist threat. FBI personnel believe that NSLs are indispensable for detecting and deterring terrorism.

In the 1960s and 1970s, the FBI secretly used its National Crime Information Center (NCIC) database to track the movements of thousands of people not wanted for any crime. Many were opponents of the Vietnam War. The FBI kept files on civil rights activists, celebrities, and many other Americans. The Defense Department maintained extensive files on Iraq war protestors. It labeled antiwar rallies and antiwar protests by Quakers as potential terrorist activities. A federal "watch list" contained 325,000 names of people (worldwide) considered to be terrorism suspects or people who aid terrorists.[36] The broad definition of terrorist activity suggests why many civil libertarians oppose exempting terrorism investigations from long-standing, constitutional protections for privacy. From the perspective of protecting the privacy of innocent people, we need appropriate oversight, careful procedures, and accurate reporting. Do the benefits of extending the FBI's powers to demand information about Americans without court supervision outweigh the risks?

2.2.3 VIDEO SURVEILLANCE

We are used to security cameras in banks and convenience stores. They help in investigations of crimes. Prisons use video surveillance systems (sometimes called CCTV, for closed-circuit television) for security. Gambling casinos use them to watch for known cheaters. Video surveillance systems monitor traffic and catch drivers who run red lights. After the 2001 terrorist attacks, the Washington, D.C. police installed cameras that zoom in on individuals a half mile away.

Cameras alone raise some privacy issues. When combined with face-recognition systems, they raise even more privacy issues. We describe applications of cameras and face recognition and some relevant privacy and civil liberties issues.

The Tampa, Florida police used a computer system to scan the faces of all 100,000 fans and employees who entered the 2001 Super Bowl (causing some reporters to dub it Snooper Bowl). The system searched computer files of criminals for matches, giving results within seconds. People were not told that their faces were being scanned. The Tampa police installed a similar system in a neighborhood of popular restaurants and nightclubs. Police in a control room zoomed in on individual faces and checked for matches in their database of suspects.[37] In two years of use, the system did not recognize anyone that the police wanted, but it did occasionally identify innocent people as wanted felons. The Tampa police stopped using the system.

The ACLU compared the use of the face-recognition system at the Super Bowl to a computerized police lineup, to which innocent people were subject without their knowledge or consent. In the early 2000s face-recognition systems had an accuracy rate of little more than 50%. (Photos in databases tend to be old, and the systems did not perform well on images taken from different angles and in different lighting conditions.) Privacy scholar David Banisar argued that the low accuracy rate could result in the detention of many innocent people.[38] Accuracy of such technologies improves over time. When is it good enough?

It is estimated that there are four million surveillance cameras in Britain, many outdoors in public places to deter crime. A Londoner is likely to be recorded dozens of times a day. Defense lawyers complain that prosecutors sometimes destroy footage that might clear a suspect. A study by a British university found a number of abuses by operators of surveillance cameras, including collecting salacious footage, such as people having sex in a car, and showing it to colleagues.[39] (A traffic monitoring system in Florida was removed after engineers were observed zooming in on individual pedestrians unrelated to traffic flow.)

Is enforcing a 9 PM curfew for young people, one of the uses of public cameras in the United Kingdom, important enough to accept the diminishing privacy and potential abuses? Even if one believes that government curfews for young people are reasonable (and many do not), this application indicates the kind of monitoring and control of specific groups of people the cameras make easy. Banisar asks whether face-recognition systems would be used to track political dissidents, journalists, and political opponents of powerful people—the kinds of people targeted for illegal or questionable surveillance in the past. More fundamentally, is this level of surveillance compatible with our notions of privacy and a free society?

The California Department of Transportation photographed the license plates on cars driving in a particular area. Then it contacted the car owners for a survey about traffic in the area. Hundreds of drivers complained. These people objected vehemently to what they considered unacceptable surveillance by a government agency even when the agency photographed only their license plates, not their faces—for a survey, not a police action. Clearly, ordinary people do not like being tracked and photographed without their knowledge. Although some cities, such as Chicago, are increasing their camera surveillance programs, other city governments considered using cameras in public places but decided not to. Several city governments gave up their systems because they did not significantly reduce crime. (Some favored better lighting and more police patrols low technology and less invasive of privacy.) Toronto city officials refused to let police take over their traffic cameras to monitor a protest march and identify its organizers. In a controversial statement, the Privacy Commissioner of Canada argued that the country's Privacy Act required a "demonstrable need for each piece of personal information collected" to carry out government programs and that therefore recording activities of large numbers of the general public was not a permissible means of crime prevention.[40]

In 2005, the British government released a report saying Britain's CCTV systems were of little use in fighting crime. The only successful use of the cameras was in parking lots where they helped reduce vehicle crime.[41] Later in 2005, photos taken by the surveillance cameras helped identify terrorists who planted bombs in the London subway. This is a reminder that it is rare for all the facts or strong arguments to support only one side of an issue. Could investigators have identified the bombers some other way? What trade-offs between privacy and identifying terrorists are we willing to make?

Some applications of CCTV and face-recognition systems are reasonable, beneficial uses of the technology for security and crime prevention. But there is a clear need for limits, controls, and guidelines. How should we distinguish appropriate from inappropriate uses? Should international events such as the Olympics, which are sometimes terrorist targets, use such systems? Should technologies like face-recognition systems be used only to catch terrorists and suspects in serious crimes, or should they be used in public places to screen for people with unpaid parking tickets? Should people be informed when and where cameras are in use? If we consider these issues early enough, we can design some privacy-protecting features into the technology, establish well-thought-out policies for its use, and pass appropriate privacy-protecting legislation before, as the Supreme Court of Canada worries in the quote below, "privacy is annihilated."

> *To permit unrestricted video surveillance by agents of the state would seriously diminish the degree of privacy we can reasonably expect to enjoy in a free society. . . . We must always be alert to the fact that modern methods of electronic surveillance have the potential, if uncontrolled, to annihilate privacy.*
>
> —Supreme Court of Canada[42]

2.3 Diverse Privacy Topics

2.3.1 MARKETING, PERSONALIZATION, AND CONSUMER DOSSIERS

Targeted and personalized marketing

> *Acxiom provides complete and accurate pictures of customers and prospects, powering all marketing and relationship efforts.*
>
> —Acxiom Web site[43]

Marketing is an essential task for most businesses and organizations. It is one of the biggest uses of personal information—by businesses, political parties, and organizations.

BEEP BEEP BEEP..
Opus
WELCOME TO PIZZA SHMIZZA, MR. OPUS! ...OF 996 MELBA LN.!
COOL! YOU KNOW ALL ABOUT ME!
RIGHT HERE ON MY SCREEN, SIR.
7-10-05
I LOVE OUR NEW INFORMATION SOCIETY!
I NEED ONE PEPPERONI, PLEASE.
NOT WITH THAT COLON, YOU DON'T.
YOUR SCREEN SHOWS MY COLONOSCOPY?
DUDE. I'VE SEEN CLEANER PIPES ON A HARLEY.
I'LL HAVE A GARDEN TOFU PIZZA THEN.
YOU CAN'T AFFORD IT. YOU MADE SOME BIG PURCHASES IN JUNE.
I DID NOT!!
"ONE DELUXE HUG-ME MOM INFLATABLE DOLL: $249.99"
HUG TIME
BERKELEYBREATHED.COM
Washington, Post, Writers & Sons
LISTEN! MY PRIVACY IS--
STOP WAVING YOUR LITTLE BATH SCRUBBIE.
YOU'RE WATCHING ME!!
AM NOT.
ARE TOO!!
NOT.
MAYBE I'M JUST PARANOID.
SOMEBODY NEEDS A BIKINI WAX!

Marketing includes finding new customers, members, or voters and encouraging old ones to continue. It also includes advertising one's products, services, or cause. Moreover, includes how to price products and when and to whom to offer discounts.

When most people lived in small communities and shopped at local stores, merchants knew the customers and their preferences and could tell them about new products or special deals that would interest them. Now, businesses use computer technology to store and analyze consumer purchases, financial information, online activity (including clicking behavior at a Web site), opinions, preferences, government records, and any other useful information to determine who might be a new customer and what new products and services an old customer might buy. We review the evolution of targeted marketing from the pre-Web 1990s to the Web era of the 2000s.

Computers and the increased storage capacity and technology of the 1980s and 1990s revolutionized targeted marketing. In 1993, an economist observed that over the previous 20 years, the cost of access to a name on a computerized mailing list dropped to about one thousandth of its earlier cost.[44] If you bought something, entered a contest, or filled out a warranty questionnaire, the information you provided was, often, made available to advertisers. If you filed a change-of-address notice with the U.S. Postal Service, your name and new address were provided to mailing list managers, who in turn sold the lists to mass mailers. Nonprofit organizations, from the Sierra Club to the National Rifle Association, use mailing lists to solicit support. Long-distance telephone companies use lists of subscribers to foreign-language newspapers or Web sites to find potential customers for special telephone service deals. They send the ads in the customer's language.

Marketers began using thousands of criteria (instead of just age, gender, and neighborhood) to decide who gets a specific catalog or promotional offer. American Express began to mine hundreds of billions of bytes of data on how customers spent hundreds of billions of dollars. Supermarket chains store a year's worth of data, or more, on the details of customer purchases. Companies sell lists of e-mail addresses organized by people's interest areas, including general interests, hobbies, religion, and "adult."

Privacy advocates and some consumers objected to mailing lists based on consumer purchase histories. At first (in the 1990s), people were disturbed by the idea that merchants were storing, and other companies buying, data on their purchasing habits. These activities threaten a key aspect of privacy: control of information about oneself. As one journalist mentioned, it "gives some people the creeps."[45]

Marketers argued that finely targeted marketing is likely to be useful to the consumer and that it reduces overhead and, ultimately, the cost of products. L.L. Bean, a big mail-order business, says it sends out fewer catalogs as it does a better job of targeting customers. A Web advertising company said users clicked on 16% of ads displayed based on the user's activity profile—many more than the 1% typical for untargeted Web ads. Another firm says that 20–50% of people used the personalized coupons it provided on screen or by e-mail, compared with the 1–5% redemption rate for newspaper inserts. The companies say targeting ads by using personal consumer information reduces the number of ads overall that people will see and provides ads that people are more likely to want.[46]

A purchase of pasta or the fact that someone reads weather reports on the Web is not particularly personal or sensitive. An immigrant might appreciate getting ads in his or her native language. But would someone like being on a list of potential customers for a product for adults who are incontinent? One company compiled such a list and made it available through a commercial list broker. (Marketers love medical information.) Would a customer be happy that a store has a record of how many packs of cigarettes, bottles of brandy, or contraceptives he or she buys? A person might not want his or her online marketing profile to include an interest in computer hacking, neo-Nazism, gambling, or various diseases.

Until the late 1990s, most businesses and Web sites had no explicit statement about using customer information. People did not realize or expect that companies would store and use their information for anything beyond the necessary tasks of completing the sale and billing. In fact, use of personal data for marketing without informing people or obtaining their consent was widespread. Sometimes, small print informed consumers that a business might use or sell data, but often consumers did not see it, ignored it, or did not understand the implications of such use or sale. Gradually, public awareness and pressure for improvement increased. Privacy policies have improved. For example, in the early 1990s, AOL's policy stated that "AOL, Inc. may use or disclose information regarding Member for any purpose" (with a few exceptions and with an opt-out option).[47] By 2000, AOL had an eight-page privacy policy stating, among other things, that it did not use or disclose any information about where a member goes in AOL or on the Web and did not give out telephone numbers or information that links screen names with real names.[48]

It has now become common for Web sites, ISPs, cable companies, magazines, retail chains, and so on to post explicit statements about what information they collect and how they use the information. Opt-out and opt-in policies are common for receiving advertising, being put on mailing lists, or distribution of personal data to other companies. (Federal laws and regulations require specific privacy protections for financial and medical information.[49]) Informed consent and choice are central issues. Although awareness varies among consumers and many do not read privacy policies, a company's privacy policy can be considered part of the agreement of doing business. How clear and obvious must an information-use policy be? Does a person's decision to interact with a business or Web site constitute consent to its policy? These questions continue to be fundamental to many privacy issues about consumer data.

With the growth of computer power, storage capacity, and sophisticated software, personalized and targeted marketing increased in sophistication. It provides new services many consumers value. It also raises new issues about uses of information. Online retailers make recommendations to you based on prior purchases made by you and other people with similar buying patterns. People like this form of personalization. The context is limited. The user registers or logs on, is greeted by name, and is presented with options based on prior activity at that Web site. Retailers send e-mail telling people about products they might want. This alerts people to products they might want but might not have been

DATA MINING AND CLEVER MARKETING

Customers of British retailing firm Tesco permit the company to collect information on their buying habits in exchange for discounts. Here are two ways, of varying complexity, Tesco used extensive and creative data mining of this information.

The company identified young adult males who bought diapers and sent them coupons for beer—assuming that, with a new baby, they would have less time to go to a pub.

To compete with Wal-Mart, the company aimed to identify those customers who were most price conscious and therefore most likely to be attracted to Wal-Mart's low prices. By analyzing purchase data, the company determined which customers regularly buy the cheapest version of products that are available at more than one price level. Then they determined what products those customers buy most often, and they set prices on those products below Wal-Mart's.[50]

From a privacy perspective, we see that customers made a voluntary trade, although many have little idea of the complex ways in which the company will use their information. Depending on one's views of business, markets, and consumers, opinions vary about whether the second example described here is desirable competition or manipulation of consumers. What do you think?

aware of or might not have found among the mass of other products available. Targeting is so popular with some people that Google advertises that its Gmail displays no *untargeted* banner ads.

Some kinds of less obvious personalization trouble people more (when they learn of them). The displays, ads, prices, and discounts you see when shopping online might be different from those others see. Some such targeting is reasonable: A clothing Web site does not display winter parkas on its home page for a shopper from Florida. Some sites offer discounts to first-time visitors (determined, perhaps, by lack of a cookie). Some display any of hundreds of variations of a page depending on time of day, gender, location, and dozens of other attributes of a person's session. If a person hesitates over a product, a Web site might offer something extra, perhaps free shipping. Is this collection and use of behavioral information an example of inappropriate invisible information gathering? Many people do not realize that a Web site can determine a visitor's approximate location. Some Web sites guess a visitor's gender based on clicking behavior.[51] Is the information "personal"; that is, is it linked to the person's name or identity? Are there privacy threats lurking in these practices?

When we shop in stores, sales clerks can see our gender and our approximate age. They can form other conclusions about us from our clothing and conversation. Good salespeople in expensive specialty stores, car dealerships, flea markets, and third-world street markets make judgments about how much a potential customer will pay. They

PRISONERS PROCESSING PERSONAL DATA

A woman, along with more than two million other consumers, filled out a detailed consumer profile form for Metromail, a major mailing-list firm, expecting to receive discount coupons and free sample products. The form included hobbies, income, buying habits, health information, investments, and much other personal information. Later, she received a frightening 12-page letter, containing graphic sexual fantasies, from a convicted rapist in a Texas prison who knew everything about her. Prisoners were contracted to enter the questionnaire data into computers.

The woman won a lawsuit against Metromail. She received a monetary award and a court order prohibiting the company and its subcontractors from using prisoners to input data.[52]

Some companies and state and local government agencies still use prisoners to process personal data, including employment and medical data. Some prisons do not permit inmates to have a pencil or other writing instrument while doing the work.

modify their price or offer extras accordingly. Is the complex software that personalizes shopping on the Web merely making up for the loss of information that would be available to sellers if we were shopping in a store? Are some people uneasy mainly because they did not realize that their behavior affected what appears on their screen? Are they uneasy because they did not realize that Web sites can determine (and store) so much about them when they thought they were browsing anonymously?

Our examples so far have been commercial situations. The next example, personalization in a noncommercial environment, uses a large amount of personal information associated with people's names. The Democratic and Republican parties use extensive databases on tens of millions of people to profile those who might vote for their candidates. The parties determine what issues to emphasize (and which to omit) in personalized campaign pitches. The databases include hundreds of details such as job, hobbies, type of car, union membership.[53] One party might send a campaign flyer to a conservative union member that emphasizes its labor policy but does not mention, for example, abortion, while the other party might do the opposite.

People dislike marketing (commercial or political) pitched at them based on a personal profile when they are not aware that the pitch is personalized for them. They feel manipulated. If they are not offered the lowest price or best deal, they might feel cheated. Deceptive practices by businesses are illegal. There is a very wide range of legal activities that include personalization, smart marketing, and manipulation.

Personal information, even when collected with consent, can leak in ways that threaten people's safety. The example of prisoners processing personal data (in the box on the preceding page) and the risks to children that we will discuss in Section 2.3.7 illustrate the importance of thinking about possible dangerous uses of personal information and the consequences of making it available to the wrong people. We will see more examples of leaks, loss, and theft of personal data in Section 2.3.3.

Paying for consumer information

Consumer information is very valuable to marketers. When businesses first began using it heavily, some privacy advocates argued that they should pay consumers for its use. In many circumstances, we are paid indirectly. For example, when we fill out a contest entry form, we trade data for the opportunity to win prizes. Many stores give discounts to shoppers who use cards that enable tracking of their purchases. A business that gets some income from selling customer information might be able to charge less for its products or services than a competitor that does not sell customer information. Many businesses offer to trade free computers, Internet connection, iPods, DVDs, or other products and services for permission to send advertising messages to people or to track their Web surfing. These offers are very popular. Free-PC started the trend in 1999 with its offer of 10,000 free PCs in exchange for providing personal information and watching advertising messages. Free-PC was swamped with applications from hundreds of thousands of people in the first day. ComScore Networks, Inc., in its first few months of operation, attracted about two million people in the U.S. and other countries with its program to track Internet use. Its incentives included contests and special software that provided faster Web access. Some privacy advocates were horrified when Google introduced Gmail: It targets ads to individual users by scanning and analyzing the user's e-mail messages. It reads people's e-mail! In exchange for permission to do so, Gmail provides free e-mail, text messaging, and file storage accounts. Many people signed up. The success of these businesses and services shows that many people do not object to retailers using their purchase history and do not consider the intrusion of online ads to be extremely bothersome, nor their Web surfing to be particularly sensitive. Some are even willing to allow automated analysis of their e-mail. They are willing to trade some privacy for other things. People who value their privacy more highly do not participate.

Some privacy advocates criticize such programs. Some oppose them altogether. Lauren Weinstein, founder of Privacy Forum, argued that less affluent people, to whom the attraction of free services may be strong, will be "coerced" into giving up their privacy.[54] People do not understand all the potential uses of their information and the long-term consequences of the agreements. On the other hand, such programs offer an opportunity for people with little money to trade something else of value (information) for goods and services they desire. Potentially negative future consequences of choices we make now (such as not getting enough exercise) are common in life. We can educate consumers and encourage responsible choices. (In the list of Web sites at the end of the chapter, we include many nonprofit organizations that help do this.) In Section 2.4.2 we consider

CREDIT RECORDS

The three major credit reporting companies, Experian, Equifax, and Trans-Union, receive and process millions of records daily. In addition to bill-paying history, a credit report may contain information from public records, such as lawsuits, bankruptcies, and liens. The primary purpose of the credit bureaus is to provide a central storehouse of information for evaluating applicants for credit. Insurance companies consult the credit reports of applicants. Credit records were among the first major sources of personal-data privacy problems. Credit companies sold information from credit reports. They sold mailing lists based on credit information to other businesses for marketing purposes. Errors in credit records have caused serious disruptions to people's finances and lives. Leaked or bought credit reports have embarrassed political candidates and undermined spouses in divorce cases. Access to a person's credit report means access to the person's credit card numbers and other account numbers, increasing the risk of fraud.

The Fair Credit Reporting Act of 1970 (FCRA) was, according to *Privacy Journal*, the first law, anywhere in the world, to establish regulations for use of consumer information by private businesses.[55] It restricts credit bureaus to disclosing credit information only to employers, the government, insurance companies, and others who need it for legitimate business purposes involving the consumer.[56] That last category was vague and easy to circumvent. In 1996, Congress amended the FCRA, setting stronger standards for access and making access under false pretenses a felony. In 2000 the FTC stopped the credit bureaus from selling consumers' credit information. After many complaints about errors in credit records and the increase in identify theft, Congress amended the FCRA in 2003 to require that credit bureaus, upon request, provide a person with a copy of his or her credit report once a year for free. This provision satisfies the personal-data principle that people should have a way to access data stored about them. Credit bureaus still sell marketing lists to credit-card companies and others that offer credit and insurance. Consumers can opt out from these lists.

Errors in credit records: Section 8.1.2

Identity theft: Section 5.3

different points of view about how far law should go in prohibiting various services and practices to protect consumers.

Data firms and consumer profiles

There is a vast world of data collection over which we have little or no direct control. When someone consents to a company's use of his or her consumer information, the person probably has no idea how extensive the company is and how far the data could travel. Many companies that maintain huge consumer databases buy (or merge with) other companies, combining data to build more detailed databases and dossiers. ChoicePoint, the data firm mentioned in Section 2.2.1, and similar firms, such as Acxiom, a large international database and direct-marketing company, collect personal data from a huge number of sources and build personal profiles. They acquire some data from public records (property, marriage and divorce, bankruptcy), some after a consumer clicks or signs a consent form, and some from transactions where consumers do not opt out from use of their information. Acxiom processes a billion records every day.[57] In addition to consumer information, ChoicePoint owns databases with records on drug tests, doctors' backgrounds, insurance fraud, and other areas. These firms sell data to businesses for marketing and "customer management." They provide services to manage and verify data and credentials for job applicants. Businesses and government agencies use them (and credit reports) for background checks on job applicants and for other sorts of investigations. Some of these services are very valuable. The point is that most people do not know that firms like ChoicePoint and Acxiom exist. Thus, although the companies provide a way for people to see their profile, most people do not know what information they hold and how it is used.

2.3.2 LOCATION TRACKING

GPS, cell phones, and other technologies and devices enable the development of a large variety of new location-based applications, that is, computer and communications services that depend on knowing exactly where a person (or object) is at a particular time. New applications for tracking/locating technologies and identification devices, such as radio frequency identification (RFID) tags, are popping up regularly. Many of the current, planned, and potential applications have significant benefits. They, however, they add detailed information about our current location and our past movements to the pool of information that computer systems store about us, with all the potential threats to privacy.

Applications include consumer services, services to others based on people's location (various kinds of tracking), behavioral and marketing research, identifying and tracking patients in hospitals (to avoid mistakes in treatment and medication), routing baggage at airports (with more accuracy than bar codes), improved inventory management for manufacturers and retailers, and manipulation of objects (robots, airplanes, etc.). Figure 2.4 shows a few services for individuals based on location detection.

❖ Providing information about nearby restaurants of a particular kind, the nearest automated teller machine, hospital, or dry cleaners, based on the location of your cell phone or laptop.

❖ Navigation aids for blind people on foot.

❖ Devices that enable locating a stolen vehicle. Navigation systems for cars. (Besides giving directions to a particular destination, a more sophisticated service can check traffic reports and suggest an alternate route to a driver headed toward a traffic jam.)

❖ Alerting you (by cell phone) if any of your friends are nearby.

❖ Providing a person's location immediately to emergency services when he or she calls 911 on a cell phone.

❖ Locating people, possibly injured or unconscious and buried in rubble, after an earthquake or bombing.

❖ Tracking children on a school outing at a park or museum.

Figure 2.4 Location-Based Services

Marketers quickly find ways to use new technologies for advertising. Recall that freedom from intrusion is one of the three aspects of privacy. Will we get calls on our cell phones announcing sales and encouraging us to shop in each store we walk by? Some expect a barrage of such advertising intrusions. There are a few reasons to expect (or hope) that this will not happen. It might so offend people that the advertising effect would be negative rather than positive. The Federal Communications Commission has already prohibited commercial e-mail to cell phones (or other wireless devices) without the device owner's consent.[58] It is likely that unsolicited advertising calls to cell phones will be illegal. It, however, is also likely that, just as many Web users trade permission to track their Web-surfing behavior for free goods and services, many companies will offer free services to users who give permission to send ads to their cell phones and laptops.

Studying behavior of customers in a store or other commercial facility is a big potential application of location tracking. For example, a supermarket or an amusement park might want to analyze customer traffic patterns within the facility in order to plan a better layout or to determine how much time people spend inside. They might use a souped-up supermarket club card, a ticket, or a person's cell phone to collect each person's movement pattern. Such businesses point out that online businesses obtain similar information by tracking how people move around a Web site, how long they stay at a particular page, and so on.

FOILING POACHERS, FOLLOWING TURTLES

Very valuable and extremely rare plants, both in the wild and in gardens, are tagged with chips so their owners can locate them if stolen.

Satellite technology and microprocessors enormously improved animal tracking. Scientists attach tiny transmitters to rare birds and other animals in order to study their behavior and learn how to protect their food sources. Researchers learned that some animals travel much farther than previously thought: sea turtles swim from the Caribbean to Africa. To get food for its young, a nesting albatross flew from Hawaii to the San Francisco Bay, a weeklong round-trip. To encourage interest among the public, many researchers have Web sites where we can follow the animals' movements.[59] These are valuable services. What happens when the same technologies track people?

The privacy implications and risks of monitoring people's movements vary from little to great, depending on how the tracking is accomplished. Suppose an amusement park such as Disneyland wants to study visitor traffic patterns, detect crowds and long lines, or gather other information about visitor behavior. It can do so with a location-emitting ticket that people get when they enter and discard when they leave. The ticket need have no information connected to the person or family. For such a system, privacy is not an issue. A supermarket card or cell phone, on the other hand, identifies a person and, thus, the tracking information is personal information and raises the usual issues of consent, potential secondary uses, risks of misuse, and so on.

RFID tags are small devices that contain a computer chip and an antenna. The chip stores identification data (and possibly other data) and controls operation of the tag. The antenna transmits and receives radio signals for communicating with devices that read the tag. RFID tags are inserted in many products to track them through the manufacturing and selling processes. If not disabled after a consumer buys the product, the tag can become a device for tracking the person.

The federal government is implementing plans to use RFID tags in various identity documents including passports. Numerous experiments and studies by computer scientists raised questions about security. One experiment demonstrated that it is relatively easy to read the information on an RFID chip and copy it to another chip to create a counterfeit document. Software viruses can corrupt the tags. If not shielded, the passport tag "announces" that the holder is an American, a fact a traveler might not want to broadcast. If shielded, so that border guards must open the passport, we lose speedy processing, one of the main original benefits of the RFID tag.[60] Computer scientists and engineers will eventually solve some of the technical problems.

What level of security and privacy protection should we expect before the tags are used?

Pets, prisoners, people with Alzheimer's disease, and children may wear devices that locate them if they wander off. Veterinarians implant ID chips under the skin of pets and farm animals. Some people have suggested that this be done for prisoners and children as well. Does the suggestion of implanting tracking chips in children make you wonder, Is that such a good idea? After heavy opposition from parents, a school dropped its proposal to require that all students wear an RFID-equipped device while on school grounds. The constant surveillance and the risks of misuse were enough, in the minds of many parents, to outweigh the benefits of a removable tracking device.

Why do people stop mail and newspaper delivery when they are away on a trip? They see this one detail about their location ("away from home") as important to protect from potential burglars. How much more serious are the security risks from access to detailed information about someone's current location at any moment?

To analyze risks, we should always consider unintended as well as intended uses. Imagine that anyone can enter a person's ID number (perhaps a cell phone number) on their cell phone or on the Internet and ask where that person is now. Or perhaps a device could sweep a particular location and detect identifying devices of the people there. Who might a person *not* want to get this information? Thieves. A violent spouse or ex-spouse. A divorce lawyer. An annoying or nosy neighbor. A stalker. Coworkers or business associates. Anyone else who might object to your religion, politics, or sexual behavior. The government. (Oh, we see that our new teacher is at a meeting of Alcoholics Anonymous.) (Who is in that medical marijuana store right now?) The ability to determine a person's current location clearly has some risks. In addition, many applications of location detection include or allow storage of information about a person's location over time. Records of *Tracking employees at work: Section 6.5.3* where we were provide more details to the ever-growing profiles and dossiers businesses and governments build about us. With fast search, matching, and analysis tools, they can add more detail about who we spend time with and what we are doing. If accessed surreptitiously, stolen, disclosed accidentally, or acquired by government agencies, records of our location and movements pose many threats to privacy, safety, and liberty.

Privacy and industry organizations are developing guidelines for using location-tracking applications to implement many of the principles in Figure 2.1 and protect against some of the risks.[61]

2.3.3   STOLEN AND LOST DATA

> *These records are blazing all over the Internet.*
>
> —Jonathan Adelstein, FCC Commissioner,
> speaking of customer telephone records[62]

One of the risks associated with databases of personal information is that criminals steal and use the information. Criminals steal personal data by hacking into computer systems, by stealing computers and disks, by buying or requesting records under false pretenses, and by bribing employees of companies that store the data. (We discuss hacking at length in Chapter 5.) Shady information brokers sell data obtained illegally or by questionable means. Software called *spyware*, often downloaded from a Web site without the user's knowledge, surreptitiously collects information about a person's activity and data on his or her computer and then sends the information over the Internet to the person or company that planted the spyware. Spyware can track someone's Web surfing for an advertising company or collect passwords and credit card numbers typed by the user. Although many of these activities are illegal, they still occur and are serious privacy threats. Businesses, government agencies, and other institutions lose computers, disks, and files containing personal data on thousands or millions of people, exposing people to potential misuse of their information and lingering uncertainty. Some businesses and organizations that make account information available to customers and members on the Web do not sufficiently authenticate the person accessing the information, allowing imposters access. We discuss these problems in this section.

Figure 2.5 shows a small sample of stolen or lost personal information of large numbers of people. In many incidents, the goal of the thieves is to collect data for use in identity theft and fraud, crimes we discuss in detail in Chapter 5. Roughly half the states in the U.S. require that companies and state agencies notify people of leaks and losses of their personal information. Federal regulations require financial institutions to do so. These relatively recent laws led to disclosure of many of the incidents in Figure 2.5, thus bringing attention to the seriousness of the problem of poor security for personal data, especially on laptops.

In most of the incidents in Figure 2.5, the lost or stolen personal information was held by businesses. Government agencies lose personal data as well. There is no law requiring federal agencies to inform people whose personal data are lost or stolen. A congressional committee investigation found that within less than four years, personal data on employees and the public were lost or stolen from government agencies in 788 incidents. A thief stole a Department of Veterans Affairs laptop and hard disk containing personal records of 26.5 million veterans, their spouses, reservists, National Guard members, and active-duty military members. (In this case, the laptop and disk were later found. Investigators concluded that the laptop itself, not the data, was the target of the theft.) More than 1,000 laptops disappeared from the Commerce Department within a few years, some with personal data from Census questionnaires. Some were stolen from the cars of temporary Census employees or simply kept by the employees. The IRS lost more than 2,000 computers in a four-year period. A report by the Treasury's Inspector General stated that the IRS did not adequately protect taxpayer information on more than 50,000 laptops and other storage media. The Federal Bureau of Prisons, the Drug Enforcement Administration, the FBI, and the U.S. Marshals Service lost 400 laptops. Congress's GAO found nearly 50 weaknesses in the operation of the government's communication network

- Records of roughly 40 million customers of TJX discount clothing stores (T. J. Maxx, Marshall's, and others), including credit- and debit-card numbers and some driver license numbers (stolen by hackers)

  More about the TJX incident: Section 5.2.4

- Student and/or alumni files from the University of California, Georgia Tech, Kent State, and several other universities, some with SSNs and birth dates. (Hackers accessed a University of California, Los Angeles, database with personal data on roughly 800,000 current and former students, faculty, and staff members.)

- Employment information, including SSNs, of more than 160,000 past and current Boeing employees (on a stolen laptop)

- Time Warner files on 600,000 employees

- Bank of America disks with account information (lost or stolen in transit)

- Records of almost 200,000 current and former employees of Hewlett-Packard (on a laptop stolen from Fidelity Investments)

- Records on millions of people stolen by a customer of huge database company Acxiom

- ChoicePoint files with personal information on hundreds of thousands of people. A fraud ring posing as legitimate businesses set up dozens of accounts with ChoicePoint and bought personal data, including credit histories, for 163,000 people. Hundreds of people became victims of identity theft as a result.

- Names, birth dates, SSNs, and medical diagnoses for 1,600 patients (laptop stolen from the University of Washington Medical Center)

- Medical data on more than 20,000 patients in MediCal, California's state health insurance system

- Confidential contact information for more than one million job seekers (stolen from Monster.com by hackers using servers in Ukraine)

- A survey of taxi drivers in London found that passengers left almost 5,000 laptops in taxicabs within a six-month period. Many, perhaps, contained only the personal information of the owner (and friends, family, and e-mail correspondants). Most likely were business laptops containing personal information of customers or others.

Figure 2.5 Lost or Stolen Personal Information[63]

for transmitting medical data in the Medicare and Medicaid programs—weaknesses that could allow unauthorized access to people's medical records.[64]

Shady data brokers will sell you someone's cell phone records, credit report, credit-card statements, mortgage payments, tax returns, medical history, employer, location of relatives, information about their financial and investment accounts, and a variety of other information. Criminals, lawyers, private investigators, spouses, ex-spouses, and law enforcement agents are among the buyers. A private investigator could have obtained much of this information in the past but not nearly so easily, cheaply, and quickly.

Investigators and data brokers get a lot of information by a process called *pretexting*, that is, by pretending to be someone with a legitimate reason for obtaining the data. Pretexters sometimes pretend to be other employees of the company from which they seek the data. Frequently, they pretend to be the person whose data they want to get. In a high-level pretexting case, a Hewlett-Packard executive hired investigators to determine which member of its board of directors leaked information to news media. Investigators impersonated journalists and members of the company's board to get their telephone records.

Pretexters often get information by telephone and usually begin with some personal information about their target to make their request seem legitimate. That is one reason why it is important to be cautious with data that are not particularly sensitive.

Banks, telephone companies, and many other businesses provide customers with online access to their accounts. Pretexters who know a person's account number and a few other details can pretend to be the person, activate online 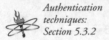 *Authentication techniques: Section 5.3.2* access (if the customer has not already done so), and then collect the account records. That is why some privacy organizations recommend that consumers activate their online access and set up their own password. Another solution would be for the businesses to improve their process for authenticating the customer before granting access.

A Canadian cable provider let customers access their accounts online by entering their name, phone number, and postal code. Such information is easily available; hence someone else could learn if, for example, a cable customer subscribes to a sexually explicit channel. Some cell phone service providers let customers retrieve voice-mail messages without entering a personal identification number (PIN) when the customers call from their phone. But someone else can fake the calling number with a Caller ID spoofing service and retrieve a person's messages. Both of these access methods are intended to make access convenient for the customer. When is the convenience worth the privacy risk?

Law and ethical responsibility

We consider some relevant laws and ethical issues both for those who obtain personal information by theft or pretexting and for those who maintain the information and have responsibility for its security.

AOL AND THE SAILOR: AN EARLY PRETEXTING CASE

AOL's terms-of-service agreement stated that their policy is "not to disclose identity information to third parties that would link a Member's screen name(s) with a Member's actual name, unless required to do so by law or legal process served on AOL, Inc. (e.g., a subpoena)." AOL reserved the right to make exceptions in special circumstances, such as a suicide threat or suspected illegal activity. In a widely publicized case in 1997 an AOL employee violated the policy. The employee gave a caller—pretending to be a friend but actually a Navy investigator—the real name of a sailor who described himself as gay in an online profile.

This incident illustrates several points. First, AOL has a very good identity-protecting policy. Second, a company must train its employees well to follow the policy and to understand that someone who calls requesting information might not be whom he claims to be. Finally, this incident illustrates the risks. The sailor might be gay—or, like many other people, he might have created a fictitious persona online—but the Navy tried to discharge him after 17 years of service with an excellent record.[65]

Pretexting to obtain financial records has been illegal since 1999 under the federal Gramm-Leach-Bliley Act. The Telephone Records and Privacy Protection Act of 2006 (passed soon after the Hewlett-Packard incident) made it a federal crime to obtain someone's telephone records without the person's permission. (There is an exception for law enforcement agencies.) Privacy groups advocate laws to explicitly criminalize pretexting for other kinds of records as well.

Data brokers who obtain consumer records by lying and then sell the data to whoever wants to buy them are acting unethically in several ways. They put at risk both the individual target and the company from which they obtain the records. They are stealing information from the company, which may have legal liability. They are irresponsibly providing the data to someone who might use them to defraud, steal from, physically harm, or harm in some other way the person who is the subject of the data. At a minimum, they are invading the person's privacy. Clearly, the person has not consented to this use of his or her information. This should all seem obvious, but it is important for anyone who copies personal information for fun—and gives or sells it to someone on the Internet—to understand the risks.

When businesses, organizations, and government agencies store personal data, we have no means of directly protecting them, as we would with files in our desk or computer. Those who collect and store personal data have an ethical responsibility (and in many cases a legal one) to protect them from misuse. Responsible data holders must anticipate risks and prepare for them. Many companies and government agencies did not realize that personal data would be such an attractive target for thieves.

Businesses and government agencies are slowly addressing the problem of poor security illustrated by the list in Figure 2.5. They need to review policies about employees taking personal information on laptops and other small, high-capacity storage devices out of the office. Do the benefits of carrying thousands of people's personal data outweigh the risks? The answer will vary depending on the kind of data and how the employees need to use them. Most often, the answer is probably no, but no one even thought about the risks. Those responsible for personal data must continually update security policies to cover new technologies and new potential threats. Employees who carry personal data must be trained to be aware of the risks and to follow proper security practices. Encryption is a particularly valuable security measure.* Other technical protections include a tracking system for laptops that includes a GPS device and a feature that allows the owner of a stolen or lost laptop to encrypt, retrieve, and/or erase files remotely. We describe more ways of protecting laptops in our discussion of responses to identity theft in Section 5.3.2.

What penalties are appropriate when businesses, organizations, or government agencies lose or disclose personal data? Legal responsibility varies depending on the kind of data, which state's laws apply, and whether the entity responsible for the data is private or a government agency. A federal law (Health Insurance Portability and Accountability Act, HIPAA) specifies strong penalties for medical organizations that do not follow detailed privacy regulations. The Privacy Act provides for payments when government agencies improperly disclose personal data. When a government agency made public the SSNs of several miners who had filed claims for black lung disease, the Supreme Court ruled that the payments were not automatic. Those whose information is released must prove that they have suffered actual harm. There are good arguments for and against this position. Payments to every person, about whom perhaps insignificant information is released and never used destructively, might amount to a ridiculously high burden. On the other hand, it might be a few years before someone is aware that criminals are using lost or stolen information to commit fraud in his or her name. Proving harm can be difficult.

2.3.4 WHAT WE DO OURSELVES

> *Broadcast Yourself.*™
> —Slogan on YouTube's home page[66]

Soon after a woman started writing a personal blog, she discovered that someone she had not seen in years read it. This horrified her. Perhaps she thought only people to whom she gave the URL read the blog. She did not realize that her blog showed up high

---

*Encrypting data means storing them in a coded form so that others cannot read them. We discuss encryption more extensively in Section 2.4.1.

in search results for her name.[67] Another woman liked the feature on a social-network site that told her which members read her profile. She was surprised and upset to find that people whose profiles she read knew she read them.

The first incident reminds us that some people do not know or understand enough how the Web works in order to make good decisions about what to put there.* The second indicates that some people do not think carefully. The second incident also illustrates a very common phenomenon: people often want a lot of information about others but do not want others to have access to the same kinds of information about themselves.

Some people include their birth date in online profiles or in résumés they post on job-hunting sites. Genealogy sites are very popular on the Web. People create family trees on genealogy sites with complete profiles of family members. Entries include birth dates and mother's maiden name. Medical and financial institutions use this information to verify a customer's identity. We can change a disclosed password; we cannot change our birth date or mother's maiden name.

Many young people post opinions, gossip, and pictures that their friends enjoy. Their posts might cause trouble if a parent, potential employer, law enforcement agent, or various others see them. An 18-year-old who posts sexy photos of herself in bathing suits is thinking about her friends viewing them, not potential stalkers or rapists. People who try to clean up their profiles before starting a job search sometimes find that it is hard to eliminate embarrassing information, photos, and videos. Some users of social-networking sites include among their network friends only people they already know offline. Others, with hundreds of network friends they never met, probably do not give enough thought to the implications of the personal information they make available.

The Web is public. Most people are decent and harmless, but a lot are evil and dangerous. Pedophiles have Web sites that link to sites of Cub Scouts, Brownies (the young version of Girl Scouts), junior-high-school soccer teams, and so on—sites with pictures of children and sometimes names and other personal information. That is scary. It does not mean that such organizations should not put pictures on their Web sites. It suggests, however, that they consider whether to include children's names, whether to require registration for use of the site, and so on.

Years ago, when many homes had answering machines connected to telephones, some people, instead, used answering services. Messages left for them resided on recording machines at the service's business site. I recall my surprise that people were comfortable with their personal messages on machines outside their control. How quaint that concern seems now. Our cell phone and e-mail messages routinely reside on computers outside our home or office. Instant messages sent to or from a cell phone are retrievable months later. After many incidents of exposure of embarrassing e-mails, individuals, politicians, lawyers, and businesspeople still write sensitive, rude, or compromising things in e-mail with the apparent belief that no one but the recipient will ever see it.

---

*In an unusual example of initiative, the woman studied the techniques used to rank search results and modified her blog so that it no longer showed up prominently in searches for her name.

We saw that businesses and government agencies lose huge numbers of files with account numbers, SSNs, and other personal data. We have no direct control over those files. What are *we* putting on computer systems outside our homes? Where do we still have choices?

Software for filling out tax forms on our PCs has been available for years and is very popular. The Web provides another option: More than ten million Americans prepare their tax returns online. Do they think about where their income and expenditure data are going? How long the data remain online? How well secured the data are? Small businesses store all their accounting information online on Web sites that provide accounting services and access from anywhere. Do the business owners check the security of the sites? Several medical Web sites provide an easy place for people to store their medical records online. Google, Yahoo, and other companies offer services where people store all their data (e-mails, photos, calendars, files) on the company's servers, instead of on their PC or laptop. There are big advantages to all these services. We do not have to manage our own system. We do not have to make backups. We can get to our files from anywhere with Internet access. We can more easily share files and collaborate with others on projects.

There are disadvantages too. We cannot access our files when the network is down or if there is a technical problem at the company that stores them. But the more serious risks are to privacy and security. We lose control of our files. Outside our home, they are at risk of loss, theft, misuse by employees, accidental exposure, uses by the service provider described in an agreement or privacy policy we did not read, uses we ignored when signing up for the service, and later uses that no one anticipated. By "sharing" our files with the service provider, we make it easier for a government agency to get them. We might decide we do not care who else sees our vacation photos. We might decide that the convenience of filling out tax forms online or storing our medical records online outweighs the risks. The point is to be aware and to consciously make the decision. For computer professionals, awareness of the risks should encourage care and responsibility in developing secure systems to protect the sensitive information people store online.

Is privacy old-fashioned?

Some people argue that young people today (in their teens and twenties) view privacy differently than people of the previous generation. The young people today are not as concerned by disclosure of personal information or videos of embarrassing behavior. They are used to being photographed frequently by surveillance cameras and cell phone cameras. They are used to their Web activity and location being tracked. They like the personalized services that depend on such tracking. Others argue that young people do not realize the risks and that they will later regret the large amount of information they and others make public about themselves.

Which point of view do you think is more accurate?

> *Polls show that people care about privacy. Why don't they act that way?*
>
> —Ian Kerr (ethics, law, and technology researcher)[68]

2.3.5 PUBLIC RECORDS: ACCESS VERSUS PRIVACY

Governments maintain "public records," that is, records that are available to the public. Examples include bankruptcy records, arrest records, marriage license applications, divorce proceedings, property-ownership records (including mortgage information), salaries of government employees, and wills. These have long been public but available on paper in government offices. Lawyers, private investigators, journalists, real estate brokers, neighbors, and others use the records. Now that it is so easy to search and browse through files on the Web, more people access public records for fun, for research, for valid personal purposes—and for purposes that can threaten the peace, safety, and personal secrets of others.

Public records include sensitive information such as SSNs, birth dates, and home addresses. Maricopa County in Arizona, the first county to put numerous and complete public records on the Web, has the highest rate of identity theft in the United States.[69] Obviously, certain sensitive information should be withheld from public-record

More about identity theft: Section 5.3

Web sites. That requires decisions about exactly what types of data to protect. It requires revisions to government software systems to prevent display of specified items. Because of the expense and lack of accountability, incentives within government agencies to do this are weak. A few have adopted policies to block display of sensitive data in files posted online, and some have laws requiring such blocking. Several software companies produced software for this purpose, using a variety of techniques to search documents for sensitive data and protect them. Until new systems—in which such security is part of the basic design—replace older systems, the patches and add-ons, while helpful, are likely to miss some sensitive data.

To illustrate more problems about public records and potential solutions, we consider a few cases of specialized information: political contributions, flight information for private airplanes, and the financial statements of judges.

Political campaign committees must report the name, address, employer, and donation amount for every donor who contributes more than $100 to a candidate for president. This information is available to the public. In the past, primarily journalists and rival campaigns examined it. Now it is on the Web and easy to search. Anyone can find out what candidate their neighbors, friends, employees, and employers support. We can also find the addresses of prominent people who might prefer to keep their address secret to protect their peace and privacy.

Pilots of the roughly 10,000 company airplanes in the U.S. file a flight plan when they fly. A few businesses have combined this flight information, obtained from government databases, with aircraft registration records, also public government records, in order to provide a service telling where a particular plane is, where it is going, when it will arrive, and so on. Who wants this information? Competitors can use it to determine with whom top executives of another company are meeting. Terrorists could use it to track movements of a high-profile target. The information was available before but not so easily and anonymously.

The Ethics in Government Act requires federal judges to file financial disclosure reports. The public can review these reports to determine whether a particular judge might have a conflict of interest in a particular case. The reports were available in print but not online. When an online news agency sued to make the reports available online, judges objected that information in the reports can disclose where family members work or go to school, putting them at risk from defendants who are angry at a judge. The reports were provided for posting online, with some sensitive information removed.[70]

The change in ease of access to information, in turn, changes the balance between the advantages and disadvantages of making some kinds of data public. Whenever access changes significantly, we should reconsider old decisions, policies, and laws. Do the benefits of requiring reporting of small political contributions outweigh the privacy risks? Do the benefits of making all property ownership records public outweigh the privacy risks?

How should we control access to sensitive public records? Under the old rules for the financial statements of judges, people requesting access had to sign a form disclosing their identity. This is a sensible rule. The information is available to the public, but the record of who accessed it could deter most people intent on doing harm. Can we implement a similar system online? Technologies for identifying and authenticating people online are developing but are not yet widespread enough for use by everyone accessing sensitive public data on the Web. We might routinely use them in the future, but that raises another question: How will we distinguish data that requires identification and a signature for access from data the public should be free to view anonymously, to protect the viewer's privacy?[71]

2.3.6 NATIONAL ID SYSTEMS

In the U.S., national identification systems began with the Social Security Card in 1936. In the 1990s, concerns about illegal immigration provided the most support for a more sophisticated and secure national ID card. Opposition, based on concerns about privacy and potential abuse, prevented significant progress on a variety of national ID proposals made by many government agencies. In this section, we review SSNs, various issues about national ID systems, and the REAL ID Act of 2005, a major step toward turning driver's licenses into national ID cards.

Social Security numbers[72]

The history of the SSN illustrates how the use of a national identification system grows. When SSNs first appeared in 1936, they were for the exclusive use of the Social Security program. The government assured the public at the time that it would not use the numbers for other purposes. Only a few years later, in 1943, President Roosevelt signed an executive order requiring federal agencies to use the SSN for new record systems. In 1961, the IRS began using it as the taxpayer identification number. So employers and others who must report to the IRS require it. In 1976, state and local tax, welfare, and motor vehicle departments received authority to use the SSN. A 1988 federal law requires that parents provide their SSN to get a birth certificate for a child. In the 1990s the FTC encouraged credit bureaus to use SSNs. A 1996 law required that states collect SSNs for occupational licenses, marriage licenses, and other kinds of licenses. Also in 1996, Congress required that all driver's licenses display the driver's SSN, but it repealed that law a few years later because of strong protests. Although we were promised otherwise, the SSN has become a general identification number.

We use our SSN for identification for credit, financial, and numerous other services, yet its insecurity compromises our privacy and exposes us to fraud and identity theft. Because the SSN is an identifier in so many databases, someone who knows your name and has your SSN can, with varying degrees of ease, get access to your work and earnings history, credit report, driving record, and other personal data. SSNs appear on public documents and other openly available forms. Property deeds, which are public records, often require SSNs. For decades, SSNs were the ID numbers for students and faculty at many universities; the numbers appeared on the face of ID cards and on class rosters. The state of Virginia included SSNs on published lists of voters until a federal court ruled that its policy of requiring the SSN for voter registration was unconstitutional. Some employers used the SSN as an identifier and put it on badges or gave it out on request. Many companies, hospitals, and other organizations to which we might owe a bill request our SSN to run a credit check. Some routinely ask for an SSN and record it in their files, although they do not need it.

More than 25 years ago, the U.S. Department of Agriculture (USDA) began including the SSN as part of the ID number for farmers who got loans or grants. In 2007, the USDA admitted that since 1996 it had inadvertently included the SSNs of more than 35,000 farmers on the Web site where it posted loan details.[73] This example illustrates how practices begun well before the Web have continuing repercussions. It also illustrates the importance of careful and thorough evaluation of decisions to put material on the Web. There are likely many similar examples that no one has yet noticed.

SSNs are too widely available to securely identify someone. Social security cards are easy to forge, but that hardly matters because people are rarely asked for the card, and numbers are rarely verified. The Social Security Administration itself used to issue cards without verification of the information provided by the applicant. Criminals have little trouble creating false identities, whereas innocent, honest people suffer disclosure of personal information, arrest, fraud, destruction of their credit rating, and so on, because of problems with the SSN.

Gradually, governments and businesses began to recognize the risks of careless use of the SSN and reasons why we should not use it so widely. In 2007, a federal report urged federal agencies to reduce unnecessary use of the SSN.[74] It will take a long time to undo the damage its widespread use has already done to privacy and financial security.

A new national ID system

> Places like Nazi Germany, the Soviet Union, and apartheid South Africa all had very robust identification systems. True, identification systems do not cause tyranny, but identification systems are very good administrative systems that tyrannies often use.
>
> —Jim Harper, Director of Information Policy Studies, Cato Institute[75]

Various national ID card proposals in recent years would require citizenship, employment, health, tax, financial, or other data, and biometric information such as fingerprints or a retina scan, depending on the specific proposal and the government agency advocating it. In many proposals, the cards would also access a variety of databases for additional information.

More about biometrics: Section 5.3.3

Advocates of national ID systems describe several benefits: you would need the actual card, not just a number, to verify identity. The cards would be harder to forge than Social Security cards. A person would need to carry only one card, rather than separate cards for various services, as we do now. The authentication of identity would help reduce fraud both in private credit-card transactions and in government benefit programs. Use of ID cards for verifying work eligibility would prevent people from working in the U.S. illegally. Criminals and terrorists would be easier to track and identify.

Opponents of national ID systems argue that they are profound threats to freedom and privacy. "Your papers, please" is a demand associated with police states and dictatorships. In Germany and France, identification papers included the person's religion, making it easy for the Nazis to capture Jews. Under the infamous pass laws of South Africa, people carried passes, or identification papers, that categorized them by race and controlled where they could live and work. Cards with embedded chips or magnetic strips and the large amount of personal information they can carry or access have even more potential for abuse. Most people would not have access to the machinery that reads the cards. Thus, they would not always know what information they are giving others about themselves. Theft and forgery of cards would reduce some of the potential benefits.

Peter Neumann and Lauren Weinstein warned of risks that arise from the databases and communication complexes that would support a national ID card system: "The opportunities for overzealous surveillance and serious privacy abuses are almost limitless, as are opportunities for masquerading, identity theft, and draconian social engineering on a grand scale."[76]

A woman in Canada could not get her tax refund because the tax agency insisted she was dead. Her identification number had mistakenly been reported in place of her mother's when her mother died. She would still have been able to get a new job, withdraw money from her bank account, pay her rent, send e-mail, and go to her doctor while she was resolving the problem with the tax agency. What if the worker verification database connected to the tax database? Or what if a mistake cancelled the one ID card required for all these transactions? A critic of a proposal for a national identification card in Australia described the card as a "license to exist."[77]

The terrorist attacks in 2001 brought new proposals for requiring everyone in the U.S. to carry a secure national ID card. (Many of the airplane hijackers had government-issued ID cards, some valid, some fake.) The REAL ID Act, passed in 2005 and effective in 2008, attempts to develop a secure national identification card by setting federal standards for driver's licenses (and state-issued ID cards, for those without driver's licenses). Licenses must meet the federal standards to be used for identification for federal government purposes. Such purposes include airport security and entering federal facilities. By implication, they likely include working for the federal government and obtaining federal benefits. It is likely that the government will add many new uses, as with the SSN. Businesses and state and local governments are likely to require the federally approved ID card for many transactions and services. The federal government pays for almost half the medical care in the U.S. (e.g., Medicare, benefits for veterans, and numerous federally funded programs). It is not hard to envision the driver's license being required for federal medical services and eventually becoming a de facto national medical ID card.

The REAL ID Act requires that, to get a federally approved driver's license or ID card, each person must provide documentation of address, birth date, SSN, and legal status in the United States. Motor vehicle departments must verify the validity of the documents submitted and scan and store them, in transferable form, for at least ten years (making motor vehicle records a desirable target for identity thieves). The licenses must satisfy various requirements to reduce tampering and counterfeiting, and they must include the person's photo and machine-readable information to be determined by the Department of Homeland Security.

The REAL ID Act puts the burden of verifying identity on individuals and the state motor vehicle departments. Many states object to the mandate and its high costs and difficulties. Several states voted not to participate. Residents in states without a federally approved driver's license could experience serious inconvenience. At this point it is unclear whether enough states and individuals will object to the REAL ID mandates to cause Congress to repeal or modify the law, or whether the huge scope of federal programs will force compliance.

Many European and Asian countries require national ID cards. An unpopular plan for an expensive mandatory national ID card in the United Kingdom stalled in 2006 when e-mails about weaknesses of the plan leaked from government offices. The government of Japan implemented a national computerized registry system that included assigning an ID number to every citizen of the country. The system is for government uses, with initially approximately 100 applications, but eventually probably thousands. It is intended to simplify administration procedures and make them more efficient. Privacy advocates and protesters complained of insufficient privacy protection, potential abuse by government, and vulnerability to hackers.

> *As soon as you are willing to put your home, your office, your safe deposit box, your bike lock, your gym key, and your desk key all onto one and ask the government to issue that one key, you will be okay with the national ID. But until then, we need to think more in terms of diversification of identification systems.*

—Jim Harper, Director of Information Policy Studies, Cato Institute[78]

2.3.7 CHILDREN

Computer technology and the Web raise several privacy issues about children. Some involve risks to the child and family from Web activity, and some involve complex family issues raised by the many surveillance tools available to parents. We consider both.

Privacy and safety are major concerns for parents. Adults can make decisions about what information they want to give out, or what degree of tracking they want to allow in exchange for discounts or access to certain services. Children are not likely to understand the risks and trade-offs. Child molesters use the Web to find children, win their confidence through e-mail and chat, and then arrange meetings. Detailed profiles about children, including their hobbies, nicknames, names of friends, and so forth, are a treasure for these predators.

In 1998, an FTC study found that 89% of Web sites aimed at children collected personal information and that only 23% of the sites asked children to get consent from their parents before providing the information. Later that year, Congress passed the Children's Online Privacy Protection Act (COPPA),* ordering the FTC to set up rules for protecting children under age 13. The rules (effective since 2000) prohibit Web sites from collecting personal information from children under 13 without "verifiable parental consent." The sites must prominently post their policy telling what information they collect and how they use it.

Concerns for privacy and safety of children increased with the advent of social-networking sites. After accusations of sexual assaults of young girls by men they met on Web sites, and after a lawsuit against MySpace for one such attack, many sites

---

*This is different from COPA, the Child Online Protection Act, a censorship law. We mentioned COPA in Section 2.1.2 and discuss it more fully in Chapter 3.

began implementing policies designed to protect members. Protections include running ads warning girls about safe practices and scanning for nudity in photos and removing them. MySpace used special software developed by an online identity and background verification company to find and delete profiles of 7000 registered sex offenders (out of 180 million profiles).*[79] Some Web sites block e-mail to members under age 16 unless the sender knows the member's real last name. MySpace removed 250,000 profiles of children under 14. Most Web sites do not verify the age of members; hence, large loopholes remain.

Parents can install software on home computers that generates logs of their children's activity on the Web, thus providing some measure of oversight and protection. Many new technologies help parents track their children's physical location. Cell phone companies offer services that enable parents to check a child's physical location on the parent's phone or on a Web site. Devices installed in a car tell parents where their teens are and how fast they are driving. A company sells wireless watchband transmitters for children, so that parents can monitor them. RFID tags in shoes and clothes can be monitored hundreds of feet away. These might be very helpful with young children who wander off in a crowded place.

Monitoring and tracking systems for children can increase safety, but there are parenting issues and risks involved in using them. At what age does Web monitoring become an invasion of the child's privacy? Should parents tell children about the tracking devices and services they are using? Informed consent is a basic principle for adults. At what age does it apply to children? Will intense tracking and monitoring slow the development of a child's responsible independence? Will parents rely more on gadgets than on talking to their children?

A monitoring system that sends easily read or easily intercepted signals could decrease rather than increase safety of a child. Child molesters and identity thieves could collect personal data. Parents need to be aware of potential for false alarms and for a false sense of security. For example, a child might lose a cell phone or leave a tagged article of clothing somewhere. Older kids might figure out how to thwart tracking systems. Clearly, how and when to use surveillance tools should involve thoughtful decisions for families.

2.4 Protecting Privacy: Technology, Markets, Rights, and Laws

2.4.1 TECHNOLOGY AND MARKETS

Many individuals, organizations, and businesses help meet the demand for privacy to some degree: Individual programmers post free privacy-protecting software on the Web. Entrepreneurs build new companies to provide technology-based privacy protections. Large businesses respond to consumer demand and improve policies and services. Organizations such as the Privacy Rights Clearinghouse provide excellent information

---

*MySpace turned over information on these people to state attorneys. This raises the question of the accuracy of the methods the software uses to identify sex offenders.

resources. Activist organizations such as the Electronic Privacy Information Center (EPIC) inform the public, file lawsuits, and advocate for better privacy protection.

Awareness

> *Most people have figured out by now you can't do anything on the Web without leaving a record.*
>
> —Holman W. Jenkins Jr., 2000[80]

Holman Jenkins got it wrong in the quotation above. In 2000, tech-savvy people were aware of the tracking of Web activity, but most ordinary people were not. In 2006, the disclosure that Google, AOL, and other companies that operate search engines store search queries shocked people. Still, each new revelation about personal data collection or loss of sensitive personal data surprises people.

Since the mid-1990s, however, television programs, newspapers, magazines, pro-privacy Web sites, and many organizations have informed the public about risks to privacy from business and government databases and the Web. As consumers, once we are aware of the problems and potential solutions, we can decide to what extent we wish to use privacy-protecting tools, be more careful about the information we give out, and consider the privacy policies of businesses and Web sites we use or visit. As business managers, we can learn and implement techniques to respond to the privacy demands of customers. As computer professionals, we can design systems with privacy protection in mind, building in protective features and designing so that others can easily be added later.

Privacy-enhancing technologies for consumers

New applications of technology often can solve problems that arise as side effects of technology. Soon after "techies" became aware of the use of cookies by Web sites, they wrote cookie disablers and posted them on the Web. Web browsers added options to alert the user whenever a Web site is about to store a cookie and to allow the user to reject it.

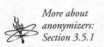 *More about anonymizers: Section 3.5.1*   Software to block pop-up ads appeared soon after the pop-ups appeared. Companies sell software to scan PCs for spyware; some versions are free. Several companies provide services, called anonymizers, with which people can surf the Web anonymously, leaving no record that identifies them or their computer.

If we want to restrict our Web site to family or a specific group of people, we can set it up to require registration and a password. A free blog service allows a blogger to specify the access group (e.g., family, friends, the world) for each posting. Of course, registration removes some privacy of the reader, a reasonable trade-off in many contexts.

Several companies offer products and services to prevent forwarding, copying, or printing of e-mail. (Lawyers are among the major customers.) A free service offers e-mail that self-destructs after a user-specified time period.

These are a very few examples of the many products and technology applications that we can use to protect our privacy. They are not panaceas. They have advantages and disadvantages; they do not solve all problems. They illustrate that individuals, businesses, and organizations are quick to respond and make privacy-protecting tools available.

Encryption is such an important technological tool for protecting privacy (as well as business and military information) that we discuss it at length next.

Encryption

> *Cryptography is the art and science of hiding data in plain sight.*
> —Larry Loen[81]

E-mail and data in transit on the Internet can be intercepted. Information sent to and from Web sites can be intercepted. Wireless transmissions can be picked out of the air. Someone who steals a computer or hacks into one can view files on it. Most eavesdropping by private citizens is illegal. Hacking and stealing laptops and credit-card numbers are crimes. The law provides for punishment of offenders who are caught and convicted, but we use technology to protect ourselves.

Encryption is a technology, often implemented in software, that transforms data into a form that is meaningless to anyone who might intercept or view it. The data could be e-mail, business plans, credit-card numbers, images, medical records, and so on. Software at the recipient's Web site (or on one's own computer) decodes encrypted data so that the recipient or owner can view the messages or files. Software routinely encrypts credit-card numbers when we send them to online merchants. Often, people are not even aware that they are using encryption. The software on PCs and Web sites handles encryption automatically. Some wireless telephones have built-in encryption.

Many privacy and security professionals view encryption as the most important technical method for ensuring the privacy of messages and data sent through computer networks. Encryption also protects stored information from intruders and abuses by employees. It is the best protection for data on laptops and other small data-storage devices carried outside an office.

Encryption generally includes a coding scheme, or cryptographic algorithm, and specific sequences of characters (e.g., digits or letters), called a *keys*, used by the algorithm. For example, a coding scheme many children learn is one where each letter of the alphabet is replaced by another specific letter. A key would be a scrambled alphabet, for example, qwertyuiopasdfghjklzxcvbnm. With this key, each *a* in the message is replaced by *q*, each *b* is replaced by *w*, each *c* by an *e*, and so on. This is not a good encryption scheme. It

PUBLIC-KEY CRYPTOGRAPHY

For all encryption methods used until the past few decades, both the sender and the recipient of an encrypted message must know the key—and keep it secret from everyone else. This presents a problem. If the key could be safely sent by the same communication method as the message, the message could be safely sent without encryption. Generally, keys must be transmitted by a more secure, hence more expensive or difficult, method—perhaps an in-person meeting of the parties. The military could afford the expense of couriers, armed guards, and other means of getting keys to a relatively small number of officers. For individuals and most businesses that communicate with a large number of people and other businesses, this would be impractical.

In the 1970s, a revolution in cryptography occurred. Whitfield Diffie and Martin Hellman developed an encryption scheme called *public-key cryptography* that eliminates the need for secure transmission of keys. Soon after, Ronald Rivest, Adi Shamir, and Leonard Adleman developed RSA, a practical implementation of the Diffie and Hellman method.* In this scheme, there are two mathematically related keys.

One is used to encrypt a message, the other to decrypt (decode) it. The feature that makes public-key cryptography so remarkable is that knowing the key used to encrypt the message provides no help at all in decrypting it. Thus, each business or person can have their own key pair, and the encrypting key can be public. The encrypting key is the *public key*. The decrypting key is the *private key*. Public keys can be made widely available. Anyone who wants to send a secret message to a person or business can encrypt the message with the recipient's public key. Even if the encrypted file and the recipient's public key are known by an outsider, the outsider cannot decrypt the message. Only the recipient, using the private key, can do that.

One major advantage of public-key cryptography is that it eliminates the need to transmit a secret encryption key between the two parties. Indeed, it eliminates the need for any prior communication between the parties. All that is needed is the recipient's public key. Thus, public-key cryptography provided suitable encryption for e-mail and for economic transactions on the Internet.

is often easy to figure out the original message without knowing the key. Military and commercial applications use much more sophisticated methods, some based on complex mathematics. Using mathematical tools and powerful computers, it is sometimes possible

---

*An engineer and two mathematicians working for a British intelligence agency developed a similar method several years earlier, but their work was classified and kept secret until 1997.[82]

to break a code, that is, to decode encrypted messages or files without the secret key. For many encryption schemes the size of the key may vary. Usually, the longer the key, the more difficult it is to break the code.

Modern encryption technology has a flexibility and variety of applications beyond protecting data. For example, it is used to create digital signatures, authentication methods, and digital cash. Digital signature technology allows us to sign documents online, saving time and paper for loan applications, business contracts, and so on. In one specialized authentication application, aimed at reducing the risk of unauthorized access to medical information online, the American Medical Association issues digital credentials to doctors that can be verified when a doctor, for instance, visits a laboratory Web site to get patient test results. There are likely to be thousands of applications of this technology.

Digital cash and other encryption-based privacy-protected transaction methods can let us do secure financial transactions electronically without the seller acquiring a credit-card or checking-account number from the buyer. Some techniques ensure that bank records contain no information linking the payer and recipient of the funds. They combine the convenience of credit-card purchases with the anonymity of cash. With such schemes, it is not easy to link records of different transactions to form a consumer profile or dossier. These techniques provide both privacy protection for the consumer with respect to the organizations he or she interacts with and protection for organizations against forgery, bad checks, and credit-card fraud. However, cash transactions make it harder for governments to detect and prosecute people who are laundering money earned in illegal activities, earning money they are not reporting to tax authorities, or transferring or spending money for criminal purposes. Thus, most governments would oppose and probably prohibit a truly anonymous digital cash system. Some digital cash systems include provisions for law enforcement and tax collection. The potential illegal uses of digital cash have long been possible with real cash. It is only in recent decades, with increased use of checks and credit cards, that we lost the privacy we had from marketers and government when we used cash for most transactions.

> *The technologies of anonymity and cryptography may be the only way to protect privacy.*
>
> —Nadine Strossen, president of the American Civil Liberties Union[83]

Business tools and policies for protecting personal data

A well-designed database for sensitive information includes several features to protect against leaks, intruders, and unauthorized employee access. Each person with authorized access to the system should have a unique identifier and a password. A system can restrict users from performing certain operations, such as writing or deleting, on some files. User IDs can be coded so that they give access to only specific parts of a record. For example, a billing clerk in a hospital does not need access to the results of a patient's laboratory tests. The computer system keeps track of information about each access, including the ID of the person looking at a record and the particular information viewed or modified. This is an *audit trail*. It can be used later to trace unauthorized activity. The knowledge that a system contains such provisions will discourage many privacy violations.

Databases with consumer information or Web-activity records are valuable assets that give businesses a competitive advantage. The owners of such lists and databases have an interest in preventing leaks and unlimited distribution. (Recall that Google fought a government subpoena for user search queries.) Thus, for example, mailing lists, often, are not actually sold; they are "rented." The renter does not receive a copy (electronic or otherwise). A specialized firm does the mailing. The risk of unauthorized copying is thus restricted to a small number of firms whose reputation for honesty and security is important to their business. Other applications also use this idea of trusted third parties to process confidential data. In some states, car-rental agencies access a computer service to check the driving record of potential customers. The service examines the motor-vehicle-department records; the car-rental company does not see the driver's record.

Public opinion and consumer preferences have a strong impact on decisions businesses make—and on the success or failure of specific products, as well as whole businesses. We saw that Facebook provided more privacy controls to members within three days of releasing new information-sharing features that members opposed (Section 2.1.3). There are search engines that do not store user search queries in a way that allows linking them together to one person.[84] In an earlier (pre-Web) incident, Lotus Development Corporation received more than 30,000 negative letters, telephone calls, and e-mail messages after it announced plans for a database with information on nearly half the population of the United States along with software that would permit users to generate mailing lists based on a variety of marketing criteria (e.g., income categories, shopping habits). Lotus dropped the project. When AOL decided to make its members' telephone numbers available to direct marketers, objections from members came swiftly, and within a few days AOL dropped the plan.

Web site operators pay thousands, sometimes millions, of dollars to companies that do *privacy audits*. Privacy auditors check for leaks of information, review the company's privacy policy and its compliance with its policy, evaluate warnings and explanations on its Web site that alert visitors when the site requests sensitive data, and so forth. Hundreds of large businesses established a new position called *chief privacy officer*. This person guides company privacy policy. Just as the Automobile Association of America rates hotels, the Better Business Bureau and newer organizations like TRUSTe offer a seal of approval, an icon companies that comply with their privacy standards can post on their Web sites.

Large companies use their economic influence to improve consumer privacy on the Web. IBM and Microsoft removed Internet advertising from Web sites that do not post clear privacy policies. Walt Disney Company and Infoseek Corporation did the same and, in addition, stopped accepting advertising on their Web sites from sites that do not post privacy policies. The Direct Marketing Association adopted a policy requiring its member companies to inform consumers when they will share personal information with other marketers and to give people an opt-out option. Many companies agreed to limit availability of sensitive consumer information including unlisted telephone numbers, driving histories, and all information about children.

There, of course, continue to be many businesses without strong privacy policies and many that do not follow their policy. The examples described here represent a strong trend, not a privacy utopia. As some problems are addressed, new ones continually arise.

> *Patient medical information is confidential. It should not be discussed in a public place.*
>
> —A sign, directed at doctors and staff, in an elevator
> in a medical office building, a reminder to prevent low-tech privacy leaks

2.4.2 RIGHTS AND LAW

In Section 2.2, and especially in Section 2.2.2, we considered some aspects of law and Fourth Amendment principles related to protection of privacy. The Fourth Amendment protects the negative right (a liberty) against intrusion and interference by government. This section focuses mainly on discussion of principles related to rights and legal protections for personal data collected or used by other people, businesses, and organizations.

We separate legal remedies from technical, management, and market solutions because they are fundamentally different. The latter are voluntary and varied. Different people or businesses can choose from among them. Law, on the other hand, is enforced by fines, imprisonment, or other penalties. Thus, we should examine the basis for law more carefully. Privacy is a condition or state we can be in, like good health or financial security. To what extent should we have a legal right to it? Is it a negative right or a positive right (in the sense of Section 1.3.2)? How far should law go, and what should be left to the voluntary interplay of markets, educational efforts of public interest groups, consumer choices and responsibilities, and so forth?

Until the late 19th-century, courts based legal decisions supporting privacy in social and business activities on property rights and contracts. There was no recognition of an independent right to privacy. In 1890, a crucial article, "The Right to Privacy," by Samuel Warren and Louis Brandeis[85] (later a Supreme Court Justice), argued that privacy was distinct from other rights and needed more protection. Judith Jarvis Thomson, an MIT philosopher, argued in a 1975 essay that the old view was more accurate, that in all cases where a violation of privacy is a violation of someone's rights, a right distinct from privacy has been violated.[86] We present some of the claims and arguments of these papers. Then we consider a variety of other ideas and perspectives about laws to protect privacy.

One purpose of this section is to show the kinds of analyses that philosophers, legal scholars, and economists perform in trying to elucidate underlying principles. Another is to emphasize the importance of principles, of working out a theoretical framework in which to make decisions about particular issues and cases.

Warren and Brandeis: The inviolate personality

The main target of criticism in the 1890 Warren and Brandeis article is newspapers, especially the gossip columns. Warren and Brandeis vehemently criticize the press for "overstepping . . . obvious bounds of propriety and decency." The kinds of information of most concern to them are personal appearance, statements, acts, and interpersonal relationships (marital, family, and others).[87] Warren and Brandeis take the position that people have the right to prohibit publication of facts about themselves and photographs of themselves. Warren and Brandeis argue that, for example, if someone writes a letter in which he says he had a fierce argument with his wife, that fact is protected and the recipient of the letter cannot publish it. They base this claim on no property right or other right except privacy. It is part of the right to be let alone. Warren and Brandeis base their defense of privacy rights on, in their often-quoted phrase, the principle of "an inviolate personality."

Laws against other wrongs (such as slander, libel, defamation, copyright infringement, violation of property rights, and breach of contract) can address some privacy violations, but Warren and Brandeis argue that there remain many privacy violations that those other laws do not cover. For example, publication of personal or business information could constitute a violation of a contract (explicit or implied), but there are many cases in which the person who discloses the information has no contract with the victim. The person is not violating a contract but is violating the victim's privacy. Libel, slander, and defamation laws protect us when someone spreads false and damaging rumors about us, but they do not apply to true personal information whose exposure makes us uncomfortable. According to Warren and Brandeis, privacy is distinct and needs its own protection. They allow exceptions for publication of information of general interest (news), use in limited situations when the information concerns another person's interests, and oral publication. (They were writing before radio and television, so oral publication meant a limited audience.)

Judith Jarvis Thomson: Is there a right to privacy?

Judith Jarvis Thomson argues the opposite point of view. She gets to her point after examining a few scenarios.

Suppose you own a copy of a magazine. Your property rights include the right to refuse to allow others to read, destroy, or even see your magazine. If someone does anything to your magazine that you did not allow, that person is violating your property rights. For example, if someone uses binoculars to see your magazine from a neighboring building, that person is violating your right to exclude others from seeing it. It does not matter whether the magazine is an ordinary news magazine (not a sensitive privacy issue) or some other magazine you do not want people to know you read. The right violated is your property right.

You may waive your property rights, intentionally or inadvertently. If you absentmindedly leave the magazine on a park bench, someone could take it. If you leave it on the coffee table when you have guests at your home, someone could see it. If you read a pornographic magazine on a bus, and someone sees you and tells other people that you read dirty magazines, that person is not violating your rights. The person might be doing something impolite, unfriendly, or cruel but not something that violates a right.

Our rights to our person and our bodies include the right to decide to whom we show various parts of our bodies. By walking around in public, most of us waive our right to prevent others from seeing our faces. When a Muslim woman covers her face, she is exercising her right to keep others from viewing it. If someone uses binoculars to spy on us at home in the shower, he or she is violating our right to our person.

If someone beats on you to get some information, the beater is violating your right to be free from physical harm done by others. If the information is the time of day, privacy is not at issue. If the information is more personal, then your privacy is compromised, but the right violated is your right to be free from attack. On the other hand, if a person peacefully asks whom you live with or what your political views are, then no rights are violated. If you choose to answer and do not make a confidentiality agreement, the person is not violating your rights by repeating the information to someone else, though it could be inconsiderate to do so. However, if the person agreed not to repeat the information, but then does, it does not matter whether or not the information was sensitive; the person is violating the confidentiality agreement.

In these examples, there is no violation of privacy without violation of some other right, such as the right to control our property or our person, the right to be free from violent attack, or the right to form contracts (and expect them to be enforced). Thomson concludes:

> I suggest it is a useful heuristic device in the case of any purported violation of the right to privacy to ask whether or not the act is a violation of any other right, and if not whether the act really violates a right at all.[88]

Criticisms of Warren and Brandeis and of Thomson

Critics of the Warren and Brandeis position argue that their arguments do not provide a workable principle or definition from which to conclude that a privacy right violation occurs. Their notion of privacy is too broad. It conflicts with freedom of the press. It appears to make almost any unauthorized mention of a person a violation of the person's right. Some critics present theories and examples, in addition to those Thomson describes, to show that other legal principles cover privacy violations without an independent privacy right.[89]

Critics of Thomson present examples of violations of a right to privacy (not just a desire for privacy), but of no other right. Some view Thomson's notion of the right to our person as vague or too broad. Her examples might be a convincing argument for the thesis that considering other rights can resolve privacy questions, but no finite number of examples can prove such a thesis.

Neither article directly refutes the other. Their emphases are different. Warren and Brandeis focus on the use of the information (publication). Thomson focuses on how it is obtained. This distinction sometimes underlies differences in arguments by those who advocate strong legal regulations on the use of personal data and those who advocate more reliance on technical and market solutions.

Applying the theories

How do the theoretical arguments apply to the privacy issues related to the vast amount of personal data that businesses and organizations use?

Throughout the Warren-and-Brandeis article, the objectionable action is publication of personal information—its widespread, public distribution. Many court decisions since the appearance of their article have taken this point of view.[90] If information in consumer databases were published (in print or by being made public on the Web), that would violate the Warren and Brandeis notion of privacy. A person might win a case if someone published his or her consumer profile. But intentional publication is not the main concern in the current context of consumer databases, monitoring of Web activity, location tracking, and so on. Warren and Brandeis and various court decisions allow disclosure of personal information to people who have an interest in it. By implication, they do not preclude, for example, disclosure of a person's driving record to a car-rental company from which he or she wants to rent a car. Similarly, it seems Warren and Brandeis would not oppose disclosure of information about whether someone smokes cigarettes to a life insurance company from whom the person is trying to buy insurance. Their view does not rule out use of consumer information for targeted marketing. (If disclosure of the information violates a trust or confidence or contract, then it is not permissible.)

An important aspect of both the Warren and Brandeis paper and the Thomson paper is that of consent. There is no privacy violation if a person consented to the collection and use of the information.

Transactions

We have another puzzle to consider: how to apply philosophical and legal notions of privacy to transactions, which automatically involve more than one person. The following scenario will illustrate the problem.

One day in the small farm community of Friendlyville, Joe buys five pounds of potatoes from Maria, and Maria sells five pounds of potatoes to Joe. (I describe the transaction in this repetitious manner to emphasize that there are two people involved and two sides to the transaction.)

Either Joe or Maria might prefer the transaction to remain secret. Joe might be embarrassed that his own potato crop failed. Or Joe might be unpopular in Friendlyville, and Maria fears the townspeople will be angry at her for selling to him. Either way, we are not likely to consider it a violation of the other's rights if Maria or Joe talks about the purchase or sale of the potatoes to other people in town. But suppose Joe asks for confidentiality as part of the transaction. Maria has three options. (1) She can agree. (2) She can say no; she might want to tell people she sold potatoes to Joe. (3) She can agree to keep the sale confidential if Joe pays a higher price. In the latter two cases, Joe can decide whether to buy the potatoes. On the other hand, if Maria asks for confidentiality as part of the transaction, Joe has three options. (1) He can agree. (2) He can say no; he might want to tell people he bought potatoes from Maria. (3) He can agree to keep the purchase confidential if Maria charges a lower price. In the latter two cases, Maria can decide whether to sell the potatoes.

Privacy includes control of information about oneself. Is the transaction a fact about Maria or a fact about Joe? There does not appear to be a convincing reason for either party to have more right than the other to control information about the transaction. Yet this problem is critical to legal policy decisions about use of consumer information. If control of the information about a transaction is to be assigned to one of the parties, we need a firm philosophical foundation for choosing which party gets it. (If the parties make a confidentiality agreement, then they are ethically obliged to respect it. If the agreement is a legal contract, then they are legally obliged to respect it.)

Philosophers and economists often use simple two-person transactions or relationships, like the Maria/Joe scenario, to try to clarify the principles involved in an issue. Do the observations and conclusions about Maria and Joe generalize to large, complex societies and a global economy, where, often, one party to a transaction is a business? All transactions are really between people, even if indirectly. So if a property right or a privacy right in the information about a transaction is to be assigned to one of the parties, we need an argument showing how the transaction in a modern economy is different from the one in Friendlyville. Later in this section, we describe two viewpoints on the regulation of information about consumer transactions: the free market view and the consumer-protection view. The free-market view treats both parties equally, whereas the consumer-protection view treats the parties differently.

Ownership of personal data

Some economists, legal scholars, and privacy advocates propose giving people property rights in information about themselves. The concept of property rights can be useful even when applied to intangible property (intellectual property, for example), but there are problems in using this concept for personal information. First, as we have just seen, activities and transactions often involve at least two people, each of whom would have reasonable but conflicting claims to own the information about the transaction. Some personal information does not appear to be about a transaction, but there still can be problems in assigning ownership. Do you own your birthday? Or does your mother own it? After all, she was a more active participant in the event.

The second problem with assigning ownership of personal information arises from the notion of owning facts. (Copyright protects intellectual property such as computer programs and music, but we cannot copyright facts.) Ownership of facts would severely impair the flow of information in society. Information is stored on computers, but it is also stored in our minds. Can we own facts about ourselves without violating the freedom of thought and freedom of speech of others?

Although there are difficulties with assigning ownership in individual facts, another issue is whether we can own our "profiles," that is, a collection of data describing our activities, purchases, interests, and so on. We cannot own the fact that our eyes are blue, but we do have the legal right to control some uses of our photographic image. In almost all states we need a person's consent to use his or her photograph for commercial purposes. Should the law treat our consumer profiles the same way? Should the law treat the collection of our search queries the same way? How can we distinguish between a few facts about a person and a "profile"?

Federal Judge Richard Posner gives economic arguments about how to allocate property rights to information.[91] Information has both economic and personal value, he points out. It is valuable to us to determine whether a business, customer, client, employer, or employee is reliable, honest, and so on. Personal and business interactions have many opportunities for misrepresentation and, therefore, exploitation of others. Posner's analysis leads to the conclusion that in some cases individuals or organizations should have a property right to information, wheras in other cases they should not. That is, some information should be in the public domain. A property right in information is appropriate where the information has value to society and is expensive to discover, create, or collect. Without property rights to such information, the people or businesses that make investments in discovering or collecting the information will not profit from it. The result is that people will produce less of this kind of information, to the detriment of society. Thus, the law should protect, for example, trade secrets, the result of much expenditure and effort by a business. A second example is personal information, such as the appearance of one's naked body. It is not expensive for a person to obtain, but virtually all of us place value on protecting it, and concealment is not costly to society. So it makes sense to assign the property right in this information to the individual. Some privacy advocates want to protect information that can lead to denial of a job or some kind of service or contract (e.g., a loan). They advocate restrictions on sharing of information that might facilitate negative decisions about people, for example, landlords sharing a database with information about tenants' payment histories. Posner argues that a person should not have a property right to negative personal information (e.g., one's criminal history or credit history) or other information whose concealment aids people in misrepresentation, fraud, or manipulation. Such information should be in the public domain. That means a person should not have the right to prohibit others from collecting it, using it, and passing it on, as long as they are not violating a contract or confidentiality agreement and do not obtain the information by eavesdropping on private communications or other prohibited means.

In recent decades, the trend in legislation has not followed Posner's position. Some critics of Posner's point of view believe that moral theory, not economic principles, should be the source of property rights.

A basic legal framework

A good basic legal framework that defines and enforces legal rights and responsibilities is essential to a complex, robust society and economy. One of its tasks is enforcement of agreements and contracts. Contracts—including freedom to form them and enforcement of their terms by the legal system—are a mechanism for implementing flexible and diverse economic transactions that take place over time and between people who do not know each other well or at all.

We can apply the idea of contract enforcement to the published privacy policies of businesses and organizations. The Toysmart case is an example. Toysmart, a Web-based seller of educational toys, collected extensive information on about 250,000 visitors to its Web site, including family profiles, shopping preferences, and names and ages of children. Toysmart had promised not to release this personal information. When the company filed for bankruptcy, it had a large amount of debt and virtually no assets—except its customer database, which had a high value. Toysmart's creditors wanted the database sold to raise funds to repay them. Toysmart offered the database for sale, causing a storm of protest. Consistent with the interpretation that Toysmart's policy was a contract with the people in the database, the bankruptcy-court settlement included destruction of the database.[92]

A second task of a legal system is to set defaults for situations that contracts do not explicitly cover. Suppose a Web site posts no policy about what it does with the information it collects. What should the Web site be legally permitted to do with the information? Many sites and offline businesses act as though the default is that they can do anything they choose. A privacy-protecting default would be that the information could be used only for the direct and obvious purpose for which it was supplied. The legal system can (and does) set special confidentiality defaults for sensitive information, such as medical and financial information, that tradition and most people consider private. If a business or organization wants to use information for purposes beyond the default, it would have to specify those uses in its policies, agreements, or contracts or request consent. Many business interactions do not have written contracts, so the default provisions established by law can have a big impact.

A third task of a basic legal structure is to specify penalties for criminal offenses *More about liability issues: Section 8.3.3* and breach of contracts. Thus, law can specify penalties for violation of privacy policies and negligent loss or disclosure of personal data that businesses and others hold. Writers of liability laws must strike a balance between being too strict and too lenient. If too strict, they make some valuable products and services too expensive to provide. If too weak, they provide insufficient incentive for businesses and government agencies to provide reasonable security for our personal data.

Regulation

Technical tools for privacy protection (like those described in Section 2.4.1), market mechanisms, and business policies are not perfect. Some privacy advocates consider this a strong argument for regulatory laws. Regulation is not perfect either. We must evaluate regulatory solutions by considering effectiveness, costs and benefits, side effects, and ease of use (clarity), just as we evaluate computer technology itself and other kinds of potential solutions to problems caused by technology. Whole books can be written on the pros and cons of regulation. We briefly describe a few points here. (We will see similar and related problems in Section 7.3.3 when we consider responses to computer errors and failures.)

There are hundreds of privacy laws. The actual laws that get passed often depend more on the current focus of media attention and special-interest pressure than on well-thought-out principles and true cost/benefit trade-offs. Government interests often conflict with privacy. Laws passed by Congress for complex areas like privacy usually state general goals and leave the details to government agencies that write hundreds or thousands of pages of regulations, sometimes over many years. It is extremely difficult to write reasonable regulations for complex situations. Laws and regulations often have unintended effects or interpretations. They could apply where they do not make sense or where people simply do not want them.

Regulations often have high costs, both direct dollar costs to businesses (and, ultimately, consumers) and hidden or unexpected costs, such as loss of services or increased inconvenience. Regulations requiring, for example, explicit consent for each secondary use of personal information instead of allowing broader consent agreements have an attribute economists call "high transaction cost." They could be so expensive and difficult to implement that they would eliminate most secondary uses of information, including those that consumers find desirable. COPPA is one of the less controversial privacy laws. It requires that Web sites get parental permission before collecting personal information from children under 13. When it passed, some Web sites deleted online profiles of all children under 13, some canceled their free e-mail and home pages for kids and some banned children under 13 entirely. (The *New York Times* does not allow children under 13 to register to use its Web site.) An attorney who helps Web sites meet COPPA's requirements estimated the cost of compliance at $60,000–$100,000 per year, a lot for a small business, not a burden for large ones like AOL and Disney.[93] Regulations often provide a relative benefit to large businesses and organizations over smaller ones because they have the legal department to deal with the rules and the revenue to absorb the added costs.

REGULATIONS FOR HEALTH RECORDS

After years of controversy, the federal government issued comprehensive medical privacy regulations under the Health Insurance Portability and Accountability Act (HIPAA). These regulations, effective in 2003, cover health records and health-payment records (both electronic and paper records). Some aspects of the regulations are big steps forward in medical privacy. For example, medical insurers now must not disclose patient medical information to lenders, employers, and marketers without the patient's consent. Health care providers must not disclose more than the minimum amount of information needed for each purpose. Also, the HIPAA rules give patients a legal right to see and copy their medical records.

Given the enormous variety of kinds of medical information and potential uses of the information, any regulations are bound to have problems. Some medical organizations described the rules, presented and explained in 1,500 pages, as "an operational nightmare." Some feared that the heavy civil and criminal penalties for serious violations might cause medical groups to adopt policies that are too restrictive. Such policies could inhibit the flow of necessary medical information among the practitioners treating a patient, leading to less-than-optimal patient care. Until the government issued additional clarifying explanations, pharmacists worried that the law might not allow them to give prescription medicines to family members or friends who came to pick them up for a sick person.

Privacy advocates object to exceptions to the consent requirement. The rules allow law enforcement agencies and various other government agencies access to patient medical records without patient consent or a court order. Some privacy advocates object that the rules do not prohibit medical organizations from using generalized consent forms. They prefer a requirement that the patient must give written permission for each disclosure.[94]

Although we must be aware of these side effects, we should remember that businesses sometimes overestimate the cost of privacy regulations. They also sometimes underestimate the costs, to themselves and to consumers, of not protecting privacy.[95]

Contrasting viewpoints

When asked "If someone sues you and loses, should they have to pay your legal expenses?" more than 80% of people surveyed said "yes." When asked the same question from the opposite perspective: "If you sue someone and lose, should you have to pay their legal expenses?" about 40% said "yes."

The political, philosophical, and economic views of many scholars and advocates who write about privacy differ. As a result, their interpretations of various privacy problems and their approaches to solutions often differ, particularly when they are considering laws and regulation to control collection and use of personal information by businesses.* We will contrast two perspectives. I call them the free-market view and the consumer-protection view.

The free-market view

People who prefer market-oriented solutions for privacy problems tend to emphasize the freedom of individuals, as consumers or in businesses, to make voluntary agreements; the diversity of individual tastes and values; the flexibility of technological and market solutions; the response of markets to consumer preferences; the usefulness and importance of contracts; and the flaws of detailed or restrictive legislation and regulatory solutions.

A free-market view for collection and use of personal information emphasizes informed consent: Organizations collecting personal data (including government agencies and businesses) should clearly inform the person providing the information if they will not keep it confidential (from other businesses, individuals, and government agencies) and how they will use it. They should be legally liable for violations of their stated policies. A free-market view emphasizes freedom of contract: People should be free to enter agreements (or not enter agreements) to disclose personal information in exchange for a fee, services, or other benefits according to their own judgment. Businesses should be free to offer such agreements. The market viewpoint respects the right and ability of consumers to make choices for themselves based on their own values. Market supporters expect consumers to take the responsibility that goes with freedom, for example, to read contracts or to understand that desirable services have costs. A free-market view includes free flow of information: The law should not prevent people (or businesses and organizations) from using and disclosing facts they independently or unintrusively discover without violating rights (e.g., without theft, trespass, or violation of contractual obligations).

We cannot always expect to get exactly the mix of attributes we want in any product, service, or job. Just as we might not get cheeseless pizza in every pizza restaurant or find a car with the exact set of features we want, we might not be able to get both privacy and special discounts. We might not be able to get certain Web sites—or magazines—without advertising, or a specific job without agreeing to provide certain personal information to the employer. These compromises are not unusual or unreasonable when interacting with other people.

Market supporters prefer to avoid restrictive legislation and detailed regulation for several reasons. They argue that the political system is a worse system than the market for determining what consumers want in the real world of trade-offs and costs. It is impossible

---

*There tends to be more agreement among privacy advocates when considering privacy threats and intrusions by government.

for legislators to know in advance how much money, convenience, or other benefits people will want to trade for more or less privacy. Businesses respond over time to the preferences of millions of consumers expressed through their purchases. In response to the desire for privacy many people express, the market provides a variety of privacy protection tools. Market supporters argue that laws requiring specific policies or prohibiting certain kinds of contracts violate the freedom of choice of both consumers and business owners.

This viewpoint includes legal sanctions for those who steal data and those who violate confidentiality agreements. It holds businesses, organizations, and government agents responsible for loss of personal data due to poor or negligent security practices. To encourage innovation and improvement, advocates of this viewpoint are more likely to prefer penalties for the loss or damage when it occurs, rather than regulations that specify detailed procedures that holders of personal information must follow.

The free-market viewpoint sees privacy as a "good," in the sense that it is both desirable and something we can obtain varying amounts of by buying or trading in the economy, like food, entertainment, and safety. Just as some people choose to trade some safety for excitement (bungee jumping, motorcycle riding), money (buying a cheaper but less safe product), or convenience, some choose different levels of privacy. As with safety, law can provide minimum standards but should allow the market to provide a wide range of options to meet the range of personal preferences.

The consumer-protection view

Advocates of strong privacy regulation emphasize the unsettling uses of personal information we have mentioned throughout this chapter, the costly and disruptive results of errors in databases (which we discuss in Chapter 7), and the ease with which personal information leaks out, through loss, theft, and carelessness. They argue for more stringent consent requirements, legal restrictions on consumer profiling, prohibitions on certain types of contracts or agreements to disclose data, and prohibitions on businesses collecting or storing certain kinds of data. They urge, for example, that the law require companies to have opt-in policies for secondary uses of personal information because the opt-out option might not be obvious or easy enough for consumers who would prefer it. They would prohibit waivers and broad consent agreements for secondary uses.

The focus of this viewpoint is to protect consumers against abuses and carelessness by businesses and against their own lack of knowledge, judgment, or interest. Advocates of the consumer-protection view emphasize that people do not realize all the ways others might use information about them. They do not understand the risks of agreeing to disclose personal data. Those who emphasize consumer protection are critical of programs to trade free computers and free Web services for personal information or consent for monitoring or tracking. Many support laws prohibiting collection or storage of personal data that could have negative consequences, if they believe the risks are more important than the value of the information to the businesses that want to collect it. Consumer advocate and privacy "absolutist" Mary Gardiner Jones does not accept the idea of consumers consenting to dissemination of personal data. She also said, that "You can't expect an ordinary consumer who is very busy trying to earn a living to sit down and understand what [consent] means. They don't understand the implications of what use of their data can mean to them." She also said that the idea that some consumers like having their names on mailing lists is a myth that the industry created.[96] A former director of the ACLU's Privacy and Technology Project expressed the view that informed consent is not sufficient protection. She urged a Senate committee studying confidentiality of health records to "re-examine the traditional reliance on individual consent as the linchpin of privacy laws."[97]

Those who emphasize the consumer-protection point of view would argue that the Joe/Maria scenario in Friendlyville, described in Section 2.4.2, is not relevant in a complex society. The imbalance of power between the individual and a large corporation is one reason. Another is that in Friendlyville the information about the transaction circulates to only a small group of people, whom Joe and Maria know. If someone draws inaccurate or unfair conclusions, Joe or Maria can talk to the person and present his or her explanations. In a larger society, information circulates among many strangers, and we often do not know who has it and what decisions about us they base on it.

A consumer cannot realistically negotiate contract terms with a business. At any specific time, the consumer can only accept or reject what the business offers. And the consumer often is not in a position to reject it. If we want a loan for a house or car, we have to accept whatever terms lenders currently offer. If we need a job, we are likely to agree to disclose personal information against our true preference because of the economic necessity of working. Individuals have no meaningful power against large companies like Google, Yahoo, and AOL. They have to use search engines whether or not they know or accept that the company stores their search queries.

In the consumer-protection view, self-regulation by business does not work. Business privacy policies are weak, vague, or difficult to understand. Businesses sometimes do not follow their stated policies. Consumer pressure is sometimes effective, but some companies ignore it. Instead, we must require all businesses to adopt pro-privacy policies. Software and other technological privacy-protecting tools for consumers cost money, and many people cannot afford them. They are far from perfect anyway, hence not good enough to protect privacy.

The consumer-protection viewpoint sees privacy as a right rather than something we bargain about. For example, a Web site jointly sponsored by EPIC and Privacy International flashes the slogans "Privacy is a right, not a preference" and "Notice is not enough."[98] The latter indicates that they see privacy as a positive right, or claim right (in the terminology of Section 1.3.2). As a negative right, privacy allows us to use anonymizing technologies and to refrain from interacting with those who request information we do not wish to supply. As a positive right, it means we can stop others from communicating about us. A spokesperson for the Center for Democracy and Technology expressed that view in a statement to Congress, saying that we must incorporate into law the principle that people should be able to "determine for themselves when, how and to what extent information about them is shared."[99]

2.4.3 PRIVACY REGULATIONS IN THE EUROPEAN UNION

The European Union (EU) has a comprehensive Data Protection Directive.[100] It covers processing of personal data, including collection, use, storage, retrieval, transmission, destruction, and other actions. The directive sets forth Fair Information Principles that EU member nations must implement in their own laws. They include the following:

1. Personal data may be collected only for specified, explicit purposes and must not be processed for incompatible purposes.
2. Data must be accurate and up to date. Data must not be kept longer than necessary.
3. Processing of data is permitted only if the person consented unambiguously, or if the processing is necessary to fulfill contractual or legal obligations, or if the processing is needed for tasks in the public interest or by official authorities to accomplish their tasks (or a few other reasons).
4. Special categories of data, including ethnic and racial origin, political and religious beliefs, health and sex life, and union membership, must not be processed without the subject's explicit consent. Member nations may outlaw processing of such data even if the subject does consent.
5. People must be notified of the collection and use of data about them. They must have access to the data stored about them and a way to correct incorrect data.
6. Processing of data about criminal convictions is severely restricted.

While the EU has much stricter regulations than the U.S. on collection and use of personal information by the private sector, some civil libertarians believe that the European Directive does not provide enough protection from use of personal data by government agencies. Although the directive says that data should not be kept longer than necessary, European countries require that ISPs and telephone companies retain records of customer communications (date, destination, duration, etc.) for up to two years and make them available to law enforcement agencies. The EU said it needs this requirement (effective since 2007) to fight terrorism and organized crime.[101]

The EU's strict privacy directive does not prevent some of the same abuses of personal data that occur in the United States. In Britain, for example, the Information Commissioner reported that data brokers use fraud and corrupt insiders to get personal information. As in the U.S., customers of illegal services include journalists, private investigators, debt collectors, government agencies, stalkers, and criminals seeking data to use for fraud.[102]

The EU Data Privacy Directive prohibits transfer of personal data to countries outside the EU that do not have an adequate system of privacy protection. This part of the directive caused significant problems for companies that do business both in and outside Europe and might normally process customer and employee data outside the EU. In 2001, the EU determined that Australia, for example, did not have adequate privacy protection. Australia allows businesses to create their own privacy codes consistent with the government's National Privacy Principles. The U.S. has privacy laws covering specific areas such as medical information, video rentals, driver's license records, but does not have comprehensive privacy laws covering all personal data. The EU agreed to the "Safe Harbor" plan, under which companies outside the EU that agree to abide by a set of privacy requirements similar to the principles in the Data Protection Directive may receive personal data from the EU.[103] After 2001, screening of air travel passengers from Europe to the U.S. raised problems. The U.S. wanted more information about the passengers than the EU wanted to provide. Negotiations for compromises continue.

Many privacy advocates describe U.S. privacy policy as "behind Europe" because the U.S. does not have comprehensive federal legislation regulating personal data collection and use. Others point out that the U.S. and Europe have different cultures and traditions. European countries tend to put more emphasis on regulation and centralization, especially concerning commerce, whereas the U.S. tradition puts more emphasis on contracts, consumer pressure, and the flexibility and freedom of the market. In the U.S., the FTC can impose penalties on businesses for deceptive and unfair business practices. The FTC sometimes uses this legal tool to restrict abuses of personal information.

When the EU passed the Privacy Directive in 1995, it required member nations to implement its principles in their own laws within three years. In 2000, the European Commission determined that many countries had not yet complied. In 2001, a study done by Consumers International found that 80% of European Web sites did not comply with the requirement that Web sites provide an opt-out option, wheras almost 60% of the most popular sites in the U.S. offered an opt-out option. The study also found that about a third of EU Web sites that collected data on users posted their privacy policies and that 62% of U.S. Web sites did. The study, although critical of privacy policies on both U.S. and EU Web sites, concluded that "despite tight EU legislation . . . U.S.-based sites tend to set the standard for decent privacy policies."[104] Consumer and privacy advocates argued that in the EU, even though enforcement was weak, people have legal recourse, whereas in the U.S. they often do not.

2.5 Communications

Law enforcement agencies intercept communications to collect evidence of criminal activities. Intelligence agencies intercept communications to collect information about the activities and plans of hostile governments and terrorists. The Fourth Amendment to the U.S. Constitution and various laws put restraints on their activities in order to protect innocent people and reduce the opportunity for abuses. In this section, we consider how changing technologies and government policies affect the ability of law enforcement agencies to intercept the contents of communications and to obtain other information about communications. We begin with background on wiretapping of telephone conversations and laws about privacy of telephone and e-mail. Then we consider the Communications Assistance for Law Enforcement Act, which requires that the technology used in communications systems be designed or modified to ensure the ability of law enforcement agencies to intercept communications. We look at secret government programs to intercept communications and collect communications records as part of the efforts to combat terrorism. We conclude with a review of government policy about use of encryption to protect communications.

2.5.1 WIRETAPPING AND E-MAIL PROTECTION

Telephone

Within ten years of the invention of the telephone, people (in and out of government) were wiretapping them.[105] Before that, people intercepted telegraph communications. Throughout the years when telephone connections were made by human operators and most people had party lines (one telephone line shared by several households), operators and nosy neighbors sometimes listened in on telephone conversations.

Increased wealth and new technology eliminated party lines and human operators, but telephones were still vulnerable to wiretapping. The legal status of wiretapping was debated throughout most of the 20th-century. Federal and state law enforcement agencies, businesses, private detectives, political candidates, and others widely used wiretapping. In 1928, the Supreme Court ruled that wiretapping by law enforcement agencies was not unconstitutional but that Congress could ban it. In 1934, Congress passed the Communications Act. This law states that no person not authorized by the sender could intercept and divulge a message; there is no exception for law enforcement agencies. A 1937 Supreme Court decision ruled that wiretapping violated the law.[106] Federal and state law enforcement agencies and local police ignored the ruling and continued to wiretap regularly for decades, sometimes with the approval of the Attorney General. In one well-publicized case, the FBI monitored the telephone calls between a defendant and her attorneys during her trial. Evidence obtained by illegal wiretapping is inadmissable in court, so the FBI kept a separate, secret file system. The FBI bugged and wiretapped members of Congress and the Supreme Court. Most states had their own laws prohibiting wiretapping. Although there was publicity about extensive use of wiretapping by police, none was prosecuted. In many cases, of course, law enforcement agencies were wiretapping people suspected of crimes, but in many other cases they tapped people with unconventional views, members of civil rights groups, and political opponents of powerful government officials.

A fierce debate on the wiretap issue continued in Congress, state legislatures, the courts, books, and the news media. Congress repeatedly rejected proposals to allow wiretapping and electronic surveillance. In 1967 (in *Katz v. United States*, discussed in Section 2.2.2), the Supreme Court ruled that intercepting telephone conversations without a court order violated the Fourth Amendment to the U.S. Constitution. In 1968, as part of the Omnibus Crime Control and Safe Streets Act, Congress explicitly allowed wiretapping and electronic surveillance by law enforcement agencies, with a court order, for the first time in U.S. history. The main argument given for this change was the necessity to combat organized crime. (The riots over race issues, the assassinations of

President John F. Kennedy, Martin Luther King Jr., and Robert Kennedy, and the antiwar demonstrations in the five years leading up to passage of the law probably contributed to its passage.)

The government needs a court order to (legally) intercept or record the content of a telephone call for a criminal investigation.* Law enforcement agents must justify the request, and the wiretap permission is granted for a limited time period. Government agents are permitted to determine the telephone numbers called from a particular telephone and to determine the number from which a call was made with less court scrutiny and justification. Agents used a device called a *pen register* to obtain numbers called. Now communications companies routinely store this information (along with the duration of calls, time of day, etc.). The term *pen register* still refers to the collection of information. A *trap and trace* logs the numbers from which incoming calls originate.

Senator Sam Ervin commented in 1968, "The mere fact of passing a law never resolves a controversy as fierce as this one."[107] He was right. Debate continued about whether the privacy protections in the Omnibus Crime Act were strong enough to be constitutional. Supreme Court justices disagreed. Wiretapping by government and politicians that was illegal or of questionable legality continued, most notably during the Vietnam War. Journalists and government employees were victims of unconstitutional wiretaps during the Nixon administration. In 1998, Los Angeles police officers admitted using wiretaps improperly in a large number of cases.

Most other countries have constitutional and legal protections for communications privacy, but police and intelligence agencies in many countries routinely perform illegal monitoring of political opponents, human rights workers, and journalists.[108]

E-mail and other new communications

Old laws did not explicitly cover e-mail and cell phone conversations, and interception was common when e-mail and cell phones were new. Driving around Silicon Valley, eavesdropping on cell phone conversations was, reportedly, a popular form of industrial spying in the 1980s. Snoops intercepted cell phone conversations of politicians and celebrities. The Electronic Communications Privacy Act of 1986 (ECPA), with amendments in 1994, extended the 1968 wiretapping restrictions to electronic communication, including e-mail, cordless and cellular telephones, and paging devices. This was a significant step toward protecting privacy in cyberspace from private and

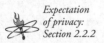 *Expectation of privacy: Section 2.2.2* governmental snooping. It requires that the government get a court order to legally intercept e-mail or read stored e-mail.† Controversy continued about the standard law enforcement agencies must meet

to obtain copies of stored e-mail. The government argued that people give up their expectation of privacy by allowing ISPs to store their e-mail on the ISP's computers.

---

*In some emergencies, the government is permitted to intercept the content of communications without a court order.

†The ECPA allows businesses to read the e-mail of employees on the business system. We discuss this issue of employee privacy in Chapter 6.

Thus, the strict requirements of the Fourth Amendment would not apply. An appeals court said in 2007[109] that the government's argument was not convincing; people do have an expectation of privacy for e-mail stored in their subscriber accounts. If upheld by the Supreme Court, the ruling will be a significant privacy protection for e-mail communications.

The USA PATRIOT Act reversed the direction of the ECPA. It loosened restrictions on government surveillance and wiretapping activities. The PATRIOT Act allows law enforcement agents to use pen-register authority to get destination and time information for e-mail. (It also allows them to get a variety of other information about people's e-mail and Internet use from ISPs, including payment information such as credit-card numbers, without a court order.) For several years (possibly continuing), the FBI operated a system to filter all the e-mail from a suspect's ISP, examining the headers to find and copy a suspect's e-mail. The main concern with such a process is that the FBI can extract anyone's e-mail (and other communications), not just that of the suspect for whom the FBI has a court order. This FBI program illustrates how technology requires reevaluation, clarification, and sometimes updating of existing laws. Does sifting through millions of e-mail headers violate the wiretapping laws and the ECPA? Instead, should the ISP provide the suspect's e-mail (and no one else's) to the FBI when presented with a court order? Is collection of e-mail headers (not contents) analogous to using a pen register to obtain telephone numbers called? An e-mail header contains more information than a telephone number. It contains a subject line, which is more like content information. Should the FBI have access to that under the lower standards for pen registers?

2.5.2 DESIGNING COMMUNICATIONS SYSTEMS FOR INTERCEPTION

New communications technologies developed in the 1980s and 1990s made access to the content of telephone calls more difficult for law enforcement agencies than it was before. When people use toll-free long-distance services or call forwarding, the first telephone number entered—the number law enforcement agents can legally get fairly easily—does not give information about the actual recipient of the call. On the Internet, e-mail, files, and Internet telephone calls are broken into pieces called packets that might travel, mingled with others, along different routes to the destination where they are reassembled. (This is called packet-mode communication.) Intercepting Internet phone calls is more difficult than attaching a clip to an old analog telephone wire. The FBI, arguing that technology was interfering with its ability to intercept telephone calls, helped draft and lobbied for the Communications Assistance for Law Enforcement Act of 1994 (CALEA). This law requires that telecommunications equipment be designed to ensure that the government can intercept telephone calls (with a court order or other authorization). In the past, engineers designed communications equipment for its communications purpose. The FBI developed its tools for interception, and communications providers had to assist. The significance of CALEA is that, previously, the government could not require the design and modification of communications equipment to meet the interception needs of law enforcement. The law itself was controversial, and, because rules for its implementation continue to evolve as communications technology changes, dispute about it continues.

New technologies, market competition, and varied customer needs have generated a great diversity of new telecommunications services, equipment, protocols, algorithms, and companies. The essential argument in favor of CALEA (and other government programs to intercept communications) is to maintain the ability of law enforcement agencies to protect us from drug dealers, organized crime, other criminals, and terrorists in a changing technological environment. "The prospect of trying to enforce laws without a nationwide standard for surveillance would turn enforcement into a nightmare," according to the FBI.[110] The problems with CALEA and other programs to intercept communications, according to critics, include threats to privacy and civil liberties, the potential for abuse by government, and side effects that threaten the security of communications systems. The idea of communications technology designed for a "nationwide standard for surveillance" is a nightmare to those who place high value on privacy and civil liberties. CALEA was a compromise. Congress made it clear that the law was not intended to extend law enforcement's surveillance power. The law contains a few limitations on government activity. For example, it limits authority to obtain tracking and location information for cell phone users. It was not supposed to apply to information services, that is, to much of the Internet.

The Federal Communications Commission (FCC) has the job of writing the actual rules and requirements to implement CALEA, in consultation with the FBI and representatives of the telecommunications industry. The FBI requested requirements that telecommunications systems permit (among other things):

- interception of all wire and electronic communications originating from or coming to a particular subscriber in real time, at any time, in ways not detectable by the parties to the communication

- performance of a large number of interceptions simultaneously

- access to numbers entered after the initial number dialed, with the looser justification standard that applies to pen registers

- determination of the physical location of cell phone users

- interception of packet-mode communications on the Internet.

There is intense disagreement about what requirements are reasonable. Over ten years or more, the FCC issued rules, and privacy and civil liberties organizations sued to block them. Critics argued that some of the rules, in particular requirements for determining the physical location of cell phone users and ensuring that the government could intercept packet-mode communications on the Internet, went beyond the scope of the law and extended the government's surveillance power. They objected to increased authority for law enforcement to get numbers entered after the initial number. Such numbers could include account numbers, passwords, and so forth. With some exceptions and revisions, courts accepted many of the rules the government requested. At the request of federal law enforcement agencies, the FCC determined that CALEA covers new services that replace old-style telephone calls. It ruled that (effective since 2007) some forms of Internet phone services and broadband Internet communications had to meet the wiretap requirements of CALEA. Internet technologists from academia and industry warned that providing the required interception capability to Internet telephony seriously compromises all Internet communications because the Internet does not distinguish voice packets from other packets.

Should the design of communications systems meet "a nationwide standard for surveillance," or should they use the best technology available for achieving speed, convenience, low cost, and privacy? How much should the needs of law enforcement activities weaken the privacy of honest and peaceful people? About 80% of the wiretaps courts authorize for criminal investigations are for drug cases. Critics claim that wiretaps are a less useful law enforcement tool than informants, detective work, witnesses, among other tools. Supporters of CALEA argue that wiretaps are essential for catching and/or convicting dangerous criminals. The focus of criminal wiretaps on drug crimes raises the question of whether the government really needs such extreme, system-wide controls on the communication systems used by 300 million Americans. If drug prohibition were to end, as alcohol prohibition did in the 1930s, would we find ourselves with a costly and privacy-threatening infrastructure of intrusion and relatively little legitimate need for it?

2.5.3 SECRET INTELLIGENCE GATHERING

The National Security Agency

The National Security Agency (NSA) collects and analyzes foreign intelligence information related to national security. It also protects U.S. government communications and information related to U.S. national security from others. It monitors communications between the U.S. and other countries and a lot of communications within other countries. Because the NSA uses methods that would not satisfy the Fourth Amendment, it is prohibited from intercepting communications within the U.S. (with some exceptions).

A secret presidential order formed the NSA in 1952. Its budget is still secret, although its Web site says the NSA/CSS (NSA and Central Security Service) is about the size of one of the larger Fortune 500 companies.[111] The NSA owns and uses the most powerful computers available. *Newsweek* estimated that it had nearly half the computing power in the world.[112]

The NSA has generated much controversy by secretly violating restrictions on surveillance of people within the United States. In 1920, the federal government's Black Chamber, a secret group of code experts and a precursor to the NSA, successfully pressured the main cable (telegram) companies to let the government routinely view foreign cables. This violated the federal Radio Communication Act of 1912, which made it illegal for a cable company employee to divulge a message without a court order to anyone except the addressee. In the 1960s and 1970s, the NSA violated its restriction to foreign intelligence by monitoring communications of specific American citizens (including civil rights leader Martin Luther King and entertainers who opposed the Vietnam War). In the 1970s, a Congressional committee chaired by Senator Church found that the NSA had been secretly and illegally collecting international telegrams, including telegrams sent by American citizens, since the 1950s and searching them for foreign intelligence information. As a result, Congress passed the Foreign Intelligence Surveillance Act (FISA) establishing oversight rules for the NSA. The Agency was prohibited from collecting masses of telegrams without a warrant and from compiling lists of Americans to be watched without a court order. The law set up a secret federal court, the Foreign Intelligence Surveillance Court, to issue warrants to the NSA to intercept communications of people it could show were agents of foreign powers or involved in terrorism or espionage.[113]

Before the USA PATRIOT Act passed in 2001, there was a sharp boundary between legal rules for terrorism investigations (involving foreigners) and criminal investigations (involving people within the U.S.). The act allows information obtained in terrorism investigations under FISA warrants to be used in criminal cases. The normal protections and rules for search warrants are not followed in terrorism cases. In addition, recordings of intercepted messages are normally provided to the defense in a criminal case. When the recordings are obtained as part of a terrorism case, the government does not have to provide copies of transcripts. Thus, the broader powers to violate privacy of communications in terrorism investigations can have serious impacts on people accused of ordinary crimes.

Although some technologies (such as fiber optic cable) make wiretapping more difficult, other changes make communications of ordinary people more vulnerable. Satellite communications were a boon to the NSA; it could pick messages out of the air. Increased wealth, travel, and trade generated more international communication—cluttering communications channels and potentially making it harder for the NSA to detect messages of interest. Vastly increased processing power of computer systems enabled law enforcement and spy agencies to filter and analyze huge quantities of communications of innocent people instead of targeting only specific suspects. The difficulty of tapping fiber optic cables (which must be cut and split to intercept communicaitons) made direct access to telecommunications company switching centers a desirable alternative from the perspective of law enforcement and intelligence agencies.

Secret access to communications and communications records

Beginning in 2005, newspapers exposed several secret programs to collect, study, and investigate terrorist communications and financing. The debates that ensued occurred in a highly contentious partisan political context. We describe two programs and summarize relevant issues and arguments.

The *New York Times* disclosed that since 2002, the NSA was intercepting international phone calls and e-mail of several hundred or several thousand people in the United States. The NSA had not sought or received approval from the FISA court that normally must approve interception of communications for foreign intelligence purposes.[114] The NSA's warrantless activity is normally restricted to communications outside the United States. In this program, one party to the communication was in the U.S. and one outside. Supporters of the program argued that the NSA must be able to quickly monitor communications to protect the U.S. from a terrorist attack and that secrecy was essential. Many people, including intelligence officials and a FISA court judge, expressed doubts about the legality of the program. About a year after disclosure of the program, the government agreed to stop warrantless wiretapping and submit terrorism-related wiretap requests to the FISA court.

In a more far-reaching program, the NSA built a huge database of telephone and e-mail records of millions of Americans, with no court order and no approval from the FISA court to obtain the records. According to news reports, the NSA obtained Internet and telephone logs from AT&T and used sophisticated data mining technology to sift through the data to learn how to detect communications of terrorist cells.[115] An AT&T employee described (under oath) a secret, secure room set up by the NSA at an AT&T switching facility. From this room, the NSA had access to e-mail, telephone, and Web communications of AT&T users.[116]

The government argued that the NSA was not intercepting or listening to telephone calls and was not collecting personal identifying information. It was only analyzing calling patterns. The analysis of calling patterns is needed because the sources of terrorism are diffuse and require broader means of detection and surveillance than old-time spy work. The NSA can no longer rely on monitoring only the telephone traffic of a few hostile governments and a small number of known suspects. It can no longer monitor just those specific physical telephone lines or communications links that connect specific military facilities or other sites of interest. Analysis of communications traffic helps the NSA determine what is suspicious. Those opposing the program argued that it is a huge intrusion on privacy. Even if the NSA did not collect customer names, it is easy to identify people from their telephone records. Opponents said the warrantless collection of the records by the NSA was illegal and that it was illegal for a telephone company to provide them. The government argued that it was legal under a broad interpretation of presidential powers. Several groups filed suits against AT&T for violating its stated privacy policies and communications privacy law by assisting the NSA in intercepting communications of millions of ordinary people. Lawsuits related to NSA's use of the secret room are in progress.

How can we evaluate these programs and similar future ones? Should the reduced privacy protections and search warrant requirements for investigating foreign agents and terrorists apply within the U.S. when agencies collect personal information about large numbers of U.S. citizens? Can we trust law enforcement and intelligence agencies to extract and use only the information for which they have a warrant or only information relevant to terrorism? Accessing data on specific suspects is a reasonable and responsible part of criminal and terrorist investigations. Broad access and data mining are more questionable because they threaten privacy of innocent people, and they threaten safety

WARTIME METHODS—BANNING FLOWER ARRANGEMENTS[117]

When trying to measure the depth of the government's concern about information passed secretly to or among enemies, it may help to consider some of the restrictions placed on communications in wartime.

During World War II, the U.S. government employed almost 15,000 people to open mail going overseas to eliminate any that contained military information of use to Germany or Japan. The censors read a million pieces of mail per day. They also listened to telephone conversations and read magazines and movie scripts. The drawings of children were suspect; they could mask a map of some sort. Crossword puzzles could contain hidden messages. And so could knitting instructions, moves in a chess game played by mail, orders of flowers that specified particular types of flowers, and phoned-in requests to radio stations to play specific songs. Any of these normally innocent things could be a form of code, giving vital information to an enemy. Many of these activities were simply banned during the war.

During the Persian Gulf War, military censors refused to allow Navajos at home to broadcast greetings on Armed Forces Radio to their relatives and friends stationed overseas. They feared that the Navajos could be transmitting secret information. (During World War II, the Marines used Navajos to do exactly that. A military code was developed using the spoken Navajo language. Because of the Navajo contribution to that war, public attention shamed the censors into lifting the ban in the Gulf War.)

In wartime, the highest priority of the government is to win the war. The fear that there might be one secret enemy message hidden in the thousands of innocent drawings, songs, flower arrangements, or Navajo greetings was enough to pry into private communications and restrict the peaceful activities of everyone. Were these actions paranoia on the government's part or a reasonable precaution? Now that billions of communications flow electronically, does the difficulty of controlling communications to enemies justify secret monitoring programs?

and freedom if investigators mistakenly decide someone's transactions look suspicious. How should we react when powerful government agencies break laws that protect privacy of communications?

The government considers these programs, and their secrecy, important in fighting terrorism. Is the secrecy justifiable? Is the secrecy essential? Exposure of the programs leads terrorists to take new measures to hide their activities, communications, and transactions. Temporary secrecy is essential for many criminal and terrorist investigations. Secrecy of government activities always presents a potential for abuse. We have seen abuses by the NSA in the past. We also have witnessed the hideous effects of terrorism. Is the fact that there have been no successful terrorist attacks in the U.S. since 2001 (up to the time this book was published) due in part to the secret communications monitoring and analysis programs of the NSA and other intelligence agencies? These important and difficult questions go beyond the impact of computer technology, the scope of this book.

2.5.4 ENCRYPTION POLICY

For centuries before the Internet, governments, their military agencies, and their spies were the main users of codes. For decades, most of the cryptographers in the U.S.

 *More about encryption: Section 2.4.1*
worked for the NSA. The NSA almost certainly could break virtually any codes that were in use before the mid-1970s.[118] The NSA exerted much effort to keeping everything about encryption secret.
The private-sector breakthrough development of public-key cryptography produced encryption that was relatively easy to use and very difficult to crack. Keeping encryption as an exclusive tool of governments and spies was no longer an option.

Throughout the 1990s, when people began using encryption for e-mail and other purposes, the U.S. government battled the Internet community and privacy advocates to restrict the availability of secure encryption (i.e., encryption that is so difficult and expensive to crack that it is not practical to do so). It maintained a costly and ultimately futile policy of prohibiting export of powerful encryption software. As one consequence of this policy, encryption products produced by U.S. companies for export were less competitive than those of foreign companies that used better encryption techniques.[119] The government interpreted anything posted on the Internet as effectively exported. Therefore, even researchers who posted encryption algorithms on the Net faced possible prosecution. The government argued that the export prohibition was necessary to keep strong encryption away from terrorists and enemy governments. At the same time, the government attempted to assure its access to the content of encrypted telephone and e-mail communications within the United States. The NSA played a major role in these efforts.

In 1996, a panel of experts from business, government, and academia prepared a study of encryption policy for the National Research Council (NRC), the research affiliate of the National Academy of Sciences. The study strongly supported the use of powerful encryption and loosening of export controls. The report stated that there should be no law barring manufacture, sale, or use of any form of encryption in the United States. It argued that strong encryption provides increased protection against hackers, thieves, and terrorists who threaten our economic, electric power, and transportation infrastructures.[120] The government appeared to ignored the NRC report.

The U.S. policy was strangely outdated. The stronger encryption schemes were available on Internet sites all over the world. By 1997, there were almost 2000 strong encryption software packages available outside the United States. Even the U.S. products were widely available—in illegal, pirated copies, for which the U.S. programmers and

PRETTY GOOD PRIVACY

Philip Zimmermann, a computer programmer, developed an encryption program for e-mail in the early 1990s. He called it PGP (for Pretty Good Privacy), and he gave it away for free.[121] PGP was widely distributed on the Internet and became the most popular program for e-mail encryption around the world. For more than two years Zimmermann was under threat of indictment for exporting encryption and could have been sent to jail for several years. Ironically, a law enforcement expert recommended PGP to police departments and estimated that hundreds of law enforcement officers were using it.[122] Although the government dropped the investigation of Zimmermann, it continued to interpret posting on the Internet as a form of export, hence illegal without a government license.

publishers received no income. A survey in 1998 estimated that U.S. industry would lose 200,000 jobs and $60 billion in the next four years because of the export controls.[123]

During this time, courts were considering legal challenges to the export restrictions based on the First Amendment. The question is whether cryptography algorithms, and computer programs in general, are speech and therefore protected by the First Amendment. In one case, cryptography researcher Daniel Bernstein wanted to publish his work, including encryption algorithms, on the Internet and discuss it at technical conferences and other public meetings. The rules required that he obtain a license from the State Department and report to the government everyone who received a copy of his work—a requirement that made distribution or discussion of the work on the Internet impossible. The government argued that software is not speech and that control of cryptography was a national-security issue, not a freedom-of-speech issue. The federal judge who heard the case thought otherwise. She stated that

> This court can find no meaningful difference between computer language...and German or French.... Like music and mathematical equations, computer language is just that, language, and it communicates information either to a computer or to those who can read it.... For the purposes of First Amendment analysis, this court finds that source code is speech.[124]

People devised many theories about why the U.S. government insisted on maintaining strict limits on export and tried to convince other countries to do the same, when strong crypto was already so widespread, so easily available to terrorists, and so important for security and electronic commerce. In their book *Privacy on the Line*, Whitfield Diffie and Susan Landau suggest that the main goal of the export rules might have been to restrict encryption to what the NSA could routinely crack in "real time," that is, as the messages are scanned.[125]

Under pressure from civil libertarians, privacy advocates, activist users of the Internet, major companies in the computer industry, court decisions on publication of cryptography research, and the obvious need for strong encryption in electronic commerce, in 2000 the U.S. government removed almost all export restrictions on encryption. Some people speculated that, with its huge budget and powerful computer systems, by 2000, the NSA might have been able to decrypt messages fast enough to scan encrypted traffic and read most of the communications it wants to read.[126]

Concurrently with the ban on export of strong encryption in the 1990s, the government attempted to ensure its access to encryption keys (or to the unencrypted content of encrypted messages) for encryption used within the United States. Pedophiles and child molesters encrypt child pornography and information about victims on their computers. Other criminals encrypt e-mail and files to hide their contents from law enforcement agents. The FBI argued that authority to intercept telephone calls or e-mail or seize computers (with a court order) meant nothing if agents could not read the contents of the messages and files they seized. Privacy advocates and civil libertarians found flaws in many of the specific proposals of the FBI and the NSA. They argued that requiring everyone to turn over their keys to government agencies threatened privacy and freedom.

In 1997, with encouragement from the FBI and other government agencies, the following statement appeared in a bill under consideration in Congress:

> After January 31, 2000, all encryption products manufactured or imported for sale or use in the United States must include features that permit immediate decryption of the encrypted data upon the receipt of a valid court order.[127]

The bill did not pass. Immediately after the terrorist attacks in 2001, support revived for a law requiring that all encryption have a "back door" for law enforcement. Technical experts argued that such a law would be extraordinarily difficult to implement because encryption is now embedded in Web browsers and many other common computing tools. Its implementation would threaten privacy and seriously weaken security of electronic commerce. They also argued that terrorists and sophisticated criminals would simply use encryption methods that did not comply with the law. The PATRIOT Act did not include a "back door" to all encryption for law enforcement.

EXERCISES

Review Exercises

2.1 What does the term *invisible information gathering* mean?

2.2 What are *cookies*? Give an example of their use.

2.3 What does the term *computer profiling* mean? Give an example.

2.4   Explain the difference between *opt-in* and *opt-out* policies for secondary uses of personal information.

2.5   Give one valuable application of encryption software, and one troublesome application.

2.6   Give one example in which release of someone's personal information threatened the person's safety.

2.7   Describe two behaviors people do on the Web that puts their privacy at risk.

2.8   What are some of the provisions of the Privacy Act of 1974? Give two examples of the databases it applies to.

General Exercises

2.9   A company that supplies filtering software to schools (to block access by children to Web sites with violence or pornography) sold statistical data about the Web sites visited by school children. The data did not identify the children or individual schools. Was this a privacy violation? Why or why not?

2.10 Caller ID is the feature that displays the telephone number of the caller on the telephone of the person he or she calls. With Caller ID now routine and widely used, it might be surprising that when the service was first made available, it was very controversial because of privacy implications. In one of my classes, it provoked the strongest argument of any topic in the course.

    a) What aspect of privacy (in the sense of Section 2.1.1) does Caller ID protect for the recipient of the call? What aspect of privacy does Caller ID violate for the caller?

    b) What are some good reasons why a nonbusiness, noncriminal caller might not want his or her number displayed?

    c) What are some (actual or possible) positive and negative business uses of caller ID?

2.11 Which of the guidelines in Figure 2.1 were violated by AOL's release of user search queries (Section 2.1.2)?

2.12 Surveillance cameras are commonplace. Give an example how they might make us safer. Give an example of how they may put us at risk.

2.13 The AOL search query database released on the Web in 2006 included the search query "How to kill your wife" and other related queries by the same person. Give arguments for and against allowing law enforcement agents to search the query databases of search engine companies periodically to detect plans for murders, terrorist attacks, or other serious crimes so that they can try to prevent them.

2.14 People who fled Hurricane Katrina left behind and lost important documents and records such as birth certificates, credit cards, property records, and employment records. A U.S. government agency proposed a new database where people could voluntarily store essential personal records in case of similar natural disasters. Discuss pros and cons of this proposal.

2.15 Prepaid cell phone service can protect privacy. One can buy a phone for cash and pay cash in advance for service. There are no billing records, and records of calls made on the phone are not linked to the owner. Cell phone carriers and governments in a few countries considered ending prepaid phone service because criminals use it; law enforcement agencies could not trace them. Should the decision about whether to provide prepaid cell phone service be left to the service providers or should governments ban it? If left to the companies, what policy do you think they should adopt? Give your reasons.

2.16 Two approaches to the problem of protecting personal information are the free market view and the consumer protection view.
   a) Briefly describe each view.
   b) How do these points of view differ on the issue of a company disclosing personal information about its customers?
   c) How do they differ on the issue of errors in the data about an individual that are distributed by a credit bureau?

2.17 The National Insurance Crime Bureau maintained a big database of suspicious insurance claims to be checked for fraud. Federal, state, and local law enforcement agencies had direct, almost unlimited access to the database. When the NICB announced plans to expand the database to include *all* insurance claims, privacy advocates objected. What are some advantages of the expanded database? What are some privacy concerns?

2.18 Describe some uses of satellite surveillance that you think are acceptable extensions of traditional law enforcement activities and capabilities. Describe some uses where the technology makes a fundamental change that is not acceptable. Explain your reasoning.

2.19 A member of the Tampa, Florida, City Council described the camera and face-recognition system installed in a Tampa neighborhood (Section 2.2.2) as "a public safety tool, no different from having a cop walking around with a mug shot."[128] Is he right? What are some similarities and differences, relevant to privacy, between the camera system and a cop walking around?

2.20 Services such as Google's Gmail offer free e-mail, text messaging, and file storage. Many individuals and some businesses use Gmail. What privacy issues does use of such a service raise for an individual? What privacy issues does use of such a service raise for a business? How are the concerns that individuals and businesses have the same? How are they different?

2.21 What are the ethical issues involved in a direct marketing company's decision or a state agency's decision about whether to contract with a prison system or use a more expensive commercial data entry service to do data entry of personal data? For what data entry tasks is it acceptable to use prisoners?

2.22 We said in Section 2.3.3 "One of the risks associated with databases of personal information is that criminals steal and use the information." How is this similar to and how does it differ from saying "One of the risks associated with buying an expensive car or stereo is that criminals steal them"? Can you draw any useful insights from the analogy?

2.23 Veterinarians implant computer chips into pets and farm animals to identify them if they get lost. Some people suggest doing so for children. Discuss the privacy implications of such proposals. What are the risks? Do the benefits outweigh the risks? If there were a bill in Congress to require ID chips in children, would you support it? Why?

2.24 The database of season subscribers at a theater uses telephone numbers as the key to access subscriber records. Box-office staff access the records when a subscriber calls. They are not available to the public online; they do not include credit-card numbers. How might someone misuse this access policy? Is the use of the telephone number as the subscriber identifier reasonable or too much of a privacy risk? Why?

2.25 An individual set up a 24-hour-a-day Webcam, on an island on the Atlantic coast, aimed at a ferry dock local people and tourists use. People could visit his Web site to check on weather conditions to find out if ferry service is likely to be canceled. But some people complained that the Webcam violated their privacy. Suppose you are asked to help settle the dispute. What solution would you suggest? What arguments would you give?[129]

2.26 Answer the question posed by Ian Kerr in the quotation at the end of Section 2.3.4. Give at least two reasonable answers.

2.27 A disgruntled employee of a county health department sent a confidential file containing the names of about 4000 AIDS patients to a newspaper.
   a) Would this have been more or less likely to have happened if the names were in paper files, not electronic files? Why?
   b) What are some ways to prevent such a leakage of sensitive data?

2.28 Implementations of digital cash can allow secure and anonymous transactions. Considering the privacy benefits and the potential for use by tax evaders, criminals, and terrorists, do you think fully anonymous digital cash should be made illegal? Give your reasons.

2.29 Section 2.4.1 gave two examples of uses of trusted third parties to reduce access to personal information. Give another example, either a real one you know of or an applicaiton you think would be useful.

2.30 A business maintains a database containing the names of shoplifters. It distributes the list to stores that subscribe.
   a) Should such a service be illegal to protect privacy? (Give reasons.)
   b) Describe the likely position of each of Warren and Brandeis, Judith Thomson, and Richard Posner (Section 2.4.2), with their reasons, on this question.
   c) Would your answer to part (a) differ if the question were about a database of tenant history available to landlords, or a database available to the public with comments from tenants about landlords? How and why?

2.31 A company called Digitizer provides service for many other companies by converting their paper documents to digital files. The documents include employee information, medical records, business records, and many others. Digitizer hires relatively unskilled employees to organize the documents and prepare them for scanning.
   a) What are some potential risks here?
   b) Describe some actions Digitizer can take or policies it can adopt to reduce the risks.

2.32 Formulate a policy about access to motor vehicle records by the news media. (News media could include both a newspaper trying to get home addresses from vehicle license plate numbers for cars parked at an abortion clinic and a newspaper trying to get home addresses from vehicle license plate numbers for cars parked at a Ku Klux Klan rally.) How would your policy apply to bloggers?

2.33 Some cities and counties post maps on their Web sites showing property lines, property ownership information, property values, locations of roads, and aerial photos of all properties. Some residents oppose putting such information on the Web. What are some benefits of posting it? What are some risks or objections? Do you think the records should be on the Web? If so, why? If not, what alternative access would you suggest?

2.34 A company planned to sell a laser device a person can wear around his or her neck that makes photographs taken of the person come out streaked and useless. The company marketed it to celebrities hounded by photographers. Suppose the device works well against closed circuit television (CCTV) cameras and many people begin to use it routinely in public places. Law enforcement agencies would probably try to ban it. Give arguments for and against such a ban.

2.35 One writer defines privacy as "freedom from the inappropriate judgement of others."[130] Is this a good definition of privacy? Why or why not?

2.36 Give an explanation, with examples and/or analogies, to describe what it would mean for privacy to be a negative right (liberty). Do the same for considering privacy a positive right (claim right). (See Section 1.3.2 for explanations of negative and positive rights.) Which kind of right, if either, seems more appropriate for privacy? Why?

2.37 Accident-data recorders for cars that record speed, braking, whether the occupants are wearing seatbelts, and so on were optional at the time of writing this text. Crash investigators use the recorders, and the National Transportation Safety Board wants them required in all cars. If such a law passes, what restrictions, if any, should it place on access to the data?

2.38 Suppose each of the following is a proposed law. For each one, choose a side, either supporting or opposing it, and defend your position.
   a) Companies that provide search engine service to members or to the public must maintain user search query records for two years in case law enforcement agencies or terrorism investigators need them.
   b) To protect privacy, companies that provide search engine service to members or to the public must not store user search queries in a way that links the queries of any one person together for more than one week.

2.39 An online book seller that provided e-mail service for a large number of book store owners and managers saved copies of thousands of e-mail messages and analyzed them to collect data on sales trends. He did not inform the e-mail users. Was this legal? Explain.

2.40 Assume you are a professional working in your chosen field. Describe specific things you can do to reduce the impact of any two problems we discussed in this chapter. (If you cannot think of anything related to your professional field, choose another field that might interest you.)

Assignments

These exercises require some research or activity.

2.41 a) Read the privacy policy of a large, popular Web site. Write a brief summary. Identify the Web site (name, URL, type of site). Give examples of parts of the policy that are, or are not, clear or reasonable.
   b) Find a Web site for a small business or organization that collects some personal information (for example, a local restaurant that takes orders or reservations on the Web). Does it have a privacy policy? If so, how does it compare to the one you summarized for part (a)?

2.42 Google introduced Street View while I was writing this book. Its cameras providing street scenes on the Web occasionally capture people in embarrassing behavior and in places they would prefer not to be seen by the whole world. Many people object that Street View violates privacy. What happened? How, and how well, did Google address the privacy concerns?

2.43 Do a Web search on yourself and four people you know. Select people with different backgrounds and interests (i.e., you may select a parent or sibling, a teacher, a neighbor, someone you do business with, etc.). What types of information did you find? Did anything you found surprise you?

2.44 As you go through your normal daily routine, locate surveillance cameras in ten different locations. Which ones did you expect to find and which ones surprised you?

Class Discussion Exercises

These exercises are for class discussion, perhaps with short presentations prepared in advance by small groups of students.

2.45 A health-information Web site has many articles on health and medical issues, a chat room where people can discuss health issues with other users, and provisions for people to send questions by e-mail for doctors to answer. You work as an intern for a company hired to do a privacy audit. The audit team will examine the site, find privacy risks (or good privacy-protection practices), and make recommendations for changes as needed. Describe at least three things you would look for, explain their significance, and tell what your recommendations would be if you do or do not find them.

2.46 Your town is considering setting up a camera and face-recognition system in the downtown area and in a neighborhood with a high crime rate. They hired you as a consultant to help design policies for use of the system. Consider a variety of aspects, for example, who will have access to the system, what databases of photos the system will use for matching, how long video will be stored, and other factors you consider important. Describe some of your most important recommendations to the city, with your reasons for them.

2.47 Several men contracted syphilis, a serious sexually transmitted disease, after arranging to meet partners through an online chat room used mostly by gay men. The public health department asked the company that hosted the Web site for the names and addresses of all people who used the chat room so that it could inform them about possible exposure to the disease. The public health department did not have a court order. The Web site's policy states that it will not release information that links screen names with real names. Should it make an exception in this case? Give arguments in favor of granting the health department request. Give arguments against granting the health department request. How do you weigh the trade-off between the possibility of an infected person's not being informed and the loss of privacy to all visitors to the chat room? How important is it that the company abide by its posted privacy policy?

2.48 An Ivy League university set up a Web site that student applicants could access, using their Social Security number and other personal information, to find out if they were accepted for admission. Officials at the university determined that computers in the Admissions Office of another Ivy League university accessed some student accounts. Many students apply to both schools. It was suspected that the university that accessed the accounts wanted to determine if students had been accepted by the other school before making its own decisions. The personal information needed to access the Web site was in the students' applications, available to the Admissions Office.

Analyze this incident. Identify the things done wrong (assuming the suspicions about the motives for the snooping are accurate). What actions should the administrations of both universities take?

2.49 Cell phone videos are popping up on the Web and the news with increasing frequency. Often the subject of the video is unaware that he or she is being recorded. With respect to cell phone videos, should people have an expectation of privacy when they are out in public? Inside a retail store or bank? Inside a public restroom? Inside their own home? What regulations, if any, would you recommend and why?

2.50 A children's hospital in the U.S. began collecting and analyzing DNA from 100,000 children for a DNA profile database. The United Kingdom plans a DNA database with data from 500,000 people. Some of the databases will be anonymous; the DNA information will not be stored with other information that identifies the individual it came from. Discuss potential valuable uses of such databases. Discuss potential risks and problems. If you were the head of a hospital, would you approve the project? As an individual, if you and your family were asked to provide DNA for the database, would you agree? Give reasons.

2.51 What restrictions should we place on the use of search techniques we described as "noninvasive but deeply revealing searches"? When should we permit government agencies to use them without a search warrant? How can they be used to enhance our security? How do they threaten our privacy?

2.52 Are businesses that provide free Internet services or other benefits in exchange for tracking Web activity offering a fair option for consumers, or are they unfairly taking advantage of low-income people who must give up some privacy for these services?

2.53 In one of Vernor Vinge's science fiction novels (*Rainbows End,* Tor, 2006), an organization scatters false information about people on the Web. Does that sound nasty? The name of the organization is Friends of Privacy. Are they?

2.54 The city of Philadelphia requires GPS systems in all taxicabs. Is a government requirement for a tracking system for private taxicabs a reasonable public safety measure or an unreasonable intrusion on the privacy of drivers and passengers? Identify several differences between such a government requirement and a taxicab company choosing to install GPS systems in its cabs. Is either more objectionable than the other? Why?

2.55 Do young people today view privacy differently from the previous generation? Discuss the ideas raised at the end of Section 2.3.4.

NOTES

1. James O. Jackson, "Fear and Betrayal in the Stasi State," *Time*, February 3, 1992, pp. 32–33.

2. Edward J. Bloustein, "Privacy as an Aspect of Human Dignity," in *Philosophical Dimensions of Privacy: An Anthology*, ed. Ferdinand David Schoeman (Cambridge University Press, 1984), pp. 156–203, quote on p. 188.

3. "Reading *Privacy Journal*'s Mail," *Privacy Journal*, May 2001, p. 2.

4. Nicole Wong, "Judge tells DoJ 'No' on search queries," Google Blog, March 17, 2006, googleblog. blogspot.com/2006/03/judge-tells-doj-no-on-search-queries.html.

5. Michael Barbaro and Tom Zeller Jr., "A Face is Exposed for AOL Searcher No. 4417749," *New York Times*, August 9, 2006, www.nytimes.com, viewed September 19, 2006. AOL acknowledged that the release was a bad mistake, fired the employees responsible, and considered improvements in internal policies to reduce the likelihood of similar errors in the future.

6. Associated Press, "Popular Software for Computer Cursors Logs Web Visits, Raising Privacy Issue," *Wall Street Journal*, November 30, 1999, p. B6.

7. The history of cookies is presented in John Schwartz, "Giving Web a Memory Cost Its Users Privacy," *New York Times*, September 4, 2001, pp. A1, C10.

8. Steven Levy, "Is It Software? Or Spyware?" *Newsweek*, February 19, 2001, p. 54. Associated Press, "Popular Software Secretly Sends Music Preferences," CNN.com, November 1, 1999.

9. The National Highway Traffic Safety Administration requires that carmakers inform owners if a car is equipped with a data recorder and specifies that the owner's consent is needed to collect data from the recorder.

10. Quoted in Theo Francis, "Spread of Records Stirs Patient Fears of Privacy Erosion," *Wall Street Journal*, December 26, 2006, p. A1.

11. The Privacy Rights Clearinghouse summarizes several specific sets of Fair Information Principles in "A Review of the Fair Information Principles," www.privacyrights.org/ar/fairinfo.htm.

12. Ruchi Sanghvi, "Facebook Gets a Facelift," September 5, 2006, blog.facebook.com/blog.php?post=2207967130; Mark Zuckerberg, "An Open Letter from Mark Zuckerberg," September 8, 2006, blog.facebook.com/blog.php?post=2208562130; and many news stories.

13. I checked Google (www.google.com), Ask.com (www.ask.com), and AOL (search.aol.com) on October 30, 2006. The information-collection policies were two clicks away.

14. Alan F. Westin, *Privacy and Freedom* (Atheneum, 1968), p. 67.

15. Steven A. Bercu, "Smart Card Privacy Issues: An Overview," *BOD-T-001*, July 1994, Smart Card Forum.

16. The GAO was called the General Accounting Office until 2004.

17. General Accounting Office, *Computers and Privacy: How the Government Obtains, Verifies, Uses, and Protects*

Personal Data (U.S. General Accounting Office, 1990), GAO/IMTEC-90-70BR; "House Panel Probes White House Database," *EPIC Alert*, September 12, 1996. OMB Watch study, reported in "U.S. Government Web Sites Fail to Protect Privacy," *EPIC Alert*, September 4, 1997; Declan McCullagh, "Feds' Hands Caught in Cookie Jar," www.wired.com/news/politics/ 0,1283,37314,00.html. *Internet Privacy: Comparison of Federal Agency Practices with FTC's Fair Information Principles*, U.S. General Accounting Office, September 11, 2000 (GAO/AIMD-00-296R); U.S. Government Accountability Office, *Data Mining* (GAO 05-866), August 2005, www.gao.gov/new.items/d05866.pdf.

18. "GAO Finds IRS Security Lacking," *EPIC Alert*, January 20, 1999; the GAO report is *IRS Systems Security*, December 1998 (AIMD-99-38). Treasury Inspector General for Tax Administration, "Increased IRS Oversight of State Agencies Is Needed to Ensure Federal Tax Information Is Protected," September 2005, Reference Number 2005-20-184, www.treas.gov/tigta/ auditreports/2005reports/200520184fr.html (accessed May 16, 2007).

19. Glenn R. Simpson, "If the FBI Hopes to Get the Goods on You, It May Ask ChoicePoint," *Wall Street Journal*, April 13, 2001, pp. A1, A6; "ChoicePoint—An Ignoble Corporate History," *Privacy Journal*, March 2005, pp. 1, 3.

20. Robert Ellis Smith, "Ominous Tracking of University Students," *Privacy Journal*, August 2006, p. 1.

21. U.S. Code, Title 13.

22. Letter from Vincent Barabba, director of Census Bureau under Presidents Nixon and Carter, and comments from Tom Clark, Justice Department coordinator of alien control, quoted in David Burnham, *The Rise of the Computer State* (Random House, 1983), pp. 23–26. Margo Anderson, *The American Census: A Social History* (Yale University Press, 1988); James Bovard, "Honesty May Not Be Your Best Census Policy," *Wall Street Journal*, August 8, 1989; Lynette Clemetson, "Homeland Security Given Data on Arab-Americans," *New York Times*, July 30, 2004, p. A14.

23. These observations were made in John Shattuck, "Computer Matching Is a Serious Threat to Individual Rights," *Communications of the ACM* 27, no. 6 (June 1984): pp. 537–545, and in J. J. Horning et al., "A Review of NCIC 2000," CPSR's report to the Subcommittee on Civil and Constitutional Rights of the Committee on the Judiciary, U.S. House of Representatives, February 1989.

24. Jeff Jonas and Jim Harper, "Effective Counterterrorism and Limited Role of Predictive Data Mining," Cato Institute Policy Analysis No. 584, December 11, 2006.

25. Quoted in David Banisar, *Privacy & Human Rights 2000: An International Survey of Privacy Laws and Developments* (EPIC and Privacy International, 2000).

26. *Marchetti v. United States*, 390 U.S. 39 (1968), quoted in Steven A. Bercu, "Smart Card Privacy Issues: An Overview," *BOD-T-001*, July 1994, Smart Card Forum.

27. Alvin Mark Domnitz, quoted in Felicity Barringer, "Using Books as Evidence against Their Readers," *New York Times*, WeekinReview section, April 8, 2001.

28. Julian Sanchez, "The Pinpoint Search," *Reason*, January 2007, pp. 21–28.

29. Ross Kerber, "When Is a Satellite Photo an Unreasonable Search?" *Wall Street Journal*, January 27, 1998, pp. B1, B7.

30. Reuters, "Critics: New Airport X-Ray Is a Virtual Strip Search," CNet News.com, February 24, 2007.

31. Sanchez, "The Pinpoint Search," p. 21.

32. The citations for the cases mentioned in this section are *Olmstead v. United States*, 277 U.S. 438(1928), *Katz v. United States*, 389 U.S. 347(1967), *Smith v. Maryland*, 442 U.S. 735(1979), *United States v. Miller*, 425 U.S. 435(1976), *Kyllo v. United States*, 99-8508(2001), and *Illinois v. Caballes*, 541 U.S. 972(2005).

33. See, for example, "My National Security Letter Gag Order," *Washington Post*, March 23, 2007, p. A17, www.washingtonpost.com/wpdyn/content/ article/2007/03/22/AR2007032201882.html.

34. Glen A. Fine, "Misuse of PATRIOT Act Powers: The Inspector General's Findings," testimony to Committee on the Judiciary, U.S. Senate, March 21, 2007, judiciary.senate.gov/testimony.cfm?id=2616&wit_ id=6193.

35. Fine, "Misuse of PATRIOT Act Powers."

36. Walter Pincus and Dan Eggen, "325,000 Names on Terrorism List," *Washington Post*, February 15, 2006, p. A1, www.washingtonpost.com/wpdyn/content/ article/2006/02/14/AR2006021402125.html.

37. Dana Canedy, "TV Cameras Seek Criminals in Tampa's Crowds," *New York Times*, July 4, 2001, pp. A1, A11.

38. An accuracy rate of 57% was reported by the National Institute of Standards and Technology, a federal government agency. Jesse Drucker and Nancy Keates, "The Airport of the Future," *Wall Street Journal*, November 23, 2001, pp. W1, W12; David Banisar, "A Review of New Surveillance Technologies," *Privacy Journal*, November 2001, p. 1.

39. Marc Champion et al., "Tuesday's Attack Forces an Agonizing Decision on Americans," *Wall Street Journal*, September 14, 2001, p. A8.

40. Ross Kerber, "Privacy Concerns Are Roadblocks on 'Smart' Highways," *Wall Street Journal*, December 4, 1996, pp. B1, B7; Banisar, "A Review of New Surveillance Technologies"; Michael Spencer, "One Major City's Restrictions on TV Surveillance," *Privacy*

Journal, March 2001, p. 3; Murray Long, "Canadian Commissioner Puts a Hold on Video Cameras," *Privacy Journal,* November 2001, pp. 3–4.

41. Robert Ellis Smith, "Cameras in U.K. Found Useless," *Privacy Journal,* March 2005, pp. 6–7.

42. Quoted in Long, "Canadian Commissioner Puts a Hold on Video Cameras."

43. Acxiom Latin America Web site, "Customer Information Management Solutions," www.acxiom.com (accessed November 26, 2006).

44. Eli M. Noam, "Privacy in Telecommunications: Markets, Rights, and Regulations," *New Telecom Quarterly,* 2nd Quarter, 1995, www.tfi.com/pubs/ntq/articles/view/95Q2_A8.pdf (accessed September 13, 2007).

45. Jonathan Berry et al., "Database Marketing," *Business Week,* September 5, 1994, pp. 56–62.

46. Julia Angwin, "A Plan to Track Web Use Stirs Privacy Concern," *Wall Street Journal,* May 1, 2000, pp. B1, B18; Paulette Thomas, " 'Clicking' Coupons On-Line Has a Cost: Privacy," *Wall Street Journal,* June 18, 1998, pp. B1, B8.

47. *Handbook of Company Privacy Codes,* Privacy and American Business, October 1994, pp. 81, 86.

48. "The AOL Privacy Policy" (accessed January 19, 2001) (current AOL Network Privacy Policy is available at about.aol.com/aolnetwork/aol_pp).

49. For example, regulations established under the Gramm-Leach-Bliley Act of 1999, which are responsible for the millions of privacy notices and opt-out forms mailed out by credit-card companies.

50. Jessica E. Vascellaro, "Online Retailers Are Watching You," *Wall Street Journal,* November 28, 2006, pp. D1, D3.

51. Cecilie Rohwedder, "No. 1 Retailer in Britain Uses 'Clubcard' to Thwart Wal-Mart," *Wall Street Journal,* June 6, 2006, p. A1.

52. The case is *Dennis v. Metromail.* "The Quintessential Abuse of Privacy," *Privacy Journal,* May 1996, pp. 1, 4; Lee Drutman, "Should Prisoners Be Processing Personal Information?" *Privacy Journal,* July 1998, p. 1; Robert Ellis Smith, "There's $1 Million Available for Privacy Activism," *Privacy Journal,* February 2001, p. 1.

53. Yochi J. Dreazen, "Democrats, Playing Catch-up, Tap Database to Woo Potential Voters," *Wall Street Journal,* October 31, 2006, pp. A1, A10.

54. Julia Angwin, "A Plan to Track Web Use Stirs Privacy Concern," *Wall Street Journal,* May 1, 2000, pp. B1, B18.

55. Robert Ellis Smith, "Privacy and Surveillance in the 20th Century," *Privacy Journal,* December 1999, p. 3.

56. Fair Credit Reporting Act of 1970, 15 U.S. Code Section 1681.

57. Acxiom Latin America Web site, "Customer Information Management Solutions," www.acxiom.com (accessed November 26, 2006).

58. "CAN-SPAM: Unwanted Text Messages and E-Mail on Wireless Phones and Other Mobile Devices," Federal Communications Commission, www.fcc.gov/cgb/consumerfacts/canspam.html (accessed November 22, 2006).

59. John L. Eliot, "Bugging Plants to Sting Poachers," *National Geographic* 189, no. 3 (March 1996): p. 148. Jon R. Luoma, "It's 10:00 P.M. We Know Where Your Turtles Are," *Audubon,* September/October 1998, pp. 52–57.

60. "RFID Passport Hacked," *EPIC Alert,* August 10, 2006.

61. See, for example, Center for Democracy and Technology, "CDT Working Group on RFID: Privacy Best Practices for Deployment of RFID Technology," May 1, 2006, www.cdt.org/privacy/20060501rfid-best-practices.php.

62. Quoted in "FCC Moves on Phone-call Info," *Privacy Journal,* March 2006, p. 4.

63. I collected many of these examples from news reports and the notification letters sent to the affected people. Some are from *Privacy Journal*'s much longer list, "Lost and Stolen Laptops Hall of Shame," July 2006, pp. 3–4. The Privacy Rights Clearinghouse (www.privacyrights.org) also maintains a list.

64. House Government Reform Committee, Associated Press, "Government Data 'Lost' in 788 Cases," *San Diego Union-Tribune,* October 14, 2006, p. A6; Kathleen Day, "IRS Found Lax in Protecting Taxpayer Data," *Washington Post,* April 5, 2007, p. D1, www.washingtonpost.com (accessed May 16, 2007); Lisa Lerer, "Lost Laptops Law," *Forbes.com,* September 27, 2006; "Information Security: The Centers for Medicare & Medicaid Services Needs to Improve Controls Over Key Communication Network," Government Accountability Office, August 2006, www.gao.gov/new.items/d06750.pdf.

65. Numerous articles in the *Washington Post, New York Times, Honolulu Star-Bulletin,* and others, December 1997–May 1998, some collected at www.gaymilitary.org/mcveigh2.htm.

66. www.youtube.com.

67. Vauhini Vara, "Covering Your Tracks In an Online World Takes a Few Tricks," *Wall Street Journal,* July 7, 2006, pp. A1, A10.

68. At University of Ottawa, Canada, quoted in *Privacy Journal,* April 2006, p. 2.

69. www.consumer.gov/idtheft; "Second Thoughts on Posting Court Records Online," *Privacy Journal,* February 2006, pp. 1, 4.

70. Tony Mauro, "Judicial Conference Votes to Release Federal Judges' Financial Records," Freedom Forum, March 15, 2000,

www.freedomforum.org/templates/document.asp?
documentID=11896 (accessed January 5, 2007).

71. The article "Can Privacy and Open Access to Records be
Reconciled?" *Privacy Journal*, May 2000, p. 6, outlines
principles and guidelines devised by Robert Ellis Smith
for access to public records.

72. Sources for this section include Chris Hibbert, "What To
Do When They Ask for Your Social Security Number,"
www.cpsr.org/cpsr/privacy/ssn/ssn.faq.html; "ID Cards
to Cost $10 Billion," *EPIC Alert*, September 26, 1997;
Glenn Garvin, "Bringing the Border War Home,"
Reason, October 1995, pp. 18–28; Simson Garfinkel,
Database Nation: The Death of Privacy in the 21st Century
(O'Reilly, 2000), pp. 33–34; "A Turnaround on Social
Security Numbers," *Privacy Journal*, December 2006,
p. 2; *Greidinger v. Davis*, U.S. Court of Appeals, Fourth
Circuit.

73. Ellen Nakashima, "U.S. Exposed Personal Data,"
Washington Post, April 21, 2007, p. A05; "USDA Offers
Free Credit Monitoring to Farm Services Agency and
Rural Development Funding Recipients,"
www.usa.gov/usdaexposure.shtml (accessed
May 24, 2007).

74. "The President's Identity Theft Task Force Releases
Comprehensive Strategic Plan to Combat Identity
Theft," U.S. Securities and Exchange Commission news
release, April 23, 2007, www.sec.gov/news/press/
2007/2007-69.htm.

75. "Understanding and Responding to the Threat of
Terrorism," *Cato Policy Report*, March/April 2007,
pp. 13–15, 19.

76. Peter G. Neumann and Lauren Weinstein, "Inside
Risks," *Communications of the ACM*, December 2001,
p. 176.

77. Quoted in Jane Howard, "ID Card Signals 'End of
Democracy,'" *The Australian*, September 7, 1987, p. 3.

78. "Understanding and Responding to the Threat of
Terrorism."

79. Caroline McCarthy, "MySpace to Provide Sex Offender
Data to State AGs," Cnet News.com, May 21, 2007,
news.com.com.

80. Holman W. Jenkins Jr., "On Web Privacy, What Are We
Really Afraid Of?" *Wall Street Journal*, August 2, 2000,
p. A23.

81. "Hiding Data in Plain Sight," *EFFector Online*,
January 7, 1993, www.eff.org/effector/effect04.05.

82. Steven Levy, "The Open Secret," *Wired*, April 1999, pp.
108–115; Simon Singh, *The Code Book: The Evolution of
Secrecy From Mary Queen of Scots to Quantum
Cryptography* (Doubleday, 1999) pp. 279–292.

83. Quoted in Steve Lohr, "Privacy on Internet Poses Legal
Puzzle," *New York Times*, April 19, 1999, p. C4.

84. Ixquick (www.ixquick.com) is one example. It is a
meta-search engine; that is, it uses several other search
engines to find results and provides what it considers the
best results to the user.

85. Samuel D. Warren and Louis D. Brandeis, "The Right
to Privacy," *Harvard Law Review* 4 (1890): p. 193.

86. Judith Jarvis Thomson, "The Right to Privacy," in
Philosophical Dimensions of Privacy: An Anthology, ed.
Ferdinand David Schoeman (Cambridge University
Press, 1984), pp. 272–289.

87. The inspiration for the Warren and Brandeis article, not
mentioned in it, was gossip columnists writing about
extravagant parties in Warren's home and, particularly,
newspaper coverage of his daughter's wedding. The
background of the article is described in a biography of
Brandeis and summarized in the critical response to the
Warren and Brandeis article by William L. Prosser:
"Privacy," in *Philosophical Dimensions of Privacy: An
Anthology*, ed. Ferdinand David Schoeman (Cambridge
University Press, 1984), pp. 104–155.

88. Thomson, "The Right to Privacy," p. 287.

89. See, for example, Ferdinand David Schoeman,
Philosophical Dimensions of Privacy: An Anthology
(Cambridge University Press, 1984), p. 15; Prosser,
"Privacy," pp. 104–155.

90. Cases are cited in Prosser, "Privacy."

91. Richard Posner, "An Economic Theory of Privacy,"
Regulation, American Enterprise Institute for Public
Policy Research, May/June 1978, pp. 19–26. Appears in
several anthologies including Schoeman, *Philosophical
Dimensions of Privacy*, pp. 333–345; Deborah G.
Johnson and Helen Nissenbaum, *Computers, Ethics &
Social Values* (Prentice Hall, 1995).

92. New York State Office of the Attorney General,
"Toysmart Bankruptcy Settlement Ensures Consumer
Privacy Protection," January 11, 2001,
www.oag.state.ny.us/press/2001/jan/jan11a_01.html
(accessed May 24, 2007).

93. John Simons, "New FTC Rules Aim to Protect Kid Web
Privacy," *Wall Street Journal*, April 21, 1999, p. B1;
"FTC Proposes Rules for Kids' Privacy Protection,"
EPIC Alert, April 22, 1999; "New Children's Privacy
Rules Pose Obstacles for Some Sites," *Wall Street Journal*,
April 24, 2000, p. B8.

94. Robert Pear, "Bush Accepts Rules to Guard Privacy
of Medical Records," *New York Times*, April 13, 2001,
pp. A1, A12. "New Federal Rule Protects Medical
Records-Or Does It?" *Privacy Journal*, January 2001,
p. 3.

95. See Robert Gellman, "Privacy, Consumers, and Costs,"
March 2002, www.epic.org/reports/dmfprivacy.html
(accessed May 24, 2007).

96. Dan Freedman, "Privacy Profile: Mary Gardiner Jones,"
Privacy and American Business 1, no. 4 (1994):
pp. 15, 17.

97. Janlori Goldman, statement to the Senate Judiciary Subcommittee on Technology and the Law, January 27, 1994.

98. www.privacy.org.

99. Deirdre Mulligan, statement to U.S. House of Representatives Committee on the Judiciary hearing on "Privacy and Electronic Communications," May 18, 2000, www.cdt.org/testimony/000518mulligan.shtml (accessed May 24, 2007). The quotation in her statement is from Westin, *Privacy and Freedom.*

100. "Directive 95/46/EC of the European Parliament and of the Council of 24 October 1995 on the protection of individuals with regard to the processing of personal data and on the free movement of such data," ec.europa.eu/justice_home/fsj/privacy/law/index_en.htm and www.cdt.org/privacy/eudirective/ EU_Directive_.html.

101. Jo Best, "EU Data Retention Directive Gets Final Nod," CNET News.com, February 22, 2006, news.com.com (accessed October 26, 2006).

102. "Just Published," *Privacy Journal*, August 2006, p. 6; the British Information Commissioner's report (May 10, 2006) www.ico.gov.uk/upload/documents/ library/corporate/research_and_reports/what_price_ privacy.pdf (accessed September 13, 2007).

103. Jacqueline Klosek, *Data Privacy in the Information Age* (Quorum Books, 2000), pp. 169–193; "Australia: We're 'Adequate'!" *Privacy Journal*, May 2001, p. 4.

104. "Privacy@net: An International Comparative Study of Consumer Privacy on the Internet," Consumers International, January 2001 (quote on p. 6), www.consumersinternational.org/news/pressreleases/ fprivreport.pdf.

105. The historic information in this section is from Westin, *Privacy and Freedom*; Alexander Charns, *Cloak and Gavel: FBI Wiretaps, Bugs, Informers, and the Supreme Court* (University of Illinois Press, 1992), Chapter 8; Edith Lapidus, *Eavesdropping on Trial* (Hayden Book Co., 1974); Walter Isaacson, *Kissinger: A Biography* (Simon and Schuster, 1992).

106. *Nardone v. U.S.*, 302 U.S. 379(1937).

107. The quote is in the foreword of Lapidus, *Eavesdropping on Trial.*

108. For examples, see U.S. Department of State, "Country Reports on Human Rights Practices," March 6, 2007, www.state.gov/g/drl/rls/hrrpt/2006 (accessed March 13, 2007).

109. *Warshak v. U.S.*, Case 1:06-cv-00357.

110. John Schwartz, "Industry Fights Wiretap Proposal," *Washington Post*, March 12, 1994, pp. C1, C7.

111. NSA FAQ, www.nsa.gov/about/about00018.cfm.

112. Gregory Vistica, "Inside the Secret Cyberwar," *Newsweek*, February 21, 2000, p. 48.

113. James Bamford, *The Puzzle Palace: A Report on NSA, America's Most Secret Agency* (Houghton Mifflin, 1982), p. 12. Statement for the Record of NSA Director Lt Gen Michael V. Hayden, USAF, House Permanent Select Committee on Intelligence, April 12, 2000, www.nsa.gov/releases/relea00059.html. James Bamford, *Body of Secrets: Anatomy of the Ultra-Secret National Security Agency, from the Cold War through the Dawn of a New Century* (Doubleday, 2001), pp. 435–440.

114. James Risen and Eric Lichtblau, "Bush Lets U.S. Spy on Callers Without Courts," *New York Times*, December 16, 2005.

115. Qwest Communications declined the NSA request for its customer records because the NSA did not have a warrant or court approval. Initial reports mentioned that Verizon and Bell South complied, but those companies denied providing records to the NSA.

116. Declaration of Mark Klein, June 8, 2006, www.eff.org/legal/cases/att/SER_klein_decl.pdf (accessed June 19, 2007).

117. Sources include David Kahn, *The Codebreakers: The Comprehensive History of Secret Communication from Ancient Times to the Internet* (Macmillan, 1967), pp. 515–517; Julian Dibbell, "Tale From the Crypto Wars", *The Village Voice*, August 3, 1993, www.juliandibbell.com/texts/code-side-2.html (accessed August 24, 2007); Nathan Aaseng, *Navajo Code Talkers: America's Secret Weapon in World War II* (Walker & Co., 1992).

118. An exception is a method called one-time pads, but it is inconvenient to use and is not significant in the issues discussed here.

119. James Bidzos, president of RSA Data Security, quoted on p. 27 of John Perry Barlow, "Decrypting the Puzzle Palace," *Communications of the ACM*, 35, no. 7 (July 1992): pp. 25–31.

120. Kenneth W. Dam and Herbert S. Lin, eds., National Research Council, *Cryptography's Role in Securing the Information Society* (National Academy Press, 1996), books.nap.edu/html/crisis.

121. RSA Data Security accused Zimmermann of violating its patents. Zimmermann signed an agreement to stop distributing PGP. The program remained available on the Internet for free and was also sold by a company that licensed RSA's technology.

122. William Sternow, quoted in Eric Dexheimer, "Police Uneasy with This Cure for the Common Code," *San Diego Union Tribune*, Computer Link section, March 1, 1994, p. 1 ff.

123. Paul Wallich, "Cracking the U.S. Code," *Scientific American*, April 1997, p. 42; Kimberley A. Strassel, "U.S. Limits on Encryption Exports Create Fans Overseas," *Wall Street Journal*, July 7, 1998, p. B5.

124. Judge Marilyn Patel, quoted in Jared Sandberg, "Judge Rules Encryption Software Is Speech in Case on Export Curbs," *Wall Street Journal*, April 18, 1996, p. B7. The Bernstein case and others continued for several more years, but in 1999 and 2000 two federal appeals courts ruled that the export restrictions violated freedom of speech. One court praised cryptography as a means of protecting privacy.

125. Whitfield Diffie and Susan Landau, *Privacy on the Line: The Politics of Wiretapping and Encryption* (MIT Press, 1998), pp. 107–108.

126. Al Qaeda encrypts files on its computers. U.S. intelligence services learned much about the activities of al Qaeda by decoding encrypted files on computers captured in Afghanistan in 2001. In several other incidents, law enforcement agencies decoded files on computers seized from terrorists.

127. From the Security and Freedom through Encryption Act (SAFE), as amended by the House Intelligence Committee, September 11, 1997.

128. Robert F. Buckhorn Jr., quoted in Dana Canedy, "TV Cameras Seek Criminals in Tampa's Crowds," *New York Times*, July 4, 2001.

129. Based on an actual case described in "Webcams in Public Called Intrusive," *Privacy Journal*, May 2001, p. 3.

130. L. D. Introna, "Workplace Surveillance, Privacy and Distributive Justice," *Proceedings for Computer Ethics: Philosophical Enquiry (CEPE2000)*, Dartmouth College, July 14-16, 2000, pp. 188–199.

BOOKS AND ARTICLES

- Bamford, James. *Body of Secrets: Anatomy of the Ultra-Secret National Security Agency, from the Cold War through the Dawn of a New Century*. Doubleday, 2001.

- Bennett, Colin J. *The Governance of Privacy: Policy Instruments in Global Perspective*. MIT Press, 2006.

- Campbell, Duncan. "Interception Capabilities 2000," www.cyber-rights.org/interception/stoa/interception capabilities_2000.htm. A report on Echelon to the European Parliament.

- Charns, Alexander. *Cloak and Gavel: FBI Wiretaps, Bugs, Informers, and the Supreme Court*. University of Illinois Press, 1992.

- Corn-Revere, Robert. "The Fourth Amendment and the Internet," Testimony before the Subcommittee on the Constitution of the House Committee on the Judiciary, April 6, 2000, www.house.gov/judiciary/corn0406.htm.

- Dorothy E. Denning, *Information Warfare and Security*, Addison-Wesley, 1999.

- Diffie, Whitfield, and Susan Landau. *Privacy on the Line: The Politics of Wiretapping and Encryption*. MIT Press, 1998.

- Harper, Jim. *Identity Crisis: How Identification Is Overused and Misunderstood*. Cato Institute, 2006.

- Klosek, Jacqueline. *Data Privacy in the Information Age*. Quorum Books, 2000. Describes the European Union data privacy directive, privacy laws in many European countries, and major U.S. privacy laws.

- Kusserow, Richard P. "The Government Needs Computer Matching to Root Out Waste and Fraud." *Communications of the ACM*, 27, no. 6 (June 1984), 446–452. An early presentation of the government's side of the computer matching controversy. See the Shattuck entry for the opposing side.

- Lapidus, Edith. *Eavesdropping on Trial*. Hayden Book Co., 1974. Contains history of wiretapping and the relevant sections of the Omnibus Crime Control and Safe Streets Act of 1968.

- National Research Council. *Protecting Electronic Health Information*. National Academy Press, 1997.

- Orwell, George. 1984. Secker and Warburg, 1949. Orwell's dystopian novel in which the totalitarian government controlled people through ubiquitous telescreens. What did he foresee accurately, and what did he miss? (Orwell introduced the term "Big Brother" for the government.)

- Posner, Steve. *Privacy Law and the USA PATRIOT Act*. LexisNexis, 2006.

- Rachels, James. "Why Privacy Is Important," *Philosophy and Public Affairs*, 4, no. 4 (1975). (Appears in several anthologies including Schoeman, *Philosophical Dimensions of Privacy*, listed below, and Johnson and Nissenbaum, *Computers, Ethics & Social Values*, Prentice Hall, 1995.)

- Rosen, Jeffrey. *The Unwanted Gaze: The Destruction of Privacy in America*. Random House, 2000.

- Schneier, Bruce. *Secrets and Lies: Digital Security in a Networked World*. John Wiley & Sons, Inc., 2000.

- Schoeman, Ferdinand David. *Philosophical Dimensions of Privacy: An Anthology*. Cambridge University Press, 1984.

- Shattuck, John. "Computer Matching Is a Serious Threat to Individual Rights." *Communications of the ACM*, 27, no. 6 (June 1984): 537–545. See the Kusserow entry for the government's arguments in favor of computer matching.

- Smith, Robert Ellis. *Ben Franklin's Web Site: Privacy and Curiosity from Plymouth Rock to the Internet*. Privacy Journal, 2004.

- Smith, Robert Ellis. *Privacy Journal*. A monthly newsletter covering news on many aspects of privacy.

- Sullum, Jacob. "Secrets for Sale." *Reason*, April 1992 (www.reason.com/9204/fe.sullum.html). Criticizes many regulatory approaches to solving privacy problems; argues for use of contracts.

- Sykes, Charles. *The End of Privacy: Personal Rights in the Surveillance Society*. St. Martin's Press, 1999.

- Volokh, Eugene. "Freedom of Speech and Information Privacy: The Troubling Implications of a Right to Stop People From Speaking About You." *Stanford Law Review*, 52, no. 1049 (2000). Also at www.law.ucla.edu/faculty/volokh/privacy.htm.

- Westin, Alan F. *Privacy and Freedom*. Atheneum, 1968.

ORGANIZATIONS AND WEB SITES

- Cato Institute: www.cato.org/tech
- Department of Homeland Security: www.dhs.gov
- Electronic Frontier Foundation: www.eff.org
- Electronic Frontiers Australia: www.efa.org.au
- Electronic Privacy Information Center: www.epic.org. See also www.privacy.org, jointly sponsored by EPIC and Privacy International

- The Federal Bureau of Investigation: www.fbi.gov

- Federal Trade Commission: www.ftc.gov

- Junkbusters: www.junkbusters.com

- The Library of Congress site for U.S. laws and bills currently going through Congress: thomas.loc.gov

- The National Security Agency: www.nsa.gov

- Privacilla: www.privacilla.org. Privacy policy from a free-market, pro-technology perspective

- Privacy Commission of Australia: www.privacy.gov.au

- Privacy Commissioner of Canada: www.privcom.gc.ca

- Privacy Forum: www.vortex.com/privacy

- Privacy International: www.privacyinternational.org. Privacy International's page on video surveillance: www.privacy.org/pi/issues/cctv/index.html. Privacy International's Frequently Asked Questions page on identity cards: www.privacy.org/pi/activities/idcard

- Privacy Rights Clearinghouse: www.privacyrights.org

- TRUSTe: www.truste.org

3

FREEDOM OF SPEECH

3.1 Changing Communications Paradigms

> *Congress shall make no law . . . abridging the freedom of speech, or of the press. . . .*
>
> —First Amendment, U.S. Constitution

As we observed in Chapter 1, the Internet brought us extraordinary opportunities for increasing free expression of ideas, easy and inexpensive communication between people of different countries, and extraordinary opportunities for access to many voices and points of view all over the world. But freedom of speech has always been restricted to some degree in the U.S. and to a large degree in many other countries. In this chapter, we examine how principles of freedom of speech from earlier media affect the Internet and how the Internet affects them.* We consider pornography on the Internet, attempts to restrict it, and attempts to restrict access by children; advertising and commerce on the Web; spam (mass, unsolicited e-mail); regulations on political campaigns; and anonymity as a protection for speakers. Some of these forms of speech have long been contentious (pornography, for example) and some are new forms that developed with the Internet (spam and links to Web sites, for example). We describe various incidents and cases and discuss issues they raise. We examine how the global nature of the Web interacts with different laws and levels of freedom of speech in different countries.

3.1.1 REGULATING COMMUNICATIONS MEDIA

It is by now almost a cliché to say that the Internet lets us all be publishers. We do not need expensive printing presses or complex distribution systems. We need only a computer and a modem—or just a cell phone. Any business, organization, or individual can set up a Web site. We can "publish" whatever we wish; it is available for anyone who chooses to read it. In 1994, shortly before the Web was widely used, Mike Godwin, then an attorney with the Electronic Frontier Foundation, described the dramatic change brought about by computer communications:

> It is a medium far different from the telephone, which is only a one-to-one medium, ill-suited for reaching large numbers of people. It is a medium far different from the newspaper or TV station, which are one-to-many media, ill-suited for feedback from the audience. For the first time in history, we have a many-to-many medium, in which you don't have to be rich to have access, and in which you don't have to win the approval of an editor or publisher to speak your mind. Usenet† and the Internet, as part of this new

---

*Although some of our discussion is in the context of the U.S. Constitution's First Amendment, the arguments and principles about the right to freedom of speech apply more widely.

†An early (pre-Web) collection of Internet discussion groups.

medium, hold the promise of guaranteeing, for the first time in history, that the First Amendment's protection of freedom of the press means as much to each individual as it does to Time Warner, or to Gannett, or to the *New York Times*.[1]

Individuals took advantage of that promise. As just one indication, the number of blogs passed 50 million by 2006. Some are as widely read and as influential as traditional newspapers. However, while computer communications technologies *might* guarantee freedom of speech and of the press for all of us, the guarantee is not certain.

Telephone, movies, radio, television, cable, satellites, and, of course, the Internet did not exist when the Constitution was written. Freedom of the press applied to publishers who printed newspapers and books and to "the lonely pamphleteer" who printed and distributed pamphlets expressing unconventional ideas. One might think the First Amendment should apply to each new communications technology according to its spirit and intention: to protect our freedom to say what we wish. Politically powerful people, however, continually try to restrict speech that threatens them. From the Alien and Sedition Acts of 1798 to regulation of Political Action Committees, such laws have been used against newspaper editors who disagreed with the political party in power and against ad hoc groups of people speaking out on issues.

Attempts to restrict freedom of speech and of the press flourish with new technologies. Law professor Eric M. Freedman sums up: "Historical experience—with the printing press, secular dramatic troupes, photographs, movies, rock music, broadcasting, sexually explicit telephone services, video games, and other media—shows that each new medium is viewed at first by governments as uniquely threatening, because it is uniquely influential, and therefore a uniquely appropriate target of censorship."[2]

In this section, we introduce the traditional three-part framework for First Amendment protection and government regulation of communications media. As we will see, modern communications technology and the Internet require that the framework be updated. The three categories are

* Print media (newspapers, books, magazines, pamphlets)

* Broadcast (television, radio)

* Common carriers (telephone, telegraph, and the postal system)

The first category has the strongest First Amendment protection. Although books have been banned in the U.S. and people were arrested for publishing information on certain topics such as contraception, the trend has been toward fewer government restraints on the printed word.

Television and radio are similar to newspapers in their role of providing news and entertainment, but the government regulates both the structure of the broadcasting industry and the content of programs. The government grants broadcasting licenses. Licensees must meet government standards of merit—a requirement that would not be tolerated for publishers because of the obvious threat to freedom of expression. The government has used threats of license revocation to get stations to cancel sexually oriented talk shows or to censor them. Cigarette ads are legal in magazines, but banned from radio, television, and all electronic media under the control of the Federal Communications Commission (FCC). Some words may appear in print but you must not speak them on the radio. The federal government frequently proposes requirements to reduce violence on television or increase programming for children, but the government cannot impose such requirements on print publishers. In recent years, the FCC imposed heavy fines on radio and television broadcast companies and threatened the broadcast of a "9/11" documentary because of profanity by firefighters. Whether you favor or oppose particular regulations, the point is that the government has more control over television and radio content than it has over communication methods that existed at the time the Bill of Rights was written. The main argument used to deny full First Amendment protection to broadcasters was scarcity of broadcast frequencies. There were only a handful of television channels and few radio frequencies in the early days of broadcasting. In exchange for the "monopoly" privilege of using the scarce, publicly owned spectrum, broadcasters were tightly regulated. With cable, satellites, hundreds of channels, and competition from the Internet, the argument based on scarcity and monopoly is irrelevant now, but the precedent of government control remains. A second argument, still used to justify government-imposed restrictions on content, is that broadcast material comes into the home and is difficult to keep from children.

Common carriers provide a medium of communication (not content) and must make their service available to everyone. In some cases, as with telephone service, the government requires them to provide "universal access" (i.e., to subsidize service for people with low incomes). Based on the argument that common carriers are a monopoly, the law prohibits them from controlling the content of material that passes through their system. Telephone companies were prohibited from providing content or information services on the grounds that they might discriminate against competing content providers who must also use their telephone lines. Common carriers had no control over content, so they had no responsibility for illegal content passing through.

Beginning in the 1980s computer bulletin board systems (BBS), commercial services like CompuServe, Prodigy, and America Online (AOL), and ultimately the World Wide Web became major arenas for distribution of news, information, and opinion. Because of the immense flexibility of computer communications systems, they do not fit neatly into the publishing, broadcasting, and common carriage paradigms. Cable television strained these categories previously. In commenting on a law requiring cable stations to carry certain broadcasts, the Supreme Court said cable operators have more freedom of speech than television and radio broadcasters, but less than print publishers.[3] But the Web does not fit between the existing categories any better than it fits within them. It has similarities to all three, and, in addition, to bookstores, libraries, and rented meeting rooms—all of which the law treats differently.

As new technologies blurred the technical boundaries between cable, telephone, computer networks, and content providers, the law began to adapt. The

Telecommunications Act of 1996 changed the regulatory structure. It removed many artificial legal divisions of service areas and many restrictions on services that telecommunications companies may provide. It also significantly clarified the question of liability of Internet service providers (ISPs) and other online service providers for content posted by third parties such as members and subscribers. Print publishers and broadcasters are legally liable for content they publish or broadcast. They can be sued for libel and copyright infringement, for example. They are legally responsible for obscene material in their products. Before passage of the Telecommunications Act, several people brought suits against BBS operators, ISPs, AOL, and other service providers for content put on their systems by others. They argued that a BBS or service like AOL provided content and was therefore not a common carrier, immune from suits for content. Similarly, service providers and content hosts might have faced criminal charges if a member posted illegal content (obscene material, for example). To protect themselves from liability, service providers would likely have erred on the side of caution and eliminated much legal content. The Telecommunications Act stated that "No provider or user of an interactive computer service shall be treated as the publisher or speaker of any information provided by another information content provider."[4]*

In 1996 the main parts of the first major Internet censorship law, the Communications Decency Act (CDA),† were ruled unconstitutional. In this decision, a federal judge commented that "as the most participatory form of mass speech yet developed, the Internet deserves the highest protection from government intrusion."[5] Will the Internet get as much protection as print media? Efforts to censor it continue. We investigate arguments about, and the impacts of, censorship and other restrictive laws in Section 3.2. In addition, we will see in Section 3.2.4 that many innovative individuals and entrepreneurs who tried to publish information, advertise products, and provide services on the Web encountered legal problems (and sometimes fines), not because of explicit censorship laws, but because of long-standing laws that restricted commerce to benefit powerful organizations, businesses, and governments. In several cases, these confrontations between new technology and old laws resulted in increased freedom.

3.1.2 FREE-SPEECH PRINCIPLES

As we proceed with our discussion of free-speech issues, it is helpful to remember several important points.

The First Amendment was written precisely for offensive and/or controversial speech and ideas. There is no need to protect speech and publication that no one objects to. The First Amendment covers spoken and written words, pictures, art, and other forms of

---

*Service providers remain at risk in many countries. For example, in 2004 the head of eBay in India was arrested because someone sold pornographic videos on eBay's Indian site. The video itself did not appear on the site, and the seller violated company policy by selling them.

†Passed as Title V of the Telecommunications Act.

expression of ideas and opinions. (It includes, for example, wearing armbands to express support of a political cause.)

The First Amendment is a restriction on the power of government, not individuals or private businesses. Publishers do not have to publish material they consider offensive, poorly written, or unlikely to appeal to their customers for any reason. Rejection or editing by a publisher is not a violation of a writer's First Amendment rights. Web sites, search engine companies, and magazines may decline specific advertisements if they so choose. That does not violate the advertiser's freedom of speech.

Over the course of many years and many cases, the Supreme Court has developed principles and guidelines about protected expression.* When a government action or law causes people to avoid legal speech and publication out of fear of prosecution—perhaps because a law is vague—the action or law is said to have a "chilling effect" on First Amendment rights. Courts generally rule that laws with a significant chilling effect are unconstitutional. Advocating illegal acts is (usually) legal; a listener has the opportunity and responsibility to weigh the arguments and decide whether or not to commit the illegal act. The First Amendment does not protect libel (making false and damaging statements) and direct, specific threats. Inciting violence, in certain circumstances, is illegal. Although the First Amendment makes no distinctions among categories of speech, the courts have had a tradition of treating advertising as "second class" speech and allowing restrictions that would not be acceptable for other kinds of speech. However, a large number of cases in recent years have gone against that trend. Courts have begun to rule that restrictions on truthful advertising do indeed violate the First Amendment.[6] Many court decisions have protected anonymous speech, but there are serious attempts to limit or prohibit anonymity on the Internet.

There is a censorship issue when the government owns or substantially subsidizes communications systems or networks (or controversial services). For example, in the 1980s federally subsidized family planning clinics were not permitted to discuss abortion. In the past, the government has made it illegal to send information through the mail that the First Amendment otherwise protects. A federal agency that provides funds for public radio stations rejected the application of a university because it broadcasts one hour a week of religious programming. In Section 3.2.2, we will see that Congress used its funding power to require censorship of the Internet in public libraries and schools. No matter what side of these issues you are on, no matter how the policy changes with different presidents or Congresses, the point is that, in many circumstances, when the government pays, it can choose to restrict speech that would otherwise be constitutionally protected.

The issues in this chapter have far-reaching implications for freedom. As Ithiel de Sola Pool wrote, in his important book *Technologies of Freedom*,

> Networked computers will be the printing presses of the twenty-first century. If
> they are not free of public [i.e., government] control, the continued application

---

*The specific laws, court decisions, and guidelines are complex in some cases. The discussion here is general and simplified.

of constitutional immunities to nonelectronic mechanical presses, lecture halls, and man-carried sheets of paper may become no more than a quaint archaism.

The onus is on us to determine whether free societies in the twenty-first century will conduct electronic communication under the conditions of freedom established for the domain of print through centuries of struggle, or whether that great achievement will become lost in a confusion about new technologies.[7]

3.2 Controlling Offensive Speech

I disapprove of what you say, but I will defend to the death your right to say it.

—Voltaire's biographer, S. G. Tallentyre (Evelyn Beatrice Hall), describing Voltaire's view of freedom of speech[8]

3.2.1 OFFENSIVE SPEECH: WHAT IS IT? WHAT IS ILLEGAL?

What is offensive speech? What should the law prohibit or restrict on the Web? The answer depends on who you are. It could be political or religious speech, pornography, racial or sexual slurs, Nazi materials, libelous statements, abortion information, anti-abortion information, advertising of alcoholic beverages, advertising in general, depictions of violence, discussion of suicide, or information about how to build bombs. There are vehement advocates for banning each of these—and more. The state of Georgia tried to ban pictures of marijuana from the Internet. A doctor argued for regulating medical discussion on the Net so that people would not get bad advice. The Chinese government restricts reporting of emergencies (such as major accidents or disasters) and how the government handles them. The French government approved a law banning anyone except professional journalists from recording or distributing video of acts of violence.

Many efforts to censor the Internet in the U.S., including several laws passed by Congress, focus on pornographic or sexually explicit material, so we use pornography as the first example. Many of the same principles apply to efforts to censor other kinds of material. In Section 3.2.5 we look at ethical considerations about posting legal, but in some way dangerous or sensitive, content on the Web.

The Internet began as a forum for research and scientific discussion, so the rapid proliferation of pornography shocked some people. It is not, however, a surprising development. The same kind of material was already available in adult magazines, bookstores, and movie theaters. As a writer for *Wired* contends, sexual material quickly invades all new technologies and art forms.[9] He points out that, from cave paintings

STRAINING OLD LEGAL STANDARDS

On the Internet, communities have no physical locations. Instead, they are defined by the people who choose to associate in cyberspace because of common interests. The definition of "community" proved critical in an early Internet case. A couple in California operated a computer BBS called Amateur Action that made sexually explicit images available to members. Legal observers generally agreed that the Amateur Action BBS operators would not be found guilty of a crime in California. A postal inspector in Memphis, Tennessee, working with a U.S. attorney there, became a member of the BBS (the only member in Tennessee[10]) and downloaded sexually explicit images in Memphis. The couple, who lived and worked in California, were prosecuted in Tennessee and found guilty in 1994 of distributing obscenity under the local community standards. Both received jail sentences. A spokesman for the American Civil Liberties Union (ACLU) commented that prosecutions like this one meant that "nothing can be put on the Internet that is more racy than would be tolerated in the most conservative community in the U.S."[11] For this reason, some courts have recognized that "community standards" is no longer an appropriate tool for determining what is acceptable material.

The Net also changed the meaning of "distribution." Did the BBS operators send obscene files to Tennessee? BBSs were accessed through the telephone system. Anyone, from anywhere, could call in if they chose. The postal inspector in Tennessee initiated the telephone call to the BBS and initiated the transfer of the files. He selected and downloaded them. Critics of the prosecution of the BBS operators argued that it is as if the postal inspector went to California, bought pornographic pictures, and brought them home to Memphis—then had the seller prosecuted under Memphis community standards.[12]

to frescos in Pompeii to stone carvings at Angkor Wat, erotica have flourished. The printing press produced Bibles and porn. Photography produced *Playboy*. Many of the first videocassettes were pornographic. The National Research Council estimated that there are roughly 400,000 subscription Web sites providing adult entertainment.[13] Whether all this is good or bad—whether it is a natural part of human nature or a sign of degeneracy and evil, whether we should tolerate it or stamp it out—are moral and political issues beyond the scope of this book. People debate pornography endlessly. In addressing the issue of pornography and of other kinds of speech that offend people, we try to focus specifically on new problems and issues related to computer systems and cyberspace.

What was already illegal?

In 1973, the Supreme Court, in *Miller v. California*, established a three-part guideline for determining whether material is obscene under the law. The First Amendment does not protect obscene material. The criteria are that (1) it depicts sexual (or excretory) acts whose depiction is specifically prohibited by state law, (2) it depicts these acts in a patently offensive manner, appealing to prurient interest as judged by a reasonable person using community standards, and (3) it has no serious literary, artistic, social, political, or scientific value. The second point—the application of community standards—was a compromise intended to avoid the problem of setting a national standard of obscenity in so large and diverse a country. Thus, small conservative or religious towns could restrict pornography to a greater extent than cosmopolitan urban areas.

Child pornography includes pictures or movies of actual minors (children under 18) in sexual positions or engaged in sexual acts. It has long been illegal to create, possess, or distribute child pornography, primarily because its production is considered abuse of the actual children, not because of the impact of the content on a viewer. It is not automatically illegal to make or distribute sexually explicit movies or photos in which an adult actor plays a minor. In other words, child pornography laws prohibit using, abusing, and exploiting children, not portraying them. (Similarly, crime reports or crime fiction describing a rape of a child, for example, would not generally be illegal.) In 1996 Congress passed the Child Pornography Prevention Act to extend the law against child pornography to include "virtual" children, that is computer-generated images that appear to be minors, as well as other images where real adults appear to be minors. The Supreme Court ruled in 2002 that the law violated the First Amendment. Justice Anthony Kennedy commented that the Act "proscribes the visual depiction of an idea—that of teenagers engaging in sexual activity—that is a fact of modern society and has been a theme in art and literature throughout the ages."[14]

3.2.2 INTERNET CENSORSHIP LAWS AND ALTERNATIVES

> *Our sole intent is to make the Internet safer for our youth.*
>
> —Department of Justice spokesman, commenting
> on the demand for millions of user search terms from Google, 2006

The Communications Decency Act

In the 1990s as more nontechnical people began using the Internet, a variety of religious organizations, antipornography groups, and others began a campaign to pass federal legislation to censor the Net. In 1995 the Federal Bureau of Investigation (FBI) reported that "utilization of online services or bulletin-board systems is rapidly becoming one of the most prevalent techniques for individuals to share pornographic pictures of minors, as well as to identify and recruit children into sexually illicit relationships."[15] Popular news magazines shocked the public with dramatic cover stories on "Cyberporn." Increasing publicity and political pressure led Congress to pass the Communications Decency Act of 1996 (CDA).[16] In the Communications Decency Act and the censorship laws that followed, Congress attempted to avoid an obvious conflict with the First Amendment by focusing on children. It provided that anyone who made available to anyone under 18 any communication that is obscene or indecent would be subject to a fine of $100,000 and two years in prison. Before looking at the arguments about the CDA and the reasons it was found unconstitutional, we consider how the Internet changed children's access to inappropriate material.

How technology created new threats to children

The distinctions between categories such as erotica, art, and pornography are not always clear, and different people have very different personal standards. But there is no doubt that there is material on the Web that most people would consider inappropriate for children. Many parents do not want their children to view hate material or sites promoting racism, anti-Semitism, and sexism. Some parents do not want their children to see violence on the Web in stories, images, games, and video. People discuss sexual activity, of conventional and unconventional sorts, including pedophilia, in graphic detail in cyberspace. Child molesters can easily communicate with children on the Web. There is much on the Web that is extremely offensive to adults. It is not surprising that some people see the Internet as a scary place for children.

Cyberspace has changed the risks to children. If a young child tried to buy a ticket for an X-rated movie or to buy an adult magazine, a cashier would see the child and refuse (at least, most of the time). On the Web, a child can access pornography without an adult observer. The Web site operator or e-mailer supplying the material does not see that the customer is a child.

In a supermarket or a playground, a parent or other observer might see a "stranger" talking to a child. A potential child molester online is not visible. The anonymity of the Net makes it easier for people to prey on children. (On the other hand, the anonymity also makes it easier for an undercover officer to pretend to be a 12-year-old girl online.)

In the early days of the Internet, one had to know how to find pornography and invoke special software to view it. Young children were not likely to come upon pornography by accident. Search engines and Web browsers changed that. Porn arrives in e-mail, and porn sites turn up in results found by search engines for innocent topics. A click displays images and video.

Schools and libraries used to be relatively safe havens from pornography and violent or hateful materials. When schools and libraries connected to the Internet, undesirable material entered. Indeed, the home used to be a safe haven from such material. Parents could relax when a child was playing in his or her bedroom. Once they had an Internet connection, they might wonder what the child is looking at or with whom he or she is chatting. The change in access by children to pornography and access to children by pornographers and pedophiles was a quick and frightening change.

Why the CDA is unconstitutional

The worst of the material threatening children is already illegal in any medium. It is attempts to protect children by reducing access to adult material by adults that generate the most controversy. Opponents of the CDA, including librarians, publishers, Internet companies, and civil liberties groups, saw it as a profound threat to freedom of expression. A broad collection of organizations, businesses, and individuals sued to block it. Two federal courts and the Supreme Court (in 1997) ruled unanimously, in *American Civil Liberties Union et al. v. Janet Reno*, that the censorship provisions of the CDA were unconstitutional. The courts made strong statements about the importance of protecting freedom of expression in general and on the Internet. The decisions against the CDA established that "the Internet deserves the highest protection from government intrusion." The courts accepted two main arguments against the CDA: that it was too vague and broad and that it did not use the least restrictive means of accomplishing the goal of protecting children. We elaborate on these arguments.

The CDA referred to "obscene, lewd, lascivious, filthy, or indecent" material. Some of these terms have legal definitions; some are vague. An enthusiastic love letter or an adult joke sent by e-mail might qualify. Opponents of the CDA gave examples of information that is legal in print but might be cause for prosecution if available online: the Bible, some of Shakespeare's plays, and serious discussions of sexual behavior and health problems like AIDS. AOL's earlier action in response to government pressure to prohibit obscene or vulgar language illustrates the difficulty in determining what to censor. AOL included the word "breast" in its list of words banned from member profiles. A week later the ban was reversed after protest, ridicule, and outrage from breast cancer patients.[17] Supporters of the CDA argued that this was overreaction. No one would be prosecuted, they said, for transmitting Shakespeare or the Bible online or for discussing health problems online. The lack of clear standards, however, can lead to uneven and unfair prosecutions. The uncertainty about potential prosecution could have a chilling effect on those who provide information for adults that might not be suitable for children.

It is sometimes difficult to design a law that keeps inappropriate material from children while allowing access for adults. The Supreme Court ruled on this problem in *Butler v. Michigan*, a significant 1957 case striking down a Michigan law that made it illegal to sell material that might be damaging to children. Justice Frankfurter wrote that the state must not "reduce the adult population of Michigan to reading only what is fit for children."[18] The CDA restricted indecent material accessible by children, but a child can access almost anything on the Net. Thus, opponents said, it would have violated Justice Frankfurter's dictum, not just in Michigan, but throughout the country.

When the government is pursuing a legitimate goal that might infringe on free speech (in this case, the protection of children), it must use the least restrictive means of accomplishing the goal. The courts found that the then newly developing filtering software was less restrictive and more desirable than censorship. The judges also commented, "The

- ❖ Distinguish speech from action. Advocating illegal acts is (usually) legal.

- ❖ Laws must not chill expression of legal speech.

- ❖ Do not reduce adults to reading only what is fit for children.

- ❖ Solve speech problems by least restrictive means.

Figure 3.1 Freedom of Speech Guidelines

government can continue to protect children from pornography on the Internet through vigorous enforcement of existing laws criminalizing obscenity and child pornography."[19]

Figure 3.1 summarizes principles courts use to help determine if a censorship law is constitutional.

The Child Online Protection Act

Congress tried again with the Child Online Protection Act (COPA) passed in 1998. This law was more limited than the CDA. COPA made it a federal crime for commercial Web sites to make available to minors material "harmful to minors" as judged by community standards. Offenses would be punishable by a $50,000 fine and six months in jail. Sites with potentially "harmful" material would have to get proof of age from site visitors. Once again, First Amendment supporters argued that the law was too broad and would threaten art, news, and health sites.

Another provision of COPA set up the Child Online Protection Commission to study and report on ways to protect children. The commission included representatives from family organizations, government, universities, and industry. Its report, issued in 2000, said that most of the material of serious concern on the Internet was already illegal. It encouraged educational efforts and the use of technological protections (including filtering software). It encouraged improvements in efforts to enforce existing law, but proposed no new laws.[20]

Several courts have ruled several times that the censorship provisions of the law are unconstitutional. The government repeatedly appealed. The courts noted that because the Web is accessible everywhere, the community-standards provision would restrict the entire country to the standards of the most conservative community. The courts said COPA restricts access to a substantial amount of online speech that is lawful for adults, and COPA's requirements that adults provide identification to view material not appropriate for minors would have an unconstitutional chilling effect on free speech. The Supreme Court ruled that the federal government had not shown that COPA is necessary to protect children, pointing out that the Commission on Child Online Protection concluded that a less restrictive means, filtering, was superior to COPA. In 2006 the government collected data from Google (with a subpoena) to try to determine how frequently inappropriate sites turn up in Web searches and how well filters screen them out. The evidence did not convince U.S. District Court Judge Lowell Reed Jr. who issued a permanent injunction against enforcement of COPA in 2007. The government planned another appeal.

The trend of judicial decisions so far is to give the Internet First Amendment protection similar to that of print media, that is, the highest degree of protection. Recall that the only remaining original argument for the government's regulation and censorship of television and radio is that broadcast material comes into the home and is more difficult to keep from children than print media. The Internet clearly also comes into the home and is difficult to keep from children. If the Internet gains strong First Amendment protection, will censorship of radio and television be eliminated? Or will the Internet replace broadcast media to such an extent that regulation and censorship of broadcast becomes irrelevant?

> *Perhaps we do the minors of this country harm if First Amendment protections, which they will with age inherit fully, are chipped away in the name of their protection.*
>
> —Judge Lowell A. Reed Jr. when granting an injunction against COPA

The quality of filters

Software filters work in a variety of ways. They can block sites with specific words, phrases, or images. They can block sites according to various rating systems. They can contain long lists of specific sites to block. Parents can choose categories to filter (e.g., sex or violence), add their own list of banned sites, and review a log of the sites their child visits. Some companies that make filters hire people to spend hours surfing the Web, reviewing sites, and classifying them according to their level of violence, sexually explicit material, and so on. Filters can be updated frequently.[21]

It should be obvious that filters cannot do a perfect job. In fact, at first, many did a very poor job. They screen out both too much and too little. Figure 3.2 lists Web pages blocked by some filters. Clearly, some contain political discussion and educational material. Subjectivity and different personal values influence decisions about what is too sexual or too violent or too critical of a religion, what medical information is appropriate for children of what age, what is acceptable to say about homosexuality, and so on. Various studies show that filters block numerous innocent, legal sites for no apparent reason. A Kaiser Family Foundation study found that filters blocked 24% of health sites. The editor of an online technology law journal intentionally misspells words like "sex" and "pornography" in his journal's articles so that filters will not block his subscribers from receiving their copies.[22]

On the other hand, filters cannot block all Web pages with pornography or other material that some parents or legislators want to exclude. New sites appear regularly. Some objectionable material may be buried in documents or low-level Web pages that are not

- Sites about Middlesex and Essex
- Pages at sites of advocacy organizations such as the American Civil Liberties Union, the Electronic Privacy Information Center, and the Electronic Frontier Foundation
- The court decision about the Communications Decency Act
- All student organizations at Carnegie Mellon University
- A page with Robert Frost's poem "Stopping by Woods on a Snowy Evening" (with the lines "My little horse must think it queer/to stop without a farmhouse near")
- The Beaver College site (The college changed its name to Arcadia University in 2001, in part because some filters blocked its Web site.)
- The National Institutes of Health's Spanish-language site about diabetes (The word "hora," meaning "hour," appears often on the site. It refers to a prostitute in Swedish.)
- Sites with information about sex education, breast cancer, feminism, or gay and lesbian rights
- The home page of Yale University's biology department
- A wrestling site and a motorcycle sport magazine site
- The Web site of a candidate for Congress containing statements about abortion and gun control
- A map of Disney World (I don't know why.)
- The Heritage Foundation (a conservative think tank) and a Quaker site

Figure 3.2 Filtering Examples

obvious to a person reviewing the site. Files transferred by some file-sharing systems are not filtered. The Kaiser Family Foundation study found that filters blocked only 91% of pornographic sites.

The weaknesses of filters, especially when they were first being developed, should not be a big surprise. Filters improved with time, but it is not possible to completely eliminate errors and subjectivity about what to block. None of the solutions we describe in this book for problems generated by new technologies are perfect. They have strengths and weaknesses and are useful in some circumstances and not others. Parents (or administrators of private schools) can carefully review the characteristics of competing products and make a choice about whether to use one. The weaknesses, however—particularly the blocking of legal material—do present a free-speech issue when legislators mandate filters. And that is what the next major law, the Children's Internet Protection Act (CIPA), did. As it applies to libraries (and schools), we describe problems raised by the Internet in libraries before the Supreme Court ruled on CIPA in 2003.

Problems in libraries

As soon as Internet terminals were installed in public libraries, some people used the terminals to look at X-rated pictures, within view of children or other library users who found them offensive. Some people tied up terminals for hours viewing such material while others waited to use the terminals. Children accessed adult sexual material. Children and adults accessed extremist political sites and racist and Nazi material. All of this activity caused problems for library staff.

Librarians tried to satisfy library users, parents, community organizations, civil libertarians, and their own Library Bill of Rights (which opposes restricting access to library materials because of age). Libraries around the country responded in different ways. Some installed polarizing filters on terminals or built walls around terminals so that the screens were visible only from directly in front (both to protect the privacy of the user and to shield other users and employees from material they find objectionable). Most set time limits on use of terminals. Some librarians asked patrons to stop viewing pornography, just as they would ask someone to stop making noise. Some revoked borrowing privileges of people viewing pornography. Some installed filtering software on all terminals, some on only terminals in the children's section. Some required parental supervision for children using the Internet, and some required written parental permission.

The efforts of the librarians did not prevent lawsuits. In a California city whose library did not use filtering software, a 12-year-old boy downloaded pornographic images and printed copies for his friends. His mother sued, arguing that the library harmed her son by exposing him to pornography. (A judge dismissed this suit.) The trustees of a Virginia county library adopted a policy requiring filters on all terminals. A group of citizens sued, arguing that the policy treated them like children and violated their First Amendment rights. They won. As in the cases of other Internet censorship laws, the judge made strong statements supporting the application of the First Amendment. She rejected the filtering policy because it was not necessary to accomplish a compelling government purpose, it was too broad, and it restricted access by adults to legal material.[23]

Library staff members in Minneapolis and Chicago filed complaints with the federal Equal Employment Opportunity Commission (EEOC) arguing that they were subjected to a "hostile work environment" in unfiltered libraries because they were forced to view offensive material on the screens of library users and pornographic printouts left on library printers. The EEOC agreed with the staff in the Minneapolis case, a reminder of the frequent conflict between sexual harassment laws and freedom of speech.

Voters and legislators showed no consistency. Voters in a Michigan town, for example, rejected a proposition to require filters in their libraries. In the same month, the Utah state senate unanimously passed a bill to deny funding for libraries unless they installed filters.[24]

The Children's Internet Protection Act

Pressure continued from organizations like the Family Research Council[25] for laws to prevent minors from obtaining sexually explicit material on the Internet. After the first rejection of COPA by a federal appeals court (in 2000), advocates of censorship laws tried a different approach. That year, Congress passed CIPA. The authors of CIPA attempted to avoid the courts' criticisms of the CDA and COPA by using the federal government's funding power. CIPA requires that schools and libraries that participate in certain federal programs (receiving federal money for technology) install filtering software on all Internet terminals to block access to sites with child pornography, obscene material, and material "harmful to minors." Of course, many schools and libraries rely on those funds. Civil liberties organizations and the American Library Association sued to block CIPA.[26] The Supreme Court ruled in 2003 that CIPA does not violate the First Amendment. CIPA does not require the use of filters. It does not impose jail or fines on people who provide content on the Internet. It sets a condition for receipt of certain federal funds. Courts often accept such conditions. The court made it clear that if an adult asks a librarian to disable the filter on a library Internet terminal the adult is using, the librarian must do so.

Alternatives to censorship

Are new restrictions on Internet content needed to protect children (and to shield adults from material that is offensive to them)? Are there other solutions that do not threaten to diminish free discussion of serious subjects or deny sexually explicit material to adults who want it? As we have seen for many problems, there are a variety of solutions based on the market, technology, responsibility, and education, as well as on enforcement of existing laws. We already noted the availability of filters as a major argument against censorship laws. The development of software filters to block access to inappropriate material on the Internet is an example of a quick market response to a new problem. Some filtering systems are now available for free. Voluntary use of filtering systems is an obvious tool for protecting children. By 2006 more than half of families with teenagers used filters on their computers. We briefly describe a variety of other approaches besides censorship laws.

Wireless carriers, such as Verizon and Cingular, set strict "decency" standards for companies providing content for their networks. Their rules are detailed and stricter than what the government can prohibit.[27]

Commercial services, online communities, and social-networking sites develop policies to protect members. A few remedies include expelling subscribers who post or e-mail material banned by law or the site's policies, removing offensive material, and aiding law enforcement with investigations of child pornography or attempts to meet and molest children. MySpace began developing technology to keep track of members who post pictures, to help trace anyone who posts child pornography. In response to market demand, companies offer online services and Web sites targeted to families and children. Some allow subscribers to lock children out of certain areas. Parents can set up accounts for

TALKING ABOUT BOMBS—OR FARMING

Within a few weeks of the bombing of the Oklahoma City federal building in 1995, the Senate's terrorism and technology subcommittee held hearings on "The Availability of Bomb Making Information on the Internet." There are many similarities between the controversy about bomb-making information on the Net and the controversy about pornography. As with pornography, bomb-making information is already widely available in traditional media, protected by the First Amendment. It also has legitimate uses. Information about how to make bombs can be found in the *Encyclopedia Britannica* (which describes how to make an ammonium nitrate and fuel oil bomb, the kind reportedly used in Oklahoma City) and in books in libraries and bookstores. Such information, again including the ammonium nitrate and fuel oil bomb, is available to the public in a booklet called the "Blaster's Handbook"—published by the U.S. Department of Agriculture. Farmers use explosives to remove tree stumps.[28]

Arguing to censor information about bombs on the Internet, Senator Dianne Feinstein said, "there is a difference between free speech and teaching someone to kill."[29] Arguing against censorship, a former U.S. attorney said that "information-plus," (i.e., information used in the commission of a criminal act) is what the law should regulate. Senator Patrick Leahy emphasized that it is "harmful and dangerous *conduct*, not speech, that justifies adverse legal consequences." This was already, in essence, established legal principle outside of cyberspace. There are, of course, existing laws against using bombs to kill people or destroy property and laws against making bombs or conspiring to make them for such purposes.

Because of the conflict with the First Amendment, there was no federal law against bomb information on the Internet until 1999—after the shootings at Columbine High School in Littleton, Colorado. The two students who killed several others were reported to have used information obtained on the Internet to make bombs they carried. Congress passed a law mandating 20 years in prison for anyone who distributes bomb-making information knowing or intending that it will be used to commit a crime. Although there have been several incidents since then in which young people have built and used bombs made with information from the Internet, no one has been tried under this law. It is difficult to determine (and prove) what a person posting the information knows and intends about its uses. Much of the information about bombs is posted by people who do not intend it to be used for a crime.[30]

their children without e-mail or set up a specified list of addresses from which e-mail will be accepted. The video game industry developed a rating system that provides an indication for parents about the amount of sex, profanity, and violence in a game.[31] Some online game sites restrict their offerings to nonviolent games and advertise that policy. Many online services distribute information with tips on how to control what children can view. The Web sites of the FBI and organizations such as the National Center for Missing and Exploited Children[32] provide information about risks to children and guidelines for reducing them. (One simple recommendation is to place the computer in the living room or family room where a parent can easily observe a child using it.)

Child pornography is illegal, and it is illegal to lure children into sexual acts. Federal agents regularly make arrests for these crimes where suspects use e-mail, chat rooms, and social-networking sites. Federal agents use surveillance, court orders to read e-mail (as the Electronic Communications Privacy Act requires), search warrants, sting operations, and undercover investigations to build their cases and make the arrests.

Parents have a responsibility to supervise their children and to teach them how to deal with inappropriate material and threats. Parents cannot always be present, of course, nor should they be watching over older children constantly, but good communication and instruction in expected behavior can avoid many problems.

> *Two-point-five million use America Online. That's like a city. Parents wouldn't let their kids go wandering in a city of 2.5 million people without them, or without knowing what they're going to be doing.*
>
> —Pam McGraw, America Online[33]
> (The number of AOL members later grew to more than 30 million.)

3.2.3 SPAM

What is the problem?

We loosely describe spam as unsolicited bulk e-mail.* Details of a precise definition, depending on how one defines "bulk" and "unsolicited," can be critical to discussions about how to deal with spam, especially when we consider laws to restrict it.

Spam has infuriated users of the Internet since the mid-1990s. It invaded cell phones and Instant Messaging in the early 2000s. Most, but not all, spam is commercial advertising. Spam developed because e-mail is extremely cheap compared to printed direct-mail advertising. Some businesses and organizations compile or buy huge lists of e-mail addresses and send their unsolicited messages. Some build lists by using automated software that surfs the Web and collects anything that looks like an e-mail address.

---

*Spam is the name of a spiced lunch-meat product sold in cans by Hormel Foods. The use of the word in the context of e-mail comes from a Monty Python skit in which some characters repeatedly shouted "Spam, spam, spam," drowning out other conversation.

Spam angers people because of both the content and the way it is sent. Content can be ordinary commercial advertising, political advertising, solicitations for funds from nonprofit organizations, pornography and advertisements for it, fraudulent "get rich quick" schemes, and scams selling fake or nonexistent products. Topics come in waves, with ads for Viagra, ads for low mortgage rates, promotions for various stocks, and Nigerian refugees who need help getting $30,000,000 out of Africa. (We consider intentionally fraudulent scams involving spam in Section 5.3.) Some spammers disguise their e-mail return address so that bounced mail from closed or invalid accounts does not bother them. ISPs filter out e-mail from known spammers, so many disguise their return address and use other schemes to avoid filters.

How much spam travels through the Internet? The first case that created an antispam furor involved advertising messages sent by a law firm to 6,000 bulletin boards or news groups in 1994. At that time, any advertising or postings not directly related to the topic of the group raised the ire of Net users. Within a few years, as e-mail use grew, one notorious spammer alone was estimated to be sending 25 million e-mails per day. In 2002 Hotmail, with 110 million members, received more than one billion spam e-mails per day. The number of spam messages filtered out by AOL peaked at about 2.4 billion per day. An antispam expert reported a rate of roughly 30 billion spam messages per day worldwide in 2006.[34]

Cases and free-speech issues

In 1996 about half of the e-mail received at AOL was spam, and a lot of it came from an e-mail advertising service called Cyber Promotions. AOL installed filters to block mail from Cyber Promotions. Cyber Promotions obtained an injunction against AOL's use of filters, claiming AOL violated its First Amendment rights. Thus began the battle over the legal status of spam.

Cyber Promotions' case was weak, and the injunction was soon removed. Why did AOL have the right to block incoming spam? The spam used AOL's computers, imposing a cost on AOL. AOL's property rights allow it to decide what it accepts on its system. AOL is a membership organization; it can implement policies to provide the kind of environment it believes its members want. Finally, AOL is a private company, not a government institution. The First Amendment prohibits government from restricting freedom of speech. On the other side, some civil liberties organizations were uneasy about allowing AOL to filter e-mail because AOL decided what e-mail to block from its members. They argued that because AOL is large, it is a lot like the post office, and it should not be allowed to block any mail.

Over the next few years, AOL filed several lawsuits and sought injunctions to stop spammers from sending unsolicited bulk mailings to members. Notice the subtle shift: Cyber Promotions sought an injunction to stop AOL from filtering out its e-mail. AOL sought injunctions to stop spammers from sending e-mail. Filters do not violate a spammer's freedom of speech, but does an order not to send the mail violate freedom of speech? We listed several arguments why a service provider should be free to filter incoming mail. Do any of the arguments support injunctions against the spammers? One does: the argument that the spam uses the recipient company's property (computer system) against its wishes and imposes a cost on the recipient. AOL and other services won multimillion-dollar settlements from Cyber Promotions and other spammers.

Over a period of less than two years, a former Intel employee, Ken Hamidi, who maintained a Web site critical of the company, sent six e-mail messages to more than 30,000 Intel employees. He disguised his return address, making it difficult for Intel to block his e-mail with a filter. Intel sought a court order prohibiting him from sending more e-mail to its employees (at work). Note that in this case, the spam was not commercial. Intel argued that freedom of speech gave Hamidi the right to operate his own Web site, but did not give him the right to intrude in Intel's property and use its equipment to deliver his messages. Intel argued that the e-mail was a form of trespass. The California Supreme Court ruled in favor of Hamidi. The court said that Hamidi's bulk e-mailing was not trespass because it did not damage Intel's computers or cause economic harm to the company. (The court said that the trespass law might apply to spammers sending commercial e-mail.) The dissenting judges argued that Intel's property rights over its computers should allow the company to exclude unwanted e-mail.[35]

Amnesty International has long used its network of thousands of volunteers to flood government officials in various countries with mail when a political prisoner is being tortured or is in imminent danger of execution. Now, volunteers can log on to its Web site and send a prewritten e-mail letter. This is not commercial mail, and it differs from most spam in that a small number of recipients receive a large number of copies of the same (or similar) mail, but it is intended to be of large volume and certainly the recipient does not solicit it.

Various political and advocacy organizations use the same kinds of systems. People can click to send prewritten e-mail to politicians or other organizations and businesses. These examples illustrate how careful we must be when designing legal restrictions on spam. Some definitions of spam include the specification that (unsolicited) identical (or almost identical) messages are sent to a large number of people. Suppose an organization's Web site sends the same e-mail to every member of Congress each time someone visits the site and clicks to send the message. Will we have different points of view about whether this is free speech or spam, depending on how sympathetic we are to the specific organization's message?

Solutions from markets, technology, and business policy

Freedom of speech does not require the intended listener, or e-mail recipient, to listen. Businesses and programmers created a variety of filtering products to screen out spam at the recipient's site, by blocking e-mail from specified addresses, by blocking messages with particular words, and by more sophisticated methods. ISPs block certain e-mail from their systems entirely and also let individual members establish their own lists and criteria for mail to block. Products are available that flag Web sites in search engine results that are known to generate spam e-mail to visitors. People can get "disposable" e-mail addresses for use with online acitivity that might generate spam. They can arrange to forward mail from that address to their real e-mail address and cancel the disposable address if it starts getting too much spam.

In one interesting approach to the spam problem, called challenge-response spam filtering, the filter program automatically "quarantines" each incoming message from any unknown return address and sends an e-mail back to the sender. The sender sees a brief explanation and is asked to do a trivial task, for example, just click to respond. When the filter gets the response, it knows the return address was real and a real person was there. It then releases the original message to the recipient's mailbox and puts the sender in the recipient's whitelist* so future messages will go through directly. Normally, the authentication message gets back to the sender almost immediately (in human time), so the delay is minimal. (This approach has some disadvantages.[36])

Many businesses subscribe to services that provide lists of spammers to block. Aggressive antispam services list not only spammers, but also ISPs, universities, businesses, and online services that do not take sufficient action to stop members of their community from sending spam. Such action encourages managers to do something, for example, limiting the number of outbound e-mail messages sent from one account. (Early in the spam wars, most ISPs refused accounts to Cyber Promotions.)

How much discretion should an antispam listing service have in deciding whom to include on its list of spammers? Harris Interactive, which conducts public opinion surveys by e-mail ("Harris polls"), sued the Mail Abuse Prevention System (MAPS) for including Harris on its blacklist. Harris claimed that the people receiving its e-mail signed up to receive it. MAPS claimed Harris did not meet its standards for assuring the recipients' consent. Harris claimed a competing polling company recommended it for the spammer list.[37] Harris claimed inclusion on the list cut it off from about half of its survey participants and harmed its business. It wanted to collect for damages. Harris dropped the suit not long after filing it, so no legal issues were settled. The case had the effect of making users more aware of criteria spam blockers use, the "gaming" of the system by competitors, and the differences of opinion that can arise about who is a spammer.

Spam is cheap. Thus one idea for reducing it is to increase its cost to the sender. Proposals include schemes in which e-mail senders pay a tiny charge to the recipient for each e-mail message they send. Such plans depend on the development of micropayment systems (that have many other uses too). For most users of e-mail, the charge would be insignificant, but for spammers who send millions of messages a day it would be a

---

*A *whitelist* is a list of e-mail addresses from which someone is willing to accept e-mail.

AN ISSUE FOR DESIGNERS AND USERS OF FILTERS

We saw that filters are not perfect. They block more or less than the material one wants blocked, and often they block both more and less. If the filter is intended to block sexually explicit material from young children, it might be acceptable to err on the side of blocking some inoffensive material to be sure of preventing the undesirable material from getting through. On the other hand, if the filter is for spam, most people would not mind a few spam messages getting through, but would be quite unhappy if some of their nonspam e-mail was thrown away.

disincentive. Some proposals make the payment an option to the recipient, with the idea that most people would not invoke the charge for most personal e-mail, but would click to charge when e-mail comes from an advertiser. Many groups object to the very idea of charging any fee to send e-mail. For example, Richard Cox of Spamhaus, an international antispam organization commented that "an e-mail charge will destroy the spirit of the Internet."[38] Critics say charges might reduce use of e-mail by poor people and nonprofit organizations.

The first significant pay-to-email scheme actually implemented is a certified e-mail service. The e-mail certifier checks out senders who sign up for the service and, for a small charge per message, certifies that their mail is not spam. The certifier makes agreements with ISPs and e-mail service providers that they deliver certified mail to their members, images and links included, without putting the mail through filters. The messages appear in the recipient's mailbox with an indication that they are "certified." In 2006 AOL and Yahoo made such an agreement with Goodmail's certified mail service. Large companies like Time Inc. signed up as senders of certified e-mail. Esther Dyson had suggested a sender-pays model for e-mail in 1997. When Goodmail brought the idea to public attention nearly ten years later, she again wrote in support of such plans. She argues that many people might like some form of "certified" e-mail, and it would be good to have competing companies offering such services. They might be more effective at reducing spam than the regulatory approaches tried so far (including the CAN-SPAM law we describe next). Dyson says we should not expect e-mail to be free forever just because it was at the beginning.[39] Critics of certified mail schemes like Goodmail's, such as Spamhaus and the Electronic Frontier Foundation, believe the service gives ISPs incentive not to improve filters. Some object particularly to schemes like this one where the service provider gets part of the fee. They argue that to make certification worthwhile to senders, ISPs who receive a percentage of the certification fee have an incentive to overfilter, that is, to filter out legitimate e-mail so that more senders will need to pay for certification. They fear that free e-mail will disappear.

It is interesting to review how attitudes about spam filtering have changed. We saw that in the late 1990s, when AOL began aggressively filtering to block spam, some Internet groups compared the filtering to censorship. Even though AOL was not a government entity, it was large and millions of people received their mail at AOL. People worried that the precedent of a large corporation filtering e-mail for any reason could lead to corporations filtering e-mail because of content they did not like. Now, many advocacy groups and customers of ISPs see spam filtering as a valuable and essential service. Now that the Internet has grown from a community of scientists and techies to a world that includes commerce and criminals, are certification services another helpful adaptation or a threat?

Antispam laws

The federal CAN-SPAM Act (whose full name is the Controlling the Assault of Non-Solicited Pornography and Marketing Act) went into effect in 2004. It targets commercial spam and covers labeling of advertising messages (for easier filtering), opt-out provisions, and methods of generating e-mailing lists. Commercial messages must include valid mail header information (that is, faking the "From" line to disguise the sender is prohibited), a valid return e-mail address, and a valid physical postal address. Deceptive subject lines are prohibited. Criminal penalties apply for some of the more deceptive practices and for sending spam from someone else's computer without authorization (a process that can be accomplished by viruses that take over another computer).[40]

Many antispam organizations opposed the CAN-SPAM Act because they preferred to see spam banned altogether (as it is in some countries), rather than legitimized by the regulation. Many businesses supported CAN-SPAM. The law has been helpful in reducing problem spam from legitimate businesses. We can filter it out and we can get off the mailing list. People who send spam that includes fraudulent "get rich quick" schemes or ads for child pornography clearly do not care about what is legal. They are not likely to obey laws to identify themselves. Such laws make it easier to fine or jail them by convicting them of violating antispam regulations in cases where there is insufficient evidence for convictions based on the content of the messages. (This is a little like sending gangster Al Capone to jail for income-tax evasion.)

The California state government passed a law banning spam to cell phones and pagers. In cell-phone and paging systems, the recipient usually pays for incoming messages. Thus the law is consistent with laws against "junk faxes." Such spam is prohibited because it imposes a cost on the recipient.

Spam continues to be a major annoyance. A wide variety of antispam tools are available to individuals and online service providers, and many of us use them. Spammers continually find new ways around spam blockers, for example hiding messages in image files (that text scanners cannot scan for spam keywords). Eventually new defenses develop. The difficulty of distinguishing spam from real mail with absolute certainty suggests that the cycle of new spam techniques and better blocking techniques will continue. Because antispam laws must avoid conflicts with freedom of speech, and because the most abusive spammers ignore laws, these laws can reduce spam but are not likely to eliminate the problem.

3.2.4 CHALLENGING OLD REGULATORY STRUCTURES AND SPECIAL INTERESTS

> *The beauty of it all is that the Internet puts my little farm on a par with a multinational company.*
>
> —Andrew Freemantles, pig farmer, whose Web site
> includes video clips of his pigs[41]

Most people would not consider investment newsletters or ads for wine and real estate to be offensive material. However, one of the points we make at the beginning of this chapter is that some people will find something offensive about almost any kind of content. Here we discuss restrictions on these and similar material on the Internet.

Several companies sell self-help software to assist people in writing wills, premarital agreements, and many other legal documents. The software includes legal forms and instructions for filling them out. It is a typical example of empowering ordinary people and reducing our dependence on expensive experts. And, in a typical example of the backlash of special interests who see threats to their income and influence, a Texas judge banned Quicken legal software from Texas. Texas authorities pursued a similar case against Nolo Press. The judge decided the software amounted to practicing law without a Texas license. The Texas legislature later changed its law to exempt software publishers.

Several similar cases illustrate how the Web challenges special interests by providing new options. Most of the cases have free-speech implications. Several involve regulatory laws that restrict advertising and sales on the Web. Such regulations have some noble purposes, such as protecting the public from fraud, but they also have the effect of entrenching large, established businesses, making it more difficult for new and small businesses to flourish, and of keeping prices high. We describe cases related to investment newsletters, wine sales, and selling a home.

The Web is a popular forum for discussing investments. In 1997 publishers of online newsletters and Web sites about commodities and futures investments discovered that they were violating 25-year-old regulations requiring government licenses. License requirements included fees, fingerprinting, a background check, and presenting a list of subscribers on demand to the Commodity Futures Trading Commission (CFTC), the federal agency that administers the regulations. Publishers who did not register with the CFTC could be fined up to $500,000 and jailed up to five years. The regulations were designed for traders who handle other people's money, but the CFTC applied them to people selling investment newsletters or software to analyze commodity-futures markets. The Institute for Justice represented several clients arguing that the licensing requirement violated the First Amendment. A federal judge ruled that the CFTC regulations were a prior restraint on speech and violated the First Amendment both for Internet publishers and for traditional newsletter publishers. In 2000 the CFTC revised its rules to exempt newsletter publishers, software developers, and Web site operators from the licensing requirements. The decision was important in eliminating a requirement for government approval to discuss certain subjects on the Net or via software. By raising an issue of free speech on the Web, this case led to termination of a long-standing unconstitutional restraint of free speech in traditional media as well.[42]

The Web provides the potential for reducing prices of many products by eliminating the "middleman." Small producers who cannot afford expensive distributors or wholesalers can set up a Web site and sell directly to consumers nationwide. But not if they operated a small winery. Thirty states in the U.S. had laws restricting the shipping of out-of-state wines directly to consumers. The laws protected large wholesaling businesses that typically get 18–25% of the price and buy mostly from large wineries or those that sell expensive wines. They also protected state revenue; state governments cannot collect sales taxes on many out-of-state sales. State governments argued that the laws were needed to prevent sales to minors. This was a weak argument in states that permit direct shipments from in-state wineries, and because states could require Internet sellers to get proof of age. Lawsuits in several states challenged the laws against out-of-state wine shipments. New York also banned *advertising* out-of-state wines directly to consumers in the state. A winery that advertised its wines on a Web site ran a risk because the Web site is accessible to consumers in New York. Winery operators challenged the New York wine law, arguing that it unconstitutionally restricted freedom of speech, interfered with interstate commerce, and discriminated against out-of-state businesses.[43] In 2005 the Supreme Court ruled that bans on out-of-state shipments directly to consumers were unconstitutional. State laws must not discriminate against sellers in other states.

In 2004 a federal court ruled that California's real estate licensing law violated the First Amendment rights of Web site operators in other states who list California homes for sale. The government of California had attempted to require that operators of Web sites like ForSaleByOwner.com get real estate licenses in California. The license requirements are irrelevant and expensive for such sites, and California law allows newspapers to publish real estate ads, in the papers and on their Web sites, without a real estate license. So the federal court ruling protects the same First Amendment rights for Web sites as for older media and also reduces the powers of a special interest (in this case, real estate brokers) to restrict competition. A similar case is in the courts in New Hampshire, where state law also allows newspapers to publish lists of homes for sale, but requires a real estate license for Web sites that do so.

3.2.5 POSTING AND SELLING SENSITIVE MATERIAL: ETHICS AND SOCIAL CONCERNS

> *Free speech is enhanced by civility.*
> —Tim O'Reilly[44]

Most of our discussion so far, and much of the debate about censorship, focuses on censorship laws, laws prohibiting distribution of or access to certain kinds of material. There are also social and ethical issues about publication and distribution of legal material that could be sensitive in some way. Examples include hoaxes, legal "adult" entertainment material, Nazi materials, vicious personal attacks by bloggers, information about how to make bombs, and even maps and other information that might be of use to terrorists. In this section, we consider some of these.

Large companies

A policy reversal by Yahoo illustrates some of the dilemmas. A few years ago, Yahoo expanded its online store for adult material (erotica, sex videos, and so forth—all legal). Many users complained. Critics objected that because Yahoo is a large, mainstream company, its action gave acceptability to pornography. It also gave adult-material sellers easy access to Yahoo's large customer base. Yahoo quickly reversed policy and removed ads for adult material. This brought complaints from other people that Yahoo "caved in" to pressure from its mainstream advertisers and users. These critics see any decision to exclude material because of its subject matter to be unprincipled censorship. Some people believe that it is wrong for a large influential business, like Yahoo or Google, for example, to ban any legal material from its services because the effect is similar to censorship by the government.

Courts have struck down as unconstitutional several state laws that would have prohibited sale or rental to minors of video games with violence, nudity, and sex. Large retailers such as Wal-Mart and Best Buy have policies that restrict sales of such games. Various online companies that host Web sites have policies against posting hate material, bomb-making information, and other unpleasant or risky material. Many auctions sites prohibit sales of some kinds of legal products.

Does the legal right of adults to purchase or read something (a negative right, to be free from arrest) impose an ethical or social obligation on a Web site or store to sell it? The main justification for an affirmative answer is, as we mentioned above, equating the large social impact of a large company with censorship. On the other hand, in a free society where the government does not decide what material we can read or view, it is more important for sellers and Web sites to take seriously their role and responsibility in deciding what material they will make available. Also, a private company has property rights in its business that include making decisions about what to sell. If most of the public considers some material inappropriate for mainstream Web sites and stores, then response to customer pressure will probably keep it from such venues. It will still be available from specialty sites and dealers.

What about search engine providers? Do they have a social or ethical obligation to provide complete search results to all queries, or do they have a social or ethical obligation to omit very offensive sites from search results? The people who set policy in such companies face difficult questions. Should a search engine display links to discussions about suicide and suicide hotlines, but not "how to" sites? How should a search engine respond to a search for "nude pictures of college students"? How should it respond to a search for graphic pictures of torture by the government of its country or by terrorists? Search engines provide an extraordinarily valuable and fundamental service. We do not want them to discriminate against unpopular opinions or most forms of controversial material. We want to find news and, sometimes, unpleasant facts. Yet recognition of antisocial or risky uses of some material might lead to ethical decisions to decline to present it prominently, or at all, in search results.

Small Web sites and individuals

To make this discussion concrete, we consider a Web site about suicide for terminally ill patients in constant, severe pain. The points we raise here apply to sites with other kinds of sensitive information as well. What should the site organizers consider?* First, even if the site is not advertised, search engines will find it. Depressed teenagers and depressed adults will find it. What we put on a public Web site is public, available to everyone worldwide. The organizers should think about potential risks, and research them. Then what? One option is to decide not to set up the site at all. Suppose the site organizers decide to proceed because they believe the planned information has significant value for the intended audience. What can they do to reduce risks? Perhaps require a password to access the site. How would someone obtain a password? Would a simple waiting period reduce the risk of use by temporarily depressed people? Would the password requirement discourage access by intended users because of privacy concerns? People who post risky material have an ethical responsibility to seriously consider questions such as these. The answers are not obvious or easy.

Similarly, individuals should exercise responsibility and discretion when posting to Web sites. Suppose someone posts a false profile of a friend as a joke. A small group of friends might have a big laugh. The funnier and cleverer it is, the more it might be copied, e-mailed, and reposted elsewhere. The friend's employer, prospective employer, or grandmother might see it. What potential damage could it do?

To summarize, here are a few guidelines for making decisions about posting sensitive material: Consider unintended readers or users. Consider potential risks. Consider ways to limit access to intended users. Remember that it can be difficult to remove material from the Net once you have posted it.

---

*Some people consider suicide itself, and any encouragement of it, to be immoral. For the sake of this discussion, we assume the people setting up the site do not.

3.3 Censorship on the Global Net

> *The coffee houses emerged as the primary source of news and rumor. In 1675, Charles II, suspicious as many rulers are of places where the public trades information, shut the coffee houses down.*
>
> —Peter L. Bernstein[45]

3.3.1 THE GLOBAL IMPACT OF CENSORSHIP

For a long time, the "conventional wisdom" among most users and observers of the Net (if anything about the Net can be called conventional) was that the global nature of the Net is a protection against censorship. Web sites with content that is illegal in one country can be set up in some other country. People in countries that censor news can access information over the Net from other countries. E-mail and fax machines played a significant role during the collapse of the Soviet Union and the democracy demonstrations in China's Tiananmen Square. After the government of Zimbabwe shut down *The Daily News*, an independent newspaper, and issued arrest warrants for dozens of its journalists in 2003, the newspaper established itself on the Web from a site in South Africa.

In some ways, however, the globalness of the Net makes it easier for one nation to impose restrictive standards on others. We saw (in the box about the Amateur Action bulletin board in Section 3.2.1) that national censorship laws applied to the Web in the U.S. would wipe out the notion of community standards. Actions by some governments threaten the notion of different national standards. The first case to indicate the problem of one nation's restrictive laws affecting content outside that country occurred in 1995, when German prosecutors told CompuServe (an early online service) to block access by German subscribers to newsgroups with indecent and offensive material. CompuServe responded by cutting off access to more than 200 newsgroups—not only for its German subscribers, but for everyone. (It later restored access to all but five.) Similarly, when the government of China objected to a particular program of the British Broadcasting Corporation (BBC) that was critical of Mao Tse-tung, the satellite provider cut the BBC completely out of its transmission to China. The area affected by the cut also included Taiwan and Hong Kong.[46] As we will see, restrictive governments are increasingly using their leverage over companies that want to do business in their countries to enforce their national standards on content available to their citizens.

3.3.2 YAHOO AND FRENCH CENSORSHIP

Display and sale of Nazi memorabilia are illegal in France and Germany, with some exceptions for historical purposes. Two antiracism organizations sued Yahoo in a French court in 1999 because French people could view Nazi memorabilia offered for sale on

Yahoo's U.S.-based auction sites. The French government also brought criminal charges against Yahoo and former CEO Tim Koogle for justifying a crime against humanity. (Yahoo's French sites, based in France, complied with the French law.) These cases were widely viewed as a threat to freedom of speech, and the civil case was not fully resolved after seven years. We consider the civil case first.[47]

The case raised technical, legal, and social issues. Yahoo argued that it was infeasible to block access from France. On the Internet at that time, one's physical location was difficult to determine. And French people could access Yahoo's sites from outside France or use anonymizing services that obscured their location. Yahoo said the use of filters to screen out Nazi material would not suffice because they would be less than 50% effective and could not distinguish references to Nazis in hate material from references in *The Diary of Anne Frank* or Holocaust memorials.[48]

At the same time, companies were recognizing that people who read, say, the *New York Times* online in Toronto or London would likely prefer to see ads from stores in their cities rather than from New York stores. A few companies were already using software, called geolocation software, to figure out where Web site visitors were located. The software uses routing information and databases of numerical Internet addresses to try to determine location. The goal is for Web site visitors to see information in their own language and advertising relevant to their own culture, country, or location. The software was fairly new at the time of the Yahoo case, but experts said Yahoo could use a variant of it to screen out 90% of French users. In 2000 the French court ordered Yahoo to make a serious effort, including using such tools, to block access by French people to its sites outside of France that contain material illegal in France.

The legal issue is whether the French law should apply to Yahoo auction sites on Yahoo's computers located outside of France. As we saw in the discussion of the Amateur Action bulletin board system case in the box in Section 3.2.1, the meaning of the term "distribution" gets fuzzy on the Internet. Should a speaker have an obligation not to make available speech that others do not want to hear (or that governments do not want the people of a country to hear), or should listeners have the task of covering their ears? Should France have the task of blocking access to material from outside its borders? The social issue concerns the impact on freedom of speech worldwide if countries with more restrictive laws can enforce them in freer countries.

Yahoo asked a U.S. court to rule that the French court decision violated the First Amendment of the U.S. Constitution and therefore would not be enforced in the United States. Yahoo won a favorable decision, but in 2006 an appeals court rejected the lower court decision and the Supreme Court declined the case.[49] This leaves Yahoo and other content providers in the difficult position of not knowing whether U.S. courts will protect them when organizations and governments in other countries challenge their exercise of freedom of speech. Even if U.S. courts do not enforce such rulings, other countries could seize foreign assets or arrest visiting executives of companies that do not comply with their censorship orders.

Tim Koogle did not go to France to attend his trial. Yahoo and Koogle were acquitted because the court decided that permitting the auctions was not "justifying" the Nazi crimes. The decision did not resolve the issue of whether one country's government could bring criminal charges against content providers based in another country for content legal in their own country. It is also worth noting that procedural laws vary significantly in different countries. In the U.S., the government may not appeal acquittals. The French government appealed Koogle's acquittal, but an appeals court upheld it in 2005.[50]

Shortly after the French court issued its order to prevent access by French people, Yahoo announced that it would ban "hate material," including Nazi and Ku Klux Klan memorabilia, from its auction sites. Perhaps Yahoo executives *More about applying conflicting national laws to the Web: Section 5.6* realized this was a necessity if they intended to continue to do business in France. EBay also announced a ban on memorabilia about Nazis, the Ku Klux Klan, and other hate groups. It cited the complex of regulations and different cultural standards of other countries in which it was expanding its business. Some saw the bans as adoption of a responsible policy, discouraging the spread of such material. Free-speech advocates worried that the policy changes demonstrate the power of one government to impose its censorship standards on other countries.

3.3.3 CENSORSHIP IN OTHER NATIONS

> *The office of communications is ordered to find ways to ensure that the use of the Internet becomes impossible. The Ministry for the Promotion of Virtue and Prevention of Vice is obliged to monitor the order and punish violators.*
>
> —Excerpt from the Taliban edict banning all Internet use in Afghanistan, 2001[51]

The vibrant communication the Internet makes possible threatens governments in countries that lack political and cultural freedom. Many governments have taken steps to cut, or seriously reduce, the flow of information and opinion on the Net (as oppressive governments have done earlier with other communications media).* We give a sampling of such restrictions.

In countries such as China and Saudi Arabia, where the national government owns the Internet backbone (the communications lines and computers through which people access information), the governments install their own computers between the Net and the people with sophisticated firewalls and filters to block what they do not want their people to see. The government of Saudi Arabia blocks pornography and gambling, as many countries might, but it also blocks sites on the Bahai faith, the Holocaust, and religious

---

*In Poland, for example, before the communist government fell, it was illegal to make a photocopy without permission from government censors.

conversion of Muslims to other faiths. It blocks sites with information about anonymizers, tools to thwart filters, and encryption. Iran, with more than seven million Internet users, at various times blocked the sites of amazon.com, Wikipedia, the *New York Times*, and YouTube. It also blocked a site advocating the end of the practice of stoning women. Generally, the government says it blocks sites to keep out decadent Western culture.[52]

Pakistan banned Internet telephony. Burma (Myanmar) banned use of the Internet or creation of Web pages without official permission, posting of material about politics, and posting of any material deemed by the government to be harmful to its policies. Under an earlier law, possession of an unauthorized modem or satellite dish was punishable by a jail term of up to 15 years. Eritrea prohibited Internet access. Many countries in the Middle East limit access. Vietnam uses filtering software to find and block anticommunist messages coming from other countries. The legality of satellite dishes in many parts of Asia and the Middle East is fuzzy.[53] (Where the technology has not caught up, governments still restrict old communications media. A rival of Zimbabwe's president Robert Mugabe in Zimbabwe's 2001 presidential election was charged with possession of an unlicensed two-way radio.)

In some long-unfree countries, governments are struggling with the difficulties of modernizing their economy and technology while maintaining tight control over information. China, so far, is managing to do both. In the 1990s, when fewer people used the Web, the government required users of the Internet to register with the police. In 1999 a Chinese court sentenced an Internet entrepreneur to two years in jail for sharing e-mail addresses with a pro-democracy Internet journal based in the United States. Now more than 130 million Chinese use the Web and 20 or 30 million write blogs. The government strictly controls and censors what people read and what they post. Chinese regulations prohibit "producing, retrieving, duplicating and spreading information that may hinder public order." Censored sites and topics include discussion of democracy, religious sites, human rights organizations including Amnesty International, news and commentary about Taiwan and Tibet, economic news, and reports of major accidents or natural disasters and outbreaks of diseases.

China banned Google in 2002. Later, access to Google's U.S.-based Chinese site was slow, incomplete, and often disrupted by Chinese firewalls and filters. The government blocked both the Chinese-language and English-language Wikipedia sites for about a year. (When unblocked, the Chinese site flourished, with thousands of volunteers contributing articles.) China blocked the blog search site Technorati. It sometimes blocks the *New York Times*. Messages and sites about censorship (and how to evade it) are filtered out. Thousands of censors monitor chat rooms and Web sites. When Chinese citizens began using text messaging to communicate about banned topics, the government set up a system to filter the messages.[54] China dropped a plan to require registration, with verification of real names, for all bloggers and prepaid (anonymous) cell phone users. It recognized that the overhead and potential loss of customers would seriously hurt Internet and phone service companies. However, it is encouraging Internet companies to require registration.

Singapore has made a great and successful effort to build a high-tech economy. In 1999 its government relaxed enforcement of Internet censorship laws but did not change them. Singapore requires that online political and religious groups register with the government. Content providers are prohibited from distributing material that could "undermine public morals, political stability or religious harmony." The government now blocks relatively few Internet sites.[55]

Criticizing or insulting current and former leaders is unacceptable in many countries. Egyptian blogger Kareem Amer was sentenced to several years in jail for harming national unity and insulting Islam and the Egyptian president.[56] Turkey and Thailand blocked YouTube because videos insulted their founder and king, respectively.

3.3.4 AIDING FOREIGN CENSORS

> *Freedom of expression isn't a minor principle that can be pushed aside when dealing with a dictatorship.*
>
> —Reporters Without Borders[57]

Internet companies, such as search engines, service providers, sellers of filtering systems, and auction sites, that are based in free countries offer services in countries with strict censorship. What are their responsibilities?

Cisco Systems Inc. helped China build its filtering system that controls access by Chinese people to the Net. Google, Yahoo, Microsoft, and other U.S. companies help China restrict access to the Internet. The Chinese sites of Yahoo and MSN comply with local law and omit news stories that offend the government. Microsoft said it censored terms like "freedom" and "democracy" on its Chinese portal. Microsoft also shut down a Chinese journalist's blog on its MSN Spaces site that criticized the Chinese government.[58] Yahoo is believed to have provided information to the Chinese government that helped identify at least one person who was then jailed for his writing. Yahoo, describing the consequences as "serious and distressing," said it was required to comply with Chinese law, and the company had not been told the reason for the government request for the information.

Google held out longer, refusing to censor its search engine, although it had taken some steps toward restricting access to information in China. Google did filter material on the Chinese version of Google News, and it had become part-owner of a Chinese search engine company that complies with the government's censorship requirements. In 2006 Google disappointed many free-speech and human rights advocates by announcing that it was introducing a Chinese version in China, google.cn, that would comply with Chinese law. Its search results will not show sites with banned content. (Google said it would include notes to users indicating that some results are not shown. Since China censors messages about censorship in China, it was not clear how well this would work.)

We consider some issues these activities and incidents raise. If companies do business within another country, they must follow the laws of that country. What are the trade-offs between providing services to the people of the country and complying with its government's censorship requirements? How do the issues in China differ from French- and German-based branches of U.S. online auction sites banning Nazi memorabilia? How do they differ from filtering out pornography in countries that have stricter antipornography laws than the U.S.? To what extent does, or should, the prospect of a huge business opportunity in a new country affect the company's decision? Should companies draw a line, perhaps agreeing to restrict access to information, but refusing to disclose information that a government can use to jail someone for publishing his or her views? A government might need to identify a person whom it suspects of stalking, fraud, posting child pornography, or other crimes. In most countries a service provider might want to, and a law might require it to, provide information in those cases. If the government does not disclose the reason for a request, or is dishonest about the reason, how can a service provider make an ethical decision?

Google has long promoted the ideal of access to information. Its mission, according to a Google attorney, is "to organize the world's information and make it universally useful and accessible."[59] Google concluded that the company could not provide a high level of service in China without a local presence. Thus the agreement to operate in China and block material the government considers sensitive was a decision that some access is better than no access. Reporters Without Borders pointed out that "A Web site not listed by search engines has little chance of being found by users. The new Google version means that even if a human rights publication is not blocked by local firewalls, it has no chance of being read in China."[60] The group said Google's action was immoral and could not be justified, a point of view many of Google's critics share.

When U.S. (or other non-Chinese) companies set up branches in China and comply with restrictive laws, should we view them as providing more access to information in China than would otherwise exist, though not as much access as is technically possible? Or should we view them as partners in the Chinese government's ethically unacceptable control of access to information by its citizens?

> *Don't be evil.*
> —Google's informal corporate motto.

3.4 Political Campaign Regulations in Cyberspace

In his run for the 2004 Democratic presidential nomination, Senator Howard Dean made news by raising a very large amount of money in many small contributions on the Web. Since then, Web sites, official campaign blogs, and online fund raising have became standard campaign tools. Unofficial blogs and Web sites supporting and opposing candidates proliferate. Hilary Clinton announced her candidacy for president on her Web site instead of in older media. Thousands of groups create their own online fund-raisers for presidential candidates.

In this section we look at problems of applying U.S. political campaign laws to the Internet. The laws were written mostly in the 1970s for media such as newspapers, television, and radio. Federal election campaign rules are quite complex. They cover contribution limits, spending restrictions, regulations on advertisements, disclosure of information about contributors, and many detailed reporting requirements. States have similar laws and regulations. The details vary for different types of political offices and different states. These laws were intended to reduce the influence on campaigns by large corporations, other large organizations, and wealthy individuals. Campaign laws put strict limits on money contributed directly to the campaigns of candidates for public offices (called "hard money"). Restrictions on money contributed to political parties and groups other than a candidate's official campaign committee (called "soft money") were much looser, but there are detailed reporting requirements.

Political speech traditionally has been recognized as the most important kind of speech protected by the First Amendment. The Supreme Court had accepted contribution limits, reporting requirements, and other restrictions on political campaigns as constitutional on the argument that lack of such regulations would threaten the democratic political system. The Court has said that the First Amendment protects the right of an individual to spend his or her money, directly, to express opinions about candidates and political issues. However, "coordinated activities," that is, activities that are in some way coordinated with an official campaign committee, are considered contributions and subject to limits and reporting requirements. Contributions other than money (called "in-kind" contributions) must be given a value by the campaign, reported as contributions, and counted against the contribution limit for the donor. Political action committees, which can consist of a few individuals organized for a short-term project, must register and follow campaign regulations.

Perhaps you can begin to see questions that come up for the Web. Is linking to a candidate's Web site a 'coordinated activity'? How much is it worth? How would you know when you have reached your contribution limit and have to take down the link? How would a campaign committee know about such contributions so that it could report them?

Meanwhile, political parties and advocacy organizations had been using a huge amount of soft money to influence elections. Corporations, unions, and organizations avoided prohibitions on paying for ads directly supporting candidates by running so-called "issue ads" supporting a candidate implicitly.

Congress passed the Bipartisan Campaign Reform Act (more commonly known as the McCain-Feingold Act) in 2002. McCain-Feingold aimed to restrict the use of soft money and to strengthen the restrictions on corporate and union ads by restricting issue ads. It prohibited corporations (which include many nonprofit organizations) and unions from paying for television or radio ads that show a candidate's name or face within 60 days of an election or within 30 days of a convention or primary. The law made sponsorship of such ads a criminal offense. How does this affect freedom of political speech? In one example, an advocacy organization halted an ad campaign asking people to contact their state's senators and encourage them to vote on a particular issue. One of the senators was running for reelection, so the ads violated the law.[61] During the 2004 campaign, distributors of a movie critical of President Bush and publishers of a book critical of candidate John Kerry asked a First Amendment attorney whether they could advertise their movie and book. The movie company and book publisher are corporations. The attorney advised them that they could not advertise within the restricted timeframes. If McCain-Feingold applied to the Internet, would amazon.com and eBay, for example, have to remove ads for books about candidates 60 days before elections, 30 days before conventions, and 30 days before primaries—exactly the times people want to learn about candidates? (Would publishers publish books and movie makers make movies about candidates if advertising them was restricted during the critical time periods before elections?) Would a corporation or union be permitted to put a link on its Web site to an ad someone else created and paid for? Could the ACLU or the National Rifle Association mention a candidate's name on its Web site during the restricted period?

Campaign laws collide with the Internet

The Federal Election Commission (FEC), established in 1975, administers election laws. It writes the detailed regulations and enforces them. The FEC recognized that applying McCain-Feingold to the Internet would raise significant problems. It interpreted the new law as designed for media such as television and newspapers and exempted the Internet from most of the troublesome requirements. However, given the growing importance of the Internet for all kinds of communications, and specifically political campaigns, exempting the Internet could soon seriously reduce the relevance and effectiveness of campaign regulations. A federal judge, in 2004, ordered the FEC to develop rules to apply McCain-Feingold to the Internet.

While the FEC worked to devise the rules, bloggers worried about both old and new rules. Would they get in trouble if they linked to campaign Web sites or reposted online ads, brochures, position papers, or news releases produced by a campaign committee? They worried that they would be silenced if their links or advocacy were interpreted as "in-kind" contributions and the value exceeded the contribution limits (which in some local elections are as low as $250).

When a few individuals or a grassroots group set up a Web site or collaborate online to promote their views on a ballot issue or candidate, do they have to register as a political action committee and file contribution and expenditure reports? What is the value of a campaign position paper e-mailed to 300 people, or 3,000 people? The fear of violating some regulation, the cost of legal advice, and the potential cost of defense and fines would chill freedom of political discussion and result in many voices shutting down. Many feared that campaign laws would disrupt the wide-open flow of political discussion and advocacy developing on the Web.

Numerous examples suggest that the concern was justified. In the 1990s there were scattered attempts to apply campaign regulations to the Web. A man had a Web page satirizing the governor of his state. The governor filed a complaint against him, suggesting that he be required to identify himself on the Web site and file financial statements. Another man set up a Web page to express his opposition to the reelection of a member of Congress. He was told that he might be subject to reporting requirements. These Web sites appear to be clear examples of speech the First Amendment protects, and the complaints appear to be harassment, attempts to scare people into refraining from speaking out. But the regulations, and the uncertainty about how they applied to the Internet, encouraged such tactics.

More recent off-line examples show that regulations are applied in unexpected ways. Opponents file complaints, so intimidation is an issue. The FEC investigated four men who put up a homemade campaign sign because the sign did not say who paid for it. When a race car driver attached a campaign sign to his car, the FEC interpreted it as an unreported campaign contribution by a corporation. Oops, like many professionals, the driver has a corporation. Ordinary individuals who volunteer for political campaigns face investigations and heavy fines because of mistakes in following the complex laws.[62] Many areas of law are necessarily complex. But, as we point out in several places in this book, complex laws tend to benefit large entities that can afford lawyers. They threaten participation of ordinary people—which is desirable in politics and which the Internet assists.

We describe one case in a bit more detail. It could have happened on the Web. Two radio talk show hosts in Washington state helped organize a campaign to repeal a gas tax increase. They supported the ballot measure on their program. Several municipalities that benefit from the tax sued the campaign. They argued that the comments by the talk show hosts were "in-kind" contributions from the radio station and that the campaign committee had to report them as such. A court ruled in their favor. Because of campaign contribution limits, the talk show hosts would have to stop talking about the initiative on their programs in the few weeks before the election. More than a year after the vote on the gas tax, the Washington state Supreme Court reversed the decision. It said the talk show hosts were not subject to the reporting requirements and contribution limits because the Washington law exempted commentary in news media. One of the judges stated "Today we are confronted with an example of abusive prosecution by several local governments. . . . This litigation was actually for the purpose of restricting or silencing political opponents."[63] Such actual abuse and the potential for abusive application of similar laws on the Web worried those who support freedom of speech.

FEC rules for the Internet and a Supreme Court ruling on McCain-Feingold

In 2006 the FEC issued rules for the Internet.[64] The FEC decided that campaign regulations would cover content (e.g., ads) placed on a Web site for a fee. Online campaign activity by individuals who are not compensated are exempt from the contribution and expenditure regulations, and the "exemption applies whether the individual acts independently or in coordination with a candidate" or political committee or party. Thus the FEC removed the worry about (uncompensated) coordinated activity. Content one puts on one's own Web site, campaign material sent in e-mail, and blogs are exempt. Creating or hosting a campaign-related Web site and providing links to campaign Web sites are exempt activities (if the site is not paid for doing so). Reproducing campaign material on one's own Web site is exempt (again, if not paid).

Campaign regulations make some exceptions for news media. The FEC ruled that the media exemption applies to news media whose only presence is online. This is an important and positive decision. (There might be problems with its application. "Alternative" newspapers, in the past, often had difficulty getting press credentials for their reporters. On the Web, an individual can be a media entity. How will the FEC select media entities that qualify for the exemption?)

The FEC devised a reasonable application of the law to the Net, perhaps the best that free-speech advocates could expect.

In 2007 the Supreme Court ruled that the McCain-Feingold restrictions on ads during campaign periods are unconstitutional. It said that issue ads are protected by the First Amendment; the restrictions may be applied only to ads that advocate for or against a candidate.[65] This decision moves in the direction of protecting freedom of political speech and removes some potential problems of extending campaign regulations to the Internet.

3.5 Anonymity

> *The Colonial press was characterized by irregular appearance, pseudonymous invective, and a boisterous lack of respect for any form of government.*
>
> —"Science, Technology, and the First Amendment," U.S. Office of Technology Assessment

3.5.1 *COMMON SENSE* AND THE INTERNET

From the description quoted above, the Colonial press—the press the authors of the First Amendment to the U.S. Constitution found it so important to protect—had a lot in common with the Internet, including controversy about anonymity.

Jonathan Swift published his humorous and biting political satire *Gulliver's Travels* anonymously. Thomas Paine's name did not appear on the first printings of *Common Sense*, the book that roused support for the American Revolution. The Federalist Papers, published in newspapers in 1787 and 1788, argued for adoption of the new U.S.

Constitution. The authors, Alexander Hamilton, James Madison, and John Jay, had already served the newly free confederation of states in important roles. Jay later became chief justice of the Supreme Court, and Madison later became president. But when they wrote the Federalist Papers, they used a pseudonym, Publius. Some opponents of the Constitution believed it gave far too much power to the federal government; they used pseudonyms as well. In the nineteenth century, when it was not considered proper for women to write books, women writers such as Mary Ann Evans and Amantine Lucile Aurore Dupin published under male pseudonyms, or pen names (George Eliot and George Sand). Prominent professional and academic people use pseudonyms to publish murder mysteries, science fiction, or other nonscholarly work, and some writers—for example, the iconoclastic H. L. Mencken—used pseudonyms for the fun of it.

On the Internet, people talk about personal things in discussion forums devoted to topics such as health, gambling habits, problems with teenage children, religion, and so on. Many people use pseudonyms ("handles," aliases, or screen names) to keep their real identity private. Victims of rape and of other kinds of violence and abuse and users of illegal drugs who are trying to quit are among those who benefit from a forum where they can talk candidly without giving away their identity. (In traditional in-person support groups and group counseling sessions, only first names are used, to protect privacy.) Whistleblowers, reporting on unethical or illegal activities within the government agency or business where they work, may choose to release information via anonymous postings (although, depending on whether the information is verifiable, credibility for such anonymous postings may be low). In wartime and in countries with oppressive governments, anonymity can be a life-or-death issue. Reporters, human rights activists, and ordinary people use anonymous e-mail to protect themselves.

To send anonymous e-mail, one sends the message to a remailer service, where the return address is stripped off and the message is re-sent to the intended recipient. Messages can be routed through many intermediate destinations to more thoroughly obscure their origins. If someone wants to remain anonymous but receive replies, he or she can use a service where a coded ID number is attached to the message when the remailer sends it. The ID assigned by the remailer is a pseudonym for the sender, which the remailer stores. Replies go to the remailer site, which forwards them to the original person. Thus people can have conversations where neither knows the identity of the other.

Johan Helsingius set up the first well-known "anonymous" remailer in Finland in 1993, originally for users in the Scandinavian countries. (Users were not entirely anonymous; the system retained identifying information.) It was extremely popular and grew to an estimated 500,000 users worldwide. Helsingius became a hero to dissidents in totalitarian countries and to free-speech and privacy supporters everywhere. He closed his remailer in 1996 after the Church of Scientology and the government of Singapore took action to obtain the names of people using it. By then, many other similar services had become available.

Several businesses, such as Anonymizer.com, provide a variety of sophisticated tools and services that enable us to send e-mail and surf the Web anonymously. Some anonymity services use encryption schemes to prevent even the company that operates them from identifying the user. Instead of storing personal information for automatic monthly billing, some companies destroy payment information after each credit-card transaction is completed and require users to pay monthly to renew. The inconvenience protects privacy. For services based in Sweden, strict privacy laws reduce access by government agencies and others.

Many people use anonymous Web browsers to thwart the efforts of businesses to collect information about their Web activity and build dossiers for marketing purposes. The founder of a company that provided anonymous Web surfing services said the company developed tools to help people in Iran, China, and Saudi Arabia get around their governments' restrictions on Internet access.[66]

We might think the main benefit of anonymizing services is protection for individuals—protecting privacy, protecting against identity theft and consumer profiling, and protecting against oppressive governments. However, businesses, law enforcement agencies, and government intelligence services are also major customers. There are several reasons for their desire for anonymity. A business might want to keep its research and planning about new products secret from competitors. If competitors can get logs of sites that a company's employees have visited, they might be able to figure out what the company is planning. Thus, businesses might choose to use anonymizing services for research on the Web.

Anonymous Web surfing aids law enforcement investigations. Suppose law enforcement agents suspect a site contains child pornography, terrorist information, copyright infringing material, or anything else relevant to an investigation. If they visit the site from their department computers, they might be blocked or see a bland, page with nothing illegal.* Also, when law enforcement agents go "undercover" and pretend to be a member or potential victim of an online criminal group, they do not want their Internet protocol (IP) address to expose them. The U.S. Central Intelligence Agency (CIA) helped fund an anonymizer start-up company. A senior CIA official commented "We want to operate anywhere on the Internet in a way that no one knows the CIA is looking at them."[67] Although anonymity can help law enforcement agents do their job, it can also mask illegal surveillance by government agencies—or legal but repressive surveillance in unfree countries. The anonymity service produced by the company funded partly by the CIA had flaws that made it possible to determine a user's identity. The company had announced that the CIA had thoroughly reviewed the product, leading to speculation that the CIA knew about the flaws and was happy to have a company distributing an anonymizing service that the CIA could easily circumvent.[68]

---

*Web sites can determine the IP addresses (that is, the sequence of numbers that identifies a particular domain or computer on the Web) of a visitor. They can block access from specified addresses or put up alternate pages for those visitors.

Introducing anonymity online from American Express. Don't leave home pages without it.

—Newspaper advertisement for American Express[69]

3.5.2 IS ANONYMITY PROTECTED?

For those not using true anonymity services, secrecy of our identity online depends both on the privacy policies of ISPs, online subscription services, and the sites we visit—and on the laws and court decisions about granting subpoenas for disclosure. What happens when someone wants to know the real identity of a person who posted something? How well protected are our real identities? How strongly should they be protected? In this section we consider political speech, controlled by state and federal laws, and attempts of corporations to learn the identities of their online critics. In the next section, we look at arguments against complete anonymity.

Political speech

In the U.S, the First Amendment protects political speech, but there are still many ways in which the government can retaliate against its critics. There are also many personal reasons why someone might not want to be known to hold certain views. Anonymity provides protection against retaliation and embarrassment.

The Web enables anyone to express political opinions to a wide audience inexpensively. Some individuals prefer to express their opinions anonymously. Can they do so? The Supreme Court has repeatedly ruled that the freedom of speech guaranteed by the First Amendment includes the right to speak anonymously (in print). In 1995 the Supreme Court invalidated an Ohio state law under which a woman was fined for distributing pamphlets against a proposed school tax without putting her name on them. The Court ruled that distribution of anonymous political leaflets (by an individual) is an exercise of freedom of speech protected by the First Amendment. The Court said "anonymous pamphleteering is not a pernicious, fraudulent practice, but an honorable tradition of advocacy and of dissent. Anonymity is a shield from the tyranny of the majority."[70] A federal court threw out Georgia's 1996 law against using a false identity on the Internet, citing the Supreme Court decision in the Ohio ase.

As we saw in Section 3.4, reporting requirements in election campaign laws restrict anonymity. The Federal Election Commission exempted the Web sites, blogs, and e-mail of individuals and organizations (that are not corporations) if they are not compensated for their campaign activity. The exemption protects anonymity of political speech by unpaid individuals, consistent with the court decisions described above.

Criticizing corporations

Internet stock message boards are to Wall Street what talk radio is to current events: Occasionally crude, often wrong, frequently useless but nonetheless a vital and widely used forum where people can speak their minds.

—Aaron Elstein, *Wall Street Journal* reporter[71]

Facebook, Yahoo, Jobster, AOL, and other services and networking sites have thousands of networks and discussion forums devoted to individual companies. Investors, employees, and others freely discuss the companies. On some, much of the discussion centers on investment issues, which include how well a company is run and its future financial prospects. Businesses have two areas of legitimate complaints: postings that spread false and damaging rumors, and postings that include confidential business documents or other proprietary information. People post false comments stating that a business is near bankruptcy or that its managers are committing fraud. They post personal accusations—for example, that the executives of the business engage in wife swapping. In one case, a former employee posted particularly nasty comments about a company and its executives, including charges of adultery. When sued, he apologized and said he made it all up.[72] We are not exempt from ordinary ethics and defamation laws merely because we are using the Internet or signing comments with an alias rather than a real name. On the other hand, many postings are simply strong criticism. This is free speech even when expressed in the flaming style common in some online forums. Should businesses be able to get real names of people posting messages they object to? If a service gives out someone's real name, should the service inform the person?

Businesses and business groups file libel lawsuits against people who post critical comments. After a lawsuit is filed, the business normally gets a subpoena ordering the service to disclose the person's real name and address. Often, the service does not inform the person that it has disclosed the information. A popular stock chat site said it received roughly one subpoena per day and did not have the staff to notify everyone. AOL gives members 14 days notice before turning over their information, so a member has an opportunity to fight a subpoena in court. Yahoo did not notify people when they were the target of a subpoena—until one person sued Yahoo for disclosing his identity to his employer (who fired him). Other people have been fired for posting comments critical of their employer. The Embroidery Software Protection Coalition subpoenaed Yahoo for the real names of embroidery hobbyists to sue them for defamation. The hobbyists had criticized the Coalition for sending more than a thousand letters threatening people with fines for buying embroidery designs that infringed copyrights. It is widely believed that businesses use the lawsuits, which they do not expect to win, as a tool to obtain the identities of people who are expressing their opinions (legally) and to intimidate them into being quiet. This general tactic—filing a lawsuit to stifle criticism by intimidation and high legal expenses—is not new to the Internet. It already had a name: a SLAPP, a Strategic Lawsuit Against Public Participation.[73]

Free-speech advocates developed legal defenses for fighting subpoenas for the names of people who are exercising freedom of speech and not committing libel or posting proprietary company material. Lawyers argued that judges should examine the individual case and determine if the evidence for defamation is strong enough that the company is likely to win—and only then issue a subpoena for the real name of the defendant. Some suggested using the same standards for requiring journalists to disclose their sources. Some recommended that the law require ISPs to notify a member when the ISP receives a subpoena for the member's identity. Gradually, as more attention focused on the threats to free speech, some courts rejected some subpoenas for real names. States passed laws to reduce frivolous suits. A California court applied an existing anti-SLAPP law to the Internet.

Lawyers proposed a general defense to defamation suits for message board comments: These forums are full of exaggeration and shrillness. Sensible people do not take the comments seriously; thus no one's reputation can truly be damaged in such a forum and there is no defamation. A federal judge ruled for a defendant saying that Internet postings are almost always opinions, which are protected speech. They are "full of hyperbole, invective, ... and language not generally found in fact-based documents."[74] Should the hyperbole of the Net protect people who intentionally libel others? Which of these suggestions or policies are useful for protecting criticism while holding people responsible for illegal speech?

3.5.3 AGAINST ANONYMITY

Anonymity versus community

In some contexts, anonymity is seen as unneighborly or risky. The WELL,* for example, takes the position that people should take responsibility for their opinions and statements by letting their identities be known. Esther Dyson, editor of *Release 1.0* and a frequent writer on the computing environment, commented that "anonymity is the opposite of community" (while also commenting that there are situations where anonymity is okay).[75] Dyson was careful to make the distinction that many overlook: People might object to something, choose not to use it, and discourage its use in certain environments, without advocating the imposition of the force of the government to stop its use. Commenting on a lawsuit challenging Georgia's anti-anonymity law, Dyson said "Anonymity shouldn't be a crime. Committing crimes should be a crime."[76]

Many Web marketplaces and product-review sites rely on users to review products. Reviews are anonymous or identified by handle or pseudonym. But sometimes publishers, authors, sellers, and their friends post multiple glowing reviews of their products using a variety of account names. Similarly, competing authors or enemies could post critical

---

*The WELL is the Whole Earth 'Lectronic Link, one of the earliest online communities.

reviews using multiple pseudonyms. Amazon addressed the problem by establishing a real-name verification system and encouraging, but not requiring, reviewers to sign reviews with their real names. Real-name reviews are marked as such, and readers can give them more weight if they choose. Other online markets, eBay and Shopping.com, for example, identify reviewers by pseudonym but provide the reviewing and shopping history of reviewers so that users can decide how to value the reviews.

Because of its potential to shield criminal activity or because they consider it incompatible with politeness and netiquette (online etiquette), some services and online communities choose to discourage or prohibit anonymity. Some require identification of all members and users. Some do not accept e-mail from known anonymous remailer sites. On the other hand, Web sites that host debate on controversial issues or discussion of socially sensitive topics often consider anonymity to be a reasonable way to protect privacy and encourage open, honest discussion. If policy decisions about anonymity are made by those responsible for individual services and Web sites, the policies can be flexible and diverse enough to adapt to specific services and clienteles.

Laws against anonymity

> *An instance of the inexplicable conservatism and arrogance of the Turkish customs authorities was recently evidenced by the prohibition of the importation of typewriters into the country. The reason advanced by the authorities for this step is that typewriting affords no clew to the author, and that therefore in the event of seditious or opprobrious pamphlets or writings executed by the typewriter being circulated it would be impossible to obtain any clew by which the operator of the machine could be traced. . . . The same decree also applies to mimeograph and other similar duplicating machines and mediums.*
>
> —*Scientific American*, July 6, 1901[77]

Anonymity on the Internet is used for criminal and antisocial purposes. It is used for fraud, harassment, and extortion. It is used to distribute child pornography, to libel or threaten others with impunity, and to infringe copyrights by posting and downloading copyrighted material without authorization. Anonymity makes it difficult to track wrongdoers. Like encryption, anonymity technology poses strong challenges to law enforcement.

The U.S. and European countries are in the process of developing laws that require ISPs to maintain records of the true identity of each user and to maintain records of online activity for a specified period of time for potential use in criminal investigations. Such laws prevent true anonymity. Civil libertarians, privacy advocates, and ISPs object that such requirements conflict with the First Amendment and privacy and that the record keeping would place an expensive burden on the ISPs. The potential for illegal access to the records by government agencies and others would also compromise freedom of speech and privacy.

Many of the core issues are the same as those in the law-enforcement controversies we discussed in Chapter 2. Does the potential for harm by criminals who use anonymity to hide from law enforcement outweigh the loss of privacy and restraint on freedom of speech for honest people who use anonymity responsibly? Is anonymity an important protection against possible abuse of government power? Should people have the right to use available tools, including anonymizers, to protect their privacy? We can send hardcopy mail without a return address. Should there be more restrictions on anonymity on the Net than in other contexts?

3.6 Protecting Access and Innovation: Net Neutrality or Deregulation?

Direct censorship is not the only factor that can limit the amount and variety of information available to us on the Internet. Businesses sometimes use the government's regulatory power to delay or prevent competition. Large companies often lobby for laws and regulations to restrict their competition. The television networks used law to delay cable for more than a decade. For decades U.S. broadcasting companies lobbied to keep low-power radio stations (called "micro radio") virtually illegal. In Section 3.2.3, we saw that there was controversy about whether paid services, such as certified e-mail, would crowd out free versions of the service, thus restricting availability to those who could or would pay. The issue we discuss here also involves, in part, lobbying for competitive advantage by large companies, in part, paying for a fundamental Internet service. Even if there is a quick resolution for this issue, the arguments are likely to be relevant when similar issues come up again.

"Net neutrality" refers to a variety of proposals for restrictions on how telephone companies interact with their broadband customers (primarily for Internet services) and how they set charges for services. Before discussing recent and current controversies, we provide some background.

Common carriers (for example, telephone and telegraph companies, as we described in Section 3.1), were prohibited from providing their own information content, and they were prohibited from discriminating against information they transmitted based on content or who the customer was. For the Internet in the late 1990s and early 2000s, the Federal Communications Commission maintained open-access requirements for telephone companies. The phone companies had to lease lines to rival broadband operators at "neutral," regulated low prices. Cable companies, providing cable television and cable modem access to the Internet, were exempt from the requirements. ISPs negotiated prices with cable companies for use of their lines. Proponents of more flexibility for phone companies argued that restraints on flexible deals and price setting reduced incentive for investment in more and improved broadband capacity. They advocated ending open-access requirements for telephone companies. Supporters of the regulations argued that market forces would lead to higher prices, exclusion of competitors by the telephone companies, and reduced access to Web content. They advocated extending the regulations to cable modem.* Between 2003 and 2005, the FCC eliminated line-sharing requirements for telephone company lines, including fiber optics lines, and regulations on residential broadband service.[78] The issue, generating much debate and lobbying in Congress, is whether this deregulation is a good thing or whether new regulations should be established.

Advocates of "net neutrality" want the government to mandate that telecommunications companies treat all content that travels through their broadband lines the same way.[†] Equal treatment includes charging all customers the same rate for sending information over the Internet and not giving priority to any particular content or customer. Net neutrality would restore part of the concept of common carrier, based partly on the view that telephone companies (now telephone and cable) have a monopoly on transmission of information and that companies that control transmission should not be permitted to control access to content as well. Many Internet content providers, including individual bloggers and large companies such as eBay, Microsoft, Amazon.com, and Google, fear that without net neutrality requirements, they will have to pay higher rates and that communications companies will give special treatment to their own content providers. Some groups argue the results will be devastating for the Internet as independent voices will be squeezed out.

There are two different but related issues here, sometimes blurred in the arguments: (1) whether the companies that provide the communications networks should be permitted to exclude or give special treatment to content transmitted based on the content itself or on the company that provides it, and (2) whether the companies that provide the communications networks should be permitted to offer content providers different levels of speed and priority at different price levels. Much debate focuses on the possibility of "tiered" service, that is different levels of service with different charges.[79]

Charging different rates for products and services is not unusual and makes economic sense in many areas. Research journals charge libraries a higher subscription rate than they charge individuals, because more people will read each library copy. Many businesses give large-quantity discounts. Some institutions and businesses, hospitals for example, pay a higher rate for services such as electricity under contracts that guarantee higher priority for repairs or emergency service when necessary. We all have a choice of paying standard delivery charges for products we buy online or paying more for faster delivery. Perhaps the best analogy is express lanes on freeways. People pay to drive in these less crowded lanes; the price might vary with the time of day and level of traffic. Thus the notion that every customer should pay the same amount does not have intrinsic merit. Does it have

---

*In a 2005 decision, the Supreme Court ruled that cable is an "information service," not subject to common carrier open-access requirements.

[†]Some make exceptions for illegal content, which may be blocked, but that is not significant to this debate.

merit for the Internet? Would it make sense for communications carriers to, say, contract with video suppliers to provide faster delivery of videos?

Supporters of neutral pricing fear that lack of pricing regulation will erode the diversity of the Internet. Only big companies and organizations will be able to afford the prices necessary to ensure that their content moves fast enough to be relevant. Content that individuals and smaller organizations provide will get lost. Some argue that flexible pricing will give telecommunications companies too much power over content on the Internet. Supporters of net neutrality see tiered service as a threat to innovation, democratic participation, and free speech online. Vinton Cerf, Vice President and Chief Internet Evangelist at Google* and a highly respected Internet pioneer, sees the neutrality of the carriers, the lack of gatekeepers and centralized control, as key factors responsible for the success of the Net and innovations like blogging and Internet telephony. He argues that there is not enough competition in the network operator industry now to protect against abuses.[80]

Opponents of net neutrality argue that neutrality regulations will slow the advance of high-speed Internet connection and improvements in infrastructure. Before the FCC relaxed regulations, telecommunications companies had little incentive to invest in broadband capacity. In the few years afterwards, they invested hundreds of billions of dollars. Speeds increased, prices fell, and the added capacity was essential for new phenomena such as video sharing. Continued investment in broadband is necessary for growth in areas such as high-definition video, online backup services, applications of remote sensors, innovations in education services, and so on. Opponents of proposed regulations say that existing laws to stop abuse by network operators are sufficient. There should be no major new regulation without evidence of harm in the current system. David Farber, another highly respected Internet pioneer, opposes neutrality legislation. He commented that "We don't want to inadvertently stall innovation by imposing rules or laws the implications of which are far from clear."[81] Some who support free markets oppose mandated uniform pricing on principle, as an unethical interference in the free choices of sellers and buyers.

Both sides argue that their position will protect innovation and outlets for free speech on the Internet. Supporters of net neutrality requirements emphasize the importance of the "level playing field" in achieving these goals. Opponents emphasize the importance of flexibility and market incentives. In 2007 AT&T agreed to follow net neutrality principles for two years (in exchange for government approval of its purchase of BellSouth). The agreement might pause the controversy and the heavy lobbying for a few years, to be renewed when the AT&T agreement expires.

---

*Really, that's his title.

EXERCISES

Review Exercises

3.1 Where, other than on the Internet, can you find bomb-making instructions? What is one legal use for a homemade bomb?

3.2 Give three examples of Web sites that were mistakenly blocked by early filtering software.

3.3 When considering laws designed to protect children on the Internet, the Supreme Court often refers to the "least restrictive means." Explain what the "least restrictive means" is, and why it is important.

3.4 Mention two methods some governments use to control access to information.

3.5 Give an example of an anonymous publication from more than 100 years ago.

3.6 Give an example of Internet censorship in a country other than the United States.

General Exercises

3.7 A large company has a policy prohibiting employees from blogging about company products. What are some possible reasons for the policy? Does it violate the First Amendment? Is it reasonable?

3.8 One of the arguments used to justify increased government control of television content is that television is "invasive." It comes into the home and is more difficult to keep from children. Do you think this argument is strong enough to outweigh the First Amendment? Give reasons. Is this argument more valid for the Internet than for television, or less valid for the Internet than for television? Give reasons.

3.9 How has the Internet changed the notion of community standards for determining if material is legally obscene? Do you think the community-standards criterion can be preserved on the Internet? If so, explain how. If not, explain why.

3.10 In many cities, one can buy both ordinary newspapers and sexually oriented publications from coin-operated machines on sidewalks. College campuses often have newspaper machines, but not the machines for sexually oriented publications. Should colleges restrict access to sexually oriented Web sites from campus computers? List several similarities and differences between coin-operated machines and Web sites that might be relevant to a college's decision.

3.11 What policy for Internet access and use of filter software do you think is appropriate for elementary schools? What policy for Internet access and use of filter software do you think is appropriate for high schools? Give your reasons.

3.12 Describe two problems associated with using filters to protect children when using the Internet. What would you recommend instead of or in addition to filters?

3.13 A bill was introduced in Congress to require that Web sites with pornography get proof of age from anyone who tries to visit the site, possibly by requiring a credit-card number or some other adult identification number. Discuss some arguments for and against such a law.

3.14 Four high school students found instructions for making a bomb on a Web site. They built the bomb and set it off in the hallway of their school. One of the students, an 18-year-old, said they had no idea how powerful the bomb would be and they had no intention of hurting anyone. He commented "These are really dangerous sites. . . . I'm not a troublemaker or anything. I'm just a regular kid."[87] Evaluate his comments.

3.15   Suppose you are writing an antispam law. What do you think is a reasonable definition of spam in this context? Indicate the number of messages and how the law would determine whether a message was unsolicited.

3.16   Do you agree with the decision in *Intel v. Hamidi* (Section 3.2.3)? Why or why not?

3.17   Describe three methods for reducing spam.

3.18   Laws in some states, some long-standing, some passed specifically for the Internet, prohibit many kinds of sales on the Web. For example, laws prohibit purchase of contact lenses on the Web, require that caskets for funerals be bought within a particular state, prohibit filling prescriptions on the Web, and prohibit auto manufacturers from selling cars directly to consumers on the Internet. The Progressive Policy Institute estimates that such state laws cost consumers at least $15 billion a year.[83]

For which of these laws can you think of good reasons? Which seem more like the anticompetitive laws described in Section 3.2.4?

3.19   Suppose that, near Christmas time, many Web sites and religious discussion groups carry a large amount of material about the religious meaning of Christmas and the religious importance of Jesus Christ. To the majority of Americans, this is not only acceptable, but valuable and positive. To members of non-Christian religions and to atheists, it might be offensive. They might not want their children to view this material. What would be your reaction to a law restricting availability of such material on the Internet? In what ways do the issues about restricting religious material, sexual material, sexist or racist comments, or bomb-making material on the Internet differ? In what ways are these issues similar?

3.20   In Section 3.2.5 we saw that people criticized Yahoo for expanding its online store for adult material, and people criticized Yahoo for responding to complaints, reversing the new policy, and removing ads for adult material. What do you think of Yahoo's decisions? What do you think of both criticisms of Yahoo?

3.21   Amateur astronomers around the world have been locating and tracking satellites—both commercial and spy satellites—and posting their orbits on the Web.[84] Some intelligence officials argue that, if enemies and terrorists know when U.S. spy satellites are overhead, they can hide their activities. What issues does this problem raise? Should posting satellite orbits be illegal? Give arguments on both sides. Which are stronger? Why?

3.22   During World War II, "Radio Free Europe" broadcast news and other information into Nazi-controlled countries. It was illegal to listen to those broadcasts in those countries. During the "Cold War," the Soviet Union jammed western radio broadcasts into that country. In the discussion of the Yahoo/France case, we asked, should a speaker have an obligation not to make available speech that others do not want to hear (or that governments do not want the people of a country to hear), or should listeners have the task of covering their ears? Does your answer for the Yahoo case differ from your answer in the Nazi and Soviet examples? If so, how and why? If not, why not?

3.23   Extremist groups use Web sites to recruit individuals to their cause. Do you think these Web sites should be protected by principles of freedom of speech? Why or why not? Does the fact that they are Web sites rather than printed and mailed newsletters make a difference? Should the people behind the Web sites be held responsible for the violence some of their followers commit even though the Web sites do not give specific directions to commit violence? Why or why not?

3.24 Canada and France have laws that restrict the number of U.S. movies, television programs, and magazines allowed into those countries. The reasons given include protecting their culture and protecting their domestic movie, TV, and magazine companies from foreign competition. How do you think the Web will affect such policies or be affected by them?

3.25 The Web sites of many tax-exempt charitable organizations have links to sites of organizations that do political lobbying—an activity illegal for tax-exempt groups. For example, a think tank has links to Handgun Control Inc. and the National Rifle Association, so visitors can find relevant research materials. The Internal Revenue Service (IRS) announced an investigation into the issue of whether such links violate the rules for tax-exempt status. What do you think they should conclude? How would various possible decisions by the IRS affect the Web?

3.26 In Section 3.2.3 we discussed proposals for charges for e-mail that would then be certified as nonspam. What are the arguments for and against such a system? Do you think such a system would work? Why or why not?

3.27 Assume you are a professional working in your chosen field. Describe specific things you can do to reduce the impact of any two problems we discussed in this chapter. (If you cannot think of anything related to your professional field, choose another field that might interest you.)

3.28 Think ahead to the next few years and describe a new problem, related to issues in this chapter, likely to develop from computing technology or the Web.

Assignments

These exercises require some research or activity.

3.29 Find out whether your college restricts access to any Web sites from its computer systems. What is its policy for determining which sites to restrict? What do you think of the policy?

3.30 Find out whether the government appealed the permanent injunction against enforcement of COPA that U.S. Court District Judge Lowell A. Reed Jr. issued in March 2007 (Section 3.2.2). If so, and if the Supreme Court has decided the case, summarize the results.

3.31 Keep a log of the e-mail you receive for one week. For each message, indicate whether it is commercial or some other form of spam (describe your criteria) and whether you solicited it.

Class Discussion Exercises

These exercises are for class discussion, perhaps with short presentations prepared in advance by small groups of students.

3.32 To what extent is violence on the Web and in computer games responsible for shootings in schools? What should be done about it, without violating the First Amendment?

3.33 *Background.* A computer system manager at a public university noticed that the number of Web accesses to the system jumped dramatically. Most of the increased accesses were to one student's home page. The system manager discovered that his home page contained several sexually oriented videos. The videos were similar to those that legally appear on many web sites. The system manager told the student to remove the videos.
      The grievance cases. A female student who accessed the videos before they were removed filed a grievance against the university for sexual harassment. The student who set up the home page filed a grievance against the university for violation of his First Amendment rights.

The hearings. Divide the class into four groups: representatives for the female student, the male student, and the university (a separate group for each grievance). A spokesperson for each group presents arguments. After open discussion of the arguments, take a vote of the class on each grievance.

3.34   Should we consider spam a form of trespass? Restaurants are open to the public but can exclude rowdy people. What rules or laws does that analogy suggest about sending spam to subscribers of an ISP? Is freedom of speech more relevant in one case than in the other?

3.35   After an incident of nasty verbal attacks and death threats to a blogger from people who disagreed with something she wrote, Tim O'Reilly and Jimmy Wales proposed a Bloggers Code of Conduct. Find a copy of the Code that developed from this proposal (or another code of conduct for bloggers). Evaluate it. Discuss its compatibility with freedom of speech. Should bloggers follow the Code?

3.36   Are campaign finance regulations compatible with freedom of political speech on the Internet? If not, is it more important to protect freedom of speech or to protect the regulations?

3.37   Should a law require ISPs to keep records of the real identity of all users? (Should true anonymity on the Internet be banned?)

3.38   What rules or standards should a court apply when an individual, business, or government agency asks it for a subpoena to get the real name of a person who has posted messages online?

NOTES

1.   From a speech by Mike Godwin at Carnegie Mellon University, November 1994, quoted with permission. (The speech is excerpted, including part of the quotation used here, in Mike Godwin, "alt.sex.academic.freedom," *Wired*, February 1995, p. 72.)

2.   Eric M. Freedman, "Pondering Pixelized Pixies," *Communications of the ACM*, 44, no. 8 (August 2001): pp. 27–29.

3.   "High Court Rules Cable Industry Rights Greater Than Broadcast's," *Investors Business Daily*, June 28, 1994.

4.   Title V, Section 230.

5.   Adjudication on Motions for Preliminary Injunction, *American Civil Liberties Union et al. v. Janet Reno.* (No. 96-963) and *American Library Association et al. v. United States Dept. of Justice* (No. 96-1458).

6.   Advertising wine on the Internet was protected in a 2006 case in Minnesota. Earlier cases concerned advertising of tobacco, legal gambling, vitamin supplements, alcohol content of beer, prices of prescription drugs, and Nike's claim that it did not use sweatshop labor. Lee McGrath, "Sweet Nector of Victory," *Liberty & Law*, Institute for Justice, 15, no. 3 (June 2006): pp. 1, 10; Robert S. Greenberger, "More Courts Are Granting Advertisements First Amendment Protection," *Wall Street Journal*, July 3, 2001, pp. B1, B3.

7.   Ithiel de Sola Pool, *Technologies of Freedom* (Harvard University Press, 1983), pp. 224–225, 10.

8.   In *The Life of Voltaire* (Smith, Elder & Company, 1904). See also Fred S. Shapiro, ed., *The Yale book of Quotations* (Yale University Press, 2007). The quotation is often incorrectly attributed to Voltaire.

9.   Gerard van der Leun, "This Is a Naked Lady," *Wired*, Premiere Issue, 1993, pp. 74, 109.

10. Mike Godwin, "Sex, Cyberspace, and the First Amendment," *Cato Policy Report*, 17, no. 1 (January/February 1995): p. 10.

11. Robert Peck, quoted in Daniel Pearl, "Government Tackles a Surge of Smut on the Internet," *Wall Street Journal*, February 8, 1995, p. B1.

12. For a commentary on the many issues in this case, see Mike Godwin, "Virtual Community Standards," *Reason*, November 1994, pp. 48–50.

13. Dick Thornburgh and Herbert S. Lin, eds., *Youth, Pornography and the Internet* (National Academy Press, 2002), books.nap.edu/catalog/10261.html.

14. In the decision striking down the Child Pornography Prevention Act (*Ashcroft v. Free Speech Coalition*). More arguments against the law are in Freedman, "Pondering Pixelized Pixies." Arguments on the other side appear in Foster Robberson, " 'Virtual' Child Porn on Net No Less

Evil than Real Thing," *Arizona Republic*, April 28, 2000, p. B11.

15. FBI statement, reported in "On-line Child-porn Probe Yields Searches, Arrests" (Associated Press), *San Diego Union-Tribune*, September 14, 1995, p. A10.

16. Passed as part of the Telecommunications Act of 1996.

17. Associated Press and New York Times News Service, "Cybercensors Reverse Ban on 'Breast,'" December 2, 1995.

18. *Butler v. Michigan*, 352 U.S. 380(1957).

19. Adjudication on Motions for Preliminary Injunction, *American Civil Liberties Union et al. v. Janet Reno* (No. 96-963) and *American Library Association et al. v. United States Dept. of Justice* (No. 96-1458).

20. "Final Report of the COPA Commission," October 20, 2000, www.copacommission.org/report.

21. For a good overview of issues and legal cases about filters, see Richard S. Rosenberg, "Controlling Access to the Internet: The Role of Filters," *Proceedings for Computer Ethics: Philosophical Enquiry*, ed. Deborah G. Johnson, James H. Moor, and Herman T. Tavani, July 14–16, 2000, at Dartmouth College, pp. 232–261.

22. Pamela LiCalzi O'Connell, "Law Newsletter Has to Sneak Past Filters," *New York Times*, April 2, 2001, p. C4.

23. Judge Leonie M. Brinkema, *Mainstream Loudoun, et al. v. Board of Trustees of the Loudoun County Library, et al.*

24. "Current State of Internet Content Filtering," *EPIC Alert*, March 2, 2000.

25. www.frc.org. On the other side, see, for example, the National Coalition Against Censorship, www.ncac.org.

26. *ALA v. United States*.

27. Amol Sharma, "Wireless Carriers Set Strict Decency Standards for Content," *Wall Street Journal*, April 27, 2006, pp. B1, B4.

28. Brock Meeks, "Internet as Terrorist," *Cyberwire Dispatch*, May 11, 1995; Brock Meeks, "Target: Internet," *Communications of the ACM*, 38, no. 8 (August 1995): pp. 23–25.

29. The quotations in this paragraph are from Meeks, "Internet as Terrorist."

30. David Armstrong, "Bomb Recipes Flourish Online Despite New Law," *Wall Street Journal*, January 18, 2001, pp. B1, B8.

31. Entertainment Software Ratings Board, www.esrb.org.

32. www.missingkids.com.

33. Quoted in David Foster, "Children Lured from Home by Internet Acquaintances," Associated Press, June 13, 1995.

34. Victoria Murphy Barret, "Spam Hunter," Forbes.com, July 23, 2007, members.forbes.com/forbes/2007/0723/054.html (accessed September 13, 2007).

35. Some case documents for *Intel v. Hamidi* are available at www.intelhamidi.com. Or see appellate-cases.courtinfo.ca.gov, case no. C033076.

36. See, for example, Wikipedia's article "Challenge-Response Spam Filtering."

37. Jayson Matthews, "Harris Interactive Continues Spam Battle with MAPS," siliconvalley.internet.com/news/article/0,2198,3531_434061,00.html, August 9, 2000 (accessed April 9, 2001).

38. Quoted in Tom Espiner, "Antispam Group Rejects E-mail Payment Plan," CNET News, February 7, 2006, news.com.com.

39. Esther Dyson, "You've Got Goodmail," *New York Times*, March 17, 2006, www.nytimes.com/2006/03/17/opinion/17dyson.html (accessed September 13, 2007).

40. Federal Trace Commission, "The CAN-SPAM Act: Requirements for Commercial Emailers," www.ftc.gov/bcp/conline/pubs/buspubs/canspam.htm.

41. Tamzin Booth, "The Web @ Work," *Wall Street Journal*, November 20, 2000, p. B6. (I could no longer find the site in 2007.)

42. John Simons, "CFTC Regulations on Publishing Are Struck Down," *Wall Street Journal*, June 22, 1999, p. A8; Scott Bullock, "CFTC Surrenders on Licensing Speech," *Liberty & Law*, Institute for Justice, 9, no. 2 (April 2000): p. 2.

43. *Swedenburg v. Kelly*.

44. Quoted in Brad Stone, "Web Gurus Aim to Bring Civility to a Bad-Tempered Blogosphere," *New York Times*, April 9, 2007, www.technewsworld.com/story/56774.html (accessed June 21, 2007).

45. Peter L. Bernstein, *Against the Gods: The Remarkable Story of Risk* (John Wiley & Sons, 1996), p. 89.

46. Stewart Baker, "The Net Escape Censorship? Ha!" *Wired*, September 1995, pp. 125–126.

47. Lisa Guernsey, "Welcome to the Web. Passport, Please?" *New York Times*, March 15, 2001, pp. D1, D8.

48. Mylene Mangalindan and Kevin Delaney, "Yahoo! Ordered To Bar the French From Nazi Items," *Wall Street Journal*, November 21, 2000, pp. B1, B4.

49. Davis Kravets, "Yahoo Nazi-Auctions Case Goes to Ninth Circuit," Associated Press, March 24, 2005; David Stout, "Whistle-Blower Protection Curbed in U.S.," *International Herald Tribune*, May 31, 2006.

50. Pinsent Masons Law Firm, "Ex-Yahoo! CEO's Nazi Auction Acquittal Upheld in France," Out-Law News, July 4, 2005, www.out-law.com/page-5510.

51. Barry Bearak, "Taliban Will Allow Access to Jailed Christian Aid Workers," *New York Times*, August 26, 2001, p. 8. In 2006 Afghanistan established a new virtue and vice ministry.

52. Reporters without Borders, "Government Filtering Makes Two Web sites Inaccessible," November 9, 2006, www.rsf.org/article.php3?id article=19678, and "New York Times Web site Unblocked, YouTube Still Inaccessible," December 7, 2006, www.rsf.org/article.php3?id article=20016.

53. *Wired*, September 1996, p. 42. James Miles, "Burma Clamps Down on Web," January 20, 2000, news.bbc.co.uk/2/hi/asia-pacific/611836.stm (accessed September 28, 2007); "State Department Releases World Human Rights Report," *EPIC Alert*, February 10, 1998; Robert Fox, "Newstracks," *Communications of the ACM*, December 1996, pp. 9–10.

54. Louisa Lim, "China to Censor Text Messages," BBC News, July 2, 2004, http://news.bbc.co.uk/2/hi/asia-pacific/3859403.stm.

55. The OpenNet Initiative, "Internet Filtering in Singapore in 2004-2005," www.opennetinitiative.net/studies/singapore. I learned of this excellent Web site, with reports on filtering the Net in many countries, from Jack Goldsmith and Tim Wu, *Who Controls the Internet?* (Oxford University Press, 2006).

56. James M. Yoch Jr., "Egypt Blogger Appeals Prison Sentence for Insulting Islam Online," *Jurist*, University of Pittsburgh School of Law, February 27, 2007, jurist.law.pitt.edu/paperchase/2007/02/egypt-blogger-appeals-prison-sentence.php (accessed February 27, 2007).

57. In "Google Launches Censored Version of Its Search-Engine," January 25, 2006, www.rsf.org.

58. Elinor Mills, "Google to Censor China Web Searches," CNET News.com, January 24, 2006.

59. Andrew McLaughlin, "Google in China," Google Blog, January 27, 2006, googleblog.blogspot.com/2006/01/googlein-china.html.

60. See n. 57.

61. The advertisements appeared on television.

62. Bradley Smith, former chair of the FEC, reports these and other incidents in "The Speech Police," *Wall Street Journal*, June 27, 2007, p. A13.

63. Justice Jim Johnson, in *San Juan County v. No New Gas Tax*, April 26, 2007, www.legalwa.org.

64. Carlin E. Bunch, "Internet Final Rules," *Record* (Federal Election Commission), 32, no. 5 (May 2006): pp. 1–3, www.fec.gov/pdf/record/2006/may06.pdf.

65. *Federal Election Commission v. Wisconsin Right to Life*.

66. Jeffrey M. O'Brien, "Free Agent," *Wired*, May 2001, p. 74.

67. Neil King, "Small Start-Up Helps CIA Mask Its Moves on Web," *Wall Street Journal*, February 12, 2001, pp. B1, B6.

68. Declan McCullagh, "SafeWeb's Holes Contradict Claims," *Wired News*, February 12, 2002, www.wired.com/politics/law/news/2002/02/50371.

69. *Wall Street Journal*, November 14, 2000, p. A11.

70. *McIntyre v. Ohio Elections Commission*, 514 U.S. 334, 115 S.Ct. 1511(1995).

71. "Defending Right To Post Message: 'CEO Is a Dodo,'" *Wall Street Journal*, September 28, 2000, pp. B1, B12.

72. *HealthSouth v. Krum*.

73. See Wikipedia (en.wikipedia.org/wiki/SLAPP) or www.cyberSLAPP.org.

74. Judge David O. Carter, *Global Telemedia International, Inc. v. Doe 1*, 00-1155 (C.D. Cal. February 23). For discussion of cases, legal background, and recommendations, see Lyrissa Barnett Lidsky, "Silencing John Doe: Defamation and Disclosure in Cyberspace," *Duke Law Journal*, 49, no. 4 (February 2000): pp. 855–946, www.law.duke.edu/journals/dlj.

75. In a speech at the Computers, Freedom, and Privacy Conference, San Francisco, March 1995.

76. Quoted in Jared Sandberg, "Suit Challenges State's Restraint of the Internet," *Wall Street Journal*, September 25, 1996, pp. B1, B4.

77. Quoted in Robert Corn-Revere, "Caught in the Seamless Web: Does the Internet's Global Reach Justify Less Freedom of Speech?" in *Who Rules The Net? Internet Governance and Jurisdiction*, ed. Adam Thierer and Clyde Wayne Crews Jr. (Cato Institute, 2003).

78. Thomas W. Hazlitt, "Broadbandits," *Wall Street Journal*, August 12–13, 2006, p. A9.

79. For Web sites of the opposing sides, see Save the Internet (SaveTheInternet.com) and Hands Off the Internet (handsoff.org).

80. Alan Davidson, "Vint Cerf Speaks Out on Net Neutrality," Google Blog, googleblog.blogspot.com/2005/11/vint-cerf-speaks-out-on-net-neutrality.html, November 8, 2005.

81. March 2006, quoted on the Web site of Hands Off the Internet (handsoff.org) (accessed July 31, 2006).

82. Armstrong, "Bomb Recipes Flourish Online Despite New Law."

83. Robert D. Atkinson, "Leveling the E-Commerce Playing Field: Ensuring Tax and Regulatory Fairness for Online and Offline Businesses," Progressive Policy Institute, www.ppionline.org, June 30, 2003.

84. Massimo Calabresi, "Quick, Hide the Tanks!" *Time*, May 15, 2000, p. 60.

BOOKS AND ARTICLES

- Abrams, Floyd. *Speaking Freely: Trials of the First Amendment.* Viking Penguin, 2005. Includes a chapter on campaign finance reform and the First Amendment and a chapter on free speech issues outside the United States.

- Corn-Revere, Robert. "Caught in the Seamless Web: Does the Internet's Global Reach Justify Less Freedom of Speech?" Cato Institute, July 24, 2002.

- Dershowitz, Alan. "The Right to Transmit Hate Anonymously," United Feature Syndicate, 1995.

- Dyson, Esther. *Release 2.1: A Design for Living in the Digital Age.* Broadway, 1998.

- Electronic Privacy Information Center. *Filters and Freedom 2.0: Free Speech Perspectives on Internet Content Controls.* www.epic.org, 2001.

- Emord, Jonathan. *Freedom, Technology, and the First Amendment.* Pacific Research Institute, 1991.

- Godwin, Mike. *Cyber Rights: Defending Free Speech in the Digital Age.* Times Books, Random House, 1998.

- Grossman, Lawrence K. "Maintaining Diversity in the Electronic Republic." *Technology Review*, November/December 1995, 23–26.

- Hazlett, Thomas W. "The Rationality of U.S. Regulation of the Broadcast Spectrum." *Journal of Law & Economics*, April 1990, 133–175.

- Heins, Marjorie. *Not In Front of the Children: "Indecency," Censorship, and the Innocence of Youth.* Hill & Wang, 2001.

- Hentoff, Nat. *Free Speech for Me—But Not for Thee: How the American Left and Right Relentlessly Censor Each Other.* Harper Collins, 1992.

- Huber, Peter. *Law and Disorder in Cyberspace.* Oxford University Press, 1997. Criticizes FCC regulation of telecommunications, showing examples where regulations have delayed the introduction of new technologies.

- Kapor, Mitchell. "Civil Liberties in Cyberspace." *Scientific American*, September, 1991, 159–164.

- Lidsky, Lyrissa Barnett. "Silencing John Doe: Defamation and Disclosure in Cyberspace." *Duke Law Journal*, 49, no. 4 (February 2000): 855–946, www.law.duke.edu/journals/dlj.

- Rosenberg, Richard S. "Controlling Access to the Internet: The Role of Filters," *Proceedings for Computer Ethics: Philosophical Enquiry*, ed. Deborah G. Johnson, James H. Moor, and Herman T. Tavani, July 14–16, 2000, at Dartmouth College, 232–261.

- "Science, Technology, and the First Amendment, Special Report," Office of Technology Assessment, U.S. Department of Commerce, Washington, DC, January 1988 (Report No. OTA-CIT-369).

- Shane, Scott, *Dismantling Utopia: How Information Ended the Soviet Union.* I. R. Dee, 1994.

- de Sola Pool, Ithiel. *Technologies of Freedom.* Harvard University Press, 1983. This book describes the history, rights, restrictions, and responsibilities of the various communications technologies in depth.

- Volokh, Eugene. "Freedom of Speech in Cyberspace from the Listener's

Perspective: Private Speech Restrictions, Libel, State Action, Harassment, and Sex," *University of Chicago Legal Forum*, 1996, 377–436.

- Walker, Jesse. *Rebels on the Air: An Alternative History of Radio in America*. New York University Press, 2001.

- Wallace, Jonathan D. "Nameless in Cyberspace: Anonymity on the Internet," Cato Institute Briefing Papers, No. 54, December 8, 1999.

4

INTELLECTUAL PROPERTY

> *The Congress shall have Power To . . . promote the Progress of Science and useful Arts, by securing for limited Times to Authors and Inventors the exclusive Right to their respective Writings and Discoveries . . .*
>
> —U.S. Constitution, Article I, Section 8

4.1 Intellectual Property and Changing Technology

4.1.1 WHAT IS INTELLECTUAL PROPERTY?

Have you ever posted on the Web a homemade video set to a popular song? Have you recorded a televised movie to watch later in the week? Have you downloaded music or a movie from the Web without paying for it? Have you e-mailed a copy of an online news article to a dozen friends? Do you know which of these actions are legal and which are illegal, and why? Is it legal for a search engine to copy video and books in order to display excerpts? How do both copyright owners and those who use or sell the works of others abuse copyright? How should intellectual-property owners respond to new technologies and the increased copying that results from them? Will strict notions of copyright smother the new creativity enabled by modern technology? We begin our exploration of these and other issues about intellectual property by explaining the concept of intellectual property and reviewing principles of copyright law.

Creative works such as books, articles, plays, songs (both music and lyrics), works of art, movies, and software are protected by copyright, a legal concept that defines rights to intellectual property. It is not necessary to apply for a copyright. If a work satisfies the requirements for copyright, it has legal protection when it is created. Patent, another legal concept that defines rights to intellectual property, protects some software. The application process for patents can be long and complex. The U.S. Patent and Trademark Office evaluates patent applications and decides whether to grant them.

In addition to copyright and patent, there are other forms of intellectual property that various laws protect. They include trademarks,* trade secrets, and others. This chapter concentrates more on copyright than other forms of intellectual property because digital technology and the Internet affect copyright so strongly. Patent issues

---

*A *trademark* is a symbol (a word, phrase, logo, or other device) that identifies a product and/or the company that produces it. Companies may register trademarks with the government in order to protect ownership and control use of their trademarks.

for software and Web technologies have become quite important. We discuss them in Section 4.7.

Why is intellectual property given legal protection? The value of a book or a song or a computer program is much more than the cost of printing it, putting it on disk, or uploading it to the Web. The value of a painting is higher than the cost of the canvas and paint used to create the painting. The value of intellectual and artistic works comes from the creativity, ideas, research, skills, labor, and other nonmaterial efforts and attributes their creators provide. Designing and developing a computer program can take months or years of work and cost thousands or millions of dollars. Our property rights to the physical property we create or buy include the rights to use it, to prevent others from using it, and to set the (asking) price for selling it. We would be reluctant to make the effort to buy or produce physical things if anyone else could just take them away. If anyone could copy a novel, a computer program, or a movie for the small price of the copying, the creator of the work would receive very little income from the creative effort and would lose some of the incentive for producing it. Protection of intellectual property has both individual and social benefits: It protects the right of artists, authors, and inventors to compensation for what they create, and by so doing, it encourages production of valuable, intangible, easily copied, creative work.

The key to understanding intellectual-property protection is to understand that the thing protected is the intangible creative work—not its particular physical form. When we buy a novel, we are buying a physical collection of paper and ink or an electronic-book file that contains a copy of the book's contents, but we are not buying the intellectual property—that is, the plot, the organization of ideas, the presentation, the characters and events that form the abstraction that is the intangible "book," or the "work." The owner of a physical book may give away, lend, or resell the physical book he or she bought but may not make copies (with some exceptions). The right to make copies belongs to the owner of the intangible "book," that is, the owner of the copyright. The principle is similar for software, music, movies, and so on. The buyer of a software package is buying only a copy of it or a license to use the software. When we buy a movie on digital video disc (DVD), we are buying one copy with the right to watch it but not to play it in a public venue or charge a fee.

The author of a particular piece of intellectual property, or his or her employer (e.g., a newspaper or a software company), may hold the copyright or may transfer it to a publisher, a music recording company, a movie studio, or some other entity. Copyrights last for a limited time, for example, the lifetime of the author plus 70 years. After that, the work is in the *public domain*; anyone can freely copy and use it. Congress has extended the time period for copyright control more than a dozen times. The extensions are controversial as they hold more material out of the public domain for a long time. For example, the movie industry lobbied for and obtained an extension of its copyright protection period from 75 years to 95 years when the first Mickey Mouse cartoon was about to enter public domain.

U.S. copyright law (Title 17 of the U.S. Code) gives the copyright holder the following exclusive rights, with some very important exceptions that we will describe:

❖ to make copies of the work

❖ to produce derivative works, such as translations into other languages or movies based on books

❖ to distribute copies

❖ to perform the work in public (e.g., music, plays)

❖ to display the work in public (e.g., artwork, movies, computer games, video on a Web site).

Restaurants, bars, shopping centers, and karaoke venues pay fees for the copyrighted music they play.* Movie makers pay for the right to base a movie on a book, even if they make significant changes to the story.

Making a copy of a copyrighted work or a patented invention does not deprive anyone else of the work's use. Intellectual property differs from physical property in this way. Thus, taking intellectual property by copying is different from theft of physical property, and copyright law does not prohibit *all* unauthorized copying, distribution, and so on. A very important exception is the "fair use" doctrine, which we discuss in Section 4.2.2. Uses of copyrighted material that the copyright owner has not authorized and that one of the exceptions in the law does not permit are infringements of the copyright and are subject to civil and/or criminal penalties.

Facts, ideas, concepts, processes, and methods of operation are not copyrightable.[†] Copyright protects creative expression, that is, the expression, selection, and arrangement of ideas. The boundary between an idea and the expression of an idea is often not clear. Hence, many cases of alleged copyright infringement involving similar, but not identical, works are legally uncertain. Many go to court.

The government grants patents (under Title 35 of the U.S. Code) for inventions of devices and processes. Patents protect new ideas by giving the inventor a monopoly on the invention for a specified period of time (e.g., 20 years). Patents differ from copyrights in that they protect the invention, not just a particular expression or implementation of it. Patent law prohibits anyone else from using the idea without authorization of the patent holder, even if another person independently came up with the same idea or invention. Thus, if the invention of a word processor, Web search engine, or e-commerce shopping cart were patentable, companies that sell or use these products would have to make agreements with, and pay royalties to, the patent holders.

Intellectual-property protection is well established in Western countries but not in all areas of the world. Most of the issues in this chapter are within a context that accepts

---

*Not all do, of course, but it is the accepted—and legal—practice.

[†]Recall, from Chapter 2, that some privacy advocates suggest giving people property rights in facts about themselves, whereas copyright law recognizes that copyrighting facts would restrict the desirable flow of information.

the legitimacy of intellectual-property protection but revolve around its extent, how new technology challenges it, and how it can or should evolve. Some people argue that there should be no copyright protection for software, that we should all be free to copy software without restrictions. We elaborate on these views in Section 4.6.*

4.1.2 CHALLENGES OF NEW TECHNOLOGIES

> *Copyright law will disintegrate.*
> —Nicholas Negroponte[1]

> *New technologies have been disrupting existing equilibria for centuries, yet balanced solutions have been found before.*
> —Pamela Samuelson[2]

Previous technologies raised challenges to intellectual-property protection. For example, photocopiers made copying of printed material easy. Earlier technologies, however, were not nearly as serious a threat as digital technology. A complete photocopy of a book is bulky, sometimes of lower print quality, awkward to read, and more expensive than a paperback. Computers and communications technologies made high-quality copying and high-quantity distribution extremely easy and cheap. Some of the technological factors are the following:

❖ storage of all sorts of information (text, sound, graphics, video) in standard digitized formats; the ease of copying digitized material and the fact that each copy is a "perfect" copy;

❖ high-volume, relatively inexpensive digital storage media, such as hard disks, compact discs (CDs), DVDs, and memory cards;

❖ scanners, which simplify converting printed text, photos, and artwork to digitized electronic form;

❖ compression formats that make music and movie files small enough to download, copy, and store;

❖ the Web, which makes it easy to find, download, and post material;

❖ broadband (high-speed) Internet connections that make transfer of huge files quick;

---

*Some people reject the whole notion of copyrights and patents. They see these mechanisms as providing government-granted monopolies, violating freedom of speech, and limiting productive efforts. This issue is independent of computer technology, so we do not directly cover it in this book. However, some arguments about free software, in Section 4.6, overlap arguments about the legitimacy of copyright in general.

❖ peer-to-peer technology, which permits easy transfer of files over the Internet by large numbers of strangers without a centralized system or service;

❖ software tools for manipulating video and sound, enabling and encouraging nonprofessionals to create new works using the works of others.

In the past, it was generally businesses (newspapers, publishers, entertainment companies) and professionals (photographers, writers) who owned copyrights, and it was generally businesses (legal and illegal) that could afford the necessary copying and production equipment to infringe copyrights. Individuals rarely had to deal with copyright law. Digital technology and the Internet empowered us all to be publishers, thus to become copyright owners (for our blogs and photos, for example), and they empowered us all to copy, and thus to infringe copyrights.

The first category of intellectual property to face significant threats from digital media was computer software itself. Copying software used to be common practice. As one writer said, it was "once considered a standard and acceptable practice (if it were considered at all)."[3] People gave copies to friends on floppy disks, and businesses copied business software. People traded *warez* (unauthorized copies of software, typically after its copy-protection has been "cracked") on computer bulletin boards long before the Web. Software publishers began using the term "software piracy" for high-volume, unauthorized copying of software. Pirated software included (and still includes) word processors, spreadsheet programs, operating systems, utilities, games, and just about any consumer software sold. Some, such as new versions of popular games, often appear on unauthorized sites or for sale in other countries before their official release. The software industry estimates the value of pirated software in billions of dollars.

Until little more than a decade ago, music and graphics files were too large to transfer conveniently. Tools for listening to music on computers were unavailable or awkward to use. In the early 1990s one could find on the Internet and download unauthorized copies of popular humor columns (copied from newspapers), lyrics of popular songs, images of Walt Disney Co. characters, Playboy pinups, and myriad Star Trek items. Technology improved, and prices of digital recording devices, like prices of computers, kept falling, making them available to the public. For example, CD recorders sold for about $1000 when introduced in 1996. Prices dropped to $99 within about three years, and millions sold. Only a few years later, the price of DVD players dropped below $100; DVD burners and iPods followed. Copying music and movies became easy, fast, cheap, and ubiquitous. The scope of the term "piracy" expanded to include high-volume, unauthorized copying of any form of intellectual property—whether by large numbers of individuals sharing files without charge or by underground groups selling unauthorized copies for high profits.

More new technology spawned services to provide music, television programs, and other entertainment in convenient ways. Video cameras and tools and video-sharing sites enabled members of the public to provide entertainment for each other—and to post and share professional videos owned by others. The entertainment industry, like the software industry, estimates that people copy, trade, and sell billions of dollars of its intellectual property without authorization.

Fearing that widespread copying and file sharing would severely reduce its income, the entertainment industry brought its ongoing battle to prevent unauthorized use of its products to the digital world and the Web. Its methods include a mix of measures: technology to detect and thwart copying, education about copyright law and the good reasons to protect intellectual property, lawsuits (both reasonable and abusive), and lobbying for expansions of copyright law, fair or not. Eventually, as we will see, some began to develop new business models to provide digital content to the public in convenient forms.

Users and observers of digital media and of the Internet debate whether copyright can survive the enormously increased ease of copying and the habits and expectations that developed about sharing information and entertainment online. Some argued that copyright would survive, mostly because of firm enforcement of copyright law. Others said the ease of copying would win out; most content will be free or almost free. These positions seem more compatible today than a decade ago. Enforcement has been fierce, but much legal content is free or cheap due to improved technology and the many services that provide free content sponsored by advertising.

4.2 Copyright Law and Significant Cases

4.2.1 A BIT OF HISTORY

A brief history of copyright law will provide necessary background and help illustrate how new technologies require changes or clarifications in law.[4]

The first U.S. copyright law, passed in 1790, covered books, maps, and charts and protected them for 14 years. Congress later extended the law to cover new technologies: photography, sound recording, and movies. The definition of an unauthorized copy in the Copyright Act of 1909 specified that it had to be in a form that could be seen and read visually. Even with the technologies of the early 20th century, this requirement was a problem. A court applied it in a case about copying a song onto a perforated piano-music roll. (Automatic pianos played such rolls.) A person could not read the music visually from the piano roll, so the copy was not judged a violation of the song's copyright, even though it violated the spirit and purpose of copyright.[5] In the 1970s a company sued for protection of its chess-playing program, implemented on a read-only memory (ROM) chip in its handheld computer chess game. Another company sold a game with the identical program; they likely copied the ROM. But because the ROM could not be read visually, a court held that the copy did not infringe the program's copyright.[6] Again, this did not well serve the purpose of copyright. The decision did not protect the creative work of the programmers. They received no compensation from a competitor's sales of their work.

In 1976 and 1980 Congress revised copyright law to cover software. "Literary works" protected by copyright include computer databases that exhibit creativity or originality[7] and computer programs that exhibit "authorship," that is, contain original expression of ideas. Recognizing that technology was changing rapidly, the revised law specifies that copyright applies to appropriate literary works "regardless of the nature of the material objects . . . in which they are embodied." A copy could be in violation of a copyright if the original can be "perceived, reproduced, or otherwise communicated by or from the copy, directly or indirectly."

One significant goal in the development of copyright law, illustrated by the examples above, has been to devise good definitions to extend the scope of protection to new technologies. As copying technologies improved, another problem arose: A lot of people will break a law if it is easy to do so and the penalties are weak. In the 1960s growth in illegal sales of unauthorized copies of recorded music (e.g., on tape) accompanied the growth of the music industry. In 1982 high-volume copying of records and movies became a felony. The software industry pressed for stiffer penalties for software copyright infringement. In 1992 making multiple copies of copyrighted work "willfully and for purposes of commercial advantage or private gain" became a felony. Making or distributing ten or more copies with retail value of more than $2,500 within six months became punishable by up to five years in jail. The copies could be of different programs (e.g., one copy each of ten programs). Fines under some circumstances could be as high as $250,000.[8] Copyright owners could sue or the government could prosecute a company if ten employees out of hundreds or thousands have an illegal copy of a program on their computers. Many intellectual-property users and attorneys believe making ten copies worth $2,500 is too small an offense to merit such severe penalties.

The No Electronic Theft Act, passed in 1997, is stricter. It was a response to the David LaMacchia case. LaMacchia, an MIT student, ran a bulletin board on a university computer. According to prosecutors, users of the bulletin board copied more than a million dollars' worth of copyrighted software, including popular applications packages and games, all in less than two months of operation in 1994. LaMacchia did not charge anyone to use the bulletin board. There was no "commercial advantage or private gain." The government dropped charges against LaMacchia after a judge ruled that the law under which prosecutors charged him did not apply. In response to the growing phenomenon of sharing files for free on the Internet, the No Electronic Theft Act made it a criminal offense to willfully infringe copyright by reproducing or distributing one or more copies of copyrighted works with total value of more than $1,000 within a six-month period.

Congress passed the Digital Millennium Copyright Act (DMCA) in 1998. This very important law has two significant parts. The anticircumvention provisions prohibit making, distributing, or using tools (devices, software, or services) to circumvent technological copyright protection systems used by copyright holders. (There are limited exceptions.[9]) The law provides for penalties up to five years in prison or a $500,000 fine for a first offense. The anticircumvention provisions are extremely controversial. They outlaw devices and software that have legitimate purposes. They criminalize actions that

CAN LAWS BE COPYRIGHTED?

State and local laws require that people follow detailed rules, specified in building codes, when constructing or remodeling a building. Professional or trade organizations of building contractors and other construction professionals write the codes. The organizations claim they hold the copyright on the building codes and charge hundreds of dollars for copies. Similarly, professional and trade organizations in other fields claim the copyright on various rules and codes they write, but which laws require the public or specific businesses to follow.

Peter Veeck bought a copy of the local building codes used in two Texas towns. He posted the codes on the Web as a public service, believing they should be in the public domain. The organization that wrote the codes, the Southern Building Code Congress International, Inc., sued him for copyright infringement. After four years in court, he won. The court ruled that when governments enact into law model building codes written by organizations, the codes enter the public domain.[10] This example, like those in Section 3.2.4 about longtime restrictions on investment newsletters and advertising, illustrates how the Web has led to reconsideration of various long-standing restrictions on flow of information.

The decision in this case seems to make sense and to obviously benefit the public. But it does raise questions: If professional or trade organizations continue to write building codes that cities and counties enact as laws, how will they be compensated? Do they need to be compensated?

do not infringe any copyrights. They can conflict with freedom of speech. We discuss them in Section 4.3.2.

The safe-harbor provisions of the DMCA, the second significant part of the law, protect Web sites from lawsuits for copyright infringement by users of the site if site operators remove infringing material when asked to do so by the copyright owners (often publishers and music and movie companies). This was a welcome protection for Web site owners and the public. The law recognized that online services, such as AOL at the time, could not review everything members post. The safe-harbor provisions of the DMCA (along with technological advances in the next several years) encouraged the development of huge numbers of Web sites that host user-generated content, including blogs, photos, recipes, articles, reviews, and the myriad other things we share on the Web. We now take this all for granted. Holding the sites legally liable for the occasional infringing material a user might post could have severely restricted this phenomenon. We discuss problems with the safe-harbor provisions in Sections 4.3.3 and 4.5.

In 2005, after huge growth in sales of unauthorized copies of movies, Congress made it a felony offense to record a movie in a movie theater—one of the ways copies get to those who reproduce and sell them illegally.

Why did copyright laws get more restrictive and punishing? Generally, creators and publishers of copyrighted works, including print publishers, movie companies, music publishers, sound recording companies (record labels), and the software industry, support stronger copyright protection. Congress often delegates the drafting of laws in complex areas to the industries involved. For most of the 20th-century, the intellectual-property industries drafted laws heavily weighted toward protecting their assets. On the other side, librarians and academic and scientific organizations generally opposed strict rules reducing the public's access to information. Most people were unaware of or indifferent to copyright issues. Digital media, and especially widespread public use of the Web and file sharing, focused attention on issues about how much control copyright owners should have. In the 1990s, cybercitizens and organizations such as the Electronic Frontier Foundation joined librarians and others to fight what they view as overly restrictive copyright law. Many court cases (some described in Section 4.2.3) began to clarify the application of copyright law to the Web. Many lawsuits over newer issues (e.g., those we discuss in Sections 4.3.3 and 4.4) are still in the courts. The challenge is to maintain the benefits of easily available material on the Web and encourage creative reuse of material while protecting the rights and investment of the owners of intellectual property.

4.2.2 THE FAIR-USE DOCTRINE

Copyright law and court decisions attempt to define the rights of authors and publishers consistent with two goals: promoting production of useful work and encouraging the use and flow of information. The fair-use doctrine allows uses of copyrighted material that contribute to the creation of new work (such as quoting part of a work in a review) and uses that are not likely to deprive authors or publishers of income for their work. Fair uses do not require the permission of the copyright holder. The notion of fair use (for literary and artistic works) grew from judicial decisions. In 1976, U.S. copyright law explicitly included it. It applies to software also. The 1976 copyright law predated the widespread use of personal computers (PCs). The software issues addressed mainly pertained to large business systems, and the law did not address issues related to the Web at all. Thus, it did not take into account many situations where questions of fair use now arise.

The law identifies possible fair uses, such as "criticism, comment, news reporting, teaching (including multiple copies for classroom use), scholarship, or research."[11] It lists four factors to consider in determining whether a particular use is a "fair use." They are the following:

1. the purpose and nature of the use, including whether it is for commercial purposes or nonprofit educational purposes. (Commercial use is less likely to be fair use.)
2. the nature of the copyrighted work. (Use of creative work, such as a novel, is less likely than use of factual work to be fair use.)

3. the amount and significance of the portion used.
4. the effect of the use on the potential market for or value of the copyrighted work. (Uses that reduce sales of the original work are less likely to be considered fair.)

No single factor alone determines whether a particular use is a fair use, but the last one generally gets more weight than the others.

Court decisions about copyright must be consistent with the First Amendment. Courts interpret the fair-use principle broadly to cover creation of parodies and similar works based on others without authorization. In many situations, it is not obvious whether a use is a fair use. Courts interpret and apply the guidelines in specific cases. Law scholars say that results of fair-use cases are often notoriously difficult to predict.

4.2.3 SIGNIFICANT CASES

The fair-use doctrine is important for different contexts. First, it helps us figure out under what circumstances we as consumers can legally copy music, movies, software, and so on. Second, developers of new software, recording devices, game players, and other products often must copy some or all of another company's software as part of the process of developing the new product. The new product might compete with the other company's product. Is such copying a fair use? We look at cases that cover these contexts. Some of the cases also involve the degree of legal responsibility a company has for copyright violations by users of its products or services. This point is important for many Web-based services, some that implicitly or explicitly encourage unauthorized uses of the works of others.

Sony v. Universal City Studios (1984)

The Sony case was the first case about private, noncommercial copying of copyrighted work that the Supreme Court decided.[12] The decision has implications for fair use involving new technologies. It is cited in Web-based entertainment cases and in cases about new kinds of digital recording devices.

Two movie studios sued Sony for contributing to copyright infringement because some customers used its Betamax video cassette recording machines to record movies shown on television. Thus, this case raised the important issue of whether copyright owners can sue makers of copying equipment because some buyers use the equipment to infringe copyrights. First we focus on the other issue the Supreme Court decided in the Sony case: whether recording a movie for personal use was a copyright infringement or a fair use. People copied the entire movie. Movies are creative, not factual, works. Thus, factors 2 and 3 of the fair-use guidelines argue against the taping. The very purpose of recording the movie was to view it at a later time. Normally the consumer reused the tape after viewing the movie, making it an "ephemeral copy." The copy was for a private, noncommercial purpose, and the movie studios could not demonstrate that they suffered any harm. The Court interpreted factor 2, the nature of the copyrighted work, to include not simply whether it was creative or factual, but also the fact that the studios receive a large fee for broadcasting movies on television, and the fee depends on having a large audience of people who view the movies for free. So factors 1, 2, and 4 argue for fair use. The Court ruled that recording a movie for viewing at a later time was a fair use.

The fact that people copied the entire work did not necessitate a ruling against fair use, although many examples of fair use apply only to small excerpts. The fact that the copying was a private, noncommercial use was significant. The Court said that private, noncommercial uses should be presumed fair unless there is a likelihood of economic harm to the copyright holder.

On the issue of the legitimacy of the Betamax machine, the Court said makers of a device with substantial legal uses should not be penalized because some people use it to infringe copyright. This is a very important principle. The DMCA (Section 4.3.2) has eroded it for tools that can circumvent copy protections.

Reverse engineering: game machines

In the Sony case, the Supreme Court's decision said that noncommercial copying of an entire movie can be fair use. In several cases involving game machines, the courts ruled that copying an entire computer program for a *commercial* use was fair, largely because the purpose was to create a new product, not to sell copies of another company's product. A federal appeals court decided *Sega Enterprises, Ltd. v. Accolade, Inc.* in 1992. Accolade made videogames to run on Sega machines. To make their games run properly, Accolade needed to figure out how part of Sega's game-machine software worked. Accolade copied Sega's program and decompiled it (i.e., translated it from machine code to a form in which they could read and understand it). This is *reverse engineering*. Sega sued; Accolade won. Accolade was making new games. The court viewed Accolade's activities as fitting the purpose of fair use, that is, to encourage production of new creative work. The fact that Accolade was a commercial entity was not critical. Although Accolade's games might reduce the market for Sega's games, that was fair competition. Accolade was not selling copies of Sega's games.[13]

In another 1992 case, *Atari Games v. Nintendo*, the court also ruled that making copies of a program for reverse engineering (to learn how it works so that a company can make a compatible product) was not copyright infringement. It is a fair "research" use.

The court applied the same arguments in 2000 in deciding in favor of Connectix Corporation in a suit by Sony Computer Entertainment, Inc. Connectix copied Sony's PlayStation BIOS (the basic input–output system) and reverse-engineered it to develop software that emulates the PlayStation console. Game players could then buy the Connectix program and play PlayStation games on their computers without buying the PlayStation console. Connectix's program did not contain any of Sony's code, and it was a new product, different from the PlayStation console. The copying of the BIOS was fair use.[14]

These decisions show how courts interpret fair use for situations not imagined when the guidelines were written. Reverse engineering is an essential process for creating new products that must interact with other companies' hardware and software. In fact, the huge PC industry and the low prices we pay for PCs owe much to reverse engineering of the IBM PC's BIOS in the 1980s. Phoenix Software, concerned about charges of copyright infringement, did not copy IBM's software. Instead, the company employed a team of engineers to painstakingly observe and document in detail how the IBM program behaved. Then, another team wrote new code to do the same functions. The court decisions permitting copying for reverse engineering make the process easier. However, the DMCA's prohibition on thwarting copy-prevention mechanisms makes reverse engineering of products with copy-protected software more difficult.

Sharing music: the Napster case

> *When Big Steel and the auto industry were under pressure during the '70s from low-cost imports, their first instinct was not to change their outmoded manufacturing plants but to beseech the courts to bar the outlanders. The record industry has taken a similar tack.*
>
> —Karl Taro Greenfeld[15]

MP3 is a file-compression format that reduced the size of files by a factor of about 10–12, so that people could download a song in a few minutes.* In 1997 and 1998, college students and other music hobbyists set up hundreds of MP3 sites on the Web, making thousands of songs available. Many songwriters, singers, and bands willingly made their music available. They considered MP3 a marvelous tool for promoting their work without the need for a contract with a large record company. But MP3 has no mechanism for preventing unlimited or unauthorized copying. Most trading of MP3 files on the Net was unauthorized. The Recording Industry Association of America (RIAA), the main record-company trade organization, shut down many MP3 sites by threatening legal action.

Napster opened on the Web in 1999 as a service allowing users to copy songs in MP3 files from the hard disks of other users. It was wildly popular and had more than 50 million users little more than a year later. Almost 100 million MP3 files were available on the service. A survey by Webnoize of more than 4,000 college students found that almost 75% of them used Napster at least once a month. It was well known that Napster users copied and distributed most of the songs they traded without authorization. Eighteen record companies sued for copyright infringement and asked for thousands of dollars in damages for each song traded on Napster. The record companies won.[16]

The Napster case is important for many reasons. The fact that so many people participated in an activity that courts decided was illegal is an indication of how new technology challenges existing law and attitudes about what is acceptable. Many people thought that the success of Napster meant the end of copyright. Instead, the court decision

---

*In the early 1990s, without MP3 and with the slower modems used then, it would have taken roughly a day to download one three-minute song.

showed that the legal system can still have a powerful impact. The arguments in the case apply to many other sites and services on the Internet.

The issues in the lawsuit against Napster were the following:

❖ Was the copying and distribution of music by Napster users legal under the fair-use guidelines?

❖ If not, was Napster responsible for the actions of its users?

Napster argued that the sharing of songs by its users was a legal fair use. Let's review the fair-use guidelines and how they apply.

Copying songs via Napster does not fit any of the general categories of purposes covered by fair use (e.g., education, research, news), but neither does copying movies or music on tapes. The *Sony v. Universal City Studios* case showed that the Supreme Court is willing to include entertainment as a possible fair-use purpose.

Napster argued that sharing songs via its service was fair use because people were making copies for personal, not commercial, use. Copyright experts said "personal" meant very limited use, for instance within a household, not trading with thousands of strangers.

Songs (lyrics and music) are creative material, and users were copying complete songs. Thus, fair-use guidelines 2 and 3 argue against fair use, but as the Sony case indicated, they do not necessarily outweigh other factors.

The final, and perhaps most important, point is the impact on the market for the songs, that is, the impact on the income of the artists and music companies that hold the copyrights. Napster argued that it did not hurt record industry sales; users sampled music on Napster and bought the CDs they liked. The music industry claimed Napster severely hurt sales. Survey and sales data did not unequivocally support either side. One of my students said he had not bought a single CD since Napster opened. How typical was that? Reports of sales data for music albums, CDs, and tapes differ, but most showed sales rising significantly during most years in the 1990s, and dropping or rising only slightly in 2000. For example, music sales in the U.S. (the largest market) dropped 1.5% in 2000. Sales of singles were down 46%, while CD album sales were up 2.5%.[17] We do not know if Napster was the only reason for the declines, but it is reasonable to conclude that the huge volume of copying on Napster had a negative impact on sales and that the impact would grow.

Many legal observers thought the large-scale copying on Napster was illegal copyright infringement, not fair use, and that is how the court ruled.

But was Napster responsible for copyright infringement by its users? Napster did not keep copies of songs on its computers. It provided lists of available songs and lists of users logged on at any time. Using peer-to-peer software downloaded from Napster, users transferred songs from each other's hard disks. Napster argued that it was similar to a search engine, and that the recently passed DMCA protected it from responsibility for copyright violations by its users. The record companies argued that the law requires companies to make an effort to prevent copyright violations, but Napster did not take sufficient steps to eliminate unauthorized songs or users who committed violations.

Napster cited the Sony Betamax case, in which the court said the maker of devices with substantial legitimate uses is not liable for users of the device who infringe copyrights, even if the maker knows some will. Napster had substantial legitimate uses in promoting new bands and artists who were willing to let users copy their songs. The recording industry argued that Napster was not a device or new technology, and it was not asking to ban a technology or shut Napster down. The record companies objected to how Napster *used* widely available technology to aid copyright infringement. They wanted Napster to stop listing songs without permission of the copyright owners.

Sony's relationship with a customer ended when the customer bought the Betamax machine. Napster interacted with its members to provide access to songs they copied. The court said Napster was liable because it had the right and ability to supervise its system, including the copyright-infringing activities, and it had a financial interest in those activities. Napster was a business. Although it did not charge for copying songs, it expected the free copying to attract users so that it would make money in other ways.

The court ruled in 2001 that Napster "knowingly encourages and assists in the infringement of copyrights."[18] The court ordered Napster to remove from its listings song titles provided by the record companies. It faced civil suits that could have required payments of billions of dollars in damages. After some ineffective attempts to manage the song lists, Napster shut down. (Another company bought the "Napster" name and now operates a legal online music service.)

File sharing: *MGM v. Grokster*

About the time of the Napster decision, new peer-to-peer software appeared, and numerous companies and Web sites sprang up to provide peer-to-peer file-sharing services (Gnutella, Morpheus, Kazaa, and others). Within months of Gnutella's appearance, for example, more than a million files were available. Many were unauthorized MP3 music files and unauthorized software. These systems presented a new challenge for the entertainment and software industries. They enabled copying of files among users on the Internet without a central service, like Napster, to sue when users infringe copyrights. In *MGM v. Grokster*, the music and movie industry sued Grokster and StreamCast Networks (the owner of Morpheus). The companies did not provide a central service or list of music files available on the disks of users (as did Napster), but they provided the software for sharing files. Technologists and supporters of file sharing argued that peer-to-peer file-transfer programs had potential for many productive, legal uses. (They were correct.) A lower court and an appeals court ruled that distribution of file-sharing software does not violate copyright laws. These rulings seemed consistent with the Supreme Court's decision in the Sony Betamax case. In 2005, however, the Supreme Court unanimously ruled that intellectual-property owners could sue the companies for encouraging copyright infringement. At about the same time, an Australian court made a similar ruling against Kazaa.

The Napster and Grokster decisions made it clear that businesses that encourage copyright infringement and provide tools to do so as a fundamental part of their business model cannot operate legally. Many file-sharing companies settled suits with the entertainment industry, paying millions of dollars. Sharman Networks, owner of Kazaa, agreed to a $115 million settlement. Grokster shut down and was sold for a token fee. Many others shut down. Critics of the decisions worried that they threatened development of new peer-to-peer technology and applications.

4.3 Copying and Sharing

Unauthorized copying and sharing of music, and now video, continue at a huge rate on the Web. Music sales have steadily dropped since about 2000. Undoubtedly, entertainment companies are losing income and potential income they could earn from their intellectual property. As we seek solutions to this problem, though, we should recognize that "the problem" looks different from different perspectives. What does it mean to solve the problems of technology's impact on intellectual-property rights? What are the problems for which we seek solutions?

To people who enjoy getting movies and music online, the problem is to get them cheaply and conveniently. To writers, singers, artists, and actors—and to the people who work in production, marketing, and management—the problem is to ensure that they are paid for the time and effort they put in to create the intangible intellectual-property products we enjoy. To the entertainment industry, to publishers and software companies, the problem is to protect their investment and expected, or hoped-for, revenues. To the millions who post amateur works using the works of others, the problem is to continue to create without unreasonably burdensome requirements and threats of lawsuits. To scholars and various advocates, the problem is how to protect intellectual property, but also to protect fair use, reasonable public access, and the opportunity to use new technologies to the fullest to provide new services and creative work. In this section, we explore problems and solutions from several perspectives. As we saw with privacy problems, solutions (some good, some not) come from technology, the market, education, and law.

4.3.1 DEFENSIVE AND AGGRESSIVE RESPONSES FROM THE CONTENT INDUSTRIES

Ideas from the software industry

Software was the first digital product to be widely copied. Individuals traded popular software on floppy disks with the view that it was okay because it was easy and the software was expensive. Software pirates sold large numbers of copied programs (and still do). In the 1980s and 1990s, employees of many businesses and organizations (including newspaper companies, architectural firms, manufacturing companies, government agencies, and schools and universities) routinely made unauthorized copies of software for large numbers of computers. A variety of techniques for protecting software were developed early, with varying success. We describe a few, including techniques to thwart copying, lawsuits, and aggressive law enforcement.

Software companies encoded an expiration date in free sample versions of software. The software destroyed itself after that date. Some business software includes a hardware *dongle*, a device that the purchaser has to plug into a port on the computer so that the software can run, thus ensuring that the software runs on only one machine at a time. Consumer software publishers use "copy protection" on diskettes to ensure that you cannot copy a diskette or, if you can, the copy will not run. Some software requires activation or registration with a special serial number.

Many companies have dropped these techniques, largely because consumers dislike them. Customers do not like the inconvenience of replacing a copy-protected diskette if something goes wrong. Some customers refuse to buy copy-protected software if there is a nonprotected competitor. Some of these systems were "cracked"; that is, programmers found ways to thwart the protection mechanisms. Some companies have sold programs that deactivate the built-in copy protection on other programs. The principle of the Sony Betamax case applied in a case where a software vendor sued a company selling a program to thwart its copy protection: The court ruled that, because the program had lawful applications (e.g., enabling someone to make backup copies), the company could sell it.*[19] Activation features irritate customers; they inconvenience people who want to move their software when they replace an old computer.

Software industry organizations, dubbed "software police," were active in business offices before they began policing cyberspace. In most cases, violations of copyright law were so clear that the business or organization agreed to fines of hundreds of thousands of dollars rather than go to trial. Software copying by businesses decreased, due in part to better understanding of the ethical issues involved and in part to fear of fines and exposure in a business climate that gradually came to view large-scale copyright violation as not acceptable. The Business Software Alliance (BSA), a software industry organization, still "busts" a few hundred companies each year for using illegally copied software. BSA offers rewards of up to $1 million for people who report serious offenders.

Law enforcement agencies raided swap meets, warehouses, and other sites and prosecuted sellers of pirated software (and, later, music CDs and movie DVDs). Penalties for organized, large-scale efforts can be severe. A leader of the group DrinkOrDie received a 46-month prison sentence, the longest sentence imposed for software piracy at the time (2002).[20] Movie and music companies pursue enforcement actions against pirate sites. A man who repeatedly recorded new movies on his camera in movie theaters and made pirate copies to sell received a sentence of seven years in jail.

---

*This case was decided before Congress passed the DMCA. Under the DMCA the decision probably would have gone the other way.

Software companies obtained court orders and filed lawsuits to shut down Internet bulletin boards and Web sites. They targeted Internet service providers (ISPs), threatening legal action against those whose subscribers operated file-sharing services or traded unauthorized files via peer-to-peer software, pressuring them to cancel accounts of alleged offenders. They continue to pursue well-publicized prosecutions of anyone infringing their copyrights. The entertainment industry has filed hundreds of lawsuits against individuals whom it accuses of sharing music. Letters to college students threaten fines of thousands of dollars.

On the early Internet, software publisher organizations searched the Internet for keywords and phrases such as "warez" and "cheap software" to find targets for their enforcement actions. As data speeds increased and video-sharing sites inspired more unauthorized copying, the entertainment industry and start-up companies (recognizing an opportunity) developed sophisticated tools to search billions of Web pages for copies of specific text, images, sound, or video. (One company announced that it could identify a segment of a song as short as four seconds.)

Banning, suing, and taxing

There has been much criticism of some of the tactics and aggressive enforcement efforts we just described. The content industries defend their actions as essential to protecting their intellectual property from the huge amount of illegal copyright infringement now common. The next approach we describe may be more threatening to innovation. Because it penalizes products, companies, and activities that do not always or necessarily infringe copyrights, it is less justifiable.

Through both lawsuits and lobbying, the intellectual-property industries have delayed, restricted, or prevented services, devices, technologies, and software that make copying easy and that people are likely to use widely in ways that infringe copyrights, although they also have many legal uses. The technology for consumer CD recording devices for music was available since 1988, but lawsuits filed by record companies delayed its introduction. Similarly, the record industry sued to block digital audio tape (DAT) and DAT recorders and lobbied for a law banning DAT machines without built-in copy protection. A group of companies, including a television network and Walt Disney Corp., sued the makers of digital video recording machines that store TV programs and can skip commercials. The movie and record industries delayed the introduction of DVD players by threatening to sue companies that make them if consumers could copy movies on the devices.

The RIAA sued and obtained a restraining order to stop Diamond Multimedia Systems from shipping its Rio machine, a portable device to play MP3 music files. Diamond eventually won, partly because the court interpreted the Rio as a player, not a recorder, that allowed people to play their music at different locations—just as the Sony decision (Section 4.2.3) said people could watch TV shows at different times.[21] Some observers believe that Apple's iPod would not have been possible if the RIAA's lawsuit against the Rio had succeeded.

As new companies introduced a variety of new products and services to deliver entertainment in flexible and convenient ways, the costs of fighting industry lawsuits effectively shut some of them down, with no trial to decide whether their products were legal.

The entertainment industry pushed hard for laws and industry agreements to require that makers of PCs and digital recorders and players build copy-protection mechanisms into their products. It pressured device makers to design their systems so that files in unprotected formats do not play well—or at all. Such requirements could reduce illegal copying, of course. They, however, interfere with the use and sharing of homemade works. They complicate sharing of material in the public domain. They restrict legal copying for personal use and other fair uses. Laws requiring or prohibiting specific features violate the freedom of manufacturers to develop and sell products they consider appropriate.

As an alternative to banning media and devices that increase the likelihood of copyright infringement, several governments, including most in the European Union, tax digital media and equipment to pay copyright holders for losses expected from unauthorized copying. In the 1960s, they introduced special taxes on photocopiers and magnetic tape and later added taxes on manufacturers of PCs, printers, scanners, and recorders. Many add significant taxes to iPods, cell phones, and blank DVDs. The taxes totaled more than a billion euros in 2005. Advocates of these taxes argue that makers of copying equipment are responsible for losses their equipment causes for intellectual-property owners, and the schemes are a reasonable compromise in a situation where it is difficult to catch each infringer. Critics argue that the taxes make equipment more expensive, penalize equipment makers unfairly, charge honest users unfairly, and politicize the difficult job of fairly distributing the money collected.

Should we ban or restrict software, a technology, a device, or research because it has the potential for illegal use, or should we ban only the illegal *uses*? This question addresses a principle covering much more than the entertainment industry fights to ban, delay, and tax electronic devices and media that make copyright infringement easier. In Chapter 2, we described the FBI's and NSA's pressure to ban telephone technology that is difficult to tap and encryption schemes that were difficult for them to crack. Law enforcement agencies advocate banning anonymous Web browsing and e-mail, because they can hide criminal activity. The issue of banning or restricting tools that have criminal uses arises in numerous areas unrelated to computer technology. Some U.S. cities prohibit the sale of spray paint to minors, because they might paint graffiti on walls. Of course, they might paint a bookcase. Some cities ban chewing gum, because some people discard the gum on the street, making a mess. Many countries prohibit ordinary people from owning guns to protect their homes or businesses, because some people misuse guns. Laws ban drug paraphernalia, because people might use it with illegal drugs. Some of these laws make prevention of specific crimes easier. For example, it might be hard to find the person who painted graffiti, but it is easy to reduce the sale of spray paint by threatening shop owners with fines.

In a free society, which should win: the freedom of people to develop and use tools for legal purposes or the prevention of potential crimes? Those who reject the policy of banning a tool that has both legitimate and illegal uses argue its absurdity by taking it to its extreme: we should ban matches because arsonists use them. Others argue that we should look at each application individually, considering the risks of harm. Proponents and lobbyists for bans on tools usually rank the damage they could cause (in general or to the interests of their clients) more highly than the loss of freedom and convenience to those who would use the tool honestly and productively. We can rarely predict all the creative and innovative (legal) uses of a new technology. Bans, delays, and expensive restrictions often cost all of society the unforeseen benefits. The technologies listed in Section 4.1.2 as causes of problems for intellectual-property protection are the foundation of the incredible benefits of the computer and communications revolution.

Digital rights management

Digital rights management (DRM) technologies are a collection of techniques that control uses of intellectual property in digital formats. Copy protection on software diskettes was an early example. DRM has become more sophisticated. It includes hardware and software schemes using encryption and other tools. Music companies, movie studios, and book publishers hesitated to deliver digital copies of their products on the Web without DRM because they could not prevent mass copying. DRM provides flexibility, allowing the producer of a file to specify what a user may do with it. With the ability to build in limits on the life or uses of digitized works, record companies began to sell songs and offer subscription services where customers could listen to a specified number of songs each month for a fixed fee. DRM implementations for various products can prevent saving, printing, making more than a specified number of copies, distributing a file, extracting excerpts, or fast-forwarding over commercials. DRM helps provide a variety of low-priced, limited-use options for authorized distribution of content while eliminating some unauthorized uses. Most people are willing to pay for what they use if the price is reasonable and the purchase is convenient.

More about encryption: Section 2.4.1

There are many criticisms of DRM. DRM prevents fair uses as well as infringing uses. It can prevent extraction of small excerpts for review or for a fair use in a new work, for example. You cannot play or view protected works on old or incompatible machines. (Apple, Microsoft, and Sony all used different DRM schemes for music.) Some DRM-protected products do not work on machines running the Linux operating system. Movie companies use DRM to prevent viewers in Europe from playing a movie on DVD legally purchased in the U.S. and vice versa.*

We have long had the right to lend and resell a physical book, record, or CD that we owned. (These activities do not require making a copy.) If we could not lend or resell a

---

*Movie companies release movies in different countries at different times and with different prices. Controls based on location help them manage their marketing.

book to a friend, the friend might buy a copy, providing income to the copyright owner. But courts and law established the principle that the copyright owner has the right only to the "first sale" of a copy. The buyer may transfer the purchased copy. Publishers, especially of textbooks, which resell often, lobbied for legislation requiring a royalty to the publisher on each resale; they were unsuccessful. DRM enables the industry to prevent lending and selling a purchased copy. DRM puts long-accepted uses of, and rights to use, intellectual property at risk. Will prevention of lending and resale lead to lower prices? So low that consumers will not care that they lose these options? Or will consumers object so much that companies provide ways to allow lending and reselling?

DRM has a serious disadvantage for the content industries: It does not really protect them. Virtually all copy-protection schemes are quickly cracked. Once one person cracks the protection and uploads a copy to a peer-to-peer network, large numbers of copies will spread all over. In an effort to address this problem, movie companies developed a particularly annoying DRM *key-revocation* scheme for movies on high-definition DVDs. Software in computers that play these DVDs match a key on the disc to a key stored in the software. When hackers figure out and distribute the key (enabling people to make copies), the companies begin using a new key in new DVDs, and consumers must install a software upgrade with the new key. An attempt to play a new disc with the old software disables the disc-playing software. This scheme irritates honest users. It is not clear if it has a significant effect on reducing movie piracy.

For years, the music industry fought against distribution of music in (unprotected) MP3 format. Steve Jobs and some people in the music industry argued that DRM was ineffective against piracy. The debate about DRM protection goes on within the movie industry as well. Some see DRM as essential for protecting against piracy. They fear the movie industry will suffer severe economic losses, as did the music industry, if they allow sharing of movie files to increase. Others point out that pirated movies, like copied songs, circulate unprotected. The controls and restrictions on legally sold movies encourage irritated consumers to seek out illegal, unprotected copies even though they are willing to pay.

In 2007, EMI Group and Universal Music Group (two of the largest music companies in the world) announced they would sell songs without DRM at numerous online outlets. This was a sharp break from the long-standing industry position. It could mark the beginning of a major shift. Its significance might become clear only after several years.

4.3.2 THE DMCA VERSUS FAIR USE, FREEDOM OF SPEECH, AND INNOVATION

> *Every time a 42-year-old figures out how to lock something up, a 14-year-old is going to figure out a new program.*
>
> —Jim Griffin, music-industry consultant[22]

Programmers and researchers frequently find ways to crack or thwart DRM and other copy-protection schemes that control uses of movies, e-books, music, among others. The DMCA prohibits making, distributing, or using tools (devices, software, or services) to circumvent technological copyright protection systems used by copyright holders. The law provides for heavy penalties and fines for violators. Before passage of the DMCA, court decisions protected technologies that have significant legitimate, noninfringing uses. The DMCA changed that for circumvention techniques. Copyright owners can sue under the DMCA even if a person or company (or device a company makes) does not infringe any copyrights. We noted that DRM controls restrict fair uses and use of material in the public domain. The DMCA ban on circumventing controls has a few exceptions, but they are limited and do not include fair use or access to material in the public domain.[23]

The first major legal cases based on the DMCA involved the Content Scrambling System (CSS), a protection scheme for movies. Three programmers, including 15-year-old Jon Johansen of Norway,* wrote and distributed a program, called DeCSS, that defeated the scrambling.[24] DeCSS could, of course, be used to create numerous unauthorized copies, and that might well be its main use. But it and other circumvention techniques have many legitimate uses. DeCSS enables users of the Linux operating system to view (legally purchased) DVDs on their computers. It enables the legal owner of a DVD to view the disk anywhere in the world. It enables someone to fast-forward through commercials if a DVD locks out the fast-forward feature.

Several Hollywood studios sued people who posted DeCSS on their Web sites. They sued Eric Corley, the operator of 2600.com, demanding removal of DeCSS from his Web site and also removal of links to other sites with DeCSS.[25] Attorneys for Corley argued that people could use DeCSS for fair uses, that banning it violated freedom of speech, and that programmers need to discuss computer code and techniques. None of these arguments mattered much. The judge ruled that DeCSS was illegal under the DMCA and ordered its removal. Soon after the decision, descriptions of DeCSS appeared on the Web in haiku, bar code, short movies, a song, a computer game, and art.[26] Most of these publications of the code were protests of the judge's decision. They demonstrate how difficult it is to distinguish between expression of an opinion, which the First Amendment strongly protects, and computer code, a form of speech the judge said the government could more easily regulate.† In a similar case (*DVD Copy Control Association v. Bunner*), courts disagreed about whether an injunction against publishing DeCSS was an unconstitutional restraint on free speech. The California Supreme Court said that prohibiting someone from publishing a company's trade secrets does not violate one's freedom of speech. Another court ruled that DeCSS was widely available when Bunner posted it. Therefore, it was not a trade secret, and the injunction *did* violate his freedom of speech. Meanwhile, Jon Johansen was tried in Norway under a Norwegian law. The court ruled that it was not

---

*The others chose to remain anonymous.

†Recall that encryption export rules (discussed in Chapter 2), like the DMCA, restricted publication of research and software, but eventually a judge ruled that software is a form of speech.

illegal to break DVD security to view legally purchased DVDs and that the prosecutors had not proved Mr. Johansen used the program to illegally copy movies.

In another case, a team of researchers responded to a challenge by the Secure Digital Music Initiative (SDMI), an industry consortium, to test its digital watermarking schemes (a form of digital copyright protection) for music files. The researchers quickly found ways to thwart several of the techniques and planned to present a paper on the flaws in the protection schemes at a conference. The head of the research group, Princeton University computer science professor Edward Felten, said SDMI threatened lawsuits based on the DMCA. He decided not to present the paper.[27] The DMCA has exceptions for actions necessary for encryption research and computer security, but the scope of the exceptions is limited and unclear. This case showed that the DMCA and the industry's threats of lawsuits have a chilling effect on publication of research. Felten and other researchers filed a suit asking a federal court to rule that the anticircumvention provisions of the DMCA (when applied to software and research) violated the First Amendment. A computer science professional organization argued that fear of prosecution under the DMCA could cause researchers and conferences to leave the U.S., eroding its leadership in the field.[28] The case ended after the recording industry and the government issued statements that lawsuits under the DMCA against scientists and researchers studying access control technologies were not appropriate.

DeCSS is widely available now, but the DMCA still prohibits its use. If a company wanted to use DeCSS or any other circumvention tools in a new DVD player, *Russian programmer arrested for violating the DMCA: Section 5.6.2* for example, with features like fast-forwarding over ads or the ability to play DVDs worldwide—or other features we have not thought of—it would be illegal. The DMCA restricts circumventing copy protection for reverse engineering to produce new products. Companies avoid the practice because the legality remains murky. The new, innovative products that might have come to market, but will not because of the DMCA, are invisible.

4.3.3 VIDEO SHARING

The first videos people posted on the Web (initially primarily on YouTube and MySpace) showed events (and nonevents) people recorded with their video cameras. Amateur creations still make up a large proportion of posted videos. Quickly, however, creativity and availability of video editing tools led to more sophisticated creations, set to music and containing clips from movies, TV shows, concerts, and so on. These components are protected by copyright and virtually all used without authorization. Often, people just post segments of TV programs or other commercial video. For example, at one point, Viacom claimed that people viewed clips from its cable TV channels on YouTube 80,000 times per day. Viewers watched an unauthorized copy of a Saturday Night Live skit millions of times.

Which of these uses of copyrighted material do the fair-use guidelines permit? Are site operators responsible for copyright-infringing material posted by users? Are there solutions

WHAT CONSUMERS WANT FROM THE ENTERTAINMENT INDUSTRY

Why was Napster so popular? When I asked my college students (in 2000, while the illegal version of Napster was thriving), many shouted out "It's free!" That's the obvious reason, but it was not the only one. My students quickly generated a list of other desirable features of Napster. They could get individual songs without having to buy a whole CD to get the ones they wanted. They could sample songs to see if they really wanted them. Through Napster, they had access to a huge "inventory," not limited to one particular store or music label. They could get songs that were not commercially available. They liked the convenience of getting their music online. They could download and play a song from anywhere; they did not need to have a physical CD with them. The Napster site provided information about singers and musicians. Users could chat online with other users while they downloaded songs in the background. Thus, Napster used a variety of then-new technologies to provide flexibility, convenience, and services, in addition to free music. A majority of Napster users in a Webnoize survey said they would be willing to pay a monthly fee for a Napster-like service.

The record companies did not embrace the new technologies. They expected their customers to continue to buy CDs from a store or order on the Web and wait a few days for shipping. They were used to the old paradigm of getting paid by each customer for each copy and were reluctant to allow or accept distribution of songs in file formats that people could easily copy.

When people began to post thousands of video clips from television shows and movies about five years later, the content owners reacted like the record companies. They did not understand that people want to view and share short clips. People often want the highlights, the funny parts, not always the entire program or movie—just as music lovers want individual songs, not necessarily a whole CD.

other than lawsuits and criminal actions that can address the problem of infringing uses in ways that do not discourage or destroy new creative forms and venues?

Let's consider the first question by reviewing a few arguments related to fair use for different kinds of videos. First, of course, when videos do not use anyone else's material, there is no problem of possible copyright infringement. Videos that use a small piece of a larger work might be within the fair-use guidelines (though the limit on the acceptable size of the copied material is not always clear). People who post such amateur videos are not receiving any payment; they are creating new entertainment (of varying quality, to be sure). Lip-synching to a popular song (a common type of video) raises more questions because the whole song is used and performed in public. It probably does not affect the market for professional recordings of the song—but even amateur theaters pay fees to perform copyrighted works, though they generally charge for admission. Unauthorized posting of professional work, especially long clips or whole works, more clearly is most often not fair use. When millions of people can easily view an unauthorized video of a band or singer performing a hit song—or the best part of a TV program—it probably does affect the market for the work. The copyright holders lose potential sales and ad revenue. Thus, some instances of posting videos containing unauthorized material are likely fair uses and many are not.

What are the responsibilities of the sites on which people post videos? Video-sharing sites do not charge the public to view the videos. They earn revenue, however, from advertising that people view because the videos attract them to the site. The Napster and Grokster cases (Section 4.2.3) show that such companies have legal responsibility for contributing to copyright infringement. The DMCA protects sites from lawsuits for copyright-infringing material posted by users if the sites remove infringing material when requested to do so by the copyright owner in a so-called takedown notice.

The first response of many entertainment companies to the video-sharing pheno- menon on legitimate sites was to send out floods of takedown notices. This is not a satisfying solution for the sites or the public, or even for the copyright holders. Copyright holders are likely to interpret fair-use principles narrowly and send takedown notices for material that might be fair use. In one incident, Wendy Seltzer, a law professor, posted a video clip from a football game. YouTube removed it after the National Football League (NFL) sent a takedown notice, then reposted it when Seltzer claimed it was an educational fair use (demonstrating issues about copyright—the clip included the NFL's copyright notice), and then took it down again after the NFL sent another takedown notice. It is often not obvious how a court will interpret the fair-use guidelines. Web site operators are likely to protect themselves by complying with requests from large entertainment companies. Large copyright holders are unhappy that they have to continually search sites for material that infringe their copyrights and send the notices. Viacom complained that it spends tens of thousands of dollars each month doing so. A more fundamental problem is that the goal of removing all unauthorized copyright-infringing material squelches creativity that new technology encourages. Individual people who create something using pieces of other works rarely know how to find copyright owners and get permission. Aside from any small fee, the overhead of managing permissions for all uses would be too burdensome for both the public and the entertainment companies. Content-sharing sites and the public want to keep popular material available on the sites. In the next section, we see some potential solutions.

Entertainment companies challenged the applicability of the safe-harbor provisions of the DMCA, requiring the takedown notices, to large commercial sites such as YouTube that host a huge number of unauthorized videos. The companies argue that the large advertising revenue these sites take in depends in part on the unauthorized content. Several companies sued YouTube, MySpace, and other content-sharing sites in 2007. The safe-harbor provision of the DMCA might have been appropriate for Web sites of the 1990s whose business plans did not depend on users posting huge amounts of copyright- infringing material. Today's sites, the companies argue, are similar to the peer-to-peer music sites (like Grokster) that made their money on the intellectual property of others

ABUSE OF TAKEDOWN NOTICES?

The takedown requirement of the DMCA is clearly open to abuse that threatens free speech (and fair competition). A study of takedown notices found that for about 30% of the notices, there is significant question whether the material actually does infringe copyright. The fair-use provisions protect much of it, for example, quotations from a book in an unfavorable book review. More than half of the notices businesses send to Google demanding removal of links to allegedly infringing Web pages come from competitors of the targeted sites.[29]

How can search engine companies and Web sites evaluate all the takedown notices they receive? How should they respond when they receive a notice that they believe is intended to silence critics or undermine competitors?

without permission. They argue that the sites should have the responsibility of filtering out copyright-infringing material. The burden should not be on the copyright holders. Viacom asked for $1 billion in damages from YouTube. The Web sites argue that they comply with the law. YouTube has pointed out that media companies sometimes post their own material to advertise. Thus, the site cannot always tell what posts are unauthorized. Supporters of the safe-harbor provisions say it would be hard to draw a line between YouTube and sites to which the safe-harbor provisions should apply. They fear that weakening this protection would threaten the many Web sites that host user-generated material. The suits were not yet settled at the time of writing this book.

Many Web sites exist primarily to distribute illegally copied videos. The Motion Picture Association of America sued YouTVpc.com and Peekvid.com. These sites do not host any videos. They provide indexes of links to sites with unauthorized popular television shows and movies on other sites, some in other countries. The movie studios argue that the sites illegally contribute to copyright infringement as did companies such as the original Napster and Grokster. These suits also were not yet settled at the time of writing this book.

4.3.4 NEW BUSINESS MODELS AND CONSTRUCTIVE SOLUTIONS

The more we attempt to provide government protection to the old ways of doing business, the less motivation we provide to the entertainment industry to adapt and benefit from new technology.

—Les Vadasz, former vice president of Intel[30]

USING IDEAS FROM THE PAST

To provide authorization and payment for uses of copyrighted material for nonelectronic media, the entertainment and publishing industries developed contracting terms and other schemes in the past. Publishers of printed academic journals have long set subscription rates for libraries higher than for individuals because more people use library copies. Organizations representing copyright holders for music, journals, and magazines made arrangements with users of such works to collect fees. For example, the American Society for Composers, Authors, and Publishers (ASCAP) and Broadcast Music, Inc. (BMI) collect hundreds of millions of dollars a year in fees for live performances and recordings of songs played in commercial places (including restaurants). In the 1960s, photocopying machines gained widespread use and led to increased copying of magazines and journals. Journal publishers formed the Copyright Clearance Center. The Center negotiates yearly fees with large companies whose employees frequently make copies of journal articles or other material. These agreements make it feasible for business or institutional users of copyrighted material to pay reasonable fees without having to go to the large expense of finding the copyright holder for each item they wish to copy and negotiating with each one individually. The organizations distribute the collected fees to authors and publishers either in accordance with the number of uses of a particular author's work or, where that is difficult to determine, by other formulas worked out by the organizations and members. Similar schemes for paying copyright fees were developed for the use of written work online. The National Writers Union established the Publication Rights Clearinghouse to provide for collection of license fees for freelance writers.

Many of these schemes include ideas that are seeds of solutions for the conflicts over copyright infringement by millions of individuals on the Web. It took, however, many years until the content industries and Web site operators began to cooperate to apply the ideas. The intellectual-property companies were afraid of losing control. Web users, file-sharing software makers, and operators of file-sharing sites held the view that copying of digital files should be free.

Music and movies—legally

The smart people in music are already working on ways to make a single playing too cheap to be worth stealing.

—Holman W. Jenkins, Jr.[31]

The success of Apple's iTunes, which has sold more than a billion songs and tens of millions of videos, showed that companies can sell digital entertainment successfully, from the point of view of the customers and the rights holders. After the Supreme Court decision in *MGM v. Grokster* (Section 4.2.3), people who wanted to operate legitimate businesses providing music realized that they had to either filter out industry-owned material or make agreements with, and payments to, music companies. Most people who copy or listen to songs online want to hear current, popular music, so the filtering option is likely to fail, as it did with the original Napster. It seemed to take a long time, but many entertainment companies came to realize that people who share music files are people who like music; they are potential customers. The industry began to explore new business and marketing models. The new Napster, for example, operates under an agreement with the music companies; the companies share in the advertising revenue for the site. This Napster offers millions of songs legally and has more than 500,000 subscribers worldwide. With appropriate technology and business arrangements, Apple, Amazon, and other companies began offering movie download services. In an attempt to reduce high rates of music piracy and sales of unauthorized concert recordings in several countries, some music companies reduced the prices of CDs and began selling DVDs of concerts almost immediately after the concert.

The entertainment industry initially viewed new distribution technologies, such as peer-to-peer file-sharing, podcasting, and streaming content, as threats—as the movie industry did with video cassette recorders in the 1980s, before it got the idea that it could earn billions by renting and selling movies on cassettes. As expected by those who work with technology, peer-to-peer systems have found many uses other than unauthorized copying. Intriguingly, the entertainment industry itself began using this technology to provide legal content. Several companies made contracts with peer-to-peer companies such as BitTorrent to deliver movies and music via peer-to-peer technology because it speeds downloads. Instead of sending all files from a central server, customers receive a movie in pieces from the computers of other customers.

The increase in legal ways to get and use content online has not, of course, eliminated unauthorized copying. Many unauthorized music- and movie-sharing services operate "underground" or in other countries. Millions of people still use these sites and services. The industries continue strong enforcement efforts against organized, large-scale "piracy" and Web sites that encourage unauthorized sharing. At the same time, it is likely that, just as retailers know they lose a percentage of goods to shoplifters, entertainment companies will adapt to forms of providing content that include some degree of copyright infringement.

Negotiated payments

Some entertainment companies and Web content-sharing sites negotiate contracts for the Web site company to pay a share of its ad revenue to the entertainment companies. YouTube and Warner Music Group, for example, worked out such an arrangement for

Warner music videos. Some sharing sites use filtering software that examines files as people upload them, looking for digital "fingerprints" of the entertainment company's properties. Depending on agreements between the companies, the site can block the post entirely or pay the entertainment company for its appearance on the site. This is a creative way to allow users to post entertainment company material or include such material in their (usually noncommercial) creations without the overhead and legal liability for getting permissions. It makes sense that the Web companies that benefit from the advertising and have the assets and expertise to develop and use the sophisticated filtering tools make the payments.

The contracts cover only the properties of a specific company, so this is not a complete solution. YouTube, for example, found it difficult to find and negotiate with all the record companies, music publishers, actors, studios, television networks, and others who have rights in material in videos on its site. But this is a sensible approach. It developed more quickly than reasonable solutions to the music-sharing issues of the late 1990s and early 2000s. If the legal challenges to the safe-harbor provisions of the DMCA (Section 4.3.3) succeed, content-sharing sites might have to filter material their users post without permission or negotiate contracts with the copyright holders and pay fees.

More uses of advertising

Some music companies adopted a clever tactic to discourage unauthorized file sharing: They put a large number of damaged music files, called "decoys," on file-sharing sites. The decoys might, for example, fail to download properly or be full of scratchy noises. The idea was that people would become frustrated and stop using the file-sharing sites if a large percentage of the songs they tried to download would not play properly. Movie companies adopted the tactic too, scattering many fake copies of new movies on the Internet. Eventually, some companies developed a new marketing model using similar techniques. Coca Cola, for example, includes advertising, not scratches, with music files distributed to peer-to-peer sites. The advertiser pays the fees to the copyright holder, and both are happy to provide the music. Thus, sharing files has become a form of viral marketing.

Some peer-to-peer sites are not happy with this development. They consider marketing messages to be a form of spam. Some peer-to-peer software attempts to detect and eliminate them.

Fan fiction: Let it be

Fan fiction includes stories written by amateurs using characters or worlds from popular fiction such as Harry Potter and Star Trek. There is a lot of it. One Harry Potter site has almost 40,000 stories and gets more than 40 million hits per month.

The characters and environments in fan fiction are creative intellectual property covered by copyright. Fan stories are not copies of copyrighted work, but they are derivative works. Thus, publication, distribution, and public display of fan fiction

TOOLS FOR SHARING

Sharing information and creative work is a major characteristic of Web culture. (Before the advent of the Web, a large community of computer programmers developed the paradigm of sharing software.) Many authors and artists, including those who sell their work on the Web, are willing to share—to a degree. How can they easily—without a publishing company's staff of lawyers and without the overhead of explicit authorization—indicate what they are willing to let others do with their work? From the user perspective, how does someone who wants to copy, for example, a photo from someone else's Web site easily determine if the photographer cares, and if he or she must get permission or pay a fee? Many people are willing to respect the preferences of an author or artist, but it is often not easy to determine what those preferences are.

Creative Commons,[32] a nonprofit organization, developed a spectrum of licensing agreements inspired by the GNU General Public License for software (Section 4.6). The licenses, which the author or artist announces to viewers by a choice of clickable icons, explicitly permit a selection of actions normally requiring authorization from the copyright owner. They provide a large degree of flexibility. For example, one can allow copying for noncommercial uses, require a specified credit line with any use, allow copies or display of the entire work only if there are no changes, allow use of pieces of the work in new works, put the entire work in the public domain, or set a shorter time limit on the copyright protection than the law provides. Like so much on the Web, the use of the licenses and associated software is free.

Enforcement is a separate issue. For most people, easy-to-use schemes like the Creative Commons licenses eliminate confusion and expensive overhead. They facilitate and encourage sharing while protecting the interests of intellectual-property owners.

generally require authorization from the copyright holder. Book and magazine publishers published little fan fiction, in part because of the copyright issue. The ease of posting on the Web and finding an audience encouraged a big growth in fan fiction, most of it unauthorized. As with blogs, quality ranges from professional to trash. With derivative works, publishers worry not only about loss of potential revenue but also about damage to their image. (For example, on the early Internet, the Walt Disney Company aggressively fought to remove modified pictures showing Disney characters in "indiscreet" poses.)

The response of writers and publishers to fan fiction was more calm than the response of the music and movie industries to unauthorized distribution of their products on the Web. Fan fiction remains controversial, and some authors and publishers threaten lawsuits, but many publishers recognized that fan fiction is not a big threat to their revenue and that amateur writers are their customers. Some authors, including J. K. Rowling, allow stories based on their works if they are noncommercial and not pornographic.

4.3.5 ETHICAL ARGUMENTS ABOUT COPYING

There is intrinsic "fuzziness" about the ethics of copying. The border between what is and what is not ethical is often unclear. Many people who get their music, movies, or software from unauthorized sources realize that they get "something for nothing." They benefit from the creativity and effort of others without paying for it. To most people, that seems wrong. On the other hand, much copying does not seem wrong. We explore some of the reasons and distinctions.

Copying or distributing a song or computer program does not decrease the use and enjoyment any other person gets from his or her copy. This fundamental distinction between intellectual property and physical property is a key reason why copying is ethical in far more circumstances than taking physical property. Most people who create intellectual property in entertainment, software, and so on, however, are doing so to earn income, not for the benefit of using their product themselves. If movie theaters could show copies of movies without paying for them, far fewer people and companies would invest money, time, energy, and creative effort in making movies. If search engines could scan any book and offer free downloads without an agreement with the publisher, publishers would probably not sell enough copies to cover costs; they would stop publishing. The value of intellectual property is not just the direct use and enjoyment one gets from a copy. Its value is also as a product offered to consumers to earn money. That is an aspect of the property that one can steal from the copyright holder. When people widely copy intellectual property without permission, they diminish the value of the work as an asset to the owner. That is why much copying is wrong.

Supporters of unauthorized file-sharing services and people who advocate loose restrictions on copying intellectual property argue that permitting copying for, say, trying out a song or computer program before buying it benefits the copyright owner because it encourages sales. Such uses seem ethical, and indeed because much of the "wrong" in unauthorized copying stems from depriving owners of income from their product, the fourth of the fair-use guidelines considers the impact on the market for the product. We should, however, be careful not to go too far in usurping a copyright holder's decisions. Many businesses give free samples and low-priced introductory offers to encourage sales, but that is a business decision. The investors and employees of the business take the risk for such choices. A business normally makes its own decisions about how it markets its product, not consumers who want free samples, nor even the courts.

People who copy for personal use or distribute works of others without charge usually do not profit financially. Personal use is, reasonably, more likely to be fair use (both ethically and legally) than is commercial use, but is personal use always fair? Is financial gain always relevant? In some contexts, a profit motive, or financial gain, is a factor in concluding that an activity is wrong. In other contexts, it is irrelevant. Vandals do not profit financially from their action, but vandalism is unethical (and a crime) because it destroys—or reduces the value of—someone's property. A profit motive is not a significant factor in determining where to protect freedom of speech.* Freedom of speech is an important social, ethical, and legal principle for book, magazine, newspaper, and Web site publishers, most of whom are in business to make profit. Many kinds of abusive or threatening speech are unrelated to financial gain but are unethical.

Here are some arguments people make in support of personal copying or posting content on the Web without authorization (in situations that are not clearly fair use) and some counterpoints to consider. The responses below do not mean that unauthorized copying or use of someone else's work is always wrong—in many cases it is not. These are brief suggestions for analyzing the arguments.

❖ *I cannot afford to buy the software (or pay the royalty for use of a song in my video).* There are many things we cannot afford. Not being able to afford something does not justify taking it.

❖ *The company is a large, wealthy corporation.* The size and success of the company do not justify taking something from it. Programmers, writers, and performing artists lose income too when copying is common.

❖ *I wouldn't buy it at the retail price (or pay the required fee) anyway. The company is not really losing a sale or losing revenue.* The person is taking something of value, getting "something for nothing," even if the something is less than the price the copyright owner would charge. There are times when we get something for nothing. Our neighborhood looks better when our neighbors paint their houses. People do us favors. It can be easy to ignore a crucial distinction: Who makes the decision?

❖ *Making a copy for a friend is just an act of generosity.* Philosopher Helen Nissenbaum argued that someone who copies software for a friend has a countervailing claim against the programmer's right to prohibit making the copy: the "freedom to pursue the virtue of generosity."[33] Surely we have a liberty (i.e., a negative right) to be generous, and we can exercise it by making or buying a gift for a friend. It is less clear that we have a claim-right (a positive right) to be generous. Is copying the software an act of generosity on our part or an act that compels involuntary generosity from the copyright owner?

❖ *This violation is insignificant compared to the billions of dollars lost to piracy by dishonest people making big profits.* Yes, large-scale commercial piracy is worse. That does not imply that individual copying is ethical. And if the practice is widespread, the losses become significant.

❖ *Everyone does it. You would be foolish not to.* The number of people doing something does not determine whether it is right. A large number of people in one peer group

---

*In Chapter 3, we mentioned that commercial speech, in particular advertising, is an exception. Some court decisions give it less First Amendment protection.

could share similar incentives and experience (or lack thereof) that affect their point of view.

❖ *I want to use a song or video clip in my video, but I have no idea how to get permission.* This is a better argument than many others. Technology has outrun the business mechanisms for easily making agreements. The "transaction costs," as economists call them, are so high that a strict requirement for obtaining permission slows development and distribution of new intellectual property.

❖ *I'm posting this video (or segment of a TV program) as a public service.* If the public service is entertainment (a gift to the public), the observations above about copying as a form of generosity are relevant here. If the public service is to express an idea or make some statement about an important issue, the posting might be analogous to creating a review or a parody. In some cases, these might be reasonable fair uses with social value. Simply posting a complete program, or a substantial portion of one, to share is probably not a fair use.

Laws are not always good guides for ethical decisions, but the fair-use guidelines do a respectable job of identifying criteria to help distinguish fair and unfair copying. Because of the complexity of the issues, there will always be uncertainty in the application of the guidelines, both ethically and legally. The guidelines might need expansion and clarification to cover new media, but they give us a good framework that corresponds to sensible ethical criteria.

4.3.6 INTERNATIONAL PIRACY

Some countries traditionally have not recognized or protected intellectual property, including copyrights, patents, and trademarks. Counterfeiting of brand name products, from blue jeans to expensive watches and medicines, is common in some parts of the world. Ignoring foreign copyrights has long been common practice in many countries. Thus, software, music, and movie piracy in these countries are variants of an old phenomenon.

Illegal businesses produce, transport, and sell unauthorized copies of the disks, documentation, and sometimes identical packaging for popular business and PC software. This is both counterfeiting (violation of trademark law) and copyright infringement. In China, factories hidden on farms produce millions of DVDs with pirated music, movies, and software, mostly for export to other countries. Raids by law enforcement agencies in the U.S. and other countries uncover millions of unauthorized copies. Pirated copies of each new version of Windows appear in other countries before the official release. Web sites that sell or share entertainment files without authorization thrive in many countries.

The Business Software Alliance (BSA) estimates that piracy accounts for 35% of PC software in use worldwide and that the value of the software is roughly $40–45 billion per year.* Obviously, it is difficult to get accurate figures for illegal activities. To make its estimates, the BSA estimates the average number of likely software applications on each computer and then uses sales information to calculate the average number of applications purchased for each. They attribute the gap between the number purchased and the estimated number installed to piracy. Figure 4.1 shows the BSA estimates of software piracy rates in various countries. These figures show decreases for many countries from previous years. China (with 82%) and Russia (80%) dropped from the top ten in 2006. The U.S. has the lowest rate, but the total amount of software used is high. The BSA estimates piracy of roughly $7 billion of software in the U.S. and more than $5 billion in China.[34]

Why has intellectual-property piracy long been more common outside the U.S.? We mentioned the general lack of a tradition of legal recognition and protection of intellectual property in some countries. There are other factors as well. Many countries with high piracy rates do not have a significant software industry. Thus, they do not have domestic programmers and software companies to lobby for protection of software. The lack of a domestic software industry may be an effect as well as a contributing cause.

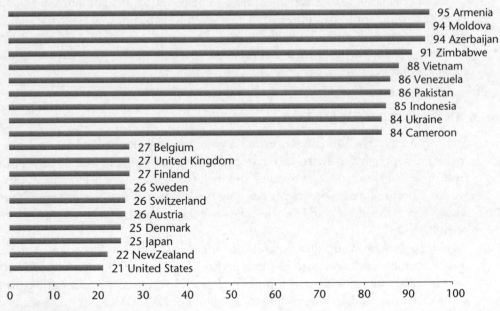

Figure 4.1 Estimated Personal Computer Software Piracy Percentage Rates for 2006 (The Ten Highest and Ten Lowest)[35]

---

*Some reports describe these figures as "losses to the software industry" from piracy. It is impossible to estimate accurately how many people using pirated software would buy full-price legal copies if the pirated copies were not available. It is reasonable to say that many would not, so the direct loss to publishers is significantly smaller than the retail value of the software.

It is difficult for such an industry to develop when it cannot recover its investment in software development. The fact that the victims of piracy are from another country, and a rich one, may make both the people and the governments less inclined to take action to reduce unauthorized sales. In the U.S., with many legitimate sellers of entertainment and software, customers are likely to know when they are buying illegal products or sharing unauthorized files. In countries where it is common to purchase food unpackaged in outdoor markets, customers may not think there is anything unusual (or wrong) about the way unauthorized vendors sell software and music. It is often easier for a consumer to find a street vendor selling, for instance, a U.S. movie on DVD, than to find an authorized dealer. Another reason for piracy in other countries is that the economies are weak and the people are poor. (Some U.S. movie companies now sell DVDs in China at relatively low prices to attract customers away from the illegal market.) Thus, culture, politics, economic development, low incomes, and lax enforcement of intellectual-property laws are all contributing factors. Recognition that poor intellectual-property protection hindered its own content industries has contributed to increased copyright protection in China.

Under pressure from the U.S. in the early 1990s, China passed laws to protect intellectual-property rights, and particularly rights for foreign works, but did not enforce the laws. Some copying of software reportedly took place in government factories. The U.S. government pressured the Chinese government to enforce copyrights by threatening high tariffs on Chinese products. Unfortunately, in international negotiations, the offenders are not necessarily those threatened with punishment: The burden of tariffs falls on legitimate Chinese businesses that produce export products, and on American consumers who buy them. In 1996, the Chinese government took steps toward reducing piracy. Some, however, involve controls that would be unacceptable threats to freedom of expression in some other countries, for example, prohibiting import of CD production equipment without government approval and requiring registration with the government of all CDs produced.[36]

More recently, as its economy has been growing, China made more effective efforts to reduce illegal production, sale, and use of intellectual property. It has increased enforcement of laws. For example, a Chinese court ruled that a Web site infringed copyright by supplying U.S. movies for download without authorization from the movie companies. Two people in Hong Kong got long jail sentences for using their disk reproduction company to make hundreds of thousands of illegal copies of music, movies, and software. Under pressure from a Chinese company that represents U.S. music companies and owns rights to thousands of Chinese songs, China's major search engine removed thousands of links to sites that offered pirated songs. In China, PC manufacturers used to sell their machines bare, without an operating system. This practice encouraged people to buy cheap, unauthorized copies. In 2006, the Chinese government required that all PCs be sold with an authorized operating system preinstalled. Also, according to the BSA, the Chinese government significantly reduced the use of unauthorized software by its own government agencies.

4.4 Search Engines and Online Libraries

Copying is essential to many of the operations and services of search engines. In response to search queries, search engines display copies of text excerpts from Web sites and copies from images or video. In order to respond to user queries quickly, the search engines copy and cache* Web pages and sometimes display these copies to users. Search engine companies copy entire books so that they can search them and display segments in response to user queries. Besides their own copying, search engines provide links to sites that might contain copyright-infringing material. Individuals and companies have sued Google for almost every search service it provides (Web text, news, books, images, and video). Should search engines need authorization for the copying essential to search services? Should they be paying fees to copyright owners? As always, uncertainties about the legal status of industry practices can delay innovation. Google boldly introduces new services amid complaints of copyright infringement, but fear of lawsuits has deterred smaller companies that cannot estimate business costs in advance if they do not know their liability. We consider arguments related to a few of the contested practices. Courts have ruled on cases for some; others remain open.

The search-engine practice of displaying copies of excerpts from Web pages seems easily to fit under the fair-use guidelines. The excerpts are short. Displaying them helps people find the Web site with the excerpted document—usually an advantage to the site. In most cases, the site from which the search engine copies the excerpt is public, available to anyone who wants to read its content. Web search services are a hugely valuable innovation and tool for the socially valuable goal of making information easily available. In *Kelly v. Arriba Soft* (2002), an appeals court ruled that copying images from Web pages, converting them to thumbnail images (small, low-resolution copies), and displaying the thumbnails to search engine users did not infringe copyrights. In *Field v. Google*, an author sued Google for copying and caching a story he had posted on his Web site. Caching involves copying entire Web pages. The court ruled that caching Web pages is a fair use. In dismissing a similar suit that challenged both caching and the practice of displaying excerpts from a Web site, a court compared Google to an ISP that makes copies of Web pages to display them to users. For ISPs, automatically and temporarily storing data to transmit to users does not infringe copyright.[37]

There are, however, some reasonable arguments on the other side. Businesses operate most search engines. They earn significant revenue from advertising. Thus, the copying accomplishes a commercial purpose. The display of short excerpts can reduce income to copyright holders in some situations. A group of Belgian newspapers claimed they lose revenue from subscription fees when Google displays headlines, photos, and excerpts from their news archives. They won a lawsuit against Google (in a Belgian court) in 2007.

---

*Caching, generally in computer science, means storing data in specialized memory, frequently updated, to optimize transfer of the data to other parts of a system that use it.

In response to similar lawsuits and disputes with other news services, Google negotiated licensing agreements to copy and display headlines, excerpts, and photos.

An adult entertainment company, Perfect 10, sued Google, arguing that Google is liable for copyright infringement because Google's search engine finds and provides links to Perfect 10 images on unauthorized sites that infringe Perfect 10's copyrights, thus raising again the issue of when it might be illegal to link to another Web page (see Section 4.3.2). Perfect 10 argued that Google's thumbnails and links to the infringing images are not fair use in part because Google could earn revenue from the infringing sites. In 2006, a lower court ordered Google to remove links to infringing sites; Google appealed. The final decision could be significant for the entertainment industry, professional photographers, and search engine companies.

Books online

In the 1970s, Project Gutenberg began converting books in the public domain into digital formats. Volunteers typed the entire text of the books—inexpensive scanners were not yet available. The University of California agreed to let Microsoft scan millions of books in its collection that are in the public domain. Google's project of scanning books in major university libraries differs in that Google scans books covered by copyright. Google provides entire books for download, but only those that are in the public domain. For books still under copyright protection, Google Book Search provides short excerpts from the books. Does Google's project infringe copyrights? How does the impact on the market for books differ from the impact of people browsing books in a library? How does the impact compare to providing excerpts from newspaper articles? Publishers and authors filed several lawsuits against Google for copying their books. The suits remained unsettled at the time of writing this book.

So far, courts have decided many—but not all—issues related to search engine copying in favor of search engines and facilitating access to information. The legal and ethical issues, however, arise again each time technology makes copying and searching of more complex content (movies, for example) possible, especially for content produced explicitly to earn revenue (again, movies, for example). Search engine companies, including Google, began negotiating contracts with major intellectual-property owners for displaying excerpts from and/or providing links to content such as images, news archives, and television programs. Such contracts recognize that the search companies benefit from the use of another company's intellectual property and that a search-engine company needs permission to copy and display intellectual property that another business owns and uses to produce income.

4.5 Free-Speech Issues

We saw that the DMCA's restrictions on the publication of circumvention software might be an unconstitutional infringement of free speech. Here, we briefly describe a few other examples of conflicts between freedom of speech and intellectual-property laws.

Domain names

Some businesses and organizations use trademark-infringement claims to sue or threaten suits against people who register domain names (Web addresses) that express criticism of the company or organization. If XYZ were the name of a big consumer products maker, XYZ might sue someone with the Internet domain name XYZIsJunk.com. The Pacifica Foundation, an operator of radio stations that, ironically, called itself "free speech radio," threatened suits against operators of several Web sites critical of Pacifica management. The sites used domain names that included "pacifica" or the call letters of a station, for example, freewpfw.org. A company name is a protected trademark, but many observers believe that its use in a domain name is a form of comment, or protected free speech.

In many cases, the company or product name is not used in a negative or critical way. For example, Ford Motor Company sued the operator of ClassicVolvo.com, a business that sells old Volvos and spare parts. (Ford owns Volvo.) Ford also sued the operator of jaguarcenter.com, a site about jaguars (the animal), not Jaguars (the car brand owned by Ford). At issue is how far control of a product name extends. Courts dismissed many of these trademark suits. Some companies use a market mechanism rather than lawsuits: They buy hundreds of domain names that include names of their products, not to use the names themselves, but to prevent others from using them.

Posting documents for criticism

Some organizations and businesses attempt to silence their critics by filing copyright-infringement lawsuits. The Church of Scientology, for example, has used this approach over many years. We describe its efforts to illustrate some of the issues.

Auxiliary organizations associated with the Church of Scientology[38] have sued critics of the Church, including several former members. They charged that the critics had posted copyrighted documents containing sacred teachings of the Church on the Internet.

The people who posted the documents argued that the postings were fair use. They made copies of entire documents but not for commercial gain. The postings were part of discussions of alleged abuses by the church. What are the arguments against accepting the postings as fair use? The copying was not commercial, but it was not for a limited, private use. Posted copies were public, where many people could see and easily recopy them. This, of course, is true of anything posted to the Internet. The Church considered some of the documents "secret" and would show them only to high-ranking members, who pay fees to move up the ranks.[39]

In one of the early cases (before the DMCA), a court ordered a bulletin board system (BBS) operator to prevent a former Scientology minister from posting messages and to screen postings for Church material. The BBS operator said that monitoring all the traffic was impossible and that small operators like him do not have the insurance or deep pockets to fight copyright-infringement lawsuits. He said he would have to shut down.[40]

The freedom-of-speech implications of such cases appear to be significant. How strong is the fair-use argument? One judge, in a ruling against the Church, said:

> [T]he dispute was presented as a straightforward one under copyright and trade secret law. However, the court is now convinced that the primary motivation of [the Church] . . . is to stifle criticism of Scientology in general and to harass its critics.[41]

However, in two cases, courts found that the men who posted material infringed the Church's copyrights. A judge fined one defendant, found him in contempt of court for posting the transcript of his trial (which included some of the Church material), and prohibited him from posting a list of Web sites containing Church material.

More recently, the Church, citing the DMCA, demanded that Google not show in search results a Norway site that contained Church documents. (Google complied, but later restored the sites to its search results.)[42]

4.6 Free Software

In Chapter 1 we talked about all the free stuff on the Web. Individuals post information and create useful Web sites. Large groups of volunteers, who do not know each other, collaborate on projects such as Wikipedia. Experts share their knowledge and contribute their work. This creation of valuable information "products" is decentralized. It has little or no "management" in the business sense. It flows from incentives other than profits and market pricing. This phenomenon, which some call "peer production," has a predecessor: the free software movement, begun in the 1970s.[43]

4.6.1 WHAT IS FREE SOFTWARE?

Free software is an idea, an ethic, advocated and supported by a large loose-knit group of computer programmers who allow and encourage people to copy, use, and modify their software. The *free* in free software means freedom, not necessarily lack of cost, though often there is no charge. Free-software enthusiasts advocate allowing unrestricted copying of programs and making the source code (the human-readable form of a program) available to everyone. Software distributed or made public in source code is *open source*, and the open-source movement is closely related to the free-software movement. (Commercial software, often called *proprietary software*, is normally sold in object code, the code run by the computer, but not intelligible to people. The source code is kept secret.)

Richard Stallman is the best-known founder and advocate of the free-software movement. Stallman began the GNU project in the 1970s (though the GNU name dates from 1983). It includes a UNIX-like operating system, Emacs (a sophisticated text editor), and many compilers and utilities. GNU programs are freely available and very popular among computer professionals and skilled amateur programmers.* With freely distributed software, more people can use and benefit from a program. With source code available, any of thousands of programmers can find and fix bugs quickly. Users and programmers can adapt and improve programs. Programmers can use existing programs to create new and better ones. Stallman compares software to a recipe. We can all decide to add a little garlic or take out some salt without paying a royalty to the person who developed the recipe.

To enforce the openness and sharing of free software within the current legal framework that provides copyright protection, the GNU project developed the concept of *copyleft*.[44] Under copyleft, the developer copyrights the program and releases it under an agreement that allows people to use, modify, and distribute it, or any program developed from it, but only if they apply the same agreement to the new work. In other words, no one may develop a new program from a copylefted program and add restrictions that limit its use and free distribution. The widely used GNU General Public License (GPL) implements copyleft.

For a long time, technically savvy programmers and hobbyists were the principal users of free software. Commercial software companies were hostile to the idea. That view changed gradually, then more dramatically, with the Linux operating system.[†] Linus Torvalds wrote the Linux kernel in 1991. Torvalds distributed it for free on the Internet, and a global network of free-software enthusiasts continued development, generally on their own time after work. At first, Linux was difficult to use, not well suited as a consumer or business product. Businesses referred to it as "cult software." Two early users were the company that did the special effects for the movie *Titanic* and the NASA Goddard Space Flight Center. Gradually, some small companies began selling a version of Linux along with manuals and technical support, and eventually, major computer companies, including IBM, Oracle, Hewlett-Packard, and Silicon Graphics, used, supported, and marketed it. Large businesses like Royal Dutch/Shell and Home Depot adopted Linux. Several movie studios adopted Linux for their special effects and digital animations. In 2007 Dell began selling PCs with Linux installed.

Other examples of popular free software include Firefox, the Web browser provided by Mozilla, and Apache, the most widely used program to run Web sites. IBM supports and distributes Apache. A lot of early free software consisted of free versions of popular proprietary software, such as Linux as an alternative for the UNIX system. Later, producers of free software innovated more. Apache's creators, for example, wrote it because there was nothing available as good and with the features they wanted.

Major companies began to appreciate the benefits of open source. Several companies now make source code for their own products public, allowing free use in noncommercial

---

*"GNU" is an acronym for "GNU's Not UNIX." (Programmers like recursive acronyms.)

†Technically, Linux is the kernel, or core part, of the operating system. Other parts are from the GNU project, but the whole operating system is often referred to as Linux.

applications. Sun Microsystems licenses the Java programming language under GPL. Adopting the view of the free-software movement, companies expected that programmers would trust the software more if they could see how it operates. Programmers might be more likely to use it and to improve it. IBM placed full-page ads in major newspapers announcing that it "embraced Linux and the open-source movement as a pillar of e-business."[45] IBM donates hundreds of its patents to the open-source community. Free software became a competitor for Microsoft, and so those who are critical of Microsoft's products and influence see it as a considerable social benefit.

Critics (and some supporters) of free software point out some of its weaknesses. Much free software is not easy for ordinary consumers to use. There is no technical support number to call for help. (Programmers and users share information about problems and fixes on very active Web sites.) Because anyone can modify free software, there are many versions and few standards, creating a difficult and confusing environment for nontechnical consumers and businesses. Many businesses want to deal with a specific vendor from whom they can request enhancements and assistance. They are uncomfortable with the loose structure of the free-software movement. Some of these weaknesses faded as businesses learned how to work with a new paradigm. Programmers created new businesses to support and enhance free software (like Red Hat for Linux), and more established businesses embraced the movement.

4.6.2 SHOULD ALL SOFTWARE BE FREE?

Some people in the free-software movement do not believe that copyright should protect software at all. They argue that all software should be open-source, free software. Thus, here we consider not the question "Is free software a good thing?" but "Should free software be the only thing?" When considering this question, we must take care to clarify the context of the question. Are we looking at it from the point of view of a programmer or business deciding how to release software? Are we developing our personal opinion about what would be good for society? Or are we advocating that we change the legal structure to eliminate copyright for software, to eliminate proprietary software? We will focus on the last two: Would it be good if all software were free software? And should we change the legal structure to require it?

Free software is undoubtedly valuable, but does it provide sufficient incentives to produce the huge quantity of consumer software available now? How are free-software developers paid? Programmers donate their work because they believe in the sharing ethic. They enjoy doing what they do. Stallman believes that many good programmers would work like artists for low pay out of commitment to their craft. Contributions, some from computer manufacturers, support some free software efforts. Stallman has suggested government grants to universities as another way of funding software.

Would the current funding methods for free software be sufficient? Most programmers work for a salary, even if they write free software on their own time. Would the extra services for which a business could charge bring in enough revenue to support all software development? Would the free-software paradigm support the kinds of consumer software sold in millions of copies? What other funding methods could developers use?

A supporter of free software used the analogy of listener-supported radio and television. It is a good analogy for free software but not one for eliminating proprietary software, because most communities have one listener-supported station and numerous proprietary ones.

Stallman believes that proprietary software—particularly, the aspect that prohibits people from making copies and changes in programs without the software publisher's approval—is ethically wrong. He argues that copying a program does not deprive the programmer, or anyone else, of use of the program. (We saw some counterarguments to this viewpoint in Section 4.3.5.) He emphasizes the distinction between physical property and intellectual property. He also points out that the primary purpose of copyright, as stated in the U.S. Constitution, is to promote progress in arts and sciences, not to compensate writers.[46]

For those who oppose copyright and proprietary software completely, the concept of copyleft and the GNU GPL provide an excellent device for protecting the freedom of free software within the current legal framework. For those who believe there are important roles for both free and proprietary software, they provide an excellent device by which the two paradigms can coexist.

4.7 Issues for Software Developers

There are many issues about copyright and patent that are of particular interest to software developers and to large companies that use complex software in their products or to manage activities on their Web sites. Fuzzy distinctions between hardware and software complicate some of the issues. Application of patents to exported products raises more issues.

Legal scholars and software industry commentators emphasize the need for clear rules so that companies can do their work without the threat of changing law and unforeseen lawsuits. Unfortunately, many questions are unresolved.

4.7.1 PATENTS FOR SOFTWARE?

Recall that patents protect inventions of devices and processes. They give the inventor a monopoly on the invention for a specified period of time (e.g., 20 years). Anyone else who wants to use the idea or process, or build a similar device, must get the authorization of the patent holder.

There is much controversy about whether patent is an appropriate protection mechanism for software. Some people are very critical of specific patents the government has granted. There are two aspects to the debate. First, what is the nature of a new program, or a new kind of program? Is it an invention, a new idea? Or is it a "writing," an expression of ideas, algorithms, techniques? Second, what are the practical consequences of each choice in terms of encouraging innovation and production of new products?

Software is so broad a field and so varied that specific programs can fit in either category—invention or writing. The first spreadsheet program, VisiCalc, introduced in 1979, was a remarkable innovation that had enormous impact on ways of doing business planning and on the sales of computer software and hardware. If the government had been willing to grant patents on software at that time, VisiCalc would likely have qualified for one. Similarly, the first hypertext system or peer-to-peer system might be a patentable invention. On the other hand, a particular computer game might have more in common with a literary work, like a novel.

The Supreme Court said in 1981 that software itself is not patentable because it is abstract. A machine that includes software, however, could be eligible for a patent. In the 1980s and 1990s, the U.S. Patent Office began to issue software patents. A federal court with jurisdiction over patents upheld them, sometimes interpreting the Supreme Court guidelines loosely.

The Patent Office is not supposed to grant a patent for an invention or method that is obvious (so that anyone working in the field would have used the same method) or if it is in wide use before the patent application is filed. The Patent Office makes mistakes. It has granted some patents for techniques that were obvious and/or were already in wide use. There is much controversy about the standard for obviousness.

4.7.2 PATENTS FOR WEB TECHNOLOGIES

To patent or not?

Commerce on the Web introduced many new tools, such as online shopping baskets and one-click shopping. Which of these are basic processes that any e-commerce site may use. Which are patentable inventions?

Various organizations, including the Electronic Frontier Foundation, argue that many patented techniques are not particularly new or innovative. For example, Amazon.com generated a lot of criticism when it sued Barnesandnoble.com for violating its patent on one-click shopping. Many in the industry objected that the government should not have granted the patent in the first place. (The companies settled the suit in 2002 without disclosing the terms.)

Critics of patents, like critics of copyright, see them as stifling innovation on the Web. Others see patents as protecting innovation. If a technique becomes widely used, does that suggest the innovator had a valuable idea that deserves compensation, or does it suggest the technique should be freely available for all to use? Do patents on Web techniques and e-commerce methods stifle innovation? Many businesses routinely pay royalties and license fees for use of intellectual property. It is a cost of doing business, like paying for electric power, raw materials, and so on. In some cases, because of the extra costs, a business might not pursue some marginally profitable uses of patented techniques. Thus, patents might stifle some innovation and new applications. On the other hand, companies invest a very large amount of money and effort to develop something new.

If one accepts the basic idea of patents for ideas and techniques implemented in software, then one issue is how to determine whether a particular patent application is worthy. Such decisions are complex. They depend on the details of particular cases, expertise in the area, and knowledge of history of related technology. A significant Supreme Court ruling in 2007 (*KSR v. Teleflex*) broadened the definition of *obvious* for rejecting patents. Many technology companies that have faced patent-infringement lawsuits welcomed the change. Critics, including companies that buy patents in order to charge for their use, argued that the broader definition could discourage inventors.

From a legal standpoint, software developers must recognize that widely used techniques implemented in software might "belong" to someone. They must research patents or consult patent attorneys if they plan to develop products using such technologies.

Some cases

The financial impact of patent decisions can be huge, and the complexity of the issues makes decisions difficult. Lawsuits often take many years.

Many Web users remember Amazon innovating the idea of recommending books to customers based on their previous purchases. But Amazon may not have been the source of the technique for doing so. After a few years of negotiations that failed to yield an agreement, IBM sued Amazon for violating several of its patents on e-commerce techniques. IBM had obtained a patent on electronic catalogs in 1994, before online retail was common. The patent covers a wide area including targeted advertising and recommending specific products to a customer. Eventually, Amazon agreed to pay IBM a licensing fee. IBM has license agreements with many other companies that use its thousands of patents.[47]

Hundreds of companies make devices that play MP3 files. Microsoft and other companies that use MP3 pay license fees to a company that developed the technology jointly with Bell Laboratories, which became part of Lucent, which was bought by Alcatel. In 2007, a jury ordered Microsoft to pay Alcatel-Lucent more than $1.5 billion for infringing two Alcatel-Lucent MP3 patents. It was one of the biggest patent awards in U.S. history. The judge rejected the jury decision, saying that Alcatel-Lucent did not prove infringement of one of the patents and that Microsoft had a license for the other from the co-owner. Alcatel-Lucent is appealing the judge's decision. The result could be significant for other companies using MP3 technology.[48]

Friendster, founded in 2002, developed many basic techniques for social-networking Web sites and filed patent applications. In the next few years, before the government approved the patents, many other social-networking sites were established and used these techniques. To the public and to Web programmers, they seem "natural"; this is what social-networking sites do, just as one-click shopping seems common and natural for retail sites. Eventual approval of Friendster's patents meant the company could demand licensing agreements and payments. Friendster has not been as successful a social-networking site as many of the sites that followed and use techniques it developed. Some companies are better at inventing new technologies than at implementing them in a successful business. Is it reasonable to expect other companies to pay for the use of the technology?

In 2007 Congress considered a major revision of patent law. The Patent Reform Act, if passed, will make it harder to get a patent and easier to challenge patents already approved. Many computer technology companies and financial companies favor the changes. Critics include biotechnology companies, manufacturing companies, and companies that buy patents in order to charge others for using them. Supporters argue that the changes will encourage innovation, reduce expensive lawsuits, and reduce the incidence of extremely high judgments against companies for patent infringement. Opponents argue that, by weakening patents, the changes will threaten innovation and make it more difficult for individual inventors and small companies to protect their inventions.

Exporting products

A patent protects intellectual property only within the country that grants the patent. Thus, to protect against foreign companies making, selling, or using its patented inventions without authorization, a company must apply for patents in many countries. This is expensive, and litigation would occur in those countries.

U.S. patent law prohibits companies in the U.S. from shipping components of a device to be assembled in another country if the device infringes a U.S. patent. In 2007 the Supreme Court ruled on a significant case between Microsoft and AT&T involving this provision. The case centered on the question of whether a master copy of software is a "component." We describe the case and then comment on it.

AT&T patented a system that encodes and compresses recorded speech (analogous to MP3 encoding and compressing music). Microsoft's Windows operating system includes software that enables a computer to encode speech using AT&T's method. Microsoft sent master copies of Windows to companies in other countries that copied the software and installed it on computers. AT&T contended that Microsoft shipped a component that was assembled into the products that infringed its patent. Microsoft contended that the foreign-made copies of Windows installed on the computers are components, but that the master software is not a component of computers onto which it was copied. The Supreme Court ruled for Microsoft.[49] It said that the prohibition on shipping components applied to companies shipping physical components that are assembled into the infringing devices. Congress would need to pass new legislation if it wished to provide protection for patent holders in cases like this, where a company ships a master copy of software.

This case reminds us of distinctions between copyright and patent. (Would Microsoft argue in a software copyright suit that the abstract software on a disk is not the essential component?) It and the other patent lawsuits we discussed in this section remind us that many basic issues about how patent applies to technology implemented in software are still unsettled. As one court said about earlier issues of copyright protection for software, the bounds of patent protection are in a state of "creative ferment."

4.7.3 COPYRIGHT AND SIMILAR SOFTWARE PRODUCTS

Subtle problems about defining and identifying copyright violations arise in disputes about whether one software company's product infringes the copyright of another's. If another work is similar, we have to determine whether it copies only ideas and functions or the copyrighted expression of the ideas and functions. This is often difficult for literary and artistic works. It is difficult for software too. Some principles about software copyright infringement emerged from court cases, but the boundaries of permissible uses are not certain.

Criteria

In a 1986 case, *Whelan Associates v. Jaslow Dental Laboratory*, the court ruled that a program that was very similar to another in structure and performance, although written in a different programming language for a different computer, infringed the copyright on the first program.[50] The ruling treated programs somewhat like novels and movies, which can infringe copyrights if they are too similar, even if they are not literal copies. That much is reasonable, and in a case where a program is simply translated to a new language for another computer system, it makes sense to treat it like an infringing translation of a book. A serious problem with the *Whelan* decision, though, was the court's interpretation of what the "idea" in a program is: the purpose of the program. Anything else in the program not essential to the purpose was copyrightable. This meant that a program that used well-known and widely used techniques and routines could infringe another program's copyright. Later decisions by other courts indicate that the *Whelan* decision went too far.

A 1987 decision took an extreme position in the other direction. A court ruled in *Plains Cotton Co-op Association v. Goodpasture Computer Service* that only literal copying of code was infringement. This is a far narrower protection than is given to literary work. Any programmer knows that there is a lot of creative expression in the organization and structure of a program, as there is in the plot and characters in a novel, but if this ruling had applied to novels it would mean that anyone else could use the plot and characters if he or she changed the words.

A reasonable interpretation of the boundaries for infringement lies somewhere between these two decisions. Such an in-between position is likely to be complicated, like the 1992 decision in *Computer Associates International v. Altai*. The court specified a complex process for deciding whether a program infringed a copyright. A brief and simplified summary is as follows: First, identify the purpose of the program, remove from consideration the parts that are in the public domain, are common practice, or are the only efficient way of accomplishing some part; copyright does not protect them.

Then compare the remaining parts of the two programs to see how similar they are. Any particular case would need expert witnesses and a complex analysis of the programs. Several subsequent court decisions used this approach.

"Look and feel"

The term *look and feel* of a program refers to the user interface: the use of pull-down menus, windows, and icons, as well as the specific commands, menus, icons, and so on used to select actions. Two programs that have similar user interfaces are sometimes called *workalike* programs. The internal structure and programming could be entirely different. One program might be faster or have other advantages. Should the look and feel of a program be copyrightable? Does a workalike program infringe the copyright of the earlier program it resembles?

In the 1986 *Whelan* decision mentioned earlier, the court found that a user interface designed for the dental profession was copyrightable.[51] In the early 1990s, Lotus Development Corp., producer of the Lotus 1-2-3 spreadsheet program, won significant copyright infringement suits against Paperback Software International and Borland International, Inc., for using its menus and commands. An appeals court reversed the *Lotus v. Borland* decision in 1995. The appeals court ruled that menu commands are "a method of operation," explicitly excluded from copyright protection. They are, the court said, like the controls of a car.[52] Other analogies offered by opponents of user-interface copyright are the arrangement of the keys on a piano—or the keys on a typewriter or computer keyboard. The trend of various court decisions has been against copyright protection for look and feel. Various courts ruled that features like overlapping windows, pull-down menus, and common operations like cut and paste are outside the scope of copyright.

The main argument in favor of protecting a user interface is that it is a major creative effort. Thus, the usual arguments for copyright and patent apply: protect the programmers who create an interface so that they profit from their effort. On the other hand, standard user interfaces increase productivity of users and programmers. We do not have to learn new interfaces for each program. Programmers do not have to reinvent the wheel, that is, design a new interface just to be different. They can concentrate on developing the truly new aspects of their programs. They can reduce development costs for new programs, keeping prices down.

EXERCISES

Review Exercises

4.1 What are the four factors to be used in deciding whether a use of copyrighted material is a fair use?

4.2 Summarize the main reasons why the court in the Sony Betamax case ruled that videotaping a movie from television to watch later was not an infringement of copyright.

4.3 Can laws be copyrighted?

4.4   Summarize the main reasons why the court in the Napster case ruled that Napster's role in distributing music violated copyright law.

4.5   Give one example where a court ordered a Web site to remove links to another site.

4.6   Give one benefit and one problem associated with free software (in the sense of Section 4.6).

General Exercises

4.7   Describe two things the entertainment industry has done to protect its copyrights. For each, tell whether you think it is justified. Give reasons.

4.8   A swap-meet owner was sued because a vendor sold pirated music CDs at the swap meet. The owner was found liable for "contributory copyright infringement." Was Napster like a swap meet? Describe some similarities and differences between a swap meet and Napster.

4.9   Your uncle owns a sandwich shop. He asks you to write an inventory program for him. You are glad to help him and do not charge for the program. The program works pretty well, and you discover later that your uncle has given copies to several friends who also operate small food shops. Do you believe your uncle should have asked your permission to give away your program? Do you believe the other merchants should pay you for the copies?

4.10   A political group organized a forum on its Web site to encourage people to post and comment on individual newspaper articles relevant to political issues of concern to the group. Other participants added their comments, and debate and discussion of the articles continued. Two newspapers sued, arguing that posting the articles violated their copyrights. Analyze the case. How do the fair-use guidelines apply? Who should win?[53]

4.11   Thousands of high schools and colleges submit student term papers and essays to a service that checks them for plagiarism by comparing them to its database of millions of student papers and to material on the Web and in journal archives. The service builds its database of student papers by adding those the schools submit for checking. Several students sued the company for infringing their copyrights by adding their papers to the database.[54]
Analyze the case. Give arguments for both sides. Which do you think should win? Why?

4.12   Software was the first digital product to be widely copied. What are some of the arguments people give to justify copying software? Do you agree with any of the arguments? If so, which ones?

4.13   Describe how the fair-use guidelines apply to making a video of oneself lip-synching to a popular song and posting the video on a social-networking site. Do you think it is ethical to do this?

4.14   You are a teacher. You would like your students to use a software package, but the school's budget does not include enough money to buy copies for all the students. Your school is in a poor neighborhood, and you know most of the parents cannot afford to buy the software for their children.
    a) List some ways you could try to obtain the software without making unauthorized copies.
    b) Suppose the methods you try do not work. Will you copy the software or decide not to use it? Give some arguments for and against your position. Explain why you think the arguments on your side are stronger.[55]

4.15   Which of the following activities do you think should be a fair use? Give reasons using copyright law and/or court cases. (If you think the ethically right decision differs from the result that follows from applying the fair-use guidelines, explain how and why.)
    a) Making a copy of a friend's spreadsheet software to try out for two weeks and then either deleting it or buying your own copy.
    b) Making a copy of a computer game, playing it for two weeks, and then deleting it.

4.16   Describe a situation involving making a copy of a computer program or an entertainment file of some sort for which you think it is difficult to decide if the copying is ethical or not. Explain the reasons for the uncertainty.

4.17   Discuss the impact technology has had on copyright infringement. What particular computer applications have contributed to the increase of copyright owners and copyright infringement?

4.18   Choose the case from this chapter that you feel is most significant. Analyze the outcome and discuss the significance of the ruling.

4.19   Patents provide protection only within the country that grants the patent. A company may have to apply for patents in several countries to protect its intellectual property. What would be the advantages and disadvantages of a global standard for patents?

4.20   A search engine company copies millions of books in a university library, including books in the public domain and books still protected by copyright. It displays segments, say a paragraph, in response to user search requests. Analyze how the fair-use guidelines apply to this practice. Should the copying and display be considered fair use, or should the company need permission from the copyright holders for the books? (If you think the ethically right decision differs from the decision that follows from applying the fair-use guidelines, explain how and why.)

4.21   The first Mickey Mouse cartoon appeared more than 75 years ago. Give ethical and/or social arguments both for and against each of the following uses of the cartoon or the Mickey Mouse character without authorization from the company that owned or owns the copyright. Tell which side you think is stronger, and why. Do not consider the copyright time period under current law or arguments about the ethics of obeying or breaking laws.
   a) Post a digitized copy of the original cartoon on a video-sharing site.
   b) Use the Mickey Mouse character as the spokesperson in an advertisement very strongly critical of a candidate running for president.
   c) Edit a digitized copy of the original cartoon to improve visual and sound quality, produce copies with the dialog dubbed in various other languages, and sell thousands of copies in other countries.

4.22   Companies selling music or movies (for example) can include digital rights management tools that cause files to self-destruct after a specified amount of time. Give some advantages and disadvantages of this practice. Do you think it is ethical for entertainment businesses to sell content with such a limitation? Why or why not?

4.23   There is much controversy about whether a patent is an appropriate protection mechanism for software. Give two arguments in favor of patents for software and two arguments against them.

4.24   Do you think taxing media and devices that aid copyright infringement (as described in Section 4.3.1) is a reasonable solution for collecting fees to pay content providers? Give your reasons.

4.25   Discuss the responsibilities of Web sites on which people post videos. What legal issues must they deal with? What are the ethical issues involved?

4.26   Debate whether copyright can survive the increased ease of copying as well as the habits and expectations that developed about sharing information and entertainment online. Will most content be free or almost free? Will firm enforcement of copyright law be sufficient for copyright to survive?

4.27   Intellectual property piracy is more common outside the United States. What are some reasons for this?

4.28 Which arguments for free software (as in Section 4.6) apply to music? Which do not? Give reasons.

4.29 A cook can modify a recipe by adding or deleting a few ingredients without getting permission or paying a royalty to the person who developed the recipe.
   a) Give an example of modifications of a professional song or a piece of software that is analogous to a cook using the recipe.
   b) Do you think your example satisfies the fair-use guidelines? That is, is it very likely courts would consider it a legal fair use? Explain why.
   c) Copyright protects cookbooks. A court would likely find that selling a cookbook in which many of the recipes are slight modifications of recipes in someone else's cookbook is copyright infringement. Give an example of modifications of a professional song or a piece of software that is analogous to selling such a cookbook.

4.30 Thomas Jefferson and several modern writers used fire as an analogy for copying intellectual property: We can light many candles from one without diminishing the light or heat obtained from the first candle. Suppose a group of people go camping in the wilderness using primitive methods. One person gets a fire started. Others want to start their fire from hers. Can you think of any ethical or practical reasons why they should be expected to trade something, perhaps some wild fruit they found, for the use of the fire?

4.31 In the 1990s, two writers suggested that software is a "public good," like public schools and national defense, that we should allow anyone to copy it, and that the federal government should subsidize it.[56] Suppose this proposal had been adopted then. How well do you think it would have worked? How would it have affected the quantity and quality of software produced? Give reasons.

4.32 Describe one kind of software or technique used in software that you think is innovative, like an invention, for which patent protection might be appropriate.

4.33 Did you know, before you read this chapter, that restaurants pay fees for the music they play, community theaters pay fees for the plays they perform, and large companies routinely pay large fees to other companies for use of patented inventions and technologies? Does this long tradition of paying for intellectual property affect your view of the legitimacy of sharing entertainment on the Web without authorization? Give your reasons.

4.34 Assume you are a professional working in your chosen field. Describe specific things you can do to reduce the impact of any two problems we discussed in this chapter. (If you cannot think of anything related to your professional field, choose another field that might interest you.)

4.35 Think ahead to the next few years and describe a new problem, related to issues in this chapter, likely to develop from computing technology or the Web.

Assignments

These exercises require some research or activity.

4.36 Read a license agreement for a software product. It could be a game, operating system, video editor, or tax preparation program, or some other kind of software.
   a) What does the license agreement say about the number of copies you can make?
   b) Does it specify penalties for making unauthorized copies?
   c) Was the agreement easy to read before purchase (e.g., on the outside of the package or available on a Web site)?
   d) Do you consider the license agreement to be clearly stated? Reasonable?

4.37   Read the member agreement or policy statement of YouTube, MySpace, or any other large site that hosts user videos. What does it say about posting files that contain or use works of others without authorization?

4.38   Find and describe the result or current status of Viacom's lawsuit against YouTube or the Motion Picture Association of America lawsuit against YouTVpc.com and Peekvid.com.

4.39   Find and describe the result or current status of any lawsuit against Google for digitizing books without permission.

4.40   Find the main provisions of the Sonny Bono Copyright Term Extension Act (1998). What is its likely impact on the availability of material on the Web?

4.41   Find and describe the result or current status of any of the patent lawsuits mentioned in Section 4.7.2 as still unresolved.

4.42   Read the articles by Esther Dyson and Lance Rose from *Wired* (listed in Books and Articles). Write a short essay telling which author's views about the future of intellectual property in the "digital age" have proved more accurate based on events in the years since they wrote the articles.

Class Discussion Exercises

These exercises are for class discussion, perhaps with short presentations prepared in advance by small groups of students.

4.43   Some people argue that digital rights management violates the public's right to fair uses.
   a) Should people or companies that create intellectual property have the right to offer it for sale (or license) in a form protected by their choice of digital rights management technology (assuming the restrictions are clear to potential customers)? Give reasons.
   b) Should people have a legal right to develop, sell, buy, and use devices and software to remove digital rights management restrictions for fair uses? Give reasons.

4.44   Debate whether Congress should repeal the Digital Millennium Copyright Act's anticircumvention provisions.

4.45   Which factor is or will be more important for protection of digital intellectual property: strict copyright laws (and strict enforcement) or technology-based protections (or neither)? Why?

4.46   With respect to copyright issues for digital media and the Web, in what ways are entertainment companies victims? In what ways are entertainment companies villains?

4.47   Debate whether software should be copyrightable or should be freely available for copying.

NOTES

1. Nicholas Negroponte, "Being Digital," *Wired*, February 1995, p. 182.

2. Pamela Samuelson, "Copyright and Digital Libraries," *Communications of the ACM*, 38, no. 3 (April 1995), pp. 15–21, 110.

3. Laura Didio, "Crackdown on Software Bootleggers Hits Home," *LAN Times*, 10, no. 22 (November 1, 1993).

4. I used several sources for the history in this section. National Research Council, *Intellectual Property Issues in Software* (National Academy Press, 1991); Neil Boorstyn and Martin C. Fliesler, "Copyrights, Computers, and Confusion," *California State Bar Journal* (April 1981), pp. 148–152; Judge Richard Stearns, *United States of America v. David LaMacchia*, 1994; Robert A. Spanner, "Copyright Infringement Goes Big Time," *Microtimes*, March 8, 1993, p. 36.

5. The piano roll case is *WhiteSmith Publishing Co. v. Apollo*, reported in Boorstyn and Fliesler, "Copyrights, Computers, and Confusion."

6. *Data Cash Systems v. JS & A Group*, reported in Boorstyn and Fliesler, "Copyrights, Computers, and Confusion."

7. In *Feist Publications, Inc. v. Rural Telephone Service Company, Inc.*, the Supreme Court ruled that Rural Telephone Service's telephone directory did not meet the requirement for copyright protection.

8. Criminal penalties for copyright infringement are in Title 18 of the U.S. Code.

9. For exemptions, see Copyright Office, Library of Congress, "Exemption to Prohibition on Circumvention of Copyright Protection Systems for Access Control Technologies," *Federal Register*, 71, no. 227 (November 27, 2006) www.copyright.gov/fedreg/2006/71fr68472.html (accessed March 15, 2007).

10. *Peter Veeck v. Southern Building Code Congress International Inc.*, No. 9940632, www.pubklaw.com/rd/courts/99-40632.html (accessed February 18, 2007).

11. U.S. Code Title 17, Section 107.

12. *Sony Corporation of America v. Universal City Studios, Inc.*, 464 U.S. 417(1984); Pamela Samuelson, "Computer Programs and Copyright's Fair Use Doctrine," *Communications of the ACM*, 36, no. 9 (September 1993), pp. 19–25.

13. "9th Circuit Allows Disassembly in *Sega vs. Accolade*," *Computer Law Strategist*, 9, no. 7 (November 1992), pp. 1, 3–5. "Can You Infringe a Copyright While Analyzing a Competitor's Program?" *Legal Bytes*, 1, no. 1 (Winter 1992–1993), p. 3; Pamela Samuelson, "Copyright's Fair Use Doctrine and Digital Data," *Communications of the ACM*, 37, no. 1 (January 1994), pp. 21–27.

14. *Sony Computer Entertainment, Inc. v. Connectix Corporation*, U.S. 9th Circuit Court of Appeal, No. 9915852, February 10, 2000.

15. Karl Taro Greenfeld, "The Digital Reckoning," *Time*, May 22, 2000, p. 56.

16. Stuart Luman and Jason Cook, "Knocking Off Napster," *Wired*, January 2001, p. 89; Karl Taro Greenfeld, "Meet the Napster," *Time*, October 2, 2000, pp. 60–68; "Napster University: From File Swapping to the Future of Entertainment," June 1, 2000, described in Mary Hillebrand, "Music Downloaders Willing to Pay," *E-Commerce Times*, June 8, 2000, www.ecommercetimes.com/story/3512.html (accessed September 6, 2007).

17. Charles Goldsmith, "Sharp Slowdown in U.S. Singles Sales Helps to Depress Global Music Business," *Wall Street Journal*, April 20, 2001, p. B8.

18. *A&M Records v. Napster*, No. 0016401, February 12, 2001, DC No. CV9905183MHP.

19. Pamela Samuelson, "The Copyright Grab," *Wired*, January 1996, pp. 134–138, 188–191. The companies were Vault and Quaid.

20. John Sankus Jr. of DrinkOrDie. "Leader of Internet Software Piracy Organization Pleads Guilty to Conspiracy," News Release, U.S. Department of Justice, February 27, 2002, www.cybercrime.gov/sankusPlea.htm.

21. *RIAA v. Diamond Multimedia*, 1999.

22. Quoted in Karl Taro Greenfeld, "The Free Juke Box," *Time*, March 27, 2000, p. 82.

23. The Library of Congress develops lists of exceptions every few years. See www.copyright.gov/fedreg/2006/71fr68472.html.

24. J. S. Kelly, "Meet the Kid behind the DVD Hack," CNN.com, January 31, 2000, archives.cnn.com/2000/TECH/computing/01/31/johansen.interview.idg/ (accessed May 10, 2007).

25. *Universal City Studios, Inc. v. Reimerdes*, 111 F.Supp.2d 294 (S.D.N.Y. 2000).

26. David S. Touretzky, a computer science professor at Carnegie Mellon University, collected many forms of expressing DeCSS on his Web site, "Gallery of CSS Descramblers," www.cs.cmu.edu/~dst/DeCSS/Gallery (accessed April 12, 2001).

27. The paper leaked and appeared on the Web. It was eventually published at a computer security conference. Scott A. Craver et al., "Reading between the Lines: Lessons from the SDMI Challenge," www.usenix.org/events/sec01/craver.pdf.

28. *Felton et al. v. RIAA, SDMI, et al.* The statement by the Association for Computing Machinery (ACM), one of the major organizations for professional and academic computer scientists, is at www.acm.org/usacm/copyright/felten_declaration.html.

29. Jennifer M. Urban and Laura Quilter, "Efficient Process or 'Chilling Effects'? Takedown Notices under Section 512 of the Digital Millennium Copyright Act," mylaw.usc.edu/documents/512Rep (accessed September 17, 2007).

30. Les Vadasz, "A Bill that Chills," *Wall Street Journal*, July 21, 2002, p. A10.

31. "Let's Give It Up for Metallica," *Wall Street Journal*, May 10, 2000, p. A27.

32. creativecommons.org.

33. Helen Nissenbaum, "Should I Copy My Neighbor's Software?" in *Computers, Ethics & Social Values*, ed. Deborah G. Johnson and Helen Nissenbaum (Prentice Hall, 1995), pp. 201–213.

34. The data in this paragraph are from Business Software Alliance, "Worldwide Software Piracy Rate Holds Steady at 35%," May 15, 2007, w3.bsa.org/usa/press/newsreleases/2007-global-piracy-study.cfm (accessed September 17, 2007); Business Software Alliance,

"Fourth Annual BSA and IDC Global Software Piracy Study," May 2007, w3.bsa.org/globalstudy/upload/2007-Global-Piracy-Study-EN.pdf (accessed September 17, 2007).

35. Business Software Alliance, "Fourth Annual BSA and IDC Global Software Piracy Study," Table 1: 2006 PC Software Piracy Rankings, p. 4.

36. R. W. Bradford pointed out the unfairness of the tactic used to pressure the Chinese to enforce copyright in "Whose Ox is Xeroxed," *Liberty*, 8, no. 5 (May 1995), pp. 8–9; William P. Alford, "A Piracy Deal Doesn't Make a China Policy," *Wall Street Journal*, July 17, 1996, p. A14.

37. *Parker v. Google*, U.S. District Court for the Eastern District of Pennsylvania, 2006; Elinor Mills, "Google Wins a Court Battle," CNET News.com, March 16, 2006, news.com.com.

38. Including the Religious Technology Center and Bridge Publications.

39. David G. Post, "New World War," *Reason*, April 1996, pp. 28–33. *EFFector Online*, 8, no. 16 (October 7, 1995).

40. Comments from the BBS operator, Tom Klemesrud, are reported in *EFFector Online*, 8, no. 2 (February 23, 1995).

41. Judge Leonie Brinkema, quoted in Jason L. Riley, "The Internet vs. the First Amendment," *Wall Street Journal*, October 25, 1999, p. A53.

42. The Google incident is reported in Jack Goldsmith and Tim Wu, *Who Controls the Internet?* (Oxford University Press, 2006), pp. 74–75.

43. See Yochai Benkler, "Coase's Penguin, or, Linux and *The Nature of the Firm*," *The Yale Law Journal*, December 2002, pp. 369–446, www.yalelawjournal.org/112/3/369_yochai_benkler.html, for an analysis of the phenomenon of peer production.

44. "What Is Copyleft?" www.gnu.org/philosophy.

45. For example in the *Wall Street Journal*, May 11, 2000, p. A7.

46. This is a brief summary of Stallman's views. See his article "Why Software Should Be Free" and many others at the GNU Web site (www.gnu.org/philosophy).

47. Charles Forelle and Suein Hwang, "IBM Hits Amazon with Ecommerce Patent Suit," *Wall Street Journal*, October 24, 2006, p. A3.

48. *Lucent Technologies Inc. v. Gateway Inc.* This and some of the other cases are described in Joe Wilcox, "Microsoft's Patent Disputes with Alcatel-Lucent, AT&T Make Waves," eWeek.com, February 23, 2007, www.eweek.com/article2/0,1895,2098063,00.asp (accessed July 3, 2007).

49. *Microsoft Corp. v. AT&T Corp.*, No. 05-1056, www.supremecourtus.gov/opinions/06pdf/05-1056.pdf (accessed September 17, 2007).

50. The source for information about the cases in this section is "When Is a Computer Program a Copy?" *Legal Bytes*, 1, no. 1 (Winter 1992–1993), pp. 1, 2, 4.

51. Anne Wells Branscomb, *Who Owns Information?* (Basic Books, 1994), p. 147.

52. David L. Hayes, "A Comprehensive Current Analysis of Software 'Look and Feel' Protection," Fenwick & West LLP, 2000, www.fenwick.com/pub/ip_pubs.

53. This exercise is based on the *Los Angeles Times v. Free Republic case*. The court's decision in favor of the newspapers seems inconsistent with the reasoning in the reverse engineering cases described in Section 4.2.3 and other fair-use cases. This decision was criticized by some scholars.

54. The students sued Turnitin in federal court in Virginia in April 2007.

55. This exercise was sparked by a brief note in Helen Nissenbaum, "Should I Copy My Neighbor's Software?" in *Computers, Ethics & Social Values*, ed. Deborah G. Johnson and Helen Nissenbaum (Prentice Hall, 1995), p. 213.

56. Barbara R. Bergmann and Mary W. Gray, "Viewpoint: Software as a Public Good," *Communications of the ACM*, 36, no. 10 (October 1993), pp. 13–14.

BOOKS AND ARTICLES

- Barlow, John Perry. "The Economy of Ideas: A Framework for Rethinking Patents and Copyrights in the Digital Age." *Wired*, March 1994, pp. 84–90, 126–129.

- Benkler, Yochai. "Coase's Penguin, or, Linux and *The Nature of the Firm*." *The Yale Law Journal*, December 2002, pp. 369–446, www.yalelawjournal.org/112/3/369_yochai_benkler.html or www.benkler.org/CoasesPenguin.html. An economic analysis of open-source software and other forms of peer production.

- Chesbrough, Henry. *Open Business Models*. Harvard Business School Press,

2006. How businesses use intellectual property, with emphasis on patents.

- Dyson, Esther. "Intellectual Value." *Wired*, July 1995, pp. 136–141, 182–185.

- Friedman, David D. *Law's Order: What Economics Has to Do With Law and Why It Matters.* Princeton University Press, 2000, Chapter 11, "Clouds and Barbed Wire: The Economics of Intellectual Property." Economic pros and cons for intellectual-property rights.

- Hayes, David L. "A Comprehensive Current Analysis of Software 'Look and Feel' Protection." Fenwick & West LLP, 2000, www.fenwick.com/pub/ip_pubs.

- Lee, Timothy B. *Circumventing Competition: The Perverse Consequences of the Digital Millennium Copyright Act.* Cato Institute Policy Analysis No. 564, March 21, 2006.

- Lessig, Lawrence. *Free Culture: The Nature and Future of Creativity.* Penguin, 2005.

- Littman, Jessica. *Digital Copyright: Protecting Intellectual Property on the Internet.* Prometheus Books, 2001.

- Moody, Glyn. *Rebel Code: Inside Linux and the Open Source Revolution.* Perseus, 2001.

- National Research Council. *The Digital Dilemma: Intellectual Property in the Information Age.* National Academy Press, 2000; books.nap.edu/html/digital_dilemma/notice.html.

- Oram, Andrew, et al. *Peer-to-peer: Harnessing the Power of Disruptive Technologies.* O'Reilly, 2001.

- Patterson, L. R. *Copyright In Historical Perspective.* Vanderbilt University Press, 1968.

- Raymond, Eric S. *The Cathedral and the Bazaar.* O'Reilly, 1999.

- Rose, Lance. "The Emperor's Clothes Still Fit Just Fine." *Wired*, February 1995, pp. 103–106.

- Thierer, Adam, and Wayne Crews, eds. *Copy Fights: The Future of Intellectual Property in the Information Age.* Cato Institute, 2002.

- Torvalds, Linus, and David Diamond. *Just for Fun: The Story of an Accidental Revolutionary.* HarperBusiness, 2001.

- Walker, Jesse. "Copy Catfight: How Intellectual Property Laws Stifle Popular Culture." *Reason*, March 2000, pp. 44–51.

ORGANIZATIONS AND WEB SITES

- Creative Commons, an organization that provides a variety of free licensing tools for both protecting and sharing intellectual property on the Web: creativecommons.org

- The DVD Copy Control Association, an industry organization that promotes digital rights management: www.dvdcca.org

- The Electronic Frontier Foundation's sites about intellectual property: (www.eff.org/IP) and the Digital Millennium Copyright Act (www.eff.org/IP/DMCA)

- The GNU project and free software: www.gnu.org/philosophy

- National Center for Technology and Law, George Mason University School of Law: www.law.gmu.edu/nctl

- The Recording Industry Association of America: www.riaa.com

- The Software & Information Industry Association: www.siia.net

5

CRIME

5.1 Introduction

Nineteenth-century bank robbers fled the scenes of their crimes on horseback. In the 20th-century, they drove getaway cars. In the 21st-century, they work from a personal computer (PC) or laptop. For generations, teenagers have committed pranks and minor crimes. Hacking into school, corporate, and government computer systems was a natural step. Employees embezzled funds from employers by "doctoring" the books. Now they modify or misuse company software. Computers and the Internet make many activities easier for us. They also make many illegal activities easier for criminals. They provide a new environment for fraud, stock manipulation, theft, forgery, industrial espionage, and many old and new scams. Hacking—intentional, unauthorized access to computer systems—includes a wide range of activities from minor pranks to huge thefts and shutdowns of important services on which lives and livelihoods depend.

Crimes committed with computers and on the Web are more devastating and harder to detect than similar crimes committed without computers. A robber who enters a bank and uses a gun gets $2,500–$5,000 on average. The average loss from a computer fraud is more than $100,000.[1] A thief who steals a credit card (or a credit-card number) gains access to a much larger amount of money than the thief of the past who stole a wallet containing only cash. A hacker who breaks into a retailer's or bank's computer might steal not one or a dozen, but thousands or millions of credit-card numbers. Identity theft affects millions of people. It can disrupt a victim's life for years. Computer vandalism by teenagers brings business operations of major companies to a halt. Terrorists could sabotage power and communications systems and other critical infrastructure. Global business networks and the Web extend the criminal's reach and make arrests and prosecutions more difficult. Some tools that aid law enforcement conflict with privacy and civil liberties.

Just as the Web changes the impact of crime, it changes the impact of law. Activities that are legal in some countries are illegal in others. But the Web is global. Businesses and individuals are sued and arrested for violating laws of countries their online business or writing reaches. Policy makers face the difficult challenge of developing ways to deal with differing national laws and cultures.

In this chapter, we examine many of these problems and issues. We examine many approaches devised for addressing them. The examples we include are representative of dozens or hundreds more.

5.2 Hacking

5.2.1 WHAT IS HACKING?

The term *hacker*, to many people, means an irresponsible, destructive criminal. Hackers break into computer systems. They intentionally release computer viruses. They steal sensitive personal, business, and government information. They steal money, crash Web sites, destroy files, and disrupt businesses. But other people who call themselves hackers do none of these things. So our first problem is to figure out what *hacker* means and what hackers do.

To organize the discussion, we describe three phases of hacking:

Phase 1—the early years (1960s and 1970s), when hacking was a positive term

Phase 2—from the 1970s to the mid-1990s, when hacking took on its more negative meanings

Phase 3—beginning in the mid-1990s, with the growth of the Web and of e-commerce and the participation of a large portion of the public online

The boundaries are not sharp, and each phase includes most of the kinds of hacking common in the earlier phases.

Phase 1: The joy of programming

In the early days of computing, a *hacker* was a creative programmer who wrote very elegant or clever programs. A "good hack" was an especially clever piece of code. Hackers were *computer virtuosos*. They created many of the first computer games and operating systems. They tended to be outside the social mainstream, spending many hours learning as much as they could about computer systems and making these systems do new things. Many hackers were high-school and college students who "hacked" the computers at their schools. Although they sometimes found a way into systems where they were not authorized users, the early hackers mostly sought knowledge and intellectual challenges—and, sometimes, the thrill of going where they did not belong. Most had no intention of disrupting services; they frowned on doing damage. The *New Hacker's Dictionary* describes a hacker as a person "who enjoys exploring the details of programmable systems and how to stretch their capabilities; ... one who programs enthusiastically (even obsessively)."[2] Jude Milhon, one of the relatively few women hackers, described hacking as "clever circumvention of imposed limits."[3] The limits can be technical limits of the system one is using, limits that someone else's security techniques impose, legal limits, or the limits of one's skills. Her definition is a good one in that it stretches over many of the uses of the term. Steven Levy captured some of the spirit of the early hackers in his book *Hackers: Heroes of the Computer Revolution*, when he said "Art, science, and play had merged into the magical activity of programming."

Nowadays, there are still examples where *hacking* has the early meaning of clever programming that reflects a high level of skill and that circumvents limits. Fans of Nintendo's Wii videogame console reprogram its remote controller to play music, make a robot hit tennis balls, and perform other tasks Nintendo never imagined. Apple built its iPhone so that none of its features would work unless the owner bought a service contract from AT&T. Within a week after Apple released the phone in 2007, hackers found ways around this restriction. They could use the phone's Web browser and other features without the service contract. Another example, of course, is software to circumvent the limits of protection schemes for digital intellectual property (discussed in Section 4.3.2). Hacking often has a whiff, at least, of challenge to powerful institutions.

Phase 2: From the 1970s to the mid-1990s

The meaning, and especially the connotations, of the word *hacker* changed as more people began using computers and more people began abusing them. Computers were and still are a mystery to most people, and it was easy for the public and the news media to lump all young people who can work magic with these machines in the same category, not seeing the distinction between good magic and bad. The word *hacking* took on its most common meaning today: breaking into computers on which the hacker does not have authorized access. By the 1980s, hacking also included spreading computer viruses, then mostly in software traded on floppy disks. Hacking behavior included pranks, thefts (of information, software, and, sometimes, money), and *phone phreaking* (manipulating the telephone system).

Hacking a computer at a big research center, corporation, or government agency was a challenge that brought a sense of accomplishment, a lot of files to explore, and respect from one's peers. In 1986, one hacker broke into at least 30 computers on the Stanford University campus, several other universities, 15 Silicon Valley companies, three government laboratories, and several other sites. It appeared that his goal was simply to get into as many computers as he could. This case was typical of the "trophy" hacking often associated with young hackers.[4] Young hackers were especially fond of breaking into Defense Department computers, and they were very successful at it. Clifford Stoll described a more serious case in his book *The Cuckoo's Egg*: A German hacker broke into dozens of U.S. computers, including military systems, in the 1980s, looking for information to sell to the Soviet Union.

Hackers obtained passwords by sophisticated techniques and by *social engineering*: fooling people into disclosing them. (A popular cover story, when calling an employee of a large company, is to pretend to be a coworker from the company's computer operations department checking on some security problem. Hackers still use this tactic.) Hackers spoofed e-mail from the premier of the province of Ontario, Canada, sending out unflattering comments about Ontario's parliament. The Secret Service reported that a 15-year-old hacked a credit reporting service and the telephone system in a scheme to get Western Union to wire money to him from other people's accounts. He is also believed to have hacked a McDonald's payroll computer and given raises to his friends. Some hackers became a serious threat to security and privacy. Using programs called *sniffers*, they read information traveling over the Internet and extracted passwords. Security analysts estimated that hackers might have compromised one million passwords in 1994.[5]

Adult criminals began to recognize the possibilities of hacking. Thus, business espionage and significant thefts and frauds joined the list of hacking activities in the 1980s and 1990s. For example, a Russian man, with accomplices in several countries, used stolen passwords to steal $400,000 from Citicorp. While unknowingly under computer

HACKING THE PHONE COMPANY

Since the 1970s, when John Draper (who called himself Captain Crunch) discovered that a whistle in a cereal box fooled the telephone system into giving free access to long-distance telephone lines, phone phreaking (hacking the phone system) has been a popular pastime of young hackers and serious criminals. Hackers infiltrated the BellSouth system for years, exploring and creating new phone numbers with no bills, until they did something overt enough to attract attention (redirecting calls for a probation office to a phone-sex line). A man manipulated telephone connections so that he would win thousands of dollars in prizes in a radio station contest. Hackers cracked private business networks and voice-mail systems and then switched to outside lines and made calls that were billed to the company. They set up their own voice mailboxes in the cracked systems to communicate with each other with less chance of being traced. They shut down companies by taking control of a company's phone system and preventing legitimate calls from getting through. A prosecutor who handled several hacker cases reported a revenge prank: Hackers rigged the system to think her home telephone was a pay phone. When she picked it up to make a call, a recording told her to deposit coins. A group of hackers routed Federal Bureau of Investigation (FBI) telephone numbers to phone-sex chat lines in Germany, Hong Kong, and Moldavia. The phone company billed the FBI about $200,000 for the calls.[6]

BellSouth described the Legion of Doom (a hacker group whose members broke into its computers in the late 1980s) as "a severe threat to U.S. financial and telecommunications industries." A U.S. attorney said, "The Legion of Doom had the power to jeopardize the entire phone network." There is, of course, a difference between having the power to do something and having the intent. Anyone with a match has the power to burn a house down. Frank Darden, one of the members of the Legion of Doom, agreed that "[i]f we'd wanted to, we could have knocked out service across the Southeastern U.S." Darden seemed as surprised as any other telephone customer might be at the vulnerability of the BellSouth computers: "The fact that I could get into the system amazed me."[7]

surveillance by authorities, he transferred another $11 million to bank accounts in other countries. (This incident also illustrates the international nature of computer crimes and some of the difficulties it creates for law enforcement. Extraditing the Russian man from London, where he was arrested, to the U.S. for trial took more than two years.)

The Internet Worm demonstrated the vulnerability of the Internet as a whole in 1988. Robert T. Morris, a graduate student at Cornell University, wrote a worm program

FINDING THE RIGHT WORDS

Some hackers of the 1960s and their intellectual heirs, who still like to use the term with its earlier respect, tried to preserve the old meaning of "hacker" by using the term *cracker* for those who break into systems without authorization, or for those who break in with intent to do damage. "Hacking is art. Cracking is revolution," said a hacker who is a professional software engineer.[8] One writer described crackers as "mean-spirited hackers."[9] The news media and the public use the word *hacker* so commonly now that trying to replace it with a different word is probably futile.

In old cowboy movies, the good guys wore white hats and the bad guys wore black hats. So some people began using the terms *white-hat hacker* and *black-hat hacker* for the cowboys of the computer frontier. White-hat hackers, for the most part, use their skills to demonstrate system vulnerabilities and improve security. Many are computer security professionals. Some spent time in jail or on probation for hacking when in their teens.

and released it onto the Internet.* The worm did not destroy files or steal passwords, and there was disagreement about whether Morris intended or expected it to cause the degree of disruption that it did. The worm, however, spread quickly to computers running particular versions of the UNIX operating system, jamming them up and preventing normal processing. The Worm affected a few thousand computers on the Internet (a large portion of the Net at the time).[10] It took a few days for systems programmers to discover, decode, and rid their systems of the worm. The worm disrupted research and other activities and inconvenienced a large number of people. This incident raised concern about the potential to disrupt critical computer services and cause social disruption. Such disruption can happen by accident, or a terrorist, extortionist, or teenager can cause it.

Phase 3: The growth of the Web

In this phase, hacking includes "all of the above" plus a variety of new threats. Beginning roughly in the mid-1990s, the intricate interconnectedness of the Web and the increased use of the Internet for e-mail and other communications, for sensitive information, and for economic transactions made hacking more dangerous and damaging—and more attractive to criminal gangs. The kind of accessible information expanded to include credit reports, consumer profiles, medical records, tax records, confidential business information, and all the other types of information we described in Chapter 2 when we discussed threats to privacy. With basic infrastructure systems (e.g., water and power,

---

*A worm is a program that copies itself to other computers. The concept was developed to make use of idle resources but was adopted by people using it maliciously. A worm might destroy files or just waste resources.

HACKERS AS SECURITY RESEARCHERS

Since well before the advent of the Web there has been a subculture of hackers who probe computer systems, most often without permission, to find security flaws as an intellectual exercise and, for some, as a public service. They sometimes call themselves "security researchers" to avoid the now negative connotation of the term *hacker*.

These people face ethical dilemmas. The most obvious is: Is it ethical to break into a system without permission, even with good intentions? We discuss this later. Here we focus on another question: How can people responsibly inform potential victims of security vulnerabilities without informing malicious hackers who would exploit these vulnerabilities? Some post details about security weaknesses on the Internet. Some quietly work with software companies. The first approach is very common. Most computer professionals are very critical of this approach. Security professionals do not announce security flaws to the public as soon as they discover them. They inform the software company or system manager responsible for the software and allow time for them to prepare patches (corrections) or close security holes before making a public announcement. Many security professionals argue that when a security-researcher hacker discovers a security weakness in a system, he or she should do the same. Publicizing the flaws only makes it easier for destructive hackers to cause serious damage.

A similar dilemma arises with respect to publication of security tools that malicious hackers could misuse. Two programmers, Dan Farmer and Wietse Venema, developed a software tool that helps system administrators find security flaws in their Internet-connected systems. The programmers made a controversial, widely debated, decision to post their program on the Net. They explained their action:

> Why wasn't there a limited distribution, to only the "white hats"? History has shown that attempts to limit distribution of most security information and tools has only made things worse. The "undesirable" elements of the computer world will obtain them no matter what you do, and people that have legitimate needs for the information are denied.[11]

The dilemma of how to treat security information is intrinsic. There is no perfect solution. Discretion is valuable.

Many security-researcher hackers are very scornful of big software companies both because of the large number of security flaws in their products and because they are slow to plug leaks even when they know of them. The hackers argue that businesses do not behave responsibly toward the public. Publicizing security problems spurs the companies to take action. This argument has some truth to it. Many system operators do not close loopholes, even well-publicized ones, until there is a break-in. Hackers and security consultants say they repeatedly warn companies of flaws that allow access by hackers, but the companies do not respond until hackers exploit the flaws and cause significant problems. Some businesses and government agencies had so much confidence in their systems that they refused to believe anyone could break in. A man who copied patient files from a medical center said he did it to publicize the system's vulnerability, not to use the information. He disclosed portions of the files to a journalist after the medical center said that no one had copied patient files. Should we view him as a whistle-blower or a criminal?[12]

Exposing security flaws is not a legitimate justification for most hacking, but as a side effect it does sometimes speed up security improvements. As software companies, financial companies, and online retailers began taking security more seriously in the early 2000s, some began treating well-intentioned hackers as allies rather than enemies.

hospitals, transportation, emergency services, in addition to the telephone system) accessible on the Net, the risk increased. Hacking for political motives increased. As the Web spread globally, so did hacking. We describe examples ranging from new pranks to serious disruptions.

Hackers modified the U.S. Department of Justice Web page to read "Department of Injustice" in protest of the Communications Decency Act. They changed the Central Intelligence Agency's (CIA's) site to read "Central Stupidity Agency" and added links to pornography sites. In 2001, attrition.org's online archive had copies of more than 15,000 defaced Web pages.[13]

A teenager crippled a computer system that handled communications between the airport tower and incoming planes at a small airport. Hackers in England impersonated air-traffic controllers and gave false instructions to pilots. In 1998, the U.S. deputy defense secretary described a series of attacks on numerous U.S. military computers as "the most organized and systematic attack the Pentagon has seen to date."[14] Two boys, aged 16 and 17, had carried them out.

A decade after the Internet Worm, several computer viruses showed that the Internet, by then much bigger, was still vulnerable. The Melissa virus of 1999 mailed copies of itself to the first 50 people in a computer's e-mail address book on systems using popular Microsoft software. Each new copy sent 50 more copies, and the virus quickly infected approximately a million computers worldwide, including those of individuals, government and military agencies, and hundreds of businesses. Many of the clogged systems shut down. In 2000, the "Love Bug," or "ILOVEYOU" virus, spread around the world in a few hours, propagating among computers using Microsoft's Windows and Outlook programs by mailing itself to people in the infected computer's address book and by other means. It destroyed digital image and music files, modified the computer's operating system and Internet browser, and collected passwords. The virus infected major corporations like Ford and Siemens and 80% of U.S. federal agencies, including the State Department, the Pentagon, and the National Aeronautics and Space Administration (NASA), along with members of the British Parliament and the U.S. Congress. Many businesses and government agencies had to shut down their e-mail servers. The virus hit tens of millions of computers worldwide and did an estimated $10 billion in damage.[15]* Later viruses and worms such as Zotob, Sasser, and MyDoom caused hundreds of millions or billions of dollars in damage.

Within about a week in 2000, *denial-of-service attacks* shut down almost a dozen major Web sites, some for several hours. Victims included Yahoo, eBay, Amazon, E*Trade, Buy.com, CNN, and others. In this kind of attack, hackers overload the target site with hundreds of thousands of requests for Web pages and other information. Programs planted on numerous other systems (many at universities), to disguise their origin, generated the requests. Thus, the attack is also called a *distributed denial-of-service attack*. Investigators traced the attack to a 15-year-old Canadian who used the name "mafiaboy"; he pleaded guilty to a long list of charges. The U.S. government estimated the cost of this incident at $1.7 billion. One disturbing aspect of this case is that mafiaboy apparently did not write the destructive programs. He found them on the Net, where other 15-year-olds can find them too. Kids who are not especially clever or technically skilled use these easily obtainable programs, called scripts. More knowledgeable hackers derisively called them *script kiddies*. In one case, a 13-year-old repeatedly shut down a site over several days because he thought, mistakenly, that the site operator had called him a script kiddy.[16]

The purposes and techniques of hacking have shifted as the Web and the amount of stored data of all kinds have grown. According to the FBI, hacker groups in Russia and the Ukraine broke into more than 40 online businesses and stole more than a million credit-card numbers. In some cases, they demanded extortion payments. After one company refused to pay for 55,000 stolen card numbers, hackers posted the numbers on Web sites in three countries. Some hackers who steal credit-card numbers are members of organized-crime groups; others sell the numbers to organized-crime groups. These and similar incidents signaled the beginning of the huge problem of credit-card fraud and identity theft that we discuss in Section 5.3. To collect credit-card numbers, hackers raid the systems of large retailers and restaurant chains. To commit identity theft, they steal huge databases of personal information.

A new type of virus became popular. The virus gives the person who distributed it the power to remotely control the infected computers. Tens of thousands of infected computers (called *zombies*) send spam, contribute to denial-of-service attacks, and participate in various kinds of online advertising fraud and other crimes. The actual owners of the zombie computers are usually unaware of what their computers are doing. In 2006, a 21-year-old California man pleaded guilty and was sentenced to almost five

---

*Damages from such virus attacks are difficult to value precisely; estimates may be rough.

years in prison (the longest hacking sentence at that time) for a collection of offenses related to such a virus. He, according to prosecutors, took over hundreds of thousands of computers (some at military sites), used the infected computers to commit fraud, and "rented" them to others for sending spam and for criminal schemes. In the same year, an antispam expert reported a sophisticated international scam. It involved 20 billion spam messages sent within a two-week period from more than 100,000 computers in more than 100 countries. The messages directed people to e-commerce Web sites where the unwary ordered products with their credit cards and received nothing. Credit-card charges went to a company in Russia. This scam illustrates the growing complexity of crime on the Web, combining hacking, spam, phony Web sites, and fraud.[17]

Early hackers exploited security weaknesses in e-mail systems and guessed or stole passwords. Now our computers are online almost constantly. We search, browse, and download, using cell phones and all sorts of new gadgets and software. Hackers have many more avenues of attack and many ways to plant spyware, viruses, and other *malware* (software that performs malicious activity). Hackers planted password-stealing programs on the Web sites of the 2007 Super Bowl teams. A virus spread through MySpace. Sites where users post content (auctions, videos, Wikipedia, for example) are new targets for malicious software. Banner ads can contain viruses.

Hackers continue to execute pranks and revenge attacks. Hackers modified the programming at an online gambling site so that everyone won. The site lost $1.9 million. In 2006 after police raided The Pirate Bay, a popular pirate music site in Sweden, an apparent retaliation attack by hackers shut down the main Web sites of the Swedish government and police.

The future

The future is full of surprises. Most of the current uses of the Web were unplanned and unexpected. But using indications from current developments, I suggest two areas where hacking will increase, with potentially dangerous and destructive impact.

We already have "things that think," that is, appliances with embedded computer chips—from microwave ovens to cars to factory machinery to heart monitors. Many such appliances are online, that is, connected to the Internet. So, while driving home from work, you can tell your stove to start cooking dinner or tell your garden sprinklers to water the lawn. Doctors access and control medical devices over the Net. Automated fleets of cars will communicate with each other to drive safely on highways. We have already seen that some hackers think misdirecting airplane pilots is fun. The potential for havoc will increase when hackers can control and disrupt devices, not just information.

Before investigators identified a 15-year-old as the source of the widespread denial-of-service attacks in 2000, some people speculated that the attacks were the work of terrorists. They could have been. Hackers stole data on 1,500 Energy Department employees whose work relates to nuclear arms. The purpose might have been identity theft, but such information could be used to kidnap, bribe, or otherwise threaten these people—and thus to threaten national security. Hacking by terrorists and by government organizations is likely to increase. The governments of the U.S., China, and other countries are using or planning such attacks (and working on defenses against attacks by others). The Japanese Defense Agency said it is developing computer viruses for military uses. After Estonia, which used to be part of the Soviet Union, removed a statue honoring Soviet soldiers, the country suffered a denial-of-service attack on government agencies, financial institutions, and other Web sites. The Estonian government traced the attack to Russia, compared it to an act of war, and complained to NATO and the European Union. We will see more hacking for political and military purposes. Countries targeted with such attacks must determine whether a foreign government or terrorist organization organized the attack and how to respond. When is a cyber attack an act of war? Are there effective responses that do not severely hurt civilians?

Is "harmless hacking" harmless?

In many cases, it is the excitement and challenge of breaking in that motivates young hackers. Some claim that such hacking is harmless. Is it?

When a system administrator for a computer system at a university, a Web site, a business, or the military detects an intruder, he or she cannot immediately distinguish a nonmalicious hacker from a thief, terrorist, or spy. The administrator must stop the intrusion. The administrator's responsibility is to protect the system and its data. Thus, at a minimum, the organization will expend time and effort to track down the intruder and shut off his or her means of access. Companies sometimes shut down their Internet connection, at great inconvenience, while investigating and defending against an intruder. Responding to nonmalicious or prank hacking uses resources that might be needed to respond to serious threats.

Uncertainty about the intruder's intent and activities has additional costs for systems that contain sensitive data. According to the head of the computer crime unit at the Department of Justice, after a hacker accessed a Boeing Corporation computer, apparently just to hop to another system, Boeing spent a large sum to verify that the intruder changed no files. Would we be comfortable flying in a new Boeing airplane if they had *not* done this? A group of young Danes broke into National Weather Service computers and computers of numerous other government agencies, businesses, and universities in the U.S., Japan, Brazil, Israel, and Denmark. Eventually police caught them. It appeared they had done little damage. But consider the risks. If they had damaged Weather Service files, for instance, they could have halted air traffic that is dependent on weather reports. In fact, their activities did cause the Weather Service computers to slow down. There was the potential that serious conditions, such as tornadoes, could have gone undetected and unreported.[18] Similarly, if system administrators detect unauthorized access in a medical records system, a credit database, payroll data, and others, they must stop the intruders and determine whether they copied or changed any records. Uncertainty causes harm, or expense, even if hackers have no destructive intent.

Another problem, of course, is that a hacker with good intentions could make a mistake and do significant damage accidentally. Almost all hacking is a form of trespass. Hackers with nonmalicious intentions must understand that others will often not view them kindly.

5.2.2   HACKTIVISM, OR POLITICAL HACKING

Hacktivism is the use of hacking to promote a political cause. What new problems does hacktivism raise? Is there ethical justification for such hacking? Should penalties for hacktivists differ from penalties for other hackers?

Some academic writers and political groups argue that hacktivism is ethical, that it is a modern form of civil disobedience. Others argue that the political motive is irrelevant or, at the other extreme, that political hacking is a form of cyberterrorism. Of course, just as hacking in general ranges from mild to highly destructive activities, so can political hacking. We consider some examples.

A hacker posted anti-Israel messages on the site of a pro-Israel lobbying organization. He also posted personal information about a few hundred of the group's members, including their credit-card numbers. Three teenagers hacked into the network of an atomic research center in India and downloaded files to protest India's tests of nuclear weapons. Hacktivists targeted the governments of Indonesia and China for their antidemocratic policies. Pro-Zapatista hackers hit Mexican government sites. Someone posted a pro-drug message on a U.S. police department antidrug Web site. Earlier we mentioned numerous cases of defacement of U.S. government Web sites; many make implicit political statements. Before investigators identified mafiaboy as the source of a denial-of-service attack against many major Web sites, some people speculated that the attack was a political act—a statement against commercialization of the Web.

Hacktivism quickly became a cover for ordinary pranks and serious crime. In several cases, hackers posted political messages on Web pages they hacked to direct suspicion at others or to divert attention from their true motives, including theft of credit-card numbers or other data.

A more fundamental problem with evaluating political hacking is that this kind of hacking can be hard to identify. People who agree with the political or social position of the hackers will tend to see an act as "activism," whereas those who disagree will tend to see it as ordinary crime (or worse). Is posting a pro-drug message on a police Web site a political statement against the futility, dishonesty, expense, and international intrusions of U.S. drug policy, or is it the act of a kid showing off? To some political activists, any act that shuts down or steals from a large corporation is a political act. To the customers and owners, it is vandalism and theft.

Suppose we know that a political cause motivates the hackers. How can we begin to evaluate the ethics of their hacktivism? Suppose a religious group, to protest homosexuality, disables a Web site for gay people. Suppose an environmentalist group, to protest a new housing development, disables a Web site of a real-estate developer. Many of the people who might argue that one of these acts is justifiable hacktivism would argue that the other is not. Yet it would be extremely difficult to develop a sound ethical basis for distinguishing between these acts.

Some writers argue that hacktivism is a legitimate form of civil disobedience and should not be subject to felony prosecution.[19] Civil disobedience has a respected, nonviolent tradition. Henry David Thoreau, Mahatma Gandhi, and Martin Luther King Jr. refused to cooperate with rules that violated their freedom. Peaceful protestors have marched, rallied, and boycotted to promote their goals. Burning down ski resorts and homes because one would prefer to see the land undeveloped is another category of activity. To evaluate incidents of hacktivism, it is helpful to fit them into a scale from peaceful resistance to destruction of other people's property and actions that risk serious harm to innocent people. Denial-of-service attacks, for example, can interfere with health and emergency services.

Freedom of speech does not include the right to hang a political sign in a neighbor's window or paint one's slogans on someone else's fence, even if that "someone else" is a group of people organized as a business or corporation. We have the freedom to speak but not the right to compel others to listen. Crashing a Web site or defacing a Web page is comparable to shouting down a speaker with whom one disagrees or stealing batches of newspapers with articles one does not like. The latter activities occur on college campuses, and those who believe that the specific content or cause is more important than the principle of freedom of speech defend them. It is common for people involved in political causes to see their side as unquestionably morally right, and anyone on the other side as morally evil, not simply someone with a different point of view. This often leads to the view that the freedom of speech, freedom of choice, and property rights of the other side deserve no respect. Peace, freedom, and civil society require that we respect such basic rights and not impose our views on those we disagree with.

Another factor to consider when evaluating hacktivism is the political system under which the hacktivists live. From both an ethical and social perspective, in free countries where almost anyone can post his or her words and video on the Web for free, it is hard to justify hacking someone else's site to promote a political cause. Activists use the Internet to organize opposition to oil exploration in Alaska that they fear will harm a caribou herd. Activists use the Internet to organize mass demonstrations against international meetings of government leaders. Human rights groups such as Amnesty International use the Web effectively. Groups supporting all kinds of nonmainstream causes, from animal rights to anarchism to odd religions, have Web sites. None of this activism requires hacktivism.

Some countries have oppressive governments that control the means of communications and prohibit open political discussion, that have secret police who kill dissenters, that ban some religions, that jail people who express opposition views. In such countries, where sponsoring one's own Web site is impossible or dangerous, there might be good arguments to justify political hacking to get one's message out to the public and, in some cases, to sabotage government activities. The nations in which hacktivism is likely to have the most ethical justification are those least likely to respect acts of civil disobedience.

5.2.3   THE LAW: CATCHING AND PUNISHING HACKERS

The law

When teenagers started hacking for the challenge of getting into off-limits computers, there was disagreement not only about whether the activity was a crime under existing law but also whether it should be. Gradually, state governments passed laws that specifically addressed computer crimes. Congress passed the main federal computer crime law, the Computer Fraud and Abuse Act (CFAA), in 1986. As a federal law, the CFAA covers areas over which the federal government has jurisdiction: government computers, financial systems, medical systems, and activities that involve computers in more than one state (because the federal government has the power to regulate interstate commerce). It covers computers connected to the Internet. Sections of the law address altering, damaging, or destroying information and interference with authorized use of a computer. These cover denial-of-service attacks and the launching of computer viruses and other malicious programs. Prosecutors use more than a dozen other federal laws to prosecute people for crimes related to computer and telecommunications systems. Access to computers by an unauthorized person (or a person exceeding his or her authorization) is now illegal in most cases. A person might accidentally interrupt the operation of a computer or cause a computer to malfunction. These actions are crimes if done while intentionally accessing a computer without authorization or when exceeding one's authorization. Other illegal actions include accessing a computer to commit fraud, disclosing passwords or other access codes to unauthorized people, and interrupting or impairing government operation, public communication, transportation, or other public utilities. State and federal antihacking laws provide for strong penalties including prison sentences and fines. Law enforcement officials complain that most sentences are too light.

The USA PATRIOT Act includes amendments to the CFAA. The PATRIOT Act expanded the definition of loss to include the cost of responding to a hacking attack, assessing damage, and restoring systems. The Act raised the maximum penalty in the CFAA for a first offense from five years to ten years. It increased penalties for hacking computers used by the criminal justice system or the military. It allows the government to monitor online activity of suspected hackers without a court order. We have seen that hacking covers a wide range of activities, some deserving serious punishment and some comparable to minor offenses kids of all generations commit. Some hackers hack to demonstrate security weaknesses and encourage fixing them. Definitions of the actions to which the tougher PATRIOT Act antiterrorism provisions apply are broad and include activity few would consider terrorism.

Catching hackers

The people responsible for almost all the hacking incidents described in Section 5.2.1 have been caught. It took only one week to catch the author of the Melissa virus. The FBI traced the denial-of-service attacks in 2000 to mafiaboy and had his real name within a week. Investigators identified the man suspected of launching the ILOVEYOU virus and four Israeli teenagers who wrote and launched the Goner worm in about the same time. How do hacker trackers do their job?

Initially, the response of law enforcement agencies was ill informed and embarrassing. John Perry Barlow, a founder of the Electronic Frontier Foundation, colorfully described how he spent two hours explaining the basics of computing and computer networks to an FBI agent who came to question him in 1990. Many civil libertarians and computer professionals believe that law enforcement agencies (and the news media) overreacted in several early cases. In a hacking investigation called Operation Sun Devil, Secret Service agents raided homes in 1990 and reportedly held families of hackers at gunpoint.[20] The paranoia, or hysteria, about hackers came in part from ignorance and in part in reaction to the discovery that teenagers could break into the computers of large corporations. Law enforcement agencies now employ people who are well informed about technical aspects of hacking and the hacker culture. Agents and security professionals read hacker newsletters and participate in online discussions of hacking, sometimes undercover. Law enforcement agents, some undercover, attend hacker conferences. Security specialists maintain logs of chat channels used by hackers. Security professionals set up *honey pots*—Web sites that look attractive to hackers—so that they can record and study everything a hacker does at the site. Law enforcement agents use wiretaps to collect evidence and build their cases against hacking suspects.

Mafiaboy was identified as a suspect, at first only by his handle, because he, like many young hackers, bragged about his exploits. Once they know a suspect's handle, hacker trackers search the vast archives of online message boards for other posts by the same person that yield clues to his real identity. Mafiaboy had posted a message including his first name and e-mail address two years earlier. Investigators identified a number of other hackers this way. Unsophisticated hackers are sometimes easy to trace because they do not hide. Attrition.org reported that many hackers who sent e-mail reporting Web sites they defaced did not disguise their own e-mail return addresses. Two Russian hackers who demanded jobs as security consultants after stealing thousands of credit-card numbers found officers waiting to arrest them when they arrived in the U.S. for job interviews. Microsoft's Anti-Virus Reward program led to the confession and conviction of the teenager who wrote the Sasser worm. (For tipping off Microsoft to the author's identity, two people received a $250,000 reward. The reward program specifically indicates that people receiving the reward must not have had any criminal involvement in the incident.)

The field of collecting evidence from computer files and disks is *computer forensics*. (Some use the term *digital forensics*.) Computer-forensics specialists can recover deleted files, often even if the user has erased the disks. In Chapter 2, we saw how easy it is to collect and save information about everything we do on the Internet and to search and match records to build consumer profiles. The same tools that threaten privacy aid in catching criminals. Investigators trace viruses and hacking attacks by using Internet service provider (ISP) records and the logs of routers, the machines that route messages through the Internet. David Smith, the man who released the Melissa virus, for example, used someone else's AOL account, but AOL's logs contained enough information to enable law enforcement authorities to trace the session to Smith's telephone line. (Smith pleaded guilty; he got a 20-month sentence in a federal prison.) In 2006, the FBI, working with law enforcement agencies in other countries, quickly traced the Zotob worm to young men in Morocco and Turkey (They received jail sentences.)

Most people are unaware that word processors, such as Microsoft Word, include a lot of "invisible information" in files—in some cases, unique identifying numbers and the author's name. Security experts used such information to trace the Melissa virus. The hidden identifying information in files appalled privacy advocates—another reminder of the tension between privacy and crime fighting.

Many of the techniques we just described worked because hackers did not know about them. When such methods receive publicity in big cases, hackers learn what mistakes to avoid. Investigators of the Code Red worm in 2001, for example, said the code held no clues to its author. Hackers, as well as people seeking privacy, learn how to remove identifying numbers from documents. Hackers learn how to forge such numbers to throw suspicion elsewhere. Thus, some of the particular methods described here will be less effective when you read this. Law enforcement and security personnel update their skills and tools as hackers change theirs.

Penalties for young hackers

Many young hackers are the modern analogue of other generations of young people who snooped where they did not belong or carried out clever pranks, sometimes breaking a law. In his book *The Hacker Crackdown*, Bruce Sterling describes the phone phreakers of 1878. That is not a typo. The new American Bell Telephone company hired teenage boys as operators. They disconnected calls and crossed lines on the switchboard, connecting people to strangers. The boys were also, like many teenage hackers, rude.[21] The phone company replaced teenage boys with woman operators.

We want young hackers to mature, to learn the risks of their actions, and to use their skills in better ways. Most of them do grow up and go on to successful, productive careers. We do not want to turn them into resentful, hardened criminals or wreck their chances of getting a good job by putting them in jail. This does not mean that we should not punish young hackers if they trespass or cause damage. Kids do not mature and become responsible without good direction, or if we reward irresponsibility. The point is that we should not overreact and overpunish. Some young hackers will become the great innovators of the next generation. Steve Wozniak created the Apple computer, cofounded Apple Computer Corporation, and, after Apple's success, donated large amounts of money to medical research and other valuable efforts. Before he was building Apples, Wozniak was building blue boxes, devices that enabled people to make long-distance phone calls without paying for them. Nobel Prize winner Richard Feynman used "hacker" techniques when he was a young physicist working on the highly secret atomic bomb project at Los Alamos National Laboratory in the 1940s. He hacked safes (not computers) containing classified work on the bomb. He found or guessed the combinations and delighted in opening the safes at night and leaving messages for the authorized users informing them that security was not as good as they thought.[22]

Many exploits of young hackers are more like pranks, trespass, and vandalism. They usually do not include financial gain for the hacker (though, in Section 4.3.5, in the context of copyright infringement, we observed that lack of financial gain is often not significant in determining whether actions are wrong). Difficult penalty issues arise for hackers who are young, hackers who do not intend to do damage, and hackers who, through accident, ignorance, or immature irresponsibility, do vastly more damage than they can pay for. Clearly, offenses related to unauthorized access vary in degree, and penalties should likewise vary, as they do for trespass, vandalism, invasion of privacy, fraud, and theft.

Sentences for hacking, as for other crimes, depend on the person's intent, the person's age, and the damage done. How can we distinguish between those who are malicious and likely to commit further crimes and those who are likely to become honest and productive professionals? What penalties are appropriate?

In many hacking cases, especially those involving young people, the hacker pleaded guilty. The evidence was clear, and the hacker and prosecutor worked out a plea bargain. At first, most hackers younger than 18 received relatively light sentences including two or three years of probation, community service, and sometimes a fine or order to pay restitution. The teens who launched the serious attack on the Pentagon in 1998 and broke into several universities received such sentences. The 15-year-old who disabled an airport radio system got probation, even though his exploits could have endangered people. In 2000, a 16-year-old was sentenced to six months in a juvenile detention facility. He was the first juvenile incarcerated for hacking. He had broken into NASA and Defense Department computers and was a member of a hacker group that vandalized government Web sites. Mafiaboy, the 15-year-old responsible for denial-of-service attacks in 2000, was sentenced to eight months of detention. As more young people caused more disruption, the severity of penalties increased.

One of the purposes of criminal penalties is to discourage people from committing crimes. Some people advocate heavy penalties for minor hacking to "send a signal" to others who might be thinking of trying something similar. There is a temptation to do this with hacking because of the costs to the victims and the potential risks to the public. On the other hand, justice requires that punishments fit the specific crime and not be increased dramatically because of the potential of what someone else might do.

Sometimes the company whose computers a hacker invaded gives him a job after catching him. Give a hacker a job instead of a jail sentence? Some computer professionals and law enforcement officials are very critical of this practice of "rewarding" hackers with security jobs. We do not reduce hacking by encouraging young people to think that breaking into a computer system is an acceptable alternative to sending a résumé. But in some cases, the job, and the responsibility and respect that go with it, and the threat of punishment for future offenses are enough to turn the hacker's energy and skills toward productive uses. Decisions about penalties must depend on the character of the particular offender. With any criminal law, there is a trade-off between having fixed penalties (for fairness, to avoid favoritism) and flexibility (to consider the particular circumstances). With young people, flexibility is probably more important. Penalties can focus on using the hacker's computer skills in a productive way and on paying victims for damage done (if possible). Deciding on what is appropriate for a particular person is delicate, one of the difficulties prosecutors and judges face with juvenile crime.

How can we dissuade young teens from breaking into computers, launching viruses, and shutting down Web sites? We need a combination of appropriate penalties, education about ethics and risks, and parental responsibility. Parents of many young hackers have no idea what their children are doing. Just as parents have responsibility for teaching their children to avoid unsafe behavior on the Web, as we discussed in Chapter 3, they have some responsibility for preventing their children from engaging in malicious, destructive hacking.

5.2.4 SECURITY

> *It's no use locking the barn door after the horse is gone.*
> —Old proverb, pre-1400

Hacking and the spread of viruses are as much a comment on the security of computers, telecommunication systems, and the Web as they are on the skills and ethics of the hackers. Hacking is a problem; so is poor security. Why was security so weak on the early Internet? How weak is it now?

A variety of factors contribute to security weaknesses. They come from the history of the Internet and the Web, from the inherent complexity of computer systems (especially the software and communications systems that run the Web and the many devices that connect to it), from the speed at which new applications develop, from economic and business factors, and from human nature. The reminder above, about the futility of locking the barn door after the horse is gone, predates cars, not just computers. This observation does not excuse poor security. Instead, it reminds us of the need for recognition and acceptance of responsibility.

In its early years, the Internet was primarily a communications medium for researchers. Open access, ease of use, and ease of sharing information were desirable qualities. It was not designed for security against malicious intruders, teenage explorers, or organized criminals. Many early systems did not have passwords. Few early systems connected to telephone networks, so protection against intruders was not an issue. Security depended primarily on trust. The World Wide Web developed as a communications tool for physics researchers. Again, security was not a primary design concern. Security on the early Web was extremely weak. When businesses and government agencies began to set up Web sites, Internet security expert Dan Farmer ran a program to probe 1,700 sites of banks, newspapers, government agencies, and pornography sellers for software loopholes that made it easy for hackers to invade and disable or damage the sites. He found that about two-thirds of the sites had such security weaknesses—and only four sites apparently noticed that someone was probing their security. Farmer's warnings had little effect.

It might not be surprising that, initially, security of computers at universities and businesses was weak. It is astonishing, however, that it was so easy to invade government and military systems. The Defense Information Systems Agency estimated that there were 500,000 hacker attacks on Defense Department networks in 1996, that 65% of them were successful, and that the Department detected fewer than 1%. Some security experts said that most of the computer systems targeted did not contain classified information and that the break-ins were the modern equivalent of a kid sneaking into a Pentagon cafeteria. This argument has some merit. On the other hand, we should expect Pentagon security to be good enough to keep a kid out of its cafeteria. The fact that files accessed by hackers are not "classified" is not reassuring. An enemy can use unclassified information such as payroll and personnel records destructively. In 1999, the Government Accountability Office (GAO) reported that computer security at NASA was so weak that hackers could easily disrupt such crucial functions as the tracking of spacecraft. The GAO reported, in 2000, that the Environmental Protection Agency (EPA) computers were "riddled with security weaknesses." Hackers had access to sensitive and confidential information and were able to modify files, use the EPA's system to launch hacking attacks on other agencies, and set up their own chat room on the EPA system. A judge found that hackers could easily hack into and steal from the government's Indian Trust fund, which manages hundreds of millions of dollars of income from land owned by American Indians. A government study in 2001 found that hackers had taken over 155 federal computer systems the previous year. A British hacker, extradited to the U.S. in 2007, was accused of breaking into almost 100 military and NASA systems. (He claimed that he was looking for information about unidentified flying objects and that security was lax.)[23]

Attitudes about security in businesses, organizations, and government agencies were slow to catch up with the risk. Security techniques and practices, however, dramatically improved in the early 2000s. Many government agencies and businesses have up-to-date, high-quality security. Businesses drastically increased their security budgets. Computer scientists responded to increased security threats with improved security technology. Entrepreneurs and the market responded with the development of many security firms and consultants offering a variety of software products and services. First developed for institutions (universities, government, and businesses), many of these tools are now available for and widely used on PCs at home as well.

Firewalls are software or separate computers that monitor incoming communications (e-mail, files, requests for services, etc.) and filter out those that are from untrusted sites or fit a profile of suspicious activity. Intrusion-detection systems monitor computer systems for unauthorized or inappropriate activity. There is software to monitor information that leaves a protected network, to check for leaks. Good system administrators for business, government, or organization computers do not rely on users to select good passwords. They run programs that make sure that user passwords meet security specifications. Encryption and antivirus software protect systems. To protect against hackers using one's system to launch attacks on others, administrators install software to monitor the volume of outgoing messages (for example, to detect denial-of-service attacks). Digital signatures, biometrics (which we discuss in Section 5.3.3), and other new tools for identification could replace or augment passwords and help reduce access by unauthorized people.

Insurance companies offer insurance for hacker attacks. Some home insurance companies give discounts for antitheft devices and fire extinguishers in a home. Similarly, some companies providing hacker insurance require that their customers use high-quality computer security technology. Some software and security companies hire hackers to attack and find flaws in systems they are developing. Some pay consulting fees to teams of students and faculty at universities to find security weaknesses in their products so that the companies can fix the flaws before destructive hackers exploit them.

Still, hackers and security professionals regularly find gaping holes, especially each time a new product, application, or online phenomenon appears. Soon after programmers adopted the popular Java programming language for Web applications, they found that it had many security weaknesses. Here are more examples. Two people figured out how to send fake traffic and weather information to navigation systems in cars using simple off-the-shelf hardware. The systems are not secure.[24] Web browsers have numerous security flaws. Microsoft has made a big effort to improve security in its software, but critics continue to assail the company for security weaknesses. Thousands of small businesses use "shopping cart" software; some of the programs have security flaws. As Google grew and offered services beyond searching, hackers found vulnerabilities in its software. Wireless networks often lack sufficient protection. Software developers are constantly finding and patching security flaws.

Many of the incidents in Figure 2.5 of lost and stolen credit-card numbers and other sensitive personal data were the work of hackers. Although attention to security has increased to a great extent, clearly many banks and large retailers still lack sufficient protection for the data and money in their care. The TJX incident is a clear example. TJX used a vulnerable, out-of-date encryption system to protect data transmitted between cash registers and store computers on its wireless network. Investigators believe hackers used high-power antennas to intercept data, decoded employee passwords, and then hacked into the company's central database. Over a period of about 18 months, the hackers stole millions of credit- and debit-card numbers and critical identification information for hundreds of thousands of people. The investigation revealed other security problems. The problems included transmission of debit-card transaction information to banks without encryption and failure to install appropriate software patches and firewalls.[25]

Responsibility for security

There are many parallels between security issues for preventing crime and security issues for protecting privacy (Section 2.3.3). There are also similarities with safety issues we discuss in Chapter 8. Principles and techniques for developing good systems exist, and responsible software designers must learn and use them. We can design systems with security from intrusion as a major goal. When a computer system contains valuable or sensitive data, or if many people depend on its smooth operation, the system administrators have a professional and ethical obligation, and in many cases a legal obligation, to take reasonable security precautions to protect the system. System developers and administrators must stay up to date about new risks and new security measures. This is often not an easy task, but it is an essential goal and a professional responsibility. No matter how well designed security software and procedures are, the complexity of computer systems means that there will be unexpected security failures. We cannot expect perfection, but we should expect professionalism.

Most individual PC users have no technical training. Many do not use firewalls and antivirus software because they do not understand the risks or because they find the security tools too confusing. It does not occur to consumers to ask, when they buy a new cell phone, if their calls are encrypted or easily interceptable. Sellers of any widely used consumer product have an ethical obligation to build in a level of safety appropriate for the general population. Software companies have an ethical obligation to design and implement their products so that they do not expose users to severe security threats.

What is the responsibility of individual computer owners? Surely, it is usually wise to install security software, such as an antivirus program, on one's computer to protect one's data and avoid the headache of dealing with a virus attack. Here is an intriguing question. Aside from protecting ourselves, do we have an ethical responsibility to take steps to prevent our computer from harming others? Given that a common hacker technique is to take over individual computers to commit crimes, is use of antivirus software an ethical responsibility, not just a personal choice?

Criminalize virus writing and hacker tools?

You can find hacking scripts and computer code for thousands of computer viruses on the Internet. Intentionally or recklessly making such programs available in a context that encourages their destructive use is irresponsible. Should the software itself be illegal? Some law enforcement personnel and security professionals propose making it a crime to write or post computer viruses and other hacking software. A law against writing or publishing viruses and hacking software could make security work and research more difficult. Security personnel and researchers must be able to possess security and hacker software to effectively do their job. Such a law would raise issues similar to some we discussed in

Chapters 2, 3, and 4 about restricting or banning strong encryption, anonymity software, and technologies to circumvent copyright protections.

We saw in Chapter 3 that writing about how to make illegal or destructive devices, such as bombs, is not (in most cases) illegal. On the other hand, as a security professional commented, "With a computer virus, the words are the bomb."[26] A federal court ruled that software is a form of speech (see Section 2.5.4), so a law against hacking software or virus software might conflict with the First Amendment. The First Amendment does not protect some kinds of speech, such as inciting a riot. Would the Supreme Court consider virus code in the same category? How do *you* think the law should treat virus code and hacking scripts?

5.3 Identity Theft and Credit-Card Fraud

5.3.1 STEALING IDENTITIES

We buy products and services from strangers in stores and on the Web. We do our banking and investing on the Web without seeing or knowing the physical location of the company we deal with. We can travel with only a passport and a credit or debit card. We can qualify for a mortgage or a car loan in minutes. All this depends on networks of computers and databases. All this is convenient and efficient. But it has risks. For many transactions and interactions, our identity has become a series of numbers (credit- and debit-card numbers, Social Security number [SSN], driver's license number, and account numbers) and computer files (credit history, work history, and driving record). Remote transactions are fertile ground for many kinds of crime, especially identity theft and, its most common result, credit and debit fraud.

Identity theft describes various crimes in which a criminal (or large, well-organized criminal group) uses the identity of an unknowing innocent person. If thieves get credit- (or debit-) card numbers, they buy expensive items or sell the numbers to others who use them. If they do not have card numbers, they use other personal information (SSN, for example) to open new accounts in the victim's name. They take out loans, buy groceries, raid the victim's bank account, pass bad checks, or use the victim's identity in various other ways for financial gain. A security company executive says, "There's a thriving underground economy that's trading stolen information . . . that will lead to identity theft. A complete identity sells for less than $20.[27]

The Federal Trade Commission receives hundreds of thousands of complaints of identity theft each year. It reports that people in the 18–29 age range are the most common victims, perhaps because they use the Web heavily or perhaps because they are less aware of the risks. The Department of Justice and research groups report that fraud losses based on identity theft amount to billions of dollars per year in the U.S., with several million victims. Businesses, not individuals, bear most of the direct monetary losses. The individual victim might lose a good credit rating, be prevented from borrowing money or cashing checks, be unable to get a job, or be unable to rent an apartment. Creditors might sue the victim for money borrowed by the criminal. The business losses increase prices for everyone.

The many tactics used for identity theft and credit- and debit-card fraud and the many solutions developed in response illustrate the continual leapfrogging between increased sophistication of security strategies and increased sophistication of criminal strategies. They also illustrate the value of the mix of technology, innovative business policies, consumer awareness, and law to solve the problems. We describe a variety of tactics for identity theft and then consider many approaches to reducing identity theft and reducing its impact on its victims. A few of the methods we describe are no longer used because the other side defeated them or consumers found them too cumbersome. Technology evolves, and clever people on both sides of the law develop new ideas. For the public and for anyone working with sensitive personal data, it is necessary to remain aware and flexible.

Have you received e-mail from PayPal, eBay, Amazon, or a bank asking you to confirm information about your account? Have you received e-mail from the Internal Revenue Service telling you the agency has a tax refund for you? These are examples of a form of spam called *phishing*: sending millions of e-mails fishing for information to use to impersonate someone and steal money and goods. The e-mail message tells the victim to click on a link to what purports to be the Web site of a well-known bank or online company. The phony site asks for account numbers, passwords, and other identifying information. Phishing is an example of social engineering, a method used by hackers: a thief or hacker directly asks a person for sensitive information with some false pretext. Identity thieves take advantage of our knowledge that there is a lot of online fraud: Several pretexts that appear frequently in phishing e-mails warn that there has been a breach in the security of your bank or PayPal account and you need to respond to determine whether someone else is misusing your account. Some e-mails tell recipients that they just made a very big purchase on eBay, and if the purchase was not really theirs, they should click a link to cancel the order. In a panic, people do—and enter their identifying information when asked for it.

The first defense against phishing is to be extremely wary of clicking on a link in an unsolicited e-mail, especially if the message is about account information. The standard antifraud advice is: If you are uncertain whether the message is authentic and want to respond, you should ignore the link in the e-mail, type the company's URL in your browser, and check your account in the usual way. As more people learned to be wary of clicking on links in e-mails that appear to be from a bank, thieves modified phishing scams; the e-mail provides a telephone number to call. Those who call hear a request for their account number and other identifying information. This variation is sometimes called *vishing*, for voice phishing. Of course, a phone number provided by phishers is as fake as the links they provide.

Pharming is another technique to lure people to fake Web sites where thieves collect personal data. Normally when we type a URL, for instance, www.yourbank.com, our browser looks up the URL on one of many domain name servers (DNS), special computers on the Internet that translate URLs into actual Internet addresses (strings of numbers called Internet protocol [IP] addresses). Pharming involves planting false Internet addresses in the tables on a DNS. (Some software, inadvertently downloaded from a dishonest or hacked Web site, plants false IP addresses in small tables maintained on individual PCs.) Thus, typing the URL of a bank or travel site, for example, might lead someone to a counterfeit site set up by identity thieves. Corrupting a DNS is more difficult than sending a huge number of phishing e-mails; hence, it is much less common.

Figure 2.5 lists many incidents of loss or theft of large databases containing personal information. In many of those incidents, identity theft and fraud were the goals. For example, shortly after the retailer TJX Companies reported the electronic break-in of its computer network and the theft of millions of customer records, many of the stolen credit- and debit-card numbers were used fraudulently in at least eight countries. Sophisticated criminal rings hack into corporate and government computer networks, steal computers and disks, or pose as legitimate businesses and buy credit records and personal dossiers to obtain information to use in identity theft.

Résumés contain a lot of personal information, and people post millions of them online on job-hunting sites. Identity thieves love them. They collect addresses, SSNs, birth dates, work histories, and all the other details that help them convincingly adopt the identity of the job seeker. To collect the information, some pose as employers and post fake job announcements; some respond to job hunters and ask for more information. (Have you posted a résumé and received a response from a prospective employer asking for information to complete a background check?) Job-hunting sites are very popular and useful. Now that identity thieves misuse them, people must adapt and be more cautious. That means omitting sensitive data from a posted résumé, not providing sensitive information until you have an actual interview, or finding other ways to determine that the potential employer is authentic. Job sites, once aware of the threat, began to offer services to keep sensitive information private.

When people connect to some Web sites, the site plants spyware on the their computer. Hackers and thieves hide malicious software in innocent-appearing programs that users willingly download. (This type of hidden malware is called a *Trojan horse*.) Such programs track keystrokes. Thieves use them to collect account numbers and passwords typed later by the user when banking or buying online.

The SSN has long been the key piece of information that criminals need to impersonate a victim or to obtain additional information to do so. Stealing these numbers was easy. A part-time English teacher at a California junior college used the SSNs of some of her students, provided on her class lists, to open fraudulent credit-card accounts. Rings of identity thieves with members working on hospital staffs obtained SSNs of hospitalized patients from their wristbands or hospital charts. Improvements in policies and practices about use and display of the numbers are reducing this kind of theft.

TACTICS AND COUNTERTACTICS IN CREDIT-CARD AND DEBIT-CARD FRAUD

Credit-card fraud began with simple crimes, for instance, an individual on a shopping spree with a lost or stolen card. At first, the main method was to steal and use (or sell) the actual credit card. Both well-organized theft rings and individual purse snatchers stole credit cards. (They still do.) Several dozen people were convicted in one case where Northwest Airlines employees stole new cards from the mail transported on Northwest's airplanes. Charges on the stolen cards ran to an estimated $7.5 million.[28]

Procedural changes helped protect against theft of new cards from the mail. To verify that the legitimate owner received the card, credit-card issuers require the customer to call in and provide identifying information to activate a card. This procedure is only as good as the security of the identifying information. At first, credit-card companies commonly used the person's SSN and mother's maiden name. According to federal prosecutors, several Social Security Administration employees provided the SSNs and mothers' maiden names of thousands of people to a credit-card fraud ring so that they could activate stolen cards.[29] Now credit-card companies use caller ID to verify that the authorization call comes from the customer's home telephone. Holograms and customer photos have made cards more difficult to counterfeit and stolen cards more difficult to use.

E-commerce has made it easier both to steal card numbers (not cards) and to use the numbers without the physical cards. Thieves use stolen numbers online or make counterfeit cards (sometimes by reprogramming the magnetic strip on stolen cards). When retail sales began on the Web, technically trained thieves used software to intercept credit-card numbers in transmission from a PC to a Web site. Encryption and secure servers solved much of that problem; without such security, e-commerce could not have thrived.

To thwart thieves who searched the trash near stores or banks for receipts with credit- or debit-card numbers on them, large stores and banks began printing only the last four digits on the receipts. Later a law required this practice.

Thieves surreptitiously install recording devices, called *skimmers*, inside the card readers in stores, gas stations, and restaurants. They collect debit-card numbers and personal identification numbers (PINs), make counterfeit cards, and raid people's bank accounts through automated teller machines (ATMs). In one such operation, a ring of thieves stole $56 million. The point-of-sale card readers in many stores are old and lack both software and physical security to prevent this scam. Some industry researchers say point-of-sale schemes account for more fraud losses than phishing and other schemes.[30]

Software for credit-card systems detects unusual spending activity. When this happens, a merchant can ask a customer for additional identification, or the credit-card company can call a card holder to verify purchases. Some banks use software to detect unusual ATM activity and alert customers.

Several companies market systems that generate a unique credit-card number for each online transaction. The credit-card issuer generates the numbers and bills all of one person's charges to one account, but once used, a number is useless to anyone who steals it.

Services like PayPal provide a trusted third party to increase confidence (and convenience) in online commerce and reduce credit fraud. A customer can buy from strangers online without giving them a credit-card number. PayPal handles the payment for a small fee. PayPal and other companies that provide online-payment services initially lost millions of dollars to fraud. Gradually, PayPal developed clever solutions and sophisticated security expertise.

5.3.2 RESPONSES TO IDENTITY THEFT

Authenticating e-mail and Web sites

E-mail programs, Web browsers, search engines, and add-on software (some free) can alert users to likely fraud. Spammers fake the apparent return address on e-mail, but some mail programs let users check the actual return address. (I find that e-mail claiming to be from PayPal came from hotmail.com, yahoo.com, Denmark, Germany, and a variety of other unlikely places.) Some mail programs will alert the user if the actual URL that a link will take you to is different from the one displayed in the text of an e-mail message.

Whether someone reaches a Web site from a link in an e-mail or by browsing or searching, various tools can help determine whether the site is safe. Sometimes, fake Web sites are easy to spot because of poor grammar and generally low quality. Software can reasonably well determine the geographic location of a site. If a Web site claims to be a U.S. bank but is located in Romania, it is wise to leave.

Some browsers (and add-on software used with browsers and search engines) will flag Web sites they consider safe or show alerts for sites known to collect and misuse personal information. Although helpful for cautious users, such tools generate potential problems. Recall that in Section 3.2.3 we observed that we might want a filter for pornography to be more restrictive even if it meant preventing a child from accessing some nonporn sites, whereas a spam filter should be less restrictive so that legitimate e-mail is not lost. How strict should a Web tool be about marking a site as safe? When a major browser marks as safe only large companies that it has certified, legitimate small businesses on the Web suffer. Mistakes in marking a legitimate site as a known or suspected phishing site could ruin a small business and could result in a lawsuit for the company that provides the rating. It is important from both an ethical and a business perspective to be cautious when designing and implementing such rating systems.

Banks and other businesses that are likely targets of phishing and pharming have developed techniques to assure customers that they are at an authentic site before they enter a password or other sensitive identifying information. For example, when a customer first sets up an account, some banks ask the customer to supply a digital image (for example, of their dog) or choose one from many at the bank site. Later, whenever the person begins the log-on process by typing his or her name (or e-mail address or other identifier that is not critical for security), the system displays the image. Thus, the site authenticates itself to the customer before the customer authenticates himself or herself by typing a password.

Hacked and stolen business and government databases

Individuals cannot directly protect their account numbers and other personal data in business and government databases. As we observed in the discussions of privacy and hacking, businesses, organizations, and government agencies that collect and store personal data have an ethical responsibility to protect those data. Responsible data holders must anticipate risks and prepare for them. Unfortunately, many have not been doing a good job.

In several major thefts of data from retailers, the databases included unencrypted credit-card numbers and other security numbers read from the magnetic strips on the cards. In many cases, the retailers were not aware that the checkout software they used stored the numbers—in violation of agreements with the companies issuing the credit cards.* Apparently, no one at the software vendors who sell the checkout software, and no one at the retailers who bought and used the software, reviewed the software to be sure it did not store card numbers. Thieves cannot get the numbers if they are not in the system. Deleting the numbers satisfies one of the key principles of privacy and, in this context, security: not storing unnecessary data. Credit-card companies set stringent security standards for merchants using their cards, including use of firewall and antivirus software and regular security audits. The card companies impose high fines on merchants that fail to meet the standards. After several incidents of theft, the credit-card companies began a program of examining and certifying checkout software supplied by software vendors.

Several of the privacy protections we described in Chapter 2 are especially important for reducing identity theft. Encryption, as we mentioned, is a particularly valuable security measure. Another useful tool is the tracking system for stolen or lost laptops that allows the owner to erase files remotely. After publicity about the large number of thefts of laptops containing sensitive personal data, laptop security became a booming business.

---

*Normally, retailers are not supposed to store credit-card numbers. Some online retailers offer a speedy checkout option that requires keeping customer credit-card numbers on file. In these cases, the retailer, of course, should store them in encrypted form.

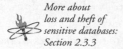
More about loss and theft of sensitive databases: Section 2.3.3

Technical protections include fingerprint readers. Companies are using more physical protections, such as cables to secure laptops to heavy furniture in offices or hotels, and training employees to be more careful with laptops.

Authenticating customers and preventing use of stolen numbers

Financial institutions have added procedures to authenticate customers, making it more difficult for a thief armed with a stolen account number and other commonly used identifying information to withdraw money from an account. Some financial institutions store an identification number for the customer's home computer or laptop and then verify the machine used when the customer logs on. Some ask the customer to provide extra information when the account is first opened and then ask for some of that information at login. Some ask the customer to select from a group of several images when the account is opened and then require the customer to identify the image at login. (Note the latter is similar to the Web site authentication method described earlier, but used in this way, it helps to authenticate the user.) Improved security guidelines and requirements from government agencies spurred some of the security improvements for online banking and investment sites.

Some security firms offer more sophisticated authentication software using artificial intelligence techniques. The software calculates a risk score based on variation from the time of day a customer usually logs in, the type of browser regularly used, the customer's typical behavior and transactions, and so on. (How would privacy advocates and the public react to the disclosure that an online bank or brokerage firm stores such information about each customer's visits to the site?)

If you send a change-of-address notification to your credit-card company, the company will probably send a confirmation to both your old and your new addresses. Why? Thieves who plan to use a stolen credit-card number for a long time do not want the owner of the card to see fraudulent charges on the bill and close the account. Thus, they send a change-of-address notice (likely using a fake address for the new one). A confirmation letter sent to the old address alerts the real card owner in such cases.

Geographic location tools, like those that tell users the physical location of a Web site, can tell an online retailer where a customer is. If the customer is not in the country where his or her credit card was issued, or if the customer is in a country with a high fraud rate, the retailer or credit-card company can require extra identification.

Credit-card issuers and merchants always make trade-offs between security and customer convenience. For purchases in stores, most customers do not want to take the time to provide identification when they use a credit card, or to wait while merchants verify it. Requests for ID might offend customers. Most merchants do not check signatures or photos on credit cards. More often, we swipe our card through a machine ourselves;

a clerk does not look at it at all. For customer convenience and to speed transactions, some stores do not require a signature for small purchases. Others have self-service checkout. Merchants and credit-card companies are willing to absorb some fraud losses as part of doing business. Such trade-offs are not new. Retail stores keep small, very expensive items in locked cabinets, but most goods are easily accessible to customers for convenience and efficiency. Openness encourages sales. Retail stores have always accepted some amount of losses from shoplifting rather than offend and inconvenience customers by keeping everything locked up or by searching customers when they leave the store. When a company perceives the losses as being too high, it improves security. When are merchants and credit-card companies irresponsibly ignoring simple and important security measures, and when are they making reasonable trade-offs for convenience, efficiency, and avoiding offense to customers?

Reducing the damage of identity theft

For many years, one of the very frustrating aspects of identity theft was that victims got little help from credit bureaus, police, motor vehicle departments, and the Social Security Administration. The motor vehicle departments and Social Security Administration are reluctant to issue a new driver's license number and SSN, respectively, to a victim because their record systems expect a person to have the same number all his or her life. Their attitude seemed to be that the fact that another person was using the number to defraud merchants and credit companies was not their problem. In 1998, Congress made it a federal crime to knowingly use another person's identification with the intent to commit a felony,[31] and government agencies began providing more assistance to victims.

Businesses and government agencies that lose personal data now often arrange for free credit-monitoring services for the people affected. Many nonprofit organizations and start-up businesses help people deal with the effects of identity theft. Laws requiring that companies and government agencies notify people of breaches of their personal information give potential victims the opportunity to take a variety of protective measures. The most common measure is a *fraud alert*. A fraud alert is a flag on your credit report that tells the credit bureau to call you for confirmation when anyone tries to open a new credit account (e.g., for a car loan or credit card) in your name. In some states, you can "freeze" your credit record. This prevents potential creditors from accessing information in your credit record. Without the information, creditors will not approve loans or open new credit accounts. We can monitor our credit-card accounts to quickly detect fraudulent charges. We can even get insurance for identity theft. Consumer advocates argue for laws requiring that companies that lose sensitive personal data pay for damages, including costs for credit monitoring and other protections for consumers whose data they lost. Some states are considering such laws.

Identity thieves are ever vigilant for more opportunities. Some pretend to be legitimate companies providing identity-verification services and services to assist identity theft victims. The consumer must provide such companies with exactly the kinds of information the identity thief wants. Consumers must always be cautious.

A few observations

Although identity theft scams are rampant on the Web, a large chunk of identity theft cases result from lost or stolen wallets and checkbooks. Friends and relatives are the culprits in many cases. It is good to remember to be careful with personal information in low-tech environments as well as on the Web.

Authenticating customers remotely is inherently difficult: information that is necessary and sufficient to identify someone or authorize a transaction must be provided to many people, businesses, and Web sites. Eventually, someone will lose, leak, or steal that information. To reduce the spread and vulnerability of SSNs, many institutions began asking customers (for example, on the telephone) for only the last four digits. Then, of course, the last four digits became the critical numbers thieves needed to impersonate someone for access to an existing account.

Reducing the incidence of fraud by identity theft—and its monetary and personal costs—requires continually evolving methods for authenticating the parties on both sides of a transaction. It requires appropriate and evolving responses from merchants, financial institutions, credit-card companies, the public, the programmers and entrepreneurs who develop technical protections and services, and the government agencies whose documents we use for identification.

5.3.3 BIOMETRICS

We have seen that to protect privacy and to reduce credit fraud, identity theft, and some kinds of hacking, it is important to identify a person accurately. Preventing terrorist access to sensitive facilities also requires accurate identification. Thieves make counterfeit credit and debit cards; they guess or steal passwords. Terrorists make counterfeit driver's licenses; they can fake airport employee tags. Is there a foolproof way to identify someone?

Biometrics are biological characteristics that are unique to an individual. They include fingerprints, voice prints, face structure, hand geometry, eye (iris or retina) patterns, and DNA. Biometric technology for identification applications is rapidly developing. It is already a multibillion dollar industry.

DNA matching has freed numerous innocent people mistakenly convicted of such serious crimes as rape and murder. Along with fingerprints, DNA has been extremely effective for identifying or eliminating suspects in crimes. Some biometric applications provide convenience that could appeal to consumers. One device lets you open the door of your house by touching a scanner with your finger. No keys to lose, forget, or drop while carrying packages. The main applications, though, are security and fraud prevention. Some states use a face scanner and digital image matching to make sure a person does not apply for extra driver's licenses or welfare benefits with different names. Some computers, especially laptops, require a fingerprint match to log on, physically or over the Net, reducing access by hackers or laptop thieves. Some cell phones (especially in Japan) use fingerprints or other biometrics to authenticate the owner and protect against theft of information and funds in "electronic wallets" in the phones. To reduce the risks of terrorism, several airports use fingerprint identification systems to ensure that only employees enter restricted areas.

It appears that the use of biometrics will increase dramatically. Do biometrics provide a foolproof identification technology?

Just as people have always found ways around other security mechanisms, from picking locks to phishing, they find ways to thwart biometric identification. Some methods seen in spy movies or science fiction movies a few years ago are serious concerns. Researchers in the U.S. and Japan fooled fingerprint readers with cadaver fingers and fingers they made from gelatin and Play-Doh. Criminals can wear contact lenses that fool eye scanners.[32]

When a thief steals a credit-card number, we can get a new account with a new number, but if a hacker gets a copy of the file with our digitized thumbprint or retina scan, we cannot get a new one. Identity theft might become easier to prevent, but much worse for a victim when it occurs. Given the weak security of the Web, it is likely that hackers will be able to steal files of biometrics from government agencies and businesses as easily as they steal files with Social Security and credit-card numbers. Then they can access other people's biometrically protected accounts by rigging their machines to transmit a copy of the file rather than scanning their own finger or eye.

We have discussed problems generated by widespread use of SSNs. Biometrics could find many more applications than SSNs, for example, all of our online purchases and Web surfing. Will biometrics make us more secure? Or will they make it easier to build dossiers on people? Like the face-matching applications described in Section 2.2.3, will biometrics increase surveillance and tracking of our activities by government agencies?

We have pointed out a few times that we cannot expect perfection. The fact that criminals can thwart biometrics or that biometrics can pose privacy risks does not condemn these technologies. As always, we must have an accurate view of the strengths, weaknesses, and risks of new technologies and compare them with alternatives to determine, carefully, for what applications we should use them. By anticipating both privacy risks and methods criminals will use to get around new security measures, we can design better systems. For example, anticipating that iris scanners can be tricked by a photo of an eye, some scanners flash a light at the eye and check that the pupil contracts, as a real one would. Similarly, some fingerprint-matching systems distinguish live tissue from fake fingers.

5.4 Scams and Forgery

Con artists and crooks of many sorts have found ample opportunity on the Web to cheat unsuspecting people. Some scams are almost unchanged from their pre-Web forms: pyramid schemes, chain letters, sales of counterfeit luxury goods, phony business investment opportunities, and so forth. Each generation of people, whatever level of technology they use, needs a reminder that, if an investment or bargain looks too good to be true, it probably is. Other scams on the Web are new, or have evolved to take advantage of characteristics of the Web, and have a bigger impact than individual pre-Web crimes. In a particularly offensive example, people set up Web sites after natural disasters or terrorist attacks to fraudulently collect credit-card donations from people who think they are contributing to the Red Cross or funds for victims.

We examine three areas of online crime (auction fraud, click fraud, and stock fraud) and one offline (digital forgery). We look at how they work and what solutions have emerged. The point is not the particular details but the patterns. Fraud and other crimes often invade new markets and then levels off or declines. People learn the risks. Businesses and individuals respond with new protection mechanisms, and law enforcement agencies combine new skills and existing law to catch and convict the crooks and discourage their activity.

5.4.1 AUCTIONS

Auction sites on the Web are extremely popular. Sellers list anything they want to sell, whether collector baseball cards, clothing, drill bits, or a whole town. Buyers bid, and the auction site gets a percentage. Auction sites illustrate the basic benefits of the Web: convenient compilation of a large amount of information and a way for strangers all over the world to communicate and make trades. eBay, founded in 1995, is the largest and best-known auction site. People spend billions of dollars on eBay each year.

Problems

Problems arose soon after auction sites opened for business. Some sellers do not send the items people paid for, or they send inferior goods that do not meet the posted description. Dishonest sellers engage in *shill bidding*, that is, bidding on one's own goods to drive up the price. The Federal Trade Commission reports that online auctions are one of the top sources of fraud complaints. Some products offered for sale are illegal or sold in illegal ways, for example, prescription drugs sold without a prescription and unauthorized copies of copyrighted material such as music and movies. Some products, though legal, are dangerous, for example, drugs that people misuse. Initially, eBay had an "anything goes" attitude about its site. The company merely served to put sellers and buyers together. The company argued that it was analogous to a common carrier or to a newspaper that publishes classified ads and that it was not responsible for fraud or illegal sales. Eventually eBay changed its viewpoint.

Solutions

In the offline world, consumers know that it might be safer to buy from an established store like Macy's or Home Depot than from someone at a swap meet. Online auctions, where one interacts with invisible strangers all over the world, became, like some swap meets, places to find both bargains and rip-offs. Thus, one of the first solutions was for customers to learn to be cautious. Later, online auction companies made improvements. Recognizing that their success, like e-commerce in general, depends on customer confidence and a good reputation, eBay and other auction sites adopted several practices and policies to address problems and complaints. Before sending a check or a product, users can consider the reputation of the seller or buyer by reviewing comments other users post on the site. Escrow services, where a trusted third party holds the payment until the buyer receives and approves the product, are available for more expensive items. Auction companies have large departments to address fraud problems. User agreements prohibit shill bidding and offering illegal items for sale. Rules prohibit certain other items, such as alcohol, firearms, fireworks, animals, stocks, and prescription drugs. Auction companies suspend users who break their rules.

eBay requires a credit-card number from sellers. This discourages fraud by making it easier to identify and trace a seller in case of complaints. Requiring a credit-card number from bidders as well would help reduce various scams, such as shill bidding by the same person under different names. Several major auction sites do not require credit-card numbers from buyers, because the practice of requiring a credit card is not popular with customers. Some buyers implicitly weigh their desire for privacy against fraud reduction. Some buyers do not have credit cards.

The solutions, of course, are not perfect. A group of dishonest sellers can write glowing recommendations for each other. Fake items still appear. Some users complain that auction sites require too much proof before removing a suspect item. Rival sellers, however, could be making false accusations, so swifter action by auction houses to remove items might not always be fair.

Fraud is illegal whether on or off the Web. There have been many prosecutions for auction fraud. In a highly publicized case, prosecutors charged three men with shill bidding to raise prices in hundreds of art auctions, including one for a painting on which one of them forged the initials of a well-known painter.[33] Two pleaded guilty. One of the men, a lawyer, was disbarred. Auction fraud has become as routine an area for law enforcement as earlier pre-Web frauds. We observed in Chapter 1 that the public can help with crime investigations on the Web. In one incident, cheated buyers tracked down two men who sold thousands of dollars of computers in online auctions but never sent them.

A few more auction issues

Companies called aggregators use automated software "bots" or "crawlers" to scan large auction sites, cull lists of products offered, and relist them on their own Web sites for comparison shopping. eBay blocked such software (unless the aggregator had a licensing agreement with eBay) and sued Bidder's Edge for trespass, unfair business practices, and impairing the performance of eBay's site. On the other side, the Justice Department's antitrust division investigated to decide whether eBay's blocking of the bots was an illegal anticompetitive action. A judge ruled that because eBay's computers are eBay's property, it could deny access to Bidder's Edge. He issued an injunction ordering Bidder's Edge to stop using its automated software on eBay's site. Recall that similar issues arose when AOL first tried to block spam (see Section 3.2.3). AOL got injunctions to stop the spammers on similar grounds.

This case raises intriguing legal and social/ethical issues. Does a Web site have a right to exclude certain visitors, including software visitors? How should the concept of trespass apply to Web sites?

5.4.2 CLICK FRAUD

Google has been extraordinarily inventive in developing new online advertising mechanisms. The methods, many now used by other search engine companies as well, help small businesses advertise more cost-effectively, generate revenue for anyone willing to let Google place ads on their Web site, and, of course, bring in revenue for the search engine company itself, helping to support all of its free services.

In newspapers and magazines and on television and radio, advertisers pay ad rates based on circulation figures or audience size. On the Web, an advertiser can pay per click. That is, the advertiser pays only for each click on their ad bringing someone to their Web site. People who host an ad receive a small fee for each click from their site.

Click fraud is an entirely new kind of fraud, based on these complex ways of selling advertising on the Web. In one type of click fraud, a competitor repeatedly clicks on its rival's ad, using up the rival's advertising budget. In another type, people who host ads on their sites click on them repeatedly to increase their fee. As with so many phenomena we have seen by now, the ingenuity of crooks took businesses by surprise at first. Google and Yahoo agreed to pay millions of dollars in disputes with advertisers because of click fraud. They and various programmers and start-up companies quickly developed responses. One technique is to check for and filter out numerous clicks on one ad from the same source. Some new businesses offer click-fraud monitoring services.

5.4.3 STOCK FRAUD

Old forms of stock fraud included posing as investment experts and luring victims to invest in worthless companies with promises of quick and easy big profits. This still happens, and now on the Net. More interesting perhaps are forms of stock fraud that developed to take advantage of specific characteristics of cyberspace. The Web reaches a huge audience immediately. It is ideal for spreading rumors. One can buy a stock, make glowing recommendations about it in chat rooms, on Web sites, and by spamming, and then sell when the price briefly and artificially rises. We describe a few cases with variations on this theme.

In the first criminal case involving Internet stock fraud, a company gave a man 250,000 shares of its stock for promoting the company in his online stock newsletter. He sold while telling his subscribers to buy. He and officials of the company received prison terms.

Some 15-year-olds hack, and some commit stock fraud. The first minor charged with securities fraud made more than $270,000 in profit by flooding the Net with hundreds of messages, under different names, touting stocks he had bought.[34]

An employee of PairGain Technologies created a fake Web page to look like the site of the Bloomberg financial news service. It displayed a positive but false announcement about PairGain. Then he posted a message about the "news" with a link to the fake site. People copied and e-mailed the link, spreading the false information quickly and widely, and causing PairGain stock to rise more than 30%. The stock quickly returned to a normal price after the hoax was uncovered, but investors who bought or sold at the wrong time lost money. The man responsible was caught within a week. Investigators traced him with tools similar to those used to trace people who release viruses and other malicious programs. A man who committed a similar fraud received a 44-month prison sentence.[35]

A law school student created a stock advice service on the Web, offered free trial subscriptions, and signed up 9,000 people. The Securities and Exchange Commission (SEC) claimed that he and several fellow law students bought stocks and then promoted them on their service. The SEC said they also sent hundreds of messages, under different names, to Yahoo and other stock message boards. They collected more than $345,000 in profits as the stocks rose on the false rumors.[36]

The type of frauds we described declined when people saw how easily investigators could trace them. Criminals adopted more sophisticated methods, including hacking and identity theft. A Russian man, using a company located in one country and registered in another, bought stock and then broke into many people's online brokerage accounts and bought the same stock in those accounts. The large number of purchases pushed the price up, and the man sold his stock at a profit. Note that criminal access to a stock account can be costly for the rightful owner even if the thief cannot get funds or stock from the account. Online brokerages report millions of dollars of losses from such scams.[37]

These examples illustrate the many ways criminals find to con people, the need for caution in evaluating any information on the Web, and the need to update law enforcement techniques. The SEC used to take months to investigate suspected securities fraud. In response to fraud on the Web, it formed an Office of Internet Enforcement and now responds more quickly. It uses specialized search engines to scan Web sites and chat rooms for suspicious cases.

5.4.4 DIGITAL FORGERY

Desktop publishing systems, color printers and copiers, and image scanners enable crooks to make fakes with relative ease—fake checks, currency, passports, visas, stock and bond certificates, purchase orders, birth certificates, identification cards, and corporate stationery, to name a few examples. A group of counterfeiters made off with $750,000 from one counterfeit check. They produced the check by scanning a real check from a corporation, changing the amount and payee, and then printing it on a laser printer. Forgers and counterfeiters used to need specialized skills; computer software and hardware dramatically reduced the requirements. Counterfeiters now produce almost all counterfeit U.S. currency passed in the U.S. by using digital technology, rather than by the old method of printing from engraved plates.

Photographs and video are evidence in legal proceedings (e.g., crime scene photos and surveillance camera video). These can be manipulated. A trusted and reliable means of authentication will be essential for the justice system.

Defenses

Defenses against forgery of printed documents include the usual array of approaches: technical tricks that make copying more difficult, education (increased training of clerks who process documents that are likely targets), business practices to reduce risk, and changes in laws.

Older antifraud techniques include microprinting, the use of paper with watermarks, and many others. The U.S. government redesigned its currency in the 1990s to include many anticounterfeiting features. For example, currency contains a security thread that a copier or scanner does not reproduce but a person can see when a bright light shines through the bill. These methods were not adequate, and the Treasury Department continues to consider more revisions, including the use of holograms and heat-sensitive materials in bills.

Embedded fibers in paper and special inks that glow under ultraviolet light increase the security of checks, money orders, and identification documents. Some copiers contain a chip that recognizes currency and prevents the copier from making a copy.

An example of a procedural change to reduce check fraud is for a business to send its bank a list with the check numbers and amounts of all checks issued. The bank can then verify incoming checks.

In the past, banks that accepted forged checks usually absorbed the loss. Changes in state laws now place some of the responsibility on the businesses whose practices make check copying easier, thus providing more incentive for them to improve security of their checks.

5.5   Crime Fighting versus Privacy and Civil Liberties

In several earlier chapters, in the context of various computer technology issues, we discussed tensions between fighting crime, on the one hand, and privacy and civil liberties, on the other. We discuss a few more such issues here.

5.5.1 SEARCH AND SEIZURE OF COMPUTERS

Privacy in group association may . . . be indispensable to preservation of freedom of association, particularly where a group espouses dissident beliefs.

—The Supreme Court, ruling against the state of Alabama's attempt to get the membership list of the National Association for the Advancement of Colored People (NAACP) in the 1950s.[38]

The NAACP's membership list was not on a computer in the 1950s. It most likely is now. We consider several issues about how the Fourth Amendment applies to searches of computers. How far does a search warrant extend when searching a computer? When is a search warrant needed? Does an automated search by software require a warrant? These questions remain at least partially open.

Recall from our discussion in Chapter 2 (Section 2.2.2) that the Fourth Amendment to the U.S. Constitution requires that search warrants be specific about what is to be searched or seized. Courts traditionally take the view that if an officer with a warrant sees evidence of another crime in plain view, the officer may seize it, and prosecutors may use it. But the amount of information or evidence that might be in plain view in a house or office is small compared to what is on a computer. A computer at a business will have information about a large number of people. Membership lists, business records, medical records, and myriad other things are on the same computer that law enforcement agents may search with a search warrant for another reason.

Suppose that while searching a computer for child pornography, with a search warrant for that purpose, investigators find evidence of tax evasion (or hacking or marijuana use or any other crime). May they use it? Suppose they find evidence of a crime by another person, not the one named in the search warrant? May they use it?

How should we interpret "plain view" for a search of computer files? A broad interpretation, for example, "all unencrypted files," invites abuse. Agents could get a warrant for a small crime for which they have supporting evidence and then go on fishing expeditions for other information. This thwarts the Fourth Amendment's requirement that a warrant be specific. Access by law enforcement agents to all the data on a computer can be a serious threat to freedom of speech, privacy, and liberty.

In one case, while searching a man's computer with a search warrant for evidence of drug crimes, an officer saw files names suggesting illegal content not related to the warrant. He opened many files and found child pornography. An appeals court said the names of files might be considered to be in plain view, but the contents of the files were not. The court overturned the man's conviction on the pornography charges.[39] Although the crime in this case is a very unpleasant one, the principle protects us from abuses by the police. In another case, however, involving a search of a computer with medical files on a large number of people, an appeals court allowed the government to use incriminating

BASEBALL, LABORATORY FILES, AND THE FOURTH AMENDMENT

In an investigation of the use of performance-enhancing drugs by professional baseball players, law enforcement agents obtained a search warrant for computer files of laboratory records on drug tests for ten specific players. The lab files they seized contained records on many more baseball players, hockey players, and ordinary people who are not athletes. The agents found that more than 100 baseball players tested positive for steroid use and intended to use this information. Several courts said the information was beyond the scope of the search warrant and that the government could not use it. A federal appeals court reversed these decisions. The players appealed the reversal. The case remained unsettled at the time of writing this book.

information from files about people who were not specified in the search warrant. (See the box above.)

Can law enforcement agents search laptops, and view personal files and confidential business files, as part of a general screening routine at airports, or do they need specific justification? We do not know yet. A U.S. Customs and Border Protection officer searched the laptop of a man arriving by airplane in the U.S. (News reports gave various reasons: he appeared nervous, he was traveling alone.) A judge ruled that, because laptops contain a large amount of personal information, the Fourth Amendment protects them. Searching a laptop requires reasonable suspicion of a crime.[40] The government appealed the ruling. Government officials say they commonly search laptops at airports and that the searches are reasonable.

> *What happened to the Fourth Amendment? Was it repealed somehow?*
> —A judge, commenting on the seizure of lab records for drug tests.[41]

Automated searches

Fraud investigators at the Federal Trade Commission and the SEC surf the Web looking for indications of illegal scams. The SEC announced a plan to use automated surveillance software to crawl through chat rooms and Web sites, looking for suspicious activity or phrases like "get rich quick." The software would build a database of suspicious material.

Is there an essential difference between human and automated surveillance? Is the SEC plan consistent with the Privacy Act and the Fourth Amendment to the Constitution?

Live agents visiting Web sites will undoubtedly miss some crimes. Surveillance software monitors constantly. Is having a (software) government agent in every chat room too intrusive in a free society? Is a chat room a public or a private forum? AOL said it prohibits the use of similar software, in order to protect the privacy of its members. We saw that court decisions allowed AOL and eBay to ban spam and information-collecting software from their sites. Should they have the right to ban government surveillance software too? Should the government need a search warrant, which requires a specific reason for a search, before running its automated surveillance software on a site? Or should we expect public Web sites to be open for all searching by law enforcement agents?

How might investigators use automated search software on PCs? Someone wrote a computer program that searches computer hard disks for child pornography and sends e-mail to a law enforcement agency if it finds any.* This particular program was distributed as a virus. Its unauthorized access to the computers it searches is illegal under the CFAA. But clearly this type of automated search software poses a challenge to the Fourth Amendment in the U.S. and to computer users anywhere.

Some lawyers suggest that automated searches do not require a search warrant because a human being is not looking at the data. They suggest that only the data presented for view by a person must meet the requirements of a search warrant. Automated search software might develop into a reasonable solution for the problem of searching a computer when a judge issues a warrant for specific information. Automated search systems would have to satisfy a number of criteria. Is the software good enough to find what it is looking for and distinguish files it must not display to the investigator? Many people do not trust the FBI to search all e-mail headers from a suspect's ISP and copy only the suspect's e-mail.[†] What supervision and privacy protection would the systems need to make their use acceptable to law enforcement agencies, the courts, civil libertarians, and the public?

5.5.2 THE ISSUE OF VENUE

Normally, prosecutors file criminal charges and a trial takes place near the location of the crime. (The Sixth Amendment to the U.S. Constitution specifies this protection for defendants in the U.S.) But where is an Internet crime committed? Laws differ in different states and countries. When computer crimes cross state and international borders, what laws apply and where should the trial take place? We discuss international cases and issues in Section 5.6. Here we briefly consider the issue of venue (that is, the place where the charges are brought or where the trial takes place) within one country, with the U.S. as our example.

Decisions about where to file charges and hold a trial have significant impact. We saw (in Section 3.2.1) that, for First Amendment cases involving distribution of obscene material, the geographical location was a critical issue, because community standards are an essential factor in determining guilt. In cases that do not explicitly involve community standards, venue is still important. The government could choose a location where prosecutors have more expertise in computer crime or where juries are more likely to

---

*Some software simply searches for filenames that suggest the files might contain child pornography. A technique called hashing can quickly compare large numbers of image files against known images.

[†]The FBI did this for a few years with a system it called Carnivore.

return "guilty" verdicts. The choice of a location far from a defendant's home adversely affects the defendant who must hire distant lawyers and travel a long distance to a trial. Defense attorneys and law professors point out that the FBI can choose where to initiate an investigation or set up a sting operation, to its own advantage. The FBI argues that it may and does seek charges in the district where it discovers the crime and does its investigation. The crime takes place in any state or district where, for example, one can purchase illegal material for sale on the Internet. Thus, the government has tried Californians in Tennessee and Pittsburgh, and a Kentuckian in New York. In several cases, courts ruled against requests by defendants to move trials to their home state. One judge did grant such a request. Judges make venue decisions at their discretion.

5.5.3 THE CYBERCRIME TREATY

The U.S. and European governments participated in drafting the Council of Europe's Convention on Cybercrime. (We call it, simply, the cybercrime treaty).[42] The purpose of the cybercrime treaty is to foster international cooperation among law enforcement agencies of different countries in fighting copyright violations, distribution of child pornography, fraud, hacking, and other crime online. It requires countries that sign the treaty to adopt laws to implement its provisions, standardizing cybercrime laws among those countries.

After years of controversy, the U.S. Senate approved the treaty in 2006. Cooperation among law enforcement agencies in different countries is essential for responding to the huge increase in international online crime. Law enforcement agencies and the Cyber Security Industry Alliance (an organization of computer security companies) strongly supported the treaty. Civil liberties organizations, ISPs, and online businesses strongly oppose some provisions. They believe that the treaty reduces protections for privacy and civil liberties. The treaty requires countries to outlaw some formerly legal activities. Requiring all countries to have laws against releasing destructive computer viruses is reasonable. But some provisions, for example, criminalizing distribution of hacking tools, raise issues we discussed near the end of Section 5.2.4.

Many international agreements related to law enforcement contain a *dual-criminality* provision. It is a provision that one country's government cannot require assistance from another unless the suspect's activity is a crime in both countries. Civil libertarians and privacy advocates argue that the cybercrime treaty's dual-criminality provisions are too weak. They fear that the treaty lets foreign governments require U.S. law enforcement agencies to assist in investigations (by, for example, providing ISP logs and real names of customers) for acts that are legal in the United States. They speculated that the U.S. government passed up an opportunity to add a stronger dual-criminality provision because it wanted to ensure cooperation from other governments for its investigations of actions that are crimes in the U.S. but not in some other countries, for example, money laundering and gambling.[43] (In Section 5.6, we discuss U.S. efforts to apply its antigambling laws to online gambling services in other countries.)

Thus, the cybercrime treaty will likely help law enforcement agencies fight some serious cybercrimes but possibly at the cost of reducing protection for civil liberties in freer countries.

5.6 Whose Laws Rule the Web?

5.6.1 WHEN DIGITAL ACTIONS CROSS BORDERS

In 2000, the ILOVEYOU virus infected tens of millions of computers worldwide, destroying files, collecting passwords, and snarling computers at major corporations and government agencies. Yet, prosecutors dropped charges against the Philippine man believed to be responsible. The Philippines had no law against releasing a virus at the time. (It passed one soon after.) Should police arrest the man if he visits Canada, the U.S., Germany, France, or any of the other countries where the virus did damage?

It is tempting to say, Yes, he should face arrest in any country where the virus caused damage and releasing viruses is illegal. It might also be reasonable that prosecutions for denial-of-service attacks, theft, fraud, and so on take place in countries where the damage is done, not solely in the country where the perpetrator acted. But we need to look carefully at the impact of applying the same policy to all laws.

Figure 5.1 lists some of the subject areas in which national laws differ. Section 3.3.3 reminds us of the kinds of content and political speech that some governments prohibit. Consider an American or French citizen of Chinese ancestry who is a journalist and publishes a blog about the democracy movement in China. The blog is legal where

---

❖ Content control/censorship (topics include politics, religion, pornography, criminal investigations and trials, and many others)

❖ Intellectual property

❖ Gambling

❖ Hacking/viruses

❖ Libel

❖ Privacy

❖ Commerce (advertising, store hours, and sales)

❖ Spam

Figure 5.1 Some Areas Where National Laws Differ

written, but much of its content is illegal in China, because, in the view of the Chinese government, discussion of democracy damages the social order. Would we consider it right if China arrests the journalist on a trip there to visit relatives? If a company sells a product or service on the Web in a country where it is legal, should its employees face arrest and jail if they visit a country where it is illegal?

The dangers are not restricted to unfree countries. We already described one case in detail, the French case against Yahoo auction content (Section 3.3.2). The U.S. government arrests employees and executives of foreign companies whose services violate U.S. laws but not their own. (We look at several cases later.) Canadian courts ban reporting court proceedings in some cases, for example, political scandals and gruesome murders. A Canadian court banned reporting in a 2005 case of alleged corruption in the Labour Party. A U.S. blogger who lived near the border reported details of the court proceedings. His blog had 400,000 hits, mostly from Canada. The blogger feared going to Canada for vacation.

Multinational corporations and tourists have always had to learn about and comply with the laws of countries they operated in or visited. At home, in the past, they had only to deal with their home country's laws. The Web changed that. Which country's laws should apply when Web content crosses borders?

In several cases so far, governments are acting on the assumption of a principle I call the "responsibility to prevent access" principle.

> *Responsibility to prevent access*   It is the responsibility of providers of services and information to make sure their material is not accessible in countries where it is illegal. They may be sued or jailed in those countries if they do not prevent access.

In the next few sections, we describe more incidents and discuss arguments for and against this point of view.

5.6.2 ARRESTING FOREIGN VISITORS

Although it might appall us when China arrests a foreign journalist, governments of democratic countries are pursuing cases based on the same principle.

Applying U.S. copyright law to foreign companies

ElcomSoft, a Russian company, sold a computer program that circumvents controls embedded in Adobe Systems Inc.'s electronic books to prevent copyright infringement. A buyer of the program could use it for legal purposes, such as making backup copies or reading an e-book on different devices—or to illegally make copyright-infringing copies. The program itself was legal in Russia and in most of the world, but not in the United States. Distribution of software that thwarts built-in copyright protection violates the Digital Millennium Copyright Act (DMCA). (We discussed the DMCA in Sections 4.2.1, 4.2.3, and 4.3.2.) When the program's author, Dmitry Sklyarov, came to the U.S. to present a talk on the weaknesses in control software used in e-books, he was arrested. He faced a possible 25-year prison term. After protests in the U.S. and several other countries, the U.S. government let Sklyarov return home but pressed a criminal case against ElcomSoft. In 2002, a federal jury acquitted the company of criminal charges. ElcomSoft claimed it did not know the program was illegal in the U.S. and it stopped distributing the program when Adobe complained. Thus, the case did not resolve the basic issue of whether a prosecution would be successful against a company for continuing to distribute a product that is legal in its own country.

A company based in Antigua sells a program that it claims defeats the controls on high-definition DVDs and Blu-ray disks. Antigua does not have a law like the DMCA making sale of such a program illegal. What action might the U.S. government or the movie studios take against this company? What action is justified?

Arresting executives of online gambling and payment companies

The U.S. arrested David Carruthers, a British citizen and then CEO of BetOnSports PLC, as he changed planes in Dallas on a flight from England to Costa Rica. The U.S. government also arrested several other executives of BetOnSports and the chairman of Sportingbook, another large British online gambling company. Online betting is legal in England. Internet gambling companies are listed and traded on the London stock exchange. The arrests caused gambling company stocks to drop by $1.5 billion, according to Reuters.*[44] The U.S. government argues that most of the companies' customers were in the U.S. where most online gambling is illegal. The companies, according to the U.S., should have blocked access by U.S. citizens. Carruthers faces a possible 20-year jail sentence. These arrests, under a 1961 law, are particularly aggressive because legal experts, gambling experts, and legislators disagree about whether the law applies to the Internet.

A foreign online gambling company might thrive with U.S. customers if its employees stay out of the U.S., so in 2006, Congress passed the Unlawful Internet Gambling Enforcement Act. It prohibits credit-card and online-payment companies from processing transactions between bettors and gambling sites. U.S. credit-card companies and online-payment companies such as PayPal had already stopped processing gambling transactions (after pressure from the government), but payment-service companies exist in other countries where online gambling and processing payments for it are legal. Within months of passing the new law, the U.S. government arrested the founders of Neteller, an Internet payment company that processes gambling transactions. The company is based in the Isle of Man, with shares traded on the London stock exchange.

---

*Reuters is a global news service that focuses on business.

> *You just don't travel to the U.S. any more if you're in that business.*
>
> —A London business analyst, after the arrests of two British online
> gambling company executives in the U.S.[45]

5.6.3 LIBEL, SPEECH, AND COMMERCIAL LAW

Differences among free countries

Under defamation law, we can sue a person, business, or organization for saying something false and damaging to our reputation in print or in other media such as television or the Web. Libel is written defamation; slander is verbal. A well-known Australian businessman, Joseph Gutnick, claimed that an article in *Barron's*, a business magazine, suggested that he had dealings with a money launderer and was involved in other shady deals. Gutnick and others in Australia who subscribe to wsj.com, the *Wall Street Journal*'s Web site, read the article online. Mr. Gutnick sued Dow Jones & Company, the owner of *Barron's* and the *Wall Street Journal*, for libel. Where should the trial be held? Should the libel laws of the U.S. or of Australia apply? Why does it matter?

Even if the laws of two countries are identical, the location of a trial is very important. A trial in a foreign country means high travel and legal expenses, time away from work and family, a foreign attorney and jury, unfamiliar forms and procedures, and a cultural disadvantage. But libel laws are not identical, even among countries that share British background and legal history. The U.S. has strong protection for freedom of speech and for expression of opinion. Public figures, such as politicians and entertainers, have less libel protection than other people. The view is that by placing themselves before the public, they must expect that people will talk about and criticize them. Vigorous, open debate, and ultimately freedom, would suffer if people could not express strong opinions about prominent people. English and Australian law and tradition, on the other hand, place more emphasis on protecting reputations. For example, Michael Jackson won a libel suit against a British newspaper for a statement that his plastic surgeries "hideously disfigured" him. He probably would not win such a suit in the United States. In England, people often sue newspapers, and it can be risky to publish details about business and political scandals.*

The burden of proof differs in different countries. In the U.S., the person who is suing has the burden of proving the case. Public figures must prove that the published information is false *and* that the publisher knew it was false or acted recklessly. Australian libel law requires the publisher of the statement in question to prove it is true or that the publisher reasonably believed it was true.

---

*In 2006, in a "landmark" ruling, the British Law Lords (similar to the U.S. Supreme Court) gave news organizations protection from libel suits for responsible journalism of value to the public.

Dow Jones argued that the Gutnick case should be moved to the U.S., where they published the article and where the wsj.com server is. Gutnick argued for a trial in Australia, where the article did the damage to his reputation. The Australian High Court ruled that the trial would be in Australia. Eventually, Dow Jones settled with Mr. Gutnick, paying him a large sum.[46]

The Gutnick case is not an extreme example of the responsibility to prevent access principle because libel is illegal in both countries, and it is conceivable that Gutnick might have won the case if tried in the United States. The implication of the case, though, like the Yahoo case described in Section 3.3.2, is that news publishers must block access to articles by people in countries where publication of the articles violates laws. The *New York Times* announced that it did so for the first time in 2006. It reprogrammed its geolocation tools, normally used for targeting advertisements, to block people in England from reading a news article. The article described the investigation of suspects arrested in the alleged plot to carry liquid explosives onto airplanes and blow them up. Publishing information damaging to defendants before a trial is illegal in England. It is not illegal in the United States.[47]

Any solution to the problem of differing national laws among free countries involves some compromise. The *New York Times*, in explaining its decision to block the terror-plot article, said that although England does not have a First Amendment protecting freedom of the press to the extent the U.S. does, England does have a free press, and it is reasonable to respect its laws.

The *New York Times* action shows that major news publishers have the legal staffs and the technical tools to handle differences in laws. Suppose someone in the U.S. sends the blocked *New York Times* article by e-mail to someone in England. Suppose a U.S. blogger with readers in England repeats some of the information in the article. What happens to these individuals, who do not have a legal staff and geolocation tools, who might not know the article is illegal in another country?

Libel law as a threat to free speech

In U.S. libel cases where the parties are in different states, courts may rule that the libel (and hence the trial) takes place where the damage happens. The Australian court's decision to hold the Gutnick case trial in Australia is consistent with that approach. It makes sense, at least for reasonably free countries like the U.S., Australia, and England. But what happens if we generalize to oppressive governments that use strict libel laws for political purposes?

Saudi Arabia bans "anything damaging to the dignity of heads of state."[48] Russia made it a crime to slander government officials. Government officials in Singapore have long used libel laws to bankrupt political opponents who criticize them. The prime minister of Singapore and his father, the former premier, demanded that the Hong Kong–based *Far Eastern Economic Review* remove from its Web site an interview with a political opponent who criticized them. They sued the publisher and editor for libel. A lawsuit or criminal charges in these countries against a foreign newspaper or a visiting journalist or blogger is more threatening to honest, critical news coverage than holding a libel trial for a U.S. publisher in Australia.

Commercial law

The European Union bans ads for medical drugs directed to consumers. Such ads are legal and common on television and on the Web in the United States. Some European countries have other restrictive laws about marketing. For example, they prohibit or restrict direct price comparisons, product giveaways, and advertising unconditional-return policies or that a business gives a contribution to charity for each sale. (The justification for these laws was that such practices and advertisements confuse or trick consumers.)[49] Should commercial Web sites with drug ads or price comparisons have to screen out shoppers from countries where they are illegal? Enforcing such laws on foreign sites does not differ, in principle, from France requiring Yahoo to prevent access by French people to auctions with Nazi memorabilia or the U.S. requiring foreign gambling sites to exclude U.S. citizens.

5.6.4 CULTURE, LAW, AND ETHICS

If publications and Web sites must comply with the laws of roughly 200 countries, would they protect themselves by avoiding anything controversial? Will the extraordinary benefits of international news blogging shrink under the burden of learning every other country's laws, the need to block potentially illegal articles, and the chilling effect of uncertainty? Some fear this would destroy the openness and global information flow of the Web, that the Web would come to reflect some combination of Muslim restrictions on discussion of religion, U.S. opposition to online gambling, and Chinese censorship. Others argue that companies would adapt and acquire software to handle the appropriate screening.

Jack Goldsmith and Tim Wu, in their book *Who Controls the Internet?*, argue that the "global network is becoming a collection of nation-state networks"[50] and that this is a good thing. The Net, Goldsmith and Wu believe, will be more peaceful and productive if each country controls content within its borders according to its own history, culture, and values. Goldsmith and Wu point

 *Enforcing community standards within the U.S.: Section 3.2.1* out that many people and governments (in both totalitarian countries and democracies) consider the freedom of speech enjoyed in the U.S. to be excessive. U.S. publishers and bloggers should respect differing national standards and laws and prevent their publications from reaching people in countries that prohibit them.

Critics of their point of view might point out that respecting culture is not the same as respecting laws. Culture evolves over time and is rarely absolute or uniform throughout a country. Governments often claim to be protecting national culture and values when they impose control on their citizens to maintain their own power or to benefit special interests within their country. Laws, as we saw in our discussion of differences between law and ethics in Chapter 1, have many ignoble sources. Who wants censorship of political discussion on the Internet in China—the people or the Communist Party, which is trying to maintain political control while it loosens economic control? The U.S. defends its ban on offshore gambling sites with the argument that it has the right to ban morally objectionable activities. Certainly, there are many valid criticisms of gambling on social and ethical grounds, but this argument from the government is not convincing. The federal and state governments allow and tax many forms of legal gambling and profit from monopolies on their state lotteries. It seems likely that anticompetitiveness—not morality—motivates the governments, casinos, and racetracks that oppose offshore gambling Web sites.

Consider Canada's and France's restrictions on showing U.S. television programs. Some defenders of these laws emphasize protecting their culture from being overrun by U.S. culture. Others (e.g., in Canada) are frank about the purpose being to provide jobs for Canadians and to protect the financial health of the small domestic broadcasting industry. Within each country that has similar protectionist laws (including the U.S.), there are strongly opposing opinions about whether such laws are unjust intrusions on freedom, whether they help some domestic industries while hurting others, or whether they are reasonable ways to help a local economy. Should they be enforced on people outside the country?

Where a large majority of people in a country support prohibitions on certain content, perhaps discussions of certain religions, is it ethically proper to abandon the basic human rights of free expression and freedom of religion for minorities? Is there a positive ethical value in thwarting a country's censorship laws and providing exactly the material that some governments ban?

5.6.5   POTENTIAL SOLUTIONS

International agreements

International treaties can set common standards or means of resolving international cases among the countries that sign them. Countries in the World Trade Organization (WTO) agree not to prevent their citizens from buying certain services from other countries if those services are legal in their own.[51] This is a good step, a generalization of the principle in the U.S. that the individual states cannot discriminate against sellers (of legal products) from other states. (Recall the wine shipment and real estate sales cases in Section 3.2.4.) But this WTO agreement does not help when a product, service, or information is legal in one country and not another.

The cybercrime treaty (Section 5.5.3) attempts to unify laws among the countries that sign it. For the crimes it covers, that is helpful. It, however, does not address many of the laws we discuss in this section, especially those that regulate the content of speech. It does not address the problem that some countries outlaw common activities that people in other countries strongly believe should be legal.

An alternative principle

An alternative to the responsibility to prevent access principle—call it the authority to prevent entry principle—says the following:

> *Authority to prevent entry* The government of Country A can act within Country A to try to block the entrance of material that is illegal there, but may not apply its laws to the people who create and publish the material, or provide a service, in Country B if it is legal there.

For example, the Soviet Union jammed radio broadcasts from Western countries during the Cold War. It did not have an internationally respected right to order the broadcasters to stop broadcasting. This principle might be particularly useful for services such as gambling, which is a prominent part of the culture in some countries, illegal in others, and regulated and taxed in still others. Within their borders, national governments have many tools to block information and activities they do not want. As we saw in Section 3.3.3, they require ISPs and search engine companies (within their country) to block access to banned sites. The government of Singapore made it a criminal offense for Singaporeans to subscribe to, import, or reproduce the *Far Eastern Economic Review* after it published an interview the government considered libelous. Of course, people who believe in freedom of speech do not approve of such actions. The authority to prevent entry principle is a compromise. It recognizes that governments are sovereign within their territories. It attempts to reduce the impact of their restrictive laws outside their borders. If influential countries like the U.S. and France, for example, adopted this principle and refrained from arresting visiting foreigners, their example could apply pressure to less free countries to do the same. They do not appear inclined to do so.

Of course, this principle has weaknesses too. Countries that lack up-to-date cybercrime laws attract people who commit international online crimes, such as major frauds. We want some sensible way for the victimized countries to take action against them. One reason for the difficulty in developing good solutions to the problem of differing laws in different countries is that there are such widely different kinds of laws. As we saw in Chapter 1, some outlaw truly bad activities that victimize other people. Some impose particular views about acceptable personal beliefs, speech, and nonviolent activities. If all laws were of the first type, there might be much agreement that such laws should be enforced. The problems would be about differences in detail (such as differences between U.S. and Australian libel law). The responsibility to prevent access principle is dangerous primarily because there are so many laws of the second type. But many people and governments strongly support such laws. It would be difficult to find agreement about which laws are the "right" laws, which a country could rightly enforce outside its borders. Compromises in this context, unfortunately, reduce freedom for the people in the country that is most free in any particular area. Thus, we still need creative development of good solutions for the problem of determining what laws apply in cross-border Internet cases.

EXERCISES

Review Exercises

5.1   What does *computer forensics* mean?

5.2   What are *script kiddies*?

5.3   What is a *honey pot*?

5.4   Describe one method financial Web sites use to convince a consumer the site is authentic.

5.5   What is one problem with using biometrics for identification?

5.6   What is one method for committing online auction fraud?

5.7   For what Web-based service did the U.S. government arrest several business executives from England?

General Exercises

5.8   Chris logs on to your computer at night while you sleep and uses some of your software. Robin takes your car at night while you sleep and drives it around for a while. (Neither has your permission; neither does damage.) List several characteristics of the two events that are similar (characteristics related to the effects of the events, ethics, legality, risks, etc.). List several characteristics of the two events that are different. Which would offend you more? Why?

5.9   Young, technically oriented hackers argued that, if the owners of a computer system want to keep outsiders out, it is their responsibility to provide better security. Ken Thompson, one of the inventors of UNIX, said, "The act of breaking into a computer system has to have the same social stigma as breaking into a neighbor's house. It should not matter that the neighbor's door is unlocked."[52] Which position do you agree with more? Give your reasons.

5.10   Some people argue that a hacker who defaces a Web page of a government entity such as the White House, Congress, or Parliament should be punished more harshly than a hacker who defaces a Web page of a private company or organization. Give some arguments for and against this view.

5.11   What are some arguments for and against the practice of hiring former hackers to help them improve security? Are you in favor of this practice? Why or why not?

5.12   One group hacks a German government Web site to protest the ban on the distribution of Nazi material in Germany. Another group hacks a German government site to protest the construction of multinational chain stores such as Wal-Mart, McDonald's, and Starbucks in Germany. Which would you consider an example of hacktivism? Explain.

5.13   Consider the analogy between occasional downtime on the Web as a result of viruses, worms, or denial-of-service attacks and vehicle traffic slowdowns on roads during rush hour or bad weather. Describe similarities; then evaluate. Are both side effects of modern civilization that we have to get used to? How can individuals and businesses reduce the negative impacts on themselves?

5.14   Suppose a 16-year-old hacker uses automatic-dialing software to flood the emergency 911 telephone system with calls, knocking out 911 service. What penalty do you think is appropriate?

5.15   Give three clues that suggest that an e-mail is a phishing attempt.

5.16 What are two tactics criminals use to commit credit fraud? What are two countermeasures financial institutions and retailers use to prevent credit fraud?

5.17 To reduce scams that steal from people banking online, some people suggest creating a new Internet domain ".bank," available only to chartered banks. Consider the identity theft and fraud techniques we discussed. Which ones would this new domain help prevent? For which would it be ineffective? Overall, do you think it is a good idea? Why or why not?

5.18 In Section 5.3.2, we gave an analogy between retailers accepting some amount of shoplifting, on the one hand, and retailers and credit-card companies accepting some amount of credit-card fraud, on the other hand. Identify a strength and a weakness of this analogy.

5.19 The meaning of the term hacker has changed over time. Describe three phases it has gone through and what it meant in each phase. Explain the terms "white-hat hacker," "black-hat hacker," and "cracker."

5.20 In Section 5.3.2, we described a customer authentication method that calculates a risk score based on many details of a customer's typical activities on a company's Web site. To use this method, the site must store many details of each customer's visits to the site. Does this violate the privacy principles in Figure 2.1 of collecting only the data needed and not storing data longer than needed? Explain your answer.

5.21 Describe the purpose of the Cybercrime Treaty (Section 5.5.3). What is the *dual-criminality provision*? Do you consider this provision to be important? Why or why not?

5.22 Commenting on constitutional objections to the SEC's plan to use surveillance software to monitor the Web for possible fraud (Section 5.5.1), an SEC official said "the Constitution doesn't give people the right to use the Internet to commit fraud."[53] Evaluate this response. Is it a good argument?

5.23 Suppose fingerprint readers are a standard feature of PCs and an ISP requires a match to log in. Would requiring a password in addition to the fingerprint be redundant and pointless, or is there a good security reason to require both? Explain.

5.24 Identify several issues raised by this scenario:

> Someone in California posts on amazon.com a very critical review of a new book written by a British author. The review says the writer is an incompetent fool without a single good idea; he can't even express the bad ideas clearly and probably did not graduate from grade school; he should be washing dishes instead of wasting paper and the reader's time. The author sues the reviewer and Amazon for libel.

5.25 If U.S. law enforcement agents in the U.S. caught the leader of a South American drug gang that smuggles drugs into the U.S., they would arrest him. Is this comparable to arresting Dmitry Sklyarov or David Carruthers? (See Section 5.6.2.) Explain similarities and differences.

5.26 Using some of the ethical principles in Chapter 1, analyze the ethics of the action of the U.S. blogger who posted details about the Canadian trial (see Section 5.6.1). Do you think he should have done it?

5.27 Assume you are a professional working in your chosen field. Describe specific things you can do to reduce the impact of any two problems we discussed in this chapter. (If you cannot think of anything related to your professional field, choose another field that might interest you.)

5.28 Think ahead to the next few years and describe a new problem, related to issues in this chapter, likely to develop from computing technology or the Web.

Assignments

These exercises require some research or activity.

5.29   Find a dozen news and/or magazine articles about hackers from mainstream media from the past few years. How are hackers described, as criminals or heroes? Give examples.

5.30   Many law enforcement agencies have developed a cold-case task force to try to solve unsolved crimes. How is technology being used to help solve these cases? Interview a cold case investigator. What technologies do they use when investigating a case?

5.31   Find a use of biometrics in your city. Describe the application and its benefits and risks.

5.32   Find the final decision or current status of the case described in the box "BASEBALL, LABORATORY FILES, AND THE FOURTH AMENDMENT" (Section 5.5.1).

5.33   This exercise explores whether the Fourth Amendment protects files on a computer during servicing. While servicing a customer's computer, a technician found material that he thought was illegal. He called police who examined some of the files without a search warrant. The trial court considered the search illegal; the state appealed. Find the final decision (or current status) of the case, *Washington State v. Westbrook* (2005). Summarize the main argument in the final or most recent decision. Do you think it is reasonable?

Class Discussion Exercises

These exercises are for class discussion, perhaps with short presentations prepared in advance by small groups of students.

5.34   Suppose a denial-of-service attack shuts down two dozen major Web sites, including retailers, stock brokerages, and large corporate entertainment and information sites, for several hours. The attack is traced to one of the following perpetrators. Do you think different penalties are appropriate, depending on which it is? Explain why. If you would impose different penalties, how would they differ?

a) A foreign terrorist who launched the attack to cause billions of dollars in damage to the U.S. economy.

b) An organization publicizing its opposition to commercialization of the Web and corporate manipulation of consumers.

c) A teenager using hacking tools he found on a Web site.

d) A hacker group showing off to another hacker group about how many sites it could shut down in one day.

5.35   Debate the following question: Is hacking into a system but not doing any damage a victimless crime?

5.36   The families of two hospital patients who died as the result of a virus in a hospital computer are suing each of the people listed below and urging the government to bring criminal charges for negligence against each of them.[54]

❖ A student in a course on computer security at a small college who posted a copy of the virus program on the class Web site, with a discussion of how it works.

❖ The student who activated the virus program and released it onto the Internet.

❖ The president of the college.

❖ The president of the college's ISP.

❖ The director of the hospital whose computer system the virus infected, causing patient medical records to be unavailable for a full day, resulting in the deaths of the two patients.

Divide the class into ten teams: five (one for each person listed above) to present arguments in favor of civil and/or criminal penalties and five (one for each person) to present defense arguments. After the presentations, use a class vote or discussion to decide which, if any, of the characters should not be considered guilty at all; which, if any, should bear a high degree of responsibility; and which are "fuzzy" cases, hard to decide.

5.37   Many viruses and denial-of-service attacks are perpetrated by minors. Some people argue for tougher penalties, claiming that light penalties (fines, community service, and probation) encourage such behavior. Some argue that young hackers have the potential to mature into responsible adults, and that incarcerating them will just turn them into criminals when they are adults. Discuss the merits of these arguments. Which side do you agree with? Why?

5.38   Suppose a local community center has invited you, a group of college students, to make a 15-minute presentation about protecting against identity theft. Plan and give the presentation.

5.39   Suppose you are on a consulting team to design a voting system for your state in which people will vote by logging on to a Web site. What are some important design considerations? Discuss some pros and cons of such a system. Overall, do you think it is a good idea?

5.40   Discuss pros and cons of law enforcement use of automated search software (described in Section 5.5.1) to find evidence of crimes on Web sites, in chat rooms, and on PCs.

NOTES

1. I have seen estimates ranging up to $500,000 for the average, some from computer security firms, which have an incentive to exaggerate. It is difficult to get precise figures, in part because victims are reluctant to report losses.

2. Eric S. Raymond, ed., *New Hacker's Dictionary* (MIT Press, 1993).

3. Quoted in J. D. Bierdorfer, "Among Code Warriors, Women, Too, Can Fight," *New York Times*, June 7, 2001, pp. 1, 9.

4. Brian Reid, "Reflection on Some Recent Widespread Computer Break-ins," *Communications of the ACM*, 30, no. 2 (February 1987), pp. 103–105; reprinted in Peter J. Denning, ed., *Computers Under Attack: Intruders, Worms, and Viruses* (Addison Wesley, 1990), pp. 145–149.

5. "Politicians and the Net," *Wired*, February 1995, p. 46; John R. Wilke, "In the Arcane Culture of Computer Hackers, Few Doors Stay Closed, *Wall Street Journal*, August 22, 1990, pp. A1, A4."; David L. Wilson, " 'Crackers': A Serious Threat," *The Chronicle of Higher Education*, August 17, 1994, pp. A23–A24; Jared Sandberg, "Security Breach at the Internet Raises Worries," *Wall Street Journal*, February 7, 1994, p. B5.

6. John Simons, "How a Cyber Sleuth, Using a 'Data Tap,' Busted a Hacker Ring," *Wall Street Journal*, October 1, 1999, pp. A1, A6.

7. All the quotes are from John R. Wilke, "In the Arcane Culture of Computer Hackers, Few Doors Stay Closed."

8. "Is Computer Hacking a Crime?" *Harper's Magazine*, March 1990, pp. 45–57; the quotation is on p. 57.

9. Wilson, " 'Crackers': A Serious Threat."

10. The early but widely repeated estimate of 6,000 infected computers was calculated from a Massachusetts Institute of Technology (MIT) staff member's guess of a 10% infection rate at MIT the day after the worm struck and an estimate of 60,000 Internet hosts at the time. A lower estimate—between 2,000 and 3,000—was reported later. Jon A. Rochlis and Mark W. Eichin, "With Microscope and Tweezers: The Worm from MIT's Perspective," *Communications of the ACM*, 32, no. 6 (June 1989), pp. 689–698.

11. Dan Farmer and Wietse Venema. The quote is from the Security Administrator Tool for Analyzing Networks (SATAN) documentation, quoted in Ted Doty, "Test Driving SATAN," in *Internet Besieged: Countering Cyberspace Scofflaws*, ed. Dorothy E. Denning and Peter J. Denning (AddisonWesley, 1998), chapter 15.

12. Larry Lange, "Corporate America: Beware Inside Job," *Electronic Engineering Times*, January 15, 1996, pp. 20, 22; Jared Sandberg, "AOL Tightens Security after Hackers Foil the Service with Fake Accounts," *Wall Street Journal*, September 8, 1995, p. B3; Marc L. Songini, "Hospital Confirms Copying of Patient Files by

Hacker," *Computerworld*, December 15, 2000,
archives.cnn.com/2000/TECH/computing/12/15/hospital.
hacker.idg/index.html (accessed September 7, 2007).

13. W. Wayt Gibbs, "Profile: Dan Farmer," *Scientific
American*, April 1997, pp. 32, 34; Jared Sandberg,
"Holes In the Net," *Newsweek*, February 21, 2000,
pp. 46–49; attrition.org.

14. "Withdrawal Ordered for U.S. Pentagon Hackers,"
San Jose Mercury News (Reuters), November 5, 1998.

15. Lev Grossman, "Attack of the Love Bug," *Time*, May 15,
2000, pp. 48–56.

16. See grc.com/dos/grcdos.htm for a firsthand report by
the victim that covers technical, sociological, and social
aspects of the attack, including e-mail from the boy who
launched it (accessed June 3, 2001).

17. Victoria Murphy Barret, "Spam Hunter," Forbes.com,
July 23, 2007, members.forbes.com/forbes/
2007/0723/054.html (accessed September 17, 2007).

18. John J. Fialka, "The Latest Flurries at Weather Bureau:
Scattered Hacking," *Wall Street Journal*, October 10,
1994, pp. A1, A6.

19. Mark Manion and Abby Goodrum, "Terrorism or
Civil Disobedience: Toward a Hacktivist Ethic," in
Readings in CyberEthics, ed. Richard A. Spinello and
Herman T. Tavani (Jones and Bartlett, 2001),
pp. 463–473.

20. John Perry Barlow, "Crime and Puzzlement," *The Whole
Earth Review*, Fall 1990, pp. 44–57. (This article
describes and comments on several early hacker cases.)
Wilke, "In the Arcane Culture of Computer Hackers,
Few Doors Stay Closed."

21. Bruce Sterling, *The Hacker Crackdown: Law and Disorder
on the Electronic Frontier* (Bantam Books, 1992),
pp. 13–14.

22. Craig Bromberg, "In Defense of Hackers," *The New York
Times Magazine*, April 21, 1991, pp. 45–49; Gary Wolf,
"The World According to Woz," *Wired*, September
1998, pp. 118–121, 178–185; Richard P. Feynman,
*Surely You're Joking, Mr. Feynman: Adventures of a Curious
Character* (W. W. Norton, 1984), pp. 137–155.

23. *Information Security: Computer Attacks at Department of
Defense Pose Increasing Risks*, GAO/AIMD9684, May 22,
1996; W. Wayt Gibbs, "Profile: Dan Farmer," *Scientific
American*, April 1997, pp. 32, 34; Robert Fox, "News
Track: NASA Computer Security Lax," *Communications
of the ACM*, July 1999, p. 10; Wade Roush, "Hackers,"
Technology Review, April 1995, pp. 32–40; Wilson,
"'Crackers': A Serious Threat"; "Interior Department
Bars Access to Internet Site," New York Times,
December 8, 2001, p. A11; Associated Press,
"U.S. Review Finds Widespread Lapses In Computer
Security," *Wall Street Journal*, April 6, 2001, p. B6;
Colin Barker, "Gary McKinnon: Scapegoat or public
enemy?" CNet News, July 13, 2005, news.com.com;

24. Joris Evers, "Don't Let Your Navigation System Fool
You," CNET News.com, April 20, 2007, news.com.com
(accessed April 30, 2007).

25. Joseph Pereira, "How Credit-Card Data Went Out
Wireless Door," *Wall Street Journal*, May 4, 2007,
pp. A1, A2.

26. Peter Tippett, quoted in Kim Zetter, "Freeze! Drop That
Download!" *PC World*, November 16, 2000,
www.pcworld.com/resource/printable/article/0,aid,
34406,00.asp (accessed September 2, 2007). The article
includes pros and cons of criminalizing virus writing and
a discussion of other means of reducing viruses.

27. Alfred Huger, vice president of Symantec Security
Response, quoted in Riva Richmond, "PC Hackers Gain
Savvy in Stealing Identities," *Wall Street Journal*,
March 21, 2007, p. B4B.

28. Barbara Carton, "An Unsolved Slaying of an Airline
Worker Stirs Family to Action," *Wall Street Journal*, June
20, 1995, p. A1, A8.

29. Saul Hansell, "U.S. Workers Stole Data on 11,000,
Agency Says," *New York Times*, April 6, 1996, p. 6.

30. Joseph Pereira, "Skimming Devices Target Debit-Card
Readers," *Wall Street Journal*, March 8, 2007, pp. B1, B2.

31. The Identity Theft and Assumption Deterrence Act of
1998, 18 U.S.C. §1028, www.consumer.gov/idtheft.

32. William M. Bulkeley, "How Biometric Security Is Far
from Foolproof," *Wall Street Journal*, December 12,
2006, p. B3.

33. Linda Harrison, "US Lawyer and Pals Indicted for Shill
Bidding on eBay," *The Register*, April 18, 2001,
www.theregister.co.uk/content/6/18354.html (accessed
April 18, 2001).

34. Daniel Kadlec, "Crimes and Misdeminors," *Time*,
October 2, 2000, pp. 52–54.

35. Christopher M. E. Painter, "Tracing in Internet Fraud
Cases: PairGain and NEI Webworld," U.S. Department
of Justice, www.usdoj.gov/criminal/
cybercrime/usamay2001_3.htm (accessed September 2,
2007); "Defendant in Emulex Hoax Sentenced," U.S.
Securities and Exchange Commission, August 8, 2001,
www.sec.gov/litigation/litreleases/lr17094.htm (accessed
September 2, 2007).

36. *SEC v. Colt*, No. 00423, March 2, 2000.

37. Robert Lemos, "Stock Scammer Gets Coal for the
Holidays," *The Register*, December 28, 2006, www.
theregister.co.uk/2006/12/28/sec_freezes_stock_
scammer_accounts (accessed February 16, 2007).

38. *NAACP v. Alabama*, 357 U.S. 449 (1958).

39. *United States v. Carey*, 1999, www.kscourts.org/CA10/
cases/1999/04/98-3077.htm (accessed May 10, 2007).

40. *U.S. v. Arnold.* Amanda Bronstad, "Computer Search Turned Back at the Border," Law.com, October 23, 2006, www.law.com/jsp/article.jsp?id=1161335118318 (accessed November 7, 2006).

41. District court judge, quoted by appellate Judge Sydney Thomas, who dissented from the appeals court ruling allowing use of the laboratory records. *USA v. Comprehensive Drug Testing*, No. 0510067.

42. The text of the treaty is at conventions.coe.int/ Treaty/en/Treaties/Html/185.htm (accessed September 2, 2007).

43. See, for example, "Cybercrime Treaty Before Senate," *EPIC Alert*, December 16, 2005, www.epic.org/ alert/EPIC_Alert_12.25.html (accessed February 21, 2007).

44. Pete Harrison, "Sportingbet Arrest Sparks Fears of Wider Crackdown," Reuters, September 8, 2006, go.reuters.com.

45. Quoted in Harrison, "Sportingbet Arrest Sparks Fears of Wider Crackdown."

46. Associated Press, "Internet Libel Case with Global Implications Ends in Settlement," November 16, 2004, accessed on the Web site of The First Amendment Center, Vanderbilt University, www. firstamendmentcenter.org/news.aspx?id=14379 (accessed August 18, 2006).

47. Tom Zeller Jr., "Times Withholds Web Article in Britain," *New York Times*, August 29, 2006, www.nytimes.com/2006/08/29/business/media/ 29times.html (accessed August 30, 2006).

48. Robert Corn-Revere, "Caught in the Seamless Web: Does the Internet's Global Reach Justify Less Freedom of Speech?" Cato Institute, Briefing Paper no. 71, July 24, 2002, p. 7.

49. Neal E. Boudette, "German Shoppers May Get 'Sale Freedom,'" *Wall Street Journal*, January 23, 2002, p. B7D. Germany recently repealed some of these laws, in force for 90 years, in part because of the influence of the Internet.

50. Goldsmith and Tim Wu, *Who Controls the Internet? Illusions of a Borderless World* (Oxford University Press, 2006), p. 149.

51. Antigua won a ruling from the WTO that the U.S. is violating WTO agreements by banning foreign gambling sites from accepting U.S. customers while allowing gambling on horse races on the Web within the United States. Antigua claims the U.S. government ignored the ruling.

52. Donn Seeley, "Password Cracking: A Game of Wits," *Communications of the ACM*, 32, no. 6 (June 1989), pp. 700–703, reprinted in Denning, *Computers Under Attack*, pp. 244–252.

53. George C. Brown, assistant general counsel, SEC, quoted in Michael Moss, "SEC's Plan to Snoop for Crime on Web Sparks a Debate over Privacy," *Wall Street Journal*, March 28, 2000, pp. B1, B4.

54. This exercise is a simplified and modified version of a scenario used in a mock hearing presentation at the Computers, Freedom, and Privacy conference, San Francisco, 1993, in a session chaired by Don Ingraham.

BOOKS AND ARTICLES

- Corn-Revere, Robert. "Caught in the Seamless Web: Does the Internet's Global Reach Justify Less Freedom of Speech?" Cato Institute Briefing Paper no. 71, July 24, 2002. (Also appears in Adam Thierer and Clyde Wayne Crews Jr., eds. *Who Rules The Net?*, listed below.) Criticizes arguments in Goldsmith and Wu, *Who Controls the Internet?*, below, and in articles published by Goldsmith earlier.

- Council of Europe Convention on Cybercrime, 2001 (the cybercrime treaty), conventions.coe.int/Treaty/EN/Treaties/ HTML/185.htm.

- Denning, Dorothy E. *Information Warfare and Security*. ACM Press/AddisonWesley, 1999.

- Denning, Dorothy E., and Peter J. Denning, cds. *Internet Besieged: Countering Cyberspace Scofflaws*. ACM Press/AddisonWesley, 1998. A collection of articles on hacking and Internet security.

- Dixon, Pam. "Medical Identity Theft: The Information Crime that Can Kill You." World Privacy Forum, May 3, 2006, www.worldprivacyforum.org/ medicalidentitytheft.html.

- Eltringham, Scott. "Prosecuting Computer Crimes." U.S. Department of Justice, February 2007, www.usdoj.gov/criminal/cybercrime/ccmanual/index.html.

- Goldsmith, Jack, and Tim Wu. *Who Controls the Internet? Illusions of a Borderless World*. Oxford University Press, 2006. Argues in favor of each country strictly enforcing its laws against foreigners to control what enters its borders via the Internet. See Robert Corn-Revere, "Caught in the Seamless Web."

- Kerr, Orin. "Searching and Seizing Computers and Obtaining Electronic Evidence in Criminal Investigations." U.S. Department of Justice, 2002, www.usdoj.gov/criminal/cybercrime/s&smanual2002.htm.

- Kruse II, Warren G., and Jay G. Heiser. *Computer Forensics: Incident Response*. AddisonWesley, 2001.

- Levy, Steven. *Hackers: Heroes of the Computer Revolution*. Doubleday, 1984.

- Manion, Mark, and Abby Goodrum. "Terrorism or Civil Disobedience: Toward a Hacktivist Ethic." *Readings in CyberEthics*. Edited by Richard A. Spinello and Herman T. Tavani. Jones and Bartlett, 2001, pp. 463–473. Argues for expanding the ethical justification for civil disobedience to include hacktivism.

- Pfleeger, Charles P., and Shari Lawrence Pfleeger. *Security in Computing*. Fourth Edition. Prentice Hall, 2007.

- Shimomura, Tsutomu, and John Markoff. *Takedown: The Pursuit and Capture of America's Most Wanted Computer Outlaw—By the Man Who Did It.* Hyperion, 1996.

- Stallings, William. *Cryptography and Network Security: Principles and Practices*. Fourth Edition. Prentice Hall, 2005.

- Stoll, Clifford. *The Cuckoo's Egg: Tracking a Spy Through the Maze of Computer Espionage*. Doubleday, 1989.

- Thierer, Adam, and Clyde Wayne Crews Jr., eds. *Who Rules The Net? Internet Governance and Jurisdiction*. Cato Institute, 2003.

ORGANIZATIONS AND WEB SITES

- Federal Trade Commission identity theft page: www.ftc.gov/bcp/edu/microsites/idtheft

- Privacy Rights Clearinghouse identity theft page: www.privacyrights.org/identity.htm

- U.S. Department of Justice cybercrime section: www.usdoj.gov/criminal/cybercrime

6

WORK

6.1 Fears and Questions

Computers free us from the repetitious, boring aspects of jobs so that we can spend more time being creative and doing the tasks that require human intelligence. Computer systems and the Internet provide quick, reliable access to information so that we work smarter and more efficiently. Nursing homes and construction sites use computers, databases, and wireless communication devices, but people care for the elderly and build buildings. Architects use computer-aided design systems, but they still design buildings. Accountants use spreadsheets and thus have more time for thinking, planning, and analysis. But will computers begin to design buildings? Will audits be automated?

The introduction of computers into the workplace generated many fears. Many social critics, social scientists, politicians, unions, and activists saw virtually all potential effects of computers on work as highly threatening. They foresaw mass unemployment due to increased efficiency. (Some argued, at first, that money spent on computers was a waste because computers *decreased* efficiency.) They argued that requiring workers to acquire computer skills was too heavy a burden, and that the need for increased technical training and skills would widen the earning gap between those who obtain the new skills and those who do not. They saw telecommuting as bad for workers and society. Many oppose offshoring (hiring people or companies in other countries to perform services that workers in one's home country used to do), arguing that it will eliminate a huge number of jobs.

Many of the fears expressed only a few years ago about the expected impact of computers on work, such as mass unemployment, probably seem surprising today. Yet the same worries arise with each new technology—or new use of technology, such as offshoring of jobs.

How do computer databases and the Web affect the way we get a job, the way we learn about potential employers, and the way they learn about us? How do we deal with the dislocations and retraining needs that result when computers and the Internet eliminate jobs?

Computers and communications networks are causing changes in the size of businesses and the number of people who are self-employed. *Telecommuting* has become part of our vocabulary, describing the phenomenon of working at a distance from the traditional company office or factory, connected by computers and telecommunications devices. What are its advantages and disadvantages? How does it affect the physical distribution of population and businesses?

At the same time that information technology is giving some workers more autonomy, computers are giving employers increased power to monitor the work, communications, movements, and Web activity of employees. These changes affect productivity, privacy, and morale. Why do employers monitor employees? Should monitoring be limited?

In this chapter, we look for answers to these questions.

6.2 The Impact on Employment

> *But nowhere is there any mention of the truth about the information highway,*
> *which is mass unemployment.*
>
> —David Noble, "The Truth About the Information Highway"[1]

6.2.1 JOB DESTRUCTION AND CREATION

Since the beginning of the Industrial Revolution, technology has generated fears of mass unemployment. In the early 1800s the Luddites (of whom we say more in Chapter 7) burned weaving looms because they feared the looms would eliminate their jobs. A few decades later, a mob of seamstresses and tailors destroyed sewing machines because of the same fears.[2]

More recently, in the 1950s and 1960s factory automation came under (verbal) fire from presidential candidate John F. Kennedy and industry and labor groups for threatening to bring the menace of increased unemployment and poverty. The quotation at the beginning of this section is about the information highway (a term commonly used for the Internet in the 1990s), but social scientists argued that it applied as well to all computer technology. Technology critics such as Jeremy Rifkin consider the reduction in the human labor and time required to produce goods and services to be one of the horrific consequences of computers and automation. Perhaps, with a narrowly focused view, they appeared to be right in the first few decades of computer use.

The number of bank tellers dropped by about 37% between 1983 and 1993. Government agencies and private financial companies predicted that more teller jobs would disappear in the next ten years because of automation and electronic banking services. Engineers used slide rules since the 17th-century. Electronic calculators made them obsolete; the jobs of manufacturing and selling them are gone. The number of telephone switchboard operators dropped from 421,000 in 1970 to 164,000 in 1996. The jobs of 35,000 electric meter readers disappeared as utility companies installed electronic devices that broadcast meter readings to company computers. Similar technology monitors vending machines and oil wells, reducing the number of people needed to check on them in person. The jobs of building, selling, and repairing typewriters have disappeared. Banks reduced the number of customer-service employees when they began using computers to handle customer inquiries. Railroads computerized their dispatch operations and eliminated hundreds of employees. The New York Stock Exchange eliminated the last 150 of its floor couriers who carried messages between brokers. "What was once done by our people is now done by technology," said an Exchange official. Travel agencies closed as consumers made airplane reservations online. During the early 1990s, newspapers were full of headlines about layoffs and corporate "downsizing." IBM, General Motors, Sears, and other large companies laid off tens of thousands of workers. Loss of jobs continues in the 2000s. Digital cameras put film processors out of work; Kodak laid off thousands of employees. Shopping on the Internet and self-service checkout systems in stores have reduced the need for sales clerks. As people bought or copied more music online, Tower Records went out of business in 2006 and laid off 3000 employees. (Hundreds of other music stores closed in 2006.) As use of cell phones increased, the number of employees in the wired telecommunications industry dropped by more than 120,000.[3]

There is no doubt that technology in general and computers in particular eliminate jobs. Human labor is a resource. By making tasks more efficient, computers reduce the number of workers required to carry out the tasks. The goals of technology include a reduction in the resources needed to accomplish a result and an increase in productivity and standard of living. If we look back at the examples of lost jobs described above, we see that many of them accompanied increased productivity. While the number of telephone operators was dropping by more than 60% between 1970 and 1996, the number of long-distance calls increased from 9.8 billion to 94.9 billion.* The railroad ships more tons per worker with its computer system. Stock brokerages and insurance companies process more orders with fewer people. Manufacturing productivity in the U.S. more than doubled between 1980 and 2002.[4] During the recession of 2001, overall productivity continued to increase at a much higher rate than in previous recessions; economists credited faster microprocessors and increased investment in technology. Productivity growth fluctuates, but the trend is upward.

A successful technology eliminates some jobs, but creates others. With a sewing machine a seamstress could make more than two shirts a day. Rather than loss of jobs, the sewing machine meant a reduction in the price of clothes, more demand, and ultimately hundreds of thousands of new jobs.[5†] It is obvious now that computers created new products and services, whole new industries, and millions of jobs. From the electronic calculators that replaced slide rules to the networks and cell phones that replaced telephone operators to the social-networking Web sites that created a new phenomenon, the new devices and services all represent new jobs. The World Wide Web contributed to the creation of about 100,000 new Internet-related jobs in 1996. By 1997 more than 109,000 people worked in the cellular communications industry in the United States. By 1998 the Semiconductor Industry Association reported that chip makers employed 242,000 workers, directly, in the U.S. and 1.3 million workers indirectly. The chip industry, which did not exist before the microprocessor was invented in the 1970s, ranked fourth among U.S. industries by annual revenue. Although e-commerce and automatic checkout in stores reduces demand for sales clerks, that does not mean there are fewer people in

---

*In the 1940s human operators, plugging wires into boards, did almost all the routing and switching of telephone calls. The volume of telephone calls in the U.S. has increased so much that, if this work were done manually instead of with computers, it would require half the adult population of the country as telephone operators.[6]

† Sewing machines were first marketed to factory owners, just as computers were first used by large companies. Isaac Singer had the insight to sell them directly to women, in a parallel to the eventual shift from corporation-owned mainframes to personal computers for consumers.

these jobs. Employment increased 3% in the retail sector between 2003 and 2006, while employment overall increased 6%, according to the Economic Policy Institute. Contrary to predictions, the number of bank tellers climbed to new highs.[7]

Countless new products based on computer technology create jobs: DVD players, iPods, medical devices, 3-D printers, navigation systems for cars, cell phones, and so on and on. New technologies and products create jobs in design, marketing, manufacture, sales, customer service, repair, and maintenance. New technical jobs also create jobs for such support staff as receptionists, janitors, and stock clerks. The enormous growth of retail sales on the Web contributed to an increase in jobs in the package shipping industry. U.S. companies sold more than $400 billion of software for personal computers in 2004. Consumers spent $4 billion on online services (such as online tax preparation). The U.S. Department of Labor's Bureau of Labor Statistics (BLS) reported more than 500,000 people working in data entry and more than 2,300,000 people working in a variety of professional level computer occupations in 2004. According to the Information Technology Association, 10.5 million people worked in information technology jobs in the U.S. by 2004. In 2005 governments, businesses, and organizations worldwide spent an estimated $1 trillion on information technology. That money paid for a very large number of jobs.[8]

A harpist described how technologies eliminated the jobs of musicians:[9] Piano rolls, automated player pianos, and recordings replaced the live piano player at silent movies. Juke boxes replaced live bands in bars. Records and CDs replaced live orchestras and bands at Broadway shows, dance performances, and weddings. There is another way to look at the same facts. A few hundred years ago, listening to professional-quality music was a rare luxury for most people. Only the wealthy could hire professional musicians to perform for them. Technology, including electricity, radio, CDs, DVDs, iPods, data-compression algorithms, and the Web, brought the cost of an individual "performance" in a private home (or out on a hiking trail) down so low that music is available to almost anyone. The effect on employment? Tens of thousands of musicians make a living, many a fortune, in jazz, country, classical, zydeco, new age, rock, and rap music. In the long term, if technology brings the cost of a product or service down far enough to expand the market, more people will work in that field, be it music or package delivery. Many new jobs created by computer technology are ones not imagined or possible before. They range from jobs of great social value (e.g., making lifesaving and life-enhancing devices) to entertainment and sports (e.g., computer game designers and even professional computer game players and video game coaches). Ten years ago, who would have imagined people would buy (and hence others would produce, market, and sell) ringtones for their phones?

What is the overall effect of computerization on employment rates? Does it create more jobs than it destroys? Measuring the effects of computers alone is difficult, because other factors influence employment trends, but we can look at overall numbers. In the U.S., in the ten years between 1993 and 2002, 309.9 million jobs ended—a huge number to anyone who has not seen these figures before. But 327.7 million jobs were added in the same period, for a net increase of 17.8 million jobs. This "job churn," roughly 30 million jobs opening and closing each year,* is typical of a flexible economy. In stagnant economies, people do not change jobs often. The BLS projects that the net increase in jobs for the period 2004 to 2014 will be 18.9 million.[10]

Long-term net social gains from new jobs are not of much interest to a person who is fired. The loss of a job is immediate and personal and can be devastating to the individual and his or her family. When large numbers of people lose their jobs in one small community or within a short time, difficult social problems occur. Thus, there is a need for people (individual workers, employers, and communities) and institutions (e.g., schools) to be more flexible and to plan for change. There are roles for education professionals who do long-range planning, entrepreneurs and nonprofit organizations that provide training programs, large companies that can retrain their employees, financial institutions that fund start-up companies, and so on. In Section 6.2.4 we look at how technology can help in the process of finding a new job.

Technology, economic factors, and employment

Unemployment rates fluctuate. We saw that new technology reduces employment in specific areas and in the short term, but it is obvious that computer technology did not cause mass unemployment. Those who continually predict mass unemployment see only the old, preexisting jobs that are lost. They lack the imagination or the knowledge of history and economics to see that people create new jobs. The next big breakthrough in technology, perhaps a major advance in artificial intelligence (AI) or robotics, will generate the same scary projections. We briefly consider other factors that affect employment levels.

Consider the times of significant unemployment in the U.S. in the last century. Technology did not cause the Great Depression in the 1930s. Economists and historians attribute the depression to a variety of factors including "business cycles," the then-new Federal Reserve Bank's inept manipulation of interest rates, and that old standby, "greed." Unemployment was very low during the Vietnam War, then high during a recession in the early 1980s and another in the early 1990s. But growth in use of computers has been dramatic and continuous, especially since the mid-1970s, when personal computers began to appear. When most of the country had recovered from the recession of the early 1990s, the California economy remained depressed. Was it because California was "computerizing" faster than the rest of the country? No. California suffered from loss of jobs in the defense and aerospace industries, as federal funding in these areas declined, and from the large number of businesses fleeing the state because California's tax and regulatory policies were more costly than those of other states. Demographics also have an impact on growth and decline of various job sectors. The BLS predicts increases in a whole range of medical jobs because of the aging Baby Boomers and the increase in the elderly population.

---

*Roughly half are seasonal jobs that appear and disappear each year.

Airplanes, automobiles, radio, television, computers, much medical technology, and so on did not exist before the 20th-century. The use of telephones and electricity was minimal. Throughout the 20th-century, there was an enormous increase in technology and a decrease in jobs in such areas as agriculture and saddle making. If technology's overall impact was to destroy jobs, there should have been fewer people working in 2000 than in 1900. But with a population that approximately quadrupled between 1900 and 2000, the U.S. unemployment rate was 4% in 2000, lower than throughout most of the century. (One segment of the population is working less: children. In 1870 the average age for starting work was 13; by 1990 it was 19.1. In the early 20th-century, children worked long days on farms and in factories and mines. Technology eliminated many of the jobs they did.)

The Organisation for Economic Co-operation and Development (OECD), an international organization whose members include most of Western Europe, North America, Japan, Australia, and New Zealand, studied employment trends in 25 countries from 1950 to 1994. OECD concluded that unemployment stems from "policies . . . [that] have made economies rigid, and stalled the ability . . . to adapt."[11] The study suggested that "unemployment should be addressed not by seeking to slow the pace of change, but rather by restoring economies' and societies' capacity to adapt to it." Unemployment in many European countries is much higher than in the U.S. and has been for a long time. But Europe is not more technologically advanced or computerized than the United States. The differences have more to do with differences in flexibility in the economies and other political, social, and economic factors. The OECD report says that history has shown that when technological progress accelerates, so do growth, living standards, and employment."[12]

But are we earning less?

Economists agree that the average hourly pay of manufacturing workers quadrupled (in constant dollars) between 1909 and the mid-1970s. They disagree about the last quarter of the 20th-century. Wages appeared to decline as much as 10% after 1970. This is sometimes cited as an indication that the value of human work is declining as computers take over tasks people used to do. Others see it as an indication that computers decreased, not increased, productivity. However, fringe benefits rose significantly, increasing total compensation by about 17% according to some experts, but other experts disagree. Some economists believe the apparent decline resulted from improper computation of the Consumer Price Index.[13] Two researchers, Michael Cox and Richard Alm, decided to avoid the problems of using income and inflation data and, instead, look at direct measures of consumption and leisure. Figure 6.1 includes a sampling of data they collected from a variety of government and industry sources. They report also that attendance at operas and symphonies doubled (per person), recreation spending more than tripled (per person), and spending on toys quadrupled (per child).[14] The data indicate that, while computerization increased, so did many measures of real income

	1970	1997[a]
Average new home size (sq. ft.)	1500	2150
New homes with central heat and air-conditioning	34%	81%
Households with two or more vehicles	29.3%	61.9%
Households with color TV	39.9%	97.9%
Households with video tape recorders (VCRs)	0	89%
Households with microwave oven	less than 1%	89.5%
Housing units lacking complete plumbing	6.9%	2.3%
Median household net worth	$27,938	$59,398
Shipments of recreational vehicles	30,300	281,000
Average household ownership of sporting equipment	$769	$1895
Americans taking cruises	0.5 million	4.7 million

[a]A few figures are for 1995 or 1996. All dollar figures in both columns are in 1997 dollars.

Figure 6.1 Living Standards and Leisure in the Computer Age[15]

and quality of life. Figure 6.2 takes a longer perspective and uses a different measure. It shows how much time an average worker had to work to earn enough money to buy food and luxuries. Technology is responsible for a large share of the dramatic reductions.[16] Simply comparing income and inflation data also misses improvements in product quality and comfort due to technology. Cars are safer now. Dentists and orthodontists can now wave a wand through a patient's mouth to make dental appliances such as retainers and

Product	1900	1920[a]	1970	1990–2000[b]
Milk (half-gallon)	56 min.	37 min.	10 min.	7 min.
Hershey chocolate bar	20 min.	6 min.	1.8 min.	2.1 min.
Chicken (3 pounds)	$2\frac{2}{3}$ hrs.	$2\frac{1}{2}$ hrs.	22 min.	14 min.
Electricity (100 kWh)	$107\frac{1}{4}$ hrs.	$13\frac{1}{2}$ hrs.	39 min.	38 min.
Bread (one pound)		13 min.	4 min.	3.5 min.
Oranges (one dozen)		69 min.	15 min.	9 min.
Gasoline (one gallon)		32 min.	6.4 min.	5.7 min.
Phone call (3 min., coast to coast)		30 hrs.	24 min.	2 min.
Air travel (100 miles)		$12\frac{3}{4}$ hrs.	102 min.	62 min.
Computing power (1 MIPS[c])			1.2 lifetimes	9 min.

[a]The air travel datum is for 1930.

[b]Figures in this column are from various years in the late 1990s and 2000.

[c]"MIPS" means *million instructions per second*.

Figure 6.2 Declining Cost Measured in Working Time[17]

dentures from 3-D images instead of stuffing a patient's mouth with wax to create wax molds. Ultrasound machines have replaced radioactive dyes for some medical tests.

Since the beginning of the Industrial Revolution, working hours have declined. We no longer routinely work 10–12 hour days, six days a week (unless we choose to). People can count working hours, like income data, in various ways, supporting different conclusions. Some economists report a significant decline in working hours since the 1950s. Others say working hours have not declined significantly since the end of World War II. Many people continue to work more hours while income rises because they have higher expectations. They consider the life style now possible to be essential. Another reason, according to labor economist Ronald Ehrenberg, is that quirks in the tax and compensation structure encourage employers to have regular workers work overtime rather than hire additional employees.[18] A third reason is that taxes take a larger percentage of income than they did in the past. People have to work more hours for the same take-home pay.* Thus it is not clear at all that we are earning less, but if we are, the causes include social, political, and economic factors as well as the impact of technology.

6.2.2 CHANGING SKILL LEVELS

Some who are concerned about the impact of computers on employment acknowledge that, in the past, technology led to new jobs and products. They argue that the impact of computers is different and more negative. Computers differ from earlier technologies in several key ways.

Computers eliminate a much wider variety of jobs than any single new technological advance in the past. The impact of new machines or technologies tended to be concentrated in one industry or activity. Earlier automation eliminated primarily manufacturing jobs, but computers automate services, such as those of telephone operators and receptionists, just as easily. The transition to new jobs will be more difficult because of the broad impact. The pace of improvement in speed, capability, and cost for computers is much faster than for any previous technology. The pace itself will cause more job disruption as people continually face job elimination and the need to retrain.

The new jobs created by computers are different from the jobs eliminated. The hundreds of thousands of new computer engineering and systems analyst jobs require a college degree. The jobs of telephone operator, bank teller, and customer-service representative do not. At the same time, computers eliminate more high-skilled jobs than older technologies. Will jobs diverge into two distinct groups: high-paying jobs for a highly skilled and highly trained intellectual elite, and fewer low-paying jobs for people without computer skills and advanced education?

Although it often seems that our times and problems are new and different from what came before, similar concerns arose for other technologies. The steam engine and

---

*Estimates vary. The Tax Foundation reported that in 2007 we paid, on average, 33% of income for all taxes, compared to 25% in 1950.[19]

WORKERS

In the exhibit "Workers" by Brazilian photographer Sebastião Salgado, a photograph shows dozens of laborers climbing out of a huge pit, a gold mine in Brazil. The men, packed tightly, one above another, climb 60-foot stick ladders carrying bags of dirt on their backs. In the pit, hundreds of workers dig and fill their sacks. Another photograph shows a worker at a sulfur mine in Indonesia holding a scarf over his mouth for protection from the thick dust. A third shows the huge earth-cutting drill, perhaps 35 feet in diameter, that bored the tunnel in the English Channel. Two skilled men are working on the drill.[20]

Aside from the extraordinary power of these photographs, one of the striking things about them is how differently someone with a positive view of technology and someone with a negative view would interpret them. To the former, the photos show dramatically how technology eliminates back-breaking, unhealthy physical labor and raises the standard of living of workers. To the latter, the photos show the evils of technology: Mines and tunnels gouge the earth and threaten the health of workers. The reduction of workers from a few hundred in the mine to two on the drill shows the unemployment caused by technology.

electricity brought enormous change in jobs, making many obsolete. When economists Claudia Goldin and Lawrence Katz researched earlier periods of rapid technological development, they found that the education system quickly adapted to train children in the necessary skills. They pointed out that a bookkeeper in 1890 had to be highly skilled, whereas a bookkeeper in 1920 was a high-school graduate using an early form of an adding machine. In the 19th-century, skilled workers earned increasingly more than manual laborers, but the trend reversed in the early 20th-century, because more people went to high school and the new technologies of that era reduced the skill level needed for white-collar jobs. As demand increases for new skills, people acquire them. For example, in 1900 only 0.5 people out of every 1000 in the U.S. worked as an engineer. After the huge growth in technology during the 20th-century, 7.6 out of every 1000 people were engineers.[21]

Complex interactive computer systems guide workers through steps of jobs that required extensive training before. Performance-support software and training software empower lower-skilled workers and make the training process for complex jobs cheaper, faster, and easier. Such systems, for example, guide auditors through an audit of a securities firm, help employees at financial institutions carry out transactions, and train salespeople. The National Association of Securities Dealers reported that its auditors were fully competent after one year using such a system, compared to two and a half years

Serra Pelada, Para State, Brazil, 1986

2002 © Sebastião SALGADO/AMAZONAS Images/CONTACT Press Images

without it. They saved more than $400,000 in annual training costs. Companies are more willing to hire people without specific skills when they can train new people quickly and use automated support systems. The benefits occur throughout a wide range of job levels. Several large companies, including Walgreen, hire previously unemployable people with mental and physical disabilities. They perform their jobs with the help of electronic gadgets and computer systems. Some of the systems are specially designed. Some are the ordinary computer and automation tools that workers use in many workplaces.[22]

The BLS expects many jobs to be available that require little, if any, computer skill. Areas in which the BLS expects the most new jobs to be created between 2004 and 2014 include retail sales, nursing, janitorial service, home health aid, and food preparation and service.[23]

Do automated systems mean fewer jobs for high-skilled workers? Will human intelligence in employment be "devalued"? Software makes decisions that used to require trained, thinking human beings. Computers could take over many white-collar, professional jobs. Computer programs analyze loan applications and decide which to approve. Some programs are better than people at predicting which applicants are likely to default on their loans. Design jobs have become automated. For example, software to design the electrical layout for new housing developments can do in half an hour a job that would have taken a high-paid employee 100 hours.[24] Even computer programming is automated. Some computer programs write computer programs, reducing the need for trained programmers. Although it still requires highly trained engineers, there is a great degree of automation in the layout of computer chips. Programming tools enable nonspecialists to do certain kinds of programming, design Web pages, and so on.

The printing press put scribes out of work when writing was a skill possessed by only a small, "highly trained" elite. Recall from Chapter 1 that machines that did simple arithmetic shocked and disturbed people in the 17th- and 18th-centuries. People thought arithmetic required uniquely human intelligence. In the past human imagination and desires continued to find new fields of work, both physical and mental, to replace those no longer needed. They continue to do so today. In spite of the trend to automate high-skill jobs, the BLS projects that the number of management, financial, software, and other professional jobs, will increase significantly between 2004 and 2014, and that computer software engineer will be one of the fastest growing occupations.[25]

6.2.3 A GLOBAL WORKFORCE

Offshoring

Over many decades in the 20th-century, as transportation and communications improved, manufacturing jobs moved from wealthier countries to less wealthy countries, especially in Asia. The difference in pay rates was large enough to make up for the extra transportation costs. The Internet and the Web reduced "transportation" costs for many kinds of information work to almost zero. With the ease of working with people and companies in other countries, *offshoring of jobs** has become a phenomenon and a political issue.

Data processing and computer programming were among the first service jobs to go offshore, many to India. The lure is the large pool of low-skilled workers, in the first case, and well-trained, English-speaking computer programmers, in the second. By 2004, 12% of U.S. information technology companies had moved some of their operations to other countries. The example best known to American consumers is the move of customer-service call centers and software help desks to India and other countries. Offshoring takes many other forms too. Companies send back-office jobs, such as payroll processing, to other countries. Some hire companies in other countries to manage their computers and networks. Actuaries in India process insurance claims for a British insurance company. Doctors in the U.S. dictate notes on patient visits and send digitized voice files to India, where medical scribes transcribe them and return text files. Rather than contracting with companies in another country, some large companies set up divisions (for example, for research and development) offshore.

India has been the most popular country for offshoring work from the U.S., but companies are moving work to Canada, China, Brazil, and other places. Before the 1990s Ireland was one of the poorest countries in the European Union. Its high-tech "boom," a side effect of U.S. offshoring, made it one of the richest. U.S. companies supply intellectual property (in pharmaceuticals as well as software and electronics), and Ireland produces products for export. Part of the lure of Ireland is its relatively low corporate tax rate.

In 2005 offshoring of skilled work, sometimes called *knowledge work*, increased dramatically, generating more worries about threats of job loss, this time for high-paying jobs held by the middle class. Companies send off work in legal services, aircraft engineering, biotechnology and pharmaceutical research, and stock analysis and other financial services. Individuals and small businesses hire people in other countries for services such as tutoring and designing logos and Web sites. Much of this work goes to India which has a large pool of highly educated people. In some fields, including computer science, one reason for offshoring is that there are not enough trained professionals in the United States. Enrollment in the computer science major dropped significantly after the "dot-com bust" in the early 2000s, but the demand for computer and network specialists remains very high.

The impact of offshoring

Many social scientists, politicians, and organizations view the globalization of the workforce as a terribly negative phenomenon, one of the negative results of information

---

*The term *outsourcing* refers to the phenomenon where a company pays other companies to build parts for its products or provide services (such as marketing, research, or customer service) instead of performing those tasks itself. This is very common. Generally the companies that do the work are in the same country as the company that hires them. The term *offshoring* refers to hiring companies or employees in other countries.

INSHORING: TWO PERSPECTIVES

Americans working for foreign companies

Americans used to import cars from Japan. Now Japanese car makers build cars in the United States. Otto Bock Health Care, a German company that makes sophisticated microprocessor-controlled artificial limbs, offshores research, development, and manufacturing to several countries including China, Estonia, and the U.S. The German software company SAP employs thousands of people in the United States. Offshoring for a German company means *inshoring* for the U.S. People in the U.S. work for Sony, Ikea, Bayer, Novartis, Unilever, Toyota. Overall, almost 5% of U.S. workers work for foreign companies, and those jobs pay 30% more than the U.S. median. In a global, interconnected economy, offshoring is one more way of providing products and services to consumers more effectively. How does it differ when a company based in one state of the U.S. moves part of its operations to another state?

Indian perspectives[26]

For many years, Indian computer scientists and engineers have flocked to the U.S. for jobs, wealth, and entrepreneurial opportunities, while Indian information technology (IT) companies perform services and provide call centers for foreign companies. Critics, from the Indian perspective, fear a talent drain. They worry that India is not growing its own high-tech industry. Some companies that had developed their own software products stopped doing so, in order not to compete with the U.S. companies for which they provide services.

Others see more positive results developing over time. India's IT companies began to provide sophisticated services well beyond the call centers many Americans encounter. They develop and service software. Offshored jobs provide professional training and experience, including experience working in a global business environment. They provide confidence and high salaries that permit the savings so helpful for taking risks and starting one's own company. An Indian entrepreneur observes that Indian culture generally had a negative view of entrepreneurs, but that has changed. Some highly trained Indian computer scientists and engineers who went to the U.S. for jobs are returning to work or start businesses at home. Providing IT services for foreign companies, from low-level services to highly sophisticated work, is now a multibillion dollar industry in India.

and communications technology and corporate greed for increased profit. From the perspective of workers in developed countries, they argue, it means millions of jobs lost, accompanied by lower pay and reduced standard of living.

Forrester Research estimates that 3.3 million white-collar jobs will have left the U.S. for other countries between 2000 and 2015. The BLS reports that 2.5% of mass layoffs (50 or more people for more than a month) come from offshoring jobs.* So the percentage of job losses due to offshoring is small. Offshoring will probably increase. What is its potential? Economist Alan Blinder, a former vice chair of the Federal Reserve, studied the types of knowledge and service jobs that could be performed at distant places—candidates for offshoring in the near future.[27] He estimated that 28–42 million people currently work in such jobs in the United States. Thus he sees offshoring as potentially very disruptive. However, Blinder emphasizes that offshoring means massive transition, not massive unemployment.

The lost jobs are obvious. The discussion in Section 6.2.1 about jobs eliminated and created by computer and communications technology in general, suggests how offshoring creates new jobs. Lower labor costs and increased efficiency reduce prices for consumers. Lower prices encourage more use and make new products and services feasible. Manufacturing of computer hardware went offshore early. That was responsible for part of the drop in the cost of hardware. The resulting lower prices contributed to the enormous growth of the industry. The U.S. is an exporter of services (banking, engineering, accounting, for example). The same technologies that facilitate offshoring make it easier and cheaper for U.S. service companies to sell more of their services to other countries. Offshoring creates jobs for both low- and high-skilled workers in less wealthy countries. The combination of increased income and reduced prices for goods and services helps the economic growth of these countries. This is likely to yield more jobs on both sides.

Blinder believes that we should plan for a major shift in the U.S. toward jobs that require presence. His examples, from taxi driver to doctor, include low-skill and high-skill jobs. He opposes attempts to stop offshoring, but warns that we must prepare by shifting emphasis in education. He expects that the flexibility of the U.S. economy will help it adapt more quickly and successfully to offshoring than developed countries with more rigid economies.[28] As we observed in Section 6.2.1 about technology-induced job loss, long-term gains from new jobs are little comfort to people who lose theirs. Helpful responses to the personal and social disruptions offshoring can cause include those we mentioned in Section 6.2.1, among them: flexibility, planning, and changes in educational programs.

Problems and side effects of offshoring

As customers and companies are finding, offshoring has problems.

Consumers have many complaints about customer-service call centers in foreign countries: Foreign accents are difficult to understand. Service personnel are not familiar with the product or service the consumer is asking about—they just read from a manual. The workers experience problems too. Because of time differences, customer service

---

*The calculation excludes farm and seasonal work layoffs. The percent of all layoffs due to offshoring is smaller.

workers in India work at night. Some find the relatively high pay worth the disruption to their lives; others quit. Problems of customer satisfaction, training, and less-than-expected savings led some companies to conclude that offshoring did not work well for them. (Some developed other cost-saving arrangements. For example, a hotel chain and flower seller agreed to share call center employees in the U.S.)

Employees in companies that send projects offshore find they need new job skills. A software engineer, for example, might need to manage people and projects in other countries. Managers and businesspeople find they must schedule meetings during the work hours of workers in another country.

Some small technology companies have found that increased demand for highly skilled workers in India has already forced salaries up. One U.S. entrepreneur said salaries of engineers he hired in India went from 25% of U.S. salaries to 75% within two years. Hiring them is no longer worthwhile for his company.

The problems of offshoring should not surprise us. A theme running through this book is that new things often have unexpected problems. We discover them and find solutions, adapt to changes, or decide not to use certain options. Simple economics tells us that salaries will rise in offshoring destinations. When the gap between salaries in the home and destination countries is no longer big enough to cover the other expenses of offshoring, the trend will decline.

> *When products cross borders, bullets don't.*
> —Unknown

Ethics of hiring foreign workers

There is much controversy about both the economics and ethics of offshoring. In this section we apply some of the ethical theories we presented in Chapter 1 to analyze the practice from an ethical perspective. This is a good example for trying to distinguish economic advantage from ethical arguments. We consider Kantian and utility approaches in the analysis. Several countries have passed legislation to restrict the hiring of foreign workers for some industries. The discussion here might provide insight into the ethics of such legislation. Here is the scenario we examine:

> You are a manager at a software company about to begin a large software project. You will need to hire dozens of new programmers. Using the Internet for communication and software delivery, you can hire programmers in another country at a lower salary than programmers in your country. Should you do this?[29]

For the discussion, we assume the software company is the U.S. and the manager is choosing between U.S. and Indian programmers.

The people most obviously affected by the decision in this case are the Indian programmers and the U.S. programmers you might hire. Before we consider other people, we will use utilitarianism and Kant's principle about treating people as ends in themselves to generate some ideas, questions, and observations about these two groups. How can we compare the impact on utility from the two choices? The number of people hired will be about the same in either case. There does not appear to be any reason, from an ethical point of view, for placing a higher value on the utility of one group of programmers merely because of their nationality. Shall we weigh the utilities of the programmers according to the number of dollars they will receive? That favors hiring the U.S. programmers. Or should we weigh utility by comparing the pay to the average salary in each country? That favors hiring the Indians. The utility obtained from a job for an individual programmer depends on the availability of other jobs. Are there more opportunities to earn a comparable income in the U.S. or in India? We see that a calculation of net utility for the programmers depends on how one evaluates the utility of the job for each group of programmers.

What happens when we apply Kant's principle? When we hire people for a job, we are interacting with them in a limited role. We are making a trade, money for work. The programmers are a means to an end: producing a marketable product at a reasonable price. Kant does not say that people must not be treated as a means to an end, but rather that they should not be treated merely as such. Kant does not seem helpful here, especially if we observe that the hiring decision does not treat the potential programmers of the two countries differently in a way that has to do with ends and means.

Are you taking advantage of the Indian programmers, perhaps exploiting them by paying them less than you would have to pay the U.S. programmers? Some people believe it is unfair to both the U.S. and Indian programmers that the Indians get the jobs by charging less money. It is equally logical, however, to argue that paying the higher rate for U.S. programmers is wasteful, or charity, or simply overpayment. What makes either pay level more "right" than the other? Buyers would like to pay less for what they buy, and sellers would like to get a higher price for their goods and services. There is nothing automatically unethical about choosing the cheaper of two products, services, or employees.

We can argue that treating the Indian programmers as ends in themselves includes respecting the choices and trade-offs they make to better their lives according to their own judgment, in particular in offering to work for lower wages than U.S. programmers. But there are special cases in which we might decide otherwise. First, suppose your company is doing something to limit the other options of the Indian programmers. If your company is lobbying for import restrictions on software produced by Indian firms, for example, thus decreasing the availability of other programming jobs in India, then you are manipulating the programmers into a situation where they have few or no other choices. In that case, you are not respecting their freedom and allowing them to compete fairly. You are, then, not treating them as ends in themselves. We will assume for the rest of the discussion that your company is not doing anything like this.

Another reason we might decide that the Indian programmers are not being treated as ends in themselves, or with respect for their human dignity, is that their working conditions would be worse than the working conditions that U.S. workers expect (or that law in the U.S. requires). The programmers might not get medical insurance. They might work in rundown, crowded offices, lacking air-conditioning. Is hiring them to work in such conditions unethical, or does it give them an opportunity to improve conditions in their country? Whether or not it is ethically required, there are several reasons why you might pay more (or provide better working conditions) than market conditions in India require: a sense of shared humanity that motivates you to want to provide conditions you consider desirable, a sense of generosity (i.e., willingness to contribute to the improvement of the standard of living of people in a country less rich than your own) and economic benefit; paying more than expected might get you high morale, productivity, and company loyalty. [30]

Governments have passed many laws to require that the same salary be paid to all workers when a large group of potential workers (foreigners, ethnic minorities, low-skilled workers, teenagers) is willing to work for lower pay. The main argument is that such laws will prevent employers from exploiting the less advantaged workers. Historically, one of the effects of these laws is that the traditionally higher-paid group gets most of the jobs. (Often that has been the intent of the law.) In this case, the almost certain result would be hiring the U.S. programmers. The law, or an ethical requirement that the pay of the Indian programmers and the U.S. programmers be the same, would protect the high incomes of programmers in the U.S. and the profits of companies that pay higher salaries. New workers or businesses that are trying to compete by lowering prices generally oppose such requirements.

Your decision affects other people besides the programmers: your customers, the owners or stockholders of your company, and, indirectly and to a smaller degree, people in other businesses. Hiring the Indian programmers increases the utility of your company and customers. The customers benefit from the lower price of the product, and the owners of the company benefit from the profits. If the product is successful, the company might pay for advertising, distribution, and so on, providing jobs for others in the United States. On the other hand, if you hire U.S. programmers, they will spend more of their earnings in the U.S. than the Indian programmers, generating jobs and income for others in the U.S. If the product is not profitable because of higher programming costs, the company could go out of business, with a negative impact on all its employees and suppliers. To which of all these people do you have responsibilities or obligations? As a manager of the company, you have an obligation to help make the product and the company successful, to manage the project to maximize profit (not in a manner independent of ethical considerations, as we noted in Chapter 1, but consistent with them). Unless the owners of the company have a policy to improve the standard of living of people in other countries or to "Buy American," your obligation to them includes hiring competent workers at the best price. You have some responsibility for the fate of other company employees who might lose their jobs if you do a poor job of managing the project. You do not have any special obligation to other service providers you could hire, nor to people seeking jobs as programmers in either country.

Although hiring lower-paid workers in other countries is often described as ethically suspect, this discussion suggests that there is no strong ethical argument for that view.

6.2.4 GETTING A JOB

Some of the same technologies that eliminate jobs make new ones easier to find. Computer technology and the Web have changed much about the process of getting a job, whether replacing one lost to technology, or finding one's first job, or for any other reason.

Learning about jobs and companies

The Web has made it much easier to find information about jobs and employers. We can learn about companies and nonprofit organizations from their Web sites. We can read company histories and annual reports online. We can learn from the many forums and networks on sites like Jobster, Yahoo, and so on, where employees discuss a company, describe what it is like to work there, and answer questions from job seekers. Companies set up recruiting pages on social-networking sites.

Since Monster.com appeared, many more sites have sprung up to provide advice and to send résumés to employers with relevant job openings. Such sites include specialized job search engines to help find job openings. You can easily search for jobs that have, or do not have, features you want, or want to avoid, such as "overtime," "dress code," or "night work." Web sites with job listings are popular in many countries. (China has several competing sites.) These sites help people find good jobs in other towns and cities if jobs at home are declining. We can learn about climate, schools, entertainment and religious facilities in distant towns on the Web before spending time and money for travel to a few good prospects. In fact, we can interview at some distant companies without traveling: Some companies conduct job interviews at online virtual communities (such as Second Life).

For people whose jobs were eliminated by technology or for people who just want to keep up with new technologies, online training programs can help them to learn new skills. Such programs are particularly convenient for people with limited hours or resources.

In the past, job seekers researched jobs and companies in libraries and by telephone. They paid for services to help write résumés and send them out. They enrolled in retraining programs. The point here is that the Web makes more information and services available to a job seeker with much more convenience and for a lower price.

Learning about applicants and employees

Companies that developed some of the first search engines for the Web collected the archives of Usenet news groups (Internet forums from the 1980s) and made them available to demonstrate the power of their search tools. Participants in the groups had thought their

VERIFYING WORKERS[31]

There are frequent proposals for programs to prevent illegal immigrants (or legal immigrants without work permits) from working in the United States. The government has done small-scale tests of several programs. The idea is that whenever an employer offers any person a job, the employer would have to verify the person's right to work by checking an automated system maintained by a government agency (the Social Security Administration or the Department of Homeland Security [DHS], for example). For such a scheme to succeed, each person needs a "fraud-proof" ID card. The immediate threat of such a system is the loss of liberty to work. "It is absolutely unprecedented," said congressman Steve Chabot, "to say that the government must grant affirmative permission every time any employee is hired."[32] The maintenance of a system that must have up-to-date information about every single person who has legal permission to work in the U.S. creates privacy threats as well. In addition to the reduction of freedom and privacy, such schemes have another serious flaw: errors in the database the government uses to verify legal status.

In experiments with an Immigration and Naturalization Service database used in one program, there was a delay of several weeks before approval for 19% of (legal) workers. This system test occurred in the 1990s. Newer systems are better. More than ten years later, however, with several bills in Congress to require that all employers get approval from government agencies for each new employee hired, problems remain. The Government Accountability Office (GAO) saw some potential in one program, the Basic Pilot Program, but it also identified several problems. A few thousand employers participate in this voluntary test program. The report shows that employers submitted roughly 657,000 verification requests in one year, and the government approved roughly 596,000. Are we confident that there were no errors among the more than 60,000 other cases? (At least one bill would have prohibited class action lawsuits against the government by workers fired because of errors.) Errors occur in both directions. The GAO said that the program could not detect identity fraud (people using valid documents, but not their own) so the program almost certainly approved many people it should not have approved. The DHS manually verified roughly 8,700 requests for work authorization that the automated systems of both the Social Security Administration and DHS had rejected. If expanded and required, the program would include more than eight million employers. How would the number of required manual verifications grow, and how many people would find their jobs delayed or lost? Approximately 65 million people in the U.S. change jobs or enter the workforce every year, so an error rate of one-tenth of 1% could mean denial of work for 65,000 people each year.

postings were as ephemeral as a conversation. Many people were stunned and horrified that some employers reviewed the old postings of job applicants. Now people post personal profiles on social-networking sites; they blog on personal and political topics. They share silly or offensive videos. Prospective and current employers look at all this. Some do quite extensive Internet searching for background information on applicants. Some read applicants' blogs to learn how well they write.

Some people, about to seek a job, try to clean up their online persona. They remove raunchy material, change their "favorite book" to one that appears intellectual, and so on. Some craft online profiles as carefully as people craft résumés. Of course, this means that some profiles are not reliable descriptions of a person, but that is no longer a surprise. On the other hand, some people naively think their blogs are invisible to prospective employers. They criticize the companies they are interviewing with, in their blogs, and wonder why they did not get the job.

Employers use other tools, beyond what people post about themselves on the Web, to learn about prospective and current employees. Some hire huge data-collection companies like ChoicePoint Inc. to run criminal-background checks. One large company fired employees and banned employees of subcontractors when searches turned up old convictions for small offenses (e.g., bouncing a $60 check, marijuana possession 14 years earlier). The policy of firing anyone with a criminal background is often a poor one, although in some sensitive businesses it might make sense. However, as we will see in Chapter 8, large databases with information going back many years are likely to contain many errors. The fired and banned employees included one with a dismissed criminal charge that still remained in the database and one who had no criminal history but who had a relative with a similar name and a criminal past. Good sense and fair treatment of applicants, employees, and contractors require that employers consider their policies carefully, understand the probability of errors, and set up a process for handling them before firing people.

6.3 The Work Environment

Computers are changing the work environment, in ways for the better, in others for the worse. We look at a few of these changes: telecommuting and the impact of computer technology on business structure, in this section, and monitoring of employees' work, physical location, e-mail, and Web activity in Section 6.5.

6.3.1 JOB DISPERSAL AND TELECOMMUTING

The Internet makes it possible for companies to locate in small towns and work with dispersed consultants instead of having hundreds or thousands of employees in larger population centers. Millions of people work without "going to work," that is, without going to their employers' (or their own) business offices. I will use the terms *telecommuting* and *telework* for several variations of such work paradigms. The most common meaning is working for an employer at a computer-equipped space in the employee's home. Some definitions include running one's own business from home using computers and telecommunications. In some jobs, such as sales and technical support, the office is mobile: The employee travels with a laptop computer and works in a car or at customer sites. Many people work on a laptop in a coffee shop, outdoors in a park, and on airplanes. In many fields, professional people, or *knowledge workers*, no longer have to live in the same city or state as their employer. Definitions of telework vary considerably; so do estimated numbers. A University of Maryland study in 2006 found that 2% of all working adults telecommuted fulltime, 9% telecommuted at least one day per week, and 8% had home businesses. Forty percent of IBM's 330,000 employees work away from the company office each day.[33]

Local governments and unions initially opposed telecommuting. Although it benefits teleworkers, their employers, and society in some ways, it also has a number of problems. Next we look at some of the pros and cons.

Benefits

Telework reduces overhead for employers and, in some cases, increases productivity. Productivity studies in areas where work is easy to measure (e.g., data entry) showed productivity gains of 15%. Replacing or shrinking large downtown offices, where real estate and office rentals are expensive, can generate significant savings. Many employees report that telecommuting has made them more productive, more satisfied with their jobs, and more loyal to their employers. One survey found that a large majority of workers whose jobs could permit teleworking would prefer to do so at least once a week.[34]

Telecommuting, and telecommunications generally, make it easier to work with clients, customers, and employees in other countries: At home, one can more easily work a few hours at night that are compatible with foreign time zones. Telecommuting reduces rush-hour traffic congestion and the associated pollution, gasoline use, and stress. Telecommuting reduces expenses for commuting and for work clothes. It saves time that workers can use for exercise, sleep, or more interaction with friends and family. It provides previously unavailable work options for some elderly or disabled people for whom commuting is physically difficult and expensive. It allows work to continue after blizzards, hurricanes, or other disasters close roads or discourage travel. Roughly 55% of woman-owned businesses are home-based businesses. Telecommuting, and the flexible hours it permits, can help reduce child-care expenses and give parents more time with their children. Employees and employers benefit when a person can accept a job with a company in a distant state without having to move. They can live in rural areas instead of big cities and suburbs if they prefer (in "electronic cottages," to use futurist Alvin Toffler's words). Two-career couples can work for companies hundreds or thousands of miles apart.

Problems

Many early telecommuters were volunteers, people who wanted to work at home. They were more likely to be independent workers. (Many were computer programmers.) As more businesses began to require employees to move their offices to their homes, problems arose, for both employees and employers.

Some employers see resentment among employees who must work at the office. Some found that the corporate loyalty of telecommuters weakened. Lacking immediate supervision, some people are less productive, while others work too hard and too long. The ease of working with people around the world leads some to work odd hours to match the time zones of clients. Some employees need better direction about what work and how much work their employer expects them to do at home. Being at home with children is an advantage for some telecommuters, but a distraction for others. In general, reducing the boundary between home and work causes stress for some workers and their families.

Some employees complain that the costs of office space and overhead that have been reduced for the employer have simply been shifted to the employee who must give up space at home for the office, learn how to maintain equipment that the company used to maintain, and so on. Some employees believe that by working at home they miss mentoring relationships and opportunities for advancement. For many people, the social interactions and camaraderie at work are a significant part of pleasant working conditions, so social isolation and low morale can be problems.

Telecommuters are likely to use their home computer for both personal and work activities. This raises a security issue. The employer might have a sophisticated firewall, antivirus software, and other security on the company network, but hackers and malicious software might more easily get into an employee's home computer. If the employee works with sensitive business information or personal information about employees or customers, the employer and employee must develop appropriate security practices and apply them conscientiously.

Problems led some companies to cut back telecommuting programs. Like many of the options provided by new technologies (or social trends), telecommuting may be very desirable for some employees and employers and of no use to others. But it is possible to reduce many problems related to telecommuting. Teleworkers use e-mail and instant messaging to stay in touch with coworkers. Employers address the social-isolation problem by holding regular meetings and encouraging other activities such as employee sports leagues, where employees interact in person. Some companies set up scattered offices in suburbs where telecommuting employees can meet and use support services and office equipment they do not have at home. Telecommuters reduce isolation by participating in activities of professional associations and other social networks. Some companies found significant improvements in employee satisfaction with their telecommuting jobs when they implemented such remedies.

Side effects

Aside from the direct advantages and disadvantages, teleworking has several side effects that might change various business and social aspects of how we live and work.

How does telework affect our sense of community? The Industrial Revolution led to a major shift in work patterns: Jobs moved to offices and factories. Working at home in the late 20th-century seemed new and unusual, but before the Industrial Revolution, most people worked at, or close to, home. Even in the past few centuries, working at home has not been uncommon. Writers traditionally work at home. Farmers work in the fields, but the farm office was in the house. Doctors, especially in small towns, had their medical offices in their homes. Shopkeepers often had an apartment behind or above the store. Perhaps writers are closest to modern information workers who telecommute in that they tend to work in isolation. Is that why we have an image of writers spending the evenings at coffee houses or at intellectual "salons" talking with other intellectuals? In the past, social isolation was not considered a problem for people who worked in or near their homes. They lived, worked, and socialized in communities. They had the grange, the church, and the community center. Urban policy researcher Joel Kotkin observes that telecommuting may encourage a return to involvement in one's local community.[35] Is he correct? Will being there all day, doing errands locally, eating in local restaurants, and so on, generate an interest in the safety, beauty, and vitality of the community that is less likely to develop when one returns home after dark, tired from a day at the office? On the other hand, now that we can communicate with people all over the world on the Internet, will home workers stay inside, communicating with unseen business and social acquaintances, and be just as unlikely to know their neighbors as many commuters are?

Restrictions on telecommuting

Telecommuting is very common now, so it might be surprising that local governments and labor unions attempted to stop it in the 1980s and that the Occupational Health and Safety Administration (OSHA) tried to regulate it. Why would they want to ban or discourage working at home?

Many communities argue that home businesses bring noise and traffic problems to residential neighborhoods. Thus local zoning laws often prohibit a home business from receiving deliveries or customers at the home. In many cities, an accountant who works in an office all day but has a tax-preparation business at home is breaking the law if clients come to the house in the evening.* These laws predate telework, but they apply to teleworkers as well. When home computers were still uncommon, the city of Chicago ordered a couple to stop using a computer at home to write textbooks and educational software because Chicago zoning laws restricted home work that used mechanical or electrical equipment.

---

*Zoning laws vary in different communities. These activities are not illegal everywhere.

Some kinds of home work have been outright illegal for a long time. For example, labor laws prohibit most home sewing work, where women sew garments for clothing manufacturers and are paid by the piece. Tens of thousands of women do this work in spite of the laws. Supporters of the laws argue that the women often get less than minimum wage, and it is difficult for the government to make sure that working conditions are safe and that children are not working in violation of child-labor laws. Critics of such laws argue that they deny the women a choice, and that unions, the main supporters of the laws, are primarily concerned with the difficulty of organizing the workers. In the 1980s various unions extended the campaign against home work to computer work. The view at the time seemed to be that most computer at-home work would be data-entry work done by low-paid women. A large union of service employees banned computer home work for its members. The AFL-CIO advocated a government ban on all computer at-home work. An AFL-CIO official warned that telecommuters might face working conditions like those of the 19th-century. A 1983 article titled "Home Computer Sweatshops" in *The Nation* reflected the same worries. The AFL-CIO official also commented that "It's very difficult to organize workers dispersed over a wide geographical area."[36]

Perhaps because telecommuters tend to be independent, middle-class workers, and perhaps because their numbers grew so fast, the efforts to stop computer work at home quickly turned futile. The mistaken views about who would do computer work at home and what the working conditions would be are reminders to be cautious about banning or restricting a new phenomenon based on guesses made before its applications and benefits, as well as problems, develop.

In 1999 OSHA declared that employers must ensure that workplaces in employees' homes meet legal regulations for workplaces at work. Regulations cover electric circuits, exit signs, hazardous chemicals, clutter, extensive reporting requirements, and so on. A furor arose over the prospect of applying workplace rules to homes and the possibility of employers and government officials inspecting people's homes. OSHA quickly backed down and said it would not hold employers responsible for conditions in the homes of telecommuters.

6.3.2 CHANGING BUSINESS STRUCTURES

There is much speculation about the impact of computer and telecommunications networks on the size and structure of business. Different observers see trends going in opposite directions.

Some see trends toward smaller businesses and more independent consultants and contractors—"information entrepreneurs," as they are sometimes called. It is easier for workers to work part time for different employers or clients, thus encouraging more information workers to become self-employed. We see an increase in "Mom and Pop multinationals," small businesses that operate globally via the Web. Many individuals have businesses on the Web. Photographers sell photos, craftsmakers sell crafts, musicians sell music, and so on. Small numbers of people start small companies constantly. Some quickly become huge successes, such as eBay, Google, Craigslist, and MySpace.

Some observers see computerization and the Web contributing to the growth of large, multinational corporations, with mergers between giant companies—communications and entertainment companies such as AOL with Time Warner, for instance. There have been many big mergers and buy outs (e.g., PayPal, Skype, MySpace, and YouTube), and more are negotiated regularly. At the same time, some large companies are splitting up into smaller units. A tremendous amount of business reorganization is taking place.

The Economist reported that the average number of employees per firm has been declining since the late 1960s. A study of a large sample of U.S. businesses found that between 1975 and 1985 the average number of employees per firm declined by 20%. It also found a correlation between high computer use and small firm size. The reason was not that computers were putting people out of work, but rather that firms narrowed the focus of their activities, purchasing more components and services from other firms. The study argued that computers and information networks reduced the cost and uncertainties of finding and relying on suppliers and consultants; hence businesses did more of it. The trend toward smaller companies continued. Between 1991 and 1995 companies with more than 5000 employees eliminated 3,377,000 jobs, but companies with fewer than 500 employees added almost 11 million employees.[37]

The legal, tax, and regulatory framework in which businesses operate has enormous impacts, sometimes quite indirect, sometimes unidentified, on business size, structure, and employment patterns. Such effects might prevent or slow changes that computers would otherwise cause. Complex regulatory laws, for example, tend to favor large firms, because they can spread the cost of a large legal department over a large sales volume—and discourage tiny firms (which are exempt from most regulations) from growing above the threshold where the regulations apply.

The availability of IT enabled many businesses to give workers more information and more decision-making authority, thus "flattening hierarchies" and "empowering workers." Manufacturing plant workers have access to online inventory and purchasing information and make decisions about production schedules. Credit-card company service representatives, with immediate access to account information, can make decisions to cancel a late charge or finance charge, for example. The need for middle managers decreased, and companies eliminated many levels of management. Management jobs changed. Some say they now think of themselves as "facilitators" rather than managers; they find the IT tools to help their workers manage their own work.

6.4 Employee Crime

Embezzlement is "fraudulent appropriation of property by a person to whom it has been entrusted."[38] With the use of computers, trusted employees have stolen hundreds of thousands—in some cases millions—of dollars from their employers. In a few spectacular cases, losses were in the hundreds of millions. (Volkswagen may have lost more than $200 million in a foreign exchange fraud perpetrated by high-level employees.[39]) Some frauds require specialized knowledge or programming skills. Others do not; employees taking advantage of poor security on their company's computer systems can commit them.

The complexities of modern financial transactions increase the opportunities for embezzlement. The complexity and anonymity of computers add to the problem and help hide scams. The victims of some of the most costly scams are banks, brokerage houses, insurance companies, and large financial institutions. Employess of insurance companies set up phony insurance policies and make claims on them. Employees transfer large sums to Swiss bank accounts and then disappear. Employees create fake purchase orders for purchases from phony companies and cash the checks themselves. They steal data from their employer's computers and sell it to competitors, crooks, spammers, and others. Employees of several banks sold account information on hundreds of thousands of customers to law firms and collection agencies.

Fired employees, or those angry at their employer for some other reason, sometimes sabotage the company computer systems. An employee fired from an insurance company destroyed more than 160,000 records with a *logic bomb*, software that destroys critical files, such as payroll and inventory records. There have been cases where an employee secretly sabotaged a system in the hopes of earning extra money to fix it. In one odd case an employee sabotaged a printing company's computer system, deleting or garbling files, jamming terminals, crashing the system, blanking screens, and generally creating havoc over a six-month period—while he continued to work at the company unsuspected. The company lost customers, and stress led some employees to quit or get fired. The owner said he believed the guilty employee (sentenced to five years in prison) just enjoyed making people miserable.[40]

The motivations for sabotage are not new. What is new with computer sabotage is the ease with which saboteurs can cause a great amount of damage.

Many practices, both technical and managerial, reduce the likelihood of large frauds. For example, management experts recommend that responsibilities of employees with access to sensitive computer systems be rotated, so that someone may notice suspicious activity. Each employee should have his or her own user ID and password and, where possible, the system should code IDs to allow only the access and actions each employee needs to perform. An employee's access should be canceled immediately after he or she quits or is fired. No one person should have responsibility for enough parts of a system to build and hide elaborate scams. (For example, in an insurance company, the same employee should not establish an insurance policy and authorize payments on claims.) Audit trails protect privacy. They also protect against fraud by providing a record of transactions and of the employee who authorized them. In one case, a brokerage firm turned off its audit trail software to speed processing of orders. An employee took advantage of the opportunity to swindle the company out of an estimated $28 million.[41]

SWINDLING CUSTOMERS

When Blaise Pascal (for whom the programming language Pascal was named) invented a calculating machine in the 1640s, he had trouble selling them. One reason was that people suspected that such machines could be rigged to give incorrect results. It is easy to modify a computer program to do so. How do you know, when a clerk scans your groceries at the supermarket checkout counter, that the prices charged are the same as the ones posted on the supermarket shelves? How do you know that your computer-generated credit-card bill is accurate? How do you know no one is robbing you?

Hertz Corporation allegedly programmed its computers to perform two calculations of the cost of repairs to cars that renters damaged: the actual cost to the company and a higher cost charged to the customer.[42] On the other hand, Walgreen, a large drugstore chain delayed implementation of a new inventory system because the checkout software sometimes generated the wrong price. Some businesses have high ethical standards and exercise care to avoid mistakes. Some businesses are complete scams. Others are unethical or sloppy. Some people assume that computer-generated statements and bills must be correct. Others are suspicious of anything that comes out of a machine. Both miss an important point: The reputation and character of the business are more important than the technology. Cheating customers is not a new phenomenon. A rigged program is the computer analog of rigged (precomputer) gas station pumps and taxi meters. Low-tech cheaters of customers included the old-time butcher who put his thumb on the scale while weighing a customer's meat.

Someone summed up the issue as "Computers don't steal—people do." The intent is not in the machine. However, the complexity of software hides scams. The complexity also hides unintended flaws that sometimes cheat customers. Responsible businesses must monitor for both.

In large impersonal institutions it is often foolish to trade security for convenience or increased efficiency.

Many people who embezzle from employers have no criminal history. Some have a gripe against the employer. Some have financial problems. Some just cannot resist the temptation. Careful screening and background checks on prospective employees can be helpful, although some laws make various kinds of screening more difficult (or completely illegal).

6.5 Employee Monitoring

> *Technology now allows employers to cross the line from monitoring the work to monitoring the worker.*
>
> —Cindia Cameron, National Association of Working Women

6.5.1 BACKGROUND

Supervisors and managers have always monitored their employees. The degree of detail and frequency of the monitoring has varied depending on the kind of work, economic factors, and available technology. Computers have made new kinds of monitoring possible and old methods more efficient.

Before we look at the new issues raised by computers, we will briefly recall some past and present monitoring that does not depend on computers. Total hours worked have long been monitored by logs or time clocks. In many jobs, the employer can count total output for a day (widgets produced, forms typed, sales concluded). In some jobs, such as factory assembly lines, the speed of the line implicitly monitors the pace of work; if a worker is not keeping up, the failure will be obvious farther down the line. Supervisors record or listen in on the work of telephone operators and customer-service representatives. Surveillance cameras have long been common in banks and convenience stores. In some of the accounts of the worst conditions in factories and clerical offices of the past two centuries, bosses patrolled the aisles watching workers, prodding them to work faster, and discouraging conversation and breaks.

Electronic monitoring capabilities are the modern version of the time clock, telephone extension, and camera. Most precomputer monitoring, however, was not constant because the supervisor had many workers to oversee and other work to do. Workers usually knew when the supervisor was present to observe them. With computers, monitoring can be constant, more detailed, and unseen by the worker. Telephone systems are now so essentially combined with computer systems that telephone monitoring has become a de *facto* computer issue.

The subjects of most precomputer monitoring were so-called blue-collar (factory) and pink-collar (telephone and clerical) workers. New monitoring capabilities, such as reading an employee's e-mail, affect white-collar (professional) workers, too. Supervisors of customer-service representatives can set their terminals to show exactly what the monitored worker sees and is doing on his or her screen. Some newspaper editors remotely monitor the computer screens of journalists, and some senior lawyers monitor other attorneys in their firm. Some companies install devices or software that secretly capture and store every keystroke typed on a keyboard. The vast growth of computer storage capabilities means that employers can store recordings of telephone conversations, e-mail, voice mail, Web activity logs, and physical surveillance information for a long time. They can also search such information more easily, with the potential of making the monitored details part of the employee's permanent record.

We discuss examples and issues in three areas of electronic monitoring:

❖ details of performance, such as keystrokes, customer-service calls, and retail-clerk operations;

❖ location and performance of scattered employees;

❖ e-mail, voice mail, and Web surfing.

6.5.2 DATA ENTRY, PHONE WORK, AND RETAIL

Monitoring systems can automatically count every keystroke of data-entry and data-processing clerks. Some employers set keystroke quotas. Some make the records of employees' performance public in the workplace to encourage competition among workers. Terminals beep if the employee pauses in his or her work. The purposes are to evaluate individual employees and to measure and increase productivity. When the quotas are unreasonable and the pace relentless, the stress can be intense. The management style that includes constant watching, very demanding work quotas, and threats of being fired is older than computers. People call the modern, computerized version of such workplaces "electronic sweatshops."

Similarly, workers who answer telephone calls all day are monitored in detail. The exact number and duration of each call, and the idle time between calls, can go into an automatic log for analysis. The log becomes part of the employee's record. (We discuss the separate issue of listening in on calls below.)

Workers complain that such constant, detailed surveillance diminishes their sense of dignity and independence and destroys confidence. It treats them like machines, not people. The surveillance causes stress, boredom, and low morale. Critics point out that the stress increases health costs for the employer. Critics also raise questions about the effectiveness of such monitoring, arguing that it puts too much emphasis on quantity instead of quality. It reduces workers' commitment to doing a good job. Pressure on telephone information operators to reduce the amount of time spent on each call, according to one critic, caused operators to cut customers off by claiming the computer was down.[43]

Telephone customer-service workers include airline and car-rental reservation clerks, catalog mail-order operators, telemarketers, credit-card and bank service representatives, and investment company representatives—to list just a few examples. Almost anytime we call customer-service numbers, we hear an announcement that the call may be monitored or recorded. The employer has a strong interest in ensuring that their service personnel handle customer calls accurately, efficiently, and courteously. Access to the recording of a call can help settle a dispute with a customer over the content of the call. Many companies with large customer-service operations have a regular program in which supervisors listen to calls periodically to train and evaluate new workers and to check on the performance of more experienced workers. Some advocacy groups argue that monitoring customer-service calls is a privacy issue: It infringes on the privacy of the employees and customers. Employers argue that there is no privacy issue: The calls are not personal; this is the worker's job, and the customer is talking to a complete stranger.

Complaints about monitoring (particularly of telephone and data-entry workers) led many large firms and industries (e.g., financial services) to establish clear and detailed monitoring policies. Certainly, employers should fully explain to employees their monitoring and evaluation procedures.

In retail environments, another purpose of employee monitoring (besides training and measuring or increasing productivity) is to reduce theft. Theft by retail-store employees amounts to 47% of retail losses ($17.6 billion in 2005), more than losses from shoplifting (33%, or $12.3 billion).[44] Some stores use software that monitors transactions at the cash registers, looking for suspicious patterns—for example, a large number of refunds, voids, or sales of cheap items. (In one scam, an employee scans and charges for cheap items, but bags expensive ones for the customer who is an accomplice.)[45] Does this kind of monitoring violate employee privacy?

Monitoring provides a good context for thinking about the distinction between policies and law. Advocates of regulation argue that it will benefit employers ("a blessing in disguise" for employers, according to Lewis Maltby of the American Civil Liberties Union[46]). Written procedures for monitoring and for use of the collected data will make monitoring more useful to the employer. Giving more freedom and respect to longtime employees will maintain their loyalty and make them more productive. Counting keystrokes is counterproductive because it increases stress, reduces worker productivity, and causes health problems and costs. These are good arguments in many cases. Employers who are convinced that proposed monitoring guidelines are beneficial to their company can adopt them. (Many, in fact, have.) What if some employers are not convinced? If the issue is whether specific practices are "good business," rather than a question of privacy rights or safety, who should make the decisions: legislators or the people responsible for a particular business? What monitoring guidelines involve issues of rights that should have legal protection, and which should be matters of internal company policy?

6.5.3 LOCATION MONITORING

In the nearby box, we illustrate some issues of location surveillance with one example—long-haul truckers. Electronic identification badges that serve as door keys raise similar issues. They provide increased security for a business, but they allow monitoring of the movements of employees. Nurses in some hospitals wear badges that track their location; a supervisor at a terminal can see where each nurse is. That means supervisors can see who someone eats lunch with and when they go to the bathroom. On the other hand, they

TRACKING TRUCKERS[47]

In the late 1980s shippers began installing tracking systems in their long-haul trucks. Now, most trucks have such devices. They communicate by satellite and can report the location and speed of the truck, as well as other detail such as when the driver turns on the headlights. Drivers communicate with dispatchers or automated systems at headquarters via a keyboard.

These systems have a number of advantages. They enable more precise planning of pickups and deliveries, increasing efficiency and saving money. Drivers no longer waste time searching for a public telephone to check in. Dispatchers can initiate communication with drivers. Communication in general, about schedule changes, road conditions, breakdowns requiring a mechanic, and so on, improved. Companies can use data on speed and rest periods to ensure that drivers follow safety rules. Trucks loaded with valuable goods are a target for thieves. Owners recovered more than a hundred stolen trucks in one year because the thieves did not know about the devices.

The main disadvantage is that many drivers saw the system as an intrusion on their privacy, a Big-Brother device watching their every move. Companies can micromanage the driver's actions and decisions, decreasing individual discretion. When the devices were first introduced, some truckers wrapped foil over the transmitter or parked for naps under highway bridges.

The truck-tracking systems predated wide use of cell phones. Perhaps simpler devices, like cell phones and wireless e-mail, can accomplish enough of the communications goals without monitoring location and performance detail. Do the benefits of monitoring outweigh privacy intrusion, or is this an example of computer technology inappropriately infringing on privacy and personal autonomy?

can also locate nurses quickly in emergencies. Would a call on a public-address system do just as well?

The Montreal city government authorized use of global positioning systems (GPS) so that supervisors can determine where employees are at all times (while at work). In Massachusetts supervisors gave cell phones with GPS to building inspectors. More than a dozen inspectors refused the phones, calling them an invasion of privacy. Is it reasonable for a nurse or a city employee working out in the field to expect his or her location, while working, to be private? Should employer policies permit employees to turn off locating devices when they are on a break?

A company that provides video surveillance services requires employees who access secure areas of the company's facility to have an identification chip implanted in their arm. Implanting chips differs in important ways from the examples above. It is a physical invasion of one's person, and it cannot be left at the office at the end of the day or turned off. For what kinds of jobs, if any, are such chips appropriate?

6.5.4 E-MAIL, BLOGGING, AND WEB USE

> *[E-mail] combines the casualness of speech with the permanence of writing. It's got a lot of potential for embarrassing the other side.*
>
> —Allan B. Taylor, attorney[48]

The use of e-mail and access to the Web at work makes a lot of work more efficient and more pleasant, benefiting both employers and employees. It also raises problems and issues about monitoring. We look at how employees use e-mail and the Web, business policies about their use and about monitoring by employers, and the issue of employee privacy. Why do employers read employee e-mail? When should they? What are reasonable policies for personal use of the Web at work and for monitoring of Web activity by employees?

E-mail and voice mail at work

Billions of e-mail messages travel within and among businesses each year. At first people thought that because they used a password to access their e-mail or voice mail, their messages were not accessible to anyone else. This is not true. In virtually all systems, the system manager can access anything on the system. Employers can read the e-mail of employees, they can listen to voice-mail messages, and they can read computer files. How many of them do? Figures from different sources vary, because of different counting methods, but roughly half of major companies in the U.S. sometimes monitor or search the e-mail, voice mail, or computer files of their employees.

Employees who have e-mail, voice mail, and their own computer files tend to be workers with more varied job functions and responsibilities than customer-service workers. They include, for example, computer programmers, managers, sales people, secretaries, lawyers, researchers, and college professors. Such workers commonly use e-mail and the telephone for communications with family and friends, especially where there is no clear policy against it. Their files and messages are more likely to include personal content. Thus, privacy is often an issue. Employers claim they have a right and a need to monitor the use of their facilities. The controversies stem from disagreements about the reasons for monitoring and the appropriate boundary between the employers' rights and the employees' privacy.

There are legitimate reasons for employers to sometimes listen to voice-mail messages or read e-mail or files on an employee's computer. Some appear in Figure 6.3. Many large companies rank leaking of proprietary information as a serious problem. Some businesses install filtering software to review all outgoing messages for content that violates laws or company policy, could damage relations with customers, or could expose the company to lawsuits. The box on page 341 describes one application of such e-mail filtering. The most common e-mail problem reported by one company was harassment (including sexual harassment, cases with pending divorces, and love triangles). Other problems include

- ❖ Find needed business information when the employee is not available.

- ❖ Protect security of proprietary information and data.

- ❖ Prevent or investigate possible criminal activities by employees. (This can be work related, such as embezzlement, or not work related, such as selling illegal drugs.)

- ❖ Prevent personal use of employer facilities (if prohibited by company policy).

- ❖ Check for violations of company policy against sending offensive or pornographic e-mail.

- ❖ Investigate complaints of harassment.

- ❖ Check for illegal software.

Figure 6.3 Reasons for Monitoring E-mail, Voice Mail, and Computer Files

mailing jokes to thousands of people, running a business using the company's address, personal communications, and running betting pools on football and basketball games. In one survey, 26% of employers surveyed said they had fired employees for misusing company e-mail. Several large companies, including the *New York Times*, Dow Chemical, Compaq (now part of Hewlett-Packard), and Xerox, made headlines by firing dozens of employees for violations of company e-mail and Web use policies, in most cases because of sexually explicit or violent content. Because businesses face liability for sexual harassment by employees, some companies believe that a harsh penalty is necessary to protect the company from lawsuits for a "hostile workplace environment." Employee e-mail led to lawsuits against more than 15% of companies surveyed in 2006.[49]

Most companies that read employee e-mail do it infrequently, primarily when there is a complaint or some other reason to suspect a problem. At the other extreme, some employers routinely intercept all e-mail entering and leaving the company site. Some supervisors snoop to find out what employees are saying about them or the company. Some snoop into personal messages.

Law and cases

There is little law controlling workplace monitoring. Monitoring for purposes listed in Figure 6.3 is generally legal. The Electronic Communications Privacy Act (ECPA) prohibits interception of e-mail and reading of stored e-mail without a court order, but the ECPA makes an exception for business systems. It does not prohibit employers from reading employee e-mail on company systems. Some privacy advocates and computer ethicists advocate a revision of the ECPA to prohibit or restrict employers from reading employee e-mail.

FILTERING PROFESSIONAL E-MAIL

Most major stock brokerage companies use e-mail filters to detect illegal, unethical, and offensive e-mail sent by their brokers. Stock brokers are not supposed to exaggerate the prospects of investments, downplay the risks, or pressure clients to buy or sell. Filters search for keywords such as *risk-free*, vulgarities, and sexist or racist terms. They use AI techniques for more sophisticated analysis of messages.[50]

Is this an example of increased monitoring made possible by new technology? Not entirely. To protect the public, the New York Stock Exchange previously required that a supervisor read all written communication from brokers to clients. When e-mail replaced mailed letters, the volume increased so much that supervisors could no longer read all the mail. E-mail filtering replaced human review of all messages with human review of only those selected by the filter. On the other hand, people tend to use e-mail for a greater variety of messages than they did printed letters—including personal messages, which are now exposed to the filters. Does routine filtering of all e-mail violate the privacy of the brokers? If it does, do the trade-offs justify it?

In one case, a company fired two employees after a supervisor read their e-mail messages criticizing him. A judge ruled that the company could read the e-mail because it owned and operated the system. In another case, a court accepted monitoring of a discussion about a boss because the discussion could affect the business environment. Courts have made similar decisions in other cases. Courts place much weight on the fact that the computers, mail, and phone systems used at work are the property of the employer who provides them for business purposes.

Courts have sometimes ruled against employers if there was a convincing case that monitoring was done to snoop on personal and union activities or to track down whistle-blowers. Court decisions sometimes depend on a conclusion about whether an employee had a reasonable "expectation of privacy," but this concept is not always clear.

More about expectation of privacy: Section 2.2.2 At a minimum, an employer should set clear policies and inform employees about whether it permits personal use of employer-provided communications and computer systems and about whether, and under what circumstances, the employer will access employee messages and files. Some large companies have explicit policies that employee e-mail is private and the employer will not read it. Others provide a notice to employees every time they log on, reminding them that the system is for business, not personal, use and that the company reserves the right to monitor messages.

A clear statement of monitoring policy by the employer removes some of the guesswork about expectations of privacy. Such a statement is essential from an ethical perspective. Respect for an employee's privacy includes warning the employee about when someone is observing his or her apparently private actions or communications (except in special circumstances such as a criminal investigation). Giving or accepting a job in which an employee will use an employer's equipment carries an ethical obligation on both parties to abide by the policy established for that use. From a practical perspective, a clear policy can reduce disputes and abuses (both by ordinary employees and by supervisors who might snoop in ways that violate the company policy).

Employees do not give up all privacy when they enter an employer's premises. The bathrooms belong to the employer too, but camera surveillance in bathrooms is generally not acceptable. Where else is there protection for privacy at a workplace? Some courts ruled that, if employers allow employees to use their own locks on their lockers, the employee has an expectation of privacy for the contents of the locker. An employee fired by Microsoft sued the company, using the locker analogy. He claimed Microsoft invaded his privacy by accessing e-mail he had stored on his computer at work in personal folders, protected by a password. Microsoft allowed the password-protected personal folders, so, the employee argued, the folders should have remained private. The court ruled against him. One of the arguments was that lockers are a discreet physical space provided for storing personal items, but the computer was for work and the messages were part of the work environment. The court also commented that "the company's interest in preventing inappropriate and unprofessional comments, or even illegal activity, over its e-mail system would outweigh [the employee's] claimed privacy interest in those communications."[51]

The National Labor Relations Board (NLRB) sets rules and decides cases about worker–employer relations. It has been a focus of controversy between unions and employers since its creation more than 60 years ago. Workers have a legal right to communicate with each other about work conditions, and the NLRB ruled in some cases that they may do so on company e-mail systems. Thus, employers may not prohibit all nonbusiness e-mail. The NLRB required that a company rehire and give back pay to an employee fired for sending an e-mail message to all employees criticizing a change in the company's vacation plan.[52] In the past, the NLRB ruled that companies must discuss policies about use of surveillance cameras, drug testing, and lie-detector tests with a union if the company has one. Some argue that it should require companies to negotiate e-mail policies with the union as well.

Many of the arguments made in legal cases are relevant to ethical decisions as well. The problem, for both ethics and law, consists of defining a reasonable boundary between, on the one hand, actions to protect the rights and needs of the employer (property rights, protection of company assets, access to business information, and monitoring for possible legal and liability problems) and, on the other hand, actions that invade personal privacy. The most reasonable policy is not always obvious, not always the same in the view of both parties, not the same for all types of businesses, and not always clear when new situations arise.

Using the Web at work

You probably first used the Web at home or at school. Ten or 15 years ago, most people who used the Web did so first at work. Employees quickly discovered they could do much more than work on the Web. One study counted 12,823 visits to *Penthouse* magazine's Web site in one month in 1996 from computers at IBM, Apple, and AT&T. (That was a large number at that time.) Various surveys found high percentages of employees at businesses and government agencies using the Web for nonwork purposes (e.g., 79.8%, 90%). Visits to "adult" and pornography sites soon gave way to visits to chat rooms and sports, shopping, gambling, and stock-investment sites. Later, workers watched videos and networked with friends on social-networking sites. Some companies found that employees spent more than two hours a week on nonwork Web activity. One found that 3% of its Web traffic was to an online investment site and another 4% went to employees downloading music.[53] Companies say access to online video slows business traffic on their networks.

Many major companies use software tools that provide reports on employee Web use. The tools rank sites by frequency of visits or create reports on an individual employee's activity, for instance. Some employers install variants of the filtering software products originally developed for parents to limit Web access by their children. They block access to social-networking and video sites. The American Management Association said 76% of 526 companies it surveyed report monitoring Internet use by employees; 65% block access to some Web sites.[54]

Is monitoring the Web activity of employees an unreasonable invasion of privacy? Is nonwork Web surfing a serious problem for employers, or is it a high-tech equivalent of reading a newspaper or listening to the radio at one's desk? Employers report a number of concerns about nonwork Web activity. The obvious one is that employees are not working the hours they are paid to work. When the employer is the government, there is the additional issue of misuse of taxpayer-funded resources. (On the other hand, a company found that one of its top-performing employees spent more than an hour a day managing his own stocks on the Web. The company did not care because his performance was good.)

Web sites can determine where a visitor is coming from. Some companies want to avoid the embarrassment of having their employees reported to be visiting pornographic sites, perhaps racist sites, or even job-hunting sites.

A major concern about Web use in general is security threats such as viruses and other malicious software with the potential to disrupt company operations or access sensitive data about the company or its customers and clients. We saw in Chapter 2 that businesses that store personal information about employees, customers, patients, or the public must be vigilant to protect against leaks and theft of such data. As we saw in Chapter 5, hackers exploit security flaws in Web applications. They target employees of companies whose systems they want to hack into. Thus control of employee Web activity is part of essential security for many companies. Some companies restrict or prohibit a variety of Internet services (at work), such as instant messaging, file sharing, blogging, Internet phone service, access to personal e-mail, and connecting iPods to company computers. So far, a relatively small number have adopted policies about blogging and instant messaging. The lack of policies could lead to major problems for employees who cause damage inadvertently or get into trouble because of misunderstandings about what is acceptable. It can also cause huge problems for employers. Employee blogs, like unmonitored e-mail, can expose a company to liability for harassment, copyright infringement, or libel. An offensive blog can damage the company's reputation. Companies also worry about leaks of product information and financial information. This is one more area, like so many others, where employers need to think ahead, develop clear, reasonable policies, and make sure employees are aware of them and understand the reasons for them.

EXERCISES

Review Exercises

6.1   List two job categories where the number of jobs declined drastically as a result of computerization.

6.2   List two job categories where the number of jobs increased drastically with increasing use of computers.

6.3   What is *offshoring*? List three problems associated with offshoring.

6.4   What are two advantages and two disadvantages of telecommuting?

6.5   What is one problem with worker verification systems that use immigration or Social Security databases?

6.6   What types of employee monitoring most affect professional (white-collar) employees?

General Exercises

6.7   List four examples from Section 1.2 that reduce or eliminate jobs. Tell specifically what jobs they reduce or eliminate.

6.8   Why is it difficult to determine the number of jobs eliminated and created by computers?

6.9   Jeremy Rifkin argues that the ability of Japanese auto mobile makers to produce a car in less than eight hours illustrates the threat of massive unemployment from computer technology and automation.[55] How do the data in Figures 6.1and 6.2 help to support or refute Rifkin's point of view? Can you cite other data on either side of this issue?

6.10   Discuss the issue of whether the U.S. programmers or the Indian programmers in the offshoring scenario in Section 6.2.3 have a negative right or a positive right to the jobs (see Section 1.4.3).

6.11   Jobs created by computers are different from the ones they eliminate. Consider the following statement:

> Jobs will diverge into two distinct groups: high-paying jobs for a highly skilled and highly trained intellectual elite and fewer low-paying jobs for people without computer skills and advanced education.

Do you agree? State your position and provide your reasons.

6.12 Should there be laws banning some kinds of home-based work and not others (e.g., sewing vs. office work)? Why or why not? If you think there should be some restrictions on home work, what principles should apply in deciding what to prohibit?

6.13 Embezzlement is defined in Section 6.4. There are several motives for embezzlement and other employee crimes. Discuss which you feel are the most serious and pose the highest risk. Propose ways a company can prevent embezzlement from occurring.

6.14 Some unions propose federal legislation to prohibit monitoring of customer-service or data-entry employees with more than five years of experience. Give reasons for and against monitoring experienced employees.

6.15 Analyze both the advantages and disadvantages to telecommuting. If you were given the opportunity to work from home or in an office for the same amount of pay, which would you choose and why?

6.16 Consider the reasons given in Figure 6.3 for employers to monitor employee e-mail, voice mail, and files. For which do you think it is appropriate to have regular, ongoing monitoring for all employees, and for which do you think an employer should access employee mail and files only when a problem occurs and only for the particular employees involved? Give reasons.

6.17 In what ways is monitoring employee use of the Web to find employees who are violating company Web-use policies similar to and different from the use of government agencies using computer matching to find people who might be breaking laws (Section 2.2.1)?

6.18 Using the Freedom of Information Act and similar state laws, some people have requested the e-mail of governors, legislators, and past and current presidents. These requests raise the issue of whether the e-mail of government employees and elected officials is personal conversation or official government documents. What do you think? Why?

6.19 Consider the following scenario.

>   An employee at an investment firm reported to a supervisor that some employees have unlicensed software on their office computers. Over a weekend, without informing the employees in advance, the company searches all computers (via its network) looking for unlicensed software.

What alternative actions could the company have taken? Give reasons why they would have been better than, or not as good as, doing the search. Do you think the search was reasonable?

6.20 Assume you are a professional working in your chosen field. Describe specific things you can do to reduce the impact of any two problems we discussed in this chapter. (If you cannot think of anything related to your professional field, choose another field that might interest you.)

6.21 Think ahead to the next few years and describe a new problem, related to issues in this chapter, that is likely to develop from computing technology or the Web.

Assignments

These exercises require some research or activity.

6.22 Use the Internet to search for information about a job that interests you. What Web sites did you use? How did you determine the credibility of the Web sites? Did you have the option to submit applications and complete forms online?

6.23 The Electronic Communications Privacy Act of 1986 (ECPA) does not prohibit universities from reading student e-mail on its computers, just as it does not prohibit businesses from reading employee e-mail on company computers. Find your university's policy about access to student computer accounts and e-mail (on university computers) by professors and university administrators. Describe and review the policy. Tell what parts you think are good and what should change.

Class Discussion Exercises

These exercises are for class discussion, perhaps with short presentations prepared in advance by small groups of students.

6.24   If someone discovers a cure for the common cold, should he or she hide it to protect the jobs of all the people who work in the huge cold-medicine industry? If there is little controversy about the answer to this question (as I suspect will be the case), try to identify reasons why so many people react negatively to advances in technology that eliminate some jobs.

6.25   Discuss ethical issues concerning offshoring jobs. How should companies deal with different pay levels, different health and safety requirements, different cultures (e.g., holidays, clothing, management styles), and so on?

6.26   Is it an invasion of privacy for a company to search the Web for information by and about a job applicant? Interviewers are trained not to ask an applicant for some kinds of information (age, marital status, disabilities) to avoid charges of discrimination. Should there be legal restrictions on what kinds of information about a candidate a company can look at on the Web?

6.27   Consider an automated system that large companies can use to process job applications. For jobs such as truck drivers, cleaning staff, and cafeteria workers, the system selects people to hire without interviews or other involvement of human staffers. Describe advantages and disadvantages of such a system.

6.28   You work for a large architectural firm. Develop a policy for blogging and other Web use by employees at work.

6.29   In the first few years of the 21st century, only about 28% of students earning college degrees in computer science were women. This is down from a peak of 38% in 1985.[56] Why do you think relatively few women major in computer science? Have you observed or experienced any behavior in classes, computer labs, or at work that would discourage women? What characteristics or images of the field might discourage women?

6.30   Walking through a public park on their way back to work after lunch, four employees of a large Internet services company begin clowning around and singing silly and raunchy songs. One of them captures the scene on his cell phone and later posts it on a major video site. In the video, the company logo is clearly visible on the T-shirts the employees are wearing. The company fires the employee who posted the video and has not yet decided on action against the others. Discuss arguments for and against the firing. What disciplinary action, if any, is appropriate for the other employees?

NOTES

1.   CPU: Working in the Computer Industry, Computer Professionals for Social Responsibility, February 15, 1995, www.cpsr.org/prevsite/program/workplace/cpu.013.html (accessed April 3, 2007).

2.   J. M. Fenster, "Seam Stresses," in *Great Inventions That Changed the World* (American Heritage, 1994.

3.   Associated Press, "Electronic Dealings Will Slash Bank Jobs, Study Finds," *Wall Street Journal*, August 14, 1995, p. A5D; W. Michael Cox and Richard Alm, *Myths of*

Rich and Poor: Why We're Better off Than We Think (Basic Books, 1999), p. 129; G. Pascal Zachary, "Service Productivity Is Rising Fast-and So Is the Fear of Lost Jobs," *Wall Street Journal*, June 8, 1995, p. A1. The quote is from Frank Zashen, in "Big Board to Lay Off All 150 Floor Couriers," *Wall Street Journal*, July 25, 2001, p. A6; Lauren Etter, "Is the Phone Company Violating Your Privacy?" *Wall Street Journal*, May 13–14, 2006, p. A7.

4. Cox and Alm, *Myths of Rich and Poor*, p. 129. Alejandro Bodipo-Memba, "Jobless Rate Skidded to 4.4% in November," *Wall Street Journal*, December 7, 1998, pp. A2, A8.

5. Fenster, "Seam Stresses."

6. George F. Gilder, *Microcosm* (Simon & Schuster, 1989), p. 46.

7. "High-Tech Added 200,000 Jobs Last Year," *Wall Street Journal*, May 19, 1998; "Chip-Industry Study Cites Sector's Impact on U.S. Economy," *Wall Street Journal*, March 17, 1998, p. A20; Andrea K. Walker, "Retailer's Mass Firing Reflects Sector's Woes," *Baltimore Sun*, March 29, 2007; Fatemeh Hajiha, "Employment Changes from 2001 to 2005 for Occupations Concentrated in the Finance Industries," U.S. Bureau of Labor Statistics, www.bls.gov/oes/2005/may/changes.pdf (accessed August 6, 2007).

8. Vauhini Vara, "As Users Go Online, Tax-Software Firms Retool Strategies," *Wall Street Journal*, April 15, 2006, pp. A1, A5. The data from the Bureau of Labor Statistics are on several pages including www.bls.gov/oco/ocos155.htm and www.bls.gov/oco/oco1002.htm; Information Technology Association of America, "Adding Value . . . Growing Careers," Annual Workforce Development Survey, September 2004, itas.org/workforce/docs/04workforcestudy.pdf; Robert N. Charette, "Why Software Fails," *IEEE Spectrum*, September 2005, www.spectrum.ieee.org/sep05/1685 (accessed December 8, 2006).

9. Kimberly Rowe, in a letter to the editor, *Wall Street Journal*, August 31, 2006, p. A9.

10. Daniel E. Hecker, "Occupational Employment Projections to 2012," *Monthly Labor Review*, February 2004, pp. 80–105 (see p. 80), www.bls.gov/opub/mlr/2004/02/art5full.pdf (accessed April 13, 2007); "BLS Releases 2004–14 Employment Projections," December 9, 2005, U.S. Bureau of Labor Statistics, www.bls.gov/news.release/ecopro.nr0.htm (accessed September 4, 2007).

11. This quote and the one that follows are from "The OECD Jobs Study: Facts, Analysis, Strategies (1994)," www.oecd.org/dataoecd/42/51/1941679.pdf (accessed April 8, 2007).

12. Ibid., p. 21.

13. Theodore Caplow, Louis Hicks, and Ben J. Wattenberg, *The First Measured Century: An Illustrated Guide to Trends in America* (AEI Press, 2001), p. 160; Cox and Alm, *Myths of Rich and Poor*, pp. 18–19.

14. Cox and Alm, *Myths of Rich and Poor*, pp. 60, 59, 10.

15. W. Michael Cox and Richard Alm, *Myths of Rich and Poor: Why We're Better off Than We Think* (Basic Books, 1999), pp. 7, 55.

16. The cost, in work time, of some products and services increased in the same time period. Increases for tax-preparation fees, Amtrak tickets, and the price of a first-class-mail stamp perhaps result from more complex tax laws and monopolies. Increases in the average cost of a new house or car are partly due to the increase in the size of new homes and the increase in the features of new cars.

17. Cox and Alm, *Myths of Rich and Poor*, p. 43

18. Paul Wallich, "The Analytical Economist," *Scientific American*, August 1994, p. 89.

19. Tax Foundation, "America's Tax Freedom Day Arrives April 30 in 2007, Two Days Later Than 2006," March 28, 2007, www.taxfoundation.org/press/show/22300.htm (accessed April 3, 2007)

20. Salgado's powerful photographic tribute to workers, many who work in extremely harsh conditions, appears in Sebastião Salgado, *Workers: An Archaeology of the Industrial Age* (Aperture, 1993). See also www.terra.com.br/sebastiaosalgado. The photos described here, and several others, also appear in Miles Orvell, "A Tribute to the World's Workers," *Technology Review*, October 1995, pp. 62–69.

21. Phillip J. Longman, "The Janitor Stole My Job," *U.S. News & World Report*, December 1, 1997, pp. 50–52; Caplow et al., The First Measured Century, p. 31.

22. Longman, "The Janitor Stole My Job." Amy Merrick, "Erasing 'Un' From 'Unemployable'," *Wall Street Journal*, August 2, 2007, pp. B1, B6.

23. U.S. Department of Labor, Bureau of Labor Statistics, "Occupations with the Largest Job Growth, 2004-14," www.bls.gov/emp/emptab3.htm (accessed April 10, 2007).

24. Zachary, "Service Productivity Is Rising Fast-and So Is the Fear of Lost Jobs."

25. U.S. Department of Labor, Bureau of Labor Statistics, "Occupational Outlook Handbook (OOH), 2006–07 Edition," www.bls.gov/oco; U.S. Department of Labor, Bureau of Labor Statistics, "Computer Software Engineers," www.bls.gov/oco/ocos267.htm.

26. The ideas in this discussion come from Corie Lok, "Two Sides of Outsourcing," *Technology Review*, February 2005, p. 33.

27. "Extended Mass Layoffs Associated With Domestic and Overseas Relocations, First Quarter 2004 Summary," Bureau of Labor Statistics, June 10, 2004,

stats.bls.gov/news.release/reloc.nr0.htm (accessed August 17, 2006); Alan S. Blinder, "Offshoring: The Next Industrial Revolution?" Foreign Affairs, March/April 2006, www.foreignaffairs.org/20060301faessay85209/alan-s-blinder/offshoring-the-next-industrial-revolution.html (accessed April 5, 2007).

28. Blinder, "Offshoring: The Next Industrial Revolution?"

29. My thanks to my student Anthony Biag, whose questions in class on this issue prompted me to include the issue in the first edition of this book.

30. Foreign-owned firms usually pay more than domestic employers. For example, a study of Indonesia, "Do Foreign-Owned Firms Pay More?" by Ann E. Harrison and Jason Scorse of the University of California, Berkeley (International Labour Office, Geneva, Working Paper #98, www.ilo.org/public/english/employment/multi/download/wp98.pdf, accessed August 17, 2006), found that foreign-owned manufacturers paid unskilled workers 5–10% more and skilled workers 20–35% more than comparable domestic employers.

31. Sources for this box include Government Accountability Office, "Immigration Enforcement: Weaknesses Hinder Employment Verification and Worksite Enforcement Efforts," GAO-05-813, August 2005, www.gao.gov/new.items/d05813.pdf (accessed April 13, 2007). "Expansion of Basic Pilot Would Steer Employment Verification Toward Disaster," Electronic Privacy Information Center, April 2006, www.epic.org/privacy/surveillance/spotlight/0406/ (accessed April 13, 2007); Kerry Howley, "Worse than a Wall," Reason, May 2, 2006; Glenn Garvin, "Bringing the Border War Home," Reason, October 1995, pp. 18–28.

32. Quoted in Joe Davidson, "House Panel Backs Telephone Process to Verify Authorization of New Hires," Wall Street Journal, September 22, 1995, pp. A2, A14.

33. Rockbridge Associates, "2005/2006 National Technology Readiness Survey," Robert H. Smith School of Business, University of Maryland, July 12, 2006, www.smith.umd.edu/ntrs/NTRS-2005-06.pdf (accessed April 13, 2007); Sue Shellenbarger, "When Working at Home Doesn't Work: How Companies Comfort Telecommuters," Wall Street Journal, August 24, 2006, p. D1.

34. Rockbridge Associates, "2005/2006 National Technology Readiness Survey."

35. Joel Kotkin, "Commuting via Information Superhighway," Wall Street Journal, January 27, 1994, p. A14.

36. David Rubins, "Telecommuting: Will the Plug Be Pulled?" Reason, October 1984, pp. 24-32. The quote at the end of the paragraph is from Dennis Chamot.

37. "The Incredible Shrinking Company," The Economist, December 15, 1990, pp. 65–66. Cox and Alm, Myths of Rich and Poor, p. 115.

38. Webster's Third New International Dictionary.

39. Tom Forester and Perry Morrison, Computer Ethics: Cautionary Tales and Ethical Dilemmas in Computing, 2nd ed. (MIT Press, 1994), p. 34.

40. William M. Carley, "As Computers Flip, People Lose Grip in Saga of Sabotage at Printing Firm," Wall Street Journal, August 27, 1992, p. A7.

41. Forester and Morrison, Computer Ethics, p. 37.

42. Peter G. Neumann et al., "Risks to the Public in Computers and Related Systems," Software Engineering Notes, 13, no. 2 (April 1988), pp. 7–8.

43. David D. Redell, "Safeguard Employees' Privacy," San Diego Union-Tribune, October 13, 1993, p. B5.

44. Richard C. Hollinger and Lynn Langton, "2005 National Retail Security Survey," University of Florida, 2006, pp. 6–8, www.crim.ufl.edu/research/srp/finalreport_2005.pdf (accessed April 11, 2007). They report that the percentages have remained fairly steady for several years.

45. Richard C. Hollinger, National Retail Security Survey 2002, reported in "Retail Theft and Inventory Shrinkage," retailindustry.about.com/od/statistics_loss_prevention/l/aa021126a.htm (accessed August 17, 2006); Calmetta Coleman, "As Thievery by Insiders Overtakes Shoplifting, Retailers Crack Down," Wall Street Journal, September 8, 2000, p. A1.

46. "A Conversation with Lewis Maltby" (director of the ACLU's Task Force on Civil Liberties in the Workplace), Privacy and American Business, September 1994, pp. 9, 12.

47. Stuart F. Brown, "Trucking Gets Sophisticated," Fortune, July 24, 2000, pp. 270B–270R.

48. Quoted in Connecticut Law Tribune, December 18, 1995.

49. American Management Association and ePolicy Institute, "2006 Workplace E-mail, Instant Messaging and Blog Survey," www.amanet.org/press/amanews/2006/blogs_2006.htm (accessed April 13, 2007).

50. Alex Markels, "I Spy: Wall Street Gets Sneaky Software to Keep an Eye on Broker-Client E-mail," Wall Street Journal, August 21, 1997, pp. C1, C23.

51. McLaren v. Microsoft, Texas Court of Appeal No. 05-97-00824CV, May 28, 1999, cyber.law.Harvard.edu/privacy/McLaren_v_Microsoft.htm.

52. Leinweber v. Timekeeper Systems, 323 NLRB 30 (1997), "E-Mail Law Expands," National Law Journal, July 19, 1999, www.wendytech.com/

articlesemaillawexpands.htm (accessed September 10, 2007).

53. Joan Rigdon, "Curbing Digital Dillydallying on the Job," *Wall Street Journal*, November 25, 1996, p. B1; *Wired*, January 2001, p. 80; Michael J. McCarthy, "Now the Boss Knows Where You're Clicking," *Wall Street Journal*, October 21, 1999, pp. B1, B4.

54. American Management Association and ePolicy Institute, "2005 Electronic Monitoring and Surveillance Survey," www.amanet.org/press/amanews/ems05.htm (accessed September 10, 2007).

55. Jeremy Rifkin, "New Technology and the End of Jobs," in *The Case Against the Global Economy and For a Turn Toward the Local*, ed. Jerry Mander and Edward Goldsmith (Sierra Club Books, 1996), pp. 108–121.

56. Cornelia Dean, "Computer Science Takes Steps to Bring Women to the Fold," *New York Times*, April 17, 2007, www.nytimes.com, viewed April 19, 2007.

BOOKS AND ARTICLES

- Brown, Clair, John Haltiwanger, and Julia Lane. *Economic Turbulence*, University of Chicago Press, 2006.

- Dertouzos, Michael L., *Computers and Productivity*. MIT Laboratory for Computer Science, 1990.

- Flynn, Nancy. *Blog Rules: A Business Guide to Managing Policy, Public Relations, and Legal Issues*. AMACOM, 2006. Workplace blogging policies from the employer perspective.

- Kutscher, Ronald. *The Impact of Technology on Employment in the United States: Past and Future*. Farmer Press, 1987.

- Nilles, Jack. "Teleworking: Working Closer to Home," *Technology Review*, April 1982, pp. 56–62. An early article that foresaw many of the advantages and disadvantages of telework.

- Rifkin, Jeremy. *The End of Work*. Tarcher, 1996 (updated edition 2004).

- Stanton, Jeffrey M., and Kathryn R. Stam. *The Visible Employee: Using Work-Place Monitoring and Surveillance to Protect Information Assets—Without Compromising Employee Privacy or Trust*. Information Today, Inc., 2006.

7

Evaluating and Controlling Technology

In this chapter we consider such questions as, Does the openness and "democracy" of the Web increase the distribution of useful information or inaccurate, foolish, and biased information? How can we evaluate complex computer models of physical and social phenomena? How do computers and telecommunications affect human interaction and community? How does access to the technology differ among different populations? What is the impact of computer technology on the quality of life? Is computer technology, overall, beneficial to us or harmful? How should technology be controlled to ensure positive uses and consequences? How soon will robots be more intelligent than people? What will happen after that?

There are entire books on most of these topics. The presentations here are necessarily brief. They introduce some of the issues and arguments.

7.1 Information, Knowledge, and Judgment

> *Where is the wisdom we have lost in knowledge?*
> *Where is the knowledge we have lost in information?*
>
> —T. S. Eliot, "Choruses from 'the Rock,'" 1934[1]

7.1.1 EVALUATING INFORMATION ON THE WEB

Expert information or the "wisdom of the crowd"?

There is a daunting amount of information on the Web—and much of it is wrong. Quack medical cures and treatments abound. Distorted history, errors, outdated information, bad financial advice—it is all available on the Web.

Search engines are replacing librarians and professionally prepared indexes to articles, but search engines rank Web pages by popularity, not by an expert evaluation of their worth. Search engines give prominent display to content providers who pay them; libraries do not. To gain a more prominent place for their Web sites, individuals and businesses continually try to dissect and outsmart ranking algorithms. A major newspaper trains its reporters to pack key phrases in their articles so that the newspaper's articles rank high. Do the methods used by search engines help or hinder access to accurate information?

Wikipedia, the online encyclopedia, is immensely popular, but can we rely on its accuracy and objectivity when anyone can edit any article at any time? On social media sites* such as Digg and Newsvine, readers submit and vote on news stories. The phenomenon is called *democratic journalism*. Is this a good way to get news? How do we know what is worth reading when there are no editors selecting the well-written and well-researched?

---

* Social media sites are sites that emphasize sharing of information, opinion, and entertainment by ordinary people.

Marketers and public relations firms post unlabeled advertisements as blogs and on social-networking and video sites. How do we know when someone is manipulating us?

While Web enthusiasts delight in the access to huge amounts of information and opinions and the easy access to audiences, some people find the huge quantity of junk, the inaccurate information, the postings by people of unknown expertise and motives, and the lack of editorial control on the Web to be serious problems. Take blogs as an example. Millions of people write blogs. Some are excellent; some are atrocious. Some provide news and insights; some provide gossip and nonsense. Bloggers are opinionated, biased. The nature of blogging (and the Internet as a whole) encourages bloggers to post their immediate thoughts and reactions, without taking time for contemplation or for checking facts. Some bloggers have rather warped views of the world, and some are just dull. Bloggers are not trained, objective journalists.

Example: Wikipedia

To explore some of these issues of quality, objectivity, and accuracy, we use Wikipedia as an example. The English edition of Wikipedia has more than 600 million words in more than 1,700,000 articles. (The long respected Encyclopædia Britannica, first published in the 18th-century, has about 40 million words.)[2] Wikipedia is huge, free, participatory, noncommercial, ad-free, and written by volunteers. But do those touted qualities make its entries necessarily true, honest, and reliable? Can we take seriously an encyclopedia in which articles about television and movie characters (e.g., the John Locke character from *Lost*) are longer than articles about important historical people with the same name (the philosopher John Locke, whose ideas helped shape the U.S. founders' beliefs about freedom and government)? Some argue that because hundreds of millions of people—anyone at all—can write or edit articles, accuracy and quality are impossible. Truth does not come from populist free-for-alls. Some articles are biased and one sided. Members of the staffs of political candidates have distorted the Wikipedia biographies of their candidates to make their bosses look better. The staff of a federal agency removed criticisms of the agency from its Wikipedia article. Discredited theories about historic events such as the terrorist attacks on September 11, 2001 and the assassination of John F. Kennedy appear regularly. Anonymity of writers encourages dishonesty. Removing false information, hoaxes, and the like requires constant effort, according to Wikipedia volunteers.

In spite of the errors, sloppiness, bad writing, and intentional distortions, most of Wikipedia is, perhaps surprisingly, of high quality and extraordinarily valuable. Why? What protects quality in large, open, volunteer projects? First, although anyone *can* write and edit Wikipedia articles, most people do not. Thousands write and edit regularly, not millions.* Most are educated and have expertise in the subjects they write about. They correct articles promptly. (Wikipedia saves old versions, so it is easy to restore an article

---

*About 4,000 experts write the articles for the Encyclopædia Britannica.

someone has vandalized.) After the manipulation of Wikipedia articles by political staffers, the people who manage Wikipedia developed new policies to reduce the likelihood of such incidents. Yes, people manage Wikipedia. They are not editors in the traditional sense, but they do exert some control. How important is the formal selection role played by editors and experts who produce traditional works like the Encyclopædia Britannica? The Encyclopædia Britannica has had errors and oddities, but because of its nature Wikipedia is prone to more. Open, volunteer, instant-publishing systems cannot prevent errors and vandalism as easily as publishers of printed books. We, as users, can (and must) learn to appropriately deal with side effects or weaknesses of new paradigms. Even though so much of Wikipedia is excellent, we learn that someone might have wrecked the accuracy and objectivity of any individual article at any hour. We learn that articles on technology, science, history, and literature are more likely to be reliable that those on politics and sensitive current events. We learn to use Wikipedia for background, but to check essential facts.

As the weaknesses of new innovations appear, creative people find solutions. Recognizing the problems that result from totally open, anonymous access to writing and editing articles, one of Wikipedia's founders began a variant called Citizendium. Reflecting the ambitious and optimistic spirit of the Web, it describes itself as a "citizens' compendium of everything." More accurately, it is a "project that combines public participation with gentle expert guidance."[3] It is much like Wikipedia but with two new levels of protection for the integrity of articles. Writers and editors must register with their real names, and chief subject editors (whose expertise is described to readers) oversee specific subject areas. Citizendium did not have to start from scratch. Anyone who wants to provide free information online may use Wikipedia articles. Thus, Citizendium can begin with what has already been created, then revise and correct as necessary, and, it is hoped, better protect the results. If Citizendium's level of control is in fact valuable and effective, perhaps when you read this book everyone will be using it instead of Wikipedia.

The "wisdom of the crowd"

People ask all sorts of questions on Yahoo! Answers about dating, makeup, food, college ("Are online college classes as good as classroom classes?"), and wide-ranging social, economic, and political issues ("If we produce enough food to feed everyone in the world, why don't we?") Of course a lot of answers are ill informed. Many are biased, or full of opinion, not fact. The questioner designates the posted answer he or she deems the best. What qualifies the questioner, presumably a person who does not know the answer, to judge the worthiness of the replies? To what extent does the ease of posting a question reduce the likelihood that a person will seek out well-researched studies or books on the subject? There are obviously questions for which this kind of forum would not provide the best results. An example might be "Are medicines safe to use past their expiration dates?" The first two sample questions I quoted above, however, are likely to generate a lot of ideas and perspectives. Sometimes, that is exactly what the questioner wants. Without the Web, if someone asked questions like those of only a few friends, the answers might be less varied and less useful.

Some health sites on the Web encourage the public to rate doctors, hospitals, and medical treatments. Are such ratings valuable or dangerous? Will they motivate doctors and hospitals to change their practices to achieve higher ratings at the expense of good medical care? Steve Case, cofounder of AOL and founder of a health site that emphasizes ratings by the public, argues that if millions of people participate, the results will be very useful. Others are extremely suspicious of "the wisdom of the crowd." And there is always concern for manipulation. We have seen auction fraud and vandalism of Wikipedia articles. New Web sites have sprung up to buy and sell votes to get prominent display for articles on social media sites. What are the implications of such practices for sites where the public rates medical care? Will providers of new or questionable medical treatments generate fake favorable reviews and votes? How can doctors respond to specific criticism from a patient without violating the patient's privacy?

Let's pause briefly to put the problems of incorrect, distorted, and manipulated information in perspective. Quack medical cures and manipulative marketing are hardly new. Unlabeled product promotions date back hundreds of years. Eighteenth-century opera stars paid people to attend performances and cheer for them or boo their rivals. *Hatchet jobs* in the form of news articles, books, ads, and campaign flyers have dishonestly attacked politicians long before the Web existed. There are plenty of poorly written and inaccurate books. Historical movies merge truth and fiction, some for dramatic purposes, some for political purposes. They leave us with a distorted idea of what really happened. Two hundred years ago, cities had many more newspapers than they do today. Most were opinionated and partisan. At supermarket counters we can buy newspapers with stories as outlandish as any in blogs. The *New York Times* is a prime example of a respected newspaper, staffed by trained journalists, with an editorial board in charge. Yet one of its reporters fabricated many stories. Numerous other incidents of plagiarism, fabrication, and insufficient fact-checking have embarrassed newspapers and television networks in the past decade.

OK, the problems of unreliable information are not new. But they are problems, and the Web magnifies them. How can we distinguish good sources of information on the Web? Search engines and other services rank sites and bloggers by the number of people who visit them. A variety of people and services review and rate sites and blogs. Critics of the quality of information on the Web and the lack of editorial control disdain such ratings as merely popularity contests. The Internet gratifies the "mediocrity of the masses."[4] For blogs, as for Wikipedia or health care sites, the critics argue that popularity, voting, and consensus do not determine truth. That is correct, but there is no magic formula that tells us what is true and reliable on the Web or off the Web. That a large number of people visit a Web site does not guarantee quality, but the number of visitors does provide some information. (Why do newspapers publish best-seller lists for books?) We can choose to read only blogs written by Nobel Prize winners and college professors, if we wish, or only those recommended by friends and others we trust. Over time, the distinction between the blog equivalents of responsible journalism and supermarket tabloids becomes clear. Good reputations develop, just as they have for decades offline. Many university libraries provide guides for evaluating Web sites and information on those sites. (URLs for two are at the end of this chapter.) One good step is to determine who sponsors the site. If you cannot determine the sponsor of a site, you can consider its information as reliable as the information on a flyer you might find under your car's windshield wiper when you park in a busy parking lot. Ultimately we must find sites, reviewers, ratings, editors, experts, and other sources we trust. Good judgment and skepticism are always useful.

> *Written by fools for the reading of imbeciles.*
>
> —An evaluation of newspapers, not blogs,
> by a character in Joseph Conrad's novel *The Secret Agent* (1907)

Vulnerable viewers

Because you are reading this book, you probably are a student, a reasonably well-educated person who is learning how to analyze arguments and make good judgments. You can develop skills to evaluate material you read on the Web. What about people who have less education or ability? What risks does bad information pose to children who find it on the Web? Some critics of the Web worry most about the impact of inaccurate information on such vulnerable people. The fears of some seem to edge toward a belief that we (or experts, or the government) should somehow prevent such information from appearing. The many strong arguments for freedom of speech are arguments against any centralized or legally mandated way of accomplishing this. What can we do to improve the quality of information? Basic social and legal forces help (to a degree): freedom of speech (to provide responses, corrections, alternative viewpoints, etc.), teachers and parents, competition, fraud and libel laws—and people who care, who volunteer to write, review, and correct online information. What else can we do to reduce access by vulnerable people to dangerously wrong information?

Responsibilities of site operators

What are the ethical responsibilities of sponsors of information sites? Obviously, they should take reasonable care to ensure that the information they provide is accurate. If the site covers a topic for which mistakes can have significant risks and includes a large amount of user-supplied content, the site should have a mechanism to review content and filter out or remove dangerous material. A site should make clear which information is supplied by users and what has, or has not, been verified.

Responsible operators of sites that display material based on rankings or votes should anticipate manipulation and prepare to protect against it.

Manipulation of images

> *Seeing is believing may soon become an anachronism of the precomputer era.*
>
> —Sanford Sherizen[5]

Forrest Gump chats with John F. Kennedy in a movie. Céline Dion sings a duet with Elvis Presley. These and many more impossible events result from digital manipulation of photographs and video. We know that Elvis died decades before Dion's performance. We know movies and videos use computerized special effects. Special effects have long added to the creativity and enjoyment of entertainment. Where is the problem?

People can use the same technology for deception and fraud. The ease with which we can modify digital images and video raises ethical and social issues about deception.

Video-manipulation tools (and increased bandwidth) provide the opportunity for "forging" people. A company developed an animation system that modifies video images of a real person to produce a new video in which the person is speaking whatever words the user of the system provides. Another system analyzes recordings of a person's voice and synthesizes speech with the voice, inflections, and tones of that person. Combined, these systems will likely have many uses, including entertainment and advertising, but clearly people can also use them to deceive.[6]

Should news organizations ever modify images and video? Many have, but have apologized and, in some cases, fired people for doing so. During the conflict between Israel and Lebanon in 2006, a freelance news photographer who had worked for Reuters news agency for many years, admitted to digitally adding and darkening smoke in photos to make damage caused by rockets look worse. Reuters withdrew hundreds of the photographer's pictures from its collection of photos for sale and said company policy was strictly against altering photos. The *Los Angeles Times* fired a staff reporter after learning that he had manipulated an Iraq war photo the newspaper had run on the front page. The *New York Times* has a policy against altering news photographs. The National Press Photographers Association has a policy that considers any alteration of a photo's editorial content to be a breach of ethical standards.[7]

Altered images have become a problem in science research. For example, an editor of the *Journal of Cell Biology* said the journal discovers unacceptable image manipulation in roughly 20% of articles it accepts for publication.[8]

Is it acceptable to alter images if the purpose is artistic, or to enhance or improve the image or video without changing the meaning? Where is the line between editorial content and aesthetics? Some magazines treat their covers as advertisements for the magazine and are more likely to manipulate cover photos than the photos inside. (*National Geographic* generated one of the first computer-era controversies about faked photos when it moved two pyramids closer together to fit them both on the cover.) Some editors realize that a reputation for manipulating photos and video, like any form of deception, makes all of one's work suspect. The art director of *Texas Monthly* commented, "The altered photographs we had done were really hurting the integrity of the magazine's cover to the point that when we had a great photograph, nobody believed it." A new director of photography at *National Geographic* said its manipulated cover was a mistake. The editor of *Audubon*, also citing the credibility problem, announced in an editorial that *Audubon* would not print any manipulated photos.[9]

Faking photos is not new. Photographers have long staged scenes, used props, and altered photos in dark rooms. Thus, the ethical issues are not new, but now many more people face them because image manipulation has become so easy. Image manipulation is no longer reserved to the specialist with a darkroom and a lot of time. Many more faked photos and video are likely to appear on the Web for many different purposes. The public must become more aware of the possibility of fakery and must develop a reasonable skepticism.

7.1.2 WRITING, THINKING, AND DECIDING

> *I have a spelling checker.*
> *It came with my PC.*
> *It plainly marks four my revue,*
> *Miss steaks aye can knot sea.*
> *Eye ran this poem threw it,*
> *I'm sure your pleased too no.*
> *It's letter perfect in it's weigh,*
> *My checker tolled me sew.*
>
> —Jerrold H. Zar, "Candidate for a Pullet Surprise"[10]

Computers, like other tools and technologies, encourage certain uses and activities by making them easier. The new tools have displaced some skills that were important before. We look at some examples of the ways computers and other technologies affect the way we do things.

The spelling-checker verse above humorously illustrates the problem of doing what the tool makes easy and ignoring other important tasks. A computer can check the spelling of all the words in a document in less time than it takes a person to find the first one by flipping through the pages of a printed dictionary. But a simple spell checker looks up each word only to discover whether it is in its dictionary. It does not check whether the writer uses the word properly.* Desktop publishing and Web page design tools lead many people to concentrate on layout, fonts, and graphics at the expense of thoughtful writing, correct grammar, word usage, correct information, and editing—the parts that

---

*Grammar checkers were not common when the poem first circulated on the Internet. They would catch some of the errors.

still require hard mental effort. The convenience of using a computer can encourage mental laziness, which can sometimes have serious consequences. A newspaper editor in Pakistan received a letter to the editor by e-mail and inserted it into the newspaper without reading beyond the title. The letter was an attack on the prophet Muhammad. Angry Muslims set fires in the newspaper office. Several editors were arrested and charged with blasphemy, sometimes punishable by death.[11] Back when newspaper content was still being typeset and copyedited, such an accident would have been unlikely. This, of course, is an extreme example, but you can probably add more common ones from your experience.

Some critics of computers see the loss of skills as part of a long trend of skill losses due to technology. Taking their cue from Socrates (through Plato's *Phaedrus*), the critics find fault with the invention of writing. It destroyed memory and oral skill and obscured the distinction between wisdom and knowledge. With reading and writing, the complaint argues, a presentation tends to be more one sided, more dogmatic, because there is no dialogue, no one to question arguments and conclusions.[12]

It is valuable to observe the changes in social patterns that occur because of the invention of a new tool or technology. These observations help us understand how human beings behave and how society evolves. Although it is valuable to be aware of changes in the relative importance of various skills, it is not obvious, as some critics suggest, that all the changes are bad. Better skills replace some old ones. How much more poetry is available to us now in books than we could have memorized? Although most of us no longer develop strong memorization skill, this skill has not been lost to those who need it, such as an actor in a one-person play that lasts two hours. Some Chinese people worry that word processors are destroying the ability to write Chinese characters by hand. A Chinese scholar, Ping Xu, reported that a similar controversy arose when pens began to replace calligraphy brushes. He argued that, if the computer is easier to use and helps people learn the Chinese language, it will prevail. Language scholar Walter Ong pointed out that the old skills are not lost. They are enhanced but not used where the new ones function better. He argued that writing made oral communication much more effective.[13]

Computers, critics argued in the 1980s and 1990s, emphasize thinking based on data, numbers, and quantifiable entities. They discourage focus on judgment and values. They encourage the making of fancy charts based on complex computations, but they discourage deep thought about the purpose to which the charts will be put or the validity and meaning of the data. They discourage discussion with others and the ability to defend a point of view in conversation. The Web has countered some of these problems but generated others. It enhances communication. Anyone who reads blogs or participates in online discussions knows that dialogue and argument survive. We can find both deep and superficial analysis of all sorts of subjects. Critics charge that a vast amount of information is available, but it comes without wisdom. The Web encourages surfing, looking for facts, without evaluation. Reading brief snippets replaces reading books and long articles.

We need to carefully evaluate the changes and identify those that truly are problems. We should be alert to the tendency to overemphasize tasks that computers can do well,

IDIOTS AND DUNDERHEADS

Many losses of skills are unintended side effects of computers, but Microsoft made a conscious decision that had the effect of diminishing language skills. The thesaurus in Microsoft Word 2000 (and later versions) lists "trick" as the only meaning for "fool." It omits synonyms "clown," "blockhead," "idiot," "ninny," "dunderhead," "ignoramus," and others—all present in earlier versions. Because of the popularity of Word and the ease of using its reference utilities, fewer people consult standard references such as dictionaries and Roget's Thesaurus (which contain some of these and more choices: "dupe," and "simpleton," for example).

Microsoft said it eliminated words "that may have offensive uses."[14] Was this a dunderheaded decision that dulls the language and reduces literacy? Do producers of widely used reference works have an ethical responsibility to report the substance of their field accurately, or a social responsibility to remove potentially offensive words from the language?

while ignoring other important tasks—that is, the tendency to mental laziness. We need to resist the temptation to emphasize data rather than analysis, facts rather than understanding and evaluation. We need to distinguish between cutting and pasting from Web sites, on the one hand, and real research and writing.

Abdicating responsibility

People are often willing to let computers do their thinking for them. Abdication of responsibility to exercise judgment, and, sometimes, a reasonable amount of skepticism, has serious consequences. Businesses make decisions about loan and insurance-policy approvals with the help of software that analyzes risks. School districts make decisions about the progress of students and the careers of administrators on the basis of computer-graded and -calibrated tests. They sometimes make bad decisions because of ignorance of the kinds of errors that limitations of the system can cause. Law enforcement agents arrested people when a check of an FBI database showed an arrest warrant for someone with a similar name. Do officers think that because the computer displayed the warrant, the system has decided that the person they are checking is the wanted person? Or does an officer know that the system simply displays any close matches and that the responsibility for the arrest decision lies with the officer?

Sometimes, reliance on a computer system rather than human judgment becomes "institutionalized," in the sense that an organization's management and the legal system can exert strong pressure on individual professionals or employees to do what the computer says. In bureaucracies, a decision-maker might feel that there is less personal risk (and less bother) in just accepting a computer report rather than doing additional checking or

CALVIN AND HOBBES © 1995 Watterson. Dist. by UNIVERSAL PRESS SYNDICATE.

making a decision the software does not support. Computer programs advise doctors on treatments for patients. It is critical to remember that, in such complex fields as medicine, the computer systems might provide valuable information and ideas but might not be good enough to substitute for an experienced professional's judgment. In environments where, when something goes wrong, "I did what the program recommended" is a stronger defense (to managers or against a lawsuit) than "I did what my professional judgment and experience recommended," there is pressure on doctors and other professionals to abdicate personal responsibility.

7.1.3 COMPUTER MODELS

> *Likeness to truth is not the same thing as truth.*
> —Peter L. Bernstein[15]

Evaluating Models

Computer-generated predictions based on mathematical models of subjects with important social impact frequently appear in the news. Figure 7.1 shows a few examples. A mathematical model is a collection of data and equations describing, or simulating, characteristics and behavior of the thing studied. The models and simulations of interest to us here require so much data and/or computation that they must be run on computers. People use computers extensively to model and simulate both physical systems, such as the design for a new car or the flow of water in a river, and intangible systems, such as parts of the economy. Models allow us to simulate and investigate the possible effects of different designs, scenarios, and policies. They have obvious social and economic benefits: They help train operators of power plants, submarines, and airplanes. They enable us to consider alternatives and make better decisions, reducing waste, cost, and risk. They enable us to project trends and plan better for the future.

❖ Population growth.

❖ The cost of a proposed government program.

❖ The effects of second-hand smoke.

❖ When we will run out of a critical natural resource.

❖ The effects of a tax cut on the economy.

❖ The threat of global warming.

❖ When a big earthquake is likely to occur.

Figure 7.1   Some Problems Studied with Computer Models

Although the models we consider are abstract (i.e., mathematical), the meaning of the word *model* here is similar to its meaning in *model airplane*. Models are simplifications. Model airplanes generally do not have an engine, and the wing flaps might not move. In a chemistry class, we could use sticks and balls to build models of molecules, to help us understand their properties. The molecule models might not show the components of the individual atoms. Similarly, mathematical models do not include equations for every factor that could influence the outcome. They often include equations that are simplified because the correct ones are unknown or too complicated. For example, we use a constant known as the acceleration of gravity in a simple equation to determine when an object dropped from a high place will hit the ground. We ignore the effect of wind in the equation, but, on some days, wind could make a difference.

Physical models usually are not the same size as the real thing. Model planes are smaller; the molecule model is larger. In mathematical models, it is time rather than physical size that often differs from reality. Computations done on a computer to model a complex physical process in detail often take more time than the actual process takes. For models of long-range phenomena, such as population growth and climate change, the computation must take less time than the real phenomenon for the results to be useful.

Predictions from expensive computers and complex computer programs impress people, but models vary enormously in quality. Some are worthless. Others are very reliable. Politicians and special interest groups use model predictions to justify multibillion-dollar government programs and laws that restrict people's freedom, with significant impact on the economy and the standard of living of millions of people. It is important for both computer professionals and the public to have some idea of what is in such computer programs, where their uncertainties and weaknesses might lie, and how to evaluate their claims. It is the professional and ethical responsibility of those who design and develop models for public issues to honestly and accurately describe the results, assumptions, and limitations of their models.

The following questions help us determine the accuracy and usefulness of a model.

1. How well do the modelers understand the underlying science or theory (be it physics, chemistry, economics, or whatever) of the system they are studying? How well understood are the relevant properties of the materials involved? How accurate and complete are the data?
2. Models necessarily involve assumptions and simplifications of reality. What are the assumptions and simplifications in the model?
3. How closely do the results or predictions of the model correspond with results from physical experiments or real experience?

After considering a few examples briefly, we will look at two examples in more depth: car crash models and climate models.

Among three models developed to predict the change in health care costs that would result if the U.S. adopted a Canadian style national health plan, the predictions varied by \$279 billion. Two of the models predicted large increases and one predicted a drastic decrease in health care costs.[16] Why was there such a difference? There are both political and technical reasons why models might not be accurate. Political reasons, especially for this example, are probably obvious. Among the technical reasons are the following:

❖ We might not have complete knowledge of the system we are modeling. In other words, we might not fully understand the basic physical or social science involved.

❖ The data describing current conditions or characteristics might be incomplete or inaccurate.

❖ Computing power could be inadequate for the number of computations needed to model the full complexity of the system.

❖ It is difficult, if not impossible, to numerically quantify variables that represent human values and choices.

Are reusable (washable cloth) diapers better for the environment than disposable diapers? When environmentalists proposed bans and taxes on disposable diapers, this controversy consumed almost as much energy as diaper manufacturing. Several modelers developed computer models to study the question. We call this particular kind of model a life-cycle analysis. It attempts to consider the resource use and environmental effects of all aspects of the product, including manufacture, use, and disposal. To illustrate how difficult such a study might be, Figure 7.2 lists a few of the questions about which the modelers made assumptions. Depending on the assumptions, the conclusions differed.[17] It is worth noting also that the models focused on one quality—environmental impact. To make a personal decision, we might consider the results of such a model (if we think it reliable), and we might also consider other factors such as cost, aesthetics, convenience, comfort, and health risks.

The U.S. Army Corps of Engineers uses mathematical models to predict how long an artificially constructed or replenished beach will last before waves wash it away.

❖ How many times do parents reuse a cloth diaper before discarding it? (Values ranged from 90 to 167.)

❖ Should the model give credit for energy recovered from incineration of waste? Or does pollution from incineration counterbalance the benefit?

❖ What value should the model assign for the labor cost of washing diapers?

❖ How many cloth diapers do parents use each time they change a baby? (Many parents use two at once for increased protection.) Numbers in the models ranged from 1.72 to 1.9.

❖ How should the model count pesticides used in growing cotton?

Figure 7.2 Factors in Diaper Life-Cycle Modeling

Two geologists explain weaknesses in these models.[18] Among other simplifying assumptions, the models assume that all waves have the same wavelength, that all waves come from the same direction, and that all grains of sand are the same size. A model uses only six of 49 parameters that might affect the amount of sand washed away. Even if these six are the most important (or if the model included all 49), the appropriate values for a particular beach are uncertain. Often, say the critics, the beaches do not last as long as the models predict, partly because the models do not accurately provide for relevant but irregular and unpredictable natural phenomena such as big storms.

Example: Modeling car crashes*

Car crash-analysis programs use a technique called the finite-element method. These programs superimpose a grid on the frame of a car, dividing the car into a finite number of small pieces, or elements. The grid is entered into the program, along with data describing the specifications of the materials making up each element (e.g., density, strength, and elasticity). Suppose we are studying the effects on the structure of the car from a head-on collision. Engineers initialize data to represent a crash into a wall at a specified speed. The program computes the force, acceleration, and displacement at each grid point and the stress and strain within each element. It repeats these calculations to show what happens as time passes in small increments. These programs require intensive computation to simulate 40–100 milliseconds of real time from the impact.

A real crash test can cost several hundred thousand dollars. It includes building and testing a unique prototype for a new car design. The crash-analysis programs allow engineers to consider alternatives, for example, to vary the thickness of steel for selected components, or change materials altogether, and discover the effect without building another prototype for each alternative. But how good are the programs?

---

*An earlier version of this section appeared in my chapter, "Social and Legal Issues," in *An Invitation to Computer Science* by G. Michael Schneider and Judith L. Gersting, West Publishing Co., 1995. (Used with permission.)

How well is the physics of car crashes understood? How accurate and complete are the data? Force and acceleration are basic principles. The physics involved in these programs is straightforward. Engineers know the relevant properties of steel, plastics, aluminum, glass, and other materials in a car fairly well. Although they understand the behavior of the materials when force is applied gradually, they know less about the behavior of some materials under abrupt acceleration, as in a high-speed impact, and their behavior near or at breaking point. There are good data on the density, elasticity, and other characteristics of materials used in the model.

What simplifications do the programs make? The grid pattern is the most obvious. A car is smooth, not made up of little blocks. Also, time is continuous. It does not pass in discrete steps. The accuracy of a simulation depends in part on how fine the grid is and how small the time intervals are. Current computer speeds allow updating the calculations on fine grids with small time intervals (e.g., one millionth of a second).

How do the computed results compare to actual crash tests on real cars? High-speed cameras record real crash tests. Engineers attach sensors to the car and mark reference points on the frame. They compare the values the sensors record with values the program computes. They physically measure the distortion or displacement of the reference points and then compare these measurements with the computed positions of the points. Starting with the results of the physical crash, the engineers use elementary physics to calculate backward and determine the deceleration and other forces acting on the car. They compare these with the values computed in the simulation. The conclusion? Crash-analysis programs do an extremely good job.

Engineers who work with the crash-analysis programs do not believe that physical crashes will be or should be eliminated. The computer program is an implementation of theory. Results could be poor if something happens that the program designers simply did not consider. The crash-analysis programs are excellent design tools that enable increases in safety with far less development cost. The physical crash test is confirmation.

In part because of the confidence that has developed over time in the validity of the results, engineers use variations of the same crash-analysis modeling programs in a large variety of other impact applications, including those in Figure 7.3.

Example: Modeling climate

Climate change is a very complex scientific phenomenon with potentially large social and economic impact. Predicting future global temperatures and other aspects of climate is an extremely difficult task. In the 1970s, after global temperatures had been dropping for about 30 years, some scientists warned that we faced serious problems from global cooling, including the possibility of a new Ice Age. Then temperatures began to rise again. The threat of excess global warming, possibly caused by human-induced increase of carbon dioxide (CO_2) and other greenhouse gases in the atmosphere, replaced global cooling in the headlines and scientific journals.

From the late 1800s to the late 1900s, the average global air temperature rose roughly 0.6°C. It is generally expected to continue to rise through the 21st-century. Scientists use

❖ Predict damage to a hazardous waste container if dropped.

❖ Predict damage to an airplane windshield or nacelle (engine covering) if hit by a bird.

❖ Determine whether beer cans would get dented if an assembly line were speeded up.

❖ Simulate a medical procedure called balloon angioplasty, where doctors insert a balloon in a blocked artery and inflate it to open the artery. The computer program helps researchers determine how to perform the procedure with less damage to the arterial wall.

❖ Predict the action of airbags and the proper location for sensors that inflate them.

❖ Design interior parts of cars to reduce injuries during crashes (e.g., from the impact of a steering wheel on a human chest).

❖ Design bicycle and motorcycle helmets to reduce head injuries.

❖ Design cameras to reduce damage if dropped.

❖ Forecast effects of earthquakes on bridges and buildings.

Figure 7.3 Other Uses of Crash-Analysis Programs

climate models to try to determine how much temperatures will rise, what is causing the rise (e.g., natural cyclic changes or human industrial activity), and what other climate changes will occur as a result. Since 1990, the Intergovernmental Panel on Climate Change (IPCC), sponsored by the United Nations and the World Meteorological Organization, has published comprehensive reports on the science of climate change roughly every five years. Much of the information in this section comes from those reports.[19]

Climate models, like the car-crash analysis models, calculate relevant variables for grid points and elements (grid boxes) for specified simulated time intervals. The grid circles the earth, rises through the atmosphere, and goes down into the ocean. Equations simulate atmospheric pressure, temperature, incoming solar energy, outgoing radiant energy, wind speed and direction, moisture, precipitation, ocean currents, and so forth.

Climate models have improved over the few decades that scientists have been developing and working with them. The models used in the 1980s and early 1990s were limited. Here is a brief sampling of simplifications, assumptions, and factors modelers did not fully understand: The models did not distinguish day and night.[20] They used a fairly coarse grid (with points roughly 500 kilometers apart). They did not include the El Niño phenomenon. They made assumptions about methane (a greenhouse gas) that scientists later determined were incorrect. They did not include aerosols (small particles in the air) that have a cooling effect. Clouds are extremely important to climate, but many processes involved with the formation, effects, and dissipation of clouds are not particularly well understood. The IPCC summarized in 2001: "As has been the case since the first IPCC Assessment Report in 1990, probably the greatest uncertainty in future projections of climate arise from clouds. . . . Clouds represent a significant source of potential error in climate simulations."[21] The extremely simplified representations of the oceans in these models were another very significant weakness. Computing power was insufficient to do the many calculations to simulate ocean behavior. When run on past data, some of the early climate models predicted temperature increases three to five times as high as what actually occurred over the previous century. Thus, it should not be surprising that there was much skepticism about the climate models and their projections.

Current models are more detailed and complex. Increased computer power allows more runs of a model with different data or assumptions. Increased computer speeds allow the use of finer grids. (That is, the models can compute variables at more points, spaced roughly 200 kilometers apart.) Increased data collection and basic science research have been improving the understanding of the behavior and interactions of climate system components. Many models now predict air temperature near the surface of the earth well, that is, close to observed temperatures, for the recent past. It is reasonable that confidence in the models had increased. Based on the calculations of the models and on comparing previous model projections with actual data from the recent past, the 2007 IPCC report finds it "extremely likely" that human activity has had a substantial warming effect on climate since 1750.[22] The report projects warming of $0.2°C$ per decade for the next few decades.

The IPCC reports that many uncertainties remain. Models project that doubling the concentration of greenhouse gases in the atmosphere from its level at the beginning of the 20th-century will cause a global temperature increase within the range $2°C$–$4.5°C$. Much of the variation in the model results comes from the still troublesome lack of full understanding of some of the effects of clouds.[23] There are still weaknesses in understanding variations in output from the sun, sources and behavior of methane, connections between CO_2 emissions and CO_2 concentration in the atmosphere, and other factors. There is insufficient data on many phenomena for the period before satellites were used for data collection. The IPCC report lists among "key uncertainties" insufficient data to draw conclusions about trends in the thickness of Antarctic sea ice. The report indicates that the accuracy of projections for future climate change is still hampered by the complexity of the problem. That is, even the extremely powerful computers of today are not sufficient to achieve an ideal level of resolution (grid size) and to include simulation of more processes that affect climate.[24] Some climate scientists who are not part of IPCC argue that the models have more fundamental weaknesses, for example, not fully considering long-term natural cycles.

A variety of studies are underway to see how sensitive the results of the climate models are to minor changes in technical assumptions. Modelers are also developing methods to quantify the uncertainty in the models.

The projections of the climate models for rise in sea level are in the range of 8 to 23 inches (between, roughly, the end of the 20th-century and the end of the 21st-century).*[25] Why do science fiction movies about global warming show the buildings of cities underwater? The entertainment industry dramatizes, of course. Why does a science-museum exhibit show water up to the middle of the Statue of Liberty (about 200 feet above sea level)? A climate scientist once said that "to capture the public's imagination," "we have to offer up scary scenarios, make simplified dramatic statements."[26] Is this a good idea? A 20-inch rise in sea level would be a very significant problem but one we can tackle. Tens or hundreds of feet of sea level rise would be an enormous disaster. Exaggeration might lead people to take constructive action. On the other hand, exaggeration might lead to overreaction and counterproductive actions. If we hope to solve real potential problems (such as flooding in low-lying areas), we must first identify them accurately.

7.2 Computers and Community

> *While all this razzle-dazzle connects us electronically, it disconnects us from each other, having us "interfacing" more with computers and TV screens than looking in the face of our fellow human beings. Is this progress?*
>
> —Jim Hightower[27]

> *Something goes on among humans that is definitely not present in human-machine relationships.*
>
> —Jerry Mander[28]

Many people spend hours online instead of with their families and in-person friends. Teenagers and young adults stay up all night in front of their computer screens, playing games, exploring systems, or surfing the Web. Some virtually eliminate direct contact with their families and other people. Some who are already socially awkward find computers easier to deal with than people; the computer provides an excuse not to overcome the social awkwardness. In an extreme case, a mother neglected her children and left them in filth while she surfed the Internet.[29]

Critics of the Internet worry that computers reduce face-to-face gathering and that the Web hurts local community vibrancy. Neil Postman says that voting, shopping, banking, and getting information at home is a "catastrophe." There are fewer opportunities for people to be "co-present," resulting in isolation from neighbors. Technology, he worries, puts a much greater emphasis on the individual and downplays the importance of

---

*The projections vary because of different assumptions in the different models and different scenarios about future greenhouse gas emissions.

community. Richard Sclove and Jeffrey Scheuer argue that electronic communication will erode family and community life to the point that people will mourn the loss of depth and meaning in their lives.[30] How serious are these problems? Does the Internet make people narrow and unsocial? Is working on a computer more isolating than reading a book, an activity that is usually applauded? Is the Internet destroying communities?

Social scientists offer various theories about what makes a strong community. Robert Putnam argues that one important factor is the number of clubs and other organizations people join and are active in.[31] As Alexis de Tocqueville observed more than 150 years ago, "Americans of all ages, all stations in life, and all types of disposition are forever forming associations."[32] We join hobby clubs, religious congregations, Boy Scouts and Girl Scouts, unions, professional organizations, service clubs, hiking and running clubs, and myriad others. Such memberships create informal personal and information networks that help solve social problems in a community. But participation in clubs has been declining. Critics of computers and the Internet blame them for this decline, but social scientists point to a number of other factors: modern transportation and communications (encouraging increased mobility), changes in family patterns (later marriage, more divorce, working mothers), and television. The loss of close, local community ties began before widespread use of personal computers and the Internet. Early studies of Net users (when they were a small part of the population) found that they were at least as likely as demographically similar nonusers to visit with family and friends and be members of a club or organization. Some studies in the 1990s found that some Internet users spent less time with family and friends. Later studies (some by the same researchers) found opposite results. Users of computers and the Internet were "voracious consumers of information," not just from online sources. They read newspapers, magazines, and books and watched serious news programs on television as much as or more than people with similar demographic characteristics who were not frequent users of computers and the Internet. A substantial number of e-mail users said e-mail brought them closer to their families. Jon Katz summarized the results of a survey by Luntz Research Companies by saying, "The Internet is not a breeding ground for apathy, disconnection, and fragmentation. Instead, the online world is home to some of the most participatory citizens we are ever likely to have."[33]

With hindsight, it might seem odd that people worried so much about the antisocial effects of computer use. Now, with the popularity of social-networking sites, cell phone conversations, instant messaging, sharing of photos and other material, the Web is a very social place. And yet, almost 6% of adults in a Stanford University study in 2006 said their relationships suffered because of their Internet use.[34] "Addiction" to the Internet is a real problem for some people. A study of so-called computer addicts found that many had other psychological problems.[35] Without computers, computer addicts might be among the people who engage in other unwise or unhealthy behavior, such as excessive gambling, alcoholism, drug abuse, eating disorders, television addiction, and even excessive shopping. These are all problems to be addressed and treated, but they are not flaws of the substances or technologies the people misuse.

WAL-MART AND E-COMMERCE VERSUS DOWNTOWN AND COMMUNITY[36]

Does electronic commerce force changes on communities that no one wants? In their article "On the Road Again? If Information Highways Are Anything like Interstate Highways—Watch Out!" Richard Sclove and Jeffrey Scheuer argued that it would.[37] They use the analogy of a Wal-Mart store draining business from downtown shops, resulting in the decline of the downtown community, a "result that no consumers wanted or intended." They generalize from the Wal-Mart scenario and warn that, as cyberspace became commercialized and we conducted more economic transactions electronically, we would lose more local stores, local professional and social services, and convivial public spaces like the downtowns of small towns. Consumers would be "compelled" to use electronic services, "like it or not." Other strong critics of technology share the underlying point of view in Sclove and Scheuer's article, so it is worth examining their argument.

The Wal-Mart analogy is a good one. The scenario is useful for illustrating and clarifying some issues about the impact of e-commerce on communities. Suppose, say Sclove and Scheuer, that a new Wal-Mart store has opened just outside of town and about half the town residents begin to do about a third of their shopping there, while the others continue to do all their shopping downtown. Everyone shops downtown, and everyone wants the downtown stores to remain. But downtown stores have lost about 16.5% of their sales, and many will not survive. Sclove and Scheuer describe this as an "involuntary transformation" that no consumer wanted or intended. It occurs, they say, because of a "perverse market dynamic." The changes, however, are not involuntary or perverse. The core of the problem with Sclove's and Scheuer's interpretation is their failure to make two important distinctions: the distinction between wanting something and willingness to pay for it and the distinction between something being coerced or involuntary, on the one hand, and being unwanted, unintended, or unexpected, on the other.

Consider a simpler situation for a moment. Suppose we poll the adult residents of a small town with a population of, for instance, 3,000, and ask if they would like to have a fine French restaurant in town. Almost everyone says yes. Will a French restaurant open in the town? Probably not. Almost everyone wants it, yet there is not enough potential business for it to survive. There is a market dynamic at work, but it is not perverse. The fact that consumers want a particular service, store, or product is irrelevant if not enough people are willing to buy it at prices that make the business viable. In Sclove's and Scheuer's Wal-Mart scenario, the downtown stores could stay in business if the people were willing to pay higher prices to make up for the 16.5% of revenue lost to Wal-Mart. But we know that if the stores raise prices, they will almost certainly lose even more customers. The town residents are not willing to pay what it costs to keep the downtown stores in business. You might object: The townspeople did not have to pay the higher prices before. Why now? Because now the people who shop at Wal-Mart (or online) *have another choice.* Whatever price advantage or convenience lured them to Wal-Mart (or to e-commerce), they were not getting that benefit before. Again there is a market dynamic at work but not a perverse one: competition.

The second issue about the Wal-Mart/ e-commerce scenario is whether the change is an "involuntary" transformation. Sclove and Scheuer say that, as local businesses decline, people will be compelled to use electronic services, like it or not. Is this accurate? No more so than Wal-Mart shoppers or cyberspace enthusiasts were compelled to shop downtown (or from other offline stores), like it or not, before they had the new option. The new status quo is no more involuntary than the previous one. Although no one wants to see the downtown decline, the actions that could lead to that result are all voluntary. When a new store opens, no one is forced to shop there. The impact on the downtown stores might not have been obvious to all the townspeople at the beginning (although now it is common enough that they might anticipate it), but an unexpected or unintended result is not the same as a coerced result. In a free society, individuals make millions of decisions based on their knowledge and preferences. This decentralized, individualized decision-making produces a constantly changing pattern of stores, services, and investments (not to mention social and cultural patterns). No one can predict exactly what the result will be, and no one

intends a particular picture of the economy or society, but (apart from government subsidies, prohibitions, and regulations) the actions of the consumers and merchants are voluntary. No one person can expect to have exactly the mix of shopping options (or other community characteristics) that he or she wants. If the result flows from the myriad decisions that consumers and producers make, it is not coerced. It is the process, not the result, that tells us whether people are being compelled.

Sclove and Scheuer propose laws and regulations to strengthen the elements they consider important to community. For example, in order to "conserve cultural space for face-to-face social engagement, traditional forms of community life, off-screen leisure activities, and time spent in nature," they give two examples of regulations they approve: adjusting charges for the Internet to discourage its use one evening a week and using revenue from a special tax on electronic shopping to subsidize (offline) local community projects. Economists point out that tax subsidies and artificial manipulation of prices waste resources by shifting production from services consumers value more highly to those they value less. Supporters of such proposals view the individual choices as less important than the strength of the community. Coming from Sclove and Scheuer, who expressed so much concern about things "involuntary" and about people being compelled to use certain services, "like it or not," their proposals are astonishing in their casual denial of freedom and choice. Like it or not, you have to pay a higher rate for

Internet access on Monday evening, even if that is the only evening you are off from your restaurant job. Like it or not, you have to subsidize community activities you do not participate in, because you prefer electronic shopping. Sclove and Scheuer do not seem to see coercion when practiced against people whose preferences differ from theirs.

Change creates new options and causes some old options to disappear. Those who prefer a new option see it as progress. Those who prefer a lost option view the change as bad. Neither side's preference is inherently or absolutely better than the other. People have different likes and dislikes, different priorities, different lifestyles. Community is important to most people. Thoughtful criticism of the impact of the Net on community can make us think about our own activities, choices, and trade-offs. Individualism and strength of community are not in opposition. Coercive manipulation of people's choices and activities breeds resentment rather than community.

Earlier critics complained that the telephone replaced true human interaction with disembodied, remote voices. It actually expanded and deepened social relationships for isolated people: women in general (farm wives, in particular) and the elderly, for example.[38] Today, the Internet provides communities focused on special interests or problems for which a person might not find many contacts in his or her local community. Some people who are socially awkward communicate more because of e-mail than they would without it. From its early years, according to the CEO of America Online, more people used AOL for "community" than for information retrieval.

To the extent that the Internet contributes to the formation of electronic relationships with people scattered around the country and the world, it might further weaken local community bonds. The degree of change, however, seems small compared to the effects on communities from other technological and social changes. Automated and online services reduce the opportunities for personal interaction with local merchants and neighbors in the course of ordinary daily activities, but they free time that we can fill with activities shared with people we know well and associate with by choice.

Many richly developed virtual communities thrive online. They include gaming communities, simulations, and alternate worlds in which our avatar (online character) can move about, interact with others, play, and learn. Some scholars who study community cannot understand the appeal of online, virtual communities. Some fear them, seeing them as symptoms of, or contributing causes of, social and psychological dysfunction. Online communities, or environments, such as Second Life, are an intriguing development. They blend online fictions with real-world realities. You can spend time in the virtual world, buy "real estate" there with virtual money, and operate a virtual business. But you can also visit the virtual store of a real-world company and buy real products. As we mentioned in Chapter 6, some companies schedule real employment interviews on Second Life. Your avatar can run around a virtual track in a fundraising event that raises real money for a real-world charity. What are the impacts of such communities? Will they attract social misfits who do not have a real life? Will people find innovative and beneficial ways to use them? What guesses or projections can we make based on what we have seen of the Internet so far?

7.3 The Digital Divide

The term *digital divide* refers to the fact that some groups of people have access to and regularly use computer, information, and communications technology, while others do not. The focus of discussion about the digital divide has shifted over time as more people acquire digital technology. In the 1990s, the focus was on access to computers and the Internet for poor people, people in rural areas, and certain demographic groups within developed countries. There is more focus now on the digital divide between developed countries and poor countries. We consider both.

7.3.1 TRENDS IN COMPUTER ACCESS

Once upon a time, everyone in the world had equal access to PCs and the Internet. They did not exist, and we all had none. Later, a small, elite minority enjoyed these new, expensive tools. As the technology began to spread and its value became clearer, people became more concerned about the gap in access. In 1994, according to a Times Mirror survey, a family in the U.S. with a college-graduate parent and family income over $50,000 was five times more likely to have a home computer and ten times more likely to have a modem than the family of a nongraduate earning less than $30,000. Almost half the children of college graduates used a computer at home. Only 17% of children of parents with high-school education or less did.[39] Poor children and children of some ethnic minorities had less access to computers both in schools and at home. In the early 1990s, only about 10% of Net users were women. By 1997, the gender gap among users had vanished,[40] but other gaps remained.* Black and Hispanic households were about half as likely as the general population to own a computer. Access in rural and remote regions lagged the cities.

Advocates of universal access to the Net argued that access might give some people such a large advantage over those without it that our society would divide sharply into the "information haves" and "information have-nots," leaving the have-nots to a lowly and unsatisfying existence. The human cost in joblessness, wasted potential, and poverty could be high. Many advocates saw access as an issue of social equity. A variety of organizations and government committees developed principles and programs for universal access. Computer Professionals for Social Responsibility (CPSR), for example, published a set of minimum requirements, including the following: that everyone in the country must

---

*Only about one-quarter of information technology professionals are women, and the percentage of women dropped between 2004 and 2006. Can you think of reasons for the drop?

have access to the Net; that hardware and software must be easy to use and fit the needs of all users, including the disabled; that training must be available; and that pricing must be structured so that everyone can afford the service.[41] Various organizations defined universal access to include e-mail, Web browsers, and interactive, multimedia equipment and software. Advocates of universal access see access as a right—in particular, a positive right (i.e., a claim right, in the terminology of Section 1.4.3)—something that society must provide for everyone who cannot afford it themselves. They advocated requirements that Internet companies subsidize access for poor people. Others argued that the gap would shrink without subsidies. Those who emphasize negative rights (liberties) over claim rights raised objections to mandatory and tax-funded programs: such programs violate the liberties of business owners and taxpayers who must pay for them.

Virtually all technological innovation is first available to the rich (or others willing to pay the initially high price). The early purchases finance improvements in design and production techniques that bring the price down. Prices of many consumer products follow this pattern. Telephones and televisions were originally luxuries of the rich. Now almost everyone (in developed countries) has them. (By 2006 there were more televisions than people in the U.S.) When first introduced in the 1980s, compact-disk music players cost $1,000. Now DVD players are cheap. Computer prices plunged more dramatically than prices of most other products, even while the memory, speed, and variety of input/output devices and software were increasing enormously.* The vast resources of the Internet are available for about what home telephone service used to cost.

Cost is one factor that affects access by the general population. Ease of use is another. At first, PCs and the Internet were difficult to use. Nearly a century ago, the electric starter for automobiles eliminated the need to crank the engine of a car. That made driving easier, and more people began driving. Similarly, software innovations, such as point-and-click graphical user interfaces, Web browsers, and search engines, made computer use significantly more comfortable for ordinary people. With lower prices, more useful applications, and ease of use, ownership and access spread quickly. The data I found about the extent of computer ownership and Web access differ in specific numbers, but all showed the same trends: In 1990, 22% of households in the U.S. owned a computer. In 2001, 63% did, and 57% had Internet access at home. At that time, 84% of homes with children in middle and high school had Internet access. That so many more homes with school children had Internet access suggests that families perceive access to be important for their children and allocate their spending accordingly. By 2004, 70%–75% of Americans, overall, had access to the Internet from their homes.[†42] Figure 7.4 shows that computer technology reached more households faster than earlier technologies.

---

*For example, the cost of disk storage fell from hundreds of dollars per megabyte in the 1980s to $5.23 per megabyte in 1991 to less than a penny a megabyte by 2001.[43] The cost continues to fall. I bought my first computer in 1983. It had less than a megabyte of memory, a 10-megabyte disk, a monochrome monitor, no modem or graphics, and a chip speed of perhaps a few megahertz. It cost $5,000.

†When I tried to find more recent figures, I found data on the percentage of homes with broadband or wireless access. Thus, the focus of the divide shifted from basic computer ownership and Internet access to higher-quality services.

Earlier technologies

- ❖ Television   25
- ❖ Radio   27
- ❖ Telephone   35
- ❖ Electricity   45
- ❖ Automobiles   55

Computer-related technologies

- ❖ Personal computers 16
- ❖ World Wide Web   7
- ❖ Cell phones   13

Figure 7.4   Number of Years (Approximately) to Reach 25% of U.S. Households[44]

Individuals, businesses, community organizations, and government programs contributed to the spread of computers and Internet access. Entrepreneurs provide options for people who want to use a product but cannot afford to buy it. For example, people who do not own a washing machine use coin-operated laundries. Internet cafés sprang up from Alaska to Cairo in the 1990s, when Net access from home was relatively uncommon. They provide access for an hourly fee, or free with purchases of food or coffee. The federal government began spending about $1.5 billion a year on technology for schools. Local governments spent several billion more. By the end of the 1990s, most public libraries provided Internet access for the public for free. By 2000, 98% of high schools had Internet access. In the early 2000s, Ford Motor Company gave free home computers to about 166,000 employees. At about the same time, African-Americans, people 65 and older, and Hispanics significantly increased their use of the Internet. Groups with low access in earlier years began to catch up. Community centers, and especially senior centers, offer classes in how to use computers. The gaps among Hispanics, Blacks, and Whites almost completely disappeared among people with the same education levels.[45] AT&T, Microsoft, Oracle, Intel, and one of Bill Gates' charitable foundations gave hundreds of millions of dollars to provide computers and Internet services for schools, universities, and libraries. But probably the most important factors in shrinking the digital divide were the incredible decline in prices of computers and the increase in services that made the Web useful and attractive to more people. The phenomenon that new technologies and inventions first are expensive luxuries, then become cheaper and spread throughout the population, has led some observers to conclude that it is more accurate to think of people as "haves" and "have-laters" rather than "haves" and "have-nots."[46]

7.3.2 THE GLOBAL DIVIDE AND THE NEXT BILLION USERS

Approximately one billion people worldwide have access to the Web. From one perspective, that is an extraordinary accomplishment in a very short a time. From another perspective, it means that about five billion people do not have access to the Web. Most people in the world have never made a telephone call and have little or no access to books. Lack of access to the Internet in much of the world has the same causes as lack of telephones, health care, education, and so on: poverty, isolation, and, sometimes, politics.

Nonprofit organizations and huge computer companies have ongoing projects to spread computer access to more people in developing countries. Some companies use the catchphrase *the next billion users* to describe the people their programs address. For the companies, these programs create goodwill and—if successful in improving the standard of living and economies of the target countries—a large future customer base. Companies have trained hundreds of thousands of teachers to use technology effectively in classrooms in China, India, and other countries. One Laptop per Child[47] is one of several nonprofit organizations working to extend access. Academic computer professionals and several companies sponsor this project to distribute inexpensive, rugged laptops with specially designed software to millions of children in developing countries.

Bringing new technology to poor countries is not simply a matter of money to buy standard equipment. PCs and laptops must work in extreme heat (or cold), extremes of humidity, and dusty or rainy environments. Power requirements must be very low. (In some areas, power is irregular and current fluctuates. In others, there is no power.) Displays must be readable in bright sunlight. One Laptop per Child aims to provide its laptop at a price of $100. It will require only two watts of power—little enough to depend on solar or human power.[48]

Intel announced plans to invest $1 billion over five years to increase access to computers and the Internet in developing countries. The goals of the program, called World Ahead, include designing low-cost computers, increasing high-speed Internet access, and training students and teachers. Microsoft and Intel are setting up thousands of computer kiosks for communities in rural areas of India. Almost every time I have read about a program to bring Internet access or cell phones to rural adults over the past several years, the most immediate uses are similar. Farmers use the Internet to learn about better farming techniques and to get up-to-date pricing information for their crops. Fishermen use their cell phones to find a nearby village where they will get a good price for their catch. As the technology spreads, food production and economic well-being improve.

Some people active in the movement to shrink the digital divide emphasize the need to provide access in ways appropriate to the local culture. For example, one Web site argues that access can hurt the poor "by loosening the bonds of tradition."[49] In many countries, access "is one-way, entertainment-oriented, commercial." It may accelerate the exodus of untrained, unprepared young people from rural areas into cities. How significant are these concerns? What can be done to alleviate them?

7.4 Evaluations of the Impact of Computer Technology

> *The microchip is . . . made of silicon, or sand—a natural resource that is in great abundance and has virtually no monetary value. Yet the combination of a few grains of this sand and the infinite inventiveness of the human mind has led to the creation of a machine that will both create trillions of dollars of added wealth for the inhabitants of the earth in the next century and will do so with incomprehensibly vast savings in physical labor and natural resources.*
>
> —Stephen Moore[50]

> *Quite apart from the environmental and medical evils associated with them being produced and used, there are two moral judgments against computers. One is that computerization enables the large forces of our civilization to operate more swiftly and efficiently in their pernicious goals of making money and producing things. . . . And secondly, in the course of using these, these forces are destroying nature with more speed and efficiency than ever before.*
>
> —Kirkpatrick Sale[51]

7.4.1 THE NEO-LUDDITE VIEW OF COMPUTERS, TECHNOLOGY, AND HUMAN NEEDS

The quotations above illustrate the extreme divergence of views about the value of computer technology. Evaluations of computers cover the spectrum from "miracle" to "catastrophe." Although most of this book discusses problems that arise with the use of computers and the Internet, the implicit (and sometimes explicit) view has been that computers are a positive development bringing us many benefits. Our discussion of failures of computer systems warns us that some potential applications can have horrifying risks. The potential for loss of freedom and privacy via government surveillance and the building of consumer dossiers is a serious danger. Computer crime is expensive, and changes in employment are disruptive. We might urgently try to prevent implementation of some applications and urgently advocate increased protection from risks and better solutions for problems, yet not consider the threats and risks as reasons for condemning the technology as a whole. For the most part, we have looked at new risks and negative side effects as problems that occur in the natural process of change, either problems we need to solve (with some combination of technology, law, education, market processes, management, and public pressure) or the price we pay for the benefits, part of a trade-off.

This attitude is shared by many people with different political views, people who disagree about the significance of specific computer-related problems and about exactly how to solve them.

On the other hand, there are people who utterly reject the view that computing technology is a positive development with many important benefits. They see the benefits as few and overwhelmingly outweighed by the damage done. The difference in perspective is illustrated by a comment made by one reviewer of this book. He objected to the "gift of fire" analogy I use to suggest that computers can be very useful and also very dangerous. The reviewer thought "Pandora's box" was more appropriate. Pandora's box held "all the ills of mankind." Kirkpatrick Sale, author of *Rebels Against the Future*, demonstrates his opinion of computers by smashing one with a sledgehammer at public appearances.

In England in 1811–1812, people burned factories and mills in efforts to stop the technologies and social changes that were eliminating their jobs. Many were weavers who had worked at home on small machines. They were called Luddites.* For almost 200 years, the memory of the violent Luddite uprising has endured as the most dramatic symbol of opposition to the Industrial Revolution. The term *Luddite* has long been a derisive description for people who oppose technological progress. More recently, critics of technology have adopted Luddite as an honorable term. Kirkpatrick Sale and many others who share his viewpoint call themselves neo-Luddites, or simply Luddites. They publish many books criticizing computers and the Internet.

Luddite criticisms of computer technology

What do the neo-Luddites find so reprehensible about computers? Some of their criticisms are problems that also trouble people whose view of computers is generally positive, problems we discussed in earlier chapters. One of the differentiating characteristics of the neo-Luddites is that they focus on these problems, seeing no solutions or trade-offs, and conclude that computers are a terribly bad development for humankind. Among their specific criticisms are the following:

❖ Computers cause massive unemployment and deskilling of jobs. "Sweatshop labor is involved in their manufacture."[52]

❖ Computers "manufacture needs," that is, we use them just because they are there, not because they satisfy real needs.

❖ Computers cause social inequity.

❖ Computers cause social disintegration; they are dehumanizing. They weaken communities and lead to isolation of people from each other.

❖ Computers separate humans from nature and destroy the environment.

❖ Computers benefit big business and big government most.

---

*The name Luddite comes from General Ned Ludd, the fictitious, symbolic leader of the movement.

- ❖ Use of computers in schools thwarts development of social skills, human values, and intellectual skills in children. They create an "ominous uniformity of knowledge" consistent with corporate values.[53]

- ❖ Computers do little or nothing to solve real human problems. For example, Neil Postman, in response to claims of the benefits of access to information, argues, "If families break up, children are mistreated, crime terrorizes a city, education is impotent, it does not happen because of inadequate information."[54]

Some of these criticisms might seem unfair. The conditions in computer factories hardly compare to conditions in the sweatshop factories of the early Industrial Revolution. In Chapter 6, we saw that computers eliminate some jobs and that the pace of computerization causes disruptions, but the case that computers, and technology in general, cause massive unemployment is not convincing. Blaming computers for social inequity in the world ignores thousands of years of history. Postman is right that inadequate information is not the source of most social problems. A computer in the classroom does not replace good parents in the home. But should this be a criticism of computers and information systems? Access to information and communication can assist in solving problems and is not likely to hurt. The main problem for ordinary people, Postman says, is how to find meaning in life. We need answers to questions like: Why are we here? How are we supposed to behave?[55] Is it a valid criticism of computing technology that it does not solve fundamental social and philosophical problems that have engaged us for thousands of years?

To the neo-Luddites, the view that computers are fundamentally malevolent is part of a wider view that almost all of technology is malevolent. To the modern-day Luddites, the computer is just the latest, but in many ways the worst, stage in the decline of what was good in human society. Computers are worse than earlier technologies because of their enormous speed and flexibility. Computers increase the negative trends that technology causes. Thus, if one points out that a particular problem blamed on computers already existed because of an earlier technology, Luddites consider the distinction to be a minor one.

The depth of the antipathy to technology in the Luddite view is perhaps made clearer by attitudes toward common devices most of us use daily. For example, Sale has said, "I find talking on the phone a physical pain, as well as a mental anguish." Sven Birkerts, another critic of computers, says that, if he lived in 1900, he would probably have opposed the telephone. Speaking of the invention of the printing press, Sale laments that "literacy . . . destroys orality." He regards not only computers but civilization as a catastrophe. Some of us see modern medicine as a lifesaving and life-enhancing boon to humanity; some Luddites point out that it gave us the population explosion and extended senility.[56]

Having read and listened to the arguments of technology enthusiasts and technology critics, I find it striking that different people look at the same history, the same society, the same products and services, and the same jobs and come to diametrically opposed conclusions about what they see. There is a fundamental difference between the world views of supporters and opponents of technology. It is more than the difference between seeing a glass as half full or half empty. The difference seems to be one of contrasting views about what should be in the glass. Supporters of technology see an upward trend in quality of life, beginning with people living at the mercy of nature with an empty glass that technology has been gradually filling. Neo-Luddites view the glass as originally full when people lived in small communities with little impact on nature; they see technology as draining the glass.

The neo-Luddite view is tied to a particular view of the appropriate way of life for human beings. For example, Sale's first point, in the quotation at the beginning of this section, makes the moral judgment that making money and producing things is pernicious. His introductory remark and his second point barely hint at the unusually high valuation he places on not disturbing nature (unusually high even in the contemporary context, where there is much awareness of the importance of protecting the environment). We explore these views further.

Business, consumers, and work

Luddites generally have a negative view of capitalism, business, markets, consumer products, factories, and modern forms of work. They see the profit-seeking goals of corporations as in fundamental conflict with the well-being of workers and the natural environment. They see work in factories, large offices, and corporations in general as dehumanizing, dreary, and bad for the health of the workers—hence, for example, the Luddite criticisms of the clock. Neil Postman describes the invention of the clock as "the technology of greatest use to men who wished to devote themselves to the accumulation of money."[57]

Choice of words, making subtle differences in a statement, sometimes illustrates the difference in perspective between Luddites and non-Luddites. What is the purpose of technology? To the Luddites, it is to eliminate jobs to reduce the costs of production. To proponents of technology, it is to reduce the effort needed to produce goods and services. The two statements say nearly the same thing, but the first suggests massive unemployment, profits for capitalists, and a poorer life for most workers. The second suggests improvements in wealth and the standard of living.

The Luddite view combines a negative attitude toward business with a high estimation of the power of corporations to manipulate and control workers and consumers. For example, Richard Sclove describes telecommuting as being "imposed by business." (Interestingly, one of the common criticisms of the Industrial Revolution was that working in factories instead of at home weakened families and local community.)

Luddites make particularly strong criticisms of automobiles, of cities, and of most technologies involved in communications and transportation. Thus, it is worth noting that most of us get both personal and social benefits from them. Cities are centers of culture, wealth production, education, and job opportunities.[58] Modern transportation and communication reduce the price of products and increase their variety and availability. For example, we can eat fresh fruits and vegetables all year. We can drive to a large discount store instead of buying from a more expensive local shop. We can phone around town or look on the Web to find a store, movie theater, or restaurant that has what we want. We can shop worldwide on the Web. We can commute a long distance to take a better job without having to sell our house and move. If we move to a new city for college or a job, airplanes, telephones, and the Internet make the separations less unpleasant. We can visit more often in person. We can share greetings and activities with friends and family members via social-networking sites and videos on the Web. Luddites and other critics of technology do not value these advantages highly. In some cases, in their point of view, the advantages are merely ameliorating other problems technology causes. For example, Postman quotes Sigmund Freud's comment, "If there had been no railway to conquer distances, my child would never have left his native town and I should need no telephone to hear his voice."[59]

Does the technology create the need for itself?

A common criticism of capitalism is that it survives by convincing us to buy products we do not need. Luddites argue, similarly, that technology causes production of things we do not need. This contrasts with the market-oriented view that sees consumer choices as determining which products, services, and businesses succeed or fail (in the absence of government favoritism, subsidies, and restrictions). We examine the issue of created needs.

Sale argued that small, portable computers do not "meet any known or expressed need," but companies produced them simply because miniaturization of computing components made it possible. People have bought many millions of laptops, palm-size computers, and cell phones. You can probably make a long list of their uses. So, does a portable computer meet a need? It depends on what we mean by "need." Do we need to do homework in the backyard or listen to music on an iPod? Does an architect or contractor need a laptop at a construction site? Those who emphasize the value of individual action and choices argue that needs are relative to goals, and goals are held by individuals. Thus, should we ask whether "we," as a society, need portable computers? Or should this be an individual decision with different responses? Many people demonstrate, by their purchases, that they want one. Anyone who does not feel a desire or need for one does not have to buy one. The Luddites, who believe buyers are manipulated by advertising, work pressure, or other forces beyond their control, reject this individual-oriented approach.

Many environmental and antitechnology groups use computers. The Web site primitivism.com attacks the technology that supports it. The editor of *Wild Earth*, who considers himself a neo-Luddite, said he "inclines toward the view that technology is inherently evil," but he "disseminates this view via E-mail, computer, and laser printer."[60] The question is, Is he using computer equipment because of an artificial need or because it is useful and helpful to him? Sale sees the use of computers by such groups as an uncomfortable compromise. The use of computers, he says, insidiously embeds into the user the values and thought processes of the society that makes the technology.[61]

The argument that capitalists or technologies manipulate people to buy things they do not really want, like the argument that use of computers has an insidiously corrupting effect on computer users, displays a low view of the judgment and autonomy of ordinary people. It is one thing to differ with another person's values and choices. It is another to conclude that, because of the difference, the other person is weak and incapable of making his or her own decisions. The Luddite view of the appropriate way of life puts little value on modern comforts and conveniences or on the availability of a large variety of goods and services. Perhaps most people value these things more highly than the Luddites do. To get a clearer understanding of the Luddite view of a proper life style, we consider some of their comments on the relationship of humans and nature.

Nature and human life styles

Luddites argue that technology has made no improvement in life, or at best improvements of little importance. Sale's list of benefits includes speed, ease, and mass access—all of which he disdains. Sale says that although individuals might feel their lives are better because of computers, the perceived benefits are "industrial virtues that may not be virtues in another morality." He defines moral judgment as "the capacity to decide that a thing is right when it enhances the integrity, stability, and beauty of nature and is wrong when it does otherwise."[62] Jerry Mander, founder of the Center for Deep Ecology and author of books critical of technology and globalization, points out that thousands of generations of humans got along without computers, suggesting that we could do just fine without them too. While some people evaluate trade-offs between negative side effects of pesticides and the benefits of reducing diseases or protecting food crops, Mander's objections to technology lead him to the conclusion that there can be no "good" pesticide. While many people work on technological, legal, and educational approaches to reducing the gasoline usage of automobiles, Mander says there can be no "good" automobile.[63]

What are the underlying premises behind these comments by Sale and Mander? We consider Sale's comment on moral judgment first. Many debates about the environment set up a humans-versus-nature dichotomy.[64] This is not the true conflict. Nature, biodiversity, forests, a hospitable climate, clean air and water, and open space away from cities are all important and valuable to humans. So is shelter from the rain, cold, and heat. So are lifesaving medicines and medical techniques. Conflicts about the environment are not conflicts between humans and nature. They are conflicts between people with different views about how to meet human needs. In contrast to Sale's statement, moral judgment—to many people, and for many centuries—has meant the capacity to choose that which enhances human life, reduces misery, and increases freedom and happiness. Sale's comment chooses nature, not humanity, as the primary standard of moral value.

Whether an automobile is "good," by a human-centered standard, depends on whether it meets our needs, how well it does so, at what cost (to the environment and society, as well as to our bank account), and how well it compares to alternatives. Critics of modern technologies point out their weaknesses but often ignore the weaknesses of alternatives, for example, the millions of acres once needed to grow feed for horses and the hundreds of tons of horse manure dropped on the streets of cities each day, a century ago.[65] Mander's comment about automobiles again raises the issues of our standard of value and our need for a product or service. Do we need electricity and hot water on tap? Do we need movies and symphony orchestras? Or do we need nothing more than food and shelter? Do we need an average life expectancy of more than 25 years? Do we want to merely exist—do we *need* even that?—or do we want long, happy, comfortable lives filled with time for love, interesting activities, and an opportunity to use our marvelously inventive brains?

> *The Web is alive, and filled with life, nearly as complex and, well, natural as a primordial swamp.*
>
> —John Perry Barlow[66]

7.4.2 ACCOMPLISHMENTS OF TECHNOLOGY

Some aspects of the neo-Luddite antitechnology view have become part of the public outlook: that living and working conditions are getting worse, that we are running out of natural resources, that the environment is deteriorating, that we are less healthy, among others. A variety of scholars find these observations to be false. (I mention only a few points here. The list of books at the end of the chapter includes some on both sides of this argument.) Economist Julian Simon argued that hard data, accepted by most economists, show that the prices of food are sharply down around most of the world, raw materials are more abundant (as measured by their price), and wages and salaries have been going up in rich and poor countries alike. Prices of natural resources (e.g., metals, raw materials, and energy) have declined over the past 100 years as a result of improvements in mining technologies and introduction of new substitutes for some minerals—for example, optical fiber for copper. (One fiber-optic cable, with about 150 pounds of silica, carries more messages than a ton of copper.) Nicholas Eberstadt, an expert on population, reported that food supplies and gross domestic product have been growing faster than population for decades in most areas of the world, in developing and developed countries. In the early 2000s, Americans spent less than 10% of family income on food, compared to approximately 47% in 1901. Agronomist Norman Borlaug, who won a Nobel Peace Prize for his work in improving agricultural productivity, reported that, when new forms of wheat and crop management were introduced in India, yields rose from 12.3 million tons in 1965 to 73.5 million tons in 1999. Between 1960 and 1990, U.S. production of its 17 most important crops increased from 252 million tons to 596 million tons, but used 25 million fewer acres. Science and technology (along with other factors such as education) reduced or almost eliminated typhoid, smallpox, dysentery, plagues, and malaria in most of the world. Deaths at work, during travel, and by accidents declined dramatically. Simon summarized by saying, "just about every single measure of the quality of life shows improvement rather than the deterioration that the doomsayers claim has occurred."[67]

Technology and the Industrial Revolution have had a dramatic impact on life expectancy. A study in 1662 estimated that only 25% of people in London lived to age 26. Records from 18th-century French villages showed that the median age of death was lower than the median age of marriage. Until recent generations, parents had to endure the deaths of most of their children. Starvation was common. In the U.S., life expectancy at birth increased from about 47.6 years in 1900 to 77.8 in 2004 for white people and from about 33 in 1900 to 73.1 in 2004 for black people. Worldwide average life expectancy increased from approximately 30 in 1900 to approximately 64 in 2006.[68]

Technology certainly is not the only factor in improving quality of life. Progress against disease, discomfort, and early death depends on the stability, freedom, and flexibility of political and economic systems as well. We have seen repeatedly that technology introduces many new problems. Measuring quality of life is subjective, and some find other measures more important than those cited above. But for many people, these data suggest that technology has contributed much to human well-being.

Who benefits most?

Technology critics recognize that many people consider computers to be useful. Mander explains one of the reasons why, in spite of this, he still considers them to be, overall, negative:

> People have them at home and find them empowering for themselves and their organizations. They are helpful in many ways and offer considerable personal control, unlike nonyielding technologies like television. Small social and political groups find computers valuable for information storage, networking, processing mailing lists, . . . and so on. Yet all this begs the question. The real issue is not whether computers can benefit you or your group; the question is who benefits most from computers in society?[69]

Mander believes the answer to his question is multinational corporations and centralized corporate power. "In capitalist society, the benefits are disproportionately allotted to the people who own the machines." Our level of empowerment, he says, is pathetic by comparison. Mander says that "small businesses would actually be better off if computers had not been invented, since they are essentially one more tool that large businesses can use better."[70]

The subtitle of John Naisbitt's book *Global Paradox: The Bigger the World Economy, the More Powerful Its Smallest Players* contrasts with Mander's view that computers are bad for small businesses. Naisbitt sees telecommunications as the driving force in creating a robust global economy and reducing the size of both political and business units. The Web and the value of information services help small (even tiny) businesses form and flourish. The benefits of telecommunications and information technology are enormous in developing countries. A report of a United Nations Conference on Trade and Development observes that developing economies can make productivity gains worth billions of dollars by encouraging the growth of electronic commerce. The report said that

> it is because the internet revolution is relevant not just to the high-tech, information-intensive sectors but also to the whole organisation of economic life that ... developing countries stand a better chance of sharing in its benefits earlier than in previous technological revolutions.[71]

Postman acknowledges that computers are very beneficial to disabled people. He sees convenient access to online information as a tremendous advantage for scholars and scientists. But he sees the main beneficiaries of computers as government and big business. In his view, computers have little value to ordinary workers.[72] This is consistent with the Luddite view that technology in general is bad for most ordinary people, but it is in stark contrast with the views of others who see technology as most benefiting the poorest and weakest people in society. Economist Julian Simon said, "The standard of living of commoners is higher today than that of royalty only two centuries ago—especially their health and life expectancy."[73] Michael Cox and Richard Alm present data showing that the poor in the U.S. had at least the same level of many appliances and luxuries that the average American had only 23 years earlier. See Figure 7.5 for a few examples.* (Luddites would probably argue that we do not need these machines.)

	% of **Poor** Households with Item in 1994	% of **All** Households with Item in 1971
Washing machine	71.7	71.3
Dishwasher	19.6	18.8
Refrigerator	97.9	83.3
Stove	97.7	87.0
Microwave oven	60.0	<1
Color television	92.5	43.3
Telephone	76.7	93.0
Air-conditioner	49.6	31.8
At least one car	71.8	79.5

Figure 7.5   Technology Benefits Spreading to the Poor[74]

---

*Cox and Alm explain that the poor can afford these items because the price of necessities declined relative to income. Households below the poverty line spent 37% of their income on food, clothing, and shelter in the 1990s, compared to 52% in the 1970s.

The number of labor-saving and entertainment appliances we can buy is only one way of measuring well-being. Consider also who benefits more from a speech-activated home-environment control system: a quadriplegic, for whom it performs basic functions and provides some independence, or a rich person for whom it is a toy or convenience. Wireless communications technologies make millions of dollars for corporate executives. How does the relative improvement in their quality of life compare to the impact of wireless communications on a third-world family living in a rural area that is not wired for telephones? When a drug company develops a new cancer cure and its stock goes way up, while people live 25 extra years after being cured of cancer, does it really matter who benefits "most"?

> *I pity the poor, and should hardly think myself innocent if any man felt more for them than I do; but the remedy for their grievances, lies not in the destruction of Machinery. They are oppressed exceedingly, but not by Machinery. Those who accuse Machinery of causing any part of the distresses of the poor, have very contracted views and narrow minds, and see but a little way. They do not seem to consider that almost every thing was new Machinery once. There was a time when corn was ground by the hand; and when Corn Mills and Wind Mills were first invented they were New Machinery; and therefore why not break and burn these as soon as any other kind of Machinery; for if they were all stopped, and corn again ground by the hand, there would be plenty of employment for many hands! Much the same observations might be made respecting every other kind of Machinery, and I have asked this question in order to show the silliness of the practice.*
>
> —George Beaumont (from "Reflections on Luddism," 1812)[75]

7.5 Making Decisions about Technology

> *No one voted for this technology or any of the various machines and processes that make it up.*
>
> —Kirkpatrick Sale[76]

7.5.1 QUESTIONS

We saw, in Section 7.4.1, that the determination of what are true needs depends on our choice of values. Throughout this book, we saw controversies about specific products, services, and applications of computer technology (e.g., personalized advertising, anonymous Web surfing, and face-recognition systems). How should decisions be made about the basic question of whether to use a whole technology, or major segments of it, at all? Who would make such decisions?

Most people in science, engineering, and business accept, almost without question, the view that people can choose to use a technology for good or ill. Some critics of technology disagree. They argue that computers, and technology in general, are not "neutral." Neil Postman says, "Once a technology is admitted [to our culture], it plays out its hand; it does what it is designed to do."[77] In a sense, this view sees the technologies themselves as being in control.

In the view of some critics of computing technology, big corporations and governments make decisions about uses of the technology without sufficient input or control by ordinary people. Kirkpatrick Sale's lament at the beginning of this section expresses this view: There was never a vote on whether we should have computers and the Internet. Some people argue that we should not use a new technology at all until we have studied it, figured out its consequences, and made a determination that the consequences are acceptable. The idea is that if the technology does not meet certain criteria, its development and use would not be permitted.

This view leads to a few basic questions. Can a society choose to have certain specific desirable modern inventions while prohibiting others or prohibiting whole technologies? How well can we predict the consequences of a new technology or application? Who would make the decisions? We consider the first question here and the others in the next section.

How finely can decisions about acceptable and unacceptable technologies be made? In response to a criticism that the tribal life he extolled would have no pianos, no violins, no telescope, no Mozart, Sale replied, "if your clan thought that the violin was a useful and nonharmful tool, you could choose to invent that."[78] Perhaps critics of computers who recognize the value of computing technology to disabled people would permit the development of such applications. The question is whether it is possible for a clan or society to choose to invent a violin or a book reader for blind people without the technological and economic base on which the development of these products depends. That base includes the freedom to innovate, a large enough economy to get materials from distant sources, and a large number of potential applications that make the research, development, and production of the basic ingredients of these products economically feasible. It is unlikely that anyone would even think of developing a book reader for the blind if some of the components did not already exist in other products (e.g., perhaps, a photocopy machine).

TELEMEDICINE: A BAD APPLICATION OF TECHNOLOGY?

In Chapter 1, we described long-distance medicine, or telemedicine, as a benefit of computer technology. Computer and communications networks make possible remote examination of patients and medical test results, and they make possible remotely controlled medical procedures. After reading Chapters 2 and 8, you should be able to think of potential privacy and safety problems with such systems. You might think of other objections as well. Should we ban telemedicine?

Several states passed laws prohibiting the practice of telemedicine by doctors who are not licensed in that state. The main argument they give for the laws is safety, or concern about out-of-state "quacks." The laws will "keep out the charlatans and snake-oil salesmen," according to one supporter.[79] Also, telemedicine could increase the influence of large, well-financed medical centers—to the detriment of local physicians in private practice. Large hospitals might become the "Wal-Marts of medicine," says one writer. Telemedicine might make medical care even more impersonal than it is already.

Was concern for patients the real reason for the laws? The arguments about charlatans and quacks seem weak, considering that the laws target doctors who are licensed, but in another state. Many doctors who support the bans see telemedicine as a significant competitive threat. As the director of one state medical board put it, "They're worried about protecting their turf."[80] The laws restrict competition and protect established special interests—a risk of any mechanism designed to prohibit a new technology or product.

7.5.2 THE DIFFICULTY OF PREDICTION

A brief look at the development of communications and computer technology suggests the difficulty of evaluating the consequences and future applications of a new technology. Computers were designed to calculate ballistics trajectories for the military. The PC was originally a tool for doing computation and writing documents. No one but a few visionaries imagined most of their current uses. Optical scanners, speech-recognition systems, touch screens, and e-mail were developed for a variety of research, business, and consumer uses, but they are major ingredients in tools for disabled people. Each new technology finds new and unexpected uses. When physicists began developing the World Wide Web, who would have predicted online auctions, social networking, or sharing home video? When people started carrying cell phones, who would have predicted that terrorists would use them to set off bombs? Postman's statement that a technology does "what it is designed to do" ignores human responsibility and choice, innovation, discoveries

❖ *The telephone is so important, every city will need one!*
—Anonymous

❖ *My personal desire would be to prohibit entirely the use of alternating currents. They are unnecessary as they are dangerous.*
—Thomas Edison, 1899

❖ *I think there is a world market for maybe five computers.*
—Thomas J. Watson, chairman of IBM, 1943

❖ *Computers in the future may . . . only weigh 1.5 tons.*
—*Popular Mechanics*, 1949

❖ *There is no reason for any individual to have a computer in their home.*
—Ken Olson, president of Digital Equipment Corp., 1977

❖ *The U.S. will have 220,000 computers by the year 2000.*
—Official forecast by RCA Corporation, 1966. (The actual number was close to 100 million.)

Figure 7.6 Predictions[81]

of new uses, unexpected consequences, and social action to encourage or discourage specific applications. Computer scientist Peter Denning takes a different view: "Although a technology does not drive human beings to adopt new practices, it shapes the space of possibilities in which they can act: people are drawn to technologies that expand the space of their actions and relationships."[82] Denning says people adopt technologies that give them more choices. Note that he does not say more choices of consumer products, but more actions and relationships. Don Norman also suggests that society influences the role of a technology when he says, "The failure to predict the computer revolution was the failure to understand how society would modify the original notion of a computational device into a useful tool for everyday activities."[83]

How well can a government committee, a think tank, or a computer-industry executive predict the consequences of a new technology? The history of technology is full of wildly wrong predictions—some overly optimistic, some overly pessimistic. Consider the quotations in Figure 7.6. Some scientists were skeptical of air travel, space travel, and even railroads. (They believed that passengers would not be able to breathe on high-speed trains.) The quotations in Figure 7.6 reflect a lack of imagination about the myriad uses people would find for each new technology, about what the public would like, and about what they would pay for. They humorously demonstrate that many experts can be utterly wrong. We examine the prediction problem more seriously and in more depth by considering arguments made by computer scientist Joseph Weizenbaum in 1975 against the development of a particular computer technology: speech-recognition systems.[84] Here are Weizenbaum's objections, accompanied by comments from our perspective today.*

❖ *"The problem is so enormous that only the largest possible computers will ever be able to manage it."* Speech-recognition software runs on PCs. We can buy pocket-sized personal organizers that take spoken commands.

❖ *"[A] speech-recognition machine is bound to be enormously expensive, . . . only governments and possibly a very few very large corporations will therefore be able to afford it."* Some computers come with simple speech-recognition software as a free bonus. The pocket organizers cost a few hundred dollars. Big companies provide voice-activated services powered by speech-recognition software to millions of consumers. Some voice-activated services on cell phones are free.

❖ *"What can it possibly be used for?"* We can search the Web from a cell phone by speaking what we want instead of typing. We can call a business, speak the name of the person we want to reach, and automatically be connected to that person's extension. Other customer-service applications include checking airline flight schedules, getting stock quotes and weather information, conducting banking transactions, and buying movie tickets on the phone by speaking naturally instead of pushing buttons.

Recall some of the applications described in Sections 1.2.5 and 1.2.6: training systems (e.g., for air traffic controllers and for foreign languages) and tools that help disabled people use computers and control appliances in their homes. Speech recognition automates transcription of dictated notes. One big application is transcription of medical notes doctors dictate. People who suffer from repetitive strain injury use speech-recognition input instead of a keyboard. IBM advertised speech-input software for poets, so they can concentrate on poetry instead of typing. People with dyslexia use speech-recognition software so they can write by dictation.

A company developed a device that recognizes speech and translates it into other languages. Full translation is still a difficult problem, but tourists, business people, social-service workers, and many others will surely find many uses for specialized versions.

Voice-activated, hands-free operation of cell phones, car stereos, and other appliances in automobiles eliminates some of the safety hazard of using these devices while driving.

The market for speech-recognition technology topped $1 billion by 2006.[85]

❖ *The military planned to control weapons by voice command, "a long step toward a fully automated battlefield."* Some argue that we should have the best possible weapons to defend ourselves. Others argue that, if wars are easier to fight, governments fight more of them. If countries fight wars with remotely controlled automated weapons

---

*We now have more than 30 years of hindsight since Weizenbaum wrote his book. Many inexpensive applications of speech recognition, however, had already appeared by the early 1990s.

and no humans on the battlefield, is that an improvement over wars in which people are slaughtered? What if only one side has the high-tech weapons? Would that cause more wars of aggression? Is there any technology that the military cannot or does not use? Should we decline to develop strong fabrics because the military can use them for uniforms? Clearly, military use of high-tech tools raises serious ethical and policy questions. Are these questions sufficient reason to abandon or condemn a particular technology?

❖ *Governments can use speech recognition to increase the efficiency and effectiveness of wiretapping.* (Abuses of wiretapping concerned Weizenbaum, for example, tapping done by oppressive governments. He does not explicitly mention wiretapping of criminal suspects.) One can argue that governments can use the same tool beneficially in legal wiretapping of suspected terrorists, but it is true that speech recognition, like many other technological tools, can be a danger in the hands of governments. Protection from such abuses depends in part on the recognition of the importance of strictly controlling government power and in part on the appropriate laws and enforcement mechanisms to do so.

Discussion of Weizenbaum's objections is important for several reasons. First, although Weizenbaum is an expert in artificial intelligence, of which speech recognition is a subfield, he was mistaken in his expectations about the costs and benefits. Second, his objections about military and government use highlight the dilemma: Should we decline to develop technologies that can be misused, or should we develop the tools because of their beneficial uses, and use other means, including our votes and our voices, to influence government and military policy? Third, Weizenbaum's argument against the development of a technology because of its expected cost is similar to arguments expressed by others about current and future computer applications and other technologies. For example, a common objection to some new medical technologies is that they are so expensive that only the rich will be able to afford them. This shortsighted view can result in the denial of benefits to the whole population. We saw that, for many new inventions, prices are high at first but quickly come down. A computer chip developed to float on the retina of the eye and send visual signals to the brain has the potential to restore sight to some blind people. The initial cost was $500,000. Should it be banned because it would be available only to the very rich? The developer of the chip expected the cost to come down to $50 with mass production.

Weizenbaum was not trying to evaluate computer technology as a whole but was focusing on one specific application area. If we are to permit the government or experts or the people via a majority vote to prohibit the development of certain technologies, it is essential at least that we be able to estimate the consequences—both risks and benefits—of the technology fairly accurately. We cannot do this. The experts cannot do it.

But what if a technology might threaten the survival of the human race? We consider such an example in the next section.

7.5.3 INTELLIGENT MACHINES AND SUPERINTELLIGENT HUMANS —OR THE END OF THE HUMAN RACE?

Prominent technologists such as Hans Moravec, Ray Kurzweil, and Vernor Vinge describe a not-very-distant future in which intelligence-enhancing devices, artificial intelligence, and intelligent robots change our society and our selves in profound ways.* The more optimistic scenarios include human use of intelligent machines and services of many kinds. People might acquire advanced mental powers through computer-brain implants and interfaces. When someone has a stroke, doctors might remove the damaged part of a brain and replace it with a chip that performs the lost functions, perhaps with a large amount of extra memory or a chip to access the Web directly. Why wait for a stroke? Once the technology is developed and tested, healthy people will likely buy and install such implants. Massachusetts Institute of Technology (MIT) robotics researcher Rodney Brooks, for example, suggests that by 2020 we might have wireless Internet interfaces that can be implanted in our heads. He says people might be just as comfortable with them as they are now getting laser eye surgery at a mall.[86] Will such implants make someone less human than a heart transplant or pacemaker does? What social problems will intelligence enhancement cause in the next few decades? What philosophical and ethical problems will arise when we combine human and machine intelligence in such intimate ways?

Going farther into the future, will we "download" our brains to long-lasting robot bodies? If we do, will we still be human?

The technological singularity

The term *technological singularity* refers to the point at which AI or some combined human–machine intelligence advances so far that we cannot comprehend what lies on the other side. It is plausible, says computer scientist Vinge, that "we can, in the fairly near future, create or become creatures who surpass humans in every intellectual and creative dimension. Events beyond such a singular event are as unimaginable to us as opera is to a flatworm."[87]

Some technologists see the human race transforming into an unrecognizable race of superintelligent, genetically engineered creatures within this century. Some see this as a welcome advance. Others find it horrifying—and others unlikely. Some technologists see potential threats to the survival of the human race. They see the possibility of the machines achieving human-level intelligence and then rapidly improving themselves to a superhuman level. Once robots can improve their design and build better robots, will they "outcompete" humans? Will they replace the human race, just as various species of animals displace others? And will it happen soon, say within the next 20 years or so?

Two estimates support these scenarios. One is an estimate of the computing power of the human brain. The other is based on Moore's law, the observation that the computing power of new microprocessors doubles roughly every 18 to 24 months. If the progress of

*I include some references at the end of the chapter.

hardware power continues at this rate, then by roughly 2030, computer hardware will be about as powerful as a human brain, sufficiently powerful to support the computation requirements of intelligent robots.

Both those who think an extreme advance in machine intelligence or human–machine intelligence is likely in the near future and those who criticize these ideas provide several reasons why it might not happen. Here are some of them. First, hardware progress might slow down. Second, we might not be able to develop the necessary software in the next few decades or at all. Developments in AI, particularly in the area of general intelligence, have been much slower than researchers expected when the field began. Third, the estimates of the "hardware" computing power of the human brain (the sophistication of the computing power of neurons) might be drastically too low. Lastly, some philosophers argue that robots programmed with AI software cannot duplicate the full capability of the human mind.

Responding to the threats of intelligent machines

Whether the singularity occurs within a few decades, or later, or not at all, many in the relevant fields foresee general-purpose intelligent machines within your lifetime. By its definition, we cannot prepare for the aftermath of the singularity, but we can prepare for more gradual developments. Many of the issues we explored in previous chapters are relevant to enhanced intelligence. Will software bugs or other malfunctions kill thousands of people? Will hackers hack brains? Will a large division open up between the superintelligent and the merely humanly intelligent? We saw that protections for safety and privacy in computer systems are often weak because they were not designed in from the start. It is valuable to think about potential problems of superintelligent systems and intelligence enhancement for humans well before they confront us so that we can design the best protections.

Bill Joy is cofounder of Sun Microsystems and a key developer of Berkeley Unix and the Java programming language. In his article, "Why the Future Doesn't Need Us,"[88] Joy describes his worries about robotics, genetic engineering, and nanotechnology. He observes that these technologies will be more dangerous than technologies of the 20th century (such as nuclear weapons) because they will be self-replicating and will not require rare and expensive raw materials and huge factories or laboratories. Joy sees profound threats, including possibly the extinction of the human race.

What protections do people who fear for the future of the human race recommend? Joy describes and criticizes some before suggesting his own. Space enthusiasts suggest creating colonies in space. Joy observes that it will not happen soon enough. If it does, it might save the human race but not the vast majority of humans on earth. If colonists take the current technologies with them, the threat goes too. A second solution is to develop protections that can stop the dangerous technologies from getting out of control. Futurist Virginia Postrel suggests "a portfolio of resilient responses."[89] Joy argues that we could not develop "shields" in time, and if we could, they would necessarily be at least as dangerous as the technologies they are supposed to protect us against. Joy recommends "relinquishment," by which he means we must "limit development of the technologies that are too dangerous, by limiting our pursuit of certain kinds of knowledge." He cites, as earlier examples, treaties to limit the development of certain kinds of weapons and the U.S.'s unilateral decision to abandon the development of biological weapons. One weakness of Joy's analysis is that he does not apply the same criterion to relinquishment as to the approaches he rejects: They are "either undesirable or unachievable or both." Enforcing relinquishment would be extraordinarily difficult, if not impossible. As Joy recognizes, intelligent robots and the other technologies that concern him have huge numbers of potentially beneficial applications, many of which will save lives and improve quality of life. At what point would governments stop pursuit of knowledge and development? Ethical professionals will refuse to participate in the development of some AI applications, but they too face the difficult problem of where to draw the line. If we develop the technology to a point where we get controlled, useful applications, how will we prevent visionary or insane scientists, hackers, teenagers, aggressive governments, or terrorists from circumventing the controls and going beyond the prohibited level?

Joy sees a relinquishment verification program on an unprecedented scale, in cyberspace and in physical facilities, with privacy, civil liberties, business autonomy, and free markets seriously curtailed. Thus, relinquishment means not only that we might lose development of innovative, beneficial products and services. We would lose many basic liberties as well.

> *Prediction is difficult, especially about the future.*[90]

7.5.4 A FEW OBSERVATIONS

We have presented arguments against the view that new technologies should be evaluated and perhaps banned at the start. Does this mean that no one should make decisions about whether it is good to develop a particular application of a new technology? No. The arguments and examples suggest two things: (1) that we limit the scope of decisions about development of new technology, perhaps to particular products, and (2) that the decision-making process be decentralized and noncoercive, to reduce the impact of mistakes, avoid manipulation by entrenched companies who fear competition, and prevent violations of liberty. We cannot often predict the decisions and the results of decisions made by individual engineers, researchers, programmers, entrepreneurs, venture capitalists, customers, and teenagers who tinker in their garages, but those decisions have a valuable robustness. The fundamental problem is not *what* decision to make about a particular technology. Rather, it is to select a decision-making *process* that is most likely to produce what people want, to work well despite the difficulty of predicting consequences, to respect the diversity of personal opinions about what constitutes a desirable life style, and to be relatively free of political manipulation.

When we consider the most extreme potential developments, such as superintelligent robots, what level of certainty of dire consequences should we require before restricting the freedom to develop technologies and products that might have marvelous benefits?

EXERCISES

Review Exercises

7.1   What is one advantage of a participatory forum written by volunteers (such as Wikipedia)? What is one disadvantage?

7.2   What ethical principle can prevent doctors from responding to criticism of their work on health sites on the Web?

7.3   What is one ethical dilemma associated with manipulating digital videos?

7.4   What is one common use of a computer and Internet access in rural areas of developing countries?

7.5   Give an example of a mistaken prediction made about computers.

General Exercises

7.6   Describe a scenario in which biased or incorrect information a child finds on the Web might harm him or her. What, if anything, might have prevented the child from finding similar information before the Web existed? Suggest and evaluate one mechanism for preventing such harm (from the Web).

7.7   Consider a "social media" Web site on which display of news stories depends on the votes of readers. Is it an ethical obligation of the site operators to ensure that votes are not bought and sold, or is it merely a good business policy? Or is it both?

7.8   Children in the current generation are becoming familiar with computers and technology at a very young age. Discuss advantages and disadvantages to this.

7.9   Rewrite the spelling-checker verse (in Section 7.1.2), correcting all the mistakes without using a computer. (There are more than a dozen mistakes.)

7.10   Some universities offer online degree programs. Do you think students get as good an education online as they do in a traditional classroom? Considering the trade-offs, do you think more students should get their college educations online? How extensive do you think university-level distance education will be in five years? Explain your answers.

7.11   Approximately 6,000 languages are spoken in the world. This number is declining rapidly, as a result of increased communication and transportation, of globalization of business and trade, and so on—all side effects of increased technology in general and of the Internet in particular. What are the advantages and disadvantages of losing languages? Overall, is it a significant problem?

7.12   What are some economic benefits of computer models? What are some risks related to relying on the computer-generated predictions? How can you judge the accuracy and usefulness of a computer model?

7.13   Consider an online poker Web site, where people bet and win or lose real money. What are the ethical obligations of the site operators toward players in a country where such businesses are legal? What are the ethical obligations of the site operators toward players in a country where such businesses are not legal?

7.14   Which of the following models do you think would produce very accurate results? Which do you think would be less reliable? Give your reasons.
   ❖ Models that predict the effect of an income tax change on government revenue.
   ❖ Models that predict the position of the moon in relation to the earth 30 years from now.
   ❖ Models that predict how much optical fiber a major city will need 30 years from now.
   ❖ Models that predict how much carbon dioxide the burning of fossil fuel for energy will emit worldwide 30 years from now.
   ❖ Models that predict the speed of a new racing-boat hull design under specified wind conditions.

7.15   Summarize the technological singularity. Do you think it is possible or likely to happen in the future? Why or why not? If so, do you see it as a potential threat to the human race?

7.16   How do the opportunities for "co-present," or in-person, social interactions today compare with those of 250 years ago?

7.17   In a debate on the impact of technology, suppose you are assigned to take the side that rejects the view that technology is a positive development. What arguments would you present? What would you argue will happen as technology continues to advance?

7.18   The number of small neighborhood bookstores is declining because of competition from both large chain megabookstores and online stores like Amazon.com. Should a law have prohibited Amazon.com from opening? If not, should we prohibit it from selling used books, to help preserve small neighborhood used-book stores? Give reasons. Suppose you like to shop in your neighborhood bookstore and fear it might go out of business. What can you do?

7.19   Some religion-based cell phone services charge less for calls to others in the same network of religion-based phones. Is this a positive way of reinforcing a community or an encouragement for insularity? Give reasons for your answer.

7.20   Recall the discussion in the box in Section 7.2 and consider these questions: Do people have a right to shop in small neighborhood stores rather than in Wal-Mart and online? Do people in a small town have a right to eat in a French restaurant? Distinguish between negative and positive rights (Section 1.4.3).

7.21   What devices or technologies, available now or in the next few years, do you think schools might ban students from using for schoolwork in order to promote fairness among students who have them and students who do not?

7.22   Many games that children used to play on boards with dice, cards, and plastic pieces are now available as computer games. Is this an example of unnecessary use of the new technology just because it is there? Describe some advantages and disadvantages of replacing a boardgame by a computer version.

7.23   In the mid-1990s, approximately 70% of the computers connected to the Internet were in the United States. Did this suggest a growing gap between "have" and "have-not" nations? Give your reasons. (Try to find out what percentage of computers or Web sites are in the U.S. now.)

7.24   The percentage of young people (18–29) who use the Internet is two or three times as high as the percentage of people above age 60 who do. What are some reasons for this digital divide? Is it a serious problem? Why or why not?

7.25   Analyze the following argument about the necessity of cell phones. Is it convincing?
Some people do not want to own a cell phone because, among other reasons, cell phones are intrusive, difficult to use, and expensive. Technology advocates say if you don't want one, you don't have to buy one. But this is not true. We have to have one. Before cell phones became popular, there were coin-operated telephones all over, on street corners, in and near stores, in restaurants, at gas stations, and so on. If we needed to make a call while away from home or work, we could use a pay phone. Now most of them are gone, so we have to have a cell phone whether we want to or not.

7.26   Which of the Luddite criticisms of computers listed in Section 7.4.1 do you consider the most valid and significant? Why?

7.27 Software originally developed to help parents and Internet service providers block access to material inappropriate for children was adapted for use by some governments to block access to political and religious discussions. In what way does this example illustrate the views that technology will inevitably have negative uses and that, as Neil Postman said, "Once a technology is admitted, . . . it does what it is designed to do"?

7.28 Speaker-recognition software analyzes speech to determine who the speaker is (not what words the speaker is saying, as in speech recognition). Describe some potentially useful and some potentially threatening or risky applications.

7.29 Assume you are a professional working in your chosen field. Describe specific things you can do to reduce the impact of any two problems we discussed in this chapter. (If you cannot think of anything related to your professional field, choose another field that might interest you.)

7.30 Think ahead to the next few years and describe a new problem, related to issues in this chapter, likely to develop from computing technology or the Web.

Assignments

These exercises require some research or activity.

7.31 Go online and find Web sites where individuals contribute news reports. Do you think this is a positive thing? How does democratic journalism relate to free speech? Does it eliminate jobs for journalists?

7.32 Find an article in Wikipedia (or Citizendium) on a subject that you already know a lot about. Read and review the article. Is it accurate, well done, complete?

7.33 Find Web sites that provide recommendations about how much vitamin C a person should consume each day. Find at least one site that is extreme in some way and at least one that you consider reasonably reliable. Describe the sites and explain the basis for your characterization of them.

7.34 With open, speedy communication on the Web, there is no easy way to prevent rumors from spreading quickly. Some urban legends persist and show up repeatedly. Find a Web site that regularly reports on myths and researches the facts about Web rumors.

7.35 Recent predictions for population growth in the 21st century have changed quite a bit from predictions made a few decades ago. Find reports of older populations models (say, from the 1960s, 1970s, or 1980s), and find reports of recent populations models. How do they differ? How have the assumptions in the models changed?

7.36 What are some problems with the "wisdom of the crowd" phenomenon? Find a Web site that presents the wisdom of the crowd. Can you verify the information that is given?

7.37 Contact a local school district and find out what computer programs are being used for instruction at different grade levels. How has the use of computer and Internet technology changed since you were in school? Do you think the technology is being used and taught well in elementary classrooms?

7.38 Some writers describe technology as our "national religion." On the other hand, the environmentalist viewpoint, often critical of technology, is quite strong in our society. Find two recent news or magazine articles, one that illustrates each of these points of view. Give a brief summary of each. Tell how it exemplifies a view of technology. In general, which view do you think is stronger in our society? Give reasons.

7.39 If you normally carry a cell phone, choose a normal day and leave it home. Did you need the phone? Was the absence of the phone a big inconvenience? Will you carry it the next day or leave it home again? Why?

7.40 Three-dimensional "printers" create 3-D structures, layer by layer, using glues and resins, under direction of a computer file. Find out what people and businesses use these devices for. Suppose someone described these devices ten years ago as a potential invention and asked: Will they fill any real needs? How do you think most people would have answered? What is your answer now?

Class Discussion Exercises

These exercises are for class discussion, perhaps with short presentations prepared in advance by small groups of students.

7.41 Describe how computer and Internet technology has changed the field of journalism. How has the way we receive our news changed? Consider democratic journalism and the impacts of blogging. Which changes are improvements and which are negative?

7.42 Do your professors allow students to use Wikipedia as a source for research and other papers? Why or why not? What are the problems with using Wikipedia as a reference?

7.43 A number of people advocate a law requiring Google to make public the algorithms it uses to rank Web sites for display in response to search queries. Considering issues in this chapter, and any other relevant issues, discuss arguments in favor of such a requirement and arguments against it.

7.44 Google has been pursuing an ambitious goal of collecting and providing vast amounts of human knowledge. Google's projects have faced a variety of criticisms, some centered on the facts that it is a private company and that it is an American company. For example, Google's databases and the wide use of its search engines give it more power over information than a private corporation should have. Google's project of scanning millions of books contributes to American and English-language domination of world culture because it is scanning books in English.

Give arguments in support of these criticisms and arguments against them.

7.45 What are some skills, traditions, and/or social conventions that have been, or might soon be, lost because of computer and Internet technology? Include at least one that you think will be a real loss (i.e., a negative consequence) and include at least one where you think the loss is not a problem. Give reasons.

7.46 What form will the digital divide likely take 10 years from now? How do digital divides differ from social divisions that occurred when other information and communication technologies were introduced?

7.47 How do sexual predators use the Internet to find young potential victims? How does law enforcement use the Internet to locate these predators? Find and compare rates of child molestation for today and for roughly 25 years ago. Has there been a significant increase? If so, what are some possible reasons for this other than the Internet? How significant a factor do you think the Internet is? If the rates have not significantly changed, what, if anything, do you think has offset the increase in predation made possible by the Internet?

7.48 Read Bill Joy's article and the reply by Virginia Postrel (see the references at the end of the chapter). Whose arguments are more convincing? Why?

NOTES

1. *Collected Poems 1901–1962* (Harcourt, Brace & World, 1963), p. 147.

2. "Wikipedia: Size comparisons," Wikipedia, en.wikipedia.org/wiki/Wikipedia:Size_comparisons (accessed March 28, 2007).

3. The quotations are from www.citizendium.org (accessed December 20, 2006), later moved to www.citizendium.org/about.html; Jonathan Sidener, "Wikipedia Cofounder Looks to Add Accountability, End Anarchy," *San Diego Union—Tribune*, September 23, 2006, pp. A1, A12.

4. Joseph Rago, "The Blog Mob," *Wall Street Journal*, December 20, 2006, p. A18.

5. "Beware of a Blizzard of Fake Documents" (letter to the editor), *New York Times*, August 16, 1991, p. 12.

6. Robert Fox, "News Track: Everybody Must Get Cloned," *Communications of the ACM*, 43, no. 8 (August 2000), p. 9; Lisa Guernsey, "Software Is Called Capable of Copying Any Human Voice," *New York Times*, July 31, 2001, pp. A1, C2.

7. "Adnan Hajj Photographs Controversy," Answers.com, www.answers.com/topic/adnan-hajj-photographs-controversy (accessed February 18, 2007); Hany Farid, a computer science professor at Dartmouth University, maintains a Web page, "Digital Tampering in the Media, Politics and Law," www.cs.dartmouth.edu/farid/research/digitaltampering (accessed April 4, 2007). He describes several examples I mention here in more detail.

8. Farid, "Digital Tampering in the Media, Politics and Law."

9. D. J. Stout, quoted in Jacques Leslie, "Digital Photopros and Photo(shop) Realism," *Wired*, May 1995, pp. 108–113; Michael W. Robbins, "The Apple of Visual Technology," *Audubon*, July/August 1994, p. 4.

10. Parts of this poem have circulated on computer networks and appeared in newspapers. The full version (36 lines), slightly different from the one I used, appeared in *Journal of Irreproducible Results*, 39, no. 1 (January/February 1994), p. 13. Zar attributes the title to Pamela Brown and the opening lines to Mark Eckman.

11. Barry Bearak, "Pakistani Tale of a Drug Addict's Blasphemy," *New York Times*, February 19, 2001, pp. A1, A4.

12. See, for example, Neil Postman, *Technopoly: The Surrender of Culture to Technology* (Alfred A. Knopf, 1992), pp. 3–8.

13. *New York Times*, February 1, 2001; Walter J. Ong, *Interfaces of the Word: Studies in the Evolution of Consciousness and Culture* (Cornell University Press, 1977).

14. From Microsoft's explanation of its policy, quoted in Mark Goldblatt, "Bowdlerized by Microsoft," *New York Times*, October 23, 2001, p. A23.

15. *Against the Gods: The Remarkable Story of Risk* (John Wiley & Sons, 1996), p. 16.

16. Amanda Bennett, "Strange 'Science': Predicting Health-Care Costs," *Wall Street Journal*, February 7, 1994, p. B1.

17. Cynthia Crossen, "How 'Tactical Research' Muddied Diaper Debate," *Wall Street Journal*, May 17, 1994, pp. B1, B9.

18. Orrin H. Pilkey and Linda Pilkey-Jarvis, "Why Mathematical Models Just Don't Add Up," *The Chronicle of Higher Education*, May 25, 2007, chronicle.com/weekly/v53/i38/38b01201.htm (accessed July 21, 2007).

19. The IPCC reports (published by Cambridge University Press): S. Solomon et al., eds., *Climate Change 2007: The Physical Scientific Basis*, 2007, Technical Summary, ipcc-wg1.ucar.edu/wg1/wg1-report.html (accessed July 17, 2007); J. T. Houghton et al., eds., *Climate Change 2001: The Scientific Basis*, 2001; J. T. Houghton et al., eds., *Climate Change 1995: The Science of Climate Change*, 1996; J. T. Houghton, B. A. Callander, and S. K. Varney, eds., *Climate Change 1992: The Supplementary Report to the IPCC Scientific Assessment*, 1992; J. T. Houghton, G. J. Jenkins, and J. J. Ephraums, eds., *Climate Change: The IPCC Scientific Assessment*, 1990. I also used a large variety of other books and articles for background.

20. One reason why this distinction is important is that temperature records for large areas of the northern hemisphere showed a larger rise in the nighttime winter lows than in the daytime summer highs (a potentially benign or beneficial form of warming). In the past few decades, according to the 2007 IPCC report (p. 36), the daily temperature range stopped shrinking.

21. D. L. Albritton et al., "Technical Summary," in *Climate Change 2001*, ed. J. T. Houghton et al., pp. 21–83 (see p. 49).

22. Solomon, Technical Summary, *Climate Change 2007*, p. 81.

23. Ibid., p. 70.

24. Ibid., TS.6: "Robust Findings and Key Uncertainties," pp. 81–91.

25. Ibid., TS.6, p. 70.

26. Stephen Schneider, quoted in Jonathan Schell, "Our Fragile Earth," *Discover*, October 1989, pp. 44–50.

27. Hightower is a radio commentator, quoted in Robert Fox, "Newstrack," *Communications of the ACM*, 38, no. 8 (August 1995), pp. 11–12.

28. Jerry Mander, *In the Absence of the Sacred: The Failure of Technology and the Survival of the Indian Nations* (Sierra Club Books, 1991), p. 62.

29. "Net Surfing Mom Charged with Ignoring Kids," CNN Interactive, June 16, 1997, www6.cnn.com/US/9706/16/briefs.pm/internet.neglect/ (accessed October 29, 2001).

30. Alexandra Eyle, "No Time Like the Co-Present" (interview with Neil Postman), *NetGuide*, July 1995, pp. 121–122. Chet Bowers, another critic, also complains that computers contribute to the view of the individual as the basic social unit. Richard Sclove and Jeffrey Scheuer, "On the Road Again: If Information Highways Are Anything Like Interstate Highways—Watch Out!" in *Computerization and Controversy: Value Conflict and Social Choices*, 2nd ed., ed. Rob Kling (Academic Press, 1996), pp. 606–612.

31. Robert D. Putnam, *Making Democracy Work* (Princeton University Press, 1993). I thank Phil Agre for bringing Putnam's work and some of the ideas in this paragraph to my attention in his talk "Networking in the Community" at the San Diego ACM chapter meeting, January 24, 1996.

32. Alexis de Tocqueville, *Democracy in America* (Alfred A. Knopf, 1945), translated by Henry Reeves.

33. "Technology in the American Household," Times Mirror Center for the People and the Press, May 1994, pp. 5–7; Jon Katz, "The Digital Citizen," *Wired*, December 1997, pp. 68–82, 274–275; Lisa Guernsey, "Cyberspace Isn't So Lonely After All," *New York Times*, July 26, 2001, pp. D1, D5; James E. Katz and Philip Aspden, "A Nation of Strangers?" *Communications of the ACM*, 40, no. 12 (December 1997), pp. 81–86; Pew Research Center, November 2000.

34. Elias Aboujaoude et al., "Potential Markers for Problematic Internet Use: A Telephone Survey of 2,513 Adults," *CNS Spectrums: The International Journal of Neuropsychiatric Medicine*, October 5, 2006, www.cnsspectrums.com/aspx/articledetail. aspx?articleid=648 (accessed March 12, 2007).

35. Robert Fox, "News Track: Disorderly Conduct," *Communications of the ACM*, 41, no. 7 (July 1998), p. 9.

36. This is a condensed version of my article "Impacts on Community," *Computers & Society*, 27, no. 4 (December 1997), pp. 15–17.

37. In Rob Kling, ed., *Computerization and Controversy: Value Conflict and Social Choices*, 2nd ed. (Academic Press, 1996), pp. 606–612.

38. From a study by sociologist Claude Fisher, reported in Charles Paul Freund, "The Geography of Somewhere," *Reason*, May 2001, p. 12.

39. "Technology in the American Household," Times Mirror Center for the People and the Press (May 1994), p. 8.

40. See, for example, Katz, "The Digital Citizen," pp. 68–82, 274–275.

41. CPSR, "Serving the Community: A Public-Interest Vision of the National Information Infrastructure," www.cpsr.org/prevsite/cpsr/nii_policy.html.

42. Most of the data in this paragraph come from polls and studies by Pew Research Center, Forrester Research, Luntz Research Companies, IpsosReid Corporation, Nielsen//NetRatings, the U.S. Commerce Department, and others, reported in various news media. The 2004 figures varied in different studies. The National Science Foundation said more than 70% ("Science and Engineering Indicators 2006," Chapter 7, www.nsf.gov/statistics/seind06); Nielsen//Netratings reported nearly 75%.

43. Richard Shim, "Thanks for the memory: 30GB Hard Drive on a Platter," *ZDNet News*, January 23, 2001, www.zdnet.com/zdnn/stories/news (accessed March 23, 2001).

44. Most data from W. Michael Cox and Richard Alm, *Myths of Rich and Poor: Why We're Better off Than We Think* (Basic Books, 1999), pp. 161–162; Theodore Caplow, Louis Hicks, and Ben J. Wattenberg, *The First Measured Century: An Illustrated Guide to Trends in America* (AEI Press, 2001), p. 276.

45. Susannah Fox and Gretchen Livingston, "Latinos Online," Pew Research Center, March 14, 2007, pewresearch.org/pubs/429/latinos-online (accessed March 21, 2007).

46. The term *have-lates*, as a substitute for *have-nots*, was first used by Marvin Minsky, to the best of my knowledge; I prefer to use *have-laters* rather than *have-lates*.

47. www.laptop.org (accessed March 19, 2007).

48. www.laptop.org; Lee Gomes, "Making a Difference, One Laptop a Child," *Wall Street Journal*, July 17, 2007, p. B4.

49. The quotes in this paragraph are from "Nine Digital Divide Truths," Digital Divide.org, www.digitaldivide.org/dd/truths.html (accessed September 7, 2007).

50. Stephen Moore, "The Coming Age of Abundance," in *The True State of the Planet*, ed. Ronald Bailey (Free Press, 1995), p. 113.

51. "Interview with the Luddite," *Wired*, June 1995, pp. 166–168, 211–216 (see pp. 213–214).

52. Kirkpatrick Sale, *Rebels against the Future: The Luddites and Their War against the Industrial Revolution: Lessons for the Computer Age* (Addison Wesley, 1995), p. 257.

53. Mander, *In the Absence of the Sacred*, p. 61.

54. Postman, *Technopoly*, p. 119.

55. Eyle, "No Time Like the Co-Present."

56. Harvey Blume, "Digital Refusnik" (interview with Sven Birkerts), *Wired*, May 1995, pp. 178–179; "Interview with the Luddite."

57. Postman, *Technopoly*, p. 15.

58. See Jane Jacob's classic *The Economy of Cities* (Random House, 1969).

59. Postman, *Technopoly*, p. 6. The Freud quote is from *Civilization and Its Discontent* (e.g., the edition edited and translated by James Strachey, W. W. Norton, 1961, p. 35).

60. John Davis, quoted in Sale, *Rebels against the Future*, p. 256.

61. Sale, *Rebels against the Future*, p. 257.

62. The quotes are from "Interview with the Luddite," p. 214 and p. 213. Sale expresses this point of view also in *Rebels against the Future*, p. 213.

63. Sale, *Rebels against the Future*, p. 256.

64. This dichotomy has always struck me as strange, because it almost suggests that humans are alien creatures who arrived on Earth from somewhere else. We evolved here. We are part of nature. A human's house is as natural as a bird's nest, though, unlike birds, we have the capacity to build both ugly and beautiful things.

65. Martin V. Melosi, *Garbage in the Cities: Refuse, Reform, and the Environment: 1880–1980* (Texas A&M University Press, 1981), p. 24–25.

66. In "George Gilder and His Critics," *Forbes ASAP*, October 9, 1995, pp. 165–181.

67. Optical fiber: Ronald Bailey, ed., *Earth Report 2000: Revisiting the True State of the Planet* (McGraw Hill, 2000), p. 51; Moore, "The Coming Age of Abundance," p. 119; Nicholas Eberstadt, "Population, Food, and Income: Global Trends in the Twentieth Century," in *The True State of the Planet*, ed. Ronald Bailey (Free Press, 1995), p. 34. Family income spent on food: Stephen Moore and Julian L. Simon, *It's Getting Better All the Time: The 100 Greatest Trends of the 20th Century* (Cato Institute, 2000), p. 53; U.S. Department of Agriculture Economic Research Service, "Food CPI, Prices and Expenditures: Food Expenditure Tables," Table 7, www.ers.usda.gov/Briefing/CPIFoodAndExpenditures/Data/ (accessed March 21, 2007); Ronald Bailey, "Billions Served" (interview with Norman Borlaug), *Reason*, April 2000, pp. 30–37; Julian L. Simon, "The State of Humanity: Steadily Improving," *Cato Policy Report*, 17, no. 5 (September/October 1995), pp. 1, 10–11, 14–15. Nonvehicular accidental deaths declined from 72 per 100,000 people in 1900 to 19 per 100,000 people in 1997 (Caplow, Hicks, and Wattenberg, *The First Measured Century*, p. 149).

68. Ian Hacking, *The Emergence of Probability* (Cambridge University Press, 1975), p. 108; C. P. Snow, *The Two Cultures* (Cambridge University Press, 1964), pp. 82–83. The population data are from National Center for Health Statistics, Center for Disease Control, www.cdc.gov/nchs/data/hus/hus06.pdf#027 (accessed March 21, 2007), and from the United Nations,

reported in Eberstadt, "Population, Food, and Income," p. 21, p. 23, and in Caplow, Hicks, and Wattenberg, *The First Measured Century*, pp. 4–5.

69. Mander, *In the Absence of the Sacred*, pp. 67–68.

70. Ibid., p. 57. Comments at the Computers, Freedom, and Privacy conference, San Francisco, 1995, panel: "Against Computers: A Systemic Critique."

71. United Nations, "E-Commerce and Development Report 2001," quoted in Frances Williams, "International Economy & the Americas: UNCTAD Spells out Benefit of Internet Commerce," *Financial Times*, November 21, 2001.

72. Eyle, "No Time Like the Co-Present"; Postman, *Technopoly*, p. 10.

73. Julian L. Simon, "The State of Humanity: Steadily Improving," *Cato Policy Report*, 17, no. 5 (September/October 1995), pp. 1, 10–11, 14–15. See the books by Cox and Alm and by Moore and Simon in the references.

74. Cox and Alm, *Myths of Rich and Poor*, p. 15.

75. Reprinted in *British Labour Struggles: Contemporary Pamphlets 1727–1850* (Arno Press, 1972).

76. Sale, *Rebels against the Future*, p. 210.

77. Postman, *Technopoly*, p. 7.

78. "Interview with the Luddite."

79. Bill Richards, "Doctors Can Diagnose Illnesses Long Distance, To the Dismay of Some," *Wall Street Journal*, January 17, 1996, pp. A1, A10.

80. Ibid.

81. Telephone: Donald A. Norman, *Things That Make Us Smart: Defending Human Attributes in the Age of the Machine* (AddisonWesley, 1993), p. 191; Edison and Watson: Chris Morgan and David Langford, *Facts and Fallacies: A Book of Definitive Mistakes and Misguided Predictions* (St. Martin's Press, 1981) (Watson: p. 44). *Popular Mechanics* (March 1949), p. 258. Olson: Christopher Cerf and Victor Navasky, *The Definitive Compendium of Authoritative Misinformation* (Pantheon Books, 1984), p. 208, 209. Olson made the comment at a convention of the World Future Society. RCA: Thomas Petzinger Jr., "Meanwhile, from the Journal's Archives," *Wall Street Journal*, January 1, 2000, p. R5.

82. Peter J. Denning, "The Internet after 30 Years," in *The Internet Besieged*, ed. Dorothy E. Denning and Peter J. Denning (AddisonWesley, 1998), p. 20.

83. Norman, *Things That Make Us Smart*, p. 190.

84. Joseph Weizenbaum, *Computer Power and Human Reason: From Judgment To Calculation* (W. H. Freeman and Company, 1976), pp. 270–272.

85. Jeanette Borzo, "Now You're Talking," *CNN Money*, March 15, 2007, money.cnn.com/magazines/business2 (accessed July 18, 2007).

86. Rodney Brooks, "Toward a Brain-Internet Link," *Technology Review*, November 2003,

www.technologyreview.com/Infotech/13349/ (accessed July 18, 2007).

87. "Superhuman Imagination," interview with Vernor Vinge by Mike Godwin, *Reason*, May 2007, pp. 32–37.

88. *Wired*, April 2000, www.wired.com/wired/archive/8.04/joy.html (accessed September 7, 2007).

89. Virginia Postrel, "Joy, to the World," *Reason*, June 2000, www.reason.com/news/show/27725.html (accessed September 7, 2007).

90. This quote has been attributed to Neils Bohr and Albert Einstein; I could not find a reliable source for either.

BOOKS AND ARTICLES

- Attarian, John. "Spiritual and Cultural Perils of Technological Progress." *The Social Critic*, Winter 1998, pp. 10–18.

- Bailey, Ronald, ed. *Earth Report 2000: Revisiting the True State of the Planet*. McGraw Hill, 2000. Includes much data on improvements in the environment, resource usage, food and energy production, and so on.

- Birkerts, Sven. *The Gutenberg Elegies: The Fate of Reading in An Electronic Age*. Faber and Faber, 1994. Birkerts is a critic of computers; he writes on a typewriter.

- Brooks, Rodney A. *Flesh and Machines: How Robots Will Change Us*. Pantheon Books, 2002 (also, Vintage, 2003).

- Brower, Kenneth. "Photography in the Age of Falsification." *The Atlantic Monthly*, May 1998, pp. 92–111. Explores views of well-known nature photographers on the ethics of altering photos.

- Caplow, Theodore, Louis Hicks, and Ben J. Wattenberg. *The First Measured Century: An Illustrated Guide to Trends in America*. AEI Press, 2001.

- Compaine, Benjamin M., ed. *The Digital Divide: Facing a Crisis or Creating a Myth*. MIT Press, 2001.

- Cox, W. Michael, and Richard Alm. *Myths of Rich and Poor: Why We're Better off Than We Think*. Basic Books, 1999.

- Denning, Peter J., ed. *Talking Back to the Machine: Computers and Human Aspiration*. Copernicus, 1999.

- Dertouzos, Michael. *The Unfinished Revolution: Human-Centered Computers and What They Can Do For Us*. Harper Collins, 2001.

- Dreyfus, Hubert L. *On the Internet*. Routledge, 2001. Criticisms of hyperlinks and the organization of information on the Internet.

- Dreyfus, Hubert. *What Computers Still Can't Do: A Critique of Artificial Reason*. MIT Press, 1992. How well did Dreyfus's arguments hold up? Can computers now do some of the things he said they could not do?

- Florman, Samuel C. *Blaming Technology: The Irrational Search for Scapegoats*. St. Martin's Press, 1981.

- Ierley, Merritt. *Wondrous Contrivances: Technology at the Threshold*. Clarkson Potter, 2002. Looks at expectations for and attitudes about many earlier technological devices.

- Jeanneney, Jean-Noel. *Google and the Myth of Universal Knowledge: A View from Europe*. University of Chicago Press, 2006. The author is president of the France's Bibliotèque Nationale (National Library).

- Joy, Bill. "Why the Future Doesn't Need Us." *Wired*, April 2000, www.wired.com/wired/archive/8.04/joy.html. A response by Virginia Postrel is listed below.

- Kotkin, Joel. *The New Geography: How the Digital Revolution Is Reshaping the American Landscape*. Random House, 2000.

- Kurzweil, Ray. *The Singularity Is Near: When Humans Transcend Biology*. Viking, 2005.

- Lappin, Todd. "Déjà Vu All Over Again." *Wired*, May 1995, pp. 175–177, 218–222. A comparison of predictions of the social impact of radio 75 years ago and the predictions for the Internet.

- Ludlow, Peter, ed. *Crypto Anarchy, Cyberstates, and Pirate Utopias*. MIT Press, 2001.

- Mander, Jerry, and Edward Goldsmith, eds. *The Case against the Global Economy and For a Turn Toward the Local*. Sierra Club Books, 1996. Extremely critical of computer technology, automation, and technology in general. Argues that globalization should be halted and reversed.

- Mander, Jerry. *In the Absence of the Sacred: The Failure of Technology and the Survival of the Indian Nations*. Sierra Club Books, 1991.

- Mokyr, Joel. *The Lever of Riches: Technological Creativity and Economic Progress*. Oxford University Press, 1990.

- Moore, Stephen, and Julian Simon. *It's Getting Better All the Time: The 100 Greatest Trends of the 20th Century*. Cato Institute, 2000.

- Moravec, Hans. *Robot: Mere Machine to Transcendent Mind*. Oxford University Press, 2000.

- Murray, Alan. *The Wealth of Choices*. Crown Business, 2000.

- Naisbitt, John. *Global Paradox: The Bigger the World Economy, the More Powerful Its Smallest Players*. William Morrow and Company, 1994.

- Norman, Donald A. *Things That Make Us Smart: Defending Human Attributes in the Age of the Machine*. AddisonWesley,1993.

- Penrose, Roger. *The Emperor's New Mind: Concerning Computers, Minds, and the Laws of Physics*. Oxford University Press, 2002. Penrose argues that artificial intelligence cannot duplicate the full range of human intelligence.

- Postman, Neil. *Technopoly: The Surrender of Culture to Technology*. Alfred A. Knopf, 1992.

- Postrel, Virginia. "Joy, to the World." *Reason*, June 2000, www.reason.com/news/show/27725.html. A response to Bill Joy's article listed above.

- Postrel, Virginia. *The Future and Its Enemies*. The Free Press, 1998.

- Putnam, Robert D. *Making Democracy Work: Civic Traditions in Modern Italy*. Princeton University Press, 1993. The observations about what makes communities work well are useful for discussions of the impact of computers on community.

- Sale, Kirkpatrick. *Rebels against the Future: The Luddites and Their War against the Industrial Revolution: Lessons for the Computer Age*. AddisonWesley, 1995.

- Snow, C. P. "The Two Cultures and the Scientific Revolution." In this speech, Snow argues that people in the humanities and people in the sciences have fundamentally different views of science and technology. The speech appears, with an update, in C. P. Snow, *The Two Cultures: And a Second Look* (Cambridge University Press, 1964).

- Stoll, Clifford. *High Tech Heretic: Reflections of a Computer Contrarian.* Anchor Books, 2000.

- Vinge, Vernor. "The Coming Technological Singularity: How to Survive in the Post-Human Era," presented at the VISION-21 Symposium (sponsored by NASA Lewis Research Center and the Ohio Aerospace Institute), March 30–31, 1993, www-rohan.sdsu.edu/faculty/vinge/misc/singularity.html.

- Wresch, William. *Disconnected: Haves and Have-Nots in the Information Age.* Rutgers University Press, 1996.

ORGANIZATIONS AND WEB SITES

- Johns Hopkins University library, "Evaluating Information Found on the Internet": www.library.jhu.edu/researchhelp/general/evaluating/

- University of California, Berkeley, library, "Evaluating Web Pages: Techniques to Apply & Questions to Ask": www.lib.berkeley.edu/TeachingLib/Guides/Internet/Evaluate.html

8

ERRORS, FAILURES, AND RISK

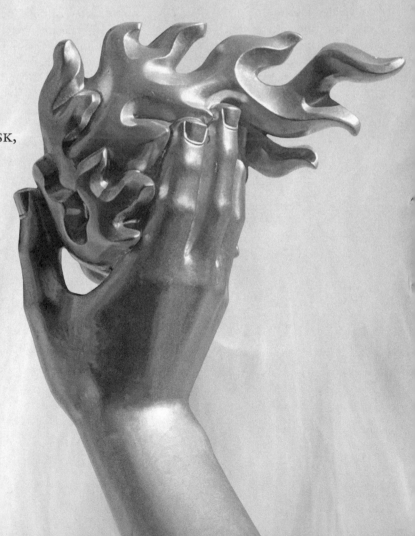

Most of this chapter is about computer systems that fail, crash, or never work at all because of software bugs, poor design, political considerations, or other factors. Some systems work as intended, but serious damage results when people misinterpret or misuse the information they provide. Errors in databases inconvenience people and disrupt lives. We consider a physical risk of computer use also: hand and arm problems. Studying these failures and risks contributes to understanding their causes and helps prevent future failures.

8.1 Failures and Errors in Computer Systems

8.1.1 AN OVERVIEW

"Navigation System Directs Car into River"
"Data Entry Typo Mutes Millions of U.S. Pagers"
"Flaws Found in Software that Tracks Nuclear Materials"
"Software Glitch Makes Scooter Wheels Suddenly Reverse Direction"
"IRS Computer Sends Bill for $68 Billion in Penalties"
"Robot Kills Worker"
"California Junks $100 Million Child Support System"
"Man Arrested Five Times Due to Faulty FBI Computer Data"

These headlines describe real incidents. Most computer applications, from consumer software to systems that control communications networks, are so complex that it is virtually impossible to produce programs with no errors. In the next few sections, we describe a variety of mistakes, problems, and failures—and some factors responsible for them. Some errors are minor. For example, a word processor might incorrectly hyphenate a word that does not fit at the end of a line. Some incidents are funny. Some are tragic. Some cost billions of dollars. All the examples can teach us something.

Are computer-controlled medical devices, factory automation systems, and airplane flight-management systems too unsafe to use? Or, like many stories on the evening news, do the headlines and horror stories emphasize the bad news—the dramatic and unusual events? We hear reports of car crashes on the news, but we do not hear that drivers completed 200,000 car trips safely in our city today. Although most car trips are safe, there is a good purpose for reporting crashes on the news: It teaches us what the risks are (e.g., driving in heavy fog) and it reminds us to be responsible and careful drivers. Just as many factors cause car crashes (faulty design, sloppy manufacturing or servicing, bad road conditions, a careless or poorly trained driver, confusing road signs, and so on), computer glitches and system failures also have myriad causes, including faulty design, sloppy implementation, careless or insufficiently trained users, and poor user interfaces. Often, there is more than one factor. Because of the complexity of computer systems, it is essential to follow good procedures and professional practices for their development and use. Sometimes, no one does anything clearly wrong, but an accident occurs anyway. Occasionally, the irresponsibility of software developers and managers is comparable to driving while very drunk.

Although millions of computers and software programs are working fine every day, it is crucial that we understand the risks and reasons for computer failures. How much risk must or should we accept? If the inherent complexity of computer systems means they will not be perfect, how can we distinguish between errors we should accept as trade-offs for the benefits of the system and errors that are due to inexcusable carelessness, incompetence, or dishonesty? How good is good enough? When should we, or the government, or a business decide that a computer is too risky to use? Why do multimillion-dollar systems fail so miserably that the firms and agencies that pay for them abandon them before completion? We cannot answer these questions completely, but this chapter provides some background and discussion that can help us in forming conclusions. It should help us understand computer-related problems from the perspective of several of the roles we play:

❖ *A computer user.* Whether we use a personal computer or a sophisticated, specialized system at work, we should understand the limitations of computers and the need for proper training and responsible use. We must recognize that, as in other areas, there are good products and bad products.

❖ *A computer professional.* Studying computer failures should help you become a better computer professional (system designer, programmer, or quality assurance manager, for example) if that is your career direction. Understanding the source and consequences of computer failures is also valuable if you will be responsible for buying, developing, or managing a complex system for a hospital, airport, or business. The discussions of the examples in this chapter include many implicit and explicit lessons about how you can avoid similar problems.

❖ *An educated member of society.* There are many personal decisions and social, legal, and political decisions that depend on our understanding of the risks of computer system failures. We could be on a jury. We could be an active member of an organization lobbying for legislation. We could be deciding whether or not to try an experimental computer-controlled medical device. Also we can apply some of the problem-solving approaches and principles in this chapter to professional areas other than computer systems.

We can categorize computer errors and failures in several ways, for example, by the cause, by the seriousness of the effects, or by the application area. In any scheme to organize the discussion, there will be overlap in some categories and mixing of diverse examples in some. For the remainder of this section, I use three categories: problems for individuals, usually in their roles as consumers; system failures that affect large numbers of people and/or cost large amounts of money; and problems in safety-critical applications that may injure or kill people. We will look at one case in depth (in Section 8.2): the Therac-25. This computer-controlled radiation treatment machine had a large number of flaws that resulted in the deaths of several patients. In Sections 8.3 and 8.4, we try to make some sense of the jumble of examples. Section 8.3 looks at underlying causes in more depth and describes some approaches to reducing problems. Section 8.4 puts the risks of computer systems into perspective in various ways, including considering risks in other systems and risks due to not using computers.

The incidents described here are a sampling of the many that occur. Robert Charette, an expert on software risk management, emphasizes that computer system errors and failures occur in all countries, in systems developed for businesses, governments, and nonprofit organizations (large and small) "without regard to status or reputation."[1] In most cases, by mentioning specific companies or products, I do not mean to single those out as unusual offenders. One can find many similar stories in news reports, in software engineering journals, and especially in the *Risks Digest* organized by Peter Neumann.[2] Neumann collects thousands of reports describing a wide range of computer-related problems.

8.1.2 PROBLEMS FOR INDIVIDUALS

Many people are inconvenienced and/or suffer losses from errors in billing systems and databases containing personal data.

Billing errors

The first few errors we look at are relatively simple ones whose negative consequences were undone relatively easily.[3]

* A woman received a $6.3 million bill for electricity. The correct amount was $63. The cause was an input error made by someone using a new computer system.

* The IRS is a constant source of major bloopers. When it modified its programs to avoid billing victims of a Midwest flood, the computer generated erroneous bills for almost 5,000 people. One Illinois couple received a bill for a few thousand dollars in taxes—and $68 billion in penalties. In one year, the IRS sent 3,000 people bills for slightly more than $300 million. One woman received a tax bill for $40,000,001,541.13.

* The auto insurance rate of a 101-year-old man suddenly tripled. Rates depend on age, but the program handled ages only up to 100. It mistakenly classified the man as a teenager.

* Hundreds of Chicago cat owners received bills from the city for failure to register dachshunds, which they did not own. The city used computer matching with two databases to try to find unlicensed pets. One database used DHC as the code for domestic house cat, and the other used the same code for dachshund.

Programmers and users could have avoided some of these errors. For example, programmers can include tests to determine whether a billing amount is outside some reasonable range or changed significantly from previous bills. In other words, because programs can contain errors, good systems have provisions for checking their results. If you have some programming experience, you know how easy it would be to include such tests and make a list of cases for someone to review. These errors are perhaps more humorous than serious. Big mistakes are obvious. They usually get fixed quickly. They are worth studying because the same kinds of design and programming errors can have more serious consequences in different applications. In the Therac-25 case (Section 8.2) we will see that including tests for inconsistent or inappropriate input could have saved lives.

Inaccurate and misinterpreted data in databases

Credit bureau records incorrectly listed thousands of New England residents as not having paid their local property taxes. An input error appeared to be the cause of the problem. People were denied loans before someone identified the scope of the problem and the credit bureau corrected it. (The credit bureau company paid damages to many of the people affected.) Like $40-billion tax bills, a systematic error affecting thousands of people is likely to get noticed. The relevant company or agency is likely to fix it quickly. More serious perhaps are all the errors in individual people's records. Critics of credit bureaus argue that incorrect information in credit records cause people to lose homes, cars, jobs, or insurance. In one case, a county agency used the wrong middle name in a report to a credit bureau about a father who did not make his child-support payments. Another man in the same county had the exact name reported. He could not get credit to buy a car or a house. It is difficult to get accurate and meaningful error rates. We

Errors in background checks of employees: Section 6.2.4

need to distinguish between a spelling error in someone's address and an incorrect report that someone bounced several checks. The results of numerous surveys and studies vary considerably, but all indicate that a high percentage of credit records have serious errors. Many people battle for years to get the credit bureaus to correct information in their records, and a few have won large settlements in lawsuits.

Federal law requires states to maintain databases of people convicted of sex crimes against children and to release information about them to the public. A family was harassed, threatened, and physically attacked after its state posted an online list of addresses where sex offenders live. The state did not know the offender had moved away before the family moved in. A lawyer reported that a man was nearly beaten to death after being mistaken for his brother. The brother was a sex offender in New Jersey's database. A man murdered two sex offenders in Washington state after getting their addresses from the state's sex offender database, and another man killed two sex offenders listed in Maine's online registry. There was no indication of database errors in these cases, but they clearly illustrate the risks. A man convicted of statutory rape for having sex with his 17-year-old girlfriend, and now married to her for many years, was in a sex offender database. While technically not an error, this case illustrates the need for careful thought about what a database includes and how it is presented to the public, especially if it involves a highly charged subject.

Florida voting officials mistakenly purged many people from its voting rolls. They could not vote in the close 2000 U.S. presidential election because their names matched names of convicted felons (who lose their voting rights). The state had hired a division of ChoicePoint, a huge database company, to supply lists of convicted felons. Apparently, the election officials used the lists without the extra verification step the company warned they would need.[4]

A high school excluded a 14-year-old boy from football and some classes without explanation. He eventually learned that school officials thought he had been using drugs while in junior high school. The two schools used different disciplinary codes in their computerized records. The boy had been guilty of chewing gum and being late. This case is very similar to the case of the dachshund/cat confusion described earlier—except that the consequences were more significant. Both cases illustrate the problems of relying on computer systems without taking the responsibility of learning enough about them to use them properly.

When errors occur in databases used by law enforcement agencies, the consequences can include arrests at gunpoint, strip searches, and time in jail with violent criminals. For example, two adults went to jail and a child to a juvenile home for 24 hours while police determined that they had really rented the rental car they were driving. The car rental company had listed the car as stolen. Studies of the FBI's National Crime Information Center (NCIC) database found that a high percentage of the arrest warrants in it were inaccurate or no longer valid. People are arrested when a check of the database shows a warrant for them—or for someone with a similar name. I will mention a few NCIC cases and other law enforcement cases. The news media and government studies reported many more. An adoption agency ran a routine check on an applicant and found a conviction for grand larceny. In fact, the applicant took part in a college prank—stealing a restaurant sign—years before. He had apologized and paid for the damage, and the charges had been dropped. The error could have caused the agency to deny the adoption. Police arrested a Michigan man for several crimes, including murders, committed in Los Angeles. Another man had assumed his identity after finding his lost wallet (or a discarded birth certificate; reports varied). It is understandable that NCIC listed the innocent man as wanted. However, he was arrested four more times within 14 months. (After repeatedly asking the city of Los Angeles to correct the records, he sued and won a judgment against the city.) The military imprisoned a man for five months because NCIC mistakenly reported that he was AWOL.* A college professor returning from London spent two days in jail after a routine check with NCIC at Customs showed that he was a wanted fugitive. NCIC was wrong—for the third time about this particular man. Police stopped and frisked an innocent driver because his license plate number incorrectly appeared as

---

*AWOL means "absent without official leave."

the license number of a man who had killed a state trooper. The computer record did not include a description of the car. (NCIC now includes digitized photographs and fingerprints to help reduce the number of incidents in which police detain an innocent person.)[5]

After September 11, 2001, the FBI gave a "watch list" to police departments and businesses such as car rental agencies, banks, casinos, and trucking and chemical firms. Recipients e-mailed the list to others, and eventually thousands of police departments and thousands of companies had copies. Many incorporated the list into their databases and systems that screened customers or job applicants. Although the list included people who were not suspects but whom the FBI wanted to question, some companies labeled the list "Suspected terrorists." Many entries did not include date of birth, address, or other identifying information, making mistaken identifications likely. Some companies received the list by fax and typed misspelled names from blurred copies into their databases. The FBI stopped updating the list but did not tell the recipients; thus many entries became obsolete.[6]

According to the Transportation Security Administration, more than 30,000 people have been mistakenly matched to names on terrorist watch lists at airports and border crossings. (The agency established a procedure to create a "cleared list" for such people so that they will not be stopped repeatedly in the future.)[7]

Several factors contribute to the frequency and severity of the problems people suffer because of errors in databases and misinterpretation of their contents:

* a large population (many people have identical or similar names, and most of our interactions are with strangers)

* automated processing without human common sense or the power to recognize special cases

* overconfidence in the accuracy of data stored on computers

* errors (some because of carelessness) in data entry

* failure to update information and correct errors

* lack of accountability for errors.

The first item is unlikely to change. It is the context in which we live. The second is partly a side effect of the speed and processing ability of computer technology, but we can reduce its negative impacts with better system specifications and training of users. Even if someone corrects an error in a database, problems may not be over for the affected person. Computer records are copied easily and often. Copies of the incorrect data may remain in other systems. The remaining factors in the list above are all within our control as individuals, professionals, and policy makers. We discuss some solutions in Section 8.3.

It is repugnant to the principles of a free society that a person should ever be taken into police custody because of a computer error precipitated by government carelessness. As automation increasingly invades modern life, the potential for Orwellian mischief grows.

—Arizona Supreme Court[8]

If you're trying to type War and Peace *with your thumbs, then you're going to have a problem.*

—Alan Hedge, director of the Human Factors and Ergonomics Lab,
Cornell University[9]

BLACKBERRY THUMB AND RSI

Millions of children play games on small electronic devices, and millions of adults answer e-mail on portable electronic gadgets with mini keypads. In many professions, people type on a computer keyboard for hours each day. Most of the risks we describe in this chapter result from errors in software, poor system design, or inaccurate and misinterpreted information. Here, we look at physical phenomena known as BlackBerry Thumb, Gamer's Thumb, Nintendonitis, repetitive strain injury (RSI), and various other terms. Repetitive strain injury, the more formal term, covers a variety of injuries or pain in thumbs, fingers, wrists, and arms (and sometimes neck and shoulders). You may have seen computer programmers, prolific bloggers, secretaries, or supermarket checkers (who move products quickly past a bar-code scanner for hours) wearing wrist braces, called splints—a common sign of RSI. These injuries can make ordinary activities painful or impossible and can prevent people from working.

RSI is not a new disease. There are references to similar problems in the 18th and 19th-centuries afflicting clerks and scribes (we used to call this writer's cramp), women who milked cows, and others whose work required repetitive hand motions. RSI problems occur among gymnasts, sign-language interpreters for the deaf, "pushup enthusiasts," auto workers, seamstresses, musicians, carpenters, meat processors, and workers in bakery factories. (An article in the *Journal of the American Medical Association* listed 29 occupations with common RSI problems.)[10] Computer game players, cell phone and keyboard users, and users of personal digital assistants (the BlackBerry is just one example) are among the newest significant group of RSI sufferers.

Thousands of people suffering from RSI sued keyboard makers and employers in the 1990s. They charged that the companies were at fault and should pay for medical costs and damages to the victims. Many of the suits resulted in dismissals or decisions for the defendants. In a few cases where plaintiffs won large awards, higher courts overturned the decisions on appeal. The uncertainty of causation (defects in the devices or improper use) made it difficult to win such suits. Some judges and others compare the complaints to ordinary aches and pains from overexercising or overusing a normally safe tool or device. What would we think of an RSI lawsuit against the maker of a tennis racket or a violin?

Attention to proper ergonomic design of keyboards and workstations reduced RSI problems for keyboard users. Laptop computer makers redesigned the machines to include a wrist rest. We can now buy split, twisted, and otherwise nontraditionally shaped keyboards—each one implementing some manufacturer's idea of what will be more comfortable and reduce strain. Modifying equipment alone does not solve the problem. RSI experts stress the importance of training in proper technique (including the importance of rest breaks, posture, and exercises). One can install free software that interrupts the user at regular intervals for rest breaks and software-guided exercises. Speech input devices might also reduce RSI caused by keyboard use. (But we might discover an increase in strain of the vocal cords.) Partly because of growing recognition of the RSI problem, and partly as protection against lawsuits, computer companies now provide information about proper use and arrangement of keyboards. Some game device makers package their product with reminders for users to take rest breaks.

Adult users of any tool or toy should learn proper techniques for its use. Young children need parental supervision or rules, as they do, for example, about wearing a helmet when riding a bicycle. Employers have a responsibility to provide training in proper and safe use of tools. Being aware of the potential for RSI might or might not encourage game players and instant messagers to take breaks and rest their hands and fingers. Mothers and doctors tell us repeatedly that we should sit up straight, exercise often, and eat our vegetables. Many people do not follow this advice—but, once we have the information, we can choose what to do with it.

Balance is very important for hand comfort. You'll be surprised at how quick your wrist will ache if the knife is not balanced properly.

—George McNeill, Executive Chef, Royal York Hotel, Toronto (on an advertisement for fine cutlery)

8.1.3 SYSTEM FAILURES

Modern communications, power, medical, financial, retail, and transportation systems depend heavily on computer systems. They do not always function as planned. We describe a lot of failures, some with indications of the causes. For computer science students and others who might contract for or manage custom software, one aim is to see the serious impacts of the failures—and to see what you want to work hard to avoid. The lessons of adequate planning, of making backup plans in case of failures, and of responsibility apply to large projects in other professions as well.

Communications, business, and transportation

Customers of AT&T lost telephone service for voice and data for nine hours because of a software error in a four-million line program. The disruption prevented roughly 50 million calls from getting through. A three-line change in a two-million line telecommunications switching program caused a failure of telephone networks in several major East Coast and West Coast cities. Although the program underwent 13 weeks of testing, it was not retested after the change—which contained a typo. A glitch in a routine software upgrade at America Online prevented subscribers from logging in all over the U.S. for several hours. American Express Company's credit-card verification system failed during the Christmas shopping season. Merchants had to call in for verification, overwhelming the call center. A majority of Skype's Internet phone users could not log in for two days in 2007. Its peer-to-peer network system had become overloaded by log-ins when a huge number of people rebooted their computers after installing routine Windows updates. (Skype has roughly 220 million users.)

When a Galaxy IV satellite computer failed, many systems we take for granted stopped working. Pager service stopped for an estimated 85% of users in the U.S., including hospitals and police departments. The failure interrupted radio and television broadcasts. Airlines that got their weather information from the satellite had to delay flights. The gas stations of a major chain could not verify credit cards. Some services were quickly switched to other satellites or backup systems. It took days to restore others.[11]

Every few years, the computer system of one of the world's largest stock exchanges or brokerages fails. An error in a software upgrade shut down trading on the Tokyo Stock Exchange. A problem in new communications software virtually shut down the NASDAQ stock exchange for two and a half hours. A glitch in an upgrade in the computer system at Charles Schwab Corporation crashed the system for more than two hours and caused intermittent problems for several days. Customers could not access their accounts or trade online. A computer malfunction froze the London Stock Exchange for almost eight hours—on the last day of the tax year, affecting many people's tax bills.[12]

A failure of Amtrak's reservation and ticketing system during Thanksgiving weekend caused delays because agents had no printed schedules or fare lists. Two large travel reservation systems that handle reservations for airlines, car rental companies, and hotels shut down for many hours because of computer problems. American Airlines could not verify electronic tickets; it delayed 200 flights. A failure of the computer that prepares flight plans for America West Airlines delayed thousands of passengers. AirTran installed a new system to handle flight check-in on the Internet, at airport self-service kiosks, and at airport check-in counters. It failed on its first day. Passengers and ticket agents could not print boarding passes; many people missed flights. Sometimes systems fail because they attempt something radically new. The AirTran failure, however, occurred in 2006, after air travelers had been checking in online and at self-service kiosks for several years.

The $125-million Mars Climate Orbiter disappeared when it should have gone into orbit around Mars. One team working on the navigation software used English measure units while another team used metric units. The investigation of the loss emphasized that while the error itself was the immediate cause, the fundamental problem was the lack of procedures that would have detected the error.[13]

Destroying businesses

Several companies have gone bankrupt after spending a huge amount of money on computer systems that failed to work. We describe one case of a system that seriously strained some businesses.

A few dozen companies that bought an inventory system called Warehouse Manager blamed the system for disastrous losses. One previously successful company saw its income decline by about half and laid off half its employees. The specific complaints were numerous. One company could not get the system to place a purchase order for several weeks. The company claimed the backlog in orders cost $2,000 per day. Processes that should have taken seconds, such as printing invoices, took several minutes. Impatient customers waited in long lines. The system gave incorrect information about inventory. It informed clerks that products were in stock when they were not and vice versa. According to users of Warehouse Manager, the system reported incorrect prices to clerks. A part that cost $114 was listed for sale at 54 cents. A $17 part was listed for sale at $30. The first error means lost money for the company. The second means lost customers—those who go elsewhere to find a better price. When two clerks tried to access the computer from their terminals simultaneously, the terminals locked up. Some companies said the system erased information needed for accounting and tax reports.[14]

What was responsible for the problems in Warehouse Manager? NCR Corporation sold the program, but another company developed it. The company originally designed and implemented the program on a different computer and operating system. It appears that there were unexpected problems when the company rewrote the program for NCR's machines and its ITX operating system. According to the *Wall Street Journal*, internal memos at NCR reported inadequate testing and poor performance in real business settings. NCR salespeople told prospective customers that Warehouse Manager was running successfully at 200 installations, but most of those were installations using the machine for which the program was originally designed. Several users claimed that although NCR was receiving complaints of serious problems from many customers,

DESTROYING CAREERS AND SUMMER VACATIONS[15]

CTB/McGraw-Hill develops and scores standardized tests for schools. About nine million students take its tests each year. An error in CTB's software caused it to report test results incorrectly—substantially lower than the correct scores—in several states. In New York City, school principals and superintendents lost their jobs because their schools appeared to be doing a poor job of teaching students to read. Educators endured personal and professional disgrace. One man said he applied for 30 other superintendent jobs in the state but did not get one. Parents were upset. Nearly 9,000 students had to attend summer school because of the incorrect scores. Eventually, CTB corrected the error. New York City's reading scores had actually risen five percentage points.

Why was the problem not detected sooner, soon enough to avoid firings and summer school? School testing officials in several states were skeptical of the scores showing sudden, unexpected drops. They questioned CTB, but CTB told them nothing was wrong. They said CTB did not tell them that other states experienced similar problems and also complained. When CTB discovered the software error,

the company did not inform the schools for many weeks, even though the president of CTB met with school officials about the problem during those weeks.

What lessons can we learn from this case? Software errors happen, of course. People usually notice significant mistakes, and they did here. But the company did not take seriously enough the questions about the accuracy of the results and was reluctant to admit the possibility—and later the certainty—of errors. It is this behavior that must change. The damage from a computer error can be small if the error is found and corrected quickly.

CTB recommended that school districts not use scores on its standardized tests as the sole factor in deciding which students should attend summer school. But New York City did so. We saw earlier that Florida state officials relied on computer-generated lists to prevent some people from voting, even though the database company supplying the lists said they needed additional verification. Relying solely on results produced by computers is temptingly easy. It is a temptation that people responsible for critical decisions in many situations should resist.

the company told them the problems they were having were unique. NCR blamed the problems on the company that developed Warehouse Manager and modified it for ITX. Eventually, NCR agreed it "did not service customers well" and the program should have undergone more extensive testing. The company settled most of the few dozen lawsuits out of court, with confidentiality agreements about the terms. The sources of the problems in this case included technical difficulties (converting software to a different system), poor management decisions (inadequate testing), and, according to the customers, dishonesty in promoting the system and responding to the problems.

Voting systems

The U.S. presidential election of 2000 demonstrated some of the problems of old-fashioned election machines and paper or punch-card ballots. Vote counters found these ballots sometimes difficult to read or ambiguous. Recounting was a slow tedious process. In 2002, Congress passed the Help America Vote Act and authorized $3.8 billion to improve voting systems. Many saw electronic systems, some using touch screens, as the solution. By the 2006 elections, a very small percent of Americans still voted with paper ballots. The rush to electronic voting machines demonstrated that they too could have numerous faults. We consider some of the problems in elections of 2002–2006.

Some electronic voting systems just crashed—voters were unable to vote. Machines in North Carolina failed to count more than 400 votes because of a technical problem. One county lost more than 4,000 votes because the machine's memory was full. A programming error generated 100,000 extra votes in a Texas county. A programming error caused some candidates to receive votes actually cast for other candidates.

Security against vote fraud and sabotage is another worry. Programmers or hackers can intentionally rig software to give inaccurate results. Depending on the structure of the system, independent recounting may be difficult. Security researchers strongly criticized voting machines made by the company that supplies a large portion of the machines. They say the machines have insecure encryption techniques, insufficient security for installation of upgrades to software, and poor physical protection of the memory card on which the system stores votes. Researchers opened the access panel on a voting machine with a standard key that is easily available and used in office furniture, electronic equipment, and hotel minibars.[16]

Independent groups of people can recount paper ballots, so more than half the states passed laws requiring some kind of paper record of votes. Poll workers in one county loaded the paper incorrectly and lost about 10% of the votes.

In some counties, election officials gave voting machines to high-school students and other volunteers to store at home and deliver to polling places on election day.

Many of the failures that occurred result from causes we will see over and over: lack of sufficient planning and thought about security issues, insufficient testing, and insufficient training. (In this application, the training task is complex. Thousands of ordinary people volunteer as poll workers and manage and operate the machines on election day.) In projects like these, the desire of states to obtain federal grants sometimes encourages haste.

One policy that can help to reduce errors and fraud is to make the software in electronic voting machines public. Then various experts and tech-savvy members of the public can examine it. Companies that produce electronic voting systems have resisted this, arguing that the software is proprietary. If they release it, they might lose an advantage over their competitors. Of course, even if the published version of the software is correct, secure, and free of intentional vote manipulation, we need procedures to ensure that the actual machines used in the voting process do not have different software installed.

Long before we voted on computers, Chicago and parts of Texas were infamous for vote fraud. In some cities, election officials found boxes full of uncounted paper ballots after an election was over. Reasonable accuracy and authenticity of vote counts are essential in a healthy democracy. Electronic systems have the potential for reducing some kinds of fraud and accidental loss of ballots, but they have not yet reached the level of security to ensure a reasonable degree of trust.

Stalled airports: Denver, Hong Kong, and Malaysia

In 1994, I flew over the huge Denver International Airport and the miles of wide highway leading to it. The airport covers 53 square miles, roughly twice the size of Manhattan. It was an eerie sight—nothing moved. There were no airplanes or people at the airport and no cars on the highway—ten months after the $3.2-billion airport was supposed to have opened. The opening was rescheduled at least four times. The delay cost more than $30 million per month in bond interest and operating costs. The computer-controlled baggage-handling system, which cost $193 million, caused most of the delay.[17]

The plan for the baggage system was quite ambitious. Outbound luggage checked at ticket counters or curbside counters was to travel to any part of the airport in less than ten minutes through an automated system of carts traveling at up to 19 miles per hour on 22 miles of underground tracks. Similarly, inbound luggage would go to terminals or transfer directly to connecting flights anywhere in the airport. Carts, bar-coded for their destinations, carried the bags. Laser scanners throughout the system tracked the 4,000 carts and sent information about their locations to computers. The computers used a database of flights, gates, and routing information to control motors and switches to route the carts to their destinations.

The system did not work as planned. During tests over several months, carts crashed into each other at track intersections. The system misrouted, dumped, and flung about luggage. Carts needed to move luggage went by mistake to waiting pens. Both the specific problems and the general underlying causes are instructive. Some of the specific problems were

❖ *Real-world problems.* Some scanners got dirty or knocked out of alignment and could not detect carts going by. Faulty latches on the carts caused luggage to fall onto the tracks between stops.

❖ *Problems in other systems.* The airport's electrical system could not handle the power surges associated with the baggage system. The first full-scale test blew so many circuits that the test had to be halted.

❖ *Software errors.* A software error caused the routing of carts to waiting pens when they were actually needed.

No one expects software and hardware of this complexity to work perfectly when first tested. In real-time systems,* especially, there are numerous interactions and conditions that designers might not anticipate. Mangling a suitcase is not embarrassing if it occurs during an early test and if the problem is fixed. It is embarrassing if it occurs after the system is in operation or if it takes a year to fix. What led to the extraordinary delay in the Denver baggage system? There seem to have been two main causes:

❖ *The time allowed for development and testing of the system was insufficient.* The only other baggage system of comparable size was at Frankfurt Airport in Germany. The company that built that system spent six years on development and two years testing and debugging. BAE Automated Systems, the company that built the Denver system, was asked to do it in two years. Some reports indicate that because of the electrical problems at the airport, there were only six weeks for testing.

❖ *Denver made significant changes in specifications after the project began.* Originally, the automated system was to serve United Airlines, but Denver officials decided to expand it to include the entire airport, making the system 14 times as large as the automated baggage system BAE had installed for United at San Francisco International Airport.

As a *PC Week* reporter said, "The bottom-line lesson is that system designers must build in plenty of test and debugging time when scaling up proven technology into a much more complicated environment."[18] Some observers criticized BAE for taking on the job when the company should have known that there was not enough time to complete it. Others blamed the city government for poor management, politically motivated decisions, and proceeding with a grandiose but unrealistic plan.

In 2005, United Airlines scrapped the complex, trouble-plagued automated baggage system. It had cost hundreds of millions of dollars. United said it would move baggage manually.

Opening day at the new airports in Hong Kong and Kuala Lumpur were disasters. The ambitious and complex computer systems at these airports were to manage *everything*: moving 20,000 pieces of luggage per hour and coordinating and scheduling crews, gate assignments for flights, and so on. Both systems failed spectacularly. At Hong Kong's Chek Lap Kok airport, cleaning crews and fuel trucks, baggage, passengers, and cargo went to the wrong gates, sometimes far from where their airplanes were. Airplanes scheduled to take off were empty. At Kuala Lumpur, airport employees had to write boarding passes by hand and carry luggage. Flights, of course, were delayed; food cargo rotted in the heat in Malaysia.

At both airports, the failures were blamed on people typing in incorrect information. In Hong Kong, it was perhaps a wrong gate or arrival time that was dutifully sent throughout the system. In Kuala Lumpur, mistakes by check-in agents unfamiliar with

---

*Real-time systems are systems that must detect and respond to or control activities of objects or people in the real world within time constraints.

the system paralyzed it. "There's nothing wrong with the system," said a spokesman at Malaysia's airport. A spokesman at Hong Kong made a similar statement. They are deeply mistaken. One incorrect gate number would not have caused the problems experienced at Hong Kong. Any system that has a large number of users and a lot of user input must be designed and tested to handle input mistakes. The "system" includes more than software and hardware. It includes the people who operate it. As in the case of the Denver airport, there were questions about whether political considerations, rather than the needs of the project, determined the scheduled time for the opening of the airports.[19]

Abandoned systems

The flaws in many systems are so fundamental that the systems end up in the trash after wasting millions, or even billions, of dollars. A large British food retailer spent more than $500 million on an automated supply management system; it did not work. The Ford Motor Company abandoned a $400-million purchasing system. The California and Washington state motor vehicle departments each spent more than $40 million on computer systems before abandoning them because they never worked properly. A consortium of hotels and a rental car business spent $125 million on a comprehensive travel-industry reservation system, then canceled the project because it did not work. The state of California spent more than $100 million to develop one of the largest and most expensive state computer systems in the country: a system for tracking parents who owe child-support payments. After five years, the state abandoned the system because it did not work. It lost data, miscalculated payments, and could not communicate with other government agencies. After spending $4 billion, the IRS abandoned a tax-system modernization plan; a GAO report blamed mismanagement. The FBI spent $170 million to develop a database called the Virtual Case File system to manage evidence in investigations, then scrapped it because of many problems. A Department of Justice report blamed poorly defined and changing design requirements, lack of technical expertise, and poor management.[20] There are many more such examples.

Many projects require much more time and money than originally planned. Some are never completed because they are beyond the capabilities of the current technology. Software expert Robert Charette estimates that from 5% to 15% of information technology projects are abandoned before or soon after delivery as "hopelessly inadequate"—out of about $1 trillion spent each year worldwide. Figure 8.1 includes some reasons he cites.[21] Such large losses demand attention from computer professionals, information technology managers, business executives, and public officials who set budgets and schedules for large projects.

Legacy systems

After US Airways and America West merged, they combined their reservation systems. The self-service check-in kiosks failed. Long lines at ticket counters delayed thousands of passengers and flights. Merging different computer systems is extremely tricky, and

---

❖ Lack of clear, well-thought-out goals and specifications

❖ Poor management and poor communication among customers, designers, programmers, and so on

❖ Institutional or political pressures that encourage unrealistically low bids, unrealistically low budget requests, and underestimates of time requirements

❖ Use of very new technology, with unknown reliability and problems, perhaps for which software developers have insufficient experience and expertise

❖ Refusal to recognize or admit that a project is in trouble

Figure 8.1 Some High-level Causes of Computer-System Failures

problems are common. But this incident illustrates another factor. According to a vice president of US Airways, most airline systems date from the 1960s and 1970s. Designed for the mainframe computers of that era, they, in some cases, replaced reservations on 3×5 paper cards. These old systems "are very reliable, but very inflexible," the airline executive said.[22] These are examples of "legacy systems"—out-of-date systems (hardware, software, or peripheral equipment) still in use, often with special interfaces, conversion software, and other adaptations to make them interact with more modern systems.

The problems of legacy systems are numerous. Old hardware fails, and replacement parts are hard to find. Old software often runs on newer hardware, but it is still old software. Programmers no longer learn the old programming languages. The programmers who wrote the software or operated the systems have left the company, retired, or died. Old programs often had little or no documentation. If there were good design documents and manuals, they probably no longer exist or cannot be found. Limited computer memory led to obscure and terse programming practices. A variable a programmer might now call "flight_number" would then have been simply "f."

Why do people still use such systems? Why do you keep an old printer, computer game, or camera when you replace an old computer? Why not buy a new one? One obvious answer is cost. Another is that you might not want the overhead of learning how to use the new one. You might have lots of old documents or applications that work with the old system, and you would need to convert them. All these reasons apply, on a large scale, to legacy business systems.

Many Windows operating systems include software that mimics the older DOS operating system so that people can run old programs written for the older environment. You can find software to run old games on new computers. Modern word processors can read "ancient" document formats. And airlines integrate Web-based reservations systems and self-service check-in kiosks with very old systems.

THE Y2K PROBLEM

Many records stored on computers include a date. Many computations use dates. Older software, designed for computers with very limited storage space, typically used two digits to represent the year (e.g., 78, 95).

Many computer systems experienced problems in the 1990s when they began using dates in or after the year 2000, ("Y2K" in the jargon of the time for "Year 2000"). For example, some credit cards with expiration dates in 2000 would not work. The software interpreted the expiration date as 1900. Software to calculate payments on loans due after 2000 failed.

People writing software in the 1960s and 1970s never considered or imagined that their code would still be in use in the year 2000. But it was. It was buried in financial systems, inventory systems, medical systems, infrastructure systems, and all sorts of other systems. Businesses and governments spent many billions of dollars on the "Y2K problem," tracking down two-digit dates in their software and making modifications, rushing to finish before January 1, 2000. Programmers took special courses in old programming languages (such as COBOL, widely used for business applications) so that they could read and patch old programs. Software customers sued software vendors for the cost of searching their software for Y2K problems and fixing them.

As January 1, 2000, approached, many people feared major disasters would result as critical computer systems failed or crashed. We awoke on January 1, 2000, to find that there had been no disasters. Some systems did not work properly, but problems were not significant. Afterward, some argued that the huge multiyear, multibillion-dollar effort to upgrade systems and fix the software had succeeded. Others argued that it was an expensive waste caused by irresponsible hype. The truth includes some of both views.

What similar problems are hiding in computer systems now? What systems are not designed with a far enough look into the future?

The major users of computers in the early days included banks, airlines, government agencies, and providers of infrastructure services such as power companies. The systems grew gradually. A complete redesign and development of a fully new, modern system would, of course, be expensive. The conversion to the new system, possibly requiring some downtime, could also be very disruptive. Thus legacy systems persist.

We will continue to invent new programming languages, paradigms, and protocols—and we will later add on to the systems we develop as they age. Among the lessons legacy systems provide for computer professionals is the recognition that someone might be using your software 30 or 40 years from now. It is important to document,

document, document your work. It is important to design for flexibility, expansion, and upgrades.

8.1.4 SAFETY-CRITICAL APPLICATIONS

There are many examples of problems in safety-critical computer systems in military applications, power plants, aircraft, trains, automated factories, medical applications, and so on. We briefly look at a few aviation cases, then at one medical-instrument case in depth in the next section.

Computers in the air

The A320 Airbus airplane was the first fully "fly-by-wire" airplane. Pilots do not directly control the plane. Their actions are inputs to computers that control the aircraft systems. Between 1988 and 1993, four A320s crashed. Although investigators decided the cause for some of the crashes was "pilot error," pilots and some observers blamed the fly-by-wire system. Pilots complained that the airplane does not respond as expected, that it seems to have "a mind of its own" and may suddenly behave in unexpected and inappropriate ways. In one crash, the pilots specified a rate of descent of 3,300 feet per minute instead of the normal 800 feet per minute. The official report on the crash indicated that reasons for the error probably included the pilots' lack of familiarity with the automation equipment and confusing design of the controls and displays. The crew left the "vertical navigation" entirely to the automatic systems although there were indications that the plane was descending too fast. Perhaps they had too much confidence in the computer's ability to detect and correct mistakes. In another crash, the computer did not recognize that the plane had landed; it prevented the pilot from reversing engine thrust to brake the airplane.[23]

The Federal Aviation Administration (FAA) installed a $1-billion system at major airports for tracking high-altitude, long-distance flights. It worked well in some of the airports where it was tested. Problems occurred within a day of modifications at other airports, causing cancellation of hundreds of flights. When the FAA installed its upgraded radar system at its traffic control center in southern California, the system crashed, grounding flights nationwide. Twice, the computer that controls flights that enter British airspace broke down. Controllers used manual backup systems. The average flight delay was three hours.[24] A computer problem at the Los Angeles airport cut capacity by 50%, causing flight delays all around the country.

Air traffic control is extremely complex. The systems that manage it include computers on the ground at airports, devices in thousands of airplanes, radar, databases, communications, and so on—all of which must work in real time, tracking airplanes that move very fast. Bureaucratic and political decision-making and funding processes compound the inherent difficulty of the task.

We discuss more incidents of failures of aircraft systems in Sections 8.3 and 8.4, where we look at solutions (including better computer systems).

8.1.5 PERSPECTIVES ON FAILURE

How close to perfection should we expect billing systems to be? A water-utility company sent a customer an incorrect bill for $22,000. A spokesman for the company pointed out that one incorrect bill out of 275,000 monthly bills is a good error rate. Is that reasonable? How accurate should the software for ATMs be? The double-withdrawal incident mentioned in Chapter 1 affected roughly 150,000 transactions. With approximately eight billion ATM transactions each year, that was one error in roughly 45,000. Is that an acceptable rate? (There were probably other ATM errors in that year, but the publicity given to this case suggests that it affected far more transactions than other errors.) How accurate should software for check processing be? 99%? 99.9%? U.S. financial institutions process roughly 250 million checks per day. Even if they made errors on 10,000 checks every day, the accuracy rate would be better than 99.99%. (How high would the accuracy rate be if checks and bills were processed without computers?) At some point, the expense of improving a system is not worth the gain, especially for applications where errors can be detected and corrected at lower cost than it would take to try to eliminate them.

Many large, complex, expensive computer systems work extremely well. We rely on them daily. Many computer systems protect lives and increase safety. To balance the examples we described of failures, we mention a few examples of successes.

The New York Stock Exchange prepared well for spikes in trading. On one day, the Stock Exchange computers processed 76% more trades than the previous record. They handled the sales without errors or delays. The Exchange managers had planned in advance, spending $2 billion on a system with hundreds of computers, 200 miles of fiber-optic cable, 8,000 telephone circuits, and 300 data routers. They had spent weekends testing the system on triple and quadruple the normal trading volume. Similarly, over one weekend, Barclays Bank replaced three incompatible computer systems with a new system to handle 25 million accounts. The transition, estimated to cost more than £100 million, was successful.[25]

A ground-proximity warning system (GPWS) helps prevent airplanes from crashing into mountains (a major cause of air travel fatalities). Older radar-based systems sometimes gave warning only ten seconds before a potential impact. The GPWS contains a digital map of the world's topography. It can give a pilot up to a minute of warning if a plane is too close to a mountain and automatically displays a map of nearby mountains. Dangerous peaks are shown in red. The system works where the older system did not: The radar-based system could not distinguish between approaching the ground for landing and a potential crash, so it did not give warnings during a landing approach. The digital maps enable the computer system to make the distinction. The GWPS is likely responsible for preventing crashes in eight incidents since 2000 (in which pilots incorrectly set an altimeter, attempted to land with poor visibility, mistook building lights for airport lights, and so on). In some airplanes, when visibility is poor, a computer system displays an accurate view of the terrain on the plane's windshield. Pilots see a view close to what they would see in clear weather.[26]

Overall, computers and other technologies have made air travel safer. In the middle of the first decade of this century, there was roughly one fatal accident per four million commercial flights, down 60% from ten years earlier.[27]

Trust the human or the computer system?

How much control should computers have in a crisis? This question arises in many application areas. We address it in the context of aircraft systems.

The Traffic Collision Avoidance System (TCAS) detects a potential in-air collision of two airplanes and directs the pilots to avoid each other. The first version of the system had so many false alarms that it was unusable. In some incidents, the system directed pilots to fly toward each other rather than away, potentially causing a collision instead of avoiding one. TCAS was improved, however. It is a great advance in safety, according to the head of the Airline Pilots Association's safety committee.[28] TCAS functioned correctly on a Russian airplane carrying many children and on a German cargo plane. The systems detected a potential collision and told the Russian pilot to climb and the German pilot to descend. Unfortunately, the Russian pilot followed an air traffic controller's instruction to descend, and the planes collided. In this example, the computer's instructions were better than the human's. A few months after this tragedy, the pilot of a Lufthansa 747 ignored instructions from an air traffic controller and followed instructions from the computer system instead, avoiding a midair collision. U.S. and European pilots are now trained to follow TCAS instructions even if they conflict with instructions from an air traffic controller.

Pilots are trained to immediately turn off autopilot systems when TCAS signals a potential collision. They manually maneuver the plane to avoid the collision. That might change. The Airbus 380, the world's largest passenger airplane, began flying in 2006. Its pilots are trained to allow its autopilot system to control the plane when a midair collision threatens. The aircraft maker says that pilots sometimes overreact to collision warnings and make extreme maneuvers that can injure passengers or cause a collision with other air traffic in the area. The policy is controversial among pilots.[29]

Some airlines (and private pilots) disable parts of computer systems in their planes because they do not trust the computer or because they believe the pilot should more actively fly the plane. However, there are circumstances where the computer can do better than most people. Like anti-lock braking systems in automobiles that control braking to avoid skidding, computer systems in airplanes control sudden sharp climbs to avoid stalling. The computers in some airplanes prevent certain actions even if the pilot tries them (e.g., banking at a very steep angle). Some people object, arguing that the pilot should have ultimate control in case unusual action is needed in an emergency. Based on accident statistics, some airlines believe that preventing pilots from doing something "stupid" can save more lives than letting them do something bold and heroic, but outside the program limitations, in the very rare cases where it might be necessary.

8.2 Case Study: The Therac-25

8.2.1 THERAC-25 RADIATION OVERDOSES

The benefits of computing technology to health care are numerous and very impressive. They include improved diagnosis, monitoring of health conditions, development of new drugs, information systems that speed treatment and reduce errors, devices that save lives, devices that increase safety of surgeries, and on and on. Yet one of the classic case studies of a deadly software failure is a medical device: a radiation treatment machine.

The Therac-25 was a software-controlled radiation-therapy machine used to treat people with cancer. Between 1985 and 1987, Therac-25 machines at four medical centers gave massive overdoses of radiation to six patients. In some cases, the operator repeated an overdose because the machine's display indicated that it had given no dose. Medical personnel later estimated that some patients received between 13,000 and 25,000 rads,* where the intended dose was in the 100–200 rad range. These incidents caused severe and painful injuries and the deaths of three patients. Why is it important to study a case as old as this? To avoid repeating the errors. Medical physicists operating a different radiation-treatment machine in Panama in 2000 tried to circumvent a limitation in the software in an attempt to provide more shielding for patients. Their actions caused dosage miscalculations. Twenty-eight patients received overdoses of radiation, and several died.[30] It seems that dramatic lessons need repetition with each new generation.

What went wrong with the Therac-25?

Studies of the Therac-25 incidents showed that many factors contributed to the injuries and deaths. The factors include lapses in good safety design, insufficient testing, bugs in the software that controlled the machines, and an inadequate system of reporting and investigating the accidents. (Articles by computer scientists Nancy Leveson and Clark Turner and by Jonathan Jacky are the main sources for this discussion.[31])

To understand the discussion of the problems, it will help to know a little about the machine. The Therac-25 is a dual-mode machine. That is, it can generate an electron beam or an X-ray photon beam. The type of beam needed depends on the tumor being treated. The machine's linear accelerator produces a high-energy electron beam (25 million electron volts) that is dangerous. Patients must not be exposed to the raw beam. A computer monitors and controls movement of a turntable that holds three sets of devices. Depending on whether the treatment is electron or X-ray, the machine rotates a different set of devices in front of the beam to spread it and make it safe. It is essential that the proper protective device be in place when the electron beam is on. A third position of the turntable uses a light beam instead of the electron beam to help the operator position the beam precisely in the correct place on the patient's body.

---

*A rad is the unit used to quantify radiation doses. It stands for "radiation absorbed dose."

8.2.2 SOFTWARE AND DESIGN PROBLEMS

Design flaws

The Therac-25 followed earlier machines called the Therac-6 and Therac-20. It differed from them in that it was fully computer controlled. The older machines had hardware safety interlock mechanisms, independent of the computer, that prevented the beam from firing in unsafe conditions. The design of the Therac-25 eliminated many of these hardware safety features. The Therac-25 reused some software from the Therac-20 and Therac-6. The software was apparently assumed to be functioning correctly. This assumption was wrong. When new operators used the Therac-20 there were frequent shutdowns and blown fuses, but no overdoses. The Therac-20 software had bugs, but the hardware safety mechanisms were doing their job. Either the manufacturers did not know of the problems with the Therac-20 or they completely missed the serious implications.

The Therac-25 malfunctioned frequently. One facility said there were sometimes 40 dose rate malfunctions in a day, generally underdoses. Thus, operators became used to error messages appearing often, with no indication that there might be safety hazards.

There were a number of weaknesses in the design of the operator interface. The error messages that appeared on the display were simply error numbers or obscure messages ("Malfunction 54" or "H-tilt"). This was not unusual for early computer programs when computers had much less memory and mass storage than they have now. One had to look up each error number in a manual for more explanation. The operator's manual for the Therac-25, however, did not include any explanation of the error messages. The maintenance manual did not explain them either. The machine distinguished between errors by the amount of effort needed to continue operation. For certain error conditions, the machine paused, and the operator could proceed (turn on the electron beam) by pressing one key. For other kinds of errors, the machine suspended operation and had to be completely reset. One would presume that the machine would allow one-key resumption only after minor, not safety-related, errors. Yet one-key resumption occurred in some of the accidents in which patients received multiple overdoses.

Atomic Energy of Canada Limited (AECL), a Canadian government corporation, manufactured the Therac-25. Investigators studying the accidents found that AECL produced very little documentation concerning the software specifications or the testing plan during development of the program. Although AECL claimed that they tested the machine extensively, it appeared that the test plan was inadequate.

Bugs

Investigators were able to trace some of the overdoses to two specific software errors. Because many readers of this book are computer science students, I will describe the bugs. These descriptions illustrate the importance of using good programming techniques. However, some readers have little or no programming knowledge, so I will simplify the descriptions.

After the operator entered treatment parameters at a control console, a software procedure called Set-Up Test performed a variety of checks to be sure the machine was in the correct position, and so on. If anything was not ready, this procedure scheduled itself to rerun the checks. (The system might simply have to wait for the turntable to move into place.) The Set-Up Test procedure can run several hundred times while setting up for one treatment. A flag variable indicated whether a specific device on the machine was in the correct position. A zero value meant the device was ready; a nonzero value meant it must be checked. To ensure that the device was checked, each time the Set-Up Test procedure ran, it incremented the variable to make it nonzero. The problem was that the flag variable was stored in one byte. After the 256th call to the routine, the flag overflowed and showed a value of zero. (If you are not familiar with programming, think of this as an automobile's odometer rolling over to zero after reaching the highest number it can show.) If everything else happened to be ready at that point, the program did not check the device position, and the treatment could proceed. Investigators believe that in some of the accidents, this bug allowed the electron beam to be on when the turntable was positioned for use of the light beam, and there was no protective device in place to attenuate the beam.

Part of the tragedy in this case is that the error was such a simple one, with a simple correction. No good student programmer should have made this error. The solution is to set the flag variable to a fixed value, say 1, rather than incrementing it, to indicate that the device needs checking.

Other bugs caused the machine to ignore changes or corrections made by the operator at the console. When the operator typed in all the necessary information for a treatment, the program began moving various devices into place. This process could take several seconds. The software checked for editing of the input by the operator during this time and restarted the setup if it detected editing. However, because of bugs in this section of the program, some parts of the program learned of the edited information while others did not. This led to machine settings that were incorrect and inconsistent with safe treatment. According to the later investigation by the Food and Drug Administration (FDA), there appeared to be no consistency checks in the program. The error was most likely to occur with an experienced operator who was quick at editing input.

In a real-time, multitasking system that controls physical machinery while an operator enters—and may modify—input, there are many complex factors that can contribute to subtle, intermittent, and hard-to-detect bugs. Programmers working on such systems must learn to be aware of the potential problems and to use good programming practices to avoid them.

8.2.3 WHY SO MANY INCIDENTS?

There were six known Therac-25 overdoses. You may wonder why hospitals and clinics continued to use the machine after the first one.

The Therac-25 had been in service for up to two years at some clinics. They did not immediately pull it from service after the first few accidents because they did not know immediately that it caused the injuries. Medical staff members considered various other explanations. The staff at the site of the first incident said that one reason they were not certain of the source of the patient's injuries was that they had never seen such a massive radiation overdose before. They questioned the manufacturer about the possibility of overdoses, but the company responded (after the first, third, and fourth accidents) that the machine could not have caused the patient injuries. According to the Leveson and Turner investigative report, they also told the facilities that there had been no similar cases of injuries.

After the second accident, AECL investigated and found several problems related to the turntable (not including any of the ones we described). They made some changes in the system and recommended operational changes. They declared that they had improved the safety of the machine by five orders of magnitude, although they told the FDA that they were not certain of the exact cause of the accident. That is, they did not know whether they had found the problem that caused the accident or just other problems. In making decisions about continued use of the machines, the hospitals and clinics had to consider the costs of removing the expensive machine from service (in lost income and loss of treatment for patients who needed it), the uncertainty about whether the machine was the cause of the injuries, and, later, when that was clear, the manufacturer's assurances that they had solved the problem.

A canadian government agency and some hospitals using the Therac-25 made recommendations for many more changes to enhance safety; they were not implemented. After the fifth accident, the FDA declared the machine defective and ordered AECL to inform users of the problems. The FDA and AECL spent about a year (during which the sixth accident occurred) negotiating about changes in the machine. The final plan included more than two dozen changes. They eventually installed the critical hardware safety interlocks, and most of the machines remained in use with no new incidents of overdoses after 1987.[32]

Overconfidence

In the first overdose incident, when the patient told the machine operator that the machine had "burned" her, the operator told her that was impossible. This was one of many indications that the makers and some users of the Therac-25 were overconfident about the safety of the system. The most obvious and critical indication of overconfidence in the software was the decision to eliminate the hardware safety mechanisms. A safety analysis of the machine done by AECL years before the accidents suggests that they did not expect significant problems from software errors. In one case where a clinic added its own hardware safety features to the machine, AECL told them it was not necessary. (None of the accidents occurred at that facility.)

The hospitals using the machine assumed that it worked safely, an understandable assumption. Some of their actions, though, suggest overconfidence or at least practices that they should have avoided. For example, operators ignored error messages because the machine produced so many of them. A camera in the treatment room and an intercom system enabled the operator to monitor the treatment and communicate with the patient. (The operator uses a console outside the shielded treatment room.) On the day of an accident at one facility, neither the video monitor nor the intercom was functioning. The operator did not see or hear the patient try to get up after an overdose. He received a second overdose before he reached the door and pounded on it. This facility had successfully treated more than 500 patients with the machine before this incident.

8.2.4 OBSERVATIONS AND PERSPECTIVE

From design decisions all the way to responding to the overdose accidents, the manufacturer of the Therac-25 did a poor job. Minor design and implementation errors usually occur in a complex system, but the number and pattern of problems in this case, and the way they were handled, suggest serious irresponsibility. This case illustrates many of the things that a responsible, ethical software developer should not do. It illustrates the importance of following good procedures in software development. It is a stark reminder of the consequences of carelessness, cutting corners, unprofessional work, and attempts to avoid responsibility. It reminds us that a complex system can work correctly hundreds of times with a bug that shows up only in unusual circumstances—hence the importance of always following good safety procedures in operation of potentially dangerous equipment. This case also illustrates the importance of individual initiative and responsibility. Recall that some facilities installed hardware safety devices on their Therac-25 machines. They recognized the risks and took action to reduce them. The hospital physicist at one of the facilities where the Therac-25 overdosed patients spent many hours working with the machine to try to reproduce the conditions under which the overdoses occurred. With little support or information from the manufacturer, he was able to figure out the cause of some of the malfunctions.

To put the Therac-25 in perspective, it is helpful to remember that failures and other accidents have always occurred and continue to occur in systems that do not use computers. Two other linear accelerator radiation-treatment machines seriously overdosed patients. Three patients received overdoses in one day at a London hospital in 1966 when safety controls failed. Twenty-four patients received overdoses from a malfunctioning machine at a Spanish hospital in 1991; three patients died. Neither of these machines had computer controls.[33]

Two news reporters reviewed more than 4,000 cases of radiation overdoses reported to the U.S. government. Here are a few of the overdose incidents they describe. A technician started a treatment, then left the patient for 10–15 minutes to attend an office party. A technician failed to carefully check the prescribed treatment time. A technician failed to measure the radioactive drugs administered; she just used what looked like the right amount. In at least two cases, technicians confused microcuries and millicuries.*

---

*A curie is a measure of radioactivity. A millicurie is one thousand times as much as a microcurie.

The underlying problems were carelessness, lack of appreciation for the risk involved, poor training, and lack of sufficient penalty to encourage better practices. In most cases, the medical facilities paid small fines or none at all.[34]

Most of the incidents we just described occurred in systems without computers. For some, a good computer system might have prevented the problem. Many could have occurred whether or not the treatment system was controlled by a computer. These examples do not excuse the Therac-25. They suggest, however, that individual and management responsibility, good training, and accountability are important no matter what technology we use.

8.3 Increasing Reliability and Safety

Success actually requires avoiding many separate possible causes of failure.

—Jared Diamond[35]

8.3.1 WHAT GOES WRONG?

Computer systems fail for two general reasons: The job they are doing is inherently difficult, and the job is often done poorly. Several factors combine to make the task difficult. Early computer programs were fed some numbers, did mathematical computations, and provided some answers. There were sometimes errors, but the task was not extremely complex. Computer systems now interact with the real world (including both machinery and unpredictable humans), include complex communications networks, have numerous features and interconnected subsystems, and are extremely large. A cell phone has several millions of lines of computer code. General Motors estimated that its cars would have 100 million lines of code by 2010.[36] Computer software is "nonlinear" in the sense that, whereas a small error in an engineering project might cause a small degradation in performance, a single typo in a computer program can cause a dramatic difference in behavior.

The job can be done poorly at any of many stages, from system design and implementation to system management and use. (This characteristic is not unique to computer systems, of course. We can say the same about building a bridge, a space shuttle, a car, or any complex system in the modern world.) Figure 8.1 (in Section 8.1.3) summarized high-level, management-related causes of system failures. Figure 8.2 lists more factors in computer errors and system failures. The examples we described illustrate most of them. We comment on a few.

Overconfidence

Overconfidence, or an unrealistic or inadequate understanding of the risks in a complex computer system, is a core issue. When system developers and users appreciate the risks,

- ❖ Design and development
    - Inadequate attention to potential safety risks.
    - Interaction with physical devices that do not work as expected.
    - Incompatibility of software and hardware or of application software and the operating system.
    - Not planning and designing for unexpected inputs or circumstances.
    - Insufficient testing.
    - Reuse of software from another system without adequate checking.
    - Overconfidence in software.
    - Carelessness.

- ❖ Management and use
    - Data-entry errors.
    - Inadequate training of users.
    - Errors in interpreting results or output.
    - Failure to keep information in databases up to date.
    - Overconfidence in software by users.
    - Insufficient planning for failures, no backup systems or procedures.

- ❖ Misrepresentation, hiding problems, and inadequate response to reported problems.

- ❖ Insufficient market or legal incentives to do a better job.

Figure 8.2   Some Factors in Computer-System Errors and Failures

they have more motivation to use the techniques that are available to build more reliable and safer systems and to be responsible users. How many PC users never back up their files until after a disk crash that destroys critical data or months of work?

Some safety-critical systems that failed had supposedly "fail-safe" computer controls. In some cases, the logic of the program was fine, but the failure resulted from not considering how the system interacts with real users or real-world problems (such as loose wires or fallen leaves on train tracks).

Can we analyze and quantify the risks of failure in a system? Yes, but we must use the techniques for developing estimates of failure rates carefully. For example, the computers on the A320 airplane each have redundant software systems designed by two separate teams of programmers. The redundancy is a safety feature, but how much safety does it provide? The failure rate was supposed to be less than one failure per billion flight hours. Designers calculated it by multiplying the estimated failure rates of each of the two systems, one in 100,000 hours. The calculation is reasonable if the systems are entirely independent. But safety experts say that even when programmers work separately, they tend to make the same kinds of errors, especially if there is an error, ambiguity, or omission in the program specifications.[37]

Unrealistic reliability or safety estimates can come from genuine lack of understanding, from carelessness, or from intentional misrepresentation. People without a high regard for honesty sometimes give in to business or political pressure to exaggerate safety, to hide flaws, to avoid unfavorable publicity, or to avoid the expense of corrections or lawsuits.

Reuse of software: the Ariane 5 rocket and "No Fly" lists

Less than 40 seconds after the launch of the first Ariane 5 rocket, the rocket veered off course and was destroyed as a safety precaution. The rocket and the satellites it was carrying cost approximately $500 million. A software error caused the failure.[38] The Ariane 5 used some software designed for the earlier, successful Ariane 4. The software included a module that ran for about a minute after initiation of a launch on the Ariane 4. It did not have to run after takeoff of the Ariane 5, but a decision was made to avoid introducing new errors by making changes in a module that operated well in Ariane 4. This module did calculations related to velocity. The Ariane 5 travels faster than the Ariane 4 after takeoff. The calculations produced numbers bigger than the program could handle (an "overflow" in technical jargon), causing the system to halt.

A woman named Jan Adams, and many other people with first initial J and last name Adams, were flagged as possible terrorists when they tried to board an airplane. The name "Joseph Adams" is on a "No Fly" list of suspected terrorists (and other people considered safety threats) given to the airlines by the Transportation Security Agency. To compare passenger names with those on the "No Fly" list, some airlines used old software and strategies designed to help ticket agents quickly locate a passenger's reservation record (e.g., if the passenger calls in with a question or to make a change). The software searches quickly and "casts a wide net." That is, it finds any possible match, which a sales agent can then verify. In the intended applications for the software, there is no inconvenience to anyone if the program presents the agent with a few potential matches of similar names. In the context of tagging people as possible terrorists, a person mistakenly "matched" will likely undergo questioning and extra luggage and body searches by security agents.

Does something about these incidents sound familiar? The Therac-25 (Section 8.2) used software from earlier machines, the Therac-6 and Therac-20. The software seemed to function acceptably in those systems but was not appropriate or safe for the Therac-25. Should we not reuse software? One of the goals of programming paradigms like object-oriented code is to make software elements that can be widely used, thus saving time and effort. Reuse of working software should also increase safety and reliability. After all, it has undergone field testing in a real, operational environment; we know it works. At least, we think it works. The critical point is that it works in a different environment. It is essential to reexamine the specifications and design of the software, consider implications and risks for the new environment, and retest the software for the new use. U.S. and

European aircraft safety experts now apply this cautious policy. They recommend that when an aircraft system uses commercial, off-the-shelf software, it be required to meet the same extensive review and testing as new custom software for aircraft. When a dispute arose about off-the-shelf software in the development of the Airbus 380 airplane, the dispute was about the level and quality of the required certification, not over whether it was a necessary step.

Failure to update

Failure to update information in databases has led to problems of varying severity. When considering the next two examples and other possible examples, think about what kinds of databases are inherently difficult to keep up-to-date. Which are extremely expensive, possibly too expensive, to keep up-to-date? For which is updating very important? For which, not so important?

The FBI maintains a database that contains criminal history records from participating states and is available to police throughout most of the country. *Privacy Journal* reported that about half the records do not indicate whether a suspect was convicted or exonerated. (In addition, there was a high inaccuracy rate.)[39]

The U.S. government spent $900 million to set up a database to track the roughly two million foreign visitors who arrive in the U.S. each month. Goals include screening for terrorists and detecting visitors who stay longer than legally permitted. The system stores photos and fingerprints of foreigners but does not have a way for visitors to check out when leaving the country. Several airports are testing a check-out system, but a full system at all border exits is likely infeasible. Without a way to update records when a visitor leaves, the system cannot meet one of its main goals.[40]

What design features in databases can encourage updating or reduce problems resulting from out-of-date information?

8.3.2   PROFESSIONAL TECHNIQUES

Software engineering and professional responsibility

The many examples of computer system errors and failures suggest the importance of using good software engineering techniques at all stages of development, including specifications, design, implementation, documentation, and testing. There is a wide range between poor work and good work, as there is in virtually any field. Professionals, both programmers and managers, have the responsibility to study and use the techniques and tools that are available and to follow the procedures and guidelines established in the various relevant codes of ethics and professional practices. (The ACM/IEEE-CS Software Engineering Code of Ethics and Professional Practice and the ACM Code of Ethics and Professional Conduct, in Appendix A, are two important sets of general guidelines for such practices.) A subfield of computer science focusing on design and development of safety-critical software is growing. Safety specialists emphasize that developers must "design in" safety from the start. There are techniques of hazard analysis that help system designers identify risks and protect against them. Software engineers who work on safety-critical applications should have special training. Software expert Nancy Leveson emphasizes that with good technical practices and good management, you can develop large systems right: "One lesson is that most accidents are not the result of unknown scientific principles but rather of a failure to apply well-known, standard engineering practices. A second lesson is that accidents will not be prevented by technological fixes alone, but will require control of all aspects of the development and operation of the system."[41]

To complete a large project successfully requires long and careful planning and good management. Companies that do well expend extensive effort to learn the needs of the client and to understand how the client will use the system. Good software developers help clients better understand their own goals and requirements, which the clients might not be good at articulating. Often some aspects of the way they work or what they need and expect are so obvious to them that they do not state them to the system developers. The long planning stage allows for discovering and modifying unrealistic goals. One company that developed a successful financial system that processes one trillion dollars in transactions per day spent several years developing specifications for the system, then only six months programming, followed by carefully designed, extensive testing.

Mistakes will happen, and unexpected problems will arise. An atmosphere of open, honest communication within the software development company and between the company and the client is essential for learning of problems early and minimizing the effort required to handle them.

In the rest of this section, we look at a few specific aspects of designing and developing good software.

User interfaces and human factors

If you are using a word processor to edit a document and you try to quit without saving your changes, what happens? Most programs will remind you that you have not saved your changes and give you a chance to do so. The designers of the programs know that people forget or sometimes click or type the wrong command. This is a simple and common example of considering human factors in designing software—one that has avoided personal calamities for millions of people.

Well-designed user interfaces can help avoid many computer-related problems. System designers and programmers need to learn from psychologists and human-factor experts who know principles and practices for doing a good job.* User interfaces should provide clear instructions and error messages. They should be consistent. They should include appropriate checking of input to reduce major system failures caused by typos or other errors a person will likely make.

The crash of American Airlines Flight 965 near Cali, Columbia, in 1995 illustrates the importance of consistency (and other aspects of good user interfaces). While approaching

---

*See, for example, the Shneiderman, Tufte, Nielsen, and Norman books in the list of references at the end of the chapter.

the airport, the pilot intended to lock the autopilot onto the beacon, called Rozo, that would lead the plane to the airport. The pilot typed "R," and the computer system displayed six beacons beginning with "R." Normally, the closest beacon is at the top of the list. The pilot selected it without checking carefully. The beacon at the top of the list was "Romeo" and was more than 100 miles away, near Bogota. The plane turned more than 90 degrees and headed for Romeo. In the dark, it crashed into a mountain, killing 159 people.[42]

In the lawsuits that followed, juries attributed blame mostly to pilot error. The pilot chose the wrong beacon without checking and continued to descend at night after the plane made a large, unexpected turn. A jury assigned some of the responsibility to the companies that provided the computer system. While it is clear that the pilot could have and should have avoided the crash, it is also clear that the inconsistency in the display—not putting the nearest beacon at the top of the list—created a dangerous situation.

As an illustration of more principles that can help build safer systems, we consider other aspects of automated flight systems. An expert in this area emphasizes the following points:[43]

❖ *The pilot needs feedback to understand what the automated system is doing at any time.* This is critical when the pilot must suddenly take over if the automation fails or if he or she must turn it off for any reason. One example is having the throttle move as a manually operated throttle would, even though movement is not necessary when the automated system is operating.

❖ *The system should behave as the pilot (or, in general, experienced user) expects.* Pilots tend to reduce their rate of climb as they get close to their desired altitude. On the McDonnell Douglas MD-80, the automated system maintains a climb rate that is up to eight times as fast as pilots typically choose. Pilots, concerned that the plane might overshoot its target altitude, made adjustments, not realizing that their intervention turned off the automated function that caused the plane to level out when it reached the desired altitude. Thus, because the automation behaved in an unexpected way, the airplane climbed too high—exactly what the pilot was trying to prevent. (The incidence of the problem declined with more training.)

❖ *A workload that is too low can be dangerous.* Clearly, an overworked operator is more likely to make mistakes. One of the goals of automation is to reduce the human workload. However, a workload that is too low can lead to boredom, inattention, or lack of awareness of the current status. That is a danger if the pilot must take over in a hurry.

Good user interfaces are essential in safety-critical applications. They are important also in ordinary applications. Customers do not return to Web sites that are confusing and difficult to navigate. It is not a coincidence that some of the most popular Web sites are, according to design experts, some of the best designed.

Redundancy and self-checking

Redundancy and self-checking are two techniques important in systems on which lives and fortunes depend. The space shuttles in the 1980s used four identical but independent computer systems that received input from multiple sensors and checked their results against each other. If one computer disagreed with the other three, it was taken out of service. If two of the three remaining judged the third to be faulty, it was taken out of service, and the rest of the flight canceled. In case of a more serious problem, perhaps caused by a common flaw in the software, there was a fifth computer, made by another manufacturer and programmed by different programmers, that could control the descent of the shuttle.[44] This degree of redundancy is expensive and there are not many applications that use it. It illustrates the kinds of precautions that system designers can take for systems that operate in dangerous physical environments where human lives are at stake or in other systems where a failure would have disastrous effects.

Complex systems collect information on their own activity for use in diagnosing and correcting errors. AT&T's telephone system handles roughly 100 million calls a day. The system constantly monitors itself and corrects problems automatically. Half of the computing power of the system goes to checking the rest for errors. When it detects a problem in a switching component, the component automatically suspends use of the switch, informs the rest of the network that it is out of service temporarily and should not receive calls, activates recovery routines that take a few seconds to correct the problem, then informs the network that the component is functioning again. But wait a minute! This is the same system that failed several years ago, disrupting telephone service for hours. In fact, it was this very part of the system that caused the breakdown. There was a bug in the routine that processed recovery messages from switches that had failed and recovered. The same software operated in each switch. Thus, each switch that received the message failed, then recovered and sent a recovery message. A chain reaction of failures occurred. The bug was in a software upgrade that had been running for about a month.[45] Even when we follow the best professional practices, with extensive testing, we have no guarantee that such complex systems are bug free.

Testing

It is difficult to overemphasize the importance of adequate, well-planned testing of software. Testing is not arbitrary. There are principles and techniques for doing a good job. Many significant computer system failures in previously working systems occurred soon after installation of an update or upgrade. Even small changes need thorough testing. Unfortunately, many cost-conscious managers, programmers, and software developers see testing as a dispensable luxury, a step you can skimp on to meet a deadline or to save money. This is a common, but foolish, risky, and often irresponsible attitude.

In his investigation of the destruction of the Challenger space shuttle, Richard Feynman concluded that development of the onboard computer systems for the space shuttle used good safety criteria and testing plans.* Ironically, he was told that, because the shuttle software usually passed its tests, NASA management planned to reduce testing to save money. Fortunately, instead, as a result of studies after the loss of the Challenger, NASA instituted a practice called independent verification and validation (IV&V). This means that an independent company (i.e., not the one that developed the program and not the customer) tests and validates the software. (Testing and verification by an independent organization is not practical for all projects, but many software developers have their own testing teams that are independent of the programmers who develop a system.) The IV&V team acts as "adversaries" and tries to find flaws. A few years later, NASA planned to eliminate IV&V but switched direction again. In response to several studies, including an extensive one done by software safety experts, NASA decided to make IV&V a permanent part of the program.[46] This example illustrates a common ambivalence about testing.

You might have used a *beta version* of a product or heard of *beta testing*. Beta testing is a near-final stage of testing. A selected set of customers (or members of the public) use a complete, presumably well-tested system in their "real-world" environment. Thus, this is testing by regular users, not software experts. Beta testing can detect software limitations and bugs that the designers, programmers, and testers missed. It can also uncover confusing aspects of user interfaces, need for more rugged hardware, problems that occur when interfacing with other systems or when running a new program on older computers, and many other sorts of problems.

8.3.3 LAW, REGULATION, AND MARKETS

Criminal and civil penalties

Legal remedies for faulty systems include suits against the company that developed or sold the system and criminal charges when fraud or criminal negligence occurs. Families of Therac-25 victims sued; they settled out of court. A bank won a large judgment against a software company for a faulty financial system that caused problems a user described as "catastrophic."[47] Several people have won large judgments against credit bureaus for incorrect data in credit reports that caused havoc in their lives.

Many contracts for business computer systems limit the amount the customer can recover to the actual amount spent on the computer system. Customers know, when they sign the contract, that there is generally no coverage for losses incurred because the system did not meet their needs for any reason. Courts have upheld such contract limitations. If people and businesses cannot count on the legal system upholding the terms of a contract, contracts would be almost useless. Millions of business interactions that take

---

*Seals that failed in cold weather caused the destruction of the Challenger, not a software error. Experts afterward studied many aspects of safety.

place daily would become more risky and therefore more expensive. Because fraud and misrepresentation are not, of course, part of a contract, some companies that suffer large losses allege fraud and misrepresentation by the seller in an attempt to recover some of the losses, regardless of whether the allegations have firm grounding.

Well-designed liability laws and criminal laws—not so extreme that they discourage innovation but clear and strong enough to provide incentives to produce good systems—are important legal tools for increasing reliability and safety of computer systems, as they are for protecting privacy and for protecting customers in other industries. After-the-fact penalties do not undo the injuries that occurred, but the prospect of paying for mistakes and sloppiness is incentive to be responsible and careful. Payments compensate the victim and provide some justice. An individual, business, or government that does not have to pay for its mistakes and irresponsible actions will make more of them. These observations about liability apply as well to accuracy of private (business) databases. The lack of market incentives makes achieving and maintaining accuracy in government databases more difficult. In addition, you often cannot sue the government. Outside of government, we are more likely to pay for accidents and carelessness.

Unfortunately, there are many flaws in liability law in the United States. People often win multimillion-dollar suits when there is no scientific evidence or sensible reason to hold the manufacturer or seller of a product responsible for accidents or other negative impacts. Abuse of the liability lawsuit system almost shut down the small-airplane manufacturing industry in the U.S. for years. The complexity of large computer systems make designing liability standards difficult, but this is a necessary task.

Warranties for consumer software

Most mass, retail consumer software, from photo-management programs to games, comes packaged with "shrink-wrap" or "click-on" licensing agreements that indicate you are buying the software "as-is." There is no guarantee that it works correctly. Some such agreements also include provisions prohibiting the user from publically criticizing the software. Some include provisions that the vendor may choose the state in which legal disputes are settled, possibly at great inconvenience to the consumer. Consumer advocates and the software industry disagree on the extent to which the law should uphold these agreements. At one extreme, the agreements would be binding contracts. At the other extreme, some consumer advocates argue for mandatory warranties on software, for making software companies pay for bugs, and for voiding provisions of licensing agreements they consider unfair to consumers.

Supporters of strict legal requirements for warranties argue that such requirements would encourage responsibility on the part of software sellers and produce better software. Consumers would have legal protection against large, indifferent companies. Consumers are paying for a product that works, and fairness dictates that they get one that does.

Opponents point out that such requirements would raise prices. The additional cost of development, testing, and insurance would hurt small companies most, putting them out of business and leading to concentration of the industry in large companies. The costs would also reduce innovation and development of new software. The inherent complexity of software makes production of error-free software infeasible. Actual use by consumers is an important part of the testing that leads to corrections and upgrades. (Some companies pay users a few dollars for each bug they find.)

Supporters of stricter laws might respond that we would not accept these arguments if we were discussing, say, microwave ovens. If we buy one, we expect it to work. A basic issue in this debate is whether legal standards and requirements for quality and warranties should be the same for software as for physical products. Some related questions are the following: How well did the first microwave ovens, the first cars, the first record players work? Are we in the early stages of software as a product? Are consumers willing to accept some bugs in software as a trade-off for other benefits? Would a warranty law speed up the process of improving software?

Having different liability standards for software and physical products raises some problems. A microwave oven has embedded software. Can the sellers of microwave ovens claim that the weaker standards for software should cover their product? Would companies making various devices and appliances add software to their products unnecessarily, just to bring the products under the lower software standards? Would this lead to a serious decline in product quality? Although there are good arguments for treating consumer software differently from physical products, laws would have to define carefully the category of products to which they apply.[48]

Regulation and safety-critical applications

Is there legislation or regulation that can prevent life-threatening computer failures? A law saying that a radiation machine should not overdose a patient would be silly. We know that it should not do that. We could ban the use of computer control for applications where an error could be fatal, but such a ban is ill advised. In many applications, the benefits of using computers are well worth the risks.

A widely accepted option is regulation, possibly including specific testing requirements and requirement for approval by a government agency before a new product can be sold. The FDA has regulated drugs and medical devices for decades. Companies must do extensive testing, provide huge quantities of documentation, and get government approval before they sell new drugs and some medical devices. Arguments in favor of such regulation, both for drugs and for safety-critical computer systems include the following: Most potential customers and people who would be at risk (e.g., patients) do not have the expertise to judge the safety or reliability of a system. It is better to prevent use of a bad product than to rely on after-the-calamity remedies. It is too difficult and expensive for ordinary people to sue large companies successfully.

If the FDA had thoroughly examined the Therac-25 before it was put into operation, it might have found the flaws before any patients were injured. However, we should note some weaknesses and trade-offs in the regulatory approach.[49] The approval process is extremely expensive and time-consuming. The multiyear delays in introducing a good product cost many lives. Political concerns affect the approval process. Competitors influence decisions. Also, there is an incentive for bureaucrats and regulators to be overcautious. Damage caused by an approved product results in bad publicity and possible firing for the regulator who approved it. Deaths or losses caused by the delay or failure to approve a good new product are usually not obvious and get little publicity.

Leveson and Turner, in their Therac-25 article, summarize some of these dilemmas:

> The issues involved in regulation of risky technology are complex. Overly strict standards can inhibit progress, require techniques behind the state of the art, and transfer responsibility from the manufacturer to the government. The fixing of responsibility requires a delicate balance. Someone must represent the public's needs, which may be subsumed by a company's desire for profits. On the other hand, standards can have the undesirable effect of limiting the safety efforts and investment of companies that feel their legal and moral responsibilities are fulfilled if they follow the standards. Some of the most effective standards and efforts for safety come from users. Manufacturers have more incentive to satisfy customers than to satisfy government agencies.[50]

Professional licensing

Another controversial approach to improving software quality is mandatory licensing of software development professionals. Laws require licenses for hundreds of trades and professions. Licensing requirements typically include specific training, the passing of competency exams, ethical requirements, and continuing education. The desired effect is to protect the public from poor quality and unethical behavior. The history of mandatory licensing in many fields shows that the actual goals and the effects were and are not always very noble. In some trades (plumbing, for example), the licensing requirements were devised to keep black people out. Requirements for specific degrees and training programs, as opposed to learning on one's own or on the job, tend to keep poorer people from qualifying for licenses. Economic analyses have shown that the effect of licensing is to reduce the number of practitioners in the field and keep prices and income for

Clashes between licensing laws and the Web: Section 3.2.4

licensees higher than they would otherwise be, in many cases without any improvement in quality.[51] Some see a legal prohibition on working for pay without a government-approved license as a fundamental violation of the freedom to work (i.e., of the negative right, or liberty, to work, in the terms of Section 1.4.3).

These objections do not apply to the many valuable voluntary approaches to measuring or certifying qualifications of software personnel, for example, a diploma from a respected school and certification programs by professional organizations, particularly for advanced training in specialized areas.

Taking responsibility

In some cases of computer errors, businesses pay customers for problems or damages. For example, Intuit offered to pay interest and penalties that resulted from errors in flawed income-tax programs. When United Airlines mistakenly posted ticket prices on its Web site as low as about $25 for flights between the U.S. and Europe, it honored tickets purchased before it corrected the error. United, at first, charged the buyers the correct fare and probably had the legal right to do so, but the airline concluded that having angry customers would cost more than the tickets. We noted that business pressures are often a reason for cutting corners and releasing defective products. Business pressure can also be a cause for insistence on quality and maintaining good customer relations. Good business managers recognize the importance of customer satisfaction and the reputation of the business. Also, some businesses have an ethical policy of behaving responsibly and paying for mistakes, just as a person would pay for accidentally breaking a neighbor's window with a misdirected softball.

Other market mechanisms besides consumer backlash encourage a quality job. Insurance companies have an incentive to evaluate the systems they insure. The insurer for the company that operated several faulty communications satellites commented that it would consider the company's lapse in testing and quality control in the future. Satellite-failure incidents illustrate another market mechanism for dealing with the risk of computer failures: Some businesses paid a higher rate for "uninterrupted" service. That is, the service company would switch their communications quickly to other satellites in case of a failure. Businesses that can withstand a few hours of interruption need not pay for that extra protection. Organizations whose communications are critical to public safety, such as police departments and hospitals, should take responsibility to ensure they have appropriate backup service, possibly paying extra for the higher level of service.

How can customers protect themselves from faulty software? How can a business avoid buying a seriously flawed program? For high-volume, consumer and small-business software, one can consult the many magazines and Web sites that review new programs. Specialized systems with a small market are more difficult to evaluate before purchase. We can check the seller's reputation with the Better Business Bureau. We can consult previous customers and ask how well they did the job. Online user groups for specific software products are excellent sources of information for prospective and current customers. In the case of the Therac-25, the users eventually spread information among themselves. If the Web had existed at the time of the accidents, it is likely that the problems would have been identified sooner and that some of the accidents would not have happened.

8.4 Dependence, Risk, and Progress

8.4.1 ARE WE TOO DEPENDENT ON COMPUTERS?

Comments about our dependence on computers appear in many discussions of the social impact of computers. Because of their usefulness and flexibility, computers are now virtually everywhere. Is this good? Or bad? Or neutral? The word "dependence" often has a negative connotation. "Dependence on computers" suggests a criticism of our society or of our use of computers. Is it appropriate?

In Holland, no one discovered the body of a reclusive, elderly man who died in his apartment until six months after his death. Eventually, someone noticed that he had a large accumulation of mail. This incident was described as a "particularly disturbing example of computer dependency." Many of the man's bills, including rent and utilities, were paid automatically. His pension check went automatically to his bank account. Thus, "all the relevant authorities assumed that he was still alive."[52] But who expects the local gas company or other "relevant authorities" to discover a death? The problem here, clearly, was the lack of concerned family, friends, and neighbors. I happened to be present in a similar situation. An elderly, reclusive woman died in her home. Within two days, not six months, the mailman noticed that she had not taken in her mail. He informed a neighbor, and together they checked the house. I do not know if her utility bills were paid automatically; it is irrelevant.

On the other hand, many people and businesses are not prepared to do without the computer systems they use every day. A BlackBerry e-mail blackout lasted nine hours. It disrupted the work of bankers, technology workers, talent agents, and others who depend on constant communication via their Blackberry—some who receive more than 500 e-mails per day. A physician commented that modern hospitals and clinics cannot function efficiently without medical-information systems. Modern crime fighting depends on computers. Some military jets cannot fly without the assistance of computers. In several incidents, computer failures or other accidents knocked out communication services. Drivers could not buy gasoline with their credit cards. "Customers were really angry," said a gas station manager. Stockbrokers could not connect to New York by telephone or computer. More than 1,000 California state lottery terminals were down; people could not buy tickets or collect winnings. A supermarket manager reported "Customers are yelling and screaming because they can't get their money, and they can't use the ATM to pay for groceries."[53]

Is our "dependence" on computers different from our dependence on electricity, which we use for lighting, entertainment, manufacturing, medical treatments—and just about everything? Is our "dependence" on computers different from a farmer's dependence on a plow? The Sioux people's dependence on their bows and arrows? Modern surgery's dependence on anesthesia?

Computers and plows are tools. We use tools because we are better off with them than without them. They reduce the need for hard physical labor and tedious routine mental labor. They help us be more productive, or safer, or more comfortable. When we have a good tool, we can forget, or no longer even learn, the older method of performing a task. If the tool breaks down, we are stuck. We cannot perform the task until someone fixes it. That can mean that no telephone calls get through for several hours. It might mean the loss of a large amount of money, and it can mean danger or death for some people. But the negative effects of a breakdown do not condemn the tool. To the contrary, for many computer applications (not all), the inconveniences or dangers of a breakdown are a reminder of the convenience, productivity, or safety the tool provides when it is working. It reminds us, for example, of the billions of communications, carrying voice, e-mail, photos, and data, that are possible or more convenient or cheaper because of computers.

We could avoid the risk of a broken plow by plowing with our hands. We could avoid the risk of losing a document file on a disk by doing all our writing by hand on paper. Even ignoring the possibility of a fire destroying our paper records, it should be clear that we reject the "safe" (nondependent) option because, most of the time, it is less convenient and less productive.

Some misconceptions about dependence on computers come from a poor understanding of the role of risk, confusion of "dependence" with "use," and blaming computers for failures where they were only innocent bystanders. On the other hand, abdication of responsibility that comes from overconfidence or ignorance is a serious problem. There are valid technical criticisms of dependence when a system design allows a failure in one component to cause a major breakdown. There are valid criticisms of dependence when businesses, government agencies, and organizations do not make plans for dealing with system failures. The wise individual is grateful for ATMs and credit cards but keeps a little extra cash at home in case they do not work.

8.4.2 RISK AND PROGRESS

Electricity lets us heat our homes, cook our food, and enjoy security and entertainment. It also can kill you if you're not careful.

—"Energy Notes" (Flyer sent with San Diego Gas & Electric utility bills)

We trust our lives to technology every day. We trust older, noncomputer technologies every time we step into an elevator, a car, or a building. As the tools and technologies we use become more complex and more interconnected, the amount of damage that results from an individual disruption or failure increases, and we sometimes pay the costs in dramatic and tragic events. If a person, out for a walk, bumps into another person, neither is likely to be hurt. If both are driving cars at 60 miles per hour, they could be killed. If two jets collide, or one loses an engine, several hundred people could be killed. However, the death rate per mile traveled is lower for air travel than for cars.

Most new technologies were not very safe when first developed. If the death rate from commercial airline accidents in the U.S. were the same now as it was 50 years ago, 8,000 people would die in plane crashes each year. In some early polio vaccines, the virus was not totally inactivated. The vaccines caused polio in some children. We learn how to make improvements. We discover and solve problems. Scientists and engineers study disasters and learn how to prevent them and how to recover from them.

When I first read about the GPWS (the system that warns pilots if they are headed toward a mountain, Section 8.1.5), it occurred to me that if American Airlines had installed it on the plane that crashed near Cali, Colombia, in 1995, they would have saved many lives. Then I read that this crash triggered adoption of the GPWS. No commercial U.S. airliner has crashed into a mountain since then. Similarly, a disastrous fire led to the development of fire hydrants—a way to get water at the scene from the water pipes under the street. Automobile engineers used to design the front of an automobile to be extremely rigid, to protect passengers in a crash. But people died and suffered serious injuries because the car frame transmitted the force of a crash to the people. The engineers learned it was better to build cars with "crumple zones" to absorb the force of impact.[54] Software engineering textbooks use the Cali crash as an example so that future software specialists will not repeat the mistakes in the plane's computer system. We learn.

What has happened to the safety record in other technologies? The number of deaths from motor vehicle accidents in the U.S. declined from 54,633 in 1970 to roughly 42,600 in 2006 (while population and the number of cars, of course, increased).[55] Why? One significant factor is increased education about responsible use (i.e., the campaign against drunk driving). Another is devices that protect people when the system fails (seat belts and airbags). Yet another is systems that help avoid accidents (many of which, like airbags, use microprocessors). Examples of the latter include rear-view cameras that help drivers avoid hitting a child when backing up and "night vision" systems that detect obstacles and project onto the windshield an image or diagram of objects in the car's path. Yet another is electronic stability systems. These systems have sensors that detect a likely rollover, before the driver is aware of the problem, and electronically slow the engine.

As use of technology, automation, and computer systems has increased in virtually all work places, the risk of dying in an on-the-job accident dropped from 39 among 100,000 workers (in 1934) to four in 100,000 in 2004.[56]

Risk is not restricted to technology and machines. It is a part of life. Sharp tools are risky. Someone living in a jungle faces danger from animals. A desert hiker faces rattlesnakes. We are safer if we know the risks and take reasonable precautions. We are never 100% safe.

There are some important differences between computers and other technologies. Computers make decisions; electricity does not. The power and flexibility of computers encourages us to build more complex systems—where failures have more serious consequences. The pace of change in computer technology is much faster than that in other technologies. Software is not built from standard, trusted parts as is the case in many engineering fields. These differences affect the kind and scope of the risks we face. They need our attention as computer professionals, as workers and planners in other fields, and as members of the public.

Observations

We have made several points:

1. Many of the issues related to reliability and safety for computers systems have arisen before with other technologies.
2. Perfection is not an option. The complexity of computer systems makes errors, oversights, and so on likely.
3. There is a *learning curve* for new technologies. By studying failures, we can reduce their occurrence.
4. We should compare risks of using computers with risks of other methods and with benefits obtained.

This does not mean that we should excuse or ignore computer errors and failures because failures occur in other technologies. It does not mean we should tolerate carelessness or negligence because perfection is not possible. It does not mean we should excuse accidents as part of the learning process, and it does not mean we should excuse accidents because, on balance, the contribution of computer technology is positive.

The potential for serious disruption of normal activities and danger to people's lives and health because of flaws in computer systems should always remind the computer professional of the importance of doing his or her job responsibly. Computer system developers and other professionals responsible for planning and choosing systems must assess risks carefully and honestly, include safety protections, and make appropriate plans for shutdown of a system when it fails, for backup systems where appropriate, and for recovery.

Knowing that one will be liable for the damages one causes is strong incentive to find improvements and increase safety. When evaluating a specific instance of a failure, we can look for those responsible and try to ensure that they bear the costs of the damage they caused. It is when evaluating computer use in a particular application area or when evaluating the technology as a whole that we should look at the balance between risks and benefits and compare the risks and benefits with those of alternative technologies.

EXERCISES

Review Exercises

8.1 List two cases described in this chapter in which insufficient testing was a factor in a program error or system failure.

8.2 A high school excluded a 14-year-old boy from football and some classes without explanation. He eventually learned that school officials thought he had been using drugs while in junior high school. What had the boy actually done in junior high school that was indicated in his record? How did this mistake occur?

8.3   What are two precautions a programmer can take to avoid errors in billing programs?

8.4   What were two technology-related problems that occurred with the voting system in the 2000 U.S. presidential election?

8.5   What is one case in which reuse of software caused a serious problem?

8.6   Describe one principle of human-interface design that is particularly important in safety-critical applications.

General Exercises

8.7   a) Suppose you write a computer program to add two integers. Assume that each integer and their sum will fit in the standard memory unit the computer uses for integers. How likely do you think it is that the sum will be correct? (If you run the program a million times on different pairs of integers, how many times do you think it would give the correct answer?)

       b) Suppose a utility company has a million customers and it runs a program to determine whether any customers have overdue bills. How likely do you think it is that the results of the program will be correct?

       c) Probably your answers to parts (a) and (b) were different. Give some reasons why the likely number of errors would be different in these two examples.

8.8   Describe two computer systems that were abandoned before they were implemented or shortly after implementation. What factors contributed to their failure?

8.9   A man applied for jobs at several retail stores. They all turned him down. Eventually, he learned that the stores used a database to screen applicants and it listed him as a shoplifter. A real shoplifter had given the police the innocent man's identification from a lost wallet.

       Would this incident have been as likely to happen 30 years ago? Why or why not? The innocent man sued the company that maintains the database and the store where the real shoplifter was arrested. Should he win? Give reasons.

8.10   In response to the lack of scientific knowledge about whether or how computer keyboards cause RSI, a plaintiff's lawyer who handled more than 1000 RSI lawsuits commented that "The law can't wait on science."[57] Give some arguments to support this statement (as it applies to RSI lawsuits). Give some arguments against it. Do you agree with the statement? Why?

8.11   When writing about the Denver International Airport baggage system failure, a *PCWeek* reporter said, "The bottom-line lesson is that system designers must build in plenty of test and debugging time when scaling up proven technology into a much more complicated environment." Explain the background of this statement. How would additional time for testing and debugging have alleviated the problems? What other factors contributed to the failure?

8.12   Suppose you are responsible for hiring drivers for a trucking company. The FBI has provided a terrorist watch list to the company. Develop a policy for how to use the list.

8.13   Consider the standardized-test score reporting error discussed in the box in Section 8.1.3. Suppose the test company had reported scores to the schools as significantly higher, rather than lower, than the correct scores. Do you think the schools would have questioned the scores? Do you think anyone would have discovered the error? If so, how? Give a few examples of situations where you think people would not report computer errors. For each example, give your reason (e.g., optimism, ignorance, gullibility, dishonesty, others).

8.14   The U.S. Immigration and Naturalization Service (INS) sent visa approval notifications for two of the September 11 hijackers six months after they crashed airplanes into the World Trade Center. No one had updated the INS database to cancel the visas (which the INS had approved before

September 11). This incident generated a lot of publicity embarrassing for the INS. What policy or process could have avoided this error? Is it reasonable to expect that the INS should have prevented it?

8.15   Figure 8.1 lists use of very new technology as a potential cause of computer system failures. Discuss the pros and cons of using new technologies. In what kinds of situations is using new technologies warranted? When is it ill advised?

8.16   Many college students attend several colleges before they eventually graduate. It would be a convenience for students if they could order a complete transcript (say, for job applications) from the federal student database discussed in Section 2.2.1*. Describe several ways in which getting transcripts from the database might be riskier than getting them from the individual colleges.

8.17   Suppose you are on a consulting team to design a computerized voting system for your state. People will vote on computers at the voting place (not over the Internet; we considered Web-based voting in an exercise in Chapter 5). What are some important design considerations?

8.18   You are the traffic manager for a small city. The City Council has directed you to buy and install a computer system to control the traffic lights. Its main purpose is to adjust the timing of the lights to improve traffic flow at rush hours and for special events.
a) List some potential risks of the system.
b) List some technical requirements and/or specifications you would put in the proposal for safety.

8.19   Find several provisions of the Software Engineering Code of Ethics and Professional Practice (Appendix A.1) that were violated in the Therac-25 case.

8.20   In California, the computer system for tracking down parents who owed child support identified a woman living in Los Angeles as the mother of an abandoned child in San Francisco. The woman provided evidence that she was living in Los Angeles at the time the abandoned child was born. She also provided a copy of a pregnancy test that showed she could not have been pregnant just three months before the child was born. Child Protective Services insisted on DNA testing. What are some reasons (good ones or bad ones) that Child Protective Services did not consider the other evidence sufficient? Do you think it was reasonable to require DNA testing?

8.21   In the scenario above, the woman eventually discovered that Child Protective Services obtained much of their data from the California motor vehicles department, which had mistakenly merged her data with that of another woman who had the same first and last name, date of birth, and birth city. They had different middle initials. Do you think the merging of the data was because of human error, computer error, or both? Eventually the motor vehicles department corrected the error, but Child Protective Services did not pay for regular updates. How did this contribute to the problem? What could have been done to prevent this problem from happening?

8.22   After making a programming change in a major bank's computer system, an employee forgot to enter certain commands. As a result, approximately 800,000 direct deposits received by the bank were not posted to the customer accounts until the next day. What are some potential consequences of the error? If you were the bank president, what would you say in a statement to the news media or your customers?

8.23   Who are the "good guys"? Pick two people or organizations mentioned in this chapter whose work helped make systems safer or reduced the negative consequences of errors. Tell why you picked them.

8.24   We mentioned that some cell phones contain a few million lines of computer code. Estimate how many pages one million lines of code would take up if printed. (State your assumptions.)

---

* The actual database proposal does not include providing services such as transcripts for individual students.

8.25   At some hospitals, doctors use a computer system to order drugs for patients. The system eliminates errors from reading doctors' handwriting, and it automatically checks for conflicts with other medicines the patient is taking. Doctors sometimes do not log out after using a terminal. When another doctor uses the same terminal, the system assigns drugs ordered by the second doctor to the first doctor's patient. Describe two features that such systems could include to reduce this kind of error.

8.26   A technician on a Navy guided-missile ship entered a zero in the wrong place in a computer program calibrating a fuel valve. The program divides another number by the entered number. It crashed because division by zero is an invalid operation. The program failure caused the ship's entire Local Area Network to fail, leaving the ship dead in the water for almost three hours.

     To what degree is each of the following people responsible: the technician, the person who wrote the fuel-valve calibration program, the person who selected and purchased the ship's Local Area Network, the software company that sells the network software, the captain of the ship? What, if anything, did each do wrong, and what could reduce the chance of such a problem in the future? Are there any other people who bear some of the responsibility? (You cannot give a full and definite answer without more detailed information. Where necessary, indicate what additional information you need and how it would affect your answer.)

8.27   A computer error in a contest sponsored by a multinational beverage company caused distribution of 800,000 winning numbers instead of the intended 18. The face value of the winnings amounted to $32 billion. Suppose you are an employee on a team given the task of deciding how to respond to this problem. Make some suggestions.

8.28   The Food and Drug Administration maintains a registry of more than 120,000 drugs. An investigation by the Department of Health and Human Services found that the information on about 34,000 drugs was incorrect or out of date. Nine thousand drugs were missing from the directory.[58] Describe several possible risks of the database being so out of date. Give as many possible reasons as you can think of why the database was out of date.

8.29   A large industrial supply company found that customer orders at one of its warehouses were frequently deleted. Normally an order would be generated by the computer system and routed to the warehouse closest to the customer. If an item was out of stock it would be placed on back order. If an item was discontinued it would be deleted from the order and the rest of the order would be filled. The warehouse in question was missing a substantial amount of its inventory. The order system had no way to account for missing inventory so the employees deleted the orders from the system. The company did not discover the problem until a customer complained that the same order had been placed four times and the items were never received. To what extent is this a computer failure? What other factors are part of the problem? What could have been done to prevent this problem?

8.30   Choose a noncomputer activity that you are familiar with and that has some risks (e.g., skateboarding, scuba diving, or working in a restaurant). Describe some of the risks and some safety practices. Describe analogies with risks related to computer systems.

8.31   Software developers are sometimes advised to "design for failure." Give some examples of what this might mean.

8.32   Assume you are a professional working in your chosen field. Describe specific things you can do to reduce the impact of any two problems we discussed in this chapter. (If you cannot think of anything related to your professional field, choose another field that might interest you.)

8.33   Think ahead to the next few years and describe a new problem, related to issues in this chapter, likely to develop from computing technology or the Web.

Assignments

These exercises require some research or activity.

8.34   Read a few items in the current issue of the *Risks Digest* (www.csl.sri.com/users/risko/risks.txt). Write a summary of two items.

8.35   Find out which (if either) of the following views is common among eye doctors: (1) Working at a computer screen for many hours permanently weakens vision. (2) Eye strain from computer use is temporary; rest breaks, ergonomic changes, or similar techniques can relieve it.

Class Discussion Exercises

These exercises are for class discussion, perhaps with short presentations prepared in advance by small groups of students.

8.36   Assume that the family of one of the victims of the Therac-25 has filed three lawsuits. They are suing a hospital that used the machine, the company that made the machine (AECL), and the programmer who wrote the Therac-25 software. Divide students into six groups: attorneys for the family against each of the three respondents and attorneys for each of the three respondents. Each group is to present a five-minute summation of arguments for its case. Then, let the class discuss all aspects of the case and vote on the degree of responsibility of each of the respondents.

8.37   Consider the following scenario. A state's highway patrol keeps records of stolen cars in its computer system. There is no routine process for updating records when stolen cars are recovered. The system still listed a car as stolen a few years after it had been recovered and the owner sold it. A highway patrol officer shot and killed the new owner of the car during a traffic stop. The officer thought the car was stolen and that the driver was acting suspiciously. An investigation concluded that the officer "acted in good faith."* To what extent should the error in the database affect the family's wrongful-death lawsuit against the highway patrol. Suggest a feature the database should have that might prevent such incidents.

8.38   A factory uses both human and robotic workers in its assembly lines. In some areas humans work with robotic arms, controlling their actions and observing the pieces as they come off the assembly line to detect any problems or failures. Humans are not allowed in other areas while the robots are in operation. Safety mechanisms automatically shut down the robots if a human enters the restricted area. The factory recently added newer and more sophisticated robots, new software to control the robots, and sensors to detect errors. These changes were expected to increase safety and production. Production did not increase and the number of accidents more than tripled. Suppose your class is a consulting team hired (by a neutral party) to investigate and write a report. What factors would you look at to determine where the problems are? What questions would you ask? What additional information would you need?

---

*I have changed some details, but this scenario was suggested by a real case.

NOTES

1. Robert N. Charette, "Why Software Fails," *IEEE Spectrum*, September 2005, www.spectrum.ieee.org/sep05/1685 (accessed December 8, 2006).

2. *The Risks Digest: Forum on Risks to the Public in Computers and Related Systems*, catless.ncl.ac.uk/risks (accessed September 7, 2007).

3. Philip E. Ross, "The Day the Software Crashed," *Forbes*, 153, no. 9 (April 25, 1994), pp. 142–156; Peter G. Neumann, "Inside Risks," *Communications of the ACM*, July 1992, p. 122.

4. Andrea Robinson, "Firm: State Told Felon Voter List May Cause Errors," *Miami Herald*, February 17, 2001.

5. Dan Joyce, e-mail correspondence, May 17, 1996 (the adoption case). Study by the Office of Technology Assessment, reported in Rothfeder, *Privacy for Sale*; "Jailing the Wrong Man," *Time*, February 25, 1985, p. 25; David Burnham, "Tales of a Computer State," *The Nation*, April 1983, p. 527; Evelyn Richards, "Proposed FBI Crime Computer System Raises Questions on Accuracy, Privacy," *Washington Post*, February 13, 1989, p. A6; "Wrong Suspect Settles His Case of $55,000," *New York Times*, March 6, 1998, p. 30; Peter G. Neumann, "Risks to the Public in Computer and Related Systems," *Software Engineering Notes*, 13, no. 2 (April 1988), p. 11. Several similar cases are reported by Peter G. Neumann in "Inside Risks," *Communications of the ACM*, January 1992, p. 186; Herb Caen, *San Francisco Chronicle*, July 25, 1991.

6. Ann Davis, "Post-Sept. 11 Watch List Acquires Life of Its Own," *Wall Street Journal*, November 19, 2002, p. A1.

7. "Terrorist Watch List Screening: Efforts to Help Reduce Adverse Effects on the Public," GAO-06-1031, September 29, 2006, p. 34, www.gao.gov/new.items/d061031.pdf (accessed December 11, 2006).

8. *Arizona v. Evans, reported in* "Supreme Court Rules on Use of Inaccurate Computer Records," *EPIC Alert*, March 9, 1995.

9. Quoted in Associated Press, " 'BlackBerry Thumb' on the Rise," CBS News, October 21, 2005, www.cbsnews.com/stories/2005/10/21/tech/main960825.shtml (accessed December 11, 2006).

10. Edward Felsenthal, "An Epidemic or a Fad? The Debate Heats up over Repetitive Stress," *Wall Street Journal*, July 14, 1994, p. A1; R. L. Linscheid and J. H. Dobyns, "Athletic Injuries of the Wrist," *Clinical Orthopedics*, September 1985, pp. 141–151; *American Annals of the Deaf* ; David M. Rempel, Robert J. Harrison, and Scott Barnhart, "Work-Related Cumulative Trauma Disorders of the Upper Extremity," *Journal of the American Medical Association*, 267, no. 6 (February 12, 1992), pp. 838–842.

11. Frederic M. Biddle, John Lippman, and Stephanie N. Mehta, "One Satellite Fails, and the World Goes Awry," *Wall Street Journal*, May 21, 1998, p. B1.

12. Reuters, "Glitch Closes Tokyo Stock Exchange," *The New Zealand Herald*, November 2, 2005, nzherald.co.nz (accessed December 12, 2006); David Craig, "NASDAQ Blackout Rattles Investors," *USA Today*, July 18, 1994, p. 2B; Associated Press, "NASDAQ Defends Its System after Stock-Pricing Errors," *New York Times*, September 13, 1994, p. D19; "Note to Readers," *Boston Globe*, October 25, 1994, p. 52; Julia Flynn, Sara Calian, and Michael R. Sesit, "Computer Snag Halts London Market 8 Hours," *Wall Street Journal*, April 6, 2000, p. A14.

13. mars.jpl.nasa.gov/msp98/orbiter (accessed December 19, 2006).

14. Thomas Hoffman, "NCR Users Cry Foul Over I Series Glitch," *Computerworld*, February 15, 1993, p. 72; Milo Geyelin, "Faulty Software Means Business for Litigators," *Wall Street Journal*, January 21, 1994, p. B1; Milo Geyelin, "How an NCR System for Inventory Control Turned into a Virtual Saboteur," *Wall Street Journal*, August 8, 1994, pp. A1, A5; Mary Brandel and Thomas Hoffman, "User Lawsuits Drag on for NCR," *Computerworld*, August 15, 1994, p. 1.

15. Jacques Steinberg and Diana B. Henriques, "When a Test Fails the Schools, Careers and Reputations Suffer," *New York Times*, May 21, 2001, pp. A1, A10–A11.

16. Ed Felton, "Hotel Minibar Keys Open Diebold Voting Machines," September 18, 2006, www.freedom-to-tinker.com/?p=1064 (accessed December 6, 2006).

17. The DIA delay was widely reported in the news media. A few of the sources I used for the discussion here are Kirk Johnson, "Denver Airport Saw the Future. It Didn't Work," *New York Times*, August 27, 2005, www.nytimes.com (accessed December 12, 2006); W. Wayt Gibbs, "Software's Chronic Crisis," *Scientific American*, 271, no. 3 (September 1994), pp. 86–95; Robert L. Scheier, "Software Snafu Grounds Denver's High-Tech Airport," *PC Week*, 11, no. 19 (May 16, 1994), p. 1; Price Colman, "Software Glitch Could Be the Hitch. Misplaced Comma Might Dull Baggage System's Cutting Edge," *Rocky Mountain News*, April 30, 1994, p. 9A; Steve Higgins, "Denver Airport: Another Tale of Government High-Tech Run Amok," *Investor's Business Daily*, May 23, 1994, p. A4; Julie Schmit, "Tiny Company Is Blamed for Denver Delays," *USA Today*, May 5, 1994, pp. 1B, 2B.

18. Scheier, "Software Snafu Grounds Denver's High-Tech Airport."

19. Wayne Arnold, "How Asia's High-Tech Airports Stumbled," *Wall Street Journal*, July 13, 1998, p. B2.

20. Charette, "Why Software Fails"; Virginia Ellis, "Snarled Child Support Computer Project Dies," *Los Angeles Times*, November 21, 1997, pp. A1, A28; Peter G. Neumann, "System Development Woes," *Communications of the ACM*, December 1997, p. 160; Harry Goldstein, "Who Killed the Virtual Case File?" *IEEE Spectrum*, September 2005, www.spectrum.ieee.org/sep05/1455 (accessed December 12, 2006).

21. Charette, "Why Software Fails."

22. H. Travis Christ, quoted in Linda Rosencrance, "US Airways Partly Blames Legacy Systems for March Glitch," *Computerworld*, March 29, 2007; Linda Rosencrance, "Glitch at U.S. Airways Causes Delays," *Computerworld*, March 5, 2007, www.computerworld.com (accessed April 24, 2007).

23. "Airbus Safety Claim 'Cannot Be Proved,'" *New Scientist*, 131, no. 1785 (September 7, 1991), p. 30; Robert Morrell Jr., *Risks Forum Digest*, 16, no. 20 (July 6, 1994); "Training 'Inadequate' Says A320 Crash Report," *Flight International*, December 22, 1993, p. 11 (on the January 1992 Strasbourg A320 crash, excerpted by Peter B. Ladkin in *Risks Forum Digest*, January 2, 1994); Ross, "The Day the Software Crashed," p. 156, on the 1993 Warsaw crash; David Learmont, "Lessons from the Cockpit," *Flight International*, January 11, 1994.

24. Alan Levin, "FAA Finally Unveils New Radar System," *USA Today*, January 20, 1999, p. 01. A; Anna Wilde Mathews and Susan Carey, "Airports Have Delays, Cancellations Due to Problems in Air-Traffic Control," *Wall Street Journal*, May 7, 1999, p. A20; "Software Glitch" (editorial), *San Diego Union Tribune*, October 23, 2000, p. B8; Robert Fox, "News Track: Air Communication Breakdown," *Communications of the ACM*, 43, no. 8 (August 2000), p. 10.

25. Raju Narisetti, Thomas E. Weber, and Rebecca Quick, "How Computers Calmly Handled Stock Frenzy," *Wall Street Journal*, October 30, 1997, pp. B1, B7; Peter G. Neumann, "System Development Woes," *Communications of the ACM*, December 1997, p. 160.

26. Alan Levin, "Airways Are the Safest Ever," *USA Today*, June 29, 2006, pp. 1A, 6A; William M. Carley, "New Cockpit Systems Broaden the Margin of Safety for Pilots," *Wall Street Journal*, March 1, 2000, pp. A1, A10.

27. FAA Commissioner Marion Blakey, "Keeping Pace with Change," speech at the National Business Aviation Association, Orlando, FL, October 17, 2006, www.faa.gov/news/speeches/news_story.cfm?newsId=7439 (accessed December 19, 2006).

28. Carley, "New Cockpit Systems Broaden the Margin of Safety for Pilots"; Barry H. Kantowitz, "Pilot Workload and Flightdeck Automation," in M. Mouloua and R. Parasuraman, eds., *Human Performance in Automated Systems: Current Research and Trends* (Lawrence Erlbaum, 1994), pp. 212–223.

29. Andy Pasztor, "Airbus to Use Computers for Avoiding Collisions," *Wall Street Journal Europe*, May 29, 2006, p. 5.

30. "FDA Statement on Radiation Overexposures in Panama," www.fda.gov/cdrh/ocd/panamaradexp.html (accessed January 4, 2007); Deborah Gage and John McCormick, "We Did Nothing Wrong," Baseline, March 4, 2004, www.baselinemag.com/article2/0,1397,1543564,00.asp (accessed January 2, 2007).

31. Nancy G. Leveson and Clark S. Turner, "An Investigation of the Therac-25 Accidents," *IEEE Computer*, 26, no. 7 (July 1993), pp. 18–41; Jonathan Jacky, "Safety-Critical Computing: Hazards, Practices, Standards, and Regulation," in Charles Dunlop and Rob Kling, eds., *Computerization and Controversy* (Academic Press, 1991), pp. 612–631. Most of the factual information about the Therac-25 incidents in this chapter is from Leveson and Turner.

32. Conversation with Nancy Leveson, January 19, 1995.

33. Jacky, "Safety-Critical Computing," p. 615; Peter G. Neumann, "Risks to the Public in Computers and Related Systems," *Software Engineering Notes*, 16, no. 2 (April 1991), p. 4.

34. Ted Wendling, "Lethal Doses: Radiation that Kills," *Cleveland Plain Dealer*, December 16, 1992, p. 12A. (I thank my student Irene Radomyshelsky for bringing this article to my attention.)

35. *Guns, Germs, and Steel: The Fates of Human Societies* (W. W. Norton, 1997), p. 157.

36. Charette, "Why Software Fails."

37. "Airbus Safety Claim 'Cannot Be Proved,'" p. 30.

38. The report of the inquiry into the explosion is at sunnyday.mit.edu/accidents/Ariane5accidentreport.html (accessed September 12, 2007).

39. *Privacy Journal*, August 1998, p. 4. The database is the Interstate Identification Index.

40. Marisa Taylor, "U.S. Struggles to Keep Tabs on Foreign Visitors Leaving," *San Diego Union-Tribune*, September 16, 2006, p. A7.

41. From an e-mail advertisement for Nancy G. Leveson, *Safeware: System Safety and Computers* (Addison Wesley, 1995).

42. A particularly good article discussing human factors and the causes of the crash is Stephen Manes, "A Fatal Outcome from Misplaced Trust in 'Data,'" *New York Times*, September 17, 1996, p. B11.

43. Kantowitz, "Pilot Workload and Flightdeck Automation," pp. 212–223.

44. Feynman, *What Do You Care What Other People Think?* The shuttle was not immune from problems. The *Risks Digest* includes reports of computer failures caused by a loose piece of solder, subtle timing errors, and other factors.

45. "AT&T Crash, 15 Jan 90: The Official Report."

46. Feynman, *What Do You Care What Other People Think?* pp. 190–194, 232–236. Aeronautics and Space Engineering Board, National Research Council, *An Assessment of Space Shuttle Flight Software Development Processes* (National Academy Press, 1993).

47. Mary Brandel and Thomas Hoffman, "User Lawsuits Drag on for NCR," *Computerworld*, August 15, 1994, p. 1.

48. Professor Philip Koopman of Carnegie Mellon University discusses these issues and others about liability for embedded software in articles posted on his Web site, www.ece.cmu.edu/~koopman/ucita.

49. These problems and trade-offs occur often with regulation of new drugs and medical devices, regulation of pollution, and various kinds of safety regulation. They are discussed primarily in journals on the economics of regulation.

50. Leveson and Turner, "An Investigation of the Therac-25 Accidents," p. 40.

51. See, for example, Walter Williams, *The State Against Blacks* (McGraw-Hill, 1982), Chapters 5–7. One year during a construction lull, a state failed everyone who took the building contractor's license exam. It is illegal in 48 states for most software engineers to call themselves software engineers because of licensing laws for engineers. One company had to spend thousands of dollars changing job titles, business cards, and marketing literature to remove the word "engineer." [Julia King, "Engineers to IS: Drop that Title!" *Computerworld*, 28, no. 22 (May 30, 1994), pp. 1, 119.]

52. Tom Forester and Perry Morrison, *Computer Ethics: Cautionary Tales and Ethical Dilemmas in Computing*, 2nd ed. (MIT Press, 1994), p. 4.

53. Heather Bryant, an Albertson's manager, quoted in Penni Crabtree, "Glitch Fouls up Nation's Business," *San Diego Union-Tribune*, April 14, 1998, p. C1; Miles Corwin and John L. Mitchell, "Fire Disrupts L. A. Phones, Services," *Los Angeles Times*, March 16, 1994, p. A1.

54. An excellent "Nova" series, "Escape! Because Accidents Happen," aired February 16 and 17, 1999, shows examples from 2000 years of history of inventing ways to reduce the injuries and deaths from fires and from boat, car, and airplane accidents.

55. "2006 Traffic Safety Annual Assessment—A Preview" (DOT HS 810 791), National Highway Traffic Safety Administration, July 2007.

56. U.S. Census Bureau, *The 2007 Statistical Abstract*, Table 638; "Workers Killed or Disabled on the Job: 1970 to 2004" (accessed December 19, 2006). "A Fistful of Risks," *Discover*, May 1996, p. 82.

57. Steven Philips, quoted in Felsenthal, "An Epidemic or a Fad?"

58. "FDA Proposes Rules for Drug Registry," *Wall Street Journal*, August 24, 2006, p. D6.

BOOKS AND ARTICLES

- Collins, W. Robert, Keith W. Miller, Bethany J. Spielman, and Phillip Wherry, "How Good Is Good Enough?" *Communications of the ACM*, 37, no. 1 (January 1994): 81–91. A discussion of ethical issues about quality for software developers.

- Dempsey, Paul Stephen, Andrew R. Goetz, and Joseph S. Szyliowicz. *Denver International Airport: Lessons Learned*, McGraw-Hill, 1997.

- Epstein, Richard. *The Case of the Killer Robot*. John Wiley and Sons, 1996.

- Feynman, Richard P. *What Do You Care What Other People Think?* W. W. Norton & Co., 1988. Includes Feynman's report on the investigation of the explosion of the Challenger space shuttle, with many insights about how to, and how not to, investigate a system failure.

- Jacky, Jonathan. "Safety-Critical Computing: Hazards, Practices, Standards, and Regulation," in Charles Dunlop and Rob Kling, eds., pp. 612–631, *Computerization and Controversy*, Academic Press, 1991.

- Leveson, Nancy G. *Safeware: System Safety and the Computer Age*. Addison Wesley, 1995.

- Leveson, Nancy G., and Clark S. Turner. "An Investigation of the Therac-25 Accidents." *IEEE Computer*, 26, no. 7 (July 1993): 18–41.

- Neumann, Peter G. *Computer-Related Risks*. Addison-Wesley, 1995.

- Nielsen, Jakob. *Designing Web Usability: The Practice of Simplicity*. New Riders Publishing, 2000.

- Norman, Donald. *The Invisible Computer: Why Good Products Can Fail, the Personal Computer Is So Complex, and Information Appliances Are the Solution*. MIT Press, 1998.

- Norman, Donald. *The Psychology of Everyday Things*. Basic Books, 1988. A study of good and bad user interfaces on many everyday devices and appliances.

- Pascarelli, Emil, and Deborah Quilter. *Repetitive Strain Injury: A Computer User's Guide*. John Wiley & Sons, Inc., 1994.

- Peterson, Ivars. *Fatal Defect: Chasing Killer Computer Bugs*. Times Books (Random House), 1995.

- Petrovski, Henry. *To Engineer Is Human: The Role of Failure in Successful Design*. St. Martin's Press, 1985. This book is more about engineering in general, not computer systems design, but the principles and lessons carry over.

- Pfleeger, Shari L., and Joanne Atlee, *Software Engineering: Theory and Practice*. 3rd ed. Pearson Prentice Hall, 2005.

- Rothfeder, Jeffrey. *Privacy for Sale*. Simon & Schuster, 1992. Although the main focus of this book is privacy, it contains many examples of problems that resulted from errors in databases.

- Shneiderman, Ben, and Catherine Plaisant, *Designing the User Interface: Strategies for Effective Human-Computer Interaction*. 4th ed. Addison Wesley Longman, 2004.

- Tufte, Edward. *Envisioning Information*. Graphics Press, 1990.

- Tufte, Edward. *Visual Explanations*. Graphics Press, 1997.

- Wildavsky, Aaron. *Searching for Safety*. Transaction Books, 1988. On the role of risk in making us safer.

ORGANIZATIONS AND WEB SITES

- Peter G. Neumann, moderator, *The Risks Digest: Forum on Risks to the Public in*

Computers and Related Systems: catless.ncl.ac.uk/risks

9

PROFESSIONAL ETHICS AND RESPONSIBILITIES

9.1 What Is Professional Ethics?

The scope of the term "computer ethics" varies considerably. It can include such social and political issues as the impact of computers on employment, the environmental impact of computers, whether or not to sell computers to totalitarian governments, use of computers by the military, and the consequences of the technological and thus economic divisions between developed countries and poor countries. It can include personal dilemmas about what to post on the Internet and what to download. In this chapter we focus more narrowly on a category of professional ethics, similar to medical, legal, and accounting ethics, for example. We consider ethical issues a person might encounter as a computer professional, on the job. Professional ethics includes relationships with and responsibilities toward customers, clients, coworkers, employees, employers, others who use one's products and services, and others whom they affect. We examine ethical dilemmas and guidelines related to actions and decisions of individuals who create and use computer systems. We look at situations where you must make critical decisions, situations where significant consequences for you and others could result.

Extreme examples of lapses in ethics in many fields regularly appear in the news. In business, we had Enron, for example. In journalism, we have had numerous incidents of journalists at prominent news organizations plagiarizing or inventing stories. In science, a famed and respected researcher published falsified stem cell research and claimed accomplishments he had not achieved. A writer invented dramatic events in what he promoted as a factual memoir of his experiences. These examples involve blatant dishonesty, which is almost always wrong.

Honesty is one of the most fundamental ethical values. We all make hundreds of decisions all day long. The consequences of some decisions are minor. Others are huge and affect people we never meet. We base decisions, partly, on the information we have. (It takes ten minutes to drive to work. This software has serious security vulnerabilities. What you post on a social-network site is available only to your designated friends.) We pick up bits and pieces of information from explicit research, from conversations, and from our surroundings and regular activities. Of course, not all of it is accurate. But we must base our choices and actions on what we know. A lie deliberately sabotages this essential activity of being human: absorbing and processing information and making choices to pursue our goals. Lies are often attempts to manipulate people. As Kant would say, a lie treats people as merely means to ends, not ends in themselves. Lies can have many negative consequences. In some circumstances, lying casts doubt on the work or word of other people unjustly. Thus it hurts those people, and it adds unnecessary uncertainty to decisions by others who would have acted on the word of people the lie contradicts. Falsifying research or other forms of work is an indirect form of theft of research funds and salary. It wastes resources that others could have used productively. It contributes to incorrect choices and decisions by people who depend on the results of the work. The costs and indirect effects of lies can cascade and do much harm.

Many ethical problems are more subtle than the choice of being honest or dishonest. In health care, for example, doctors and researchers must decide how to set priorities for organ transplant recipients. Responsible computer professionals confront issues such as, How much risk (to privacy, security, safety) is acceptable in a system? What uses of another company's intellectual property are acceptable?

Suppose a private company asks your software company to develop a database of information obtained from government records, perhaps to generate lists of convicted shoplifters or child molesters or marketing lists of new home buyers, affluent boat owners, or divorced parents with young children. The people who will be on the lists did not have a choice about whether the information would be open to the public. They did not give permission for its use. How will you decide whether to accept the contract? You could accept on the grounds that the records are already public and available to anyone. You could refuse in opposition to secondary uses of information that people did not provide voluntarily. You could try to determine whether the benefits of the lists outweigh the privacy invasions or inconveniences they might cause for some people. You could refuse to make marketing lists, but agree to make lists of people convicted of certain crimes, using Posner's principle that negative information, such as convictions, should be in the public domain (see Section 2.4.2). The critical first step, however, is recognizing that you face an ethical issue.

The decision to distribute software to convert files from formats with built-in copy protection to formats that can be copied more easily has an ethical component. So too does the decision about how much money and effort to allocate to training employees in the use of a new computer system. We have seen that many of the related social and legal issues are controversial. Some ethical issues are also.

There are special aspects to making ethical decisions in a professional context, but the decisions are based on general ethical principles and theories. Section 1.4 describes these general principles. It would be good to reread or review it now. In Section 9.2 we consider ethical guidelines for computer professionals. In Section 9.3, we consider sample scenarios.

9.2 Ethical Guidelines for Computer Professionals

9.2.1 SPECIAL ASPECTS OF PROFESSIONAL ETHICS

Professional ethics have several characteristics different from general ethics. The role of the professional is special in several ways. First, the professional is an expert in a field, be it computer science or medicine, that most customers know little about. Most of the people affected by the devices, systems, and services of professionals do not understand how they work and cannot easily judge their quality and safety. This creates special responsibilities for the professional. Customers rely on the knowledge, expertise, and honesty of the professional. A professional advertises his or her expertise and thus has an obligation to provide it. Second, the products of many professionals (e.g., highway bridges, investment advice, surgery protocols, and computer systems) profoundly affect large numbers of people. A computer professional's work can affect the life, health, finances, freedom, and future of a client or members of the public. A professional can cause great harm through dishonesty, carelessness, or incompetence. Often the victims have little ability to protect themselves. The victims, often, are not the direct customers of the professional and have no direct control or decision-making role in choosing the product or making decisions about its quality and safety. Thus, computer professionals have special responsibilities not only to their customers, but also to the general public, to the users of their products, regardless of whether they have a direct relationship with the users. These responsibilities include thinking about potential risks to privacy and security of data, safety, reliability, and ease of use. They include taking action to diminish risks that are too high.

In Chapter 8, we saw some of the minor and major consequences of flaws in computer systems. In some of those cases, people acted in clearly unethical or irresponsible ways. In many cases, however, there was no ill intent. Software can be enormously complex, and the process of developing it involves communications between many people with diverse roles and skills. Because of the complexity, risks, and impact of computer systems, a professional has an ethical responsibility not simply to avoid intentional evil, but to exercise a high degree of care and follow good professional practices to reduce the likelihood of problems. That includes a responsibility to maintain an expected level of competence and be up-to-date on current knowledge, technology, and standards of the profession. Professional responsibility includes knowing or learning enough about the application field to do a good job. Responsibility for a noncomputer professional using a sophisticated computer system includes knowing or learning enough about the system to understand potential problems.

In Section 1.4.1, we observed that although courage is often associated with heroic acts, we have many opportunities to display courage in day-to-day life by making good decisions that might be unpopular. Courage in a professional setting could mean admitting to a customer that your program is faulty, declining a job for which you are not qualified, or speaking out when you see someone else doing something wrong.

9.2.2 PROFESSIONAL CODES OF ETHICS

Many professional organizations have codes of professional conduct. They provide a general statement of ethical values and remind people in the profession that ethical behavior is an essential part of their job. The codes provide reminders about specific professional responsibilities. They provide valuable guidance for new or young members of the profession who want to behave ethically but do not know what is expected of them, people whose limited experience has not prepared them to be alert to difficult ethical situations and to handle them appropriately.

There are several organizations for the range of professions included in the general term *computer professional*. The main ones are the ACM and the IEEE Computer Society

(IEEE CS).[1] They developed the Software Engineering Code of Ethics and Professional Practice (adopted jointly by the ACM and IEEE CS) and the ACM Code of Ethics and Professional Conduct (both in Appendix A). We refer to sections of the Codes in the following discussion and in Section 9.3, using the shortened names SE Code and ACM Code. The Codes emphasize the basic ethical values of honesty and fairness.* They cover many aspects of professional behavior, including the responsibility to respect confidentiality,† maintain professional competence,‡ be aware of relevant laws,§ and honor contracts and agreements.¶ In addition, the Codes put special emphasis on areas that are particularly (but not uniquely) vulnerable from computer systems. They stress the responsibility to respect and protect privacy,‖ avoid harm to others,** and respect property rights (with intellectual property and computer systems themselves as the most relevant examples).†† The SE Code covers many specific points about software development. It is translated into several languages, and various organizations have adopted it as their internal professional standard.

Managers have special responsibility because they oversee projects and set the ethical standards for employees. Principle 5 of the SE Code includes many specific guidelines for managers.

9.2.3 GUIDELINES AND PROFESSIONAL RESPONSIBILITIES

We highlight a few principles for producing good systems. Most concern software developers, programmers, and consultants. A few are for professionals in other areas who make decisions about acquiring computer systems for large organizations. Many more specific guidelines appear in the SE Code and in the ACM Code, and we introduce and explain more in the scenarios in Section 9.3.

Understand what success means. After the utter foul-up on opening day at Kuala Lumpur's airport, blamed on clerks typing incorrect commands, an airport official said, "There's nothing wrong with the system." His statement is false, and the attitude behind the statement contributes to the development of systems that will fail. The official defined the role of the airport system narrowly: to do certain data manipulation correctly, assuming all input is correct. Its true role was to get passengers, crews, planes, luggage, and cargo to the correct gates on schedule. It did not succeed. Developers and institutional users of computer systems must view the system's role and their responsibility in a wide enough context.

---

*SE Code: 1.06, 2.01, 6.07, 7.05, 7.04; ACM Code: 1.3, 1.4

†SE Code: 2.05; ACM Code: 1.8

‡SE Code: 8.01–8.05; ACM Code: 2.2

§SE Code: 8.05; ACM Code: 2.3

¶ACM Code: 2.6

‖SE Code: 1.03, 3.12; ACM Code: 1.7

**SE Code: 1.03; ACM Code: 1.2

††SE Code: 2.02, 2.03; ACM Code: 1.5, 1.6, 2.8

Include users (such as medical staff, technicians, pilots, office workers) in the design and testing stages to provide safe and useful systems. Recall the discussion of computer controls for airplanes (Sections 8.1.4 and 8.3.2), where confusing user interfaces and system behavior increased the risk of accidents. There are numerous "horror stories" in which technical people developed systems without sufficient knowledge of what was important to users. For example, a system for a newborn nursery at a hospital rounded each baby's weight to the nearest pound. For premature babies, the difference of a few ounces is crucial information.[2] The responsibility of developers to talk to users is not limited to systems that affect safety and health. Systems designed to manage stories for a news Web site, to manage inventory in a toy store, or to organize documents and video on a Web site could cause frustration, waste a client's money, and end up in the trash heap if designed without sufficient consideration of the needs of actual users.

The box on the next page illustrates more ways to think about your users.

Do a thorough, careful job when planning and scheduling a project and when writing bids or contracts. This includes, among many other things, allocating sufficient time and budget for testing and other important steps in the development process. Inadequate planning is likely to lead to pressure to cut corners later. (See SE Code 3.02, 3.09, and 3.10.)

Design for real users. We have seen several cases where computers crashed because someone typed input incorrectly. In one case, an entire pager system shut down because a technician did not press the Enter key (or did not hit it hard enough). Real people make typos, get confused, or are new at their job. It is the responsibility of the system designers and programmers to provide clear user interfaces and include appropriate checking of input. It is impossible for computers to detect all incorrect input, but there are techniques for catching many kinds of errors and for reducing the damage that errors cause.

Don't assume existing software is safe or correct. If you use software from another application, verify its suitability for the current project. If the software was designed for an application where the degree of harm from a failure was small, the quality and testing standards might not have been as high as necessary in the new application. The software might have confusing user interfaces that were tolerable (though not admirable) in the original application but could have serious negative consequences in the new application. We saw in Chapter 8 that a complete safety evaluation is important even for software from an earlier version of the same application if a failure would have serious consequences. (Recall the Therac-25 and Ariane 5.)

Be open and honest about capabilities, safety, and limitations of software. In several cases described in Chapter 8, there is a strong argument that the treatment of customers was dishonest. Honesty of salespeople is hardly a new issue. The line between emphasizing your best qualities and being dishonest is not always clear, but it should be clear that hiding known, serious flaws and lying to customers are on the wrong side of the line.

Honesty includes taking responsibility for damaging or injuring others. If you break a neighbor's window playing ball or smash into someone's car, you have an obligation to pay for the damage. If a business finds that its product caused injury, it should not hide that fact or attempt to put the blame on others.

REINFORCING EXCLUSION

A speaker-recognition system is a system (consisting of hardware and software) that identifies the person speaking. (This is different from speech recognition, discussed in Section 7.5.2, which identifies the words spoken.) One application of speaker recognition is teleconferencing for business meetings. The computer system identifies who is speaking and displays that person on everyone's screens. Some speaker-recognition systems recognize male voices much more easily than female voices. Sometimes when the system fails to recognize female speakers and focus attention on them, they are effectively cut out of the discussion.[3] Did the designers of the system intentionally discriminate against women? Probably not. Are women's voices inherently more difficult to recognize? Probably not. What happened? There are many more male programmers than female programmers. There are many more men than women in high-level business meetings. Men were the primary developers and testers of the systems. The algorithms were optimized for the lower range of male voices.

In his book *The Road Ahead*, Bill Gates tells us that a team of Microsoft programmers developed and tested a handwriting recognition system. When they thought it was working fine, they brought it to him to try. It failed. All the team members were right-handed. Gates is left-handed.[4]

In some applications, it might make sense to focus on a niche audience or ignore a special audience, but that choice should be conscious (and reasonable). These examples show how easy it is to develop systems that unintentionally exclude people—and how important it is to think beyond one's own group when designing and testing a system. Besides women and left-handed people, other groups to consider are nontechnical users, different ethnic groups, disabled people, older people (who might, for example, need a large-font option), and children.

In these examples, doing "good" or "right" in a social sense—taking care not to reinforce exclusion of specific groups of people—coincides with producing a good product and expanding its potential market.

Honesty about system limitations is especially important for *expert systems*, or decision systems, that is, systems that use models and heuristics incorporating expert knowledge to guide decision making (for example, medical diagnoses or investment planning). Developers must explain the limitations and uncertainties to users (doctors, financial advisors, and so forth, and to the public when appropriate). Users must not shirk responsibility for understanding them and using the systems properly.

Require a convincing case for safety. One of the most difficult ethical problems that arises in safety-critical applications is deciding how much risk is acceptable. Burning gases that leaked from a rocket shortly after launch destroyed the space shuttle Challenger, killing the seven people aboard. A comment from one of the engineers who opposed the launch sheds some light on how subtle shifts in attitude can affect a decision. The night before the scheduled launch, the engineers argued for a delay. They knew the cold weather posed a severe threat to the shuttle. We cannot prove absolutely that a system is safe, nor can we usually prove absolutely that it will fail and kill someone. The engineer reported that, in the case of the Challenger, "It was up to us to prove beyond a shadow of a doubt that it was not safe to [launch]." This, he said, was the total reverse of a usual Flight Readiness Review.[5] For the ethical decision maker, the policy should be to suspend or delay use of the system in the absence of a convincing case for safety, rather than to proceed in the absence of a convincing case for disaster.

Pay attention to defaults. Everything, it seems, is customizable: the level of encryption on a cell phone or wireless network, whether consumers who buy something at a Web site will go on an e-mail list for ads, the difficulty level of a computer game, the type of news stories your favorite news site displays for you, what a spam filter will filter out. So the default settings might not seem important. They are. Many people do not know about the options they can control. They do not understand issues of security. They often do not take the time to change settings. System designers should give serious thought to default settings. Sometimes protection (of privacy or from hackers, for example) is the ethical priority. Sometimes ease of use and compatibility with user expectations is a priority. Sometimes priorities conflict.

Develop communications skills. A computer security consultant told me that often when he talks to a client about security risks and the products available to protect against them, he sees the client's eyes glaze over. It is a tricky ethical and professional dilemma for him to decide just how much to say so that the client will actually hear and absorb it.

There are many situations in which a computer professional has to explain technical issues to customers and coworkers. Learning how to organize information, distinguishing what is important to communicate and what is not, engaging the listener actively in the conversation to maintain interest, and so on, will help make one's presentations more effective and help to ensure that the client is truly informed.

9.3 Scenarios

9.3.1 INTRODUCTION AND METHODOLOGY

The cases we present here, some based on real incidents, are just a few samples of the kinds that occur. They vary in seriousness and difficulty, and they include situations that illustrate professional responsibilities to potential users of computer systems in the general public, customers or clients, the employer, coworkers, and others. More scenarios appear in the exercises at the end of the chapter.

In most of this book, I have tried to give arguments on both sides of controversial issues without taking a position. Ethical issues are often even more difficult than some of the others we have covered, and there could well be disagreement among computer-ethics specialists on some points in the cases considered here. In any real case, there are many other relevant facts and details that affect the conclusion. In spite of the difficulty of drawing ethical conclusions, especially for brief scenarios, for some of these cases I give conclusions. You might face cases like these where you have to make a decision. I do not want to leave the impression that, because a decision is difficult or because some people benefit or lose either way, there is no ethical basis for making the decision. (It seems ethically irresponsible to do so.)

On the other hand, in Section 1.4 we emphasized that there is not always one right answer to an ethical question. Often many responses or actions are ethically acceptable. We also emphasized that there is no algorithm that cranks out the correct answers. We often must use our knowledge of how people behave, what problems have occurred in the past, and so on, to decide what choices are reasonable. Throughout this book we have approached many issues as problem-solving situations. Identity thieves get information in a certain way. How can we make it harder for them while maintaining varied and convenient services for consumers? The Internet exposes children to pornography. How can we reduce that exposure while protecting freedom of speech and access to information for adults? We will see the same approach in some of these ethical scenarios. Rather than concluding that a particular service or product or action is right or wrong, we, as responsible, ethical professionals, look for ways to reduce its negative consequences.

How shall we analyze specific scenarios? We now have a number of tools. We can try to apply our favorite ethical theory, or some combination of the theories. We can ask questions that reflect basic ethical values: Is it honest? Is it responsible? Does it violate an agreement we made? We can consult a code of professional ethics. Ethical theories and guidelines might conflict, or we might find no clause in the Codes specifically applicable. The Preamble of the SE Code, in Appendix A.1, recognizes this problem and emphasizes the need for good judgment and concern for the safety, health, and welfare of the public.

Although we will not follow the outline below step by step for all the scenarios, our discussions will usually include many of these elements:

1. *Brainstorming phase*

   ❖ List all the people and organizations affected. (They are the *stakeholders*.)

   ❖ List risks, issues, problems, and consequences.

   ❖ List benefits. Identify who gets each benefit.

   ❖ In cases where there is no simple yes or no decision, but rather one has to choose some action, list possible actions.

2. *Analysis phase*

   ❖ Identify responsibilities of the decision maker. (Consider responsibilities of both general ethics and professional ethics.)

❖ Identify rights of stakeholders. (It might be helpful to clarify whether they are negative or positive rights, in the sense of Section 1.4.3.)

❖ Consider the impact of the action options on the stakeholders. Analyze consequences, risks, benefits, harms, costs for each action considered.

❖ Find sections of the SE Code or the ACM Code that apply. Consider the guidelines in Section 9.2.3. Consider Kant's and Mill's approaches. Then, categorize each potential action or response as ethically obligatory, ethically prohibited, or ethically acceptable.

❖ If there are several ethically acceptable options, select an option, considering the ethical merits of each, courtesy to others, practicality, self-interest, personal preferences, and so on. (In some cases, plan a sequence of actions, depending on the response to each.)

The brainstorming phase can generate a long discussion with humorous and obviously wrong options. In the analysis phase, we might reject some options or decide that the claims of some stakeholders are irrelevant or minor. The brainstorming effort in generating these ideas was not wasted. It could bring out ethical and practical considerations and other useful ideas that one would not immediately think of. And it is as helpful to know why some factors do not carry heavy ethical weight as it is to know which ones do.

9.3.2 PROTECTING PERSONAL DATA

Your customer is a community clinic. The clinic works with families that have problems of family violence. It has three sites in the same city, including a shelter for battered women and children. The director wants a computerized record system, networked for the three sites, with the ability to transfer files among sites and make appointments at any site for any other. She wants to have an Internet connection for routine Web access and e-mail communication with other social service agencies about client needs. She wants a few laptop computers on which staffers can carry records when they visit clients at home. At the shelter, staffers use only first names for clients, but the records contain last names and forwarding addresses of women who have recently left. The clinic's budget is small, and she wants to keep the cost as low as possible.

The clinic director is likely to be aware of the sensitivity of the information in the records and to know that inappropriate release of information can result in embarrassment for families using the clinic and physical harm to women who use the shelter. But she might not be aware of the risks of a computer system. You, as the computer professional, have specialized knowledge in this area. It is as much your obligation to warn the director of the risks as it is that of a physician to warn a patient of side effects of a drug he or she prescribes. (See, for example, ACM Code 1.7 and SE Code 2.07 and 3.12.)

The most vulnerable stakeholders here are the clients of the clinic and their family members, and they are not involved in your negotiations with the director. You, the director, the clinic employees, and the donors or agencies that fund the clinic are also stakeholders.

Suppose you warn the director about unauthorized access to sensitive information by hackers and the potential for interception of records and e-mail during transmission. You suggest measures to protect client privacy, including, for example, an identification code system (not Social Security number) for clients of the clinic to use when real names are not necessary and encryption for e-mail and transmission of records. You recommend security software to reduce the threat of hackers who might steal data. You tell the director that carrying client records on laptops has serious risks, citing examples of loss and theft of laptops containing large amounts of sensitive personal data. You advise that records on laptops be encrypted and suggest that the director buy laptops with thumbprint readers so that only authorized employees can access the data. You warn that staffers might be bribed to sell or release information from the system. (Suppose a client is a candidate for the city council or a party in a child-custody case.) You suggest procedures to reduce such leaks. They include a user ID and password for each staff member, coded to allow access only to information that the particular worker needs, a log function that keeps track of who accessed and modified the records, and monitoring and controls on employee e-mail and Web activity. Note that your ability to provide these suggestions is dependent on your professional competence, currency in the field, and general awareness of relevant current events.

The features you recommend will make the system more expensive. If you convince the director of the importance of your recommendations, and she agrees to pay the cost, your professional/ethical behavior has helped improve the security of the system and protect client privacy.

Suppose the director says the clinic cannot afford all the security features. She wants you to develop the system without them. You have several options. You can develop a cheap, but vulnerable, system. You can refuse and perhaps lose the job (although your refusal might convince the director of the importance of the security measures and change her mind). You can add security features and not charge for them. You can work out a compromise that includes the protections you consider essential. All but the first option are pretty clearly ethically acceptable. What about the first? Should you agree to provide the system without the security you believe it should have? Is it now up to the director alone to make an informed choice, weighing the risks and costs? In a case where only the customer would take the risk, some would say yes, it is your job to inform, no more. Others would say that the customer lacks the professional expertise to evaluate the risks. In this scenario, however, the director is not the only person at risk, nor is the risk to her the most significant risk of an insecure system. You have an ethical responsibility to consider the potential harm to clients from exposure of sensitive information and not to build a system without adequate privacy protection.

The most difficult decision may be deciding what is adequate. Encryption of personal records on the laptops might be essential. Monitoring employee Web access is probably not. There is not always a sharp, clear line between sufficient and insufficient protection. You will have to rely on your professional knowledge, on being up-to-date about current risks and security measures, on good judgment, and perhaps on consulting others who develop systems for similar applications (SE Code 7.08).

Note that, although we have focused on the need for privacy protection here, you can overdo such protection. You also have a professional ethical responsibility not to scare a customer into paying for security measures that are expensive but protect against very unlikely risks.

9.3.3   DESIGNING AN E-MAIL SYSTEM WITH TARGETED ADS

Your company is developing a free e-mail service that will include targeted advertising based on the content of the e-mail messages—similar to Google's Gmail. You are part of the team designing the system. What are your ethical responsibilities?

Obviously you must protect the privacy of e-mail. The company plans a sophisticated text analysis system to scan e-mail messages and select appropriate ads. No human will read the messages. Marketing for the free e-mail will make clear that users will see targeted ads. The privacy policy will explain that the content of the e-mail will determine which ads appear. So, the marketing director contends, you have satisfied the first principle of privacy protection, informed consent. What else must you consider to meet your ethical responsibility in offering this service to the public?

The fact that software, not a person, scans the e-mail messages and assigns the ads reduces privacy threats. However, we now know that companies store huge amounts of data. What will this system store? Will it store data about which ads it displayed to specific users? Will it store data about which key words or phrases in e-mails cause particular ads to be selected? Will it store data about who clicked on specific ads?

Release of search query data: Section 2.1.2 Why are these questions of ethical concern? Because we know that leaks, theft, or demands by a government agency might compromise the privacy of such data. The set of ads displayed to a particular user could provide a lot of information about the person, just as one's search queries do. Some of it will be incorrect or misleading information because of quirks in the ad-targeting methods.

Should we insist that no such data be stored? Not necessarily. Some of it might have important uses. Some records are necessary for billing advertisers, some for analysis to improve ad-targeting strategies, and perhaps some for responding to complaints from e-mail users or advertisers.

The system design team needs to determine what records are necessary, which need to be associated with individual users, how long the company will store them, how it will protect them (from hackers, accidental leaks, and so on), and under what conditions it will disclose them.

Now, back up and reconsider informed consent. Telling customers that they will see ads based on the content of their e-mail is not sufficient if the system stores data that can link a list of ads with a particular user. You must explain this to potential users in a privacy policy or user agreement. But we know that most people do not read privacy policies and user agreements, especially long ones. A click might mean legal consent, but ethical responsibility goes farther. Independent of what is in the agreement, the designers must think about potential risks of the system, consider privacy throughout the planning process, and design in protections.

9.3.4 SPECIFICATIONS

> You are a relatively junior programmer working on modules that collect data from loan application forms and convert them to formats required by the parts of the program that evaluate the applications. You find that some demographic data are missing from some forms, particularly race and age. What should your program do? What should you do?

Consult the specifications for the program. Any project should have specification documents approved by the client or managers of the company developing the project (or both). Your company has an ethical and business obligation to ensure that the specifications are complete and to produce a program that meets them. Ethical reasons for this include, but go beyond, doing what the company has agreed to do and had been paid to do.

Suppose you do not find anything in the specs that cover your problem. The next step is to bring the problem to the attention of your manager. Suppose the manager tells you "Just make the program assume 'white' for race if it's missing. Banks shouldn't discriminate based on race anyway." Do you accept your manager's decision? You should not. You do not have the authority to make a decision not covered by the specifications without consulting the client or higher level managers in your company who are responsible for the program design. Probably your manager does not either. The manager's quick and simplistic response suggests that he or she is not acting with informed responsibility. In addition, your company must document whatever decision it makes. That is, the specifications need a revision so that they will be complete (SE Code 3.11).

Why is it important, from an ethical point of view, to consult someone else? Decisions about how a program handles unusual situations might have serious consequences. You (and your manager) might not know enough about the uses of the program to make a good decision. In this example, it is possible that the modules of the program that evaluate the loan application do not use the data on race at all. The lender or the government might want data on race to ensure compliance with nondiscrimination policies and laws.

What other consequences could the manager's decision have? Suppose the company later uses some of your modules in another project, say one that evaluates patients for inclusion in research studies on new drugs. Some diseases and drugs affect people in different ethnic groups differently. Inaccurate data could threaten the health or life of people in the studies and distort the conclusions in ways that harm other people who later use the drugs. But, you might say, we emphasized in Chapter 8 and Section 9.2.3 that people who reuse existing software, especially in a safety critical project, should review the software and its specifications to ensure that it meets the safety standards of the new project. That is their responsibility, you say. But if your way of handling missing data is not in the specifications, how will they know about it? Perhaps someone will notice that the specs are incomplete. Perhaps they will test the modules thoroughly before reusing them and discover what the code does. However, we have seen enough examples of human error to derive a lesson for a responsible professional: Do not count on everyone else to do their jobs perfectly. Do your best to make sure your part is not one of the factors that contribute to a failure.

9.3.5 SKIPPING TESTS

As we observed in Chapter 8, there are often pressures for reducing testing of software. Testing is one of the last steps in development, so when deadlines approach, testing schedules often shrink.

A safety-critical application

> Your team is working on a computer-controlled device for treating cancerous tumors. The computer controls direction, intensity, and timing of a beam that destroys the tumor. Various delays have put the project behind schedule, and the deadline is approaching. There will not be time to complete all the planned testing. The system has been functioning properly in the routine treatment scenarios tested so far. You are the project manager, and you are considering whether to deliver the system on time, while continuing testing, and to make patches if the team finds bugs.

The central issue here is safety. Your company is building a machine designed to save lives, but if it malfunctions, it can kill or injure patients. Perhaps the situation seems obvious: Delivering the system on time benefits the company but could endanger the patients—a case of profits versus safety. But we will defer a conclusion until after we analyze the case further.

Who are the people affected? (Who are the stakeholders?) First, the patients who will receive treatment with the machine. A malfunction could cause injury or death. On the other hand, if you delay release of the machine, some patients it might have cured could undergo surgery instead. We will assume treatment with the new machine is preferable because it is less invasive, requires less hospitalization and recovery time, and overall is less expensive. For some patients, surgery might be impossible, and they could die from their cancer without the new device. Second, there is an impact on the hospitals and clinics who will purchase the machine. Delay could cause financial losses if they have planned on having the machine at the scheduled time. However, it is reasonable for them to expect that the design and testing are professional and complete. You are deceiving the customers if you do not tell them that you have not completed testing. Third, your decision affects you and your company (including its employees and stockholders). Negative consequences of delaying delivery could include damage to your reputation for managing a project (with possible impact on salary and advancement), loss of reputation, a possible fall in stock price for the company, and loss of other contracts, resulting in reduction of jobs for the company's programmers and other employees. As a project manager, you have an obligation to help the company do well. On the other hand, if the system injures a patient, the same negative consequences are likely to occur, in addition to the human feelings of guilt and remorse and significant monetary losses from lawsuits.

This brief examination shows that delivering the system without complete testing could have both negative and positive impacts on patients and also on the manager and the company. The issue is not simply profits versus safety. We assume you are honestly trying to weigh the risks of delivering the system against the costs of delay. However, we must consider a few aspects of human nature that can influence the decision. One is to put more weight on short-term and/or highly likely effects. Many of the costs of delay are fairly certain and immediate, and the risk of malfunction is uncertain and in the future. Also, people tend to use the inherent uncertainties of a situation and the genuine arguments for one side to rationalize making the wrong decision. That is, they use uncertainty to justify taking the easy way out. It might take experience (with both professional and ethical issues), knowledge of cases like the Therac-25, and courage to resist the temptation to put short-term effects ahead of longer-term risks.

Now that we have seen that there are arguments on both sides, we must decide how to weigh them and how to avoid rationalization. First, the machine works well in the routine tests performed so far. The Therac-25 case illustrates that a complex system can function correctly hundreds of times, but fail with fatal consequences in unusual circumstances. Your customer might not know this. You, as a computer professional, have more understanding about the complexity of computer programs and the potential for errors, especially in programs that interact with real-world events such as operator input and control of machinery. We assume that careful thought went into devising the original test plan for the machine. You should delay delivery and complete the tests. (See SE Code 1.03 and 3.10 and ACM Code 1.2.)

Some patients will benefit from on-time delivery. Should their interests bear equal weight with those of the patients whom a malfunction might harm? Not necessarily. The machine represents an improvement in medical treatment, but there is no ethical obligation that it be available to the public on a certain date. You are not responsible for the disease of people who rely on existing treatments. Your obligation to the people who will use the machine is to be sure that it is as safe as good professional practice can make it, and that includes proper testing. You do not have an ethical obligation to cure people of cancer. You do have an ethical obligation to use your professional judgment in a way that does not expose people, without their knowledge, to additional harm.*

What about your responsibility to your company? Even if we weigh the short-term effects of the delay more highly than the risks of losses that would result from a malfunction, the ethical arguments are on the side of fully testing the machine. Yes, you have a responsibility to help your company be successful, but that is not an absolute obligation. (Recall the discussion of goals and constraints in Section 1.4.3.) Perhaps the distinction would be more obvious if the issue were stealing (from a competitor or a customer perhaps). Your responsibility to the financial success of the company is secondary to ethical constraints. In the present case, avoiding unreasonable risk of harm to patients is the ethical constraint (SE Code 1.02).

Getting a product to market[6]

Most products are not safety-critical ones where flaws might threaten people's lives. Consider this scenario:

> You are a programmer working for a very small start-up company. The company has a modest product line and is now developing a truly innovative new product. Everyone is working 60 hour weeks and the target release date is nine months away. The bulk of the programming and testing is done. You are about to begin the beta testing. (See Section 8.3.2 for an explanation of beta testing.) The owner of the company has learned about an annual industry show that would be ideal for introducing the new product. The show is in two months. Packaging must start within a week in order to have the product on the shelves for the show. The owner talks with the project manager. They decide to skip the beta testing and start making plans for an early release.

Should you protest? Students discussing this scenario generally recognize that the decision is a bad one and that the company should do the beta testing. They ask, however, if the programmer is even in a position to protest. Are you supposed to do what the project manager, your direct supervisor, says? Should you say nothing, speak up, or quit?

Consider this possible outcome: The programmer asks for a meeting with the owner. He explains that the product is not ready, that beta testing is a very important stage of development, and they should not skip it. The owner (who is not a programmer) accepts what the programmer tells him and drops the idea of an early release. The new product, released when originally planned, is a success. The programmer eventually becomes the head of quality control for the growing company.

---

*There are many situations where patients knowingly try risky drugs or treatments. Here, we are assuming that doctors and hospitals do not present the device as risky or experimental but as a new, presumably safe, treatment device.

This is not a fairy tale. It is an actual case, and the outcome I just described is what actually happened. This case makes a very important point: Sometimes people will listen to you, provided, of course, you are respectful, thoughtful, and well prepared. In another actual case, a manager within a company, but not in the software division, asked a programmer to do something the programmer knew was not a good idea. Although she feared that she might lose her job for refusing a manager's request, she said no and gave a brief explanation. The manager accepted the explanation, and that was the end of the incident. People often ask for things they do not necessarily expect to get. It is important to keep in mind that others might respect your opinion. You might be the only one who recognizes the problem or understands a particular situation. Your responsibilities to your company include applying your knowledge and skill to help avoid a bad decision. In the start-up scenario, speaking up might have had a significant impact on the success of the product and the company. Many people are reasonable and will consider a good explanation or argument. Of course, not all cases end this well.

The CEO of a small electronics company proposed producing a new version of a product within three months. The director of engineering (an excellent, experienced software engineer) wrote up a detailed schedule of all the necessary steps and told the CEO that the project would take more than a year. Note that the software engineer did not simply tell the CEO that the three-month plan was unreasonable. He documented his claim. (SE Code 2.06 and 3.09 apply.) The CEO replaced him with someone who had a "can do" attitude. This is one of many cases where doing what is professionally responsible corresponds with doing what is good for oneself. The software engineer did not want the stress of working under an extremely unreasonable schedule and the responsibility for the inevitable failure. Leaving the company was not a bad thing.

9.3.6 COPYRIGHT VIOLATION

> Your company has 25 licenses for a computer program, but you discover that it has been copied onto 80 computers.

The first step here is to inform your supervisor that the copies violate the license agreement. Suppose the supervisor is not willing to take any action? What next? What if you bring the problem to the attention of higher level people in the company and no one cares? There are several possible actions: Give up; you did your best to correct the problem. Call the software vendor and report the offense. Quit your job.

Is giving up at this point ethically acceptable? My students thought it depended in part on whether you are the person who signed the license agreements. If so, you have made an agreement about the use of the software, and you, as the representative of your company, are obligated to honor it. Because you did not make the copies, you have not broken the agreement directly, but you have responsibility for the software. Your name on the license could expose you to legal risk, or unethical managers in your company could make you a scapegoat. Thus, you might prefer to report the violation or quit your job and have your name removed from the licenses to protect yourself. If you are not the person who signed the licenses, then you observed a wrong and brought it to the attention of appropriate people in the company. Is that enough? What do Sections 2.02, 6.13, and 7.01 of the SE Code and 1.5 and 2.6 of the ACM Code suggest?

9.3.7 GOING PUBLIC

Suppose you are a member of a team working on a computer-controlled crash-avoidance system for automobiles. You think the system has a flaw that could endanger people. The project manager does not seem concerned and expects to announce completion of the project soon. Do you have an ethical obligation to do something?

Given the potential consequences, yes (see SE Code 1.04; ACM Code 1.2, 2.5). We consider a variety of options. First, at a minimum, discuss your concerns with the project manager. Voicing your concerns is admirable and obligatory. It is also good for your company. Internal "whistle-blowing" can help protect the company, as well as the public, from all the negative consequences of releasing a dangerous product. If the manager decides to proceed as planned with no examination of the problem, your next option is to go to someone higher up in the company.

If no one with authority in the company is willing to investigate your concerns, you have a more difficult dilemma. You now have the option of going outside the company to the customer, to the news media, or to a government agency. There is personal risk of course: You might lose your job. There is also the ethical issue of the damage you might do to your company, and ultimately to the people who would benefit from the system. You might be mistaken. Or you might be correct, but your method of whistle-blowing might produce negative publicity that kills a potentially valuable and fixable project. As the ACM Code (1.2) says, "misguided reporting of violations can, itself, be harmful." At this point it is a good idea to consider whether you are confident that you have the expertise to assess the risk. It could help to discuss the problem with other professionals. If you conclude that the management decision was an acceptable one (and that you are not letting your concern for keeping your job sway your conclusion), this might be the point at which to drop the issue. If you are convinced that the flaw is real, or if you are aware of a careless, irresponsible attitude among the company managers, then you must go further (SE Code 6.13). You are not an uninvolved bystander, for whom the question of ethical obligation might be more fuzzy. The project pays your salary. You are part of the team; you are a participant. Note also that this is the kind of situation suggested in the SE Code 2.05, where you may violate a confidentiality agreement.

There have been several dramatic cases where professionals faced this difficult situation. Computer engineers who worked on the San Francisco Bay Area Rapid Transit system (BART) worried about the safety of the software designed to control the trains. Although they tried for many months, they were not successful in their attempts to convince their managers to make changes. Eventually, a newspaper published some of their critical memos and reports. The engineers were fired. During the next few years, when several crashes occurred, there were public investigations and numerous recommendations made for improving safety of the system.[7]

One of the BART engineers made these comments about the process:

> If there is something that ought to be corrected inside an organization, the most effective way to do it is to do it within the organization and exhaust all possibilities there . . . you might have to go to the extreme of publishing these things, but you should never start that way.[8]

It is important, for practical and ethical reasons, to keep a complete and accurate record of your attempts to bring attention to the problem and the responses from the people you approach. The record protects you and others who behave responsibly and could help avoid baseless accusations later.

9.3.8   RELEASE OF PERSONAL INFORMATION

We will look at two related scenarios. Here is the first:

> You work for the IRS, the Social Security Administration, a movie-rental company, or an Internet service provider. Someone asks you to get a copy of records about a particular person. He will pay you $500.

Who are the stakeholders? You: You have an opportunity to make some extra money. The person seeking the records: Presumably he has something to gain. The person whose records the briber wants: Providing the information invades his or her privacy. All the people about whom the company or agency has personal information: If you sell information about one person, chances are you will sell more if asked in the future. Your employer (if a private company): If the sale becomes known, the victim might sue the company. If such sales of information become common, the company will acquire a reputation for carelessness and will potentially lose business and lawsuits.

There are many alternative actions open to you: Sell the records. Refuse and say nothing about the incident. Refuse and report the incident to your supervisor. Refuse and report to the police. Contact the person whose information the briber wants and tell him or her of the incident. Agree to sell the information, but actually work with the police to collect evidence to convict the person trying to buy it.

Are any of these alternatives ethically prohibited or obligatory? The first option, selling the records, is clearly wrong. It almost certainly violates rules and policies you have agreed to abide by in accepting your job. As an employee, you must abide by the guarantees of confidentiality the company or agency has promised its customers or the public. Depending on the use made of the information you sell, you could be helping to cause serious harm to the victim. Disclosing the information might be illegal. Your action might expose your employer to fines. If someone discovers the leak, the employer and the police might suspect another employee, who could face arrest and punishment. (See ACM Code: 1.2, 1.3, 1.7, 2.6; SE Code: 2.03, 2.05, 2.09, 4.04, 6.05, 6.06.)

Some would argue that selling the records is wrong because it violates the privacy of the victim, but recall that the boundaries of privacy are unclear because they can conflict with freedom of speech and reasonable flow of information. If you happened to know the victim, and knew some of the same information in the records, you might not be under an ethical obligation to keep the information secret. The essential element that makes selling the information wrong in this scenario is your position of trust as an employee in a company or agency that maintains the information. The risks are greater for sensitive information, but your obligation extends to any information the company has promised to keep confidential.

What about the second alternative: refusing to provide the records, but not reporting the incident? Depending on policies of the employer (and laws related to certain government agencies; see SE Code 6.06 and ACM Code 2.3), you might be obligated to report any attempt to gain access to the records. There are other good reasons for reporting the incident. Reporting could lead to the capture of someone making a business of buying sensitive information without the knowledge or consent of the person the information concerns and without the knowledge and consent of the companies and agencies responsible for the information. It could protect you and other innocent employees if someone later discovers the sale of the records and does not know who sold them. (Some ethicists, for example, deontologists, argue that taking an action because it benefits you is not ethically meritorious. However, one can argue that taking an action that protects an innocent person is meritorious, even if the person is yourself.)

ACM Code 1.2 and 1.7 suggest an obligation to report, but it is not explicit. There might be disagreement about whether you are ethically bound to do more than refuse to sell the information. It is difficult to decide how much you must do to prevent a wrong thing from happening if you are not participating in the wrong act. A recluse who ignores evils and pains around him might not be doing anything unethical, but he is not what we would consider a good neighbor. Acting to prevent a wrong is part of being a good neighbor, good employee, or good citizen—it is ethically admirable—even in situations where it is not ethically obligatory.

Now consider a variation of this scenario.

You know another employee sells records with people's personal information.

Your options include doing nothing, talking to the other employee and trying to get him or her to stop selling files (by threats of exposure or ethical arguments), reporting to your supervisor, or reporting to an appropriate law-enforcement agency. The question here is whether you have an obligation to do anything. This scenario differs from the previous one in two ways. First, you have no direct involvement; no one has approached you. This difference might seem to argue for no obligation. On the other hand, in the first scenario, if you refused to sell the file, the buyer might give up, and the victim's information would remain protected. In this case, you know that a sale of confidential, sensitive information occurred. Thus the argument in favor of an obligation to take action is stronger (see SE Code 6.13 and 7.01).

9.3.9 CONFLICT OF INTEREST

> You have a small consulting business. The CyberStuff company plans to buy software to run a new collaborative content-sharing Web site. CyberStuff wants to hire you to evaluate bids from vendors. Your spouse works for NetWorkx and did most of the work in writing the bid that NetWorkx plans to submit. You read the bid while your spouse was working on it and you think it is excellent. Do you tell CyberStuff about your spouse's connection with NetWorkx?

Conflict-of-interest situations occur in many professions. Sometimes the ethical course of action is clear. Sometimes, depending on your connection with the people or organizations your action affects, it can be more difficult to determine.

I have seen two immediate reactions to scenarios similar to this one (in discussions among professionals and among students). One is that it is a simple case of profits versus honesty, and ethics requires that you inform the company about your connection to the software vendor. The other is that if you honestly believe you can be objective and fairly consider all bids, you have no ethical obligation to say anything. Which is right? Is this a simple choice between saying nothing and getting the consulting job or disclosing your connection and losing the job?

The affected parties are the CyberStuff company, yourself, your spouse, your spouse's company, and the other companies whose bids you will be reviewing. A key factor in considering consequences is that we do not know whether CyberStuff will later discover your connection to one of the bidders. If you say nothing about the conflict of interest, you benefit, because you get the consulting job. If you recommend NetWorkx (because you believe its bid is the best), it benefits from a sale. However, if CyberStuff discovers the conflict of interest later, your reputation for honesty—important to a consultant—will suffer. The reputation of your spouse's company could also suffer. Note that even if you conclude that you are truly unbiased and do not have an ethical obligation to tell CyberStuff about your connection to your spouse's company, your decision might put NetWorkx's reputation for honesty at risk. The appearance of bias can be as damaging (to you and to NetWorkx) as actual bias.

Suppose you take the job and you find that one of the other bids is much better than the bid from NetWorkx. Are you prepared to handle that situation ethically?

What are the consequences of disclosing the conflict of interest to the client now? You will probably lose this particular job, but they might value your honesty more highly and that might get you more business in the future. Thus, there could be benefits, even to you, from disclosing the conflict of interest.

Suppose it is unlikely that anyone will discover your connection to NetWorkx. What are your responsibilities to your potential client as a professional consultant? When someone hires you as a consultant, they expect you to offer unbiased, honest, impartial professional advice. There is an implicit assumption that you do not have a personal interest in the outcome or a personal reason to favor one of the bids you will review. The conclusion in this case hangs on this point. In spite of your belief in your impartiality, you could be unintentionally biased. It is not up to you to make the decision about whether you can be fair. The client should make that decision. Your ethical obligation in this case is to inform CyberStuff of the conflict of interest. (See SE Code Principle 4, 4.03, and 4.05, and ACM Code 2.5.)

9.3.10 KICKBACKS AND DISCLOSURE

> You are a programmer on the programming staff of a major university. The office that plans freshman orientation is selecting one or two brands of security software for laptops and cell phones to recommend to all new students. Your supervisor has asked you to evaluate software from a dozen companies and make recommendations. One of the companies takes you out to dinner, gives you free software (in addition to the security software you are evaluating), offers to pay your expenses to attend a professional conference on computer security, and offers to give the university a percentage of the price for every student who buys its security package.

You are sensitive to the issue of bribery, but the cost of the dinner and software the company gave you is relatively small. The university cannot pay to send you to conferences. Attending one will improve your knowledge and skills and make you better at your job, a benefit to both you and the university. The percentage from the sales benefits the university and thus all the students. This sounds like a good deal for all.

It also might sound a bit familiar. Universities recommend loan companies to students seeking student loans. A flurry of news reports disclosed that several universities and their financial-aid administrators gave special privileges and preferred recommendations to particular lending companies in exchange for payments to the universities and consulting fees, travel expenses, and other gifts for the administrators. Some financial aid officers defended the practices. Professional organizations scurried to write new ethical guidelines. Some lenders paid heavy fines. The reputations of the universities suffered. The government heavily regulates the lending industry, so we return to the security software scenario to discuss ethical issues, not primarily legal ones.

First of all, does your employer have a policy about accepting gifts from vendors? Even if gifts appear small to you and you are confident that they do not influence your judgment, you are obligated to follow your employer's policy. Violating the policy violates an agreement you have made. Violating the policy could expose the employer to negative publicity (and possibly legal sanctions). (See SE Code 6.05 and 6.06. SE Code 1.06, 4.03, and 4.04 are also relevant to this case.)

Who does not benefit from the arrangement with the software company? Any company that charges less for software of comparable quality. Any company that charges the same or perhaps a little more for a better product. All the students who rely on the recommendation. The university's obligation in making the recommendation is primarily to the students. Will the benefits the programmer and university receive sway their choice of company to the point where they do not choose the product best for the students?

People want to know when a recommendation represents an honest opinion and when someone is paying for it. We expect universities and certain other organizations to be impartial in their recommendations. When a programmer selects software to recommend, the presumption is that it is, in the programmer's opinion, the best for the buyer. If there are other reasons for the selection, the programmer should disclose them. Disclosure is a key point. Many organizations encourage their members to get a credit card that provides a kickback to the organization. This is not unethical primarily because the kickback is made clear. It is even a selling point: Use this card and help fund our good cause. However, even if the university makes clear in its recommendation that it benefits financially from sales of the product, there are good arguments against the arrangement. They are not computer professional issues, so we leave them for you to think about.

9.3.11 A TEST PLAN

> A team of programmers is developing a communications system for firefighters
> to use when fighting a fire. Firefighters will be able to communicate with each
> other, with supervisors near the scene, and with other emergency personnel.
> The programmers will test the system in a field near the company office.

What is the ethical issue? The test plan is insufficient and this is an application where lives could be at risk. Testing should involve real firefighters inside buildings or in varied terrain, perhaps in an actual fire (perhaps a controlled burn). The programmers who work on the system know how it behaves. They are experienced users with a specific set of expectations. They are not the right people to test the system. Testing must address issues such as: Will the devices withstand heat, water, and soot? Can someone manipulate the controls wearing heavy gloves? Are the controls clear and easy to use in poor light conditions? Will a building's structure interfere with the signal?

In an actual case, the New York City fire commissioner halted use of a $33 million digital communications system after a fireman called for help on his radio and no one heard. Firefighters reported other problems during simulation tests. The commissioner commented "We tested the quality, durability, and reliability of the product, but we didn't spend enough time testing them in the field or familiarizing the firefighters with their use."[9]

9.3.12 ARTIFICIAL INTELLIGENCE AND SENTENCING CRIMINALS

> You are part of a team developing a sophisticated program using artificial
> intelligence (AI) techniques to make sentencing decisions for convicted
> criminals.

Maybe, in the future, we will have computer systems capable of doing this well without human intervention. It is helpful for judges to review sentencing in cases with similar characteristics, but judges use their discretion in deciding sentences (within bounds established in law). Prosecutors and defense lawyers present arguments that a judge considers, but software cannot. A judge can consider unusual circumstances in the case, characteristics of the convicted person, and other factors that a program cannot handle. Judges sometimes innovate creative new aspects of sentencing. A program that analyzes and chooses from prior cases cannot. On the other hand, some judges have a reputation for giving extremely tough sentences, while others are very lenient. Some people argue that software might be more fair than a judge influenced by personal impressions and biases. At this point, however, most of the legal community, and probably the public, would prefer to have human judges make sentencing decisions. Years of experience provide insights that are, at this time, difficult to encode into software. For now, we modify the scenario by adding two words:

> You are part of a team developing a sophisticated program using AI techniques
> to help judges make sentencing decisions for convicted criminals.

The system will analyze characteristics of the crime and the criminal to find other cases that are similar. Based on its analysis of cases, should it then make a recommendation for the sentence in the current case, or should it simply display similar cases, more or less as a search engine would, so that the judge can review them? Or should it provide both a recommended sentence and the relevant cases?

This is clearly an application where it is essential to have experts and potential users involved in the design. The expertise and experience of judges and lawyers are essential for choosing criteria and strategies for selecting the similar cases on which the program bases its recommendation or on which a judge bases a decision. The system's recommendations, if it makes them, must comply with sentencing requirements specified in laws.

The involvement of lawyers can improve more subtle decisions. Consider the question of the ordering of the cases the system displays. Should it order them by date or by the length of the sentence? If the latter, should the shortest or longest sentences come first? This last question suggests that the project's consultants should include both prosecutors and defense lawyers. But probably none of these orderings is best. Perhaps you should order the cases according to an evaluation of their similarity or relevance to the current case. That is a fuzzier criterion than date or length of sentence. Again, it is important to include a variety of experts, with different perspectives, in the design process.

Is the ordering of the selected cases so important? When you are researching some topic, how many pages of search-engine results do you look at? Many people rarely go beyond the first page. We expect a judge making a sentencing decision to be more thorough. Experience and human factors research, however, remind us that people sometimes are tired or rushed. Sometimes they have too much confidence in results from computer systems. (We saw examples in Chapter 8. County election officials and school districts ignored warnings that they should not rely solely on results from computer systems when making decisions about voter eligibility and about assigning students to summer school.) Even when people are deliberate and careful in interpreting output from a computer system, the manner in which the viewers see the data can influence their perceptions. Thus careful planning, including much consultation with relevant experts, is an ethical requirement in a system that will have significant impact on people's lives.

A company or government agency that develops or installs this system must consider how it will maintain and update the system. Clearly there will be new cases to add. How will the system handle changes in sentencing laws? Should it discard cases decided under the old law? Include them but flag them clearly as predating the change? How much weight should the system give such cases in its selection criteria?

We have not yet answered the question about whether the system should recommend a sentence. A specific recommendation from the system that differs from the judge's initial plan might lead a judge to give a case more thought. Or it might influence a judge more than it should. If the system presents a recommendation, legislators or administrators might begin to think that a clerk or law student, not a judge, can operate the system and handle sentencing. This is not likely in the short term—judges and lawyers would object. It is, however, a possible consequence of apparently sophisticated AI systems making apparently wise decisions in any professional area. A potential drop in employment for judges (or other professionals) is not the main issue. The quality of the decisions is. Thus an answer to the question will depend in part on the quality of AI technology (and the specific system) at the time of development and on the sensitivity of the application. (See Exercise 6.27 for another application area.)

> Suppose judges in your state use a sentencing decision system that displays similar cases for the judge to review. You are a programmer working for your state government. Your state has just made it a criminal offense to use a cell phone while taking a college exam. Your boss, a justice department administrator, tells you to modify the program to add this new category of crime and assign the same relevancy weights to cases as the program currently does for using a cell phone while driving a car (already illegal in your state).

The first question, one for your boss, is whether the contract under which the system operates allows the state to make changes. For many consumer products, guarantees and service agreements become void if the consumer takes the product apart and makes changes. The same can be true for software. Let us assume the boss knows that the state's contract allows the state to modify the system.

Suppose you know that your boss made the decision quickly and independently. You should say no, with appropriate politeness and reasons. SE Code 3.15 states a very important, often ignored principle: "Treat all forms of software maintenance with the same professionalism as new development." That includes developing specifications, in this example in consultation with lawyers and judges who understand the law and its subtleties. We raised a sampling of the complex and sensitive issues that go into the design of a system such as this. Modifications and upgrades should undergo as thorough planning and testing.

9.3.13 A GRACIOUS HOST

> You are the computer system administrator for a mid-sized company. You can monitor the company network from home, and you frequently work from home. Your niece, a college student, is visiting for a week. She asks if she can use your computer to check her e-mail. Sure, you say.

You are being a gracious host. What is the ethical problem?

Maybe there is none. Maybe you have an excellent firewall and excellent antivirus software. Maybe your files are password protected, and you created a separate account on your computer for your niece. But maybe you did not even think about security when your niece asked to use the computer.

Your niece is a responsible person. She would not intentionally snoop or harm you or your company. But after checking e-mail, she might visit MySpace, then look for someone selling cheap concert tickets, then ... who knows? Maybe her own computer crashed twice in the past six months because of viruses.

Your company network contains employee records, customer records, and plenty of information about company projects, finances, and plans. Depending on what the company does, the system might contain other very sensitive information. Downtime, due to a virus or similar problem, would be very costly for the company. In an actual incident, someone in the family of a mortgage company employee signed up for a peer-to-peer file sharing service and did not properly set the options indicating which files were to be shared. Mortgage application information for a few thousand customers leaked and spread on the Web.

The point of this scenario is that you must always be alert to potential risks. Mixing family and work applications poses risks.

EXERCISES

Review Exercises

9.1 What special responsibilities do software project managers have?

9.2 Why did a program to read handwriting, developed by Microsoft programmers, fail?

9.3 What is one important policy decision a company should consider when designing a system to target ads based on e-mail content?

9.4 You are a programmer, and you think there is a serious flaw in software your company is developing. Who should you talk to about it first?

General Exercises

9.5   *Understand what success means* is a key guideline for programmers. Explain this guideline and why it is important.

9.6   Review the description of the inventory system called Warehouse Manager in Section 8.1.3. Find specific guidelines in Section 9.2.3 and the ethics codes in Appendix A that, if followed carefully, might have avoided problems in this system.

9.7   You are setting up a small business with a Web site and considering what privacy policy to adopt for the information you will collect about your customers. You will choose either informed consent (stating how you use the information, with no opt-out options), an opt-out option, or opt-in box to click (as described in Section 2.1.3). Your site will clearly and fully explain your policy. Are any of the three choices ethically obligatory or ethically prohibited, or are all ethically acceptable? Justify your answers.

9.8   You work as a database programmer for a company that provides exercise and diet advice via the Internet. The customers must register, providing not only name, address, and credit card number, but also a wide variety of health information in order to customize their exercise and diet plan. The advice your system provides is based on accepted standards and research in the field. A large company that owns many subsidiaries, including a vitamin and dietary supplement manufacturer, has bought your company. You have been asked to merge the data from your company with the manufacturer's database and reprogram the exercise and diet plans to include specific recommendations for the products made by the manufacturer. Using the methodology of Section 9.3.1, analyze the ethics of doing so.

9.9   Looking at the scenario above, suppose the new parent company has decided to sell the health information to pharmaceutical companies. Your company's privacy policy has always stated that the information is for internal use only and will not be sold or shared with others. It also said the policy was subject to change without notice. The new parent company has already changed the policy to state that information collected may be sold or shared with trusted third party business partners. You have been asked to develop a program that allows the marketing department to pull this health information for sale to the pharmaceutical companies. Using the methodology of Section 9.3.1, analyze the ethics of doing so.

9.10   A factory manager has hired your company to develop and install a surveillance system in the factory. The system includes cameras small enough not to be noticed. Supervisors and security personnel can view images in real time on monitors in a control room. The system will store the video. The factory manager says the purposes are to watch for safety problems and for theft of materials by workers. What issues, specifications, and policies will you discuss with the manager? Would you set any conditions on taking the job? Explain.

9.11   You work for a company that develops security products. You helped write software for a car door lock that operates by matching the driver's thumbprint. The manager for that project is no longer at the company. A local power station wants your company to develop a thumbprint-operated lock for secure areas of the power station. Your boss says to use the software from the car locks. What is your response?

9.12   Write a scenario to illustrate SE Code 2.05 and ACM Code 1.8.

9.13   You are a manager at a health-maintenance organization. You find that one of your employees has been reading people's medical records without authorization. What is your response?

9.14   You work for a company that produces software to assist computer technicians. The software allows the technician to remotely take control of a computer to diagnose problems, install software, and remove viruses. You have been informed that the company is going to branch out into the employee monitoring market. You have been asked to modify the software so that someone can record all activity on a desktop computer without the user knowing. It would not take much to modify the software for this purpose, and some of the capabilities are already there. What are the ethical issues in this case? What principles of the SE Code would apply?

9.15 The monitoring software described in the previous exercise has legitimate uses but also potential for abuse. Suppose you discover that a minor modification in the software would prevent many potential abuses but would also disable one feature in the software. Should you make the modification? Should the company make the modification? What are the ethical considerations? Suppose customer feedback indicates that most clients do not use the feature that would be disabled? Suppose the feature is a popular and heavily used feature?

9.16 You are offered a job with a company that is developing software for a new generation of space shuttles. You do not have any training in the specific techniques used in the programs you will be working on. You can tell from the job interview that the interviewer thinks your college program included this material. Should you take the job? Should you tell the interviewer that you have no training or experience in this area? Analyze this scenario, using the methods in Section 9.3.1. Find relevant sections from the ethics codes in Appendix A.

9.17 You are a programmer for a company that manages large investment portfolios. You have been working on a project to develop a program to decide how to invest a large amount of money according to criteria that balance risk and potential gain according to the client's preferences. The program is complete and has performed well in preliminary testing, but the planned full-scale testing has not yet been done. It is Friday afternoon, and one of the investment managers has just received a large amount of money from a client to invest. The investment manager wants to get the money into the stock market before the weekend. He tells you that there is not enough time to use the old investment-planning method. He wants a copy of your program to run. Your supervisor, the software manager, has gone away for the weekend. What do you do? Analyze this scenario, using the methods in Section 9.3.1.

9.18 A small company offers you a programming job. You are to work on new versions of its software product to disable copy-protection and other access controls on electronic books. The company's program enables buyers of e-books to read their e-books on a variety of hardware devices (fair uses). Customers can also use the program to make many unauthorized copies of copyrighted books. The company's Web page implicitly encourages this practice. Analyze the ethics of accepting the job. Find relevant sections from the ethics codes in Appendix A. (For this exercise, assume you are in a country that does not outlaw tools to circumvent copy protection as the Digital Millennium Copyright Act does in the United States.)

9.19 Find at least two examples described in this book where there was a violation of Clause 3.09 of the SE Code.

9.20 Clause 1.03 of the SE Code says "Approve software only if" it does not "diminish privacy or harm the environment." Search engines can diminish privacy. Do they violate this clause? Should the clause say something about trade-offs, or should we interpret it as an absolute rule? The concluding sentence of Clause 1.03 says, "The ultimate effect of the work should be to the public good." Does this suggest trade-offs? Give another example in which the dilemma in this exercise would be relevant.

9.21 Clause 8.07 in the SE Code says we should "not give unfair treatment to anyone because of any irrelevant prejudices." The guidelines for Section 1.4 of the ACM Code say "Discrimination on the basis of ... national origin ... is an explicit violation of ACM policy and will not be tolerated." Analyze the ethical issues in the following scenario. Do you think the decision in the scenario is ethically acceptable? How do the relevant sections from the two Codes apply? Which Code has a better statement about discrimination? Why?

> Suppose you came to the U.S. from Iraq 15 years ago. You now have a small software company. You will need to hire six programmers this year. Because of the devastation by the war in your homeland, you have decided to seek out and hire only programmers who are refugees from Iraq.

9.22 Consider the following statements.

1. In addition to a safe social environment, human well-being includes a safe natural environment. Therefore, computing professionals who design and develop systems must be alert to, and make others aware of, any potential damage to the local or global environment.[10]

2. We cannot assume that a computer-based economy automatically will provide enough jobs for everyone in the future. Computer professionals should be aware of this pressure on employment when designing and implementing systems that will reduce job opportunities for those most in need of them.[11]

Compare the two statements from the perspective of how relevant and appropriate they are for an ethical code for computer professionals. Do you think both should be in such a code? Neither? Just one? (Which one?) Give your reasons.

9.23 You are the president of a small computer-game company. Your company has just bought another small game company that was developing three new games. You look them over and find that one is complete, ready to reproduce and sell. It is very violent and demeaning to women. It would probably sell 200,000–400,000 copies. You have to decide what to do with the game. Give some options, and give arguments for and against them. What will you do? Why?

9.24 Suppose there are two large competing telecommunications firms in your city. The companies are hostile to each other. You have worked for one of the companies for five years in a position that gives you access to company trade secrets. You are now interviewing for a job with the other company; it would be a substantial step up in your career. During the interview, you get the impression that the company expects you to share your knowledge, including the trade secrets, if they hire you. What are the ethical issues involved? What are the legal issues? Are they the same as the ethical issues? You have signed a nondisclosure agreement as part of your condition of employment with your current company. Does this change the ethics involved? Suppose the first company fired you. Would the ethics involved change?

9.25 A Dutch hacker who copied patient files from a University of Washington medical center (and was not caught) said in an online interview that he did it to publicize the system's vulnerability, not to use the information. He disclosed portions of the files (to an individual, not the public) after the medical center said that no patient files had been copied.[12] Analyze the ethics of his actions using the methodology of Section 9.3.1. Was this honorable whistle-blowing? Irresponsible hacking?

9.26 Consider the scenario in Section 9.3.5. Suppose that the company has decided to deliver the device before completing the testing and that you have decided you must inform the hospitals that are purchasing it. Discuss ethical arguments about whether to include your name with the information you give to the hospitals or to send it anonymously.

9.27 The first case in Section 9.3.5 concerns safety-critical systems. Suppose the software product in the second scenario is an accounting system, or a game, or a photo-sharing system for the Web. Which principles or ideas in the analysis of the first scenario apply to the second one? Which do not? Explain your answers.

9.28   You run a small company that developed and markets a filter program that enables parents to block access to Internet sites they do not want their children to visit. A large corporation has asked you to customize the program to install on its machines to block access by employees to various game sites, sites containing pornography, and video-sharing sites. A foreign government has asked you to customize the program to install on its Internet gateways to block access by people in the country to sites containing pornography and sites containing political discussion critical of the government. Will you accept either or both jobs? If one but not the other, make clear the reasons for the distinction.

9.29   Several professional associations of engineers opposed increased immigration of skilled high-tech workers. Was this ethical? Give arguments for both sides. Then give your view and defend it.

Assignments

These exercises require some research or activity.

9.30   Watch a science fiction movie set in the near future. Describe a computer or telecommunications system in the movie that does not currently exist. Suppose, in the years before the movie takes place, you are on the team that develops it. Identify issues of professional ethics the team should consider.

Class Discussion Exercises

These exercises are for class discussion, perhaps with short presentations prepared in advance by small groups of students.

9.31   You are the programmer in the clinic scenario (Section 9.3.2). The director has asked you to rank your suggestions for security and privacy protection measures so that she can choose the most important ones while still trying to stay within her budget. Group the suggestions into at least three categories: essential, recommended, and least important. Include explanations you might give her and assumptions you make (or questions you would ask her) to help determine the importance of some features.

9.32   You are an experienced programmer working on part of a project to bring automation to a pharmacy, automatically filling the most common prescriptions, leaving the pharmacists to focus on the more complex and less common prescriptions. The project is behind schedule and risks losing some sales that have already been made with a promised delivery date. In order to make the delivery date it has been proposed that documentation be finished after the delivery, and the testing schedule be condensed to half the allotted time. Any problems not caught in testing will be dealt with in patches and updates. Discuss the implications of this proposal. What are the ethical issues involved? Would the ethical considerations be the same if the software was to automate an auto parts store? A stationery store?

9.33   The faculty at a large university requested that the campus store sell an electronic device, AutoGrader, that students would use when taking machine-scorable tests. Students would enter test answers into this personal electronic device. When done, they send the answers via infrared signal to the instructor's computer in the classroom. Once the instructor's computer receives the answers, it immediately grades the test and sends each student's score back to the student's device.

     Suppose you are a university dean who must decide whether to allow use of this system. Analyze the decision as both an ethical and practical problem. Discuss potential benefits and problems or risks of using the system. Discuss all the issues (of the kind relevant to the topics of this book) that are relevant to making the decision. Mention any warnings or policies you might include if you approve use of the system.

9.34   As we saw in Section 7.5.3, many people, including Sun Microsystems cofounder Bill Joy, fear that development of intelligent robots could have devastating consequences for the human race.[13] Is it ethical to do research aimed at improving artificial intelligence?

NOTES

1. The full names are the Association for Computing Machinery and the Institute of Electrical and Electronics Engineers.

2. Bob Davis and David Wessel, *Prosperity: The Coming 20-Year Boom and What It Means to You* (Random House, 1998), p. 97.

3. Charles Piller, "The Gender Gap Goes High-Tech," *Los Angeles Times*, August 25, 1998, p. A1.

4. Bill Gates, *The Road Ahead* (Viking, 1995), p. 78.

5. Roger Boisjoly, quoted in Diane Vaughan, *The Challenger Launch Decision: Risky Technology, Culture, and Deviance at NASA* (University of Chicago Press, 1996), p. 41.

6. I thank Cyndi Chie for giving me this scenario.

7. Robert M. Anderson et al., *Divided Loyalties: Whistle-Blowing at BART* (Purdue University, 1980).

8. Holger Hjortsvang, quoted in Anderson et al., *Divided Loyalties*, p. 140.

9. Robert Fox, "News Track," *Communications of the ACM*, 44, no. 6 (June 2001), pp. 9–10; Kevin Flynn, "A Focus on Communication Failures," *New York Times*, January 30, 2003, p. A13.

10. Guidelines of the ACM Code of Ethics and Professional Conduct (Section 1.1).

11. Tom Forester and Perry Morrison, *Computer Ethics: Cautionary Tales and Ethical Dilemmas in Computing*, 2nd ed. (MIT Press, 1994), p. 202.

12. Marc L. Songini, "Hospital Confirms Copying of Patient Files by Hacker," *Security Informer*, December 14, 2000 (accessed June 4, 2001). The article is no longer accessible on the Security Informer Web site. A version of it from *Computerworld*, dated December 15, 2000, is at archives.cnn.com/2000/TECH/computing/12/15/hospital.hacker.idg (accessed April 20, 2007).

13. Bill Joy, "Why the Future Doesn't Need Us," *Wired*, April 2000, www.wired.com/wired/archive/8.04 (accessed September 6, 2007).

BOOKS AND ARTICLES

- Anderson, Robert M., Robert Perrucci, Dan E. Schendel, and Leon E. Trachtman. *Divided Loyalties: Whistle-Blowing at BART*. Purdue University, 1980.

- Anderson, Ronald E., Deborah G. Johnson, Donald Gotterbarn, and Judith Perrolle. "Using the New ACM Code of Ethics in Decision Making." *Communications of the ACM*, 36, no. 2 (February 1993): 98–107.

- Bayles, Michael D. *Professional Ethics*. Wadsworth, 1981.

- Cerf, Vint. "Ethics and the Internet." *Communications of the ACM*, 32, no. 6 (June 1989): 710. An early attempt to establish a standard of ethics for the Internet.

- Collins, W. Robert, Keith W. Miller, Bethany J. Spielman, and Phillip Wherry. "How Good Is Good Enough?" *Communications of the ACM*, 37, no. 1 (January 1994): 81–91.

- Ermann, M. David, Mary B. Williams, and Michele S. Shauf, eds. *Computers, Ethics and Society*. 2nd ed. Oxford University Press, 1997.

- Gotterbarn, Donald, Keith Miller, and Simon Rogerson. "Software Engineering Code of Ethics Is Approved." *Communications of the ACM*, 42, no. 10 (October 1999): 102–107.

- Johnson, Deborah G. *Computer Ethics*. 3rd ed. Prentice Hall, 2001.

- Rachels, James. *The Elements of Moral Philosophy*. McGraw Hill, 1993.

- Spinello, Richard. *CyberEthics: Morality and Law in Cyberspace*. Jones and Bartlett, 2000.

- Vaughan, Diane. *The Challenger Launch Decision: Risky Technology, Culture, and Deviance at NASA*. University of Chicago Press, 1996.

ORGANIZATIONS AND WEB SITES

- ACM: www.acm.org
- Computer Professionals for Social Responsibility: cpsr.org

- IEEE Computer Society: www.computer.org

EPILOGUE

Although most of this book focuses on problems and controversial issues, we celebrate the enormous benefits that computer technology and the Internet have brought us.

Critics of computer technology predicted many very negative consequences that did not occur (for example, mass unemployment). Critics, especially those without a technical background, were less likely to anticipate some of the problems that do occur: hacking, identity theft, spam. Very few people anticipated some of the marvelous benefits and whole new phenomena such as social media and content sharing by millions of members of the public.

The human mind, and hence technology, does not stand still. Change always disrupts the status quo. Technology is always shifting the balance of power—between governments and citizens, between hackers and security experts, between people who want to protect their privacy and businesses that want to use personal information. Entrenched powers such as governments or dominant companies in an industry will fight to maintain their prior position. We can look to governments for solutions to some problems caused by technology, but we should remember that governments are institutions, like businesses and other organizations, with their own interests and incentives.

Because technology brings change, it often brings new problems. With time, we solve or reduce many of the problems, using more or better technology, the market, innovative services and business arrangements, laws, education, and so on. We cannot eliminate all negative effects of computer technology. We accept some and adapt to a new environment. We always make trade-offs in life.

In some areas, such as privacy of personal data and activities, computer technology has brought profound changes that could fundamentally alter our interactions with the people around us and with our governments. It is essential to think about personal choices and their consequences. It is essential for businesses and computer professionals to think about appropriate guidelines for use of the technology. It is essential to think ahead—to anticipate potential problems and risks and to design products and policies to reduce them. On the other hand, we must be careful not to regulate too soon in ways that would stifle innovation and prevent new benefits.

The issue of banning a tool or technology arose in several contexts. These included encryption, anonymity on the Web, devices and software that copy music and movies, software to circumvent copyright protection, intelligent robots, and so on. The difficulty of predicting future beneficial uses of technologies is a strong argument against such bans.

We learn from experience. System failures, even disasters, lead to better systems. However, the observation that perfection is not possible does not absolve us of responsibility for sloppy or unethical work.

There are many opportunities for computer professionals to develop wonderful new products and to use their skills and creativity to build solutions to some of the problems we have discussed. I hope that this book has sparked a lot of ideas. I hope also that the discussion of risks and failures encourages you to exercise the highest degree of professional and personal responsibility.

Appendix A

A.1 The Software Engineering Code of Ethics and Professional Practice*

Preamble

Computers have a central and growing role in commerce, industry, government, medicine, education, entertainment, and society at large. Software engineers are those who contribute by direct participation or by teaching, to the analysis, specification, design, development, certification, maintenance, and testing of software systems. Because of their roles in developing software systems, software engineers have significant opportunities to do good or cause harm, to enable others to do good or cause harm, or to influence others to do good or cause harm. To ensure, as much as possible, that their efforts will be used for good, software engineers must commit themselves to making software engineering a beneficial and respected profession. In accordance with that commitment, software engineers shall adhere to the following Code of Ethics and Professional Practice.

The Code contains eight Principles related to the behavior of and decisions made by professional software engineers, including practitioners, educators, managers, supervisors, and policy makers, as well as trainees and students of the profession. The Principles identify the ethically responsible relationships in which individuals, groups, and organizations participate and the primary obligations within these relationships. The Clauses of each Principle are illustrations of some of the obligations included in these relationships. These obligations are founded in the software engineer's humanity, in special care owed to people affected by the work of software engineers, and the unique elements of the practice of software engineering. The Code prescribes these as obligations of anyone claiming to be or aspiring to be a software engineer.

* Version 5.2, prepared by the ACM/IEEE-CS Joint Task Force on Software Engineering Ethics and Professional Practices, Executive Committee: Donald Gotterbarn (Chair), Keith Miller, and Simon Rogerson. Jointly approved by the ACM and the IEEE-CS as the standard for teaching and practicing software engineering. ©1999 by the Institute for Electrical and Electronics Engineers, Inc. and the Association for Computing Machinery, Inc.

It is not intended that the individual parts of the Code be used in isolation to justify errors of omission or commission. The list of Principles and Clauses is not exhaustive. The Clauses should not be read as separating the acceptable from the unacceptable in professional conduct in all practical situations. The Code is not a simple ethical algorithm that generates ethical decisions. In some situations, standards may be in tension with each other or with standards from other sources. These situations require the software engineer to use ethical judgment to act in a manner that is most consistent with the spirit of the Code of Ethics and Professional Practice, given the circumstances.

Ethical tensions can best be addressed by thoughtful consideration of fundamental principles, rather than blind reliance on detailed regulations. These Principles should influence software engineers to consider broadly who is affected by their work; to examine if they and their colleagues are treating other human beings with due respect; to consider how the public, if reasonably well informed, would view their decisions; to analyze how the least empowered will be affected by their decisions; and to consider whether their acts would be judged worthy of the ideal professional working as a software engineer. In all these judgments concern for the health, safety and welfare of the public is primary; that is, the "Public Interest" is central to this Code.

The dynamic and demanding context of software engineering requires a code that is adaptable and relevant to new situations as they occur. However, even in this generality, the Code provides support for software engineers and managers of software engineers who need to take positive action in a specific case by documenting the ethical stance of the profession. The Code provides an ethical foundation to which individuals within teams and the team as a whole can appeal. The Code helps to define those actions that are ethically improper to request of a software engineer or teams of software engineers.

The Code is not simply for adjudicating the nature of questionable acts; it also has an important educational function. As this Code expresses the consensus of the profession on ethical issues, it is a means to educate both the public and aspiring professionals about the ethical obligations of all software engineers.

Principles

PRINCIPLE 1: PUBLIC

Software engineers shall act consistently with the public interest. In particular, software engineers shall, as appropriate:

1.01. Accept full responsibility for their own work.

1.02. Moderate the interests of the software engineer, the employer, the client, and the users with the public good.

1.03. Approve software only if they have a well-founded belief that it is safe, meets specifications, passes appropriate tests, and does not diminish quality of life, diminish privacy, or harm the environment. The ultimate effect of the work should be to the public good.

1.04. Disclose to appropriate persons or authorities any actual or potential danger to the user, the public, or the environment, that they reasonably believe to be associated with software or related documents.

1.05. Cooperate in efforts to address matters of grave public concern caused by software, its installation, maintenance, support, or documentation.

1.06. Be fair and avoid deception in all statements, particularly public ones, concerning software or related documents, methods, and tools.

1.07. Consider issues of physical disabilities, allocation of resources, economic disadvantage, and other factors that can diminish access to the benefits of software.

1.08. Be encouraged to volunteer professional skills to good causes and contribute to public education concerning the discipline.

PRINCIPLE 2: CLIENT AND EMPLOYER

Software engineers shall act in a manner that is in the best interests of their client and employer, consistent with the public interest. In particular, software engineers shall, as appropriate:

2.01. Provide service in their areas of competence, being honest and forthright about any limitations of their experience and education.

2.02. Not knowingly use software that is obtained or retained either illegally or unethically.

2.03. Use the property of a client or employer only in ways properly authorized, and with the client's or employer's knowledge and consent.

2.04. Ensure that any document upon which they rely has been approved, when required, by someone authorized to approve it.

2.05. Keep private any confidential information gained in their professional work, where such confidentiality is consistent with the public interest and consistent with the law.

2.06. Identify, document, collect evidence, and report to the client or the employer promptly if, in their opinion, a project is likely to fail, to prove too expensive, to violate intellectual property law, or otherwise to be problematic.

2.07. Identify, document, and report significant issues of social concern, of which they are aware, in software or related documents, to the employer or the client.

2.08. Accept no outside work detrimental to the work they perform for their primary employer.

2.09. Promote no interest adverse to their employer or client, unless a higher ethical concern is being compromised; in that case, inform the employer or another appropriate authority of the ethical concern.

PRINCIPLE 3: PRODUCT

Software engineers shall ensure that their products and related modifications meet the highest professional standards possible. In particular, software engineers shall, as appropriate:

3.01. Strive for high quality, acceptable cost, and a reasonable schedule, ensuring significant tradeoffs are clear to and accepted by the employer and the client, and are available for consideration by the user and the public.

3.02. Ensure proper and achievable goals and objectives for any project on which they work or propose.

3.03. Identify, define, and address ethical, economic, cultural, legal, and environmental issues related to work projects.

3.04. Ensure that they are qualified for any project on which they work or propose to work by an appropriate combination of education and training, and experience.

3.05. Ensure an appropriate method is used for any project on which they work or propose to work.

3.06. Work to follow professional standards, when available, that are most appropriate for the task at hand, departing from these only when ethically or technically justified.

3.07. Strive to fully understand the specifications for software on which they work.

3.08. Ensure that specifications for software on which they work have been well documented, satisfy the users' requirements, and have the appropriate approvals.

3.09. Ensure realistic quantitative estimates of cost, scheduling, personnel, quality, and outcomes on any project on which they work or propose to work and provide an uncertainty assessment of these estimates.

3.10. Ensure adequate testing, debugging, and review of software and related documents on which they work.

3.11. Ensure adequate documentation, including significant problems discovered and solutions adopted, for any project on which they work.

3.12. Work to develop software and related documents that respect the privacy of those who will be affected by that software.

3.13. Be careful to use only accurate data derived by ethical and lawful means, and use it only in ways properly authorized.

3.14. Maintain the integrity of data, being sensitive to outdated or flawed occurrences.

3.15. Treat all forms of software maintenance with the same professionalism as new development.

PRINCIPLE 4: JUDGMENT

Software engineers shall maintain integrity and independence in their professional judgment. In particular, software engineers shall, as appropriate:

4.01. Temper all technical judgments by the need to support and maintain human values.

4.02. Only endorse documents either prepared under their supervision or within their areas of competence and with which they are in agreement.

4.03. Maintain professional objectivity with respect to any software or related documents they are asked to evaluate.

4.04. Not engage in deceptive financial practices such as bribery, double billing, or other improper financial practices.

4.05. Disclose to all concerned parties those conflicts of interest that cannot reasonably be avoided or escaped.

4.06. Refuse to participate, as members or advisors, in a private, governmental, or professional body concerned with software related issues, in which they, their employers, or their clients have undisclosed potential conflicts of interest.

PRINCIPLE 5: MANAGEMENT

Software engineering managers and leaders shall subscribe to and promote an ethical approach to the management of software development and maintenance. In particular, those managing or leading software engineers shall, as appropriate:

5.01. Ensure good management for any project on which they work, including effective procedures for promotion of quality and reduction of risk.

5.02. Ensure that software engineers are informed of standards before being held to them.

5.03. Ensure that software engineers know the employer's policies and procedures for protecting passwords, files, and information that is confidential to the employer or confidential to others.

5.04. Assign work only after taking into account appropriate contributions of education and experience tempered with a desire to further that education and experience.

5.05. Ensure realistic quantitative estimates of cost, scheduling, personnel, quality, and outcomes on any project on which they work or propose to work, and provide an uncertainty assessment of these estimates.

5.06. Attract potential software engineers only by full and accurate description of the conditions of employment.

5.07. Offer fair and just remuneration.

5.08. Not unjustly prevent someone from taking a position for which that person is suitably qualified.

5.09. Ensure that there is a fair agreement concerning ownership of any software, processes, research, writing, or other intellectual property to which a software engineer has contributed.

5.10. Provide for due process in hearing charges of violation of an employer's policy or of this Code.

5.11. Not ask a software engineer to do anything inconsistent with this Code.

5.12. Not punish anyone for expressing ethical concerns about a project.

PRINCIPLE 6: PROFESSION

Software engineers shall advance the integrity and reputation of the profession consistent with the public interest. In particular, software engineers shall, as appropriate:

6.01. Help develop an organizational environment favorable to acting ethically.

6.02. Promote public knowledge of software engineering.

6.03. Extend software engineering knowledge by appropriate participation in professional organizations, meetings, and publications.

6.04. Support, as members of a profession, other software engineers striving to follow this Code.

6.05. Not promote their own interest at the expense of the profession, client, or employer.

6.06. Obey all laws governing their work, unless, in exceptional circumstances, such compliance is inconsistent with the public interest.

6.07. Be accurate in stating the characteristics of software on which they work, avoiding not only false claims but also claims that might reasonably be supposed to be speculative, vacuous, deceptive, misleading, or doubtful.

6.08. Take responsibility for detecting, correcting, and reporting errors in software and associated documents on which they work.

6.09. Ensure that clients, employers, and supervisors know of the software engineer's commitment to this Code of ethics, and the subsequent ramifications of such commitment.

6.10. Avoid associations with businesses and organizations which are in conflict with this code.

6.11. Recognize that violations of this Code are inconsistent with being a professional software engineer.

6.12. Express concerns to the people involved when significant violations of this Code are detected unless this is impossible, counterproductive, or dangerous.

6.13. Report significant violations of this Code to appropriate authorities when it is clear that consultation with people involved in these significant violations is impossible, counterproductive, or dangerous.

PRINCIPLE 7: COLLEAGUES

Software engineers shall be fair to and supportive of their colleagues. In particular, software engineers shall, as appropriate:

7.01. Encourage colleagues to adhere to this Code.

7.02. Assist colleagues in professional development.

7.03. Credit fully the work of others and refrain from taking undue credit.

7.04. Review the work of others in an objective, candid, and properly-documented way.

7.05. Give a fair hearing to the opinions, concerns, or complaints of a colleague.

7.06. Assist colleagues in being fully aware of current standard work practices including policies and procedures for protecting passwords, files, and other confidential information, and security measures in general.

7.07. Not unfairly intervene in the career of any colleague; however, concern for the employer, the client, or public interest may compel software engineers, in good faith, to question the competence of a colleague.

7.08. In situations outside of their own areas of competence, call upon the opinions of other professionals who have competence in that area.

PRINCIPLE 8: SELF

Software engineers shall participate in lifelong learning regarding the practice of their profession and shall promote an ethical approach to the practice of the profession. In particular, software engineers shall continually endeavor to:

8.01. Further their knowledge of developments in the analysis, specification, design, development, maintenance, and testing of software and related documents, together with the management of the development process.

8.02. Improve their ability to create safe, reliable, and useful quality software at reasonable cost and within a reasonable time.

8.03. Improve their ability to produce accurate, informative, and well-written documentation.

8.04. Improve their understanding of the software and related documents on which they work and of the environment in which they will be used.

8.05. Improve their knowledge of relevant standards and the law governing the software and related documents on which they work.

8.06. Improve their knowledge of this Code, its interpretation, and its application to their work.

8.07. Not give unfair treatment to anyone because of any irrelevant prejudices.

8.08. Not influence others to undertake any action that involves a breach of this Code.

8.09. Recognize that personal violations of this Code are inconsistent with being a professional software engineer.

A.2   The ACM Code of Ethics and Professional Conduct*

Preamble

Commitment to ethical professional conduct is expected of every member (voting members, associate members, and student members) of the Association for Computing Machinery (ACM).

---

* This Code and the supplemental Guidelines were developed by the Task Force for the Revision of the ACM Code of Ethics and Professional Conduct: Ronald E. Anderson, Chair, Gerald Engel, Donald Gotterbarn, Grace C. Hertlein, Alex Hoffman, Bruce Jawer, Deborah G. Johnson, Doris K. Lidtke, Joyce Currie Little, Dianne Martin, Donn B. Parker, Judith A. Perrolle, and Richard S. Rosenberg. The Task Force was organized by ACM/SIGCAS, and funding was provided by the ACM SIG Discretionary Fund. This Code and the supplemental Guidelines were adopted by the ACM Council on October 16, 1992. It was updated on January 16, 1998. ©1997, Association for Computing Machinery, Inc.

This Code, consisting of 24 imperatives formulated as statements of personal responsibility, identifies the elements of such a commitment. It contains many, but not all, issues professionals are likely to face. Section 1 outlines fundamental ethical considerations, while Section 2 addresses additional, more specific considerations of professional conduct. Statements in Section 3 pertain more specifically to individuals who have a leadership role, whether in the workplace or in a volunteer capacity such as with organizations like ACM. Principles involving compliance with this Code are given in Section 4.

The Code shall be supplemented by a set of Guidelines, which provide explanation to assist members in dealing with the various issues contained in the Code. It is expected that the Guidelines will be changed more frequently than the Code.

The Code and its supplemented Guidelines are intended to serve as a basis for ethical decision making in the conduct of professional work. Secondarily, they may serve as a basis for judging the merit of a formal complaint pertaining to violation of professional ethical standards.

It should be noted that although computing is not mentioned in the imperatives of Section 1, the Code is concerned with how these fundamental imperatives apply to one's conduct as a computing professional. These imperatives are expressed in a general form to emphasize that ethical principles which apply to computer ethics are derived from more general ethical principles.

It is understood that some words and phrases in a code of ethics are subject to varying interpretations, and that any ethical principle may conflict with other ethical principles in specific situations. Questions related to ethical conflicts can best be answered by thoughtful consideration of fundamental principles, rather than reliance on detailed regulations.

Contents and Guidelines

1.   GENERAL MORAL IMPERATIVES.

As an ACM member I will . . .

1.1 Contribute to society and human well-being.

This principle concerning the quality of life of all people affirms an obligation to protect fundamental human rights and to respect the diversity of all cultures. An essential aim of computing professionals is to minimize negative consequences of computing systems, including threats to health and safety. When designing or implementing systems, computing professionals must attempt to ensure that the products of their efforts will be used in socially responsible ways, will meet social needs, and will avoid harmful effects to health and welfare.

In addition to a safe social environment, human well-being includes a safe natural environment. Therefore, computing professionals who design and develop systems must be alert to, and make others aware of, any potential damage to the local or global environment.

1.2 Avoid harm to others.

"Harm" means injury or negative consequences, such as undesirable loss of information, loss of property, property damage, or unwanted environmental impacts. This principle prohibits use of computing technology in ways that result in harm to any of the following: users, the general public, employees, employers. Harmful actions include intentional destruction or modification of files and programs leading to serious loss of resources or unnecessary expenditure of human resources such as the time and effort required to purge systems of "computer viruses."

Well-intended actions, including those that accomplish assigned duties, may lead to harm unexpectedly. In such an event the responsible person or persons are obligated to undo or mitigate the negative consequences as much as possible. One way to avoid unintentional harm is to carefully consider potential impacts on all those affected by decisions made during design and implementation.

To minimize the possibility of indirectly harming others, computing professionals must minimize malfunctions by following generally accepted standards for system design and testing. Furthermore, it is often necessary to assess the social consequences of systems to project the likelihood of any serious harm to others. If system features are misrepresented to users, coworkers, or supervisors, the individual computing professional is responsible for any resulting injury.

In the work environment the computing professional has the additional obligation to report any signs of system dangers that might result in serious personal or social damage. If one's superiors do not act to curtail or mitigate such dangers, it may be necessary to "blow the whistle" to help correct the problem or reduce the risk. However, capricious or misguided reporting of violations can, itself, be harmful. Before reporting violations, all relevant aspects of the incident must be thoroughly assessed. In particular, the assessment of risk and responsibility must be credible. It is suggested that advice be sought from other computing professionals. See principle 2.5 regarding thorough evaluations.

1.3 Be honest and trustworthy.

Honesty is an essential component of trust. Without trust, an organization cannot function effectively. The honest computing professional will not make deliberately false or deceptive claims about a system or system design, but will instead provide full disclosure of all pertinent system limitations and problems.

A computer professional has a duty to be honest about his or her own qualifications, and about any circumstances that might lead to conflicts of interest.

Membership in volunteer organizations such as ACM may at times place individuals in situations where their statements or actions could be interpreted as carrying the "weight" of a larger group of professionals. An ACM member will exercise care to not misrepresent ACM or positions and policies of ACM or any ACM units.

1.4 Be fair and take action not to discriminate.

The values of equality, tolerance, respect for others, and the principles of equal justice govern this imperative. Discrimination on the basis of race, sex, religion, age, disability, national origin, or other such factors is an explicit violation of ACM policy and will not be tolerated.

Inequities between different groups of people may result from the use or misuse of information and technology. In a fair society, all individuals would have equal opportunity to participate in, or benefit from, the use of computer resources regardless of race, sex, religion, age, disability, national origin or other such similar factors. However, these ideals do not justify unauthorized use of computer resources nor do they provide an adequate basis for violation of any other ethical imperatives of this code.

1.5 Honor property rights including copyrights and patent.

Violation of copyrights, patents, trade secrets and the terms of license agreements is prohibited by law in most circumstances. Even when software is not so protected, such violations are contrary to professional behavior. Copies of software should be made only with proper authorization. Unauthorized duplication of materials must not be condoned.

1.6 Give proper credit for intellectual property.

Computing professionals are obligated to protect the integrity of intellectual property. Specifically, one must not take credit for other's ideas or work, even in cases where the work has not been explicitly protected by copyright, patent, etc.

1.7 Respect the privacy of others.

Computing and communication technology enables the collection and exchange of personal information on a scale unprecedented in the history of civilization. Thus there is increased potential for violating the privacy of individuals and groups. It is the responsibility of professionals to maintain the privacy and integrity of data describing individuals. This includes taking precautions to ensure the accuracy of data, as well as protecting it from unauthorized access or accidental disclosure to inappropriate individuals. Furthermore, procedures must be established to allow individuals to review their records and correct inaccuracies.

This imperative implies that only the necessary amount of personal information be collected in a system, that retention and disposal periods for that information be clearly defined and enforced, and that personal information gathered for a specific purpose not be used for other purposes without consent of the individual(s). These principles apply to electronic communications, including electronic mail, and prohibit procedures that capture or monitor electronic user data, including messages, without the permission of users or bona fide authorization related to system operation and maintenance. User data observed during the normal duties of system operation and maintenance must be treated with strictest confidentiality, except in cases where it is evidence for the violation of law, organizational regulations, or this Code. In these cases, the nature or contents of that information must be disclosed only to proper authorities.

1.8 Honor confidentiality.

The principle of honesty extends to issues of confidentiality of information whenever one has made an explicit promise to honor confidentiality or, implicitly, when private information not directly related to the performance of one's duties becomes available. The ethical concern is to respect all obligations of confidentiality to employers, clients, and users unless discharged from such obligations by requirements of the law or other principles of this Code.

2. MORE SPECIFIC PROFESSIONAL RESPONSIBILITIES.

As an ACM computing professional I will . . .

2.1 Strive to achieve the highest quality, effectiveness and dignity in both the process and products of professional work.

Excellence is perhaps the most important obligation of a professional. The computing professional must strive to achieve quality and to be cognizant of the serious negative consequences that may result from poor quality in a system.

2.2 Acquire and maintain professional competence.

Excellence depends on individuals who take responsibility for acquiring and maintaining professional competence. A professional must participate in setting standards for appropriate levels of competence, and strive to achieve those standards. Upgrading technical knowledge and competence can be achieved in several ways: doing independent study; attending seminars, conferences, or courses; and being involved in professional organizations.

2.3 Know and respect existing laws pertaining to professional work.

ACM members must obey existing local, state, province, national, and international laws unless there is a compelling ethical basis not to do so. Policies and procedures of the organizations in which one participates must also be obeyed. But compliance must be balanced with the recognition that sometimes existing laws and rules may be immoral or inappropriate and, therefore, must be challenged. Violation of a law or regulation may be ethical when that law or rule has inadequate moral basis or when it conflicts with another law judged to be more important. If one decides to violate a law or rule because it is viewed as unethical, or for any other reason, one must fully accept responsibility for one's actions and for the consequences.

2.4 Accept and provide appropriate professional review.

Quality professional work, especially in the computing profession, depends on professional reviewing and critiquing. Whenever appropriate, individual members should seek and utilize peer review as well as provide critical review of the work of others.

2.5 Give comprehensive and thorough evaluations of computer systems and their impacts, including analysis of possible risks.

Computer professionals must strive to be perceptive, thorough, and objective when evaluating, recommending, and presenting system descriptions and alternatives. Computer professionals are in a position of special trust, and therefore have a special responsibility to provide objective, credible evaluations to employers, clients, users, and the public. When providing evaluations the professional must also identify any relevant conflicts of interest, as stated in imperative 1.3.

As noted in the discussion of principle 1.2 on avoiding harm, any signs of danger from systems must be reported to those who have opportunity and/or responsibility to resolve them. See the guidelines for imperative 1.2 for more details concerning harm, including the reporting of professional violations.

2.6 Honor contracts, agreements, and assigned responsibilities.

Honoring one's commitments is a matter of integrity and honesty. For the computer professional this includes ensuring that system elements perform as intended. Also, when one contracts for work with another party, one has an obligation to keep that party properly informed about progress toward completing that work.

A computing professional has a responsibility to request a change in any assignment that he or she feels cannot be completed as defined. Only after serious consideration and with full disclosure of risks and concerns to the employer or client, should one accept the assignment. The major underlying principle here is the obligation to accept personal accountability for professional work. On some occasions other ethical principles may take greater priority.

A judgment that a specific assignment should not be performed may not be accepted. Having clearly identified one's concerns and reasons for that judgment, but failing to procure a change in that assignment, one may yet be obligated, by contract or by law, to proceed as directed. The computing professional's ethical judgment should be the final guide in deciding whether or not to proceed. Regardless of the decision, one must accept the responsibility for the consequences.

However, performing assignments "against one's own judgment" does not relieve the professional of responsibility for any negative consequences.

2.7 Improve public understanding of computing and its consequences.

Computing professionals have a responsibility to share technical knowledge with the public by encouraging understanding of computing, including the impacts of computer systems and their limitations. This imperative implies an obligation to counter any false views related to computing.

2.8 Access computing and communication resources only when authorized to do so.

Theft or destruction of tangible and electronic property is prohibited by imperative 1.2 - "Avoid harm to others." Trespassing and unauthorized use of a computer or communication system is addressed by this imperative. Trespassing includes accessing communication networks and computer systems, or accounts and/or files associated with those systems, without explicit authorization to do so. Individuals and organizations have the right to restrict access to their systems so long as they do not violate the discrimination principle (see 1.4). No one should enter or use another's computer system, software, or data files without permission. One must always have appropriate approval before using system resources, including communication ports, file space, other system peripherals, and computer time.

3. ORGANIZATIONAL LEADERSHIP IMPERATIVES.

As an ACM member and an organizational leader, I will . . .

BACKGROUND NOTE: This section draws extensively from the draft IFIP Code of Ethics, especially its sections on organizational ethics and international concerns. The ethical obligations of organizations tend to be neglected in most codes of professional conduct, perhaps because these codes are written from the perspective of the individual member. This dilemma is addressed by stating these imperatives from the perspective of the organizational leader. In this context "leader" is viewed as any organizational member who has leadership or educational responsibilities. These imperatives generally may apply to organizations as well as their leaders. In this context "organizations" are corporations, government agencies, and other "employers," as well as volunteer professional organizations.

3.1 Articulate social responsibilities of members of an organizational unit and encourage full acceptance of those responsibilities.

Because organizations of all kinds have impacts on the public, they must accept responsibilities to society. Organizational procedures and attitudes oriented toward quality and the welfare of society will reduce harm to members of the public, thereby serving public interest and fulfilling social responsibility. Therefore, organizational leaders must encourage full participation in meeting social responsibilities as well as quality performance.

3.2 Manage personnel and resources to design and build information systems that enhance the quality of working life.

Organizational leaders are responsible for ensuring that computer systems enhance, not degrade, the quality of working life. When implementing a computer system, organizations must consider the personal and professional development, physical safety, and human dignity of all workers. Appropriate human-computer ergonomic standards should be considered in system design and in the workplace.

3.3 Acknowledge and support proper and authorized uses of an organization's computing and communication resources.

Because computer systems can become tools to harm as well as to benefit an organization, the leadership has the responsibility to clearly define appropriate and inappropriate uses of organizational computing resources. While the number and scope of such rules should be minimal, they should be fully enforced when established.

3.4 Ensure that users and those who will be affected by a system have their needs clearly articulated during the assessment and design of requirements; later the system must be validated to meet requirements.

Current system users, potential users and other persons whose lives may be affected by a system must have their needs assessed and incorporated in the statement of requirements. System validation should ensure compliance with those requirements.

3.5 Articulate and support policies that protect the dignity of users and others affected by a computing system.

Designing or implementing systems that deliberately or inadvertently demean individuals or groups is ethically unacceptable. Computer professionals who are in decision making positions should verify that systems are designed and implemented to protect personal privacy and enhance personal dignity.

3.6 Create opportunities for members of the organization to learn the principles and limitations of computer systems.

This complements the imperative on public understanding (2.7). Educational opportunities are essential to facilitate optimal participation of all organizational members. Opportunities must be available to all members to help them improve their knowledge and skills in computing, including courses that familiarize them with the consequences and limitations of particular types of systems. In particular, professionals must be made aware of the dangers of building systems around oversimplified models, the improbability of anticipating and designing for every possible operating condition, and other issues related to the complexity of this profession.

4.   COMPLIANCE WITH THE CODE.

As an ACM member I will . . .

4.1 Uphold and promote the principles of this Code.

The future of the computing profession depends on both technical and ethical excellence. Not only is it important for ACM computing professionals to adhere to the principles expressed in this Code, each member should encourage and support adherence by other members.

4.2 Treat violations of this Code as inconsistent with membership in the ACM.

Adherence of professionals to a code of ethics is largely a voluntary matter. However, if a member does not follow this code by engaging in gross misconduct, membership in ACM may be terminated.

INDEX

519